People and Buildings

PEOPLE AND BUILDINGS

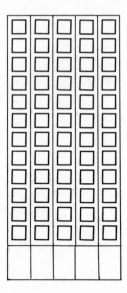

EDITED BY ROBERT GUTMAN

Basic Books, Inc., Publishers

NEW YORK   LONDON

© 1972 by Basic Books, Inc.
Library of Congress Catalog Card Number 75–174827
SBN 465–05456–0
Manufactured in the United States of America
Designed by the Inkwell Studio

To the Memory

of

JOHN MADGE (1914–1968)

Contributors

CHRISTOPHER ALEXANDER is Professor of Architecture at the College of Environmental Studies at the University of California, Berkeley. He is the author of *Notes on the Synthesis of Form* (1964) and one of the co-authors of *A Pattern Language Which Generates Multi-Service Centers* (1968).

BERNARD BARBER is Professor and Chairman of the Department of Sociology at Barnard College. His works include *Science and Social Order* (1952), *Social Stratification* (1957), and *Drugs and Society* (1967).

MAURICE BROADY is Professor of Social Administration at the University College of Swansea, England. Several of his articles have been collected in *Planning for People: Essays on the Social Context of Planning* (1968).

JOHN CASSEL is Professor and Chairman of the Department of Epidemiology in the School of Public Health at the University of North Carolina. He is a specialist in the epidemiology of chronic and non-infectious diseases and has written many articles on that subject.

ALAN COLQUHOUN is an architect in private practice in London. He has taught at the Architectural Association School, at Cambridge University, and at Princeton University.

DERK DE JONGE, a research sociologist, is with the Housing and Planning Research Section at the Technical University in Delft, the Netherlands.

LEE E. FARR, currently Chief of the Bureau of Emergency Health Services for the city of Berkeley, has published articles on nuclear medicine, nuclear reactors, and protein metabolism.

NANCY JO FELIPE is Assistant Professor of Psychology at the American University in Washington, D.C. She has written articles on personal space and the significance of seating patterns.

LEON FESTINGER is Else and Hans Staudinger Professor of Psychology at the New School for Social Research. He is the author of *Conflict, Decision and Dissonance* (1964) and senior author of the classic *Social Pressures in Informal Groups* (1950).

JAMES MARSTON FITCH is Professor of Architecture at Columbia University and the author of several books, including *Architecture and the Esthetics of Plenty* (1961) and *American Building* (1966).

MARC FRIED is Research Professor at the Institute of Human Sciences at Boston College, a lecturer in psychology at the Harvard Medical School, and a psychologist at the Massachusetts General Hospital. His special fields of interest are the epidemiology of mental health and illness and the relationship between personality and sociocultural patterns.

ROBERT GUTMAN is Professor of Sociology at Rutgers University and currently Class of 1913 Lecturer in Architecture at Princeton University. He recently coedited *Neighborhood, City, and Metropolis* (1970).

EDWARD T. HALL is Professor of Anthropology at Northwestern University and the author of *The Silent Language* (1959) and *The Hidden Dimension* (1966).

JOHN N. HAZARD is Professor of Public Law at Columbia University and is well known as a specialist in Soviet law.

ALEXANDER KIRA is Professor of Architecture at Cornell University. He is preparing a revised edition of *The Bathroom* (1967) and is planning a similar volume on the bedroom.

STANFORD M. LYMAN is Associate Professor of Sociology at the University of Nevada and the author of articles on deviant behavior.

ABRAHAM H. MASLOW (1908–1970) was for many years Professor of Psychology at Brandeis University. Among his books are *Toward a Psychology of Being* (1962) and *Religion, Values, and Peak Experiences* (1964).

THE MINISTRY OF HOUSING AND LOCAL GOVERNMENT in Great Britain maintains The Architects Research and Development Group, which has designed a number of demonstration housing projects for selected local authorities. It also conducts programming and evaluation studies in connection with these projects.

NORBETT L. MINTZ is currently a psychologist at McLean Hospital. His fields of interest include personality, abnormal psychology, and esthetics.

THOMAS C. PINKERTON is a psychologist and biophysicist who presently holds a research appointment at the University of California, San Diego.

LEE RAINWATER is Professor of Sociology at Harvard University and a faculty associate of the Joint Committee for Urban Studies of Massachusetts Institute of Technology and Harvard University. His recent book, *Behind Ghetto Walls: Black Family Life in a Federal Slum* (1970), also deals with the housing project described in his article.

AMOS RAPOPORT is a member of the Department of Architecture at the University of Sydney and the author of *House Form and Culture* (1969), as well as many articles dealing with the relation of the behavioral sciences to architecture.

BARRY SCHWARTZ is a doctoral candidate in sociology at the University of Pennsylvania, whose special fields of interest are crime and delinquency and social psychology.

MARVIN B. SCOTT is Associate Professor and Chairman of the Department of Sociology at Sonoma State College in California. He is a specialist in theory and social psychology.

MURRAY SILVERSTEIN teaches in the School of Architecture at the University of Washington and is currently engaged in an examination of the teenager's place in urban culture.

ROBERT SOMMER is Professor and Chairman of the Department of Psychology at the University of California, Davis, and is the author of *Personal Space* (1969) and of numerous articles on the effects of the physical setting on attitudes and behavior.

MATTHEW TAYBACK is presently Assistant Secretary of the Department of Health and Mental Hygiene of the state of Maryland.

SIM VAN DER RYN is Associate Professor of Architecture at the College of Environmental Design at the University of California, Berkeley.

THORSTEIN VEBLEN (1857–1929), American sociologist, economist, and social critic, was the author of many well known and influential books, including *The Theory of the Leisure Class* (1899), *The Theory of Business Enterprise* (1904), *The Higher Learning in America* (1918), and *The Vested Interests and the State of the Industrial Arts* (1919).

ROSABELLE PRICE WALKLEY is Lecturer in Behavioral Sciences and Associate Research Behavioral Scientist at the University of California, Los Angeles.

NEWTON WATSON is Professor of Architecture in the School of Environmental Studies at University College in London.

B. W. P. WELLS is a member of the Department of Psychology at the University of Strathclyde, Scotland, and a member of the research staff of the Building Performance Research Unit at that university.

BARBARA WESTERGAARD is a Research Associate of the Built Environment Research Project in the Department of Sociology at Rutgers University.

DANIEL M. WILNER is Professor of Public Health and Professor of Preventive and Social Medicine and Chairman of the Department of Public Health at the University of California, Los Angeles. He is the co-author of the influential *Human Relations in Interracial Housing* (1955) and author of *Narcotics* (1965).

JOACHIM F. WOHLWILL is Professor of Psychology at Pennsylvania State University. He is the author of many articles on environmental and developmental psychology.

Preface

There is at the present time an enormous interest in relating the behavioral sciences to the design disciplines. Most schools of architecture now require their students to take courses in the behavioral sciences, with particular attention being paid to urban sociology. Sociologists and social psychologists are being added to the faculties of architecture schools, where they offer lectures and seminars and participate as programming specialists and design critics in studio courses. For a number of years sociologists and other behavioral scientists in many European countries have collaborated with architects and planners in the design work undertaken by governmental ministries, and more recently have been participating in the work of private design firms. Similar developments are now occurring in the United States. Within the last few years, in both this country and abroad, several new magazines and journals have been published that are specifically devoted to reporting on the interaction between the behavioral sciences and the design professions.

The demand for collaboration was initiated by the design professions. The behavioral science disciplines have not always responded helpfully, but reciprocity is now beginning to occur. A few graduate departments in the behavioral sciences have begun to offer specialized doctoral training programs in what is coming to be called "environmental psychology" or "environmental sociology," and papers and monographs dealing with this subject have begun to appear in increasing numbers. The meetings of the American Sociological Association, the American Psychological Association, and the Society of Applied Anthropology now regularly include sessions in which the problems of environmental studies are discussed. Each of these organizations has developed liaison activities with the Interprofessional Council on Environmental Design, an organization representing six design groups, including the American Institute of Architects, the American Institute of Planners, and the American Society of Landscape Architects.

The interest in joining the resources of the social and design disciplines arises from several sources. Probably the major factor in this process is the realization by the design professions that the intellectual traditions of architecture and planning are simply not adequate for grasping the complexity of the building needs of urbanized and industrialized societies. Architects find themselves facing tasks and clients for which their training did not prepare them. Instead, for example, of designing villas and palaces for the wealthy, architects must now design projects to house the black and disadvantaged populations. Where once they were hired by a college to propose a scheme for one or two dormitories, a library, or an administration building, very often now designers are expected to take charge of the design of a complete campus. In these settings architects encounter questions that they are unable to answer through informal programming techniques—questions about the life styles of the poor, about the housing needs of different racial groups, about the ultimate purposes of a college or university—and they turn to the behavioral scientist in the hope that he can provide the answers.

The design professions are also setting higher standards of social responsibility for themselves. The modern movement in architecture has been characterized by a utopian thrust, but the aspiration to increase welfare and improve justice demands more than good intentions. Architects evidence an increasing desire to be sure ahead of time that the buildings they design will have a beneficial effect upon the ultimate users. Of course, the architect's greater interest in the users' requirements is also a response to the increasing articulateness of clients and users. With building resources becoming scarcer at the same time that unmet needs for shelters are apparently increasing, those who pay for and use buildings want clear evidence that the final product will satisfy their needs.

At the same time that designers have become more self-conscious, behavioral scientists have developed a new concern for the practical applications of their research. During the years immediately following World War II, sociologists and psychologists often argued that their main task was to describe and explain the principles that govern human behavior, whereas the application of that knowledge was the responsibility of the policy makers, administrators, and the public. It became evident, however, to many behavioral scientists that their reports were being used in pursuit of goals they did not support. Furthermore, they came to realize that much of their research, for all of its contribution to knowledge, was not really apposite to the problems of industrialized society. As a result, many more behavioral scientists now wish to focus their research efforts on contemporary social problems and to try to maintain control over the development and use of their investigations.

The social disciplines also exhibit a renewed awareness of the relevance of environmental factors to human behavior. A body of coherent theory and research is now emerging that examines those needs of the human organism and of group functioning that are best satisfied through the provision of specific conditions in the physical, as distinguished from the social, environment. Examples of such studies are those based on the need for personal space and for territory. Both of these needs, it is coming to be thought, must be met if organisms and groups are to function effectively, and both needs imply certain constraints on the form of buildings and urban settlements. Investigations are also being carried out, particularly within the field of anthropology, on the communication function of symbol systems. Some of these investigations take into account the role of architecture and urban form as "languages," through which men and groups define the boundaries of relevant social interaction and through which the social values and norms that produce social order and integration are reinforced. One can also point to the expansion of research in social biology, epidemiology, and social control. Studies in these fields consider the influence of the physical environment on physiological stress, mental illness, and symptoms of social pathology, such as family disorganization, urban violence, and delinquency.

It is important to emphasize that these developments are not taking place primarily because of demands from the design professions for useful behavioral knowledge. In large part they reflect the sense within the behavioral sciences that the tradition that assumed that human personality was formed by culture and that the causes of social distress could therefore be found in social and cultural conditions was an extreme overreaction against an earlier period of evolutionary and biological determinism in American social theory. As in many other fields concerned with human behavior, the idea has suddenly taken hold that many of our social problems may stem from a failure to be sensitive to the limits on human progress and perfectability. To put the same thought in a less negative light, civilization can advance further only by respecting the constraints that the nature of the organism and the nature of the environment impose on human adaptability.

Those of us who have tried to work in the middle ground between environmental design and sociology are aware of the many issues about which little is known and of how much about the interaction between men, society, and architecture remains to be understood. A tremendous investment in research must be forthcoming if the potential utility of the behavioral sciences to design is to be fully exploited. But the situation is not as impoverished as some critics and skeptics would have us believe. A good deal of empirical research has been undertaken on many problems, and many potentially productive ideas and concepts have been developed. This work, however, is not widely known or easily accessible. It is this fact that constitutes the rationale for this collection of articles, essays, and selections from books and research monographs.

I have tried to assemble some of the most illuminating material in five important areas of converging interest between the social and design disciplines. The first of these areas deals with current research and theory on human anatomy and physiology, on man's sensory apparatus and his behavior in space, and on the requirements that these characteristics generate for the design of buildings. The second area deals with the impact of spatial organization on social interaction and group relationships, as revealed through studies of friendship patterns, communication and privacy. Part Three of the book discusses environmental influences on physical and mental health, with particular attention to the role of housing conditions, noise, esthetic surroundings, urban relocation and overcrowding. A fourth area is concerned with the work that anthropologists, functional sociologists, and psychologists have done in demonstrating the significance of architecture as the expression of social values and the reinforcement for cultural patterns. Part Five includes a series of readings that illustrate the ways in which architects and behavioral scientists are applying a variety of these ideas and approaches to the practical problems of the design process.

The selections have been written primarily by behavioral scientists and designers working in the behavioral science mode. The selections within each part have been arranged to provide an ordered argument or exploration of the general topic with which the part as a whole deals. To facilitate the reader's appreciation of the argument, each selection is preceded by a short prefatory statement. In view of the fact that a single article or preface can hardly be representative of the depth of the literature that has developed around an argument, I have included an annotated bibliography, which is keyed to the selections through the use of subheadings.

The resulting collection is not intended as a manual or handbook to guide design decisions on specific projects, nor is it intended to be just an assemblage of interesting articles dealing with the intriguing issues that arise when the behavioral sciences confront architecture. It has a polemical aim as well: namely, by the selection, organization, and arrangement of the readings and introductory notes, to urge both architects and behavioral scientists to recognize certain features of the phenomena to which their work is addressed. These points can be summarized as follows:

1. Architecture is a legitimate topic of inquiry for the social sciences. It is an element in human culture and social organization to which all people are responding even when they are unaware of it.

2. Architectural phenomena involve a range of properties—from the subtle and elusive features of symbolism and sensual qualities at one end to the utilitarian qualities of measurable space and ambient conditions at the other—and *all* of these properties must be kept in view if one is to achieve a comprehensive understanding of the effect of the built environment on man and society.

3. Sensitivity to the totality of buildings and environments implies, in turn, recognition of the fact that architecture connects with the full range of human qualities, capacities, instincts, feelings, needs, and dispositions, including the measurable needs for light and air, the experimentally observable functions of seeing and hearing, and the experientially observable demands for communication and group membership, as well as the cultural need for strong integrative symbols and the individual need for a sense of place. The latter requirements probably cannot be directly observed or measured, but they can be inferentially determined from the study of human actions and the linguistic and symbolic products of society.

4. Designers and others who are anxious to apply the insights and findings of the behavioral sciences to the creation of built environments must be careful to recognize the variety of interconnections between buildings and men. They should not merely use the findings from a selected sample of studies to justify an approach to architecture that may in its concern for behavioral requirements be just as restrictive as the older design methodology was in its concern for symbolic and esthetic features.

5. Finally, behavioral scientists and architects who collaborate in joint efforts should realize that full appreciation of the behavioral science tradition demands using its critical apparatus not only to consider the spatial organization and building specifications that are appropriate for reinforcing existing behavior patterns and preferences but also to evaluate and, if necessary, to

encourage the reform of the goals and purposes that the existing patterns imply.

This volume grows out of my experience in working with architects, in teaching sociology to architecture students, and in discussing architectural problems with sociologists. I am especially grateful to Peter Cowan, Peter Eisenman, Kenneth Frampton, Robert Geddes, and Robertson Ward Jr. for many valuable discussions about architecture, building, design, and society; to William L. Gum and Irving Kristol for encouraging me to put this volume together; and to Angela G. Irby for her guidance in making available the resources of Princeton University's Urban and Environmental Studies library. The editorial and bibliographical assistance of Barbara Westergaard has been invaluable. My wife, Sonya Rudikoff Gutman, has been a sympathetic critic and reader. I owe a special debt to the late John Madge for his help in getting me to appreciate the sociology of architecture and I would like to dedicate this book to his memory.

R. G.

Princeton, New Jersey
March, 1971

Contents

PART FIVE
The Application of Behavioral Science to Design

PART ONE
Behavioral Constraints on Building Design

The Aesthetics of Function

JAMES MARSTON FITCH

It is common in design circles to claim that architectural phenomena are enormously complex. Usually what this assertion means is that a building is made up of so many different kinds of systems and is subject to such a wide variety of technological, esthetic, and social constraints that it is often exceedingly difficult to resolve a design problem. The notion of architectural complexity, however, also applies to the relations between the built environment and society. Many different aspects of architecture and a variety of human needs and group processes are interconnected. For example, the visual qualities of architecture, its geometrical forms, the environmental control systems of buildings, the sheer provision of two-dimensional surfaces and three-dimensional spaces—all these aspects of architecture may become meaningful to people and influence their behavior. In the other direction, there are a great number of biological, psychological, and cultural needs that architecture and the environment have the capacity to satisfy. At the least, many of these needs can be satisfied through social mechanisms and social forms that architecture can help to organize and regulate. These needs are related to specific characteristics of the human organism, including man's anatomical structure and physiology, his personality and unconscious mental life, his perceptual apparatus, his use of symbol systems for communication, and his dependence upon group interaction for civilized survival.

Fitch's selection is an attempt to provide a conceptual framework that will alert the student of architectural phenomena to the many different ways in which the built environment and man are related. His argument is particularly directed against the traditional emphasis in architectural training and criticism on the visual qualities of buildings. Fitch counters this view by describing the linkages between the human being's response to the environment and his full perceptual mechanism. The full perceptual mechanism includes not only the visual and auditory senses but the gustatory, olfactory, and haptic responses, and the sense of spatial orientation as well. This perspective leads Fitch to a definition of architecture as a "third environment" that mediates between the hazards of the natural world and of civilized society and the internal breathing, feeling, seeing, and hearing processes of man.

Two additional polemical thrusts underlie Fitch's argument. One is the

Reprinted from James Marston Fitch, "The Aesthetics of Function," *The Annals of the New York Academy of Sciences* 128, article 2 (September 27, 1965): 706–714.

view, repeated in several selections in this book, that until basic anatomical and physiological needs are better satisfied through building designs, human societies cannot really afford the luxury of an interest in the esthetic properties of architecture. The second is the demand for an experimental architecture that will also be experiential, that is to say, that will be responsive to the full range of human needs and will call upon the total sensory capacity of the human organism.

□

A fundamental weakness in most discussions of aesthetics is the failure to relate it to experiential reality. Most literature on aesthetics tends to isolate it from this matrix of experience, to discuss the aesthetics process as though it were an abstract problem in logic.

Art and architectural criticism suffers from this conceptual limitation. This finds expression in a persistent tendency to discuss art forms and buildings as though they were exclusively visual phenomena. This leads to serious misconceptions as to the actual relationship between the artifact and the human being. Our very terminology reveals this misapprehension: we speak of art as having "spectators," artists as having "audiences." This suggests that man exists in some dimension quite separate and apart from his artifacts; that the only contact between the two is this narrow channel of vision or hearing; and that this contact is unaffected by the environmental circumstances in which it occurs. The facts are quite otherwise and our modes of thought should be revised to correspond to them.

Art and architecture, like man himself, are totally submerged in an exterior environment. Thus they can never be felt, perceived, experienced in anything less than multi-dimensional totality. A change in one aspect or quality of the environment inevitably affects our response to, and perception of, all the rest. The primary significance of a painting may indeed be visual; or of a concert, sonic: but perception of these art forms occurs in a situation of experiential totality. Recognition of this is crucial for aesthetic theory, above all for architectural aesthetics. Far from being based narrowly upon any single sense of perception like vision, architectural aesthetics actually derives from the body's *total* response to, and perception of, its external physical environment. It is literally impossible to experience architecture in any "simpler" way. *In architecture, there are no spectators: there are only participants.* The body of architectural criticism which pretends otherwise is based upon photographs of buildings and not actual exposure to architecture at all.

Life is coexistent and coextensive with the external natural environment in which the body is submerged. The body's dependence upon this external environment is absolute—in the fullest sense of the word, *uterine*. And yet, unlike the womb, the external natural environment does not afford optimum conditions for the existence of the individual. The animal body, for its survival, maintains its own special internal environment. In man, this internal environment is so distinct in its nature and so constant in its properties that it has been given its own name, "homeostasis." Since the natural environment is anything but constant in either time or space, the contradictions between internal requirements and external conditions are normally stressful. The body has wonderful mechanisms for adjusting to external variations, e.g., the eye's capacity to adjust to enormous variations in the luminous environment or the adjustability of the heat-exchange mechanism of the skin. But the limits of adaptation are sharp and obdurate. Above or below them, an ameliorating element, a "third" environment, is required.

Before birth, the womb affords this to the foetus. But man, once born into the world, enters into a much more complex relationship with his external environment. Existence now is on two distinct levels, simultaneously and indissolubly connected, the metabolic and the perceptual. (Figure 1–1.) The metabolic process remains basic. It is at once a "preconscious" state and the material basis of consciousness. Many of life's fundamental processes transpire at this level: heart beat, respiration, digestion, hypothalmic heat exchange controls, etc. Metabolic disturbance occurs only when the external environment begins to drop below the minimal, or rise above the maximal, requirements of existence. And sensual perception of the external environment comes into play only *after* these minimal requirements are met. (As a matter of fact, loss of consciousness is one of the body's characteristic responses to environmental stress—drop in oxygen or pressure, extremes of heat and cold, etc.)

Metabolic process then is clearly the precondition to sensory perception, just as sensory perception is the material basis of the aesthetic process. But the aesthetic process only begins to operate maximally, i.e., as a uniquely human faculty, when the impact upon the body of all environmental forces are held within tolerable limits (limits which, as we have said, are established by the body itself). Thus, we can construct a kind of experimental spectrum of stress. The work of psychiatrists like Dr. George Ruff at the University of Pennsylvania establishes the lower end of this spectrum: sensory overloading is destructive, first of balanced judgments, then of rationality itself.[1] But

5

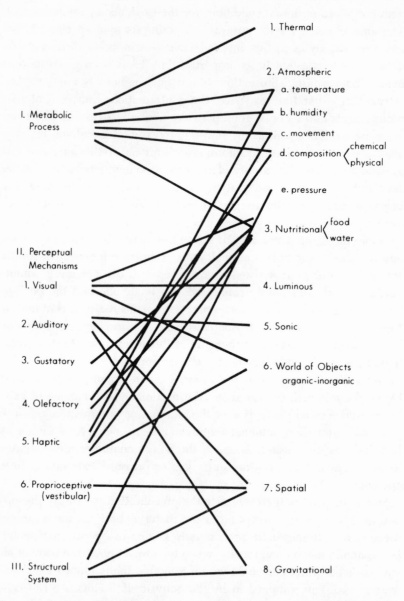

Organism   Environmental Factors

Figure 1–1 The relationship of the metabolic process to its environmental support is literally uterine. And since the process is the substructure of consciousness, sensory perception of changes in the environment in which the body finds itself is totally dependent upon satisfaction of the body's minimal metabolic requirements.

the other end of this spectrum proves equally destructive. Investigations of the effects of sensory deprivation, such as those carried on by Dr. Philip Solomon of the Harvard Medical School, indicate that too little environmental stress (and hence too little sensory stimulation) is as deleterious to the body as too much. Volunteer subjects for Dr. Solomon's experiments were reduced to gibbering incoherence in a matter of a few hours by being isolated from all visual, sonic, haptic and thermal stimulation.[2]

Psychic satisfaction with a given situation is thus directly related to physiologic well-being, just as dissatisfaction must be related to discomfort. A condition of neither too great nor too little sensory stimulation permits the fullest exercise of the critical faculties upon that situation or any aspect of it. But even this proposition will not be indefinitely extensible in time. As one investigator has observed in a recent paper (significantly entitled *The Pathology of Boredom*)[3]: "variety is not the spice of life; it is the very stuff of it." The psychosomatic equilibrium which the body always seeks is dynamic, a continual resolution of opposites. Every experience has built-in time limits. Perception itself has thresholds. One is purely quantitative; the ear cannot perceive sounds above 18,000 cycles per second; the eye does not perceive radiation below 3,200 Angstroms. But another set of thresholds are functions of time: constant exposure to steady stimulation at some fixed level will ultimately deaden perception. This is true of many odors, of "white" sounds and of some aspects of touch.

Of course, even more important facts prevent any mechanistic equating of physical comfort with aesthetic satisfaction. For while all human standards of beauty and ugliness stand ultimately upon a bedrock of material existence, the standards themselves vary astonishingly. All men have always been submerged in the environment. All men have always had the same sensory apparatus for perceiving changes in its qualities and dimensions. All men have always had the same central nervous system for analyzing and responding to the stimuli thus perceived. The physiological limits of this experience are absolute and intractable. Ultimately, it is physiology, and not culture, which establishes the levels at which sensory stimuli become traumatic. With such extremes—high temperatures, blinding lights, cutting edges and heavy blows, noise at blast level, intense concentrations of odor—experience goes beyond mere perception and becomes somatic stress. Moreover, excessive loading of any one of these senses can prevent a balanced assessment of the total experiential situation. (A temperature of 120 degrees F. or a sound level of 120 decibels can render the most beau-

7

tiful room uninhabitable.) But as long as these stimuli do not reach stressful levels of intensity, rational assessment and hence aesthetic judgments are possible. Then formal criteria, derived from personal idiosyncrasy and socially-conditioned value judgments, come into play.

The value judgments that men apply to these stimuli, the evaluation they make of the total experience as being either beautiful or ugly, will vary: measurably with the individual, enormously with his culture. This is so clearly the case in the history of art that it should not need repeating. Yet we constantly forget it. Today, anthropology, ethnology and archaeology alike show us the immense range of aesthetically satisfactory standards which the race has evolved in its history: from cannibalism to vegetarianism in food; from the pyramid to the curtain wall in architecture; from polygamy and polyandry to monogamy and celibacy in sex; from hoopskirt to bikini in dress. Yet we often act, even today, as if our own aesthetic criteria were absolutely valid instead of being, as is indeed the case, absolutely relative for all cultures except our own.

Our aesthetic judgments are substantially modified by non-sensual data derived from social experience. This again can be easily confirmed in daily life. It is ultimately our faith in antiseptic measures that make the immaculate white nurses, uniforms and spotless sheets of the hospitals so reassuring. It is our knowledge of their cost which exaggerates the visual difference between diamonds and crystal, or the gustatory difference between the flavor of pheasant and chicken. It is our knowledge of Hitler Germany which has converted the swastika from the good luck sign of the American Indians to the hated symbol of Nazi terror. All sensory perception is modified by consciousness. Consciousness applies to received stimuli, the criteria of digested experience, whether acquired by the individual or received by him from his culture. The aesthetic process cannot be isolated from this matrix of experiential reality. It constitutes, rather, a quintessential evaluation of and judgment on it.

Once in the world, man is submerged in his natural external environment as completely as the fish in water. Unlike the fish in his aqueous abode, however, he has developed the capacity to modify it in his favor. Simply as an animal, he might have survived without this capacity. Theoretically, at least, he might have migrated like the bird or hibernated like the bear. There are even a few favored spots on earth, like Hawaii, in which biological survival might have been possible without any modification. But, on the base of sheer biological existence, man builds a vast superstructure of institutions, processes and activities: and these could not survive exposure to the natural environment even in those climates in which, biologically, man could.

Thus man was compelled to invent architecture in order to become man. By means of it he surrounded himself with a new environment, tailored to his specifications; a "third" environment interposed between himself and the world. Architecture, is thus *an instrument whose central function is to intervene in man's favor.* The building—and, by extension, the city—has the function of lightening the stress of life; of taking the raw environmental load off man's shoulders; of permitting *homo fabricans* to focus his energies upon productive work.

The building, even in its simplest forms, invests man, surrounds and encapsulates him at every level of his existence, metabolically and perceptually. For this reason, it must be regarded as a very special kind of container. (Figure 1–2.) Far from offering solid, impermeable barriers to the natural environment, its outer surfaces come more and more closely to resemble permeable membranes which can accept or reject any environmental force. Again, the uterine analogy; and not accidentally, for with such convertibility in the container's walls, man can modulate the play of environmental forces upon himself and his processes, to guarantee their uninterrupted development, in very much the same way as the mother's body protects the embryo. Good architecture must thus meet criteria much more complex than those applied to other forms of art. And this confronts the architect, especially the contemporary architect, with a formidable range of subtle problems.

All architects aspire to give their clients beautiful buildings. But "beauty" is not a discrete property of the building: it describes, rather, the client's response to the building's impact upon him. This response is extremely complex. Psychic in nature, it is based upon somatic stimulation. Architecture, even more than agriculture, is the most environmental of man's activities. Unlike the other forms of art— painting, music, dance—its impact upon man is total. Thus the aesthetic enjoyment of an actual building cannot be merely a matter of vision (as most criticism tacitly assumes). It can only be a matter of total sensory perception. And that perceptual process must in turn have adequate biological support. To be truly satisfactory, the building must meet *all* the body's requirements, for it is not just upon the eye but upon the whole man that its impact falls.

From this it follows also that the architect has no direct access to his client's subjective existence: the only channels of communication open to him are objective, somatic. Only by manipulating the physical properties of his environment—heat, air, light, color, odor, sound, sur-

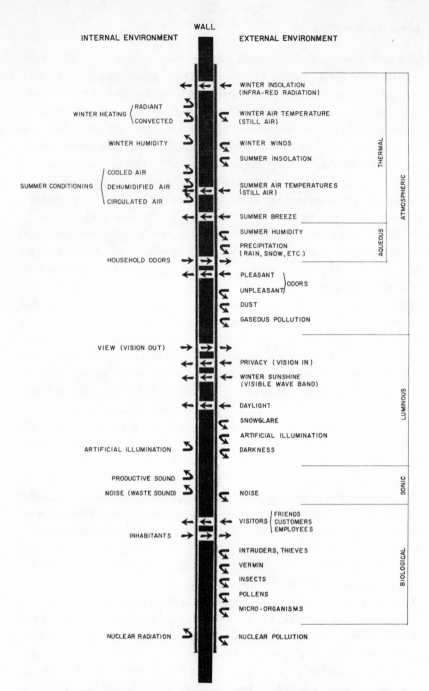

Figure 1–2 The building wall can no longer be considered as an impermeable barrier separating two environments. Rather, it must be designed as a permeable filter, capable of sophisticated response to the wide range of environmental forces acting upon it. Like the uterus, its task is the modulation of these forces in the interests of its inhabitants—the creation of a "third environment" designed in man's favor.

face and space—can the architect communicate with his client at all. And only by *doing it well,* i.e., meeting all man's requirements, objective and subjective, can he create buildings which men may find beautiful.

The matter by no means ends here, however. The architect builds not merely for man at rest, man in the abstract. Typically, he builds for man at work. And this confronts him with another set of contradictions. For work is not a "natural" activity, as Hannah Arendt has brilliantly reminded us.[4] Labor, according to her definition, is "natural" —that is, the use of the whole body to meet its biological needs, to feed it, bathe it, dress it, protect it from attack. Work, on the other hand, is "unnatural"—the use of the hand and the brain to produce the artificial, non-biological world of human artifice (skyscrapers, textbooks, paintings, space ships, highways, symphonies and pharmaceuticals). Both levels of human activity are, of course, fundamental to civilization, and the world of work can only exist as a superstructure on the world of labor. But insofar as we share the world of labor with the beasts, it can fairly be described as both natural and subhuman. Only the world of work, of human thought and artifice, is truly human.

This distinction is not so fine as it might at first appear: it has important consequences for architectural design. For if the architect ever builds for the wholly "natural" man, it will be only in his house, at his biological activities of resting, eating, lovemaking and play. Most other modern building types involve man at work, engaged in a wide spectrum of "unnatural" processes. Each of these involves stress. Stress, as we have seen, comes either from too much or too little stimulation, from sensory "overloading" and "underloading" alike. Biological man requires a dynamic balance, a golden mean between extremes. But modern work knows no such requirements: on the contrary, for maximum output and optimum quality, it sometimes implies environments of absolute constancy (e.g., pharmaceuticals, printing) and often requires extreme conditions never met in nature (e.g., high-temperature metallurgy, cobalt radiation therapy, etc.).

When plotted, these two sets of requirements will seldom lie along the same curve. From this it follows that architecture must meet two distinctly different sets of environmental criteria—those of man at some "unnatural" task, and those of the "unnatural" process itself.

Variety may indeed be the very stuff of man's natural life. But most of our human activities are, to a greater or lesser extent, "unnatural." From the moment we place the young child in kindergarten, we are imposing "unnatural" tasks upon him—placing his eyesight, his posture, his capacity for attention under quite abnormal stress. And this situation grows more acute throughout his education and his normal working life. As an adult, his biological existence is linked to processes which are never completely congruent with his own. Often they involve work which is fractionalized, repetitive and hence often unintelligible to the individual; often, the processes are actually dangerous to him. Only in agriculture does he confront work whose "natural" environment, rhythms and wholeness correspond to his own; but only six out of one hundred American workers are involved nowadays in this work.

The child at school faces a situation not qualitatively different from his father on the job: namely, to accomplish a given amount of work in a given time. Ideally, his physical growth and intellectual development should be steady and parallel. His rate of development should be as high at the end of his school day as at its beginning. In reality, of course, this is impossible. His energies flag as the day advances and nothing but play, food and rest will restore them. The question for architects is how should the classroom intervene in his favor? How to manipulate his external environment so that his learning advances with optimum speed and minimum stress?

It should be immediately apparent that the child's requirements are dynamic and imply a dynamic relationship with his classroom. No classroom should confront the child with a fixed set of day-long environmental norms, e.g., 72°F. air, 50 per cent humidity, 60 foot lamberts at desk top, 45 decibels of sound. Far from being held at some fixed level, the probability is that environmental conditions should be continually changing. *But this change cannot be casual or statistically indeterminate* (if change alone were all that was required, the class could be held in a nearby meadow). It must be a *designed* response to the child's changing requirements. The child may well need less heat at 2 p.m. than at 9 a.m. At day's end he may need less humidity and more oxygen; he may require more light and a different color; he may need a chair that gives a different posture or sound levels higher or lower than the morning. Whatever the requirements are, they could only derive from the child himself, in the experiential circumstances of study. They cannot be met by mechanistic engineers (windowless classrooms, "steady state" controls) nor by formalistic architects who design as though visual perception is the whole of experience.

But the symbiotic relationship between the architectural container and the men and processes contained is nowhere clearer than in the modern hospital. Here we find every degree of biological stress, including that of birth and of death. Here we find a wide range of highly specialized technologies, each with its own environmental requirements. And here we find the narrowest margins for error of any building type: here success or failure are literally matters of life or death. Here, if anywhere, we can observe the integral connections of metabolic function and aesthetic response as shown in Figure 1-1.

The seriously ill patient—above all, the major surgery case—will traverse the full experiential spectrum during his stay at the hospital. Stress will be greatest under surgery. His relationship with his environment can be almost wholly defined in somatic terms. Since he is under total anesthesia, there is no aesthetic aspect to his experience. (It is interesting, in this connection, to note that the two words anesthesia and aesthetic have a common origin in the Greek word meaning "to feel" or "to perceive.")

His gradual process of convalescence—through the recovery room, intensive nursing, regular nursing and ambulatory state, on up to discharge—traverses the full spectrum of experience. Precisely as the metabolic crisis diminishes so will his aesthetic response rise to the front of consciousness. Colors, lights, noises and odors which he was too ill to notice can now become major factors of experience. And their satisfactory manipulation becomes matters of active therapy.

The surgeon and his staff too will meet their greatest period of stress during surgery. At this juncture their requirements will be opposed to those of the patient. Where the latter requires warm moist air (and anti-explosive measures demand even higher humidities), the staff under nervous tension should ideally be submerged in dry, cool air. But since stress for them is of limited duration while any added load might be disastrous for the patient, the room's thermo-atmospheric environment is usually designed in the latter's favor. The staff sweats and suffers and recovers later. On the other hand, the luminous environment of the operating room must be wholly designed in the surgeon's favor (and no contradiction is raised because of the patient's lack of consciousness). The color of the walls, of the uniforms, even of the towels is quite as important to visual acuity of the surgeon as the lighting fixture themselves.

Thus, every decision made in design of the operating room will be based upon functional considerations, objectively evaluated. The very nature of the intervention prohibits any abstractly "aesthetic" considerations. The margin of safety is too narrow to allow the architect the luxury of any formalistic decisions based upon subjective prefer-

13

ences. In varying degrees, this situation will obtain in other specialized areas of the hospital. And it will increase as the hospital comes to be regarded not merely as a container for men and processes but as being itself an actual instrument of therapy. There are many evidences of this tendency already: the hyperbaric chamber where barometric pressure and oxygen content are manipulated in the treatment of both circulatory disorders and gas gangrene; the metabolic surgery suites where body temperatures are reduced to slow the metabolic rate before difficult surgery; the use of saturated atmospheres for serious cases of burn; artificially-cooled, dry air to lighten the thermal stress on cardiac cases; the use of electrostatic precipitation and ultraviolet radiation to produce completely sterile atmospheres for difficult respiratory ailments or to prevent cross-infection from contagious diseases. Here the building is not merely manipulating the natural environment in the patient's favor but actually creating totally new environments with no precedent in nature as specific instruments of therapy.

The exact point in hospitalization at which these environmental manipulations cease to be purely therapeutic and become merely questions of comfort or satisfaction, i.e., the point at which they cease to be functional and become aesthetic problems, is not easy to isolate. Objectionable odors, disturbing noises and lights; uncomfortable beds; lack of privacy; hot, humid atmosphere—all these will work against "beauty" in the hospital room. They may also delay convalescence. We cannot hope to make modern medical procedures "pretty" and the well-adjusted patient will probably want to leave the hospital as soon as possible under any circumstances. All the more reason, then, that every external factor be analyzed as objectively as possible, with a view to removing all unnecessary stress.

All of this suggests the possibility of establishing, much more precisely than ever before, an objective basis for aesthetic decision. It would be mistaken to attach too much importance to aesthetics in hospital design; but it would be equally foolish to minimize it. It cannot, in any case, be avoided. Everything the architect does, every form he adopts or material he specifies, has aesthetic repercussions. His problem is thus not Hamlet's: to act or not to act. It is rather to act wisely, understanding the total consequences of his decision.

If the architect's aesthetic standards are to be placed on a firmer factual basis than the one on which they now stand, he will need the help of physiologists and psychologists to do it. Architecture needs a much more systematic and detailed investigation of man's actual

14

psychosomatic relationship with his environment than has yet been attempted, at least in architecture. It is not at all accidental that we can find the broad lines of such research appearing in the field of aerospace medicine. For man can only penetrate space by encapsulating himself in a container of terrestrial environment. And to accomplish this he must ask fundamental questions: what, actually, *is* this environment? What specifically is its effect upon us? What *is* its relation to human pleasure and delight?

In the design of the space vehicle, for example, it is no longer possible to say where problems of simple biological survival leave off and more complex questions of human satisfaction begin. Clearly, they constitute different ends of one uninterrupted spectrum of human experience. It is very probable that the upper end of this spectrum, involving as it does man's innermost subjective existence, can never be fully explored or understood. But it could certainly be far better understood than it is today, even among architects and doctors.

American society today employs some 270 distinct building types to provide the specialized environments required by its multiform activities. Most of them embody contradictions which must be resolved at two different levels: first between the persons and processes contained and then between their container and the natural environment. Respect for these two conditions is mandatory if the building is to be operationally successful. And yet, respect for these two conditions will often leave the architect with little room in which he can manipulate the building for purely formal, i.e., aesthetic, ends.

Most contemporary failures in architecture (and they are very many) stem either from a failure to understand this situation or else from a refusal to come to terms with it. Of course, no building can grow like an organism. Architects do not work with living tissue, with its powers of cellular division and genetic memory. In this sense, buildings must always be designed by men and these men will always bring to the task preconceived ideas of what forms they ought to assume. As Ernst Fischer, the Austrian philosopher has said, a good honey bee will often put a bad architect to shame. "But what from the very first distinguishes the most incompetent of architects from the best of bees is that the architect has built a cell in his head before he constructs it in wax." [5] Good or bad, beautiful or ugly, the building is always the expression of somebody's creative ambitions. Today, more than ever in history, these ambitions must be contained, structured and disciplined by objectively verifiable terms of reference.

NOTES

1. Lecture. 29 October 1963. School of Architecture, Columbia University, New York.

2. Lecture. 12 November 1963. Sensory Deprivation and Psychological Stress. Columbia University, New York.

3. Heron, Woodburn. 1957. Scientific American. N.Y. 196: 1 (52).

4. Arendt, Hannah. 1959. The Human Condition, Doubleday, New York.

5. Fischer, Ernst. 1963. The Necessity of Art. Pelican Book, New York, p. 17.

Physiology and Anatomy
of Urination

ALEXANDER KIRA

Although Fitch is probably correct in claiming that discussions of architecture have often proceeded as if the only important human or social dimension of architecture was how a building looked to the educated eye, the fact is that buildings, if they are to meet even the minimal requirements of functional adequacy, must necessarily respect the anatomical and physiological characteristics of the organism. Indeed, the importance of human biology as a constraint on design is an ancient architectural notion, having been discussed by Vitruvius, who in the first century A.D. advised practitioners of architectural design to acquire a basic knowledge of medicine. Some architects, for example Leonardo and Alberti in Renaissance Italy and Le Corbusier in our own time, have worked with the idea of basing a formal geometry of design on the dimensions of the human figure.

However, it is possible to conclude that respect for the constraining power of man's biological nature has declined since the Industrial Revolution, and that contemporary architecture, partly because of its technical prowess, has tended to overlook the role of biological factors. As a result, for several decades now, there has been a growing sentiment in architectural and environmental design circles, particularly in schools of design, to reintroduce a deliberate concern for anatomical and biological studies.

This new emphasis on the role of biology in the practice of architecture has taken form in the development of specialized fields of scientific inquiry, such as ergonomics, or human factors engineering, and anthropometrics. Ergonomics is concerned primarily with developing work environments that are compatible with human physiological processes. Anthropometrics compiles anatomical measurements for different age groups and populations, thus providing an objective basis for determining the size of spaces and equipment. Both specialties examine in minute detail the characteristics of the human organism at rest and in movement, often in laboratory environments. These data are then used to design equipment and spaces that will fit the human body, not only in static terms but also when performing the move-

Reprinted from Alexander Kira, "Physiology and Anatomy of Urination," and "Design Considerations for Urination," in *The Bathroom, Criteria for Design* (New York: Bantam Books, 1967), pp. 138–151. © 1966 by Cornell University. Reprinted by permission of Bantam Books, Inc.

ments necessary to the task at hand. These studies have been applied with greatest effect to the design of industrial and military equipment and to the design of highly specialized environments that impose unusual stress on the organism, such as space capsules and submarines.

The significance of Kira's research is that he has applied to a domestic facility, the bathroom, the same careful method of investigating the requirements for comfortable and efficient operation ordinarily used in the study of industrial and military equipment. The selection reprinted deals with the design of equipment for urination within the home. In the book from which it is taken, Kira also analyzes facilities for washing, bathing, and defecation. The study was based on a thorough review of the previous anthropometric and ergonomic literature; a field survey of user attitudes, practices, and preferences; and detailed observations of personal hygiene activities in a laboratory specially constructed for the research.

☐

The Process of Urination

Urination, or micturition, is the process of excreting from the body the waste fluids produced by the kidneys. The kidney is a highly discriminating organ which processes the body's supply of blood. It eliminates varying amounts of waste substances according to the body's needs. The urine, which is the final excretory product, is a composite not only of waste products which may have been in the blood but also of foreign substances and the excess products of the metabolic processes. Because the kidneys function to maintain the constancy of the body's internal environment, the composition of urine may vary considerably from one discharge to another. The quantity of urine which is produced over a 24-hour period varies directly with the amount of fluid intake but generally averages between 1,000 and 1,400 cc. Normal urine has an amber color and a very faint odor unless allowed to stand at room temperature for any length of time. As the urine is produced, it is carried through the ureters, or ducts, to the bladder where it accumulates until discharged from the body through the urethral openings.

Inasmuch as body posture has an effect on blood circulation, it can also affect urine composition and volume. The effect, however, is not significant unless there is considerable change or considerable stress from one posture and there is no evidence to suggest that posture has any appreciable bearing on the act of urination itself, either in terms of comfort or facilitating or hindering the process as is the case for defecation.[1]

Although the process of toilet training with respect to urination does not appear to be as complex and fraught with psychological overtones as defecation, it does, nevertheless, demand a similar period of training and requires a similar degree of neuromuscular differentiation and control. The development of voluntary bladder control is generally not achieved until from 18 to 30 months. Usually nighttime control takes longer. Full control and the ability to void without any assistance is usually not achieved until well into the third or fourth year. Because of the differences in the positioning of the bladder, males generally have greater difficulty in developing proper control since the anal and urethral sphincters are so close together as to require a particularly fine neuromuscular differentiation.[2] In the female the two sphincters are separated by the vagina. While this simplifies the problem of learning to control each of the sphincters separately, the relation of the vagina to the bladder and the urethral sphincter often results in a sympathetic stimulation leading to urination. This is particularly true during the later months of pregnancy when the ever increasing pressure on the bladder results in more and more frequent urges to urinate. It may also be caused by vaginal stimulation prior to, or during, intercourse, especially if the bladder is at all full.

In this connection it may also be noted that the urge to urinate frequently is also very common among the aged. Largely this is due to an atrophying of the kidneys and bladder and a weakening of the sphincter muscles. Another fairly common problem among the aged is incontinence, particularly among prostate patients. This gradual degeneration of body functions may be regarded in some respects as a reversal of the initial developmental processes as, for example, in the loss of neuromuscular controls, which in some instances causes aged men to be as inept at urinating as small boys.

Anatomy

Anatomical differences between the male and female result in certain aspects of the urination process being different for each of the sexes. Aside from the problem of developing controls, the most significant and obvious difference is in the location and nature of the actual urethral openings from which the urine is discharged. In the female, the urethra is located just in front of the vagina, within the labial folds, and well inside the body envelope. As a consequence, for all practical purposes, she has no control over the direction of the urine stream. As we shall see later, this has certain consequences which restrict the posture assumed and the kind of facilities which might be provided. In the male, on the other hand, the urethral opening is located in the penis, thus lying outside the body envelope and permitting control of the urine stream within the entire volume circumscribed by its possible trajectory.

Design Considerations for Urination

Female Urination. The nearly universal custom in Western societies is for females to urinate in a sitting position (or squatting, if no support is available). From a purely physiological viewpoint, females could perform in a standing position as well. Urinating in such a position, however, inevitably results in soiling oneself, both directly and from splash, since the female's urine stream cannot be directed away from its essentially vertical axis. In addition, the complications of present-day clothing present varying degrees of handicap to comfortable, or possible, urinating in any position other than sitting, without virtually disrobing, because of the present tendency for some form of girdle, or otherwise restrictive and elasticized undergarment, to be worn virtually universally and constantly—even by teenagers. In this connection, it may be noted that attempts have been made over the years to provide a "stand-up" urinal for females similar to the standard men's wall-hung urinal, except for a longer projecting basin, primarily with the aim of improving the traffic capacity and particularly the sanitation of public facilities. In using these fixtures, a woman would have to partially disrobe and then straddle the projecting lip of the fixture in more or less a standing position. The practical difficulties of using the fixture in terms of clothing, combined with the psychological resistances to being publicly uncovered, have resulted in relatively little acceptance of it. The problem of exposure has been resolved by placing the fixture in a stall, but this has negated the potential advantages of economy and rapid turnover in use.

It seems obvious, however, that under present circumstances, particularly in the home where the problem of sanitation, compared with public facilities, can be considered for practical purposes to be nonexistent, the most convenient and comfortable position for a woman to assume for urination is a sitting one. If we accept this premise, the problem then is largely one of making appropriate minor modifications in whatever fixtures might evolve for defecation since the basic requirements are very similar. Accordingly, the rest of this discussion, since we are concerned primarily with facilities in the home, focuses on the particular problems posed by male urination which is almost overwhelmingly accomplished from a standing position and which poses major sanitary problems.

Male Urination. Males can urinate equally conveniently and comfortably from either a sitting/squatting, or standing, position. However, the restrictive effects of clothing, the sexual considerations which are involved, and the extreme convenience have caused men to favor the standing position almost universally. In general, men will urinate in a sitting/squatting position only when this activity takes place in conjunction with defecation and they have already assumed a sitting position. Insofar as urination, per se, is concerned, we must regard it as primarily a standing activity.

Because of the male's anatomy and his early learned ability to control the trajectory of the urine stream, there is, in some respects, relatively little problem of any substantial self-soiling in a standing position.[3] The qualification depends upon the nature of the facilities available. That there are serious soiling problems associated with the use of current home facilities may be attested to by any housewife or cleaning woman. The soiled fixtures and the soiled, discolored, and rotted floors and walls, which everyone is familiar with, stem from the use of the water closet, which is completely inadequate for this purpose, instead of a separate "urinal." The key to these problems lies in understanding the particular characteristics of the male urine stream.

Urine passing through the slit-like urethral opening is emitted in the form of a thin sheet which twists and spirals for several inches and then disintegrates into a centrifugal spray. (See Figure 2–1.) Both the point of disintegration and the maximum diameter of the spray are directly proportional to the velocity of the stream, which is a function of the bladder pressure. A low velocity produces an increment (each twist in the integrated phase of the stream) of approximately ⅜ of an inch; extreme velocity an increment of almost 2 inches. Normal velocity produces an increment of approximately 1 inch. In every instance, however, the centrifugal action causes the stream to disintegrate and assume a roughly conical shape. It is this dispersion which is responsible for a substantial share of the soiling both of the self and of the surroundings which can occur when urinating from a standing position, and when the receiving container is not as close as, for example,

22

Figure 2–1 Typical Dispersion and Splash Pattern of a Simulated Male Urine Stream.

a wall-hung urinal which intercepts the stream before the point of dispersion.

Another aspect which must be considered is the inability of the male to predict, or accurately position, the *initial* point of impact of the urine stream. Although the degree of accuracy is reasonable in most instances, there are a sufficient number of "accidents," or gross distortions, attributable generally to temporary and unnoticed dermal adhesions of the urethral opening. Once the activity has begun, however, most adult males can, by a process of successive corrective maneuvers, exercise fairly accurate control thereafter. The notable exceptions are the ill and intoxicated, the very young, or the very old and infirm.

The normal water closet, however, presents a relatively poor target, particularly because of the psychological resistances involved in its use. Because of the general taboos on the elimination processes, and the particular aversions to being directly and actively aware of elimination taking place, most men will try to avoid urinating into the standing pan water—the easiest and most natural target—in order to avoid the embarrassment of being heard, since the noise, particularly with a full bladder, can be quite considerable and easily identified. Once this decision is made, the choice of target areas is limited to the sides and front and back walls of the bowl. In the majority of water closets the bowl configurations are such that these areas are quite small and difficult to hit with any degree of accuracy. Because of the necessity to stand up close to the front of the bowl to catch the dribble at the end of the action, the possibilities are further limited to the sides and the back. However, since the back wall in most cases is vertical or nearly so, the target area presented is quite small and is useful for only a brief period since the length of the stream trajectory continuously varies. This leaves only the side walls which present a feasible elongated target. Since this area rarely exceeds 2 inches by 7 or 8 inches it becomes obvious that not only is the proper trial and error maneuvering difficult to accomplish successfully, but also half of the stream spray inevitably falls outside the bowl.

Still another problem which arises in the use of the water closet is the back splash which results when the urine stream hits a hard surface. (See Figure 2–1.) This problem will, of course, arise and have to be dealt with in any container. However, it poses a particular problem with respect to use of the water closet since this fixture has obviously been primarily designed to accommodate defecation, and urination has been left to be accomplished as best it can.

Any stream of relatively nonviscous liquid hitting a hard surface (including a body of liquid) will result in a considerable splash. The direction and extent of this rebound, or splash, is determined not only by the force with which the stream strikes the surface, but also, and more importantly, by the configuration of the surface and the angle at which the stream hits the surface. Proper manipulation of this latter factor can appreciably reduce the quantity of splash and can control its direction.

DESIGN CONSIDERATIONS

For a fixture to adequately accommodate male urination from a standing position, the following criteria should be observed. The receiving container must be so positioned, relative to the point of origin, as to intercept the urine stream before the point of appreciable disintegration. The container must be of a size and shape which will present an adequate "target" under a variety of circumstances. Use of the fixture should be relatively noiseless. The internal configuration of the container should be such as to avoid or minimize back splash, and the production of aerosols. The resulting fixture should not be obvious in appearance, and should probably look as little like the urinal found in "men's rooms" as possible.

In order to adequately provide for male urination in the home there are several possible approaches which may be taken. The first, and most obvious, is to provide a standard wall-hung urinal since this satisfies all the necessary functional criteria. It is unlikely, however, to meet with general acceptance, chiefly because of various psychological reasons. In addition, it may be argued on practical grounds that such a fixture would entail too much extra space and expense even if the standard urinal were to be adapted for household tank-type operation. In view of all the evidence, this solution might as well be dismissed for the moment, even though it represents the simplest and most direct one.

A second approach is to try to make appropriate modifications to the water closet. This would offer the advantage of being relatively unobvious and at the same time relatively inexpensive. Extensive investigation, however, indicates that this is a next to impossible task. This is particularly true with respect to the low water closet since, as will shortly be made clear, the farther the container is from the point of origin, the greater the problem of containment of the stream. As is so often the case, in trying to accomplish several functions, each is compromised. The more the fixture is modified to accommodate urination the poorer it becomes for its primary function of defecation.

A third possibility, which might be mentioned in passing, is that, instead of accommodating the standing male, perhaps things should somehow be so arranged so that he would have to sit. From all practical and psychological viewpoints, this would seem, however, to be totally unworkable. Aside from changing a natural and age-old habit, it is likely to meet with strong resistance, from the aspect of convenience, particularly since in recent years the male has become ever more accustomed to the speed and effortlessness of the urinal, which is now almost universal. The idea of having to substantially undress for an operation which is presently so simple would certainly meet with considerable opposition. There is also not much question but that it would encounter a great deal of psychological resistance since it would, in effect, deny the male the free use of his greatest glory and would condemn him to assume the position of a woman.

The final and most logical possibility is to attempt to evolve a totally new fixture which will satisfy all of the criteria described.

Stream Characteristics and Positioning of Container. As pointed out earlier, the major problem posed by the standing male urinating in a water closet is the centrifugal breakup and dispersion of the urine stream which results in considerable soiling of the self and the surrounding area.

The behavior of a simulated stream was studied, assuming a point of origin of 29 inches above the floor, relative first, to an intercepting plane at a height of 16 inches (standard water closet), and then to an intercepting plane at a height of 9 inches (point of assumed interception of a floor mounted urinal and of the proposed squat closet). In

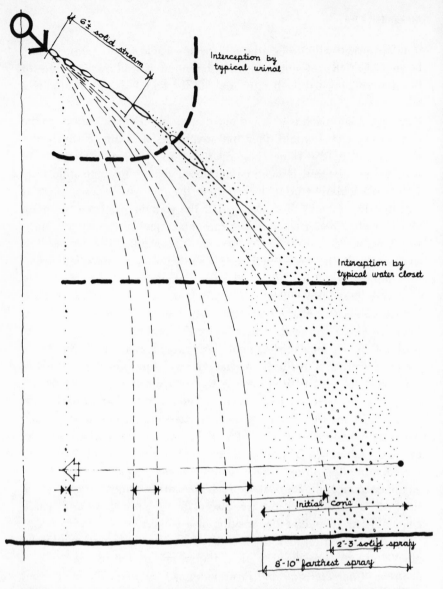

Figure 2–2 Dispersion and Containment Characteristics of Simulated Male Urine Stream. The stream at any given moment assumes the form of a warped conical solid which shrinks and shifts its base over a period of time. The size of the receiving container is also directly related to its distance from the point of origin.

every instance, the full extent of the spray indicated in Figure 2–2 could be measured within a 30-second period, the assumed average time of urination. Graus cites 45 seconds as the average time in military situations.[4] This higher figure is undoubtedly due to the opportunities for urination or rather, the lack of them. The actual range, however, is quite considerable and can vary from 10 or 15 seconds up to a minute and a half, or longer, depending on how full the bladder is. It should be noted that these dispersion figures for a simulated stream represent minimums which are rarely achieved in actuality. Depending upon the particular angle of the stream trajectory, there is likely to be a greater dispersion the flatter the trajectory and the greater the pressure. In addition, incidental dermal adhesions can result in an immediate and erratic dispersion of the stream.

When we consider that the stream assumes the form of a warped conical solid with a shifting base, it is obvious, as indicated in Figure 2–2, that the size and shape of the necessary container or enclosure is directly related to its distance from the point of origin in order to completely contain the stream. The closer the container is to the point of origin, the more compact it can be and the less the danger of accidental soiling. In view of the range of heights of adult males, the front lip of the container should be set at a minimum height of 24 inches from the floor, the height at which regular wall-hung urinals are commonly set. At this height, the container needs to have a minimum opening dimension approximately 10 inches by 10 inches.

The container must also be so shaped and positioned that it can be more or less straddled in order to catch the dribble and drip at the conclusion of urination, again, in a fashion similar to existing wall-hung urinals.

Size and Shape of Container. The particular combination of size and shape may vary over a considerable range, so long as the container meets the criteria of presenting an adequate target area and of minimizing and containing back splash as well as dispersion.

In terms of shape, the most crucial point is that the contouring be such as to keep back splash to a minimum. To allow for variable bladder pressures and/or variable stream trajectories, the cross section should be continuously variable so that the surface maintains a constant relationship to the stream. (See Figure 2–3.) The effect of this angular relationship between the stream and the impact surface is shown in Figure 2–3, which reports the results of a series of tests with a simulated vertical stream at maximum pressure (twist length of 2 inches). As indicated, the smaller the angle between the stream and the impact surface the less the resulting splash. In general, it would be desirable to keep this relationship within a 30-degree limit in both a lateral and a longitudinal direction. While a properly designed single warped planar surface can keep splash within reasonable limits, it

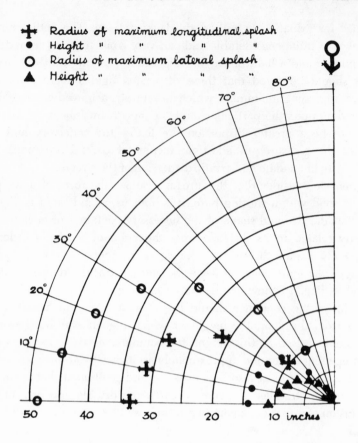

Figure 2–3 Variations in Splash Effects according to Angular Relationship between Stream and Contact Surface.

would obviously be desirable to warp both surfaces. Offhand, this would suggest that a spherical configuration might be the most appropriate. However, if we take into account the effect of the continuously varying angle between the stream and the surface, it becomes apparent that the ideal shape is one which approximates a funnel. (See Figure 2–4.) Such a form would result in a minimum of splash and would direct most of it forward. It is also critical that the axis of the container be set at an appropriate angle. In the course of normal urination the angle formed by a maximum trajectory rarely exceeds 60 degrees from the vertical. Accordingly, the angle at which the container should be set lies in the 40 to 50 degree range. This is the "critical" range in the sense that maximum trajectory equals maximum pressure, which in turn equals maximum dispersion and splash. As the stream trajectory

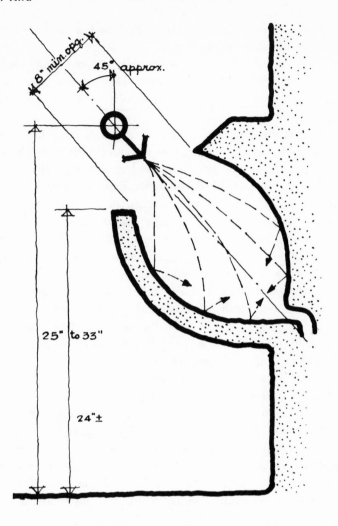

Figure 2–4 Sectional View of Stream Showing Necessary Dimensions and Configurations for Containment.

drops off into the 20 and 10 degree range it begins to form a larger angle with the surface, but the problems at this range are considerably less.

Experiments have also suggested that a single ridge placed in the longitudinal plane of the stream can assist in further reducing the problem of containment since it has the effect of dividing the stream and deflecting it laterally. As a result, it would be possible in some circumstances to provide a smaller container. A divider is likely to be particularly useful in the area of greatest pressure impact. Many models of wall-hung urinals have, in fact, such a divider as a result of the trap protruding into the bowl.

Another feature which may be desirable is something which would serve as a "target" in the critical area. This might conceivably be the ridge just described or possibly some very obvious marker set in the surface.

Insofar as the precise determination of a size for the container is concerned, this is again a function of both the shape of the container and its positioning and can be arrived at only after these other variables have been established within the limits set forth.

Avoidance of Noise. The avoidance of a distinctive and clearly recognizable noise should be a major consideration in any design. Pan water such as exists in water closets is the most obvious thing to be avoided unless it is normally missed as in wall-hung urinals. It may well be that a dry container which is flushed is the best way to cope with this problem, since the noise of flushing, while it meets with some objections, is not nearly so embarrassing to most people as the direct noise of urination.[5] In the event that materials other than chinaware are used, attention should be paid to their denseness, or mass, in terms of drumming and generating sound.

Controls. Since we are considering a fixture intended solely for stand-up use, the controls for flushing should be easily reached from a standing position. This is perhaps best accomplished by a hand operated control located approximately 36 to 48 inches from the floor. A foot operated control unless it is simple to clean is apt to be undesirable from a cleaning standpoint. Again, caution should be observed with respect to ambiguous or dual (hand or foot) operated controls which are both awkward to use and unsanitary as a result.

SUMMARY: DESIGN POSSIBILITIES

In order to illustrate the application of the criteria developed in this paper, one possible approach to a home urinal is shown in Figure 2–5 in outline form. The fixture is assumed to be a funnel-like container which pulls down, or out, from a recess in the wall, much like a pullman lavatory. In order to save space and utilize other existing plumbing it has also been assumed that this fixture would be mounted over the water closet and would use the same tank for flushing, the same vent space, and other features. In the illustration, the urinal is shown in combination with the low-squat water closet suggested and illustrated in a previous section. Use of this water closet assumes that it can be straddled so that the dimensions of the urinal can be kept at a

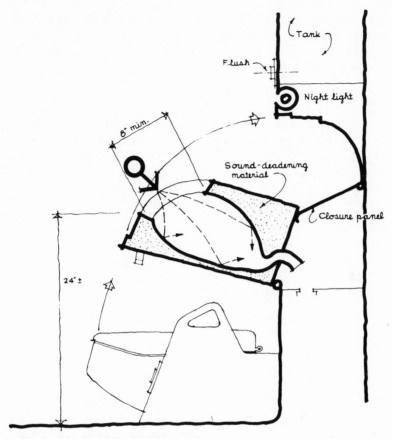

Figure 2–5 Experimental Home Urinal Incorporating Suggested Criteria.
One possible approach to the home urinal might be in the form of a pull-down funnel-like fixture set over the toilet.

minimum. It has also been assumed that the fixture would normally be dry and that it might be either manually or automatically flushed when closed up into the wall.

As proposed, this combination of fixtures might also lend itself fairly readily to some form of prefabricated assembly, complete with the necessary electrical controls, night-light, and so forth.

The criteria upon which this particular proposal rests are that: the fixture be available, be functional, and be obvious as to its purpose, but only when needed and in use. Undoubtedly, these same criteria might be met in a variety of other ways. In some instances, it may be preferable to provide a regular separate urinal similar to that illustrated in Figure 2–4.

31

NOTES

1. Smith, H. W., *The Kidney—Structure and Function in Health and Disease,* New York: Oxford University Press, 1951.
2. Despert, J. L., "Urinary Control and Enuresis," *Psychosomatic Medicine,* Vol. 6, No. 4, 1944, p. 294.
3. On the other hand the relatively minor but inevitable problem which does exist, is still significant enough to have been memorialized in the scatological rhyme familiar to every American male: "No matter how much you jiggle and squeeze, the last drop always goes down your knees."
4. Graus, H., "A Scientific Approach to Military Plumbing Fixture Requirements," *Air Conditioning, Heating and Ventilating,* February 1957, p. 96.
5. Langford, Marilyn, *Personal Hygiene Attitudes and Practices in 1000 Middle-Class Households,* Memoir 393, Ithaca, N.Y.: Cornell University Agricultural Experiment Station, 1965, pp. 29, 30.

3

Cultural Variability in Physical Standards

AMOS RAPOPORT AND NEWTON WATSON

Kira's research into bathroom design provides a good illustration of the difficulties inherent in the methodology of equipment studies, which often assume that information about universal biological characteristics can be used to project new and more efficient environmental designs. What Kira's selection demonstrates is that even when one is dealing with criteria that relate to so called hard information, it is important for the designer to respect the interpretations that different groups of users put on the particular facilities and design forms and the biological activities to which they relate. For example, Kira found it necessary to modify his designs to take account of the clothing styles of Western women, feelings of shame about urinary activity, attitudes toward urine odor, and the high valuation placed on toilet privacy.

The same general principle, but applied to a broader range of environmental situations, is illustrated by Rapoport and Watson's survey of physical standards in Western nations, India, and Japan. Physical and environmental standards are those rules or norms institutionalized in a society that define acceptable levels of daylight, heat, noise, and room and furniture size. They are written down in the form of building codes established by governmental ordinance or are described in handbooks of architectural practice. To some degree these standards have been derived from ergonomic and anthropometric studies carried out by building research organizations in each country, although in large part they also derive from unconscious cultural processes.

Rapoport and Watson make several points about the degree of cultural variability in these standards. (1) The situations for which it is judged necessary to establish standards differ between societies. For example, American charts show a number of activities, such as drinking at a bar or eating at a counter, that are missing in Indian handbooks. (2) Given the fact that a group of countries will have standards applying to similar conditions, the standards will vary widely. This generalization applies not only to space standards, which architects have known for a long time possess "low criticality," but applies as well to standards for heat, light, and noise, which usually have

Reprinted from Amos Rapoport and Newton Watson, "Cultural Variability in Physical Standards," *Transactions of the Bartlett Society*, Bartlett School of Architecture, University College, London 6 (1967–1968): 63–83.

been assumed to be biologically determined and thus to have "high criticality." (3) Finally, Rapoport and Watson point out that standards differ not only across cultures but within them, depending upon the social context in which the facility is used. Standards for tread and riser dimensions in stair design differ for interior, exterior, domestic, and ceremonial staircases.

The authors conclude their selection by asserting that an awareness of the cultural component present in standards that relate to biological factors should be an important aid to architects and designers who practice in different societies.

☐

Recent attempts to develop user requirements as a basis for physical design in building reflect the desire for a more rational approach in the light of the increasing complexity of the problems involved in design and the increasing separation between designer and user. In seeking for hard data it is understandable that physical determinants such as anthropometrics and ergonomics, as well as comfort needs with regard to light, heat and sound should until recently have received more attention than topics within the more complex socio-cultural and psychological realms. Recently, however, a growing interest in the socio-cultural and psychological forces involved in the development and use of space organizations has led to work on these aspects in a number of places.

E. T. Hall [1] was among the first to draw attention to the cultural variability of the use of space, the scale of spaces, needs for privacy, tolerance of noise and overcrowding, and the like. Similarly, in his recent work on the bathroom, Alexander Kira [2] has pointed out that while the problems of personal hygiene have remained constant, the ways in which people have coped with them have varied widely depending on the beliefs, fears and values which have motivated them at any particular time and place. He gives many examples of different attitudes to privacy, cleanliness, odors and comfort, and suggests that it is such attitudes rather than mere utility which give insights into, for example, the preference for showers rather than baths and other significant planning decisions regarding personal hygiene.

It is the thesis of this selection that even physical standards which might be regarded as "hard" and quantifiable data are themselves affected by cultural attitudes and social forces prevailing at the time and place of their inception. Such standards, in common with most human activities and institutions, are the result of a combination of

34

constant and variable factors. In the area which we are discussing, the constant aspects which set certain possible ranges and limits are man's physiological and anatomical characteristics, while the variables are *culturally defined choices.* The fact that choice exists is due to what one could term the low *criticality* of architecture [3] since choice plays a major role only where criticality is low. In this paper we will discuss a number of examples of physical standards of apparently high criticality—*anthropometrics, noise, thermal comfort and lighting*—and try to show that they contain a rather important component of choice. It is not, of course, our intention to deny the need for the existence of standards and ranges of acceptability and non-acceptability but rather to suggest that the physical determinants of built form are a more complex and subtle matter than is commonly accepted.

That this is so is better known outside the design professions than it is within them. René Dubos,[4] for example, has pointed out that we respond actively and often creatively to environmental stimuli—we shut out some, modify others through symbolic and other socio-cultural mechanisms and our responses to these stimuli depend on the meaning which we attach to them, depending on our cultural background. Man can therefore use the effects of these stimuli for his own purposes which he selects.

Douglas H. K. Lee has similarly discussed "the role of attitude in response to environmental stress" [5] pointing out that the influence of attitude increases as the severity of the stress decreases, i.e., as the criticality goes down. However, even in highly critical situations the influence of cultural attitudes can be quite striking. For example, it has even been suggested, although not universally accepted, that cultural attitudes "can determine such basic physiological responses as glandular secretions, sexual appetites, the pulse rate, the direction of peristalsis and so on." [6] The fact that responses to pain, whether caused by injury or disease, seem to be affected by cultural attitudes as expressed in child-rearing practices, expectations of roles and the like seems, however, to have been well documented.[7]

Anthropometrics

In establishing a starting-point for physical design, the size of the human body is often considered in relation to the equipment which it uses and the swept volumetric zones which it occupies when in movement. It is known that there are variations of human size due to heredity. A

35

comparison of the body sizes of American Whites and Negroes with Japanese (for example) shows the following differences:

	Mean Height	Mean Weight
American Whites	68.4 in.	155 lb. (11 st. 1 lb.)
American Negroes	68.0 in.	152 lb. (10 st. 12 lb.)
Japanese	63.5 in.	121 lb. (8 st. 9 lb.)[8]

These variations concern the manufacturers of "off-the-peg" clothing for civilian and military use. NATO, for example, was forced into making comparative anthropometric studies of American and Southeast European troops from Italy, Greece and Turkey in order to establish ranges of equipment sizes which would be required.[9] This variability of the human body has been taken seriously by services supply branches in spite of the jokes about ill-fitting clothing which surround quartermasters' stores. The variation within groups has been considered along a normal curve and the stress has been on establishing ranges of dimensions and tolerance limits rather than precise data.[10] Less commonly considered has been variability over time. It has recently been pointed out that US soldiers in World War II were 0.7 in. taller and 13 lb. heavier on average than World War I GIs (67.7 in. compared with 68.4, 142 lb. compared with 155).[11] The changes in size among the Japanese since the end of the war have also received attention. While these increases over time have been attributed to improved diet, fashion probably also plays a part. A comparison of the ideals of feminine beauty as revealed in paintings and advertising are a clear indication of this; compare, for example, the currently fashionable slim and boyish figures with those of Rubens, or the deliberately distorted feet, ears, lips, head shapes and degree of obesity of various cultures.

Variations in size and body shape between different sub-cultural groups within a single culture is another aspect which has recently been discussed. There are the rather obvious differences between military and civilian populations due to the selection process involved and there are even variations between different branches of the armed forces.[12] A curious difference, more difficult to explain, is that, for example, between American lorry drivers and research workers; as a group the former average 68.5 in. and 167 lb. while the latter average 70.6 in. and 167 lb.—with consequent very different body proportions.[13]

36

All these variations in body size suggest the fallacy of the "average man" concept. But the influence of anthropometrics on design is made even more complex by the effects of the way man moves and uses equipment. Since motor habits and gestures vary considerably with culture,[14] we may well expect this to introduce further variations into anthropometric data leading to variations in the types, sizes and arrangements of anthropometric space requirements. That this is indeed the case is shown by the differences between the recommended space standards for certain basic and similar activities as well as the great number of activities found in certain cultures and not in others. For example, American standards recommend a minimum width of 5 ft. 4 in. for two people facing each other in a dining booth. This dining pattern is not shown at all in Indian data, but for two people facing each other across a dining *table* the American dimension is 6 ft. 2 in., while in India it is 5 ft. 6 in. (i.e., 8 in. less). The Indian data show additional requirements for eating in a squatting position (6 ft. 6 in.) and also distinguish between informal and formal situations with different dimensions, both for dining at a table and in a squatting position [15] (see Figures 3–1 and 3–2).

The American charts also show a number of activities which are missing in the Indian examples (drinking at a counter, drinking at a bar, etc.), while the Indian charts show many examples missing in Western charts (squatting for both toilet and eating, meditation positions, Yogi exercise position, braiding hair, worshipping positions, receiving various vendors at the door, story-telling to a group of many children, etc.). For any given activity the variety of positions in India seems greater, involving formal and informal situations, different types of furniture (traditional and Western) and other variations. Food preparation, washing and toilet activities are totally different because the ways of doing things and equipment used differ. For example, double beds in India are 4 ft. 9½ in. × 6 ft. 2½ in., in Britain 4 ft. 6½ in. × 6 ft. 6 in. Kitchen counters in India are 2 ft. 4 in. for traditional equipment, 2 ft. 9 in. for Western equipment, and in the US 3 ft. 0 in. While these differences are perhaps to be expected between Eastern and Western cultures, they are also found *within* Western cultures. For example, in Germany we find anthropometric data for a woman beating out a rug outdoors [16] which, not surprisingly, is missing in US data. There are also marked differences between the standards recommended for similar activities between more comparable ways of life.

For example, the domestic WC cubicle is usually reduced to a mini-

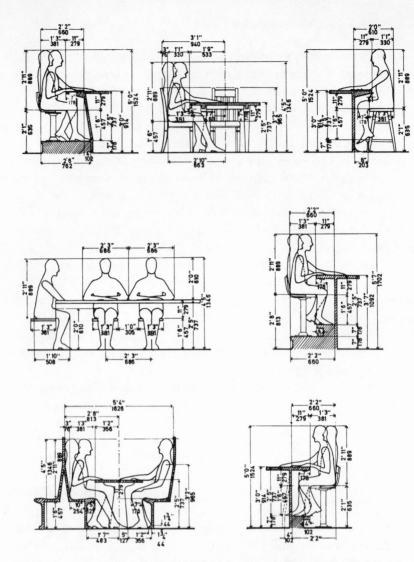

Figure 3–1 American Anthropometric Standards. Source: Timesaver Standards (New York: McGraw-Hill, 4th ed., 1966), p. 15.

mum, and any oversizing by the designer is regarded as waste space. Yet we find a variation of 20 cm. (8 in.) between the widths recommended by German, US and British standards which amounts to about 25% of the width.

British	70-75 cm.	(*Space in the Home*. London: HMSO, 1968.)
	2 ft. 3¼ in.-2 ft. 5¼ in.	
US	80-90 cm.	(*Timesaver Standards*. New York: McGraw-Hill,
	2 ft. 7¼ in.-2 ft. 11 in.	4th ed. 1966.)
Germany	80 cm.	(Rainer Wolff, *Das Kleine Haus*. Munich:
	2 ft. 7¼ in.	Callway, 1959.)

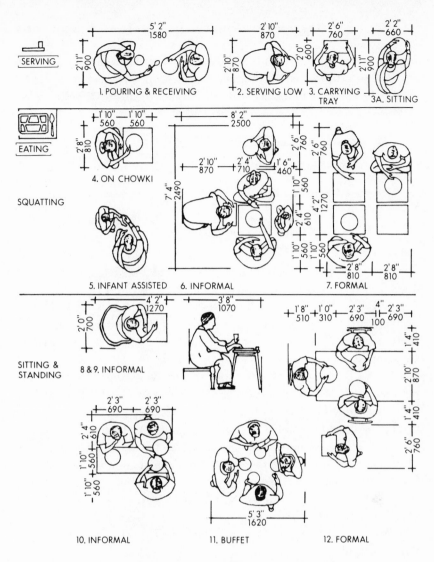

Figure 3–2   Indian Anthropometric Standards. Source: CIB Bulletin, 1, 2 (1966):16.

Even between England and Scotland we find differences, for example, in the recommended volumes for linen storage:

Scotland	0.9 m.³ (31.9 cu. ft.)
England	0.4-0.6 m.³ (14.1-21.2 cu. ft.)
Sweden	0.14-0.33 m.³ (4.9-11.6 cu. ft.)[17]

One wonders why the thrifty Scots collect so much linen!

Stairs might be thought to represent an area of particularly high criticality yet even here we commonly find rather considerable variations. In the United States 2 storeys is the maximum allowed for walking up, as it is in the UK (where 3 is allowed for maisonettes), while in France 4–5 storeys is still commonly used. If we examine rules of thumb formulae, handbooks and regulations regarding tread-riser relationships, we find a great variability and possible range.

Common rule of thumb (in Britain)	riser X tread = 66 in.
	2 riser + tread = 23 in.
Britain (*Specification*, 1968, Vol. 1, p. 252)	2 riser + tread = 22½-25 in.
Germany (Neufert, op. cit.)	2 riser + tread = 23.8-25 in.
	(norm 24.4 in.)
US (NY City Code and National Board of Fire Underwriters cited in *Timesaver Standards*)	riser X tread = 70-75 in.

None of these suggest optima but give "acceptable" ranges which vary a good deal. If maxima and minima for both riser and tread are fixed, the range is still great. For R between 7–9 in. and T between 8½–11½ in. there are 35 configurations possible using ½ in. intervals only, and these recommended maxima and minima themselves can be seen to vary a great deal.

Alberti (Book 1 ch. 3) was quite specific when he stated that the number of steps had to be odd so that "we always set our right foot into the temple first" saying that "the best architects never put above 7 or at most 9 steps together in one flight; imitating I suppose the number of either the planets or the heavens . . ." but his recommendations as to height of steps were more liberally defined "never higher than 9 in. nor lower than 6 in." Figure 3–3 shows the spread of recommended stairs and was prepared from data published in *Specification* (Britain), 1968, Vol. 1, Neufert's *Bauentwurfslehre* (Germany), *Timesaver Standards* (USA) and the *Uniform Building Regulations* (State of Victoria, Australia).

It is interesting to note that while the English *normal* stair has a rise of 19 cm. (7.4 in.) and a tread of 21 cm. (8.2 in.), in Germany a rise of 20 cm. (7.8 in.) and tread of 22 cm. (8.5 in.) is regarded as too steep and a *normal* stair in Germany (Rainer Wolff, *Das Kleine Haus*) has a rise of 17 cm. (6.6 in.) and a tread of 28 cm. (10.7 in.).

In testing and questioning English people about stairs no optimum was found. The stairs preferred were, surprisingly, *not* those which used the least energy but rather those which were "comfortable" (a subjective measure) and gave safe support to the shoe. There were variations between men and women regarding stairs using the least amount of energy, and stairs preferred, and there were also variations within these groups even for the limited sample tested.[18]

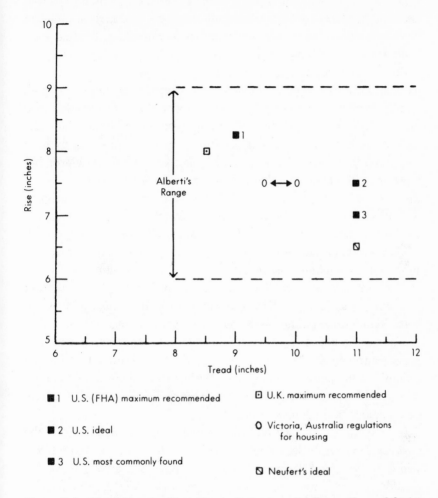

Figure 3–3   Chart Showing Variation in Recommended Proportions of Stairs in the U.K., U.S., and Australia.

In the various designers' guides to staircase design the suggested proportions change depending on whether stairs are interior or exterior, domestic or "grand," which suggests that the limits set are not *physical* but *contextual*.

Noise

We have already referred to Hall's point that the tolerance of noise varies with culture. There seems to be evidence that some cultures may

41

actually prefer high noise levels, and Hall suggests that Italians in general, and southern Italians in particular, prefer rather high noise levels whereas Germans have stringent requirements for quiet. On that scale Americans come somewhere between.

Beranek has pointed out that European standards for noise control tend to be rather higher than American ones. He attributes this both to the greater experience of flat dwelling in Europe and also to a greater stress on the quality of life rather than on gadgets.[19] Countries such as the Netherlands, the Soviet Union, Sweden and Germany have well developed codes; Britain has only "recommended" standards but these are still higher than those of the proposed New York City code— the only one being considered by any American city. For airborne sound the Dutch code requires a 54 dB reduction at 2,000 cycles; the British recommendation is 56 dB for grade I and 54 dB for grade II, while New York proposes 45 dB at the same frequency. Figure 3–4 shows some comparative curves derived from various sources.

The current noise-reduction performance of buildings in New York and other American cities is worse still. Part of the difficulty in setting better standards is political—the number of jurisdictions with their own codes and the like. It is also interesting to note that the concern with noise control in the US began as a result of an insurance claim—an example of the point made by Boris Pushkarev that insurance requirements and frequent law-suits are important design constraints and form determinants in the United States.[20]

If we consider the 1963 recommendations on noise reduction by the Federal Housing Administration we find that, for structure-borne sound, the range of recommendations for reduction among the codes considered is rather sizable.[21] Figure 3–5 shows the FHA recommendations, the range of recommendations in the overseas codes considered, and some specific European curves which we have superimposed. It is clear that there is agreement only within fairly wide limits, and that once again, the specific standards seem to be related to attitudes and choices rather than any definite physical needs.

Temperature

Thermal comfort, the *raison d'être* for heating and other environmental controls is also variable. Not only does it vary due to adaptation, as experiences with people moving to both tropics and arctic conditions have shown, but it also seems to have different values in different cul-

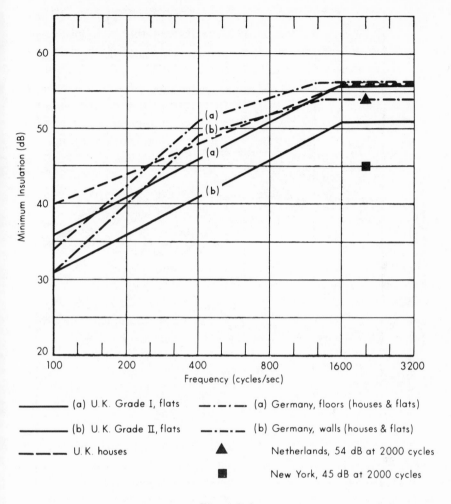

Figure 3–4

tures. Consider, for example, the case of Australian airmen training in Canada during World War II. One would have expected that Australians, unused to cold weather, would suffer from the cold. The main problem, however, was the "overheated" atmosphere in the barracks. There are possibly apocryphal stories of airmen in Alberta in midwinter breaking fixed windows to reduce temperatures in barracks with uncontrolled radiators.

There are figures relating to the comfort zones for different groups which clearly show these differences. In light industry in Great Britain the optimum in the summer is about 63° F. (ET) [22] with a range be-

43

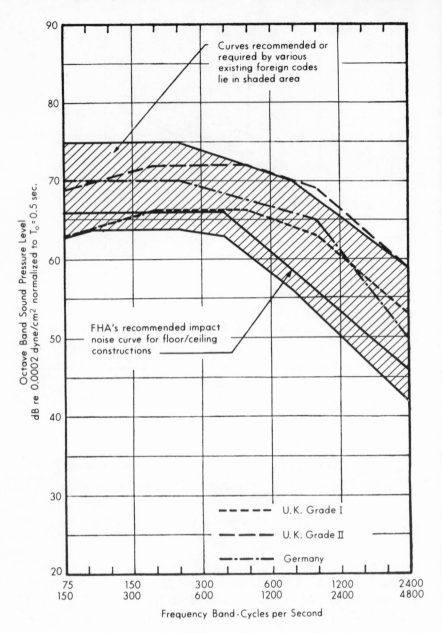

Figure 3–5

tween 57–63° F. (ET). The corresponding comfort zones for American workers are 65–69° F. (ET) for winter and 69–74° F. (ET) for summer with the optimum somewhere around 67° F. (ET) for winter and 71° F. (ET) for summer.[23]

44

Great Britain	sedentary work	65° F. (60-68° F. range)
	light work	60° F. (60-65° F. range)
	heavy work	55° F. (55-60° F. range)
South Africa	sedentary work	68-70° F.
	light work	65-68° F.
	heavy work	60-65° F.[24]

In Australia the figure for office workers is 80–82° F. (DBT) with a range between 77–90° F.[25]

Even within one country there are differences between groups. In Australia, for example, outdoor manual workers were comfortable at 87° F. compared with 80–82° F. for office workers. In the US there are differences between men and women (due, in part, to the clothing worn), age groups, geographic location, winter and summer seasons, diet, etc. Winter comfort in the US at 66° F. rises to 73° F. (ET) in summer, although the range in that case is 69–73.[26]

As one would expect, the difference in temperatures at which people are comfortable result in different recommendations for temperatures to be maintained. Within the figures given (see Table 3–1), comparing Great Britain, the United States and Germany, it is noticeable that there are particularly great differences for certain spaces. For example, bedrooms in Britain are kept colder than American bedrooms by a greater amount than other spaces, and the differences generally are greater for houses than for other building types. This is also reflected in the differentiation between different parts of the house in the United Kingdom but *not* in the United States. The generally higher American temperatures are due not only to higher comfort zones generally but also because American design temperatures are largely for women who tend to be more lightly dressed than men and are dominant in the design requirements, unlike Britain until very recently. Standards in Britain are also going up, as they tend to do with the growth of affluence and technology [27]—possibly as status symbols and partly influenced by advertising.

For example, the need for air conditioning in summer may not always be due to physiological needs but rather to the living standards which society expects. This is shown by the new hotels and motels in the San Francisco Bay Area which need to be air conditioned if rooms are to be let, although the climate certainly does not require it. Similar points have also been made regarding the cleanliness of bathrooms [28] and also light levels (which are discussed in the next section).

TABLE 3-1
Comparative Recommended Temperatures (°F.) in UK, USA and Germany

	UK (IHVE guide 1965)	Germany	USA (ASHRAE guide 1963)	
Living Room	65°	68°		*Homes** Note:
Bedroom	60°	68°		*(a)* no
Bed-Sitting Room	65°		73-75°	differentiation
Kitchen	60°	68°		*(b)* major
Bathroom	60°	71.6°		difference with
				UK, especially
				bedrooms
School: Assembly Halls	65°		68-72°	
Gymnasium	55°	59°	55-65°	
Teaching Rooms	65°	68°	72-74°	
Changing Rooms		71.6°	65-68°	
Hotels: Bedrooms	60°		75° *	
Ballroom	65°		65-68°	
Dining Room	65°		72°	
Theatre Auditorium	65°		68-72°	
Hospital:	65°		72-74°	
Operating Room	65-70°		70-95°	
Shops, Stores	65°		65-68°	
Offices: Conference				
Rooms		64.4°		
Typing Rooms		68°		
Circulation		59°		

*Indicates major differences.

Sunlight, Daylight and Artificial Light

SUNLIGHT

The lighting committee of the Building Research Board have pressed for a minimum standard with regard to sunlighting "because there is an evident desire of people to have it." [29] It has been suggested that past regulations were "framed to allow excessively easy legislative control and/or to allow for inadequate education of the designer with the result that *the underlying functional principles have been completely obscured.*" [30] The authors of this selection draw attention to the pseudo-functional status given to abstracted standards in design manuals and criticize the tendency of designers to derive functional criteria from "relatively imprecisely defined data." They go on to consider a standard of sunshine from which the "designer can find the penalty for not orientating the room in the preferred direction"; this penalty being, of

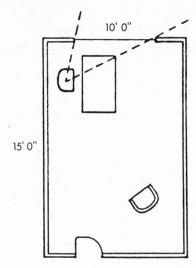

Figure 3–6 Room Layout as Designed—Furniture Turned to Light, Sun, and View.

course, the partial or total deprivation of sunlight. This assumes that sunshine in rooms is a desirable feature in northern temperate climates, although there is in fact, little scientific evidence to show that behavior in buildings is affected by sunlight in temperate zones.

A recent study carried out in the Bartlett School of three large London "tower" office blocks examined precisely this point—the effect which sunlight (and view) might have on the way office workers in single rooms arranged their furniture.[31] Similar rooms were studied for each orientation, in which the designers had intended the occupant to arrange himself as in Figure 3–6 so that he could enjoy sun and view. From the results of the survey there would seem to be stronger influences than environmental factors at work in these particular rooms. The most commonly found arrangement was that shown in Figure 3–7 in which the occupant had positioned his desk diagonally across the corner of the room. The reasons for this might be twofold: (a) it seems critical for the user of the room to have complete visual coverage of the door so that anyone entering may be immediately recognized, (b) it seems important to establish a public zone and a private one which the "intruder" rarely penetrates. These considerations were dominant to the extent of some occupiers sitting with their back to view and sun. It is possible that if the same study was replicated in other cultures other patterns of space organizations might be found based on other criteria—possibly even giving priority to sun and view.

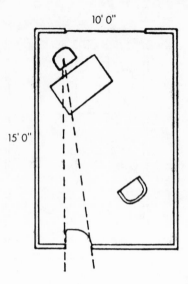

Figure 3–7   Room Layout as Used—Furniture Turned to Give Visual Control of the Door and to Create a Private Zone.

DAYLIGHT

In England, daylight standards have been given more importance than in most countries. A school designer, for example, has to comply with a statutory requirement which states that a minimum daylight factor of 2% must be provided on the working plane—the daylight factor being expressed as a percentage of sky brightness. The intention behind this regulation was to ensure that, in addition to receiving adequate daylight to work by, children and teachers were given the opportunity of viewing the world outside. The regulations, in fact, assumed that adequate daylight and view were inextricably linked.

Earlier regulations presumably relate to then current teaching techniques, economic conditions and cultural attitudes. In 1863 it was recommended that windows be placed so that "full light" should fall on the *faces* of the children and teacher, no doubt indicating the great importance placed on verbal communication and discipline at that time and also related to the static conditions with positions of both teachers and pupils fixed. In 1888 the regulations required classrooms to be lit from two sides—an indication of a felt need for cross ventilation, possibly as part of the "healthy mind in a healthy body" trend linked with the then current interest in improved public health. 1901 saw the regulations requiring no desk to be more than 20 ft. from a window and related the area of window to floor space (⅕ was required). At that time there was clearly much more desk work involved.

The 1945 post-war regulations established a 2% minimum daylight factor, but 5% was "preferred." As a result of this, schools were overglazed and classrooms became overheated in summer from solar gain and were cold in winter due to rapid heat loss.[32] The present regulations, in force since 1951, dropped the references to 5% because of this tendency to overglaze.

We are at present seeing further changes in teaching techniques: the greater freedom shown to children in primary education and "involvement teaching" are currently fashionable attitudes which are finding their way into secondary education. The formal classroom seems to be on its way out, and educational methods now call for more open spaces and, as a result, deeper plans in which it is impossible to achieve the statutory daylight factors by sidelighting alone. Designers are employing techniques of top-lighting and permanent artificial supplements to achieve the recommended levels. Social, cultural and economic determinants may soon cause a further change in our approach to daylighting standards in this country, although it is unlikely that total daylight exclusion, already tried in the US where there have been a number of windowless schools built, will be accepted in England—another example of differences based on cultural attitudes rather than any clear objectively established needs.

It is, in fact, varying cultural needs which seem to lead to standards. "The establishing of levels [of daylight] depends upon the indigenous culture. If the current fashion is for 'picture windows' and for a seeking after outdoor life, the standard of daylight considered necessary for amenity will be far higher than in a society which considers the outdoor elements to be cruel and inimical to human well-being. Hence an arrangement of windows which may appeal to one may be disliked by another, depending on his training or upon the *environmental culture from which he springs.*" [33]

ARTIFICIAL LIGHT

Standards for artificial light seem to have been rising constantly since the English optometrist Trotter wrote in 1908: "one foot-candle is a very convenient and comfortable illumination . . . and more than 3 foot-candles is seldom obtained in artificial illumination." The output of a 5 ft. fluorescent tube is now around 4,500 lumens and it seems reasonable to suppose that mechanical efficiency will increase. Although de-

49

signers recognize that good lighting is not just the provision of ever higher lighting levels it seems that increasing wealth, advertising and changing cultural habits of a particular country bear more closely on the recommended artificial lighting than "real" psycho-physiological needs.

By its nature artificial lighting can be designed to finer tolerances than can daylighting and most countries specify precise values in lux

TABLE 3-2

	U.S.A.[1]	Great Britain[2]	France[3]
	lux	lux	lux
Most Difficult Seeing Tasks Finest precision work. Involving: finest detail; poor contrasts; long periods of time. Such as: extra-fine assembly; precision grading; extra-fine finishing.	10000-20000	1500-3000	1500-3000
Very Difficult Seeing Tasks Precision work. Involving: fine detail; fair contrasts; long periods of time. Such as: fine assembly; high-speed work; fine finishing.	5000-10000	700-1500	700-1500
Difficult and Critical Seeing Tasks Prolonged work. Involving: fine detail; moderate contrasts; long periods of time. Such as: ordinary benchwork and assembly; machine shop work; finishing of medium-to-fine parts; office work.	1000-5000	300-700	300-700
Ordinary Seeing Tasks Involving: moderately fine detail; normal contrasts; intermittent periods of time. Such as: automatic machine operation; rough grading; garage work areas; switchboards; continuous processes; conference and life rooms; packing and shipping.	500-1000	150-300	150-300
Casual Seeing Tasks Such as: stairways; reception rooms; washrooms, and other service areas; inactive storage.	200-300	70-150	70-150
Rough Seeing Tasks Such as: hallways; corridors-passageways; inactive storage.	100-200	30-70	30-70

1 footcandle = 1 lm/sq. ft. = 10.8 lux

SOURCE: From Leslie Larson, *Lighting and Its Design*, New York, Whitney Library of Design, 1964, p. 22. © 1964 Whitney Library of Design, New York, N.Y.

[1] I.E.S. Handbook 1959, Table 9-53, pp. 9-76 to 9-84.
[2] I.E.S. Code 1961, Interior Lighting, p. 41.
[3] L'Ass. Française des Eclairagistes, Recomm. 1961, p. 33.

for a range of seeing tasks. In spite of this precision in the recommended levels there are considerable variations between countries (see Table 3–2). For example, for machine shop and office routines, the ratio between recommended levels in Switzerland, Great Britain and the United States is 1:3:9. While there may be minor physiological differences between the inhabitants of these countries, as we have discussed earlier in this selection, these differences alone would not ac-

TABLE 3-2 *(continued)*

Germany[4]	Sweden[5]	Finland[6]	Belgium[7]	Switzer-land[8]	Australia[9]
lux	lux	lux	lux	lux	lux
4000	1000-2000	1000-2000		over 1000	over 2000
600-1000	300-500	500	500-1000	300-1000	700-1500
250-500	300	300	250-500	150-300	300-700
120-250	150	150	100-250		150-300
60	40-80	80	50-80	40-80	70-150
30	20	40	20-30		50-70

[4]Deutsche Industrie Normen. Blatt 5053, Table 1, 1953.
[5]Svenska Belysningssälskapet, Lux table 1949.
[6]Proceedings, C.I.E. Stockholm 1951, report 62b, p. 31.
[7]Com. Nat. Belge de l'Eclairage, Code preliminaire 1951, p. 12.
[8]Schw. Elektr. Verein, Leitsätze 1947, S. 6.
[9]Australian Standard Code No. CA. 30-1957.

count for variations of this magnitude. The range of levels considered desirable must be related to economic and cultural factors. American standards are invariably the highest for all the tasks in the table. What the table does not show are the *attitudes towards* artificial lighting design. In England, in spite of pressure from certain quarters for continual increases in light levels, a good deal of effort has gone into the introduction of qualitative standards such as the "glare index" which to some extent controls the design of fittings. In the US no such controls exist and the trend is for higher levels *per se*. There are also differences among various countries in the preference for fluorescent versus incandescent light, and other variations in lighting design—all linked, it would seem, to cultural factors.

Conclusion

In this selection we have sought to show that even physical standards (supposedly the only "hard" information designers possess) are greatly affected by values and culturally based choice. The study of comparative standards, their relation to physiological and psycho-physical experiments in different cultures and to differing value systems may help to define those areas of requirements which are based on constant needs, i.e., the ranges of feasibility and criticality, while the variations for different cultures would enable standards to be compared and would also help designers working in other cultures, especially in the developing countries. A monitoring of the rate of change would enable forecasts to be made of possible developments in standards and also to isolate these aspects of change which are due to real improvements in environmental quality, due to rising standards of wealth and demand, and those which are due to changing fashion and the impact of advertising and hard-pressure salesmanship. This would seem to be an essential component in the development of a meaningful understanding of user requirements and the relation of man to his environment.

NOTES

1. E. T. Hall, *The Silent Language.* Garden City, N.Y.: Doubleday, 1959. *The Hidden Dimension.* Garden City, N.Y.: Doubleday, 1966.

2. Alexander Kira, *The Bathroom.* New York: Bantam Books, 1967.

3. This concept is described in Amos Rapoport, *House Form and Culture.* Englewood Cliffs, N.J.: Prentice-Hall, 1969.

4. René Dubos, *Man Adapting.* New Haven: Yale University Press, 1966; "Humanistic biology," *American Scientist,* 53, 1965, pp. 4–19.

5. *Journal of Social Issues*, Vol. XXII, No. 4, 1966, pp. 83–91.

6. See Harry C. Bredemeier and Richard M. Stephenson, "The analysis of culture," in Peter I. Rose (ed.), *The Study of Society*. New York: Random House, 1967, p. 120.

7. See Mark Zborowski, "Cultural components in responses to pain," *Journal of Social Issues*, 8, 1953, pp. 16–31. For a review of the literature on this topic see B. B. Wolff and S. Langley, "Cultural factors and response to pain: a review," *American Anthropologist*, Vol. 70, No. 3, June 1968, pp. 494–501.

8. A. Damon, H. W. Stoudt and R. A. McFarland, *The Human Body in Equipment Design*. Cambridge, Mass.: Harvard University Press, 1966, pp. 10 ff.

9. Ibid., p. 11.

10. Ibid., p. 38.

11. Ibid., p. 11.

12. Ibid., p. 11.

13. Ibid., p. 11.

14. Clyde Kluckhohn, "Culture and behavior," in G. Lindzey (ed.), *Handbook of Social Psychology*, Vol. 2. Cambridge, Mass.: Addison-Wesley, 1954.

15. For American data, see *Timesaver Standards*. New York: McGraw-Hill, 4th ed., 1966, p. 15; for Indian data see *CIB Bulletin*, 1–2, 1966, p. 16.

16. Ernst Neufert, *Bauentwurfslehre*. Ullstein Fachverlag, 1962, p. 169.

17. *A.J. Metric Handbook*, para. 17.42 and Table X.

18. J. S. Ward and P. Randall, "Optimum dimensions for domestic stairways," *Architects' Journal*, 5 July 1967, pp. 29–34.

19. Leo L. Beranek, "Noise," *Scientific American*, December 1966, pp. 66–76.

20. Boris Pushkarev in J. B. Holland (ed.), *Who Designs America?* Garden City, N.Y.: Doubleday, 1966, pp. 113–15.

21. *Impact Noise Control in Multifamily Dwellings*, FHA No. 750, Washington, D.C., January 1963.

22. Within the range of 20–60° relative humidity at the hot time of day the dry-bulb temperature can be used interchangeably with effective temperature. See W. V. McFarlane, *Tropical Building Studies*, Vol. 1, No. 2, 1962 (University of Melbourne), p. 102.

23. Van Straaten, *Thermal Performance of Buildings*. Amsterdam: Elsevier, 1967, p. 32.

24. Ibid.

25. McFarlane, op. cit., Vol. 1, No. 4, 1962, p. 7.

26. T. S. Rogers, *Thermal Design of Buildings*. New York: Wiley, 1964, p. 4.

27. See Douglas H. K. Lee, op. cit., p. 86, where he points out that the acceptable indoor winter temperature has gone up from 68° F., still beloved by the British [*sic*—see Table 3–1], to 72° F., 74° F. and now even 78° F.

28. Ibid.

29. "Sunlight in building," *Proc. CIE International Conference*, 5–9 April 1965, Newcastle-on-Tyne: Paper 1, R. G. Hopkinson, "The Psychophysics of sunlighting."

30. Ibid. Paper 4, J. H. Ritchie and J. K. Page, "Sunshine and sun control standards."

31. Duncan Joiner and Newton Watson. This forms part of a Ph.D. thesis not yet published.

32. R. G. Hopkinson, P. Petherbridge, J. Longmore, *Daylighting*. London: Heinemann, 1966, p. 401.

33. Ibid., p. 404 (our italics).

4

Invasions of Personal Space

NANCY JO FELIPE AND ROBERT SOMMER

Previous selections have indicated that data drawn from human biology become fully useful to designers only when they are interpreted in terms of the cultural context in which men live. A respect for the importance of suprabiological factors in design is now showing itself in other ways, too, especially in the interest that architects and planners have evinced in understanding the psychological roots of environmental response. This new interest goes beyond the architect's traditional concern with the psychology of perception and is focused instead on the areas of psychology dealing with the dynamics of personality functioning.

In attending to the implications of depth psychology for environmental design, two questions are, in effect, being asked. The first is whether or not there are any personality needs that are specifically environmental, in the sense that they are best satisfied by the provision of a physical object rather than a social pattern. The second issue is to determine whether or not such needs, if they exist, are universal, that is to say, characteristic of the human organism, regardless of the cultural or social setting in which he lives.

One of the few such personality needs to have been successfully identified thus far is the need for personal space. Personal space is usually defined as an area with invisible boundaries surrounding a person's body into which no one may intrude. It is sometimes described metaphorically as an invisible snail shell, a soap bubble, or breathing room. The need to maintain such a space is apparently deeply rooted in the human personality, even though the volume of space varies between cultures and for different persons and situations in the same culture.

The concept of personal space was first formulated by Simmel in the early 1900s and was investigated empirically by social psychologists in the 1930s, but it has received its most extensive development much more recently. In the following selection Felipe and Sommer discuss one of the many ways in which the existence of the need has been inferred experimentally. Their method was to approach naïve subjects living in mental hospitals or studying in library reading rooms and to observe the subjects' reactions to the invasion of their personal space. Most of the subjects first tried to accommodate themselves to the intruder, but eventually most fled, even though in the case

Reprinted from Nancy Jo Felipe and Robert Sommer, "Invasions of Personal Space," in *Social Problems* 14, no. 2 (1966): 206–214. Reprinted by permission of The Society for the Study of Social Problems.

of the students using the reading rooms, this meant interrupting their work. The authors conclude their article by relating their findings to studies of animal behavior and by speculating about the variety of factors likely to modify the human response to the invasion of personal space.

It should be noted that the concept of personal space has been utilized in the design of many types of small-scale, intimate environments, including dormitory rooms, school classrooms, mental hospital wards, subway car seating, dining tables, and park benches.

□

The last decade has brought an increase in empirical studies of deviance. One line of investigation has used the case study approach with individuals whom society has classified as deviants—prostitutes, drug addicts, homosexuals, mental patients, etc. The other approach, practiced less frequently, has involved staged situations in which one individual, usually the investigator or one of his students, violates the norm or "routine ground" in a given situation and observes the results.[1] The latter approach is in the category of an experiment in that it is the investigator himself who creates the situation he observes and therefore has the possibility of systematically varying the parameters of social intercourse singly or in combinations. From this standpoint these studies have great promise for the development of an experimental sociology following the model set down by Greenwood.[2] With topics such as human migration, collective disturbance, social class, the investigator observes events and phenomena already in existence. Control of conditions refers to modes of observations and is largely on an *ex post facto* statistical or correlational basis. On the other hand, few staged studies of deviance have realized their promise as experimental investigations. Generally they are more in the category of demonstrations, involving single gross variations of one parameter and crude and impressionistic measurement of effect without control data from a matched sample not subject to the norm violation. Of more theoretical importance is the lack of systematic variation in degree and kind of the many facets of norm violation. The reader is left with the impression that deviancy is an all-or-none phenomenon caused by improper dress, impertinent answers, naïve questions, etc. It cannot be denied that a graduate student washing her clothes in the town swimming pool is breaking certain norms. But we cannot be sure of the norms that are violated or the sanctions attached to each violation without some attempt at isolating and varying single elements in the situation.

The present selection describes a series of studies of one norm violation, sitting too close to another individual. Conversational distance is affected by many things including room density, the acquaintance of the individuals, the personal relevance of the topic discussed, the cultural backgrounds of the individuals, the personalities of the individuals, etc.[3] There are a dozen studies of conversational distance which have shown that people from Latin countries stand closer together than North Americans,[4] eye contact has important effect on conversational distance,[5] introverts stand farther apart than extraverts,[6] friends place themselves closer together than strangers,[7] and so on, but there is still, under any set of conditions, a range of conversational distance which is considered normal for that situation. Several of these investigators, notably Birdwhistell,[8] Garfinkel,[9] Goffman,[10] and Sommer[11] have described the effects of intruding into this distance or personal space that surrounds each individual. The interest shown in the human spacing mechanisms as well as the possibilities of objective measurement of both norm violation and defensive postures suggests that this is an excellent area in which to systematically study norm violations.

The present selection describes several studies of invasions of personal space that took place over a 2-year period. The first was done during the summer of 1963 in a mental hospital. At the time it seemed that systematic studies of spatial invasions could only take place in a "crazy place" where norm violation would escape some of the usual sanctions applied in the outside world. Though there is a strong normative control system that regulates the conduct of mental patients toward one another and toward staff, the rules governing staff conduct toward patients (except cases of brutality, rape, or murder), and particularly higher status staff, such as psychiatrists, physicians, and psychologists, are much less clear. At times, it seems that almost anything can be done in a mental hospital provided it is called research, and one can cite such examples as psychosurgery, various drug experiments, and recent investigations of operant conditioning as instances where unusual and sometimes unproven or even harmful procedures were employed with the blessings of hospital officialdom. To call a procedure "research" is a way of "bracketing" it in time and space and thus excluding it from the usual rules and mores. This is one reason why we supposed that spatial invasions would be more feasible inside a mental hospital than outside. We had visions of a spatial invasion on a Central Park bench resulting in bodily assault or arrest on a sex deviant or "suspicious character" charge. It seemed that some studies of norm violation were deliberately on a one-shot basis to avoid such difficulties. After the first study of spatial invasions in a mental hospital had been completed, however, it became apparent that the method could be adapted for use in more typical settings. We were then able to undertake similar intrusions on a systematic basis in a university library without any untoward consequences, though the possibilities of such problems arising were never far beyond the reaches of consciousness in any of the experimental sessions.

Method

The first study took place on the grounds of Mendocino State Hospital, a 1500-bed mental institution situated in parklike surroundings. Most wards were unlocked and many patients spent considerable time outdoors. In wooded areas it was common to see patients seated underneath trees, one to a bench. Because of the easy access to the outside as well as the number of patients involved in hospital industry, the ward areas were relatively empty during the day. This made it possible for the patients to isolate themselves from other people by finding a deserted area on the grounds or remaining in the almost empty wards. The invasions of personal space took place both indoors and outdoors. The victims were chosen on the basis of these criteria: the victim would be a male, sitting alone, and not engaged in any clearly defined activities such as reading, card playing, etc. All sessions took place near the long stay wards, which meant that newly admitted patients were largely omitted from the study. When a patient meeting these criteria was located, E walked over and sat beside the patient without saying a word. If the victim moved his chair or moved farther down the bench, E would move a like distance to keep the space between them about 6 inches. There were two experimental conditions. In one, E sat alongside a patient and took complete notes of what ensued. He also jiggled his keys occasionally and looked at the patient in order to assert his dominance. In the second experimental condition, E simply sat down next to the victim and, three or four times during the 20-minute session, jiggled his keys. Control subjects were selected from other patients seated at some distance from E but still within E's visual field. To be eligible for the control group, a patient had to be sitting by himself and not reading or otherwise engaged in an activity as well as be visible to E.

Each session took a maximum of 20 minutes. There were sixty-four individual sessions with different patients, thirty-nine involved the procedure in which E took notes and twenty-five involved no writing.[12] One ward dayroom was chosen for additional, more intensive observations. During the daylight hours this large room was sparsely populated and the same five patients occupied the same chairs. These patients would meet Esser's criteria of territoriality in that each spent more than 75 per cent of his time in one particular area.[13]

Results

The major data of the study consist of records of how long each patient remained seated in his chair following the invasion. This can be compared with the length of time the control patients remained seated. Figure 4-1 shows the cumulative number of patients who had de-

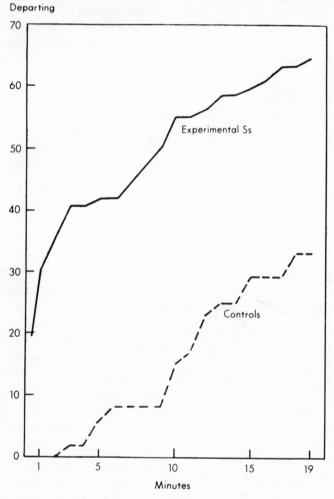

Figure 4-1 Cumulative Percentage of Patients Having Departed at Each 1-Minute Interval.

parted at each 1-minute interval of the 20-minute session. Within 2 minutes, all of the controls were still seated but 36 per cent of the experimental subjects had been driven away. Within 9 minutes fully half of the victims had departed compared with only 8 per cent of the controls. At the end of the 20-minute session, 64 per cent of the experimental subjects had departed compared with 33 per cent of the controls. Further analysis showed that the writing condition was more potent than the no-writing condition but that this difference was significant only at the .10 level ($\chi^2 = 4.61$, df $= 2$). The patient's actual departure from his chair was the most obvious reaction to the intrusion. Many more subtle indications of the patient's discomfort were evident. Typically the victim would immediately face away from E, pull in his shoulders, and place his elbows at his sides. Mumbling, irrelevant laughter, and delusional talk also seemed to be used by the victim to keep E at a distance.

Repeated observation of the same patients took place on one particular ward where the patients were extremely territorial in their behavior. Five patients generally inhabited this large room and sat in the same chairs day after day. There were gross differences in the way these particular territorial patients reacted to the writer's presence. In only one case (S_3) was E clearly dominant. At the other extreme with S_1 and S_2, it was like trying to move the Rock of Gibraltar. E invariably left these sessions defeated, with his tail between his legs, often feeling the need to return to his colleagues and drink a cup of coffee before attempting another experimental session. S_5 is a peculiar case in that sometimes he was budged but other times he wasn't.

Study Two

These sessions took place in the study hall of a university library, a large room with high ceilings and book-lined walls. The room contains fourteen large tables in two equal rows. Each table is 4×16 feet, and accommodates six chairs on each long side. Because of its use as a study area, students typically try to space themselves as far as possible from others. Each victim was the first female sitting alone in a pre-determined part of the room with at least one book in front of her, two empty chairs on either side (or on one side if she was at the end of the table), and an empty chair across from her. An empty chair was also required to be across from E's point of invasion. The second female to meet these criteria and who was visible to E served as a control. The control was observed from a distance and no invasion was attempted. Sessions took place between the hours of 8–5 on Mondays through Fridays; because of time changes between classes and the subsequent turnover of the library population, the observations began between 5 and 15 minutes after the hour. There were five different experimental conditions.

Condition I: E walked up to an empty chair beside an S, pulling the chair out at an angle, and sat down, completely ignoring S's presence. As E sat down, she unobtrusively moved the chair close to the table and to S, so that the chairs were approximately within 3 inches of one another. The E would lean over her book, in which she surreptitiously took notes, and tried to maintain constant shoulder distance of about 12 inches between E and S. To use Crook's terms, E tried to maintain the arrival distance, and to keep the S from adjusting to a settled distance.[14] This was sometimes difficult to do because the chairs were 18½ inches wide and an S would sometimes sit on the other half of her chair, utilizing its width as an effective barrier. However, E tried to get as close to the Ss as possible without actually having any physical contact. If the S moved her chair away, E would follow by pushing her chair backward at an angle and then forward again, under the pretense of adjusting her skirt. At no time did she consciously acknowledge S's presence. In this condition E took detailed notes of the S's behavior, as well as noting time of departure.

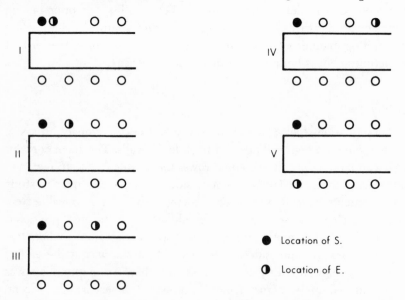

Figure 4–2 Seating of Intruder Vis-à-vis Victim in Each Experimental Condition.

Condition II: E went through the same procedure, except instead of moving the adjacent chair closer to S, E sat in the adjacent chair at the expected distance, which left about 15 inches between the chairs or about 2 feet between the shoulders of E and S.

Condition III: One empty seat was left between E and S, with a resulting shoulder distance of approximately 3½ feet.

Condition IV: Two empty seats were left between E and S with a resulting shoulder distance of about 5 feet.

Condition V: E sat directly across from S, a distance of about 4 feet.

In all conditions E noted the time of initial invasion, the time of the S's departure (or the end of the 30-minute session, depending on which came first), and any observable accommodation to E's presence such as moving books or the chair. For the controls E noted the time the session began and the time of the C's departure if it occurred within 30 minutes after the start of the session.

Results

Figure 4–3 shows the number of subjects remaining after successive 5-minute periods. Since there was no significant difference between the scores in Conditions II–V, these were combined in the analysis. At the end of the 30-minute session, 87 per cent of the controls, 73 per cent of the Ss in the combined conditions remained, compared to only 30 per cent of the experimental Ss in Condition I. Statistical analysis shows that Condition I produced significantly more flight than any of the other conditions, while there was a slight but also significant difference between the combined conditions (II to V) and the control condition. Although flight was the most clearly defined reaction to the invasion, many more subtle signs of the victim's discomfort were evident. Frequently an S drew in her arm and head, turned away from E exposing her shoulder and back, with her elbow on the table, her face resting on her hand. The victims used objects including books, notebooks, purses, and coats as barriers, and some made the wide chair into a barrier.

Discussion

These results show clearly that spatial invasions have a disruptive effect and can produce reactions ranging from flight at one extreme to agonistic display at the other. The individual differences in reacting to the invasion are evident; there was no single reaction among our

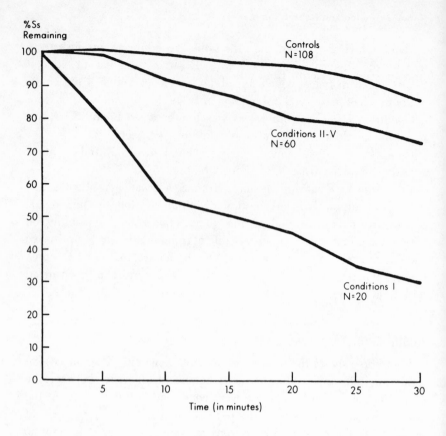

%Ss Remaining

Controls
N=108

Conditions II-V
N=60

Conditions I
N=20

Time (in minutes)

Figure 4–3 Per cent of Victims Remaining at Each 5-Minute Interval after the Invasion.

subjects to someone "sitting too close." The victim can attempt to accommodate himself to the invasion in numerous ways, including a shift in position, interposing a barrier between himself and the invader, or moving farther away. If these are precluded by the situation or fail because the invader shifts positions too, the victim may eventually take to flight. The methods we used did not permit the victim to achieve a comfortable *settled distance*. Crook studied the spacing mechanisms in birds, and found three component factors that maintain individual distance, which he defined as the area around an individual within which the approach of a neighboring bird is reacted to with either avoidance or attack.[15] A number of measurements may be taken when studying individual distance—the arrival distance (how far away from settled birds a newcomer will land), settled distance (the resultant distance after adjustments have occurred), and the distance after departure. The conditions in Study One and in Condition I of the second study called for E to maintain the arrival distance, and to keep the victim from adjusting to a settled distance. In these conditions, the victim was unable to increase the arrival distance by moving away (since the invader followed him down the bench in Study One and moved her chair closer in Study Two), and the greatest number of flight reactions was produced by these conditions. McBride, who has studied the spatial behaviors of animals in confinement, has found that avoidance movements and turning aside are common reactions to crowding,[16] particularly when a submissive animal is close to a dominant animal. Literally the dominant bird in a flock has more space and the other birds will move aside and look away when the dominant bird approaches. Looking away to avoid extensive eye contact was also a common reaction in the present studies. This probably would not have occurred if a subordinate or lower status individual had invaded the personal space of a dominant or higher status individual. There was also a dearth of direct verbal responses to the invasions. Only two of the mental patients spoke directly to E although he sat right beside them, and only one of the eighty student victims asked E to move over. This is some support for Hall's view that "we treat space somewhat as we treat sex. It is there but we don't talk about it." [17]

We see then that a violation of expected conversational distance produces, first of all, various accommodations on the part of the victim. The intensity of his reaction is influenced by many factors including territoriality, the dominance-submission relationship between invader and victim, the locus of the invasion, the victim's attribution of sexual motives to the intruder (in this case all victims and intruders were like-sex individuals), etc. All of these factors influence the victim's definition of the situation and consequently his reaction to it. In the present situation the first reaction to the invasion was accommodation or adaptation: the individual attempted to "live with" the invasion by turning aside, interposing a notebook between himself and the stranger, and pulling in his elbows. When this failed to relieve the tension produced by the norm violation, flight reactions occurred.

There are other elements in the invasion sequence that can be varied systematically. We have not yet attempted heterosexual invasion sequences, or used invaders of lower social standing, or explored more than two unusual and contrasting environments. We are making a start toward using visual rather than spacial invasions, in this case staring at a person rather than moving too close to him. Preliminary data indicate that visual invasions are relatively ineffective in a library where the victims can easily retreat into their books and avoid a direct visual confrontation. There are many other types of intrusions, including tactile and olfactory, that have intriguing research potentialities. It is important to realize that the use of staged norm violations permits these elements to be varied singly and in combination, and in this sense to go beyond the methods of *ex post facto* or "natural experiments" or single-point demonstrations. It is noteworthy that the area of norm violation provides one of the most fruitful applications for the experimental method.

NOTES

1. See for example Harold Garfinkel, "Studies of the Routine Grounds of Everyday Activities," *Social Problems,* 11 (Winter, 1964), pp. 225–250.
2. Ernest Greenwood, *Experimental Sociology,* New York: Kings Crown Press, 1945.
3. Edward T. Hall, *The Silent Language,* Garden City, N.Y.: Doubleday, 1959.
4. Edward T. Hall, "The Language of Space," *Landscape,* 10 (Autumn, 1960), pp. 41–44.
5. Michael Argyle and Janet Dean, "Eye-Contact, Distance, and Affiliation," *Sociometry,* 28 (September, 1965), pp. 289–304.
6. John L. Williams, "Personal Space and its Relation to Extraversion-Introversion," unpublished M.A. thesis, University of Alberta, 1963.
7. Kenneth B. Little, "Personal Space," *Journal of Experimental Social Psychology,* 1 (August, 1960), pp. 237–247.
8. Birdwhistell, R. L. *Introduction to Kinesics,* Washington, D.C.: Foreign Service Institute, 1952.
9. Garfinkel, *op. cit.*
10. Erving Goffman, *Behavior in Public Places,* New York, N.Y.: The Free Press, 1963.
11. Robert Sommer, "Studies in Personal Space," *Sociometry,* 22 (September, 1959), pp. 247–260.
12. Four incomplete sessions are omitted from this total. On two occasions a patient was called away by a nurse and on two other occasions the session was terminated when the patient showed signs of acute stress. The intruder in Study One was the junior author, a 35-year-old male of slight build. It is likely that invasions by a husky six-footer would have produced more immediate flight reactions.
13. Aristide H. Esser, *et al.,* "Territoriality of Patients on a Research Ward," *Recent Advances in Biological Psychiatry,* Vol. 8, in Joseph Wortis, ed., New York: Plenum Press, 1965.
14. J. H. Crook, "The Basis of Flock Organization in Birds," in W. H. Thorpe and O. L. Zangwill (eds.), *Current Problems in Animal Behaviour,* Cambridge: Cambridge University Press, 1961, pp. 125–149.
15. Crook, *op. cit.*
16. Glen McBride, *A General Theory of Social Organization and Behaviour,* St. Lucia: University of Queensland Press, 1964; also McBride, *et al.,* "Social Forces Determining Spacing and Head Orientation in a Flock of Domestic Hens," *Nature,* 197 (1963), pp. 1272–1273.
17. Hall, *The Silent Language, op. cit.*

5

Territoriality: A Neglected
Sociological Dimension

STANFORD M. LYMAN AND MARVIN B. SCOTT

Territoriality, defined as the need of individuals and groups to claim some geographical area as their own, is another need of the human personality that can best be satisfied through the provision of specific environmental or spatial conditions. The specific environmental condition that can fulfill this need is the availability of a fixed, circumscribed area, which the individual or group has the capacity to control. A territory, because it is a fixed area, can be said to exist even when the individual identified with it is not physically present. Territory thus differs from personal space, which is something an individual carries around with him. (Personal space is sometimes referred to as portable territory.)

Most discussions of the concept of territoriality note that it was first developed to explain the spatial behavior of animals. As a consequence, the application of the concept to human behavior has usually proceeded by crude analogy, and thus people have tended to overlook the fact that concern for territory and the response to its invasion are linked to the symbolic and cultural dimensions of human psychology as well as to the biological. The great merit of the selection by Lyman and Scott is that it makes these connections clear. Territoriality is by definition a spatial phenomenon, but the way its boundaries are defined, the uses to which it is put, the manner in which groups cope with invasions, and the consequences of territorial deprivation for social order are all highly variable. The authors, for example, distinguish four different types of human territories (public territories, home territories, interactional territories, and body territories); three types of territorial encroachment (violation, invasion, and contamination); and three types of reaction to encroachment (turf defense, insulation, and linguistic collusion).

Lyman and Scott's discussion is redolent with implications for housing and urban design. Especially interesting is the distinction they make between public territories, which are accessible to all citizens but in which users are under public scrutiny and must conduct themselves according to official norms, and home territories, which are private areas in which users are relatively free to behave in their own individual fashion. Both types of territory serve a purpose in cities. They mention that the need for a home

Reprinted from Stanford M. Lyman and Marvin B. Scott, "Territoriality: A Neglected Sociological Dimension," in *Social Problems* 15, no. 2 (1967): 236–249. Reprinted by permission of the Society for the Study of Social Problems.

territory can be met through erecting walls and doors, but that invaders can also be excluded by the confusion of odd gestures, strange ethnic dialects, and other manifestations of linguistic collusion. Designers presumably must be sensitive to the possibility that these insulating and defensive mechanisms can operate at the urban scale.

☐

All living organisms observe some sense of territoriality,[1] that is, some sense—whether learned or instinctive to their species—in which control over space is deemed central for survival.[2] Although man's domination over space is potentially unlimited, in contemporary society it appears that men acknowledge increasingly fewer *free* territories for themselves.[3]

Free territory is carved out of space and affords opportunities for idiosyncrasy and identity. Central to the manifestation of these opportunities are boundary creation and enclosure. This is so because activities that run counter to expected norms need seclusion or invisibility to permit unsanctioned performance, and because peculiar identities are sometimes impossible to realize in the absence of an appropriate setting.[4] Thus the opportunities for freedom of action—with respect to normatively discrepant behavior and maintenance of specific identities—are intimately connected with the ability to attach boundaries to space and command access to or exclusion from territories.

In American society where territorial encroachment affects nearly all members of society, certain segments of the population are particularly deprived, namely, Negroes, women, youth, and inmates of various kinds. With these categories in mind, this selection re-introduces a neglected dimension of social analysis important to understanding deprived groups.

Our strategy is twofold: first, to bring together under a new set of organizing concepts the notions of types of territory, types of territorial encroachment, and types of responses to encroachment; and second, to specify the reactions of spatially deprived groups.

The Types of Territories

We can distinguish four kinds of territories, namely, *public territories, home territories, interactional territories* and *body territories*.

PUBLIC TERRITORIES

Public territories are those areas where the individual has freedom of access, but not necessarily of action, by virtue of his claim to citizenship.[5] These territories are officially open to all, but certain images and expectations of appropriate behavior and of the categories of individuals who are normally perceived as using these territories modify freedom. First, it is commonly expected that illegal activities and impermissible behavior will not occur in public places. Since public territories are vulnerable to violation in both respects, however, policemen are charged with the task of removing lawbreakers from the scene of their activities and restricting behavior in public places.[6]

Second, certain categories of persons are accorded only limited access to and restricted activity in public places. It is expected, for instance, that children will not be playing in public playgrounds after midnight; that lower-class citizens will not live—although they might work—in areas of middle-class residence; and that Negroes will not be found leisurely strolling on the sidewalks of white neighborhoods, though they might be found laying the sewer pipe under the streets.

Since the rights of such discrepant groups to use these territories as citizens sometimes contradicts the privileges accorded them as persons, such territories are not infrequently the testing grounds of challenges to authority. The wave of sit-ins, wade-ins, and demonstrations in racially segregated restaurants, public beaches, and schools constitutes an outstanding recent example. Informal restrictions on access to public territories often violate unenforced or as yet untested rights of citizens. Since the informal delineation of some of these territories implies the absence of certain persons, their presence stands out. Policemen frequently become allies of locals in restricting citizenship rights when they remove unseemly persons from territories which they do not regularly habituate, or when they restrict certain categories of persons to specific areas.[7]

Public territories are thus ambiguous with respect to accorded freedoms. First, the official rights of access may be regularly violated by local custom. Second, status discrepancy may modify activity and entrance rights. For example, the ambiguity in the distinction between minors and adults is a source of confusion and concern in the regulation of temporal and access rights to those whose status is unclear. Finally, activities once forbidden in public may be declared permissible, thus enlarging the freedom of the territory; or activities once licit may be proscribed, thus restricting it. Hence display of female breasts is now permitted in San Francisco nightclubs, but not on the streets or before children. Nude swimming enjoys police protection at certain designated beaches, but watching nude swimmers at these same beaches is forbidden to those who are attired.

67

HOME TERRITORIES

Home territories are areas where the regular participants have a relative freedom of behavior and a sense of intimacy and control over the area. Examples include makeshift club houses of children, hobo jungles, and homosexual bars. Home and public territories may be easily confused. In fact "the areas of public places and the areas of home territories are not always clearly differentiated in the social world and what may be defined and used as a public place by some may be defined and used as a home territory by others." [8] Thus, a home territory that also may be used as a public one is defined by its regular use by specific persons or categories of persons and by the particular "territorial stakes" or "identity pegs" that are found in such places. The style of dress and language among the patrons at a bar may immediately communicate to a homosexual that he has arrived in home territory, while a heterosexual passerby who pauses for a drink may be astonished or outraged when he is accosted for sexual favors by the stranger seated next to him. Large-scale clandestine brotherhoods indoctrinate their members in secret codes of dress and demeanor so that regardless of their later travels they can unobtrusively communicate their fraternal identity and ask for assistance from one another in otherwise public places. Home territories sometimes enjoy a proactive status, beyond the presence of their inhabitants, in the form of reserved chairs, drinking mugs, signs or memorabilia that serve to indicate special and reserved distinctions.

Home territories may be established by "sponsorship" or "colonization." An example of the former is found in the merchant emigrants from China who established caravansaries in certain quarters of Occidental cities which served as public trading establishments but also as living quarters, employment agencies, meeting places, and courts for their *Landsmänner*.[9] Colonization occurs when a person or group lays claim to a formally free territory by virtue of discovery, regular usage, or peculiar relationship. Thus certain restaurants become home territories to those who are impressed with their first meal there; to those who eat there on specific occasions, such as luncheons, birthdays, or after sporting events; and to those who are intimate with the waitress.

Loss of home status may be occasioned by the death or resignation of a sponsor, by violation of the previously established usages, by rejection, or by conquest. Erstwhile "regulars" at a bar may discover they are no longer warmly greeted nor eligible for a free drink when the proprietor dies or when their patronage becomes irregular. Homosexuals may desert a "queer bar" when it becomes a place which heterosexuals frequent to observe deviant behavior.

It is precisely because of their officially open condition that public areas are vulnerable to conversion into home territories. The rules of openness are sufficiently broad and ambiguous so that restrictions on time, place, and manner are difficult to promulgate and nearly impossible to enforce. Armed with a piece of chalk children can change the public sidewalk into a gameboard blocking pedestrian traffic. Despite building codes and parental admonitions youngsters convert abandoned buildings or newly begun sites into forts, clubs, and hideaways.[10]

But children are not the only colonizers on the public lands. Beggars and hawkers will stake out a "territory" on the sidewalks or among the blocks and occupy it sometimes to the exclusion of all others similarly employed. The idle and unemployed will loiter on certain streetcorners, monopolizing the space, and frightening off certain respectable types with their loud, boisterous, or obscene language, cruel jests, and suggestive leers. Members of racial and ethnic groups colonize a portion of the city and adorn it with their peculiar institutions, language, and rules of conduct.[11] Ethnic enclaves, like certain notorious homosexual bars and prisons on open-house day, are often "on display" to non-ethnics who thus grant legitimacy to the colony's claim for territorial identity.

Among the most interesting examples of colonizing on the public lands are those attempts by youths to stake out streets as home territories open only to members of their own clique and defended against invasion by rival groups. Subject always to official harassment by police and interference by other adults who claim the streets as public territories, youths resolve the dilemma by redefining adults as non-persons whose seemingly violative presence on the youth's "turf" does not challenge the latter's proprietorship. Streets are most vulnerable to colonizing in this manner and indeed, as the early studies of the Chicago sociologists illustrated so well, streets and knots of juxtaposed streets become unofficial home areas to all those groups who require relatively secluded yet open space in which to pursue their interests or maintain their identities.[12]

INTERACTIONAL TERRITORIES

Interactional territories refer to any area where a social gathering may occur. Surrounding any interaction is an invisible boundary, a kind of social membrane.[13] A party is an interactional territory, as are the several knots of people who form clusters at parties. Every interactional territory implicitly makes a claim of boundary maintenance for the duration of the interaction. Thus access and egress are governed by rules understood, though not officially promulgated, by the members.

Interactional territories are characteristically mobile and fragile. Participants in a conversation may remain in one place, stroll along, or move periodically or erratically. They may interrupt only to resume it at a later time without permanently breaking the boundary or disintegrating the group. Even where "settings" are required for the interaction, mobility need not be dysfunctional if the items appropriate to the setting are movable. Thus chemists may not be able to complete a discussion without the assistance of a laboratory, but chess players may assemble or disassemble the game quite readily and in the most cramped quarters. Similarly, so long as Negroes were chattel slaves slaveholders might move them anywhere their services or appearance were needed.

The fragility of interactional territories is constantly being tested by parvenus and newcomers. The latter, even when they possess credentials entitling them to entrance into the interactional circle, break down ongoing interaction and threaten it by requiring all to start over again, end it instead, and begin a new subject of common interest, or disintegrate.[14] Parvenus are a greater threat since their presence breaks the boundaries of the interaction and challenges the exclusiveness of the group. They may be repulsed, or accepted fully, though the latter is less likely than the granting of a "temporary visa," i.e., rights to interact for the instant occasion with no promise of equal rights in the future.

BODY TERRITORIES

Finally, there are body territories, which include the space encompassed by the human body and the anatomical space of the body. The latter is, at least theoretically, the most private and inviolate of territories belonging to an individual. The rights to view and touch the body are of a sacred nature, subject to great restriction. For instance, a person's rights to his own body space are restricted where norms govern masturbation, or the appearance and decoration of skin. Moreover, rights of others to touch one's body are everywhere regulated, though perhaps modern societies impose greater restrictions than others.[15]

Body territory is also convertible into home territory. The most common method is marriage in a monogamous society in which sexual access to the female is deemed the exclusive right of the husband so long as he exercises propriety with respect to his status. Ownership, however, is not necessarily or always coterminous with possession, so that sexual rivalry might continue illegitimately after a marital choice has been made and erupt in trespass on the husband's sexual property.[16] Under situations where women are scarce, such as nineteenth-century overseas Chinese communities in the United States, sexual property was institutionalized through organized prostitution, and the few Chinese wives among the homeless men were carefully secluded.[17]

Body space is, however, subject to creative innovation, idiosyncrasy, and destruction. First, the body may be marked or marred by scars, cuts, burns, and tattoos. In addition, certain of its parts may be inhibited or removed without its complete loss of function. These markings have a meaning beyond the purely anatomical. They are among the indicators of status or stigma. They can be signs of bravado as was the dueling scar among German students, or of criminality as is a similar scar on Italians and Negroes in America. Loss of an eye may prevent one's entrance into dental school, but at least one clothing manufacturer regards one-eyed men as status symbols for starched shirts. Tattoos may memorialize one's mother or sweetheart as well as indicate one's seafaring occupation.

The human organism exercises extraterritorial rights over both internal and external space. In the latter instance the space immediately surrounding a person is also inviolate.[18] Thus conversations among friends are ecologically distinguishable from those between acquaintances or strangers. A person who persists in violating the extraterritorial space of another of the same sex may be accused of tactlessness and suspected of homosexuality, while uninvited intersex invasion may indicate unwarranted familiarity.[19] Moreover, eye contact and visual persistence can be a measure of external space. Thus two strangers may look one another over at the proper distance, but as they near one another, propriety requires that they treat one another as non-persons unless a direct contact is going to be made.[20]

Control over "inner space" is the quintessence of individuality and freedom. Violations of "inner space" are carried out by domination, ranging in intensity from perception of more than is voluntarily revealed to persuasion and ultimately hypnosis.[21] Demonstration of idiosyncrasy with respect to "inner space" is exemplified by the modifications possible in the presentation of self through the uses of the several stimulants and depressants.

Territorial Encroachment

We can distinguish three forms of territorial encroachment: violation, invasion, and contamination.

Violation of a territory is unwarranted use of it. Violators are those who have repulsed or circumvented those who would deny them access. Violators are also, by virtue of their acts, claimants in some sense to the territory they have violated. Their claim, however, may vary in scope, intensity, and objective. Children may violate the graves of the dead by digging "for treasure" in the cemetery, but unlike ghouls, they are not seeking to remove the bodies for illicit purposes. Some territories may be violated, however, merely by unwarranted entrance into them. Among these are all those territories commonly restricted to categorical groups such as toilets, harems, nunneries, and public baths —areas commonly restricted according to sex. Other territories may not be necessarily violated by presence but only by innovative or prohibited use. Thus some parents regard family-wide nudity as permissible, but hold that sexual interest or intercourse among any but the married pair is forbidden. Interactional territories are violated when one or more of the legitimate interactants behaves out of character.[22]

Invasion of a territory occurs when those not entitled to entrance or use nevertheless cross the boundaries and interrupt, halt, take over, or change the social meaning of the territory. Such invasions, then, may be temporary or enduring.

Contamination of a territory requires that it be rendered impure with respect to its definition and usage. Cholera may require that a portion of the city be quarantined. In a racial caste society the sidewalks may be contaminated by low caste persons walking upon them. Home territories may be contaminated by pollution or destruction of the "home" symbols. Orthodox Jews may destroy their dinnerware when an unwary maid has accidentally mixed the milk and meat dishes. Heterosexuals who regularly congregate at a bar sometimes discontinue their patronage when known homosexuals begin frequenting the bar. (This example illustrates a continuum in the process of territorial encroachment from invasion to contamination.) Interactional territories may be contaminated by sudden odors, especially if they emanate from one of the interactants, or by indiscreet language, e.g., obscenity, among those for whom identification with such language constitutes a loss of face or a reduction in status.[23]

Contamination of bodily territories occurs whenever the immediate space of or around the body is polluted. The removal by bathing of

material involuntarily attached to the skin constitutes a ritualized purification rite of considerable importance in industrial societies.[24] However, body space may be contaminated in many ways, by smell, look,
touch, and by proximity to contaminated persons or things. The sensitivity with respect to touch illustrates the complex nature of this contamination and also its peculiarly social character. The rules regarding
touch are highly developed in American society and are clear indicators
of social distance between individuals and groups.[25] Typically, older
people can touch younger ones, but suspicions of sexual immorality
modify such contacts. Women who are friends or relatives may greet
one another with a light kiss (commonly called a "peck") on the cheek,
but not on the lips. Men who are long absent may be greeted by male
friends and relatives with a hearty embrace and a touching of the
cheeks, but the embrace must not be overlong or tender. Indeed,
"rough-housing," mock-fighting, and pseudo-hostility are commonly
employed in masculine affective relationships. Touch which would
otherwise be contaminating is exempt from such designation when it
takes place in situations of intense social action, e.g., on a dance floor,
or in situations when the actors are not privileged to interact, e.g.,
crowded buses. At other times bodies contaminated by impermissible
contacts are restored to their pure state by apologies.

Body space may be contaminated by a kind of negative charismatic
contact whereby objects, though neutral in themselves, carry a contaminating effect when transferred directly to the body. Thus a comb
or toothbrush may not be lent or borrowed in certain circles since
to use someone else's tools of personal hygiene is to contaminate
oneself. Typically, when clothing, especially clothing that will directly
touch the skin, is lent, it is proper for the lender to assure the bor-
rower that the apparel is clean, and that it has not been worn by anyone since its last cleaning.[26] A more striking example involves the rule
of some shops forbidding Negroes from trying on clothes—their skin
being regarded as a source of pollution. Similarly, drinking from the
same glass as another is discouraged as a matter of hygiene among
the middle class and as a source of pollution if it occurs among persons
of different races or castes.

Reaction to Encroachment

We have already suggested that something of a reciprocal relation
exists between the territorial types. For example, a public swimming
pool—while officially open to all persons—might be conceived by cer-

tain regular users as an exclusive area. Strangers seeking access by virtue of their diffuse civic rights might be challenged by those whose sense of peculiar propriety is thus violated. Such a confrontation (sometimes called "when push meets shove") could result in retreat on the part of the party seeking admittance, flight on the part of those favoring denial, or strategy and tactics on the part of the contending parties to expand the area of legitimate access on the one hand, and withhold entirely or restrict the meaning of entry on the other.

Of course, the occupants of a territory may extend its use to others whose presence is not regarded as a threat. The most common situation is that in which common usage will not destroy or alter the value of the territory.[27] When public territories have been colonized by users who do not fully monopolize the space, who embroider it by their presence, or whose occupancy still allows for other public and colonizing usages, the colonists will not be seriously opposed. Delinquent gangs who often define the streets of a neighborhood as a home territory do not usually regard the presence of local adults and children as an encroachment on their own occupancy. Unwarranted intrusion on interactional territories may be countenanced if the unwelcome guest indicates his willingness to be present on this occasion alone with no future rights of reentry, or to listen only and not to interrupt the proceedings. Bodies usually invulnerable to feel and probe by strangers may be violated if circumstances render the act physically safe, socially irrelevant, or emotionally neutral. Thus female nurses may massage their male patients with mutual impunity, and striptease dancers may perform unclothed upon a raised stage out of reach of the audience.[28] However, all such contacts will tend to be defined as territorial encroachment when the claimants threaten obliteration, monopoly, or fundamental alteration of a territory. Under these conditions, the holders of territory are likely to react to unwelcome claimants in terms of *turf defense, insulation,* or *linguistic collusion.*

TURF DEFENSE

Turf defense is a response necessitated when the intruder cannot be tolerated. The animal world provides a multitude of examples which are instructive with respect to the human situation.[29] Here we may be content however, to confine ourselves to the human scene. When Chinese merchants sought "colonizing" rights among the urban merchants of San Francisco, they were welcomed and honored. A few years later, however, the appearance of Chinese miners in the white

Americans' cherished gold fields called forth violent altercations and forced removals.[30] In contemporary American cities delinquent gangs arm themselves with rocks, knives, tire irons, and zip guns to repel invaders from other streets.[31] Among the "primitive" Kagoro the choice of weapons is escalated in accordance with the social distance of the combatants; poison spears and stratagems are employed exclusively against hostile strangers and invaders.[32]

Turf defense is an ultimate response, however. Other more subtle repulsions or restrictions are available to proprietors wishing to maintain territorial control.

INSULATION

Insulation is the placement of some sort of barrier between the occupants of a territory and potential invaders. The narrow streets, steep staircases, and regularized use of Cantonese dialects in Chinatowns serve notice on tourists that they may look over the external trappings of Chinese life in the Occidental city but not easily penetrate its inner workings. Distinct uniforms distinguishing status, rights, and prerogatives serve to protect military officers from the importunities of enlisted men, professors from students, and doctors from patients.[33] Bodily insulation characteristically takes the form of civil inattention and may be occasioned by a subordinate's inability to repel invasion directly. Another common form of insulation involves use of body and facial idiom to indicate impenetrability. It may be effected by the use of sunglasses,[34] or attained accidentally, by dint of culturally distinct perceptions of facial gestures, as, for example, often happens to orientals in Western settings.[35] It can also be attained by conscious efforts in the management and control of the mouth, nostrils, and especially the eyes.[36]

LINGUISTIC COLLUSION

Linguistic collusion involves a complex set of processes by which the territorial integrity of the group is reaffirmed and the intruder is labeled as an outsider. For example, the defending interactants may engage one another in conversation and gestures designed to so confuse the invader that he responds in a manner automatically labeling him eligible for either exclusion from the group or shameful status diminution. In one typical strategy the defending interactants will speak to one another in a language unfamiliar to the invader. Ethnic enclaves provide numerous examples. Jewish and Chinese storekeepers will speak Yiddish and Cantonese respectively to their clerks when

75

discussing prices, bargaining rights, and product quality in the presence of alien customers. Negroes may engage one another in a game of "the dozens" in the presence of intruding whites, causing the latter considerable consternation and mystification.[37] And teenagers develop a peer group argot (frequently borrowed from Negro and jazz musician usages) which sets them apart from both children and adults, and which, incidentally, is most frequently cited as proof for the claim that a distinctive youth culture does exist in the United States.

In another recognizable strategy, the participants continue to engage in the same behavior but in a more exaggerated and "staged" manner. Mood and tone of the voice are sometimes regulated to achieve this effect. Thus persons engaged in conversation may intensify their tone and include more intra-group gestures when an outsider enters the area. Professors may escalate the use of jargon and "academese" in conversations in the presence of uninvited students or other "inferiors." Homosexuals engaged in flirtations in a "gay" bar may exaggerate their femininity when heterosexuals enter the establishment. Such staged displays call attention to the exclusive culture of the interactants and suggest to the outsider that he is bereft of the cards of identity necessary to participate.

Reaction to the Absence of Free Space

There are some segments of society that are systematically denied free territories. One outstanding example is that of lower-class urban Negro youth. Their homes are small, cramped, and cluttered and also serve as specialized areas of action for adults; their meeting places are constantly under surveillance by the agents of law enforcement and social workers; and, when in clusters on the street, they are often stopped for questioning and booked "on suspicion" by the seemingly ever-present police.[38]

What is the condition of Negro youth in particular appears to be an exaggerated instance of the trend with respect to denial of freedom among youth in general. Thus it has been suggested that youth are adrift somewhere between humanism and fatalism, i.e., between situations in which they feel they have control over their destinies and those in which such control is in the hands of forces outside youth's individual direction and influence.[39] In such a situation one response is to seek to maximize the area of freedom, the situations in which one can exercise liberty and license, the times one can be cause rather than effect. Among lower-class youth the carving of home territories out of the space provided as public ones is common and has already been noted. Note also, however, the frequency with which youth-created home territories are subject to invasion, violation, and contamination and the relative vulnerability of youth home territories to such encroachments.

Exercising freedom over body territory provides a more fruitful approach to those for whom public territories are denied and home territories difficult or impossible to maintain. The body and its attendant inner and external space have an aura of ownership and control about them that is impressed upon the incumbent. The hypothesis we wish to suggest here is that as other forms of free territory are perceived to be foreclosed by certain segments of the society, these segments, or at least those elements of the segments not constrained by other compelling forces, will utilize more frequently and intensively the area of body space as a free territory. Three forms of such utilization are prominent: *manipulation, adornment,* and *penetration.*

Manipulation rests upon the fact that the body is adjustable in a greater number of ways than are positively sanctioned and that by modifying the appearance of the self one can establish identity, and flaunt convention with both ease and relative impunity. Thus children, separated from one another for being naughty and enjoined from conversation, may sit and "make faces" at one another, conforming to the letter of their punishment but violating its principle. Teenagers, denied approval for the very sexual activity for which they are biologically prepared, and also enclosed more and more from private usage of public territories for such purposes, have developed dance forms which involve little or no body contact but are nevertheless suggestive of the most intimate and forbidden forms of erotic interaction. Further, male youth—enjoined from verbal scatological forms by customs and by rules of propriety—have developed a gesture language by which they can communicate the desired obscenity without uttering it.

Adornment of the body is another response.[40] By covering, uncovering, marking, and disfiguring the body individuals can at least partly overcome whatever loss of freedom they suffer from other encroachments. Both the French "bohemians" of the nineteenth century and the disaffected American Negro youths of the twentieth have exhibited themselves as "dandies," [41] while the ascetic Doukhobors of British Columbia disrobe entirely and in public when challenged by authority.[42] Body space may also be attended by filling in the apertures in nose, mouth and ears by rings, bones, and other emblematic artifacts; by marking upon the skin with inks and tattoos; and by disfigurements, scars, and severance of non-vital members. An alternative mode of adornment, that appears to be directed definitely against elements of the core culture, is the refusal to use instruments of personal hygiene. We have already noted how these instruments acquire a peculiar aspect of the personal charisma of the user so that people do not customarily borrow the comb, toothbrush, and razor of another unless the contamination that occurs thereby is neutralized. Here, however, adornment occurs by simply *not* washing, combing, shaving, cutting the hair, etc. Like public nudity this form of assertiveness and reaction to oppression has the advantage of inhibiting a like response among those who are offended by the appearance created thereby, but, unlike stripping in public, has the added advantage of being legal.

Penetration refers to the exploitation and modification of inner space in the search for free territory. One might hypothesize that the greater the sense of unfreedom, the greater the exercise of body liberty so that penetration is an escalated aspect of manipulation and adornment. There is, as it were, a series of increasing gradations of body space. The ultimate effort is to gain freedom by changing one's internal environment. The simplest form of this is cultivating a vicarious sense of being away, of transporting the self out of its existential environment by musing, daydreaming, or relapsing into a reverie.[43] However, voluntary reorganization of the inner environment can be assisted by alcohol and drugs. Contemporary college youth sometimes partake of hallucinogenic and psychedelic drugs in order to make an inner migration (or "take a trip" as the popular idiom has it).

Conclusion

The concept of territoriality offers a fruitful approach for the analysis of freedom and situated action. Although the early school of ecology in American sociology provided a possible avenue for this kind of exploration, its practitioners appear to have eschewed the interactionist and phenomenological aspects of the subject in favor of the economic and the biotic. Nevertheless, much of their work needs to be examined afresh for the clues it provides for understanding the nature and function of space and the organization of territories. Similarly the work done by the students of non-human animal association provides clues to concept formation and suggestions for research. Here we may mention several potentially fruitful areas. The first involves cross-cultural studies of territoriality. Such studies would attempt to describe in greater specificity the constituent features of types of territoriality, the ways in which they vary, and their interrelationships. Using a cross-cultural perspective would also serve to specify generic forms of reactions to territorial encroachment and to establish how certain contexts predispose one type of response rather than another. A second area of research would focus on a variety of deviant behaviors (e.g., crime, juvenile delinquency, drug addiction) with the purpose of understanding the part the territorial variable plays in the etiology of such behaviors. Finally, we may suggest that micro-sociological studies of territoriality—which are perhaps more amenable to rigorous research design—may be extrapolated to an analysis of macro-sociological inquiries, especially in the realm of international affairs.

NOTES

AUTHOR's NOTE: We are grateful to Donald Ball and Edwin Lemert for their critical reading of the manuscript.

1. The concept of territoriality was introduced into sociological analysis in the twenties under the label of "the ecological school." For an early statement see Robert E. Park, Ernest W. Burgess, and R. D. McKenzie, The City, Chicago: University of Chicago Press, 1925. For a summary and bibliography of the school see Milla Aissa Alihan, Social Ecology, New York: Columbia University Press, 1938. An updated version of this school is found in James A. Quinn, Human Ecology, New York: Prentice-Hall, 1950 and Amos H. Hawley, Human Ecology, A Theory of Community Structures, New York: The Ronald Press, 1950.

Originating in animal studies, "territoriality" still looms large as an organizing concept in ethology. For a summary statement see C. R. Carpenter, "Territoriality: A Review of Concepts and Problems," in A. Roe and G. Simpson, eds., Behavior and Evolution, New Haven, Conn.: Yale University Press, 1958, pp. 224–250.

For a challenging argument that sociological investigation can fruitfully employ the techniques of comparative ethology—especially to such subjects as territoriality—see Lionel Tiger and Robin Fox, "The Zoological Perspective in Social Science," Man, I., 1, (March, 1966), esp. p. 80.

Only very recently have sociologists revived ecological thinking to include a truly interactional dimension. The outstanding contributor is, of course, Edward T. Hall. See his The Silent Language, Garden City, New York: Doubleday and Co., 1959, and The Hidden Dimension, Garden City, New York: Doubleday and Co., 1966. For a masterful application of the concept of territoriality in interactional terms see Erving Goffman, Asylums, Garden City, New York: Doubleday and Co., Anchor Books, 1961, pp. 227–248. In a slightly different vein see the interesting efforts of Robert Sommer, "Studies in Personal Space," Sociometry, 22 (September, 1959), pp. 247–260, and the writings of Roger Barker, especially his "Roles, Ecological Niches, and the Psychology of the Absent Organism," paper presented to the conference on the Propositional Structure of Role Theory, University of Missouri, 1962.

2. For the argument that human territoriality is a natural rather than a cultural phenomenon see Robert Ardrey, The Territorial Imperative, New York: Atheneum, 1966, pp. 3–41.

3. The idea of "free territory" is derived from Goffman, loc. cit.

4. See Erving Goffman, The Presentation of Self in Everyday Life, Garden City, New York: Doubleday and Co., Anchor Books, 1959, p. 22.

5. The term "citizenship" is used in a sense similar to that employed by T. H.

Marshall in *Class, Citizenship and Social Development*, Garden City, New York: Doubleday and Co., Anchor Books, 1965, esp. pp. 71–134.

6. See Harvey Sacks, "Methods in Use for the Production of a Social Order: A Method for Warrantably Informing Moral Character." Center for the Study of Law and Society, University of California, Berkeley, 1962; and Aaron Cicourel, *The Social Organization of Juvenile Justice*, unpublished manuscript.

7. See Jerome Skolnick, *Justice Without Trial*, New York: John Wiley, 1966, pp. 96–111 *et passim;* and Sacks, *op. cit.*

8. Sherri Cavan, "Interaction in Home Territories," *Berkeley Journal of Sociology*, 5 (1963) p. 18.

9. See Stanford M. Lyman, *The Structure of Chinese Society in Nineteenth Century America*, unpublished, Ph.D. dissertation, Berkeley: University of California, 1961.

10. Indeed, children are among the most regular and innovative creators of home territories from the space and material available to the public in general. Speaking of their peculiar tendency to violate the rules governing trespass, William Prosser has aptly observed, "Children, as is well known to anyone who has been a child, are by nature unreliable and irresponsible people, who are quite likely to do almost anything. In particular, they have a deplorable tendency to stray upon land which does not belong to them, and to meddle with what they find there." "Trespassing Children," *California Law Review* (August, 1959), p. 427.

11. Ethnic groups in the process of assimilation sometimes discover to their astonishment that the isolated slum wherein they have traditionally and unwillingly dwelt is in fact a home territory possessed of cherished values and irreplaceable sentiments. A militant Negro thus writes: "For as my son, Chuck, wrote me after exposure to the Negro community of Washington: 'I suddenly realized that the Negro ghetto is not a ghetto. It is home.' " John Oliver Killens, *Black Man's Burden*, New York: Trident Press, 1965, p. 94.

12. Harvey W. Zorbaugh, *The Gold Coast and the Slums*, Chicago: University of Chicago Press, 1929. See also Jane Jacobs, *The Death and Life of Great American Cities*, New York: Vintage Books, 1961, pp. 29–142.

13. See Erving Goffman, *Behavior in Public Places*, New York: The Free Press, 1963, pp. 151–165 *et passim.*

14. An excellent illustration of the several facets of this process and attendant issues in social gatherings is found in David Riesman, *et al.*, "The Vanishing Host," *Human Organization*, (Spring, 1960), pp. 17–27.

15. Talcott Parsons notes that "the very fact that affectionate bodily contact is almost completely taboo among men in American society is probably indicative of [the limited nature of intra-sex friendship] since it strongly limits affective attachment." *The Social System*, Glencoe, Ill.: The Free Press, 1951, p. 189. For an empirical study and analysis of touching relations see Erving Goffman, "The Nature of Deference and Demeanor," *American Anthropologist*, 58 (June, 1956), pp. 473–502.

16. See Kingsley Davis, *Human Society*, New York: Macmillan, 1948, pp. 19–193.

17. Lyman, *op. cit.*, pp. 97–111.

18. The perceptions of Simmel on this subject surpass all others and we are indebted to his work. Thus Simmel has noted:

In regard to the "significant" [i.e., "great"] man, there is an inner compulsion which tells one to keep at a distance and which does not disappear even in intimate relations with him. The only type for whom such distance does not exist is the individual who has no organ for perceiving distance. . . . The individual who fails to keep his distance from a great person does not esteem him highly, much less too highly (as might superficially appear to be the case); but, on the contrary, his importune behavior reveals lack of proper respect. . . . The same sort of circle which surrounds a man—although it is value-accentuated in a very different sense —is filled out by his affairs and by his characteristics. To penetrate this circle by taking notice, constitutes a violation of personality. Just as material property is, so

Stanford M. Lyman and Marvin B. Scott

to speak, an extension of the ego, there is also an intellectual private property, whose violation effects a lesion of the ego in its very center.

[Georg Simmel, "Secrecy and Group Communication," reprinted in T. Parsons, et al., *Theories of Society*, New York: The Free Press, 1961, p. 320.] For an updated statement of Simmel's point see Goffman, *Behavior in Public Places, op. cit.*

19. An interesting dilemma in this respect arises for the deaf and myopic. In attempting to appear as "normals" they may overstep another's territorial space and thus call attention to the very stigma they wish to conceal. On the problems of those who are stigmatized see Goffman, *Stigma*, Englewood Cliffs, New Jersey: Prentice-Hall, 1963.

20. Goffman refers to this as "civil inattention." See *Behavior in Public Places, op. cit.*

21. Compare the remarks by Simmel, *op. cit.*, p. 321.

In the interest of interaction and social cohesion, the individual must know certain things about the other person. Nor does the other have the right to oppose this knowledge from a moral standpoint, by demanding the discretion of the first: he cannot claim the entirely undisturbed possession of his own being and consciousness, since this discretion might harm the interests of his society. . . . But even in subtler and less unambiguous forms, in fragmentary beginnings and unexpressed notions, all of human intercourse rests on the fact that everybody knows somewhat more about the other than the other voluntarily reveals to him; and those things he knows are frequently matters whose knowledge the other person (were he aware of it) would find undesirable.

See also Goffman, *The Presentation of Self in Everyday Life, op. cit.*, pp. 1–16.

22. The structural properties and parameters of interactional territories in unserious gatherings have been admirably presented by Georg Simmel. See his "The Sociology of Sociability," *American Journal of Sociology*, (November, 1949), pp. 254–261. Reprinted in Parsons, et al., *Theories of Society, op. cit.*, pp. 157–163.

23. Here perhaps it is worth noting that language has a "tactile" dimension, in the sense that to be "touched" audially by certain terms is to be elevated or reduced in status. For Southern Negroes to be publicly addressed as "Mr.," "Miss," and "Mrs.," and by last names is considered so relevant for removal of caste barriers that legal action to require these usages has been undertaken. We may also note that genteel persons are polluted by audial contact with slang, obscenity, and, on occasion, idiomatic expression.

24. See Horace Miner, "Body Ritual Among the Nacirema," *American Anthropologist, 55, 3 (1956).*

25. Note such phrases as "I wouldn't touch him with a ten-foot pole," "She's under my skin," "He's a pain in the neck," and "Look, but don't touch." For the rules regarding touch see Erving Goffman, "The Nature of Deference and Demeanor," *op. cit.*

26. Robin Williams has shown that one test of social distance among the races in America is their unwillingness to try on clothing at an apparel shop when they have witnessed that clothing tried on and rejected by members of another—and supposedly inferior—race. Robin Williams, *Strangers Next Door*, Englewood Cliffs, New Jersey: Prentice-Hall, 1964, pp. 125–130.

27. Our usage is similar to that employed in describing the relationships in plant-communities.

The majority of individuals of a plant-community are linked by bonds other than those mentioned—bonds that are best described as commensal. The term commensalism is due to Van Beneden, who wrote "Le commensal est simplement un compagnon de table," but we employ it in a somewhat different sense to denote the relationship subsisting between species which share with one another the supply of food-material contained in soil and air, and thus feed at the same table.

[Robert E. Park and Ernest W. Burgess, *Introduction to the Science of Sociology*, Chicago: University of Chicago Press, 1921, p. 175. (Adapted from Eugenius Warming, *Oecology of Plants*, London: Oxford University Press, 1909, pp. 12–13, 91–95.)]

28. Ann Terry D'Andre, "An Occupational Study of the Strip-Dancer Career," paper delivered at the annual meetings of the Pacific Sociological Association, Salt Lake City, Utah, 1965.

29. See Ardrey, *op. cit.*, p. 210, who writes: "Biology as a whole asks but one question of a territory: Is it defended? Defense defines it. Variability becomes the final description." See also Konrad Lorenz, *On Aggression*, New York: Harcourt, Brace and World, 1966, pp. 33–38 *et passim*.

30. See Mary Coolidge, *Chinese Immigration*, New York: Henry Holt, 1909, pp. 15–26, 255–256.

31. See Lewis Yablonsky, *The Violent Gang*, New York: Macmillan, 1962, pp. 29–100 for a good ethnography of urban gangs. For an analytical treatment see Frederic M. Thrasher, *The Gang*, Chicago: University of Chicago Press, 1927, pp. 97–100, 116–129.

32. See M. G. Smith, "Kagoro Political Development," *Human Organization*, (Fall, 1960), pp. 137–149.

33. It is now a commonplace of sociological irony that persons thus insulated are vulnerable once the insulating material is removed or ubiquitously available. Thus non-coms will insult officers in clubs when both are out of uniform, psychiatrists will be mistaken for patients at dances held in the recreation room of an insane asylum, and students will adopt an inappropriate familiarity with professors not wearing a coat and tie.

34. See Goffman, *Behavior in Public Places, op. cit.*, p. 85 for a succinct account of the elements of this process as a form of civil inattention.

35. Kathleen Tamagawa, *Holy Prayers in a Horse's Ear*, New York: Long, Smith, Inc., 1932, pp. 144–151 *et passim*. André M. Tao-Kim-Hai, "Orientals are Stoic," in F. C. Macgregor, *Social Science in Nursing*, New York: Russell Sage, 1960, pp. 313–326.

36. See Georg Simmel, "The Aesthetic Significance of the Face," in Kurt H. Wolff, ed., *Georg Simmel 1858–1918*, Columbus, Ohio: Ohio State University Press, 1959, pp. 280–281.

37. The usual situation is quite the reverse, however. The "dozens" and other verbal contest forms are most frequently used by Negroes within the ethnic enclave out of earshot and view of whites. See Roger D. Abrahams, *Deep Down in the Jungle*, Hatboro, Penn.: Folklore Associates, esp. pp. 41–64.

38. See Carl Werthman, *Delinquency and Authority*, M.A. Thesis, Berkeley: University of California, 1964.

39. David Matza, *Delinquency and Drift*, New York: John Wiley, 1964.

40. Many suggestive essays on this subject can be found in *Dress, Adornment, and the Social Order*, M. E. Roach and J. B. Eicher, eds., New York: John Wiley, 1965.

41. See Cesar Grana, *Bohemian vs. Bourgeois*, New York: Basic Books, 1964, and Harold Finestone, "Cats, Kicks, and Color," *Social Problems*, 5, 1 (1957), pp. 3–13.

42. See Harry B. Hawthorn, ed., *The Doukhobors of British Columbia*, Vancouver, B.C.: The University of British Columbia and Dent & Sons, 1955.

43. Goffman, *Behavior in Public Places, op. cit.*, pp. 69–75.

6

The Physical Environment:
A Problem for a Psychology
of Stimulation

JOACHIM F. WOHLWILL

There has been growing interest among architects and other students of
environmental phenomena in the question of whether or not complex,
ambiguous, noisy, and otherwise stimulating urban environments are beneficial or harmful. In some cases designers and planners have urged that noise
levels and population densities be reduced on the grounds that sensory
overloads are causing apathy and personality decay; at the same time other
members of the same professions have been arguing that urban landscapes
are harmfully monotonous and that there is a need for greater diversity in
the urban landscape, for an architecture that is more complex and
contradictory.

It is difficult to assess the validity of these points of view, in large part
because the concepts being used are poorly defined, but even when they are
more clearly defined, they deal with phenomena that are not really comparable. Nevertheless, discussion of this issue is at least potentially capable
of greater clarification, because it is obviously related to serious research
now taking place in psychology to identify and define the need for sensory
stimulation and the function of sensory arousal in the development of a
healthy personality.

Wohlwill's selection is an attempt to summarize current data and theory
on the psychology of stimulation and to discuss the implications of this
material for environmental design, in terms of three important but unresolved issues. The first issue is: which dimensions of stimulation are most
important for arousing the organism and maintaining its curiosity? Many
stimulus characteristics have been investigated, including intensity, novelty,
complexity, temporal change, and surprisingness, but no experimental means
have yet been found for establishing the relative significance of these dimensions. The second issue is: for a particular group, is there an optimal level of
stimulation, and if so, how can it be determined operationally? Most interesting in this regard is the theory that an individual establishes an adaptation
level for himself and that deviations from the level in either direction are

Reprinted from Joachim F. Wohlwill, "The Physical
Environment: A Problem for a Psychology of Stimulation,"
Journal of Social Issues 22, no. 4 (1966): 29–38. © The Society
for the Psychological Study of Social Issues.

evaluated positively within a certain range, whereas outside this range stimuli are experienced as unpleasant. Although it is not specifically discussed in Wohlwill's selection, there has been some experimental effort to explain the popularity of the golden section as a measure of architectural proportion in terms of a similar theoretical proposition. The final issue is the relation between short-run and long-run effects. Even when an individual seems to have adjusted successfully to a particular level of sensory stimulation, there may be a long-run damage that he is not aware of.

It is obvious, as Wohlwill points out, that a good deal more research must be done on the effects of sensory stimulation or deprivation before answers can be found that can be applied to the problems of environmental design. Indeed, a similar conclusion is justifiable with respect to the other two psychological needs discussed in this section—personal space and territoriality.

□

Introduction

As a psychologist this writer has been struck by a curious paradox. Psychologists never tire to point out the importance of stimulus factors as a determinant of behavior, and of the role of environmental influences in behavior. Yet, as a group they have had relatively little to say on the important problems relating to man's response to his physical environment. We may hope that the valuable contributions now being made to this area by many psychologists portend a change in this state of affairs in the foreseeable future. Meanwhile it may be instructive to examine briefly, at the outset, some of the likely reasons for this seeming lack of attention given to these problems by psychologists; our primary aim, however, is to point more positively to some recent developments in the experimental psychology of motivation which appear to have interesting implications for the study of the impact of the physical environment on behavior and for approaches to environmental design.

That child psychologists, personality psychologists and social psychologists with an environmentalist bias should have neglected the role of the physical environment in behavior is readily understandable. For the most part they have been interested in the interpersonal, social and cultural aspects of the environment, in line with the prevalent drive theory of motivation, built on the concepts of appetitive and aversive reinforcement, which has featured much of their thinking. According to this conception, it is *people* who administer rewards and punishments; the natural and artificial surroundings in which people live thus have little power to influence behavior. Not surprisingly, this has been true of those working outside of a stimulus-response reinforcement model, notably within a field-theoretical framework. Yet even here, where the vocabulary of boundaries, barriers and field forces might seem to favor attention to variables of the physical environment, primary interest has remained in the analysis of interpersonal interaction, social encounters, and the like.

Turning now to the side of experimental psychology, ever since the appearance in 1949 of Hebb's influential *The Organization of Behavior,* the role of sensory stimulation from the environment, not only for the normal development of perceptual and cognitive functions but for motivational processes as well, has become of increasing concern. Yet, starting from the premise that stimulation is good, indeed essential for the development and maintenance of normal behavior, most of the efforts of workers in this area have been devoted to demonstrating the deleterious effects of drastic reductions in level of stimulation, whether as a short-term condition with human adults (cf. the work on "sensory deprivation," [10]) or as a more prolonged condition of the early experience of animals (e.g., 11, 1961). Where attempts have been made to enhance the behavioral effectiveness of animals, e.g., their problem-solving ability, by providing for "enriched" stimulus environments, the research has typically started from a straightforward "the more, the better" assumption. The success of such efforts is not surprising, if one bears in mind the impoverished level of stimulation provided by the typical laboratory environment used as the base of comparison for most of these studies, but its relevance to the living conditions under which modern man operates is doubtful.

A recent extension of this stimulus-enrichment approach to the study of "imprinting" in newly hatched chicks, that is, the development of the following response to the mother, is particularly instructive in revealing the psychologists' conception of an optimal set of stimulus conditions. The authors describe the treatment to which the experimental animals were subjected immediately after hatching as follows:

The complex environment . . . consisted of a black-walled enclosure with random stripes and blotches of white paint. Above was a bank of six 200-w light bulbs which flashed on and off at 1-sec. intervals. Two metronomes produced a constant ticking. A radio, tuned to a local AM station, played constantly at high volume. Every 30 min. E stroked each chick's back with a foam rubber brush and with a whisk broom for 15 sec., rang a bicycle bell for 2 min., and gave a gentle puff of air from an air compressor (5, p. 654).

Let it be recorded that this treatment apparently worked wonders on the imprinting response of these chicks, which developed both earlier and more strongly than did chicks who started life amidst more humdrum environmental conditions. Yet this positive result will not be altogether reassuring to some who may see in the treatment described above only a slight caricature of the frenetic bombardment from stimuli of all kinds encountered in certain urban environments. After all, newborn chicks, even of the Vantress Broiler variety used in this study, are not to be equated to human beings, and the imprinting response hardly constitutes a valid model of human behavior and adjustment. Such doubting Thomases could derive support for their skepticism, moreover, by pointing to the case of the typical "culturally deprived" child from the slums, who is apt to grow up under just such conditions of overstimulation, without great profit to his general intellectual development or emotional well being.

A whole host of questions arise at this point: Is there a particular level of stimulation conducive to optimal development? Does patterned stimulation differ in its effects on development from unpatterned (e.g., noise)? Above all, what is the role of meaning (as invested in language and in object stimuli) in modulating the effects of stimulation on development, and what conditions promote the sifting out of meaningful from meaningless stimuli by the child? Though some research with animals has been carried out relative to the first of these questions, the others have remained virtually untouched, so that in the aggregate the evidence available thus far is probably of limited significance for an understanding of the effects of the stimulus conditions characterizing our typical physical environments on the development of the individual.

Once we turn away from the study of the effects of stimulus experience on development, however, we find a considerable body of recent work that is of direct relevance for us, dealing with the stimulus correlates of the arousal of human attention and with human activity involving the seeking out of stimulation. Psychologists have come to recognize what persons in the amusement and recreation industries —to say nothing of observant parents—have known all along: that a large part of the everyday activity of the human (or of the animal, for that matter) has as its aim not to *reduce* unpleasant tensions, e.g., from the hunger or sex drives, but rather to heighten the level of incoming stimulation, by voluntary exposure to stimulus objects or situations that are novel, incongruous, surprising or complex. Man, it seems, is ever curious, ever eager to explore, and unlike the proverbial cat, appears generally to thrive on such activity.

This is not the place to review the extensive literature in this area, dealing with the motivational and arousal properties of stimulation, or to enter into a discussion of the complex theoretical issues raised by this work (1, 3, 4, 13). Let us rather examine its possible relevance to problems of man's response to his physical environment, and some of the questions raised by an attempt to apply such notions to this problem area. We will confine ourselves to a discussion, necessarily oversimplified, of three main questions.

Dimensions of Stimulation

What are the chief dimensions of stimulation that are of concern to the student of environmental psychology? Those most frequently discussed by psychologists include simple intensity, novelty, complexity, and temporal change or variation; to these we may add surprisingness and incongruity, which have been more specifically emphasized by Berlyne (1). If only in an illustrative sense, all of these can be shown to touch on important aspects of our physical environment. To start with intensity, questions of level of noise and illumination have been of concern to industrial designers, architects and planners for some time, although outside of an industrial context there has been little systematic research on the effects of different levels of auditory or visual intensity on behavior. The importance of *novelty* is well known to observers of that favorite pastime, sightseeing, a facet of behavior which can play an important role in questions of urban design (e.g., the role of San Francisco's cable-cars), as well as in the administration of our natural recreation areas. *Complexity* of stimulation may well be a major factor in differential evaluation of urban, suburban and rural environments, as it is in the response to more particular features of our environment, e.g., samples of modern architecture or highway layouts. *Variation* in the stimulus input enters into diverse problems in environmental design that in one way or another have concerned the need to reduce boredom or monotony, from the subtle variations in design introduced into the construction of housing à la Levittown to the layout of highways, e.g., the avoidance of long, straight stretches.[1]

Surprisingness and *incongruity* are likewise of interest to us, notably in architecture and landscape design. As an example, the pleasing effect of surprise in the exploration of a building complex is nicely brought out by Nairn in his perceptive analysis of the layout of the entrance to the Wellesley College campus (8, p. 33ff). The same author lays a good deal of stress on the role of incongruity, though mainly in a negative sense, i.e., by bringing out the jarring effect of the juxtaposition of different structures lacking in any relationship to one another. Whether some degree of incongruity may nevertheless serve a positive function (in the sense of heightening our attention, if not necessarily our affective evaluation of a scene) must remain an unanswered question at this time. (We may note, in any event, that some degree of incongruity in our environment is inevitable, if only because architectural styles change—cf. the contemporary look of the area around Harvard Square.)

While it may thus be easy to illustrate the relevance of these "collative" variables (as Berlyne calls them) to our response to the physical environment, systematic research in this area will have to come to grips with the problems of operational definition and measurement of these variables, in situations not permitting their control or manipulation by the investigator. Even in the laboratory air-tight definitions allowing for consistent differentiation of the effects of novelty from surprise, on the one hand, or temporal variation on the other are difficult to formulate. Similarly the measurement of novelty (particularly in the long-term sense) and of complexity poses considerable problems. All of these are of course greatly magnified when dealing with ready-made stimuli taken from the actual physical environment, such as landscapes, or urban scenes. In such a situation it may be necessary to compromise to a certain extent with scientific rigor, but this is no reason to shy away from research in such real-life settings. If it is impossible to manipulate variables independently, their relative contributions can generally still be assessed through techniques of statistical control and multivariate analysis.

A more critical problem is that of the measurement of these variables, in the absence of systematic, controlled manipulation. Here we will have to resort to indirect methods based on ratings or other subjective scaling methods. It is worth noting in this connection, that a recent study utilizing judges' ratings to assess complexity of landscapes, still showed consistent relationships between this variable and the relative interest (i.e., fixation times) of these stimuli (7). More recent developments in the area of stimulus scaling techniques, some of which allow for the construction of a metric scale even with purely subjective judgments, lessen the need for independent, objective measures of the physical stimulus (12).

Joachim F. Wohlwill

The Concept of an Optimal Level of Stimulation

A number of psychologists working in this area have advanced an optimal-level hypothesis, postulating an inverted-U shaped relationship between magnitude of stimulation along the dimensions considered above and the arousal value of, interest in, or preference for a given stimulus. Except for variables representing continua of stimulus intensity, systematic evidence on this point is actually fairly meager.[2] Nevertheless the concept deserves our consideration, in view of its patent relevance to man's response to the wide range of stimulation encountered in the physical environment. It ties in directly, furthermore, with Helson's Adaptation-level theory, which represents a much more general framework for the study of the most diverse responses to any stimuli varying along some assumed dimension (6). In a nutshell, this theory maintains that for any specified dimension of stimulus variation the individual establishes an AL (adaptation-level) which determines his judgmental or evaluative response to a given stimulus located on that dimension. In particular, with reference to an evaluative response, the principle is that deviations from the AL in either direction are evaluated positively within a certain range, while beyond these boundaries they are experienced as unpleasant.

Let us try to apply this hypothesis to a person's choice of a vacation spot. To this end, let us conceive of a hybrid dimension of "closeness to civilization," which probably represents a composite of such variables as intensity, complexity, temporal variation and novelty. Take a person living in a small eastern city, so that his AL may be assumed to be somewhere in the middle of our dimension. Where will he go for his vacation? He may either be drawn to the kaleidoscopic attractions of a big metropolis like New York, or, alternatively, to the restful vistas of Vermont or the Cape Cod seashore. However, in accordance with the notion that beyond a certain range marked discrepancies from the AL are no longer experienced as pleasant or desirable, we may hypothesize that, in the first case, our vacationer will tend to avoid or be repelled by places representing the more extreme levels of stimulation to be found in the big city (e.g., Times Square at New Year's Eve; the subway during rush hour).[3] If, on the other hand, he chooses the open country, he is apt to want a motel room with TV, or to stick to the more populated resort areas.

This would seem to represent a plausible research hypothesis,

89

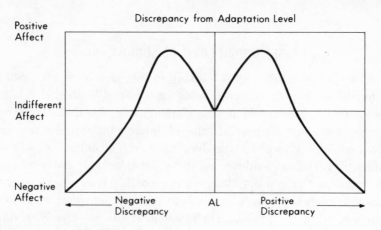

Figure 6-1 Changes in Affective Response to Stimuli as a Function of Extent of Deviation from Adaptation Level (after Helson, H., Adaptation-Level Theory, New York: Harper & Row, 1964).

though there are bound to be exceptions from this norm, e.g., hardy souls preferring a more nearly total isolation from civilization, or on the contrary a more intensive immersion in the stimulation offered by the big city. If so, this would show that not only the AL itself, but the degree of departure from it that would be experienced as pleasurable may vary considerably from one person to the next. This would admittedly make life more complex for the researcher investigating these problems, but would not pose any insuperable difficulties, provided independent measures of these parameters were available. It may also be noted that our model implies that such wilderness-fanciers would be least likely to come from a big metropolitan area; conversely, among those most strongly attracted to the excitement of the bustling metropolis, we should expect to find the visitor from a small town relatively underrepresented.

The Question of Long-Term Adaptation Effects

The concept of adaptation-level itself brings up a further question: What are the long-range effects of exposure to a given environment featured by a particular level of intensity, complexity, incongruity, etc., of stimulation? (In the very nature of the case, if the environment remains constant, novelty and surprisingness effectively cease to be relevant variables.) According to AL theory, the individual's AL will be shifted to a value corresponding more nearly to that environment.[4] This is of course no more than an expression of the

90

fact of adaptation. The question arises, however, whether in spite of the individual's capacity to adapt to an astonishingly wide range of environmental conditions, such prolonged exposure to stimulus environments falling near the extreme of the complexity or intensity dimension, for instance, may not leave its mark nevertheless. That is, it is possible that the arousal value or the subjective evaluation of the stimulus environment by the individual may become assimilated to some normal range, and his behavior become effectively adapted to it; yet more subtle long-term effects on behavior may nevertheless occur. For instance, a commuter subjected morning and evening to rush-hour traffic conditions on the New York subways may come to experience them as no more arousing than would his wife taking a quiet, uncrowded bus ride through suburban streets (though his evaluation of the experience is apt to remain rather more negative). He may even develop the knack of reading and assimilating "all the news that's fit to print," unaware of the din and shoving around him. Yet the cumulative effect of the exposure to these conditions may still leave a residue detectable in his behavior, which might take the form of heightened arousal thresholds, lessened frustration tolerance, or the like, representing the price being paid for this surface adaptation. Or take the child growing up among a steady backdrop of high-intensity TV signals, rattling subway trains and yells from neighbors: he may well adapt to these conditions of noise, but perhaps only by shutting out from awareness much of the input—notably speech—to which in fact he needs to become sensitized for his optimal development.

Admittedly we are operating largely on hunches in our estimates of such long-term behavioral effects of exposure to particular levels of stimulation, but their possible reality can hardly be discounted, especially in view of the considerable evidence in this respect uncovered at the physiological level (2). There are, furthermore, undoubtedly large individual differences in tolerance of or adaptability to extreme levels of stimulation; for example, much migration behavior may be interpretable as an individual's response to his experienced level of stress emanating from the physical as well as the social environment (14).

Conclusion

In closing, we may express the hope that ultimately attention to questions such as these will lead to the creation of a science of environmental esthetics as a branch of psychology concerned with man's

91

effective response to the qualitative and quantitative features of the world of natural and man-made stimuli surrounding him. Esthetics, to be sure, has not been a particularly flourishing branch of psychology in the past, no more than it has, until recently, represented an area of concern in our social, political and economic life. But it is perhaps not an entirely fortuitous coincidence that the attention which leaders in our public life have most recently been giving to the beautification of our artificial environment, as well as to the preservation of natural beauty, comes at the very time that the "new look" in the field of motivation is bringing psychologists ever closer to the realm of esthetics. (It is significant that the two books which are the primary sources with respect to this "new look," i.e., Berlyne (1); Fiske and Maddi (3), both include a chapter on esthetics.) The time would thus seem most auspicious for experimental psychologists to take their place alongside their colleagues in social psychology, sociology, geography, architecture, planning, etc., in a broadside attack on the problems facing us in improving the quality of our environment.

NOTES

1. Other ways in which the variable of temporal change, as well as of complexity of the stimulus input affect our perception of and locomotion within our geographical environment are brought out succinctly by A. E. Parr (9). Many of the points made in his paper are quite apposite to the kind of analysis of the stimulus properties of our environment being presented here.
2. As Fiske and Maddi (3, p. 9) note, most of their book is concerned with understimulation, rather than overstimulation, which they identify with stress. But in view of the emphasis given in their own formulation to the concept of an optimal level of activation, their readiness to dismiss the problem of overstimulation as unimportant is difficult to understand.
3. Though this proposition might seem to lack surface plausibility, it derives some limited support from the results of a pilot study carried out by two Clark undergraduates, Kenneth Holm and Harlan Sherwin, who interviewed tourists at Penn. Station to obtain their reactions to New York City. Of those who lived in suburban districts, one-third expressed some degree of positive reaction to the New York subways, whereas less than 10% of those residing in either small-town or country areas or in a metropolitan area gave any positive responses. It is also interesting to note that, in another sample of suburbanites, only 40% picked the crowds and noise as the aspects they disliked most about New York City, whereas 80% of the country-, small-town- or city-dwellers chose these aspects. (The suburbanites responded almost as frequently to the *dirt* of the city.)
4. It should be noted that for environmental settings characterized by either very low or very high levels of stimulation, the AL should be expected to fall considerably short of this extreme value, since the effects of exposure to a given environment on the AL are superimposed on factors of a more intrinsic sort, relating to the individual's assumed needs for a certain modal level of stimulation lying within some intermediate range.

REFERENCES

1. Berlyne, D. E. *Conflict, Arousal and Curiosity.* New York: McGraw-Hill, 1960.

2. Dubos, R. *Man Adapting.* New Haven: Yale University Press, 1965.

3. Fiske, D. W. and S. R. Maddi, eds. *Functions of Varied Experience.* Homewood, Ill.: Dorsey Press, 1961.

4. Fowler, H. *Curiosity and Exploratory Behavior.* New York: Macmillan, 1965.

5. Haywood, H. C., and D. W. Zimmerman. Effects of early environmental complexity on the following response in chicks. *Percept. mot. Skills,* 1964, **18**, 653–658.

6. Helson, H. *Adaptation-Level Theory.* New York: Harper & Row, 1964.

7. Leckart, B. T. and P. Bakan. Complexity judgments of photographs and looking time. *Percept. mot. Skills,* 1965, **21**, 16–18.

8. Nairn, I. *The American Landscape.* New York: Random House, 1965.

9. Parr, A. E. Psychological aspects of urbanology. *Journal of Social Issues,* 1966, **22**, no. 4, 39–45.

10. Solomon, P., et al., eds. *Sensory Deprivation.* Cambridge: Harvard University Press, 1961.

11. Thompson, R. W. and T. Schaefer, Jr. "Early environmental stimulation." In *Functions of Varied Experience.* D. W. Fiske and S. R. Maddi, eds. Homewood, Ill.: Dorsey Press, 1961, 81–105.

12. Torgerson, W. S. *Theory and Methods of Scaling.* New York: John Wiley and Sons, 1958.

13. White, R. W. "Motivation reconsidered: the concept of competence." In *Functions of Varied Experience.* D. W. Fiske and S. R. Maddi, eds. Homewood, Ill.: Dorsey Press, 1961, 278–325.

14. Wolpert, Julian. Migration as an adjustment to environmental stress. *Journal of Social Issues,* 1966, **22**, no. 4, 92–102.

PART TWO

Spatial Organization and Social Interaction

7

The Psycho-Social Influence of Building Environment: Sociometric Findings in Large and Small Office Spaces

B. W. P. WELLS

One of the principal interests of environmental designers today is the role that architecture can play in fostering social interaction. When architecture is considered in terms of this goal, the aspect of the built environment that is usually examined is spatial organization. What is the horizontal distribution of people and activities across the plane of the earth, as in a site plan or floor plan, or, in a vertical structure, the distribution of rooms and activities from floor to floor? In such discussions spatial organization is measured in terms of the physical and functional distance between persons, groups, and activities.

That architecture does have some influence on social interaction cannot be disputed. A building, or a group of buildings, has the capacity to serve as a communications network. The arrangement of rooms, walls, doors, partitions, driveways, and streets does affect the opportunities people have to see and hear each other and thus to respond to one another. By the location of barriers, apertures, and paths, physical arrangements can provide opportunities for communication, or hinder it. It is only a short step from the chance to communicate to the act of communicating, and therefore, to social interaction.

Wells' study of the formation of cohesive work groups in an office building illustrates the effect of spatial arrangements on communications networks. His measure of the existence of cohesive work groups is the degree of reciprocity in friendship choices among the workers in an insurance company office in Manchester, England. Wells collected data from 295 office workers on one floor about which clerks they preferred to work next to. Of the respondents 214 worked in a large open area, while 81 worked in 1 of 3 smaller enclosed areas. Wells' findings were (1) that choices were directly related to the distances between employees, with both men and women preferring office mates who already were working next to or close to them; (2) that workers in the smaller partitioned areas were likely to prefer office

Reprinted from B. W. P. Wells, "The Psycho-Social Influence of Building Environment: Sociometric Findings in Large and Small Office Spaces," in *Building Science* 1(1965): 153–165.

mates from their own section; and (3) that the percentage of individuals who were not chosen by any of their colleagues, that is who were social isolates, was larger in the smaller work spaces. Wells concludes that internal group cohesion in the smaller areas was greater than in the open plan sections, even though the smaller areas included more isolates and had fewer links with those outside the small area.

It should be noted that Wells' research, although it deals with a general issue in the relation of architecture to behavior, was undertaken in response to a practical design problem. Deep office blocks of the kind discussed in his selection are becoming increasingly common because they are less expensive to construct. However, since most workers prefer daylight and an outside view, deep blocks require large, open plan offices. In his concluding discussion, Wells raises the issue of how the designer and client can achieve a proper balance between the presumed advantages in morale of the more cohesive groups in the smaller spaces and the greater building efficiency and broader departmental ties of the open plan.

☐

The approach made in this study is that of sociometry—a complex methodology but one yielding utterly simple data—consisting merely of the preferences or rejections expressed by members of a given group towards other members of that group. These are termed socioprefer-ential choices and are usually written down in reply to a highly specific question about the circumstances of the choice. The method has proved extremely interesting in connection with the sort of research that psychologists may come to use extensively on architectural problems, and with this justification, the methodology has been presented in detail.

However, before describing the experimental work so far completed, a consideration of the background to the psycho-social component of environmental studies would be in order.

Background of Theory and Research

In 1963 John Noble (1) wrote an article in the *Architects' Journal* entitled "The How and Why of Behaviour: Social Psychology for the Architect" in which he wrote "as architects we help to shape people's future behaviour by the environment we create." This is a belief very widely held amongst architects and one, if true, of very great importance not only to architects, but also to the public in general and the human sciences in particular. However, at the present time, the empirical evidence for such a belief (except in the most trivial sense) is sparse indeed: the influence of the building environment remains very much an unknown quantity.

Psychologists spend a great deal of time defining and examining the concept of "environment" and in describing the influence of the environment on the human being. The clearly defined aspects of physical environment such as heat, light and sound; the internal physical environmental features such as hormonal function; the family and the larger social environments, are all matters of the deepest concern to the psychologist. It is, however, an extremely curious fact that the most prominent and obvious feature of our environment, the very buildings, towns and cities in which we act out our entire lives have so far attracted scarcely any attention whatsoever.

At any point *lower* than man on the phylogenetic scale, the biological scientist would regard habitat as a fundamentally important feature in determining an animal's behavior. However, at the level of man, the psychologist and other behavioral and social scientists concentrate their attention on learning and the acquired behavior patterns which have given man a large measure of mastery of his environment. He creates the conditions he feels he needs or wants and is no longer so much influenced by his physical environment. Instead, the greater environmental pressures are applied by the social milieu and organization created from his relative freedom from instinctive behavior patterns. This not to say that there is a complete, or anything like complete, freedom from the influence of the created physical environment. The influence of habitat may be relatively smaller in the case of man, but it may still be a potent factor in influencing certain types of behavior.

Where environmental studies *have* been made, though, they have rather tended to be concerned with the most simple—and probably least influential—aspects. That is, discrete studies of optimal heating, lighting and ventilation, and acoustical conditions. It has further been felt that these factors, taken collectively and in conjunction with subjective preferences for layout and finish, exhaust the topic of the internal environment of buildings—at least so far as the designer is concerned.

However, it is the thesis of this paper that the *social* factors of environment are amongst the most important, and that these are very much the concern of designers where their designs affect the way in which space may be used. This, of course, would be so in almost every case.

One way of thinking about a building is as a catalyst; that is, a relatively inert agent, but one vital to a particular process—in the present context the work of an office. However, if the building *is* a catalyst, it is one which differs in a very important respect from the catalytic agents of chemistry. They facilitate only *one* kind of reaction between substances. The building, on the other hand, may facilitate *many* reactions. For example, common entrances to different departments mean that there are many more opportunities for inter-departmental contacts than if there were separate ones. The results of these interactions must be studied both from the personal-social and from the company point of view. The individual's potential social world is perhaps widened, and it may well be that inter-departmental working is facilitated by such informal contacts. The size of the rooms themselves also sets the limits and range of working, and therefore, social intercourse. Another consequence of room size may follow from the introduction of very large clerical areas which would seem to offer chances for the introduction of more autocratic measures in supervision and management.

The sort of questions which arise in relation to room size are, what happens when a clerk moves from a small office setting to the large open one? In what way do his group sentiments change *vis à vis* both the group and the department or company as a whole? Which group sizes tend to have cohesive and which disintegrative effects on social and working groups? Are they affected at all? How does the individual's concept of himself change; does the worker regard himself as reduced in stature by being given less obvious prominence in a larger group? Does he feel more or less ambitious in the new setting? Are there more far-reaching social consequences? No such systematic work on the influence of office size on the clerical worker has yet been done, and it is some aspects of this fundamentally important problem which will be considered by means of the sociometric approach.

The methods of judging the social conditions within open plan offices are often questionable in the extreme and thus many of the conclusions which are derived must be treated with some caution.

The literature on the open plan design is replete with comment which, in the absence of good supportive evidence, can only be regarded as an attempt on the part of the writer to identify with the clerical worker. The very terms used in stating the problem are heavily weighted with the attitudes of their authors. In an address to the Association of Industrial Medical Officers, McGirr (2) referring to the open plan offices, spoke of "herding clerical staff into them" and described them as "soulless subtopia of impersonalization." He rejected the counter-evidence of their acceptance in America on the grounds that open planning is congruent with the American national aim of "togetherness," whereas it is a "principle fundamentally at variance with our national concepts of individuality and personal privacy."

McGirr's position has clearly been derived from reference to his own standards. His beliefs in the need for individuality and personal privacy are middle class sentiments which are not necessarily relevant to the majority of workers in the large clerical organizations. As Lockwood (3) has pointed out, recent social and economic forces have created paperwork industries manned not by the nonprofessional members of the middle classes, but mainly by members of lower socio-economic groups. The nature of the work is also different: it has been mechanized and de-skilled and is now largely in the hands of young female workers. It has currently more in common with light industrial assembly work than with the clerical work of a generation ago. It may very well be then that the sentiments expressed by McGirr are not those of the modern office worker, but only research will settle the issue.

Unfortunately, the research has usually not been done before the conclusions are anticipated. Even such respected figures as McGirr (who was a member of the Institute of Directors' Main Committee in the publication of "Better Offices" 1962) (4) reach far beyond the evidence when discussing open office planning. For example, later in the paper already referred to, he went on to say:

. . . *by neglecting the social studies already existing in small group performances, these gentleman (i.e. methods engineers and business efficiency experts), may be sowing the seeds of future frustration and breakdown. I believe that as doctors in commerce and industry we have a duty to protect those entrusted to our care against the potential evils of an entirely mechanistic approach by work study.*

This, of course, constitutes a clarion call for industrial medical officers to oppose innovation on exceedingly slender evidence and grounds. Almost nothing is known of the consequences of open plan organization and it is premature to claim that it may be the cause of future frustration and breakdown. However, because the chain of evidence is not a strong one, and is probably colored by personal feelings, one certainly cannot disregard McGirr's apprehensions; indeed they are shared by many planners, managements, and their staffs.

McGirr concluded his paper by saying:

We must make ourselves familiar with studies in group dynamics and breakdown; if satisfied that the human element is being neglected for a wholly mechanical approach to work, we ought to be fearless in our denunciations.

This is, of course, a sentiment with which few people would disagree, but the links connecting human happiness and psychic balance with space utilization and staff deployment have yet to be shown. The whole question is so important from not only a personal point of view, but also from that of management and designers, that prompt research into the subject is clearly necessary.

Of the little objective research which has been done in connection with building design, perhaps the most celebrated attempt to apply the methods of social psychology has been that of Festinger *et al.* (5). They studied sociometrically the effects of different types of housing and spatial relationship upon group and friendship formation, and concluded that:

the relationship between ecological and sociometric structures is so very marked that there can be little doubt that in these communities passive contacts are a major determinant of friendship and group formation.

Similarly, Gullahorn (6) showed in an office setting that frequency of social interaction and friendship choice were closely related to spatial relationships. This raises the question of whether, in an organization such as the one in which this research was done,[1] and where departments are broken into smaller sections working side by side, informal groups arise more easily between individuals assigned to different formal (i.e. working and administrative) groupings. The study to be described contrasts some of the friendship patterns found in open working areas with those of some relatively small and enclosed ones.

In view of the research findings on the social consequences of spatial contiguity, one might expect a number of important managerial consequences from the decision to adopt either the open or the closed office plan. One might, for example, expect that the single section occupying a small office would offer the greatest opportunity for the formation of a stable work group. In a small office, cohesive forces would derive from the fact that each member of the primary, or face to face, group shares the common working objectives of that group. The small office area produces a closeness of the group determined not only by the physical distances between working spaces, but also by functional distances involved. That is, people are brought close together by the passive interactions taking place as a result of using a common entrance and common circulation space, and also by the non-business interactions at

102

such foci as the filing cabinets, postal trays, and telephones. Unlike the open office, all these interactions will take place on a working unit basis. Thus the small office arrangement produces the best possibility for the formation of a group with a clear identity and concept of itself as a discrete and simple entity.

On the other hand, the open plan office allows for more *possibilities* of interpersonal contact and group formation. Common entrances and circulation spaces will increase the number of inter-group contacts (that is, contacts between different working groups). Without partitions, both the physical and functional distance between groups is reduced and one might expect, from the research findings previously referred to, that the number of intergroup friendships would increase. The individual may then find himself a member of two groups—the formal group of his work section, and an informal friendship group composed of members of *different* sections.

The existence of large numbers of intra-group friendships (i.e. friendships existing within the formal work unit), is a factor which has been shown to be related to group effectiveness and morale (7, 8). However, unlike the small office, the open plan area allows for the easy formation of between section friendships. If these are made at the expense of the within section ones, then one might expect on theoretical grounds that the morale and effectiveness of the work unit might suffer.

The proliferation of friendship groups between work units is also a potential force working against managerial control. The status roles, lines of communication, and group loyalties intended to operate within a working group may well be undermined by the competing claims of the informal group. The influences exerted by the immediate primary group can be very strong indeed, influencing the attitudes, expectations, and behavior of not only the pliable individual, but also the average and strong personality (9-12). An appraisal of these effects should therefore be a prerequisite to the management decision of whether to adopt the open plan: whether the advantages are outweighed by the disadvantages. But this first requires that the research should be done in order to establish the *actual* influence of office size.

THE STATUS OF THE HYPOTHESES

The present investigation of the psycho-social consequences of large and small office areas started with a few specific hypotheses which were derived from the previously referred to literature. They were of the kind that there would be more mutual friendship choices in small areas than large, and that there would be more friendship choices directed outside of people's own formal work group in the large area than in the small. These were, though, only conceptual guide lines: the study was much more empirical and exploratory than it was theoretical and so the hypotheses are relatively unimportant compared with the findings as no existing theoretical issues were being critically tested.

POPULATION AND SAMPLES USED

As has already been referred to, the investigation took place within the head office building of an insurance company. The experimental area was limited to a single floor of 36,000 sq. ft., containing more than three hundred clerks, supervisors and managers.

The floor taken as the experimental one was selected as being the only one which met the criteria of having both large and small work areas with personnel who were closely comparable in terms of their supervision, formal group membership and nature of the work. There were only general clerical areas on the floor—no typing pools or machine rooms—thus there was considerable homogeneity amongst the clerical workers. This homogeneity was increased by the fact of the whole floor being part of the same department: little internal partitioning was used—just sufficient to mark the boundaries of the three sub-departments. These open areas were vast (of the order of one hundred clerks within partition lines which themselves were not wall to wall).

Three small working areas (of approximately thirty clerks) were taken as ones to contrast with the remaining open ones. They were fairly well defined from the open areas as they were sited between partition walls and the walls of enclosed stair wells. All the desks in the small areas faced the window wall and thus the clerks had little opportunity for even visual contact with other members of their department although they were occupied on similar work.

All of the people working on the experimental floor were invited to participate in the study and, with the exception of those away sick or on holiday, all did. They composed 295 general clerks in the grades below section clerk (or supervisor). The sample was therefore fairly homogeneous as it did not include any other such categories as machine operators, typists, managers or supervisors.

Of the 295 respondents, 214 worked in the large open areas, and 81 in the smaller enclosed areas referred to above: age and sex categories were comparable. The youngest group of 15–19 year olds composed 43 per cent of the population, and older workers, the age groups over 40, accounted for 21 per cent. The age groups between 20 and 39 were

104

fairly evenly distributed minorities. The ratio of females to males was of the order 2:1. These proportions are closely similar to the overall distribution of the company's staff.

METHOD OF INVESTIGATION

The method of collecting the sociometric data was dependent, to some extent, upon the need to use the experimental opportunity to collect other material about the attitudes and feelings of the subjects towards large and small offices.[2] This latter material involved the presentation of verbal and visual material (tape recorded instructions and slide projections), the responses to which were to be written in a reply booklet. It was decided to include the sociometric item with this other, less emotionally toned, material.

The experimental setting of the study was a recreation hall which had been made available by the company, and in which there were facilities for projecting slides and presenting tape recorded instructions.

The total sample of 295 was divided into 4 groups of approximately 75; each group taking just under half an hour to process. By taking the subjects as groups and carefully dispersing them within the experimental room it was possible to deal with them as aggregates rather than groups, giving essentially isolated conditions for the individual (thus avoiding interpersonal influence), and having the advantage of processing large numbers at one time. The data collection was completed by lunch time and thus the dangers inherent in subjects discussing experiments were greatly reduced.

ANALYSIS OF DATA

From the point of view of construction, devising a sociometric reply sheet is a perfectly common-sense procedure. Moreno (13) who was principally responsible for the development of the sociometric method, gives a general background to the preparation of such a document in his book "Who shall survive?" The most fundamental prerequisite in using such a technique is, of course, having the confidence of the respondents. In the present instance, the request for sociometric data came as the culmination of a 2-year research project within the company. The investigator was therefore very well known to the respondents and on good personal terms with many of them, having spent a great deal of time working on the floor in question and mixing socially in the coffee lounges and recreation rooms. One might also expect that the study

105

would derive a certain amount of acceptance from the fact that it was supported by the trade union, of which every employee was a member. At all stages in the project great care had been taken to promote the goodwill of the union so that it should continue to recommend the investigations to its members.

As Moreno, and many others since, have pointed out, it is essential to be specific about the conditions under which the preference choice is to be made. That is, whether the choice is a work choice, a dining choice, a choice of sports companion, or what. One must also specify the population from which the choices may be drawn if the pattern of interactions is to be interpretable. The criterion of the sociopreferential choice for this study was the people beside which the respondent would like to work. The universe of choice was limited to those people also working on the same floor. In this case, taking the whole of one floor allowed for most of the possible face to face social interactions which occur during working hours as most between-floor communication must take place either by means of the telephone or the document conveyor.

Selltiz *et al.* (14) have drawn attention to the desirability of stating, where feasible, that the investigator will arrange for the individual's preferences to be met if possible. This was not possible in the present case, and instead the experimenter took the alternative course recommended by Bjerstedt (15).

It may therefore often be advantageous to make the situation cognitively experimental, to stress that nothing will happen as a result of the findings. If there is no need for report-distortion the subject is likely to give a true answer that is after all, most natural and least laborious.

As well as having the general goodwill and support of the subjects, it is also absolutely vital that they be reassured of their anonymity and the fact that their reply forms will be treated in an absolutely confidential manner. The written and spoken instructions made this abundantly clear, and also that the data was to be coded and transferred to punched cards and the questionnaires immediately destroyed. It is though, the investigator's belief that the greatest reassurance came not from promises made at the time, but from people's experience of the way in which other confidences, derived from 2 years of contact, had been maintained.

No limit was set to the number of choices that a respondent could make. Preferences were to be given in ranked order, and spaces were allowed for up to ten names on the reply form. As an additional motivator to the hesitant, the tape recorded instruction "Please try to list

at least three people" was given half a minute after the first set of instructions. A total of 2 minutes was allowed to list the preferential
choices, and one further minute to complete the additional information
about friendships with people on other floors.

FORM OF ANALYSIS OF DATA

The sociometric method is used principally as a tool for the examination of the social structure of groups of less than about forty people,
and more usually still, for smaller ones. The techniques of analysis are
therefore most developed for the small group. The original method described by Moreno (13) and still the most popular, entails drawing a
diagram in which preferences or rejections are represented by lines
between the individuals forming the group. (See Figure 7–1.)

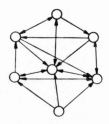

Figure 7–1   Simple Sociometric Diagram.

7 subjects   2 stars
21 preference choices   1 isolate
6 mutual preferences

The diagram is then rearranged in such a way as to make it perceptually more simple. It then remains to look for any trends; to establish
who are the isolates in a group, and who are the "stars." The procedures involved are not systematic and the pattern tends to be exceedingly difficult to comprehend with large numbers. (See Figure 7–2.)

To simplify the analysis, methods were developed in which the
diagram was replaced by the matrix. Forsyth and Katz (16) developed
a method in which the individuals of the group were listed in the same
order down the rows and along the columns.

The matrix was completed by entering the choices made by individuals in the row bearing his name and in the column of the person receiving that choice. This gave a picture almost as complicated as the
diagram, but it could be simplified by rearranging the order of the columns and rows so that the entries in the matrix clustered as closely as
possible about the main diagonal. The diagonal is, of course, composed

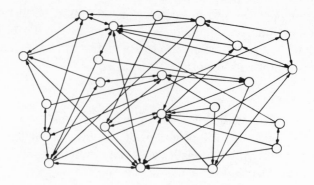

Figure 7–2   More Complex Sociometric Diagram.

22 subjects   3 stars
66 preferences (3 each)   1 isolate
16 mutual preferences

of empty cells as it is formed by the point at which the individual's name appears in both the column and the row. The arrangement shows, in the clusters, those people who have chosen one another relatively frequently. The well separated entries represent the people who have not chosen one another. (See Figure 7-3.)

However, the method of matrix analysis so far described is, as Festinger (17) pointed out, most useful for establishing changes within a group from one time to another and is of little value in demonstrating the existence of subgroups or for comparing two groups. Festinger's own special contribution was to suggest a technique to allow for the determination of cliques within a group.

The above represent the three main types of analysis applied to sociometric data. There are almost innumerable variations of them, but none allows for a comparison of the social organization of physically separated groups, both of which form part of the same universe of choice. The usual situation involves taking two groups, each of which represents a separate universe, and comparing their internal sociometric structures. However, the present study is specifically concerned with the between group relationships and so it must be possible for the respondent to express his choices within his actual universe of choice, rather than an arbitrarily limited one. Therefore the results for the entire floor were treated together, with a corresponding gain in the validity of the data and loss in the rigor of the analytic techniques available.

The main objectives of the analysis were threefold. In the first place to establish the number of choices directed outside of the section in

Subject	1	2	3	4	5	6	7	8	9	10	11	12	13	14	15	16	17	18	19	20	Total Given
1		1									1								1		3
2	1				1											1					3
3		1		1		1															3
4	1			1					1												3
5			1	1			1														3
6							1	1			1										3
7				1		1							1								3
8						1			1	1											3
9											1	1	1								3
10											1	1	1								3
11			1						1	1											3
12					1								1				1				3
13								1				1		1							3
14	1							1								1					3
15													1				1	1			3
16								1						1			1				3
17								1								1		1			3
18																1	1		1		3
19								1	1											1	3
20								1										1	1		3
Total Received	3	2	2	2	3	3	2	8	3	3	4	3	5	0	2	4	4	3	2	2	60

Figure 7–3   Example of a Sociometric Matrix.

20 Individuals   1 Star
60 Preferences (3 each)   1 Isolate
9 Mutual Preferences

which they were made. Secondly, to compare the number of reciprocated choices [3] made within the open areas and the three smaller partitioned ones. Thirdly, to compare the numbers of isolates found in the
open and the partitioned areas.[4]

Results

The analysis of results was undertaken in two stages: the first to
determine the effect on preference choices of personal variables: the
second to determine the effect of the spatial ones, though much of the
data for each is given in both stages.

109

STAGE 1: THE EFFECT OF PERSONAL VARIABLES

The initial task in the analysis was the manual cross-tabulation of the total number of sociometric preferences made by each sex and age group. In the course of the cross-tabulation it was found that 18 per cent of the respondents completing the rest of the reply form had left this particular item blank. They were therefore not included in the analysis, though their number is shown in column 4 of Table 7–1. Their names were also excluded from the preferences made by other people; thus they effectively cease to exist as members of the population studied.

Against the left hand column of Table 7–1 is summarized the number and proportion of preference choices made and received by each sex and age group, and thus the influence of these variables as determinants of choice. It is therefore convenient to consider separately the influence of each.

(1) *Sex as a determinant of preference choice*—Column 3 shows that the average number of choices made by men and women is approximately the same (i.e. 4.4 to 4.2) though columns 4 and 5 show that the men are more likely to refuse to record their preferences than are the women.

It was found that the men, who represent 31 per cent of the sample, in fact received 36 per cent of all the stated preferences; whereas the women, who represent 69 per cent of the sample, received 64 per cent of the total choices made. However, as columns 6 and 7 show, the great majority of choices made by a given sex were directed towards members of the same sex. This held for the entire range of age groups, and it therefore appears that sex is an important determinant of choice pattern. This is not, of course, a novel or unexpected finding; indeed one would have been surprised at any other result. The value of the findings is not therefore intrinsic but they do establish the relative amount of weight to be given to the sex variable when considering the influence of other determinants.

(2) *Age as a determinant of preference choice*—The youngest age group, the 15 to 19 year olds, composed the numerically largest group and made the greatest absolute number of choices. In all, they made 48 per cent of the total preference choices recorded, but they received only 35 per cent of the total choices themselves. Conversely, with the exception of the over 40 age group, all other groups received more choices than they made. It appears therefore that older working companions are generally more acceptable than younger ones.

110

Summary Table of Sociometric Preferences Cross-Tabulated by Age Group and Sex

Age Groups and Sex	(1) Number of Respondents Completing Form	(2) Number of Named Preferences Given	(3) Average Number of Named Preferences Given	(4) Number of Respondents Not Replying	(5) Percentage of Respondents Not Replying (of cols. 1+4)	(6) Choices to Males Num-ber	(6) Per-centage (of col. 2)	(7) Choices to Females Num-ber	(7) Per-centage (of col. 2)	(8) Choices to 15-19 Year Group Num-ber	(8) Per-centage (of col. 2)	(9) Choices to 20-24 Year Group Num-ber	(9) Per-centage (of col. 2)	(10) Choices to 25-29 Year Group Num-ber	(10) Per-centage (of col. 2)	(11) Choices to 30-34 Year Group Num-ber	(11) Per-centage (of col. 2)	(12) Choices to 35-39 Year Group Num-ber	(12) Per-centage (of col. 2)	(13) Choices to 40+ Age Group Num-ber	(13) Per-centage (of col. 2)
15-19 Years																					
Male	21	91	4·3	2	8·7	64	70·3	27	29·7	48	52·7	19	20·9	14	15·4	2	2·2	5	5·5	3	3·3
Female	95	378	4·0	9	8·7	53	14·0	325	86·0	227	60·1	103	27·2	9	2·4	8	2·1	10	2·6	21	5·6
Totals	116	469	4·0	11	8·7	117	24·9	352	75·1	275	58·6	122	26·0	23	4·9	10	2·1	15	3·2	24	5·1
20-24 Years																					
Male	21	103	4·9	1	4·5	76	73·8	27	26·2	23	22·3	50	48·5	17	16·5	4	3·9	5	4·9	4	3·9
Female	36	158	4·4	6	14·3	22	13·9	136	86·1	52	32·9	74	46·8	5	3·2	9	5·7	7	4·4	11	7·0
Totals	57	261	4·6	7	10·9	98	37·5	163	62·5	75	28·7	124	47·5	22	8·4	13	5·0	12	4·6	15	5·7
25-29 Years																					
Male	3	18	6·0	1	25·0	14	77·8	4	22·2	2	11·1	3	16·7	5	27·8	6	33·3	0	0·0	2	11·1
Female	9	45	5·0	3	25·0	11	24·4	34	75·6	5	11·1	9	20·0	9	20·0	9	20·0	6	13·3	7	15·6
Totals	12	63	5·3	4	25·0	25	39·7	38	60·3	7	11·1	12	19·0	14	22·2	15	23·8	6	9·5	9	14·3
30-34 Years																					
Male	6	27	4·5	2	25·0	23	85·2	4	14·8	0	0·0	1	3·7	6	22·2	15	55·5	1	3·7	4	14·8
Female	3	21	7·0	1	20·0	6	28·6	15	71·4	0	0·0	1	4·8	5	23·8	9	42·9	2	9·5	4	19·0
Totals	9	48	5·4	3	25·0	29	60·4	19	39·6	0	0·0	2	4·2	11	22·9	24	50·0	3	6·2	8	16·7
35-39 Years																					
Male	5	21	4·2	3	37·5	17	81·0	4	19·0	0	0·0	2	9·5	1	4·8	6	28·6	6	28·6	6	28·6
Female	4	13	3·3	1	20·0	0	0·0	13	100·0	1	7·7	1	7·7	0	0·0	3	23·1	2	15·4	6	46·2
Totals	9	34	3·8	4	30·8	17	50·0	17	50·0	1	2·9	3	8·8	1	2·9	9	26·5	8	23·5	12	35·3
40 or More																					
Male	19	69	3·6	12	38·7	58	84·1	11	15·9	2	2·9	6	8·7	1	1·4	8	11·6	21	30·4	31	44·9
Female	19	76	4·0	13	40·6	27	35·5	49	64·5	1	1·3	7	9·2	3	3·9	14	18·4	14	18·4	37	48·7
Totals	38	145	3·8	25	39·7	85	58·6	60	41·4	3	2·1	13	9·0	4	2·8	22	15·2	35	24·1	68	46·9
All Age Groups Combined																					
Male	75	329	4·4	21	21·9	252	76·6	77	23·4	75	22·8	81	24·6	44	13·4	41	12·5	38	11·6	50	15·2
Female	166	691	4·2	33	16·6	119	17·2	572	82·8	286	41·4	195	28·2	31	4·5	52	7·5	41	5·9	86	12·5
Grand Totals	241	1020	4·2	54	18·3	371	36·4	649	63·6	361	35·4	276	27·0	75	7·4	93	9·2	79	7·7	136	13·3

It is interesting to note from columns 6 and 7 that there is a tendency for the proportion of men being chosen by women to rise with the women's age group. On the other hand, the proportion of women chosen by men declines with the older age groups. The reasons for this are not apparent from the results and so one must postulate some other factor; for example, differences in the relative attractiveness of the two sexes for one another at different ages.

Inspection of the blocked-off cells in the center of the table shows that each age group tends to choose predominantly from the members of its own age group. This is most marked for the numerically larger age groups: members of the smaller ones presumably being more cut-off from members of their own age group. With the single exception of the 30–34 year age group it is members of the adjacent age group who are next most frequently chosen. That is, the ones to the immediate left or right of the blocked-off diagonal. In fact, the percentage of choices made to members of the same age group plus those immediately adjacent are as follows:

15-19 years	85 per cent	30-34 years	79 per cent
20-24 years	80 per cent	35-39 years	85 per cent
25-29 years	65 per cent	40 or more	71 per cent

As in the case of the sex variable, it is clear that age group also is a very potent factor in determining the preference choices. Again, the finding is neither novel nor unexpected, but a necessary step in evaluating the factors responsible for preference choices.

STAGE 2: THE EFFECT OF SPATIAL VARIABLES

Tables 7–2 and 7–3 are concerned with the sheer effect of physical distance on the different age and sex groups and are therefore more clearly connected with the designers' and clients' interests. They were prepared by measuring, on a scale floor plan, the distance between the person making the preference choice and the person receiving it. The name of every individual participating had previously been written against his desk position on the plan in order to facilitate such cross-referencing.

The Totals row of Table 7–2 shows a very clear pattern: the number of sociopreferential choices decreases steadily with distance. The only exception to the trend is the case of distances of more than 36 ft., where the number is slightly above that for the 25–36 ft. group, and is

Distance of Respondents from Sociometric Choice Cross-Tabulated with Age Group

	(1) Number of Choices Made by Group	(2) 12 Ft. or Less		(3) 13-18 Ft.		(4) 19-24 Ft.		(5) 25-36 Ft.		(6) More Than 36 Ft.	
Distance of Respondent from Choice											
Age Group		Number	Percentage (of col. 1)	Number	Percentage (of col. 1)	Number	Percentage (of col. 1)	Number	Percentage (of col. 1)	Number	Percentage (of col. 1)
15-19	469	187	39·9	129	27·5	64	13·6	41	8·7	48	10·2
20-24	261	111	42·5	78	29·9	34	13·0	22	8·4	16	6·1
25-29	63	20	31·8	12	19·0	12	19·0	11	17·5	8	12·7
30-34	48	18	37·5	10	20·8	12	25·0	4	8·3	4	8·3
35-39	34	12	35·3	6	17·6	7	20·6	4	11·8	5	14·7
40 or More	145	46	31·8	28	19·1	19	13·1	19	13·1	33	22·8
Totals	1020	394	38·6	263	25·8	148	14·5	101	9·9	114	11·2

TABLE 7-3

Distance of Respondents from Sociometric Choice Cross-Tabulated with Sex

	(1) Number of Choices Made by Group	(2) 12 Ft. or Less		(3) 13-18 Ft.		(4) 19-24 Ft.		(5) 25-36 Ft.		(6) More Than 36 Ft.	
Distance of Respondent from Choice											
Sex		Number	Percentage (of col. 1)	Number	Percentage (of col. 1)	Number	Percentage (of col. 1)	Number	Percentage (of col. 1)	Number	Percentage (of col. 1)
Male	329	114	34·7	75	22·8	63	19·1	40	12·2	37	11·2
Female	691	280	40·5	188	27·2	85	12·3	61	8·8	77	11·1
Totals	1020	394	38·6	263	25·8	148	14·5	101	9·9	114	11·2

TABLE 7-4

*Summary Table of Sociometric Choices Made and Reciprocated within
Sections and Departments, Including the Number of Isolates in Each*

Type of Office Space	(1) Number of Respondents Completing Form	(2) Number of Named Preferences Given	(3) Average Number of Preferences Given	(4) Number of Respondents Not Replying	(5) Percentage of Respondents Not Replying (of cols. 1 + 4)
Open Areas	174	779	4·5	40	18·7
Small Areas (X, Y and Z)	67	241	3·6	14	17·3
Totals	241	1020	4·2	54	18·3

*The percentage is calculated from twice the actual number of reciprocated choices. in column 2.

presumably a consequence of grouping together several possible distance categories.

One interesting effect apparent from the results in column 2 is that the younger age groups choose the highest proportion of people from those within one desk distance, and the general trend is for this proportion to fall with age. Conversely, inspection of column 6 shows that there is a general trend for older groups to select a higher proportion of their workmate choices from the over 36 ft. distance. This is an effect that one might expect from the tendency, already demonstrated, for choices to be made from members of the same age group. As the older age groups are in a minority, the individuals composing them must be relatively more isolated from one another, and thus the number of choices to greater distances relatively higher.

Table 7-3 compares the distances involved in the preference choices made by men and women. The frequency distribution of choices at various distances is broadly the same, but there is a slight tendency for men to draw a higher proportion of their choices from further away. As with the older age groups, men being a minority, are relatively more isolated from one another. Sex, having been shown to be an important determinant of sociopreferential choice, would therefore be expected to result in choices being made over somewhat greater distances.

114

TABLE 7-4 *(continued)*

(6) Choices to Members of Respondent's Own Section		(7) Choices to Members of Respondent's Own Department		(8) Reciprocated Choices within Single Section		(9) Reciprocated Choices within Single Department		(10) Unchosen Individuals (Isolates)	
Num-ber	Percen-tage (of col. 2)	Num-ber	Percen-tage (of col. 2)	Num-ber	Percen-tage (of col. 2)*	Num-ber	Percen-tage (of col. 2)*	Num-ber	Percen-tage (of col. 1)
498	63·9	710	91·1	147	37·7	207	53·1	8	4·6
195	80·9	229	95·0	80	66·4	84	69·7	6	9·0
693	67·9	939	92·1	227	44·5	291	57·1	14	5·8

This was done because each reciprocal choice involves two choices taken from the total

Workmate choice seems, therefore, to be a result of the simultaneously acting influences of age, sex and physical distance.

Table 7–4 summarizes the sociometric choices made and reciprocated within sections and departments, and the number of isolates found in each. The data from the small partitioned areas is compared with that from the remainder of the floor. Column 1 shows the number of subjects who completed the sociometric question; column 4 shows the number of those who did not. Column 5 shows that the percentage of workers in the large and small areas who did not state their preferences was almost identical.[5] Column 3 shows that there exists a very substantial difference between the average number of choices made by workers in the open areas and those in the small. People working in the larger office spaces produced the greater outgoing choice volume: in sociometric terms exhibiting a higher level of "expansivity" than workers in the small areas.

Columns 6 and 7 show that the preference choices of workers in the small areas are very much more frequently made from amongst members of their own section, and somewhat more frequently from members of their own department, than are those of the open area personnel. Columns 8 and 9 show that this greater proportion of choices made within a single section or department is also paralleled by a much greater proportion of choices reciprocated within them. That the pro-

115

portion of within-department reciprocated choices is much higher for workers in the small areas than for those in the large is, though, a consequence of the great number of within-section reciprocated choices. In fact, the number of reciprocated choices with members of the same department, other than members of the same section, is very much lower.

The results therefore show that there exists a much greater degree of internal cohesion amongst the members of the sections working within the smaller areas than amongst those working in the open ones. However, the number of isolates is greater. Column 10 shows that, though their numbers are small, there are proportionately almost twice as many in the small areas. If spatial relationships *are* important factors in determining the sociopreferential choice, then one might anticipate such a result because a higher proportion of workers in a small area must perforce be relatively physically isolated by working in a corner or beside a wall.

To summarize the results, it was found that both age and sex were important determinants of sociopreferential choice but, allowing for this, they tend to operate within the framework of spatial relationships. As the sections working in both the open and the small areas were essentially similar in respect of the nature of the work and composition of the subsamples, differences in sociometric pattern must be attributable to differences in the size of area in which they worked.

It was found that the social organization of the sections working in small areas was internally more cohesive, though the proportion of isolates was higher, and the number of wider links with other members of the same department much smaller.

The higher average number of preference choices made by members of the open areas, coupled with the lower proportion of reciprocations, shows that the social-occupational network existing in the two types of area are fundamentally different. In the small areas there exists a fairly tight social group, whereas the social links connecting people in the open areas are much less tightly knit.

Discussion of Results and Conclusions

Objective differences have been shown to result from locating working sections in large and small areas, and the existence of these differences now raises the management question of which one is to be preferred. The internal cohesiveness of the sections in the small area meets many of the criteria for small group effectiveness. On the other hand, the sections in the open areas have better interconnections with other parts of the department and may therefore constitute a more effective total working unit than the sum of individual sections.

It may be that individuals working in small areas enjoy better morale as a result of their internal cohesiveness or, alternatively, that they inbreed greater tensions as a result of the relative lack of contact with a wider working group. Managements may wish to promote small and exclusive work groups of high morale and efficiency, and this may prove to be one way of doing it. On the other hand, they may wish to promote the department as the more important work unit, to encourage cooperation between the subunits rather than competition. All of these different alternatives are possible results of different types of spatial arrangements. The exact results of particular arrangements cannot yet be predicted, but it *is* clear that they must be investigated as a part of management's effective method of control. Thus, because of the relationship between the spatial organization of the building and socio-occupational relationships, organizational and man-management problems might be expected to become a more substantial part of the architectural and design problem.

Earlier in this paper, the possible psychological factors influencing the decision to opt for deep block and open office design were discussed, and it has since been shown that the social milieu, and thus the psychological climate, of large and small offices are in fact radically different.

Having established an empirical basis for these psycho-social differences, it now remains to examine further McGirr's assumptions about the possible medico-psychological consequences of the deep and open office. If undesirable effects are found, then clearly the arguments for and against different types of accommodation must ultimately be measured against the criterion of human needs. This may also be so even though the psycho-social effects are nonclinical but are influential on morale and job performance. As yet, no such information is available but the appropriate research has already begun in the Department of Building Science, in Liverpool.

In conclusion, and by way of a justification for having dealt with the techniques of sociometry in such detail, it should be stressed just what promise they hold. They offer the chance to extend beyond the physical and simpler psychological studies to a point much closer to the understanding and control of the *total environment*—a concept which neces-

117

sarily includes a substantial psycho-social component. With the increasing professional interaction of behavioral and building scientists, sociometry will come to be applied not only to offices and factories but to building complexes such as in town planning and neighborhood design. This selection will have fulfilled its purpose if it has adequately introduced the subject.

NOTES

1. The head office of a large insurance company, housed in new office block.
2. The attitudinal study does not form part of this selection.
3. A reciprocated choice is where two individuals mutually choose one another.
4. An isolate is defined as a person unchosen, on the criterion of the test, by any of the other members of his group.
5. Many of the refusals were of the form "no particular preference," or "I get along quite well with most people." They are not, therefore, necessarily a refusal to co-operate but may reflect a genuine lack of strongly held preferences.

REFERENCES

1. J. Noble, The how and why of behaviour: social psychology for the architect. *Architects' J.*, **137**, 531–546 (1963).
2. P. O. M. McGirr, Environmental targets in offices and commercial premises. *Trans. Ass. Industr. Med. Offrs.*, Vol. 9, No. 3 (1959).
3. D. Lockwood, *The black-coated worker.* London: Allen & Unwin, 1958.
4. *Better Offices.* London: An Institute of Directors Publication, 1962.
5. L. Festinger, S. Schachter and K. Back, *Social pressures in informal groups: a study of human factors in housing.* London: Tavistock Publications, 1963.
6. J. T. Gullahorn, *Distance and friendship as factors in the gross interaction matrix.* In the Sociometry Reader, ed. J. L. Moreno. Glencoe: The Free Press, 1960.
7. D. M. Goodacre, Group characteristics of good and poor performing combat units. *Sociometry*, **16**, 168–178 (1953).
8. D. Cartwright and M. Herwitz, A projective method for the diagnosis of group properties. *Hum. Relat.*, **6**, 397–410 (1953).
9. M. Sherif, A study of some social factors in perception. *Arch. Psychol.*, **27**, 187 (1935).
10. M. Sherif, *The psychology of social norms.* New York: Harper & Row, 1936.
11. S. E. Asch, *Effects of group pressure upon the modification and distortion of judgments.* In Readings in Social Psychology, eds. E. E. Maccoby, T. M. Newcomb and E. L. Hartley. London: Methuen, 1959.
12. F. J. Rothlisberger and W. J. Dickson, *Management and the worker:* an account of a research program conducted by the Western Electric Company, Hawthorne Works, Chicago. Cambridge, Mass.: Harvard University Press, 1939.
13. J. L. Moreno, Who shall survive? A new approach to the problem of human interrelations. *Nervous and Mental Disease Monograph*, Washington. Series No. 58 (1934).
14. C. Selltiz, M. Jahoda, M. Deutsch and S. W. Cook, *Research methods in social relations.* London: Methuen, 1959.

15. A. Bjerstedt, The methodology of preferential sociometry. *Sociometry Monogr.* No. 37, p. 51 (1956).

16. E. Forsyth and L. Katz, A matrix approach to the analysis of sociometric data: preliminary report. *Sociometry, 9,* 340–347 (1946).

17. L. Festinger, *The analysis of sociograms using matrix algebra.* In the Sociometry Reader, ed. J. L. Moreno. Glencoe: The Free Press, 1960.

8

Architecture and Group Membership

LEON FESTINGER

The previous selection by Wells demonstrates the capacity of architecture to serve as a communications network and to generate simple forms of interaction among office workers. However, the concern of environmental designers and planners over the influence of spatial organization is usually addressed to more intensive and more enduring forms of group life. For example, much of the discussion of the consequences of spatial organization is concerned with its power to generate a sense of community, a feeling of shared values, attitudes, and beliefs; or at a still more complex level of interaction, its role in stimulating organized community action aimed at achieving a specific political goal. Furthermore, in such discussions the environments under consideration are also complex—housing projects, suburban developments, and urban neighborhoods—and the residents come from different social and cultural backgrounds and are not usually constrained to spend a good deal of time in close proximity to other people as is the usual fate of office workers.

Festinger's selection is addressed to the question of the effectiveness of architecture in determining such group structures and membership patterns in residential environments. In general he concludes that, when looked at from the perspective of complex forms of social life, the influence of spatial organization is uncertain and variable. In one of the housing developments that he and his colleagues studied, the Westgate project at M.I.T., friendship patterns were directly related to the distance between dwelling units. An active and vital group life began in the project almost as soon as the graduate student tenants moved in. The residents were enthusiastically favorable toward their environment, even in the face of its physical inconveniences and material defects. However, in another project, Regent Hill, with a similar layout and in which assignments to housing were also involuntary, social cohesion and user satisfaction were both absent. Rather than choosing to associate with each other, neighbors were hostile, and residents did not even have good relations with people in the surrounding community.

Festinger uses the experience of these two projects to discuss the factors that occasion the different responses of users to their environments. He con-

Reprinted from Leon Festinger, "Architecture and Group Membership," in *Journal of Social Issues* 7, nos. 1 and 2 (1951): 152–163. © The Society for the Psychological Study of Social Forces.

centrates on the phenomenon of homogeneity: the similarity or presumed similarity of residents in terms of their cultural values, family and child-rearing norms, and social interests. In Westgate the residents were all graduate students, already in or destined to become members of the technically educated professional upper-middle class. The tenants in Regent Hill were divided: 40 per cent were old-timers, the others had moved in after the war. The newcomers assumed that the established residents belonged to a lower social class. When the tenants of a housing community are socially heterogeneous, it is apparently not so easy to encourage social cohesion by means of spatial organization.

□

The architect and planner have traditionally concerned themselves with supplying physical convenience and satisfying physical needs. They have, for example, been able to specify minimum standards for things like the number of square feet of floor space necessary for a given size family. They have acquired a great deal of knowledge concerning arrangements of rooms for maximum convenience, arrangement of streets for easy accessibility and the like. They must now, or in the very near future, also concern themselves with supplying *social* convenience and satisfying social needs. This growing emphasis on the social consequences of architecture and city planning results from two parallel developments:

1. New housing is more and more being built in planned developments. That is, communities are being built rather than homes. The architect under these circumstances assumes the responsibility for planning much that is important for the social as well as the physical life of people.

2. Basic research on social processes, the behavior of persons in groups, and the effects of group membership has proceded far enough to show the great importance of these things in the lives of people. The problems have begun to be clearly formulated and facts have begun to emerge which can be used by the architect.

These two independent developments must be brought together. In the face of the new problems with which the architect must cope and the new responsibilities he has assumed, he cannot afford to ignore the facts, present and potential, which offer help in carrying out his task. Let us examine in detail some of the points at which the research of the social scientist on group processes has bearing on what the architect does.

The Importance of Group Membership

A significant aspect of our society is that persons desire membership in groups. It is extremely rare to find a person who does not seek such membership and is content to live with a minimum of social contact with other people. It is more common to find people with membership in a wide variety of different kinds of groups, both formal and informal.

The process of entering and leaving groups is a continuing one for most people. The small informal social groups to which they belong change their membership; some friends drift away and new ones are made; a person will leave a club and, perhaps, join a different one.

To understand the significance of acquiring group memberships and of belonging to groups, it is first necessary to understand why people seek membership in groups and how groups acquire power over their members.

SOURCES OF ATTRACTION TO GROUPS

Social life, interpersonal relationships, and membership in groups are important aspects of person's lives because so many goals and satisfactions are attainable most easily in groups, and in some cases, only through association with other people. The multitude of attractions which draw people into groups and into associations with others may be conveniently summarized under three general headings:

Groups frequently mediate the attainment of important individual goals. This source of attraction is recognized by groups and used to attract members. Along these lines, a club will offer different facilities for use only by recognized members. While the overt use of such attractions is generally available only to organized, formal groups, informal groups also frequently attract members because of the goals which they mediate. Thus a person who seeks to be regarded as "upper class," for example, will be strongly attracted to associations whose members are regarded as having such status. By establishing such associations he then may achieve the goal of being himself included in this category.

It is, of course, unlikely that any social group has the mediation of goals as its sole attraction. Yet the mediation of goals should be separated from the other attractions for a number of reasons. First, the attraction of group membership is not so much in sheer belonging, but rather in attaining something by means of this membership. With some types of goals the attraction to the group may cease once the goal is attained. Secondly, with respect to such sources of attraction, a specific group is rarely indispensable. There will generally be other, perhaps more difficult, means of attaining these goals. Thus the group, on both these counts, holds its members on a rather tenuous basis to the extent that the mediation of personal goals is the source of attraction.

The activities in which the group engages are frequently attractive to the member. Many groups form simply on the basis of a common activity which the members like to engage in, and the attraction to this activity may remain one of the major sources of attraction to the group. Thus both formal and informal groups will form to play bridge, tennis, poker, to discuss books or political issues, to have parties and dances, and so on. Here again, it is rare to find a group where this would be the sole source of attraction. Other sources of attraction will also be present, but it seems worthwhile to distinguish this one from the others on a theoretical basis.

Generally, no single group to which a person may belong has relevance for every aspect of his life. A group such as the family has a relatively wide realm of relevance. At the other extreme, groups with exceptionally narrow realms of relevance depend primarily on the activities in which they engage to attract and hold their members. In general, the realms of relevance of such groups are identical with the activities which are the source of attraction to the group. To the extent that this is true, the group may have relatively little importance in the lives of its members.

Almost all groups are, at least in part, attractive because people have needs that can be satisfied only by personal relationships with other people. Some of these needs are friendship, approval and support from other persons, respect and prestige from those with whom one associates, and the like. We are undoubtedly not yet aware of all the personal needs that fall into this general category, nor are we aware of why such needs exist and why they are as powerful as they seem to be. There is no question, however, that they are powerful motivators of human behavior. Since satisfaction of these needs can only occur in the course of personal associations with others, belonging to groups which offer the possibility of satisfying them is virtually a necessity for most humans. Indeed, the state of loneliness, of not knowing other people and having no close personal relationships, is a state of extreme psychological hardship.

THE PROCESS OF ENTERING AND LEAVING GROUPS

Having examined the attractions to groups, we may now look at the process by which people enter and leave groups and the circumstances under which such movement takes place. It is obvious that a person will attempt to move into groups which offer the possibility of satisfying his particular needs. It is also clear that persons will attempt to move out of groups which no longer satisfy their needs or whose negative aspects outweigh the positive satisfactions of belonging to the group. Disapproval by other members, low status in the group, and other such states of affairs can produce pressure to leave the group.

Moving out of one group and into some other one is, however, not an entirely unrestricted matter. While there are some groups out of which one may move at will and some groups into which one may move with relatively little difficulty, most groups exert some restraints against their members leaving and many groups exert even greater restraints against new members entering. Formal, organized groups frequently have rules governing the admission of new members. Informal groups also have such rules which, although not formalized, are frequently even more restrictive. An additional difficulty in entering some informal groups is the lack of an easy way of making contact with the group.

We have then the simultaneous existence of forces tending to move people in and out of groups and forces restraining such movement. Groups differ in their attraction for members, and members differ in how satisfying the group membership is for them.

Groups can influence the attitudes, opinions, and behavior patterns of their members. The manner in which these influences are exerted is most often informal and subtle. The expression of some opinion receives approval or disapproval; a certain manner of behaving gains acceptance; a certain way of looking at things becomes the normal and "correct" way. When pressures for uniformity arise among the members, the group may bring about such uniformity. Since we shall elaborate some of these powers of the group in the specific context of housing, we content ourselves here with summarizing some of the conditions under which they are effective.

The extent to which the group can produce lasting change in opinions, attitudes, and behavior in its members depends on the strength of the attraction to the group, that is, on the extent to which the group satisfies the needs of its members. The force on a member to remain in the group is the force which, in a sense, he applies upon himself to accept the opinions, and behaviors of others in the group as correct.

The areas where the group most easily exerts influence correspond to those areas relevant to the functioning of the group and to those

124

needs which the group can and does satisfy in its members. If the exertion of influence becomes an overt, formalized process, the group can extend its influence to a broader area, but as long as the influence process remains subtle, informal, and unrecognized, influence will only be exerted within the group's realm of relevance.

Groups which are difficult for the member to leave, either because the group itself erects restraints against leaving or because outsiders do not easily permit members to leave the group, can exert power over members by threats of punishment. Such power is exercised in overt and recognized manner and is effective in producing overt change in members; it may not necessarily be effective in producing changes in opinions or attitudes which are not open to public examination.

The Social Importance of Architecture

In our discussion of entering and leaving groups we have omitted one major aspect, namely, involuntary membership in groups. Many group memberships are involuntary. One is born into a certain family and ethnic group, and, be it satisfactory or not, one remains a member.

Living in a house also means involuntary membership in a group. The decisions of the architect in designing the house, in laying out the site plan for a group of houses, and in deciding who will live in the houses determine to a large extent the nature of the group memberships which will be imposed upon the residents of the houses. When a person moves into a house, his social life and the group membership that will be attributed to him by outsiders will already have been determined to some extent by these decisions.

Even within the general community in which he lives and with which he is identified by other people, the specific site plan of the group of houses in which his own is located further affects the amount and nature of his social contacts. To illustrate these effects, let us refer to a number of empirical studies.

A study of group formation (3) was conducted in a housing project built by the Massachusetts Institute of Technology for occupancy by married veteran students. The development consisted of 100 single or semi-attached small houses arranged in courts consisting of from eight to thirteen houses. Each court was a U-shaped affair with the houses facing into a grassy area; the open end of each U faced onto a street which bisected the housing project. The project was rather unusual in that a great degree of homogeneity existed among the residents, who were all married veteran students at M.I.T. There was no freedom of choice of dwelling unit within the project, since all were assigned to houses in the order in which their names appeared on the waiting list. The study in question began soon after the project was fully occupied and, consequently, was able to trace the development of friendships and informal social groups quite thoroughly.

It is a fair summary to say that two major factors affecting the friendships which developed were (a) sheer distance between houses and (b) the direction in which a house faced. Friendships developed more frequently between next-door neighbors, less frequently between people whose houses were separated by another house, and so on. As the distance between houses increased, the number of friendships fell off so rapidly that it was rare to find a friendship between persons who lived in houses that were separated by more than four or five other houses. People also tended to make friends with those whose houses faced their own. Because of the arrangement of the courts in the housing project, these two factors combined to make it easy for social groups to develop within the court and difficult for social groups to develop on any other basis. Each court in the project became a more or less cohesive group with a social life of its own. The relatively little social contact that did exist between one court and another, was almost entirely limited to contact between adjacent courts. Because of the design of the project the social groups which developed were determined by the order in which the names happened to appear on the waiting list.

There were instances in which the site plan of the project had more profound effects than merely to determine with whom one associated. Indeed, on occasion the arrangement of the houses severely limited the social life of their occupants. It will be recalled that the open end of the U of each court faced a street which bisected the project. In order to have the street appear "lived on," ten of the houses near the street had been turned so that they faced the street rather than the court area like the other houses. This apparently small change in the direction in which a house faced had a considerable effect on the lives of the people who, by accident, happened to occupy these end houses. They had less than half as many friends in the project as did those whose houses faced the court area. The consistency of this finding left no doubt that the turning of these houses toward the street had made involuntary social isolates out of the persons who lived in them.

The same study investigated the development of social groups in an adjoining project that was also maintained for married veteran students of the same school. This project consisted of thirteen apartment buildings with ten apartments in each building. Each building had two floors with five apartments in a row on each floor. The same types of effects of architecture on friendship formation were found here. Once more, sheer physical distance between apartments within the same building was a major factor determining which friendships developed. Needless to say, there were relatively few friendships between residents of different floors of the same building and even fewer between residents of different buildings. Even along the same floor of the same building, the number of friendships decreased rapidly as one went from adjoining apartments to apartments separated by one, two, or three others.

Again, slight architectural features had important effects on the social life of the apartment residents. The positions of the stairways leading to the second floor enabled the residents of some apartments to make more friends, while leaving other apartments in relative social isolation. The position of the mailboxes in each building added to the social life of the residents of the apartment near which they were located. The social activity of some residents and the relative social isolation of others could largely be traced to such minor architectural features.

Results like these have been confirmed in other kinds of communities (4, 1). Living in a certain house in a certain neighborhood determines many of a person's group memberships, not only as others see them, but also as they are actually lived. Since such group memberships have much to do with how people behave toward each other, and since these group memberships are potential sources of satisfaction for many important needs, it is important that groups formed on a relatively involuntary basis be satisfying ones. If a group which one can easily leave is unsatisfying, one may find another group which provides more satisfaction, if such a group is easily accessible. But one can not easily avoid the group memberships that come with residence in a specific location unless one is prepared to suffer relative social isolation. Social isolation or continued group membership of an unsatisfying sort can seriously affect the total context within which the person lives. We shall discuss below two studies of general housing satisfaction and social functioning as examples of the wider effects of satisfactory and unsatisfactory involuntary group memberships occasioned by living in particular housing projects.

Effects of Involuntary Group Membership in a Housing Project

AN EXAMPLE OF SATISFYING GROUP MEMBERSHIP

The previously mentioned study by Festinger, Schachter and Back, in addition to investigating the determinants of group formation, concerned itself with the social life of the residents. It was clear that the group memberships provided in the housing community were satisfying ones for the residents. This may have been because of the homogeneity and common interests of the residents; it may have been affected by the temporary nature of residence in the project and perhaps by other factors. Whatever the basis for this satisfactory group life, we have here an example of involuntary group membership which does provide the satisfactions generally desired of group membership. Let us examine the results of this state of affairs.

Social and Emotional Aspects of Living in the Project. One of the most prominent aspects of life in Westgate was the ease with which friendships formed. Most people remarked about it in the interviews, emphasizing that it was one of the most satisfactory aspects of living there. On the whole, they felt it was easy to make friends, that the friendships they had made would probably be lasting ones, and that the resulting social life was satisfactory. The following comments from Westgate residents are typical:

There are wonderful people in this court. We have a lot of social life and do almost everything together.

We don't very often go out of Westgate for amusements. Almost all of our friends are here, and there is really so much to do here.

About two-thirds of the residents reported that their social life was entirely or primarily within the Westgate community. More than 90 per cent of the residents felt that they had enough friends in Westgate and had as much social life as they wanted.

There were several general consequences of this. The most prominent was a general satisfaction with the homes and with living in the community. Only one or two residents expressed any desire to leave Westgate and live elsewhere. More than half of the residents were vigorous in their statements that they would not consider leaving Westgate at all.

This general satisfaction existed in spite of, and seemed to compensate for, many physical inadequacies of the houses. At the time of our study there were many physical nuisances in the houses. Some were incompletely equipped, the grounds were muddy and had not yet been landscaped, they were difficult to heat in the winter, and the like. One example of the reaction to such physical inadequacies will suffice, however, to illustrate the point. At the time of the investigation, many of the houses had trouble with the roofs. The houses were prefabricated, and many of the roofs had not been assembled properly. All the roofs have since been fixed, but in the interviews about one third of the residents reported that the roofs leaked. Any rain accompanied by a moderately strong wind would apparently raise the roof slightly, and water would pour down the walls. One family reported that in a particularly strong rain the roof had started to blow off; the husband had to go outside and hold the roof down until the wind subsided.

It is remarkable, however, that even such serious physical inconvenience did not create a strong impression on the residents. Typically the reaction was, "Oh yes, there are many things wrong with these houses, but we love it here and wouldn't want to move."

The adequate and satisfying social life was sufficient to override many inconveniences. The result was a rather happy social and psychological existence. The phenomenon may perhaps best be summed up by the expression which many of the people in Westgate used: "We're all in the same boat."

Group Action and Group Standards in the Community. There are grounds for believing that successful community action is possible only under conditions like those found in Westgate where there is considerable identification with the community, and where people find satisfying social life and want to continue to belong to the community.

One late afternoon an unoccupied building adjoining Westgate caught fire and burned down. Sparks fell on some of the closer Westgate houses, and there was much concern about the fire spreading to the project. That evening a group of tenants made plans for starting a tenant organization which would try to obtain more adequate fire protection. Once started, the tenant organization also dealt with many other aspects of life in the project, including social activities. A tenant council of representatives from each of the courts in Westgate was established, and this council continued to function fairly successfully. This spontaneous beginning of a community organization which received enough active support in the community to enable its continued successful functioning in a number of activities is rather unusual, considering the difficulty of starting such community activities in other situations.

The attitudes of the tenants toward the community organization and its activities, and their active participation in the tenant organization were to a major extent determined by their small group memberships within the Westgate project. It will be recalled that the physical structure of the project was such that small social groups tended to form along court lines. Each court became a more or less cohesive social group, somewhat separated from the other groups in the project. Each of these small court groups within the project tended to react to the tenant organization as a unit. In one court all but two or three of the residents might be favorably inclined to the organization and active in its affairs. In another court all but two or three of the residents would be quite hostile to the tenant organization and would be entirely inactive with respect to its activities.

The reactions of individual residents to the tenant organization were so influenced by the small informal groups to which they belonged as to produce relative uniformity within each of these groups. Within each group the degree of uniformity depended on how attractive the group was for its members. Those groups which were very attractive to their members showed high uniformity of opinion and behavior with respect to the tenant organization. Those groups which were relatively less attractive to their members showed correspondingly less uniformity. In other words, the degree to which a group was able to influence the attitudes, opinions, and behavior of its members depended on how much the members wanted to remain in the group. These small social groups, whose specific composition derived from the architectural design of the project, were a major influence on the thinking and behavior of the residents and were important in determining the structure of the community as a whole.

With this close relationship between social life and opinions about community-wide affairs, one might also expect that persons whose opinions and behavior differed from those prevailing around them would feel the effects of this divergence in their social life within the project. This was found to be the case. Those persons within each court who could be called deviates—that is, whose attitudes toward the tenant organization or whose behavior with respect to it, differed substantially from the norm of their social group—were relatively rejected by the other members. The deviates were infrequently mentioned as close friends.

Let us summarize the results of this study. There was a good deal of social life and a resultant satisfaction with living in the project. The social groups which formed exerted influences on the relationships of members to the total community, and social relationships within the

130

project were affected by the similarity or difference of attitudes among the residents. Some of these effects, namely, the satisfying emotional life and the power of the group to influence its members, are results that we would expect from the general considerations about group membership which were discussed earlier in this selection. Where group membership is satisfying, it tends to lose its character of involuntary membership. But whether or not group memberships in Westgate were satisfying, it would have been difficult or impossible for most residents to escape from the memberships thrust upon them as a result of living in Westgate. The fact that the memberships were satisfying was fortuitous.

A government housing project built for shipyard workers in 1942 was studied by Festinger and Kelley (2). It illustrates the effect of involuntary group membership that is not satisfying. The project consisted of 100 single and semi-attached permanent housing units. It was built in the middle of a residential area of a town about fifteen miles from a large city. At the time of the study, 1947, about 40 per cent of the population of Regent Hill were older residents who had once worked in the shipyards and had remained in the project after the end of the war. The others were persons who had moved in later during the period of acute housing shortages. The great majority of the residents keenly felt that they had been forced to live in the project by circumstances beyond their control. For those who had moved in during the war, it was the shipyards and war exigencies that had forced them to live there. For the others, it was the acute housing shortage and impossibility of finding other places to live that had made them come to Regent Hill.

The group memberships forced upon them by living in the project were resented, and attempts were made to avoid them. Many residents stated that they had not expected to like the type of person who lived in a government housing project. They expected to find the other residents rather low-class people and did not want to be forced to associate with them. Thus, irrespective of the actual potentialities which these group memberships may have had, they were unsatisfying because the residents never encouraged the development of any group life and indeed tried to dissociate themselves from the community in which they were forced to live. Let us examine the consequences of this state of affairs.

The Social and Emotional Aspects of Membership in the Regent Hill Project. The residents of the project had on the whole an inadequate social life. Indeed, for many residents the state of affairs might be described as self-imposed social isolation. Most residents reported only one or two friends in the community, and about one-fourth did not have any friends there.

There was, in addition, a surprisingly great amount of hostility expressed toward neighbors in the project. In one interview survey more than 60 per cent of those interviewed expressed belief that their neighbors were low-class people with whom it was undesirable to associate. In other words, the residents had come to the project expecting to find undesirable neighbors in "a government housing project." They feared the group memberships forced upon them; choosing between such undesirable and unsatisfying group membership and no membership at all, they tended to choose the latter.

One might expect from such a state of affairs that the residents of the project would have tended to make friends and belong to groups in the surrounding community. This, however, was not the case. While they may have desired such group membership in the surrounding community, there were a number of factors which prevented their achieving it. Since they looked down on the project and its residents, they imagined that outsiders would also have the same attitudes toward people from the project. Thus, in any contact which they had with the people in the surrounding community they strove to detach themselves from the project. This, of course, placed severe limitations on the kinds of contacts they could have with the surrounding community and severely limited the number of channels available to them for making such contacts. The result was that the project residents were also rather isolated from the surrounding town. Only about 20 per cent of the project residents were members of any town clubs or organizations. There were relatively few friendships between project residents and townspeople. Compared to residents of the surrounding community who had been living there the same length of time, the project residents were clearly in a state of relative social isolation.

We thus have practically the opposite state of affairs from that of Westgate. Instead of a full and satisfying social life there was here a very unsatisfactory state of little social life and great difficulty in achieving group memberships which had the possibility of being satisfying. As one might expect, this state of affairs generalized into attitudes toward their homes and toward the community. Most residents were dissatisfied with living in the Regent Hill project. Many wanted to leave and expressed the intention of doing so as soon as they could find a suitable place elsewhere. The physical inconveniences which did exist in the project became very important and were major sources of irritation to the residents.

Group Standards and Group Action. The investigators in this study, after assessing and attempting to diagnose the state of affairs in the Regent Hill project, tried experimentally to change the pattern of social life within the project and to change the seemingly dominant pattern of hostility among neighbors. The experiment tried to stimulate contacts among the residents by getting them to cooperate on a program of community activities. In contrast to the spontaneity and ease with which a community organization and community activities had arisen in Westgate, such a program in Regent Hill, even with the help of skilled community workers, was by no means an easy affair. Feelings of noncooperation, hostility, threatened status and prestige, and reluctance to enter into contact with other project residents all made such a program difficult to start and carry on. We do not need to dwell here on the success of the program and the changes of various kinds that were created. The point we wish to make is that, in the absence of real need-satisfaction from the group memberships, the whole context of social and personal life was adversely affected.

In the preceding pages we have done little more than indicate in general the contribution which present and potential knowledge in the area of group membership and group life can make to the field of housing. It is clear that group membership has a very important place in the lives of people. It is also clear that the decisions of the architect, planner, or housing administrator will affect group memberships and, directly or indirectly, the total context of the lives of the people. We have described an instance in which the design of the houses and the physical and spatial relations among houses had an important influence on the formation of social groups. We have also described instances in which these involuntary group memberships were satisfying and others in which they were not satisfying. This difference in satisfaction affected the social life within the community and the satisfaction with living in the houses.

With the aid of a vigorous program of research we can learn much more about these phenomena. Before the social psychologist can materially affect the decisions of the architect and the planner, it is necessary to accumulate this additional knowledge. How do architectural design and site planning variations affect social intercourse among people? What kinds of social interactions exist among neighbors in a community? How does the nature of the group memberships affect

133

family living patterns and other aspects of the functioning of individuals? How do the characteristics of the residents—their interests, backgrounds, anticipations of permanency, and the like—affect the formation and functioning of community groups? And how do community facilities interact with these other factors?

Many more questions like these can be asked, and they can be phrased specifically enough so that answers can be obtained. The more of these questions we answer, the more we will be able to build houses and communities which provide for people the satisfactory social and private lives we would like to see.

REFERENCES

1. Caplow, Theodore, and Forman, R. "Neighborhood interaction in a homogeneous community," *American Sociological Review*, 1950 **15**, 357–366.

2. Festinger, Leon, and Kelley, Harold H. *Changing Attitudes through Social Contact: An Experimental Study of a Housing Project*. Ann Arbor, Research Center for Group Dynamics, Institute for Social Research, University of Michigan, 1951.

3. Festinger, Leon, Schachter, Stanley, and Back, Kurt. *Social Pressures in Informal Groups*. New York: Harper & Brothers, 1950.

4. Merton, Robert K. "The social psychology of housing," in Dennis, W., ed., *Current Trends in Social Psychology*. Pittsburgh: University of Pittsburgh Press, 1948.

9

Silent Assumptions in Social Communication

EDWARD T. HALL

Any consideration of the influence of spatial organization on social interaction inevitably recalls developments in the field of "proxemics." Hall, who is the major inventor and exponent of this field, defines proxemics in the following selection as "the study of ways in which man gains knowledge of the content of other men's minds through judgments of behavior patterns associated with varying degrees of proximity to him."

Proxemics is usually of interest to architects and designers because it emphasizes the concept that spatial distance is a "silent language" through which men unwittingly convey attitudes, feelings, and judgments about their fellows. This emphasis fits naturally with the wish of architects to find in the behavioral sciences evidence that design variables are objectively meaningful.

In the context of the issues discussed in this section, proxemics has other significance. First, it provides a useful typology of distances, defined in terms of the kind of information or sentiment being communicated. Hall identifies four classes of distance, or as he calls them distance-sets: intimate, casual-personal, social-consultative, and public. Second, and this is really the obverse of the previous point, proxemics suggests that in order for certain sentiments to be communicated successfully, people must be located in particular degrees of proximity to each other. For example, the communication of the sentiment of love demands closer proximity than the expression of respect. Third, a model is developed for locating the mechanisms available for the exchange of particular kinds of messages at specific distance sets. These mechanisms are sensory and involve tactile-kinesthetic, visual, olfactory, heat-radiation, and oral-aural sensory systems. Finally, the proxemics approach indicates that the reliance on these mechanisms at any particular distance is culturally determined. Thus, according to Hall, Americans rely on eye contact to define a particular distance as an intimate distance, but presumably depend less than other people on olfactory and heat-radiation systems for this purpose.

Although the insights of proxemics suggest a relationship between its concerns and our understanding of how spatial organization influences social interaction, the ideas available in this field have unfortunately not really

Reprinted from Edward T. Hall, "Silent Assumptions in Social Communication," in *Disorders of Communication*, Research Publications, Association for Research in Nervous and Mental Disease 42 (1964): 41–55.

been applied in site planning, office design, or any of the other fields in which spatial organization is an important design factor. It would be interesting to know, for example, whether user response to high or low density housing and the capability of people in different societies to form viable communities in these settings bear any relation to cultural definitions of the kind of communication and interaction appropriate to different distances.

☐

The investigations reported briefly in this selection deal with *proxemics,* the study of ways in which man gains knowledge of the content of other men's minds through judgments of behavior patterns associated with varying degrees of proximity to him. These behavior patterns are learned, and thus they are not genetically determined. But because they are learned (and taught) largely outside awareness, they are often treated as though they were innate. I have found this type of behavior to be highly stereotyped, less subject to distortion than consciously controlled behavior and important to individuals in the judgments they form as to what is taking place around them at any given moment in time.

Thoreau wrote *Walden* (1) over 100 years ago. Yet in a section entitled "Visitors" he describes how conversational distance and subject matter are functions of each other and, what is even more remarkable, he names some of the variables by means of which people unconsciously set distances.

One inconvenience I sometimes experienced in so small a house, is the difficulty of getting to a sufficient distance from my guest when we began to utter the big thoughts in big words. You want room for your thoughts to get into sailing trim and run a course or two before they make their port. The bullet of your thought must have overcome its lateral and ricochet motion and fallen into its last and steady course before it reaches the ear of the hearer, else it may plough out again through the side of his head. Also our sentences wanted room to unfold and form their columns in the interval. Individuals, like nations, must have suitable broad and natural boundaries, even a considerable neutral ground, between them. I have found it a singular luxury to talk across the pond to a companion on the opposite side. In my house we were so near that we could not begin to hear—we could not speak low enough to be heard; as when you throw two stones into calm water so near that they break each other's undulations. If we are merely loquacious and loud talkers, then we can afford to stand very near together, cheek by jowl, and feel each other's breath; but if we speak reservedly and thoughtfully we want to be farther apart, that all animal heat and moisture may have a chance to evaporate. If we would enjoy the most intimate society with that in each of us which is without, or above, being spoken to, we must not only be silent, but commonly so far apart bodily that we cannot

136

possibly hear each other's voice in any case. Referred to this standard, speech is for the convenience of those who are hard of hearing; but there are many fine things which we cannot say if we have to shout. As the conversation began to assume a loftier and grander tone, we gradually shoved our chairs farther apart till they touched the wall in opposite corners, and then commonly there was not room enough.

The insights and sensitive observations of Thoreau are helpful in pointing up certain consistencies in behavior in heretofore unsuspected areas, such as perceptions of body heat. They strengthened my original premise that man's behavior in space is neither meaningless nor haphazard. Yet there are paradoxes associated with proxemic behavior that need explaining.

Some Paradoxes

A casual observer confronted with American reactions to being touched or approached too closely by foreigners is likely to dismiss such reactions as minor annoyances that will disappear as people get to know each other better. More careful investigation reveals, however, several puzzling questions, or anomalies, which suggest that there is more to behavior patterns based on interpersonal distance than meets the eye.

An anthropologist becomes accustomed to resistance to and denial of the idea that there are regularities in human behavior over which the individual has little or no control. But why do so many people, when faced with other people's behavior, take "interference" with space patterns so personally? And why is there apparently so little that they can do to relieve their feelings?

One of my interview subjects, a colleague, quite typically explained that, after 12 years of working with French culture, he still could not accustom himself to the French conversational distance. He found it "uncomfortably" close, and he found himself annoyed with Frenchmen, possibly because he felt they were getting too familiar. Like other Americans who have been brought up to resent being crowded, he used the device of barricading himself behind his desk.

Another anomaly is associated with architecture. Why is it that, even with a history of building dating back to predynastic Egypt, with surveying developed somewhere around 2500 B.C. and with the magnificence of the Parthenon achieved by the fifth century before Christ, architects have failed to develop a way of describing the experience of space? Recently Philip Thiel (2) published a notation system for describing open spaces.

By what means do people make spatial distinctions? How do people judge distance from each other and teach it to their young with such uniformity and still apparently not know that they are teaching it at all? Technically the work of transactional psychologists answered some questions and raised others (3), while Gibson's approach (4) is the most comprehensive treatment of how man perceives space visually. Asking subjects how they differentiate between distances or why they feel so strongly about matters of space, doesn't help—even the most cooperative subjects can give you only bits of information. Most people have only the vaguest notion of the rules governing the use of their immediate and distant receptors.

In approaching any new problem, the anthropologist must constantly remind himself that, even though he is faced with complexity on all sides, the components that go to make up the complexity must of necessity not be overly complex. Cultural systems are organized in such a way that the basic components (structure points) can be controlled by all *normal* members of the group. For example, varied and rich as languages are, all normal members of a group learn to speak and understand them.

In essence, one looks for simple distinctions that can be made by any normal person and that go beyond individual differences.

This is a report of a study in progress. Additional data will undoubtedly result in revisions. If the data seem obvious, I can only say that to me they seemed obvious *after* I had identified the principal structure points of the system. Then I wondered why it had taken so long to reach this particular point. Recently Bruner (5) stressed something the linguistic scientist has known for a long time: that people do not necessarily have to know the structure of a system of behavior in order to control it.

Research Strategy

A combination of research strategies was employed during this study. Techniques included observation, participant's observations, interviews—structured and unstructured—and biweekly sessions with four blind subjects.[1] Normal subjects were drawn predominantly from the Washington area from the educated-professional group. Fifteen Americans and 18 foreign subjects were interviewed in depth. Interviews lasted from 3 to 15 hours in units of 2 to 3 hours. Data were gathered from 100 additional subjects in unstructured, natural situations. Foreign subjects included English, French, German, Swiss, Dutch, Spanish, Arab, Armenian, Greek and West Africans studying in the United States. These subjects were used in much the same way as subjects are used by the linguist, *i.e.*, as examples of their own particular systems. A few hours with one subject does little more than provide some of the basic and most obvious structure points as well as contrasting examples of proxemic behavior.

Since people apparently cannot describe the patterns that enable them to discriminate between one distance and another, it is next to useless to question them directly about how they go about perceiving spatial relations. It has been necessary to resort to various projective-type devices as a means of getting subjects started thinking about their own spatial experiences. Some of the most valuable leads were gathered as a result of casual conversations when a subject would "warm up" and begin talking about an experience he had had with a particular person.

"Boy, you ought to see a guy we have in our office; everybody talks about it. They even kid him a lot. He comes right up to you, breathes in your face. I sure don't like seeing his face so close, with pop eyes and nose distorted all over the place. He feels you a lot, too. Sometimes we wonder if there isn't something wrong with him."

"He breathes down my neck; why can't he keep his hands off you?"

"Did you ever notice how close he stands to you—it gives me the willies."

"She's one of those who's always pawing you; did you ever notice how some people stand much too close?"

Many of these utterances are virtually stream-of-consciousness. They are valuable because they provide clues to what specific events in other people's behavior stand out as significant.

The Arabs and the English complain (for different reasons) because Americans do not listen. Greeks experience a great flatness in our interaction with them—like eating unsalted rice, they say. In each complaint there lie valuable data concerning the nature of the feedback mechanisms used by *both* parties.

In research of this sort one is faced with a paradox, namely, it is the commonplace that makes the difference when confronted with someone else's "commonplace." Another paradox is that, in writing and talking about one's reactions to being touched and breathed upon by a stranger, the description loses much of the immediate effect. The reactions are so obscure, so small and so seemingly inconsequential that at times it is difficult to realize they may add up to something.

The distinction that Hediger (6) makes between "contact" and "non-contact" species can also be made for man or groups of men. Indeed, it seems to be the first and possibly the most basic distinction between groups.

As the term implies, the "contact" group is characterized by considerable touching, both in private and public. The "non-contact" group perceives the contact group as overly familiar and sometimes "pushy," while the contact group refers to the non-contact as "standoffish," "high-hat," "cold," or "aloof."

In addition to the contact, non-contact category, man seems to share a number of features of the generalized mammalian pattern described by Hediger (6). Personal distance and social distance are certainly present though—inasmuch as a certain amount of confusion exists because of misunderstanding of Hediger's terminology—it may eventually become necessary to define operationally what is meant by these terms. The observations which follow refer to the non-contact group.

Distance Sets

For the American non-contact group, and possibly for others as well, four distance sets seem to encompass most, if not all, behavior in which more than one person is involved. These are referred to as intimate, casual-personal, social-consultative and public. Each distance set is characterized by a close and a far phase.

The perception of distance and closeness apparently is the result of an interplay of the distant and immediate receptor systems (visual, auditory, olfactory), the systems in the skin that record touch and heat flow and those in the muscles that feed back information concerning where a part of the body is at any given moment in time. *The transition from one group of receptors to another is the boundary point between distance sets,* as will be shown subsequently.

For Americans, space judgments seem to depend principally on the tactile-kinesthetic and visual senses, although the olfactory, heat-radiation and oral-aural systems are also involved.

The two most commonly observed sets are *casual-personal distance* and *social-consultative distance.*[2] The descriptions which follow are idealized stereotypes for subjects in non-excited or non-depressed states with 20–20 vision, without excessive background noise, and at average comfortable temperature (55° to 85° F.).

SOCIAL-CONSULTATIVE DISTANCE

The distinguishing features of this distance (close phase: 4 to 7 feet plus or minus 6 inches at each end; far phase: 7 to 12 feet plus or minus 6 inches at each end) are that intimate visual detail in the face is not perceived and that nobody touches or expects to touch unless there is some special effort. Voice level is normal for Americans. There is little change between the far and the close phases, and conversations can be overheard at a distance of up to 20 feet. (There is no loudness scale for the voice that is adaptable to descriptions such as these.)

I have observed that in over-all loudness, the American voice at these distances is under that of the Arab, the Spaniard, the South Asian Indian and the Russian; and it is somewhat above that of the English upper class, the Southeast Asian and the Japanese.

Close Phase: Social-Consultative Distance. The boundary between social-consultative and casual-personal distance lies at a point just beyond where the extended arms can no longer touch (4 to 7 feet).

Foveal vision (area of sharpest focus of the eye) at 4 feet covers an area of just a little larger than one eye (Table 9–1); at 7 feet the area of sharp focus extends to nose and parts of eyes, or mouth; eye and nose are sharply seen. In many Americans, this sharp vision shifts back and forth, or around the face. Details of skin texture and hair are clearly perceived. At 60° visual angle, head, shoulders, and upper trunk are seen at 4 feet distance; the same sweep includes the whole figure at 7 feet. Feet are seen peripherally, even if standing. Head size is perceived as normal. As one moves away from the subject, the foveal area can take in an ever-increasing amount.

A good deal of impersonal business takes place at this distance. In the close phase there is much greater implication of involvement than in the distant phase. People who work together a good deal tend to use close social-consultative distance. It is also a very common distance for people who are attending a casual social gathering.

Looking down at a person at this distance is to dominate him almost completely, as when a man talks to his secretary or receptionist on leaving or entering the office.

Distant Phase: Social-Consultative Distance. Business and social discourse conducted at this distance (7 to 12 feet) has a more formal character than in the close phase. Desks in offices of "important" people are large enough to hold anyone at this distance. In most instances, even with more or less standard desks, the chair opposite the desk is at about 8 or 9 feet from the man behind the desk.

141

TABLE 9-1
Areas Covered at Eight Distances by Four Visual Angles

Distances		1° *	15° X 3° †	60° Sweep‡	180°
			Visual Angles		
Intimate					
	6"	0.1"	2.5" X 0.3" eye, mouth	6" the face	head and shoulders
	18"	0.3" central iris	3.75 X 1" upper or lower face	18" head	upper body and arms
Casual-Personal					
Close	30"	0.5" tip of nose	6.25" X 1.5" upper or lower face	30" head, shoulders	whole figure
Far	48"	0.8" one eye	10" X 2.5" upper or lower face	48" waist up	
Social Con-sultative					
Close	7'	1.7" mouth, eye plus nose; nose plus parts of eye	20" X 5" the face	7' whole figure	
Far	12'	2.5" two eyes	31" X 7.5" faces of two people	12' figure w/ space around it	
Public					
	30'	6.3" the face	6'3" torso of 4 or 5 people	30'	
	340'	6'			
	500'	9'			
	1500'	26'			

*Computed to nearest 0.1 inch.
†Computed to nearest 0.25 inch.
‡Varies with culture.

At social-consultative distance, the finest details of the face, such as the capillaries in the eyes, are lost. Otherwise skin texture, hair, condition of teeth and condition of clothes are all readily visible. Neither heat nor odor from another person's body is apparently detectable at this distance. At least, none of my subjects mentioned either factor.

The full figure—with a good deal of space around it—is encompassed in a 60° angle. This is the distance which people move to when someone says "Stand away so I can look at you." Also, at around 12 feet, accommodation convergence ceases (4, 8); the eyes and the mouth are contained in the area of sharp vision so that it is not necessary to shift the eyes to take in the face. During conversations of any significant length, visual contact has to be maintained and subjects will peer around intervening objects.

If one person is standing and another seated, the seated person may push his or her chair back to about 12 feet in order to reduce the tilt of the head. Several subjects mentioned that "looking up" accentuated the higher status of the other person. In the days of servants it was taken for granted that none would approach a seated employer so close as to make him look up. Today it may be that motorcycle policemen use the device of resting one foot on a running board and looking down on an offender as a way of increasing their psychological leverage. Judges' benches often accentuate differences in elevation.

The voice level is noticeably louder than for the close phase and can usually be heard easily in an adjoining room if the door is open. As the term implies, social-consultative distance is employed for professional and social transactions as long as there is an emotionally neutral effect. Raising the voice or shouting can have the effect of reducing social-consultative distance to personal distance.

I have observed some interviews start at the far end of this scale and move in; in others this process is reversed.

One of the functions of this distance is to provide for flexibility of involvement so that people can come and go without having to talk.[3] A receptionist in an office can usually work quite comfortably if she is 10 or more feet from people waiting to see her boss; if she is any closer, she will feel she should talk to those waiting.

A husband coming back from work often finds himself sitting and relaxing reading the paper at 10 or more feet from his wife. He may also discover that his wife has arranged the furniture back-to-back (a favorite device of the cartoonist, Chick Young, creator of *Blondie*). The back-to-back arrangement is an appropriate solution to minimum space, or a shortage of reading lights.

The social-consultative distance has the advantage of permitting an easy shifting back and forth between one's activity and whoever else is in the room. Participation with others at this distance is spotty and brief. Questions and answers and introductory or opening remarks are what one hears most often. Likewise, it is easy for one of several participants to disengage himself without offending.

CASUAL-PERSONAL DISTANCE

"Personal distance" (close phase: 18 to 30 inches; far phase: 30 to 48 inches) is the term originally used by Hediger to designate the distance consistently separating the members of non-contact species. It might be thought of as a small protective sphere that an organism maintains between itself and others (6).

Far Phase: Casual-Personal Distance. Keeping someone "at arm's length" is one way of expressing this distance (2½ to 4 feet). It begins at a point that is just outside easy touching distance on the part of one person to a point where two can touch easily if they extend both arms.

Details of subject's features are clearly visible. Fine detail of skin, gray hair, "sleep" in eye and cleanliness of teeth are easily seen. Head size is perceived as normal.

Foveal vision covers only an area the size of the tip of the nose or one eye, so that the gaze must wander around the face; 15° clear vision covers the upper *or* lower face. Details of clothing—frayed spots, small wrinkles or dirt on cuffs—can be seen easily; 180° peripheral vision takes in the hands and the whole body of a seated person. Movement of the hands is detected, but fingers cannot be counted.

The voice is moderately low to soft.

No body heat is perceptible. The olfactory factor is not normally present for Americans. Breath odor can sometimes be detected at this distance, but Americans are trained to direct it away from others.

The boundary line between the far phase of the casual-personal distance and the close phase of social-consultative distance marks, in the words of one subject, "the limit of domination."

This is the limit of physical domination in the very real sense, for beyond it, a person cannot easily get his hands on someone else. Subjects of personal interest and involvement are talked about at this distance.

For a woman to permit a man inside the close personal zone when they are by themselves makes her body available to touch. Failure to withdraw signifies willingness to submit to touching.[4]

Close Phase: Casual-Personal Distance. There appears to be a distinct shift from the far phase to the close phase of casual-personal distance (1½ to 2½ feet). The distance roughly is only half that of the former. Olfaction begins to enter in, as well as heat gain and loss from the other person. The kinesthetic sense of closeness derives from the possibilities that are opening up in regard to what each participant can do to or with the other's body. At this distance one can hold or grasp the extremities.

A visual angle of 15° (clear vision) takes in the upper or lower face which is seen with exceptional clarity. The planes of the face and its

144

roundness are accentuated; the nose projects and the ears recede; fine hair of the face and back of neck, eyelashes and hair in nose, ears and pores are clearly visible.

This is as close as one can get without real distortions of the features. In fact, it is the distortion and the enlargement of the features that one encounters in the next closer zone—the intimate—that make it intimate.

INTIMATE DISTANCE

At intimate distance (full contact to 18 inches), two subjects are deeply involved with each other. The presence of the other person is unmistakable and may at times be overwhelming because of the greatly stepped-up sensory inputs. Olfaction, heat from the other person's body, touch or the possibility of touch, not only by the hands but also by the lips and the breath, all combine to signal in unmistakable ways the close presence of another body.

Far Phase: Intimate Distance. Hands can reach and grasp extremities but, because of the space between the bodies (6 to 18 inches), there is some awkwardness in caressing. The head is seen as enlarged in size and its features are distorted.

Ability to focus the eye easily is an important feature of this distance for Americans.[5]

In foveal vision the iris of the eye is enlarged over life size. Small blood vessels in the sclera are seen. Pores are enlarged. This is the distance at which personal services, such as removal of splinters, are provided. In apes it is the "grooming distance."

Fifteen-degree clear vision includes the upper or lower portion of the face which is perceived as enlarged. When looking at the eye, the nose is overlarge, distorted and exaggerated. So are other features, such as lips, teeth and tongue. During conversations, the hands tend to come in and move up toward the face so they will be included in the peripheral field.

Peripheral vision, 180°, includes the outline of head and shoulders and very often, hands.

The voice is normally held at a low level, and Joos' "intimate style" (9) prevails.[6]

Heat as well as odor of breath may be detected, even though it is directed away from the subject's face. Heat loss or gain from the other person's body begins to be noticed by some subjects if their attention is directed to heat.

145

Sensory input from all previously used sources has been stepped up considerably. New channels (such as the olfactory) are just beginning to come into play.

Close Phase: Intimate Distance. This is the distance (full contact to 6 plus or minus 2 inches) of lovemaking and wrestling, comforting and protecting. Physical contact is featured. Use of the distance receptors is greatly reduced except for olfaction and sensitivity to radiant heat, both of which are stepped up.

Vocalization at intimate distances plays a very minor part in the communications process, which is carried mainly by other channels. A whisper has the effect of expanding the distance. The moans, groans and grunts that escape involuntarily during fighting or sex are produced by the action. The two parties act as one as it were.

In the most close (maximum contact) phase, the muscles communicate. Pelvis, thighs and head can be brought into play, arms can encircle. Except at the outer limits, sharp vision is blurred at this distance, although this is not true of the highly plastic eye of the very young or or the extraordinarily nearsighted.

Much of the physical discomfort that Americans experience when others are inappropriately inside the intimate sphere is expressed as distortions of the visual system. One subject said in regard to people that got "too close"—"these people get so close, you're crosseyed! It really makes me nervous they put their face so close it feels like they're *inside you.*"

The expressions, "get your face out of mine," and "he shook his fist in my face" apparently express how many Americans perceive their body boundaries. That is, there is a transition between inside and the outside. At that point where sharp focus is lost, one feels the uncomfortable muscular sensation of being crosseyed from looking at something too close.

When close vision is possible within the intimate range—as with the young—the image is greatly enlarged and stimulates a significant portion (if not the total) of the retina. The detail that one sees at this distance is extraordinary. This, plus the felt pull of the eye muscles, structures the visual experience in such a way that it cannot be confused with the less intense personal, social-consultative and public distances.

Intimate distance is not favored in public among the American middle class. However, it is possible to observe the young in automobiles and on beaches using intimate distances. Crowded subways and buses may bring strangers into what would ordinarily be coded as intimate spatial relations, if it were not for several characteristically isolating compensatory devices. The correct behavior is to be as immobile as possible and, when part of the trunk or extremities contact another, to withdraw if possible. If this is not possible, the muscles in the affected area are kept tense. For members of the non-contact group it is taboo to relax and enjoy the contact. In crowded elevators the hands are kept at the side or used to steady the body by grasping railings and overhead straps. The eyes are fixed at infinity and should not be brought to bear on anyone for more than a passing glance. Men who take advantage of the crowded situation in order to feel or pinch women violate an important cultural norm dealing with the privacy of the body and the right of a person to grant or withhold from others access to it. Middle Eastern subjects do not express the outraged reactions to palpation in public places that one encounters among the non-contact American group.

PUBLIC DISTANCE: OUTSIDE THE CIRCLE OF INVOLVEMENT

Several important shifts occur in the transition from the personal, consultative and social distances to public distances (close phase: 12 feet to 25 feet plus or minus 5 feet; far phase: 30 feet to maximum carrying distance of voice).

Close Phase: Public Distance. In this phase of public distance (12 to 25 feet) participants cannot touch or pass objects to each other. Possibly some form of flight reaction may be present subliminally. At 12 feet an alert subject can take evasive or defensive action if a threatening move is made.

The voice is loud but not full volume. Rice (10) suggests that choice of words and phrasing of sentences is much more careful and there may be grammatical (or syntactic) shifts that differentiate speech at this distance from that at closer, less formal distances. Joos' choice of the term "formal style" (9) is appropriately descriptive: "formal texts . . . demand advance planning . . . the speaker is correctly said to think on his feet."

Because angular accommodation of the eyes is no longer necessary, there is an absence of feedback from the ocular muscles. The angle of sharpest vision (1°) covers the whole face. Fine details of the skin and eyes are no longer visible. The color of the eyes begins to be imperceivable (at 16 feet only the whites of the eyes are visible). Also at 16 feet the body begins to lose its roundness and to look flat.

Head size is perceived as considerably under life size. The 15° cone of clear vision includes the faces of two people (at 12 feet), 60° the

147

whole body with a little space around it. Peripheral vision includes other persons if they are present.

Far Phase: Public Distance. The far phase of public distance begins somewhere around 30 feet. It is the distance that is automatically set around important public figures. White's description of the spatial treatment accorded John F. Kennedy when his nomination became certain is an excellent example:

Kennedy loped into the cottage with his light, dancing step, as young and lithe as springtime, and called a greeting to those who stood in his way. Then he seemed to slip from them as he descended the steps of the split-level cottage to a corner where his brother Bobby and brother-in-law Sargent Shriver were chatting, waiting for him. The others in the room surged forward on impulse to join him. Then they halted. A distance of perhaps 30' separated them from him, but it was impassable. They stood apart, these older men of long-established power, and watched him. He turned after a few minutes, saw them watching him, and whispered to his brother-in-law. Shriver now crossed the separating space to invite them over. First Averell Harriman; then Dick Daley; then Mike DiSalle; then, one by one, let them all congratulate him. Yet no one could pass the little open distance between him and them uninvited, because there was this thin separation about him, and the knowledge they were there not as his patrons but as his clients. They could come by invitation only, for this might be a President of the United States (11).

At this distance body stance and gestures are featured; facial expression becomes exaggerated as does the loudness of the voice. The tempo of the voice drops; words are enunciated more clearly. Joos' *frozen style* (9) is characteristic: "Frozen style is for people who are to remain strangers." The whole man may be perceived as *quite small* and he is *in a setting.* Foveal vision takes in more and more of the man until he is entirely within the small cone of sharpest vision. At this point, contact with him as a human being begins to diminish.

The 60° cone of vision takes in the setting. Peripheral vision seems to have as its principal function the alerting of the individual to movement at the side, which may represent danger.

Meaning and Distance

What significance do people attach to different distances? The very term "closeness" conjures up different images than "distance." "Getting *next to*" someone implies a number of things about your relationship. The expression, "I can't get together with him on that," has a literal, in addition to a figurative, meaning. In the world of actions from which

148

words take their meaning, a wife who sees another woman standing too close to her husband gets the message loud and clear.

For that matter, anyone confronted with a person whose space pattern varies from his own, finds himself asking the following questions: Who does this man think he is? What is he trying to say? Is he trying to push me around, or why does he have to be so familiar?

Yet one of the first things one discovers in this research is that very similar spatial relationships can have entirely different meanings. What one makes of how others treat him in space is determined by one's ethnic past. This is *not* a matter, however, of generalizing about Latinos' standing closer than North Americans, of moving each space zone up a notch as it were. Rather it is a matter of entirely different systems, in which some items are shared but many others are not, including the order and selection of transactions that occur in the different distance sets (12). Thus, it does not necessarily imply any existing or intended relationship if an Arab walks up and places himself inside one's personal sphere in a public place. It may only mean that he wants the spot you are standing on for himself. Since there is no relationship or chance of one, he does not care what you think. The point, however, is so basic and so subtle that it is apt to be lost.

Summary

This selection has dealt with some rather specific aspects of how we gain knowledge as to the content of the minds of other men by means which function almost totally outside awareness. Proxemics represents one of several such out-of-awareness systems which fall within the general rubric of paracommunication.[7]

Communication of this sort, operating outside awareness as it does, appears to be an extraordinarily persistent form of culturally specific behavior which is responded to with considerable effect whenever people encounter patterns which are at variance with their own. It is also apparently a rather basic form of communication, many features of which are shared with other vertebrates.

How man codes distance is a function of which combinations of receptors he uses. These do not always seem to be the same from culture to culture and vary even within subcultures. Visual and kinesthetic cues are prominent in non-contact Americans. Olfactory and tactile cues are emphasized in Eastern Mediterranean urban Arab culture.

Recording of cues used to distinguish one distance from another is possible. It should be noted however, that proxemic research is in its infancy and suffers from many obvious flaws. This report represents a summary of some of what has been accomplished to date rather than a definitive statement of the field.

NOTES

1. These sessions were conducted in cooperation with Dr. Warren Brodey of the Washington School of Psychiatry in the winter of 1961 to 1962.

2. Not to be confused with "social distance," a term used by both Hediger (6) and Bogardus (7). "Social-consultative distance" as used here is not at all like Bogardus' "social distance," which is the distance separating two members of a group in a social hierarchy. It is much closer in meaning to Hediger's term "social distance."

3. In other countries the circle of involvement cannot be counted on to be the same as in the United States.

4. One female subject from a Mediterranean country repeatedly miscued American men who misinterpreted her failure to respond quickly (virtually with reflex speed) to a reduction in distance from *personal* to *close-personal*.

5. American Optical Company Phoroptor Test Card no. 1985-IA (20–20 vision at 0.37 M.) was used to test subjects in a variety of situations including subjects chosen from audiences during lectures. The distance at which the smallest type (0.37 M.) could be read was in all cases the same distance at which the investigator was told that he was now "too close." Twenty diopter lenses fitted to the eye reduced this distance from 15 inches to 19 inches to as little as 7 inches. Subjects were chosen in the 35- to 45-year age bracket. Two subjects with presbyopia failed to respond in this way. With them sharp vision ceased to be featured in the intimate zone.

6. ". . . an intimate utterance pointedly avoids giving the addressee information from outside of the speaker's skin. The point . . . is simply to remind (hardly 'inform') the addressee of some feeling . . . inside the speaker's skin."

7. "Paracommunication" is the term suggested as an appropriate designation by Joos (9) and George Trager (13) to refer to communicative behavior which does not have its base in language but is often synchronized with linguistic and paralinguistic phenomena.

REFERENCES

1. Thoreau, H. D.: Walden. The Macmillan Company, New York, 1929.

2. Thiel, P.: A sequence-experience notation for architectural and urban space. Town Planning Review, April 1961.

3. Kilpatrick, F. P., ed.: Explorations in Transactional Psychology. New York University Press, New York, 1961.

4. Gibson, J. J.: The Perception of the Visual World. The Riverside Press, Cambridge, 1950.

5. Bruner, J.: The Process of Education. Harvard University Press, Cambridge, Mass., 1959.

6. Hediger, H.: Studies of the Psychology and Behavior of Captive Animals in Zoos and Circuses. Butterworth Scientific Series, London, 1955.

7. Bogardus, E. S.: Social Distance. Antioch Press, Yellow Springs, Ohio, 1959.

8. Whitcomb, M.: Vision Committee, National Academy of Sciences, personal communication.

9. Joos. M.: The five clocks. Internat. J. Am. Linguistics, April, 1962.

10. Rice, F.: Institute for Applied Linguistic Research, personal communication.

11. White, T. H.: The Making of the President 1960. Atheneum Publishers, New York, 1961. (Reprinted by permission of the publisher.)

12. Hall, E. T.: Sensitivity and Empathy at Home and Abroad. Three Leatherbee Lectures, given at Harvard University Graduate School of Business Administration, Boston, Spring, 1962.

13. Trager, G. L.: Paralanguage: a first approximation. Stud. Linguistics, 13: 1–12, 1958.

10

The Social Psychology
of Privacy

BARRY SCHWARTZ

The concern for the impact of architecture on group cohesion, community development, and worker morale first emerged in the late nineteenth century in response to growing public anxiety over the violence and disorder of urbanized society. Higher population densities, the destruction of peasant and farm life, and the separation of home and work were seen as forces that were breaking up the basic social relationships that held cities together. Garden city planners, utopian architects, industrial technocrats—all made proposals for the organization of the physical environment that they hoped would restore the social bond.

In recent decades a new emphasis has emerged in urban design theory, namely a concern with preserving individuality and protecting people from the conformist pressures of group life. This emphasis is a response to the later stages of industrial society, which, with its mass culture and electronic media and surveillance systems, has an unprecedented technological power to invade privacy and destroy political liberty. In terms of design this concern takes the form of plans that promise to achieve a proper balance between community *and* privacy. Whereas garden city theorists aimed to provide village greens and open spaces to be used and maintained by all the residents of a neighborhood unit, the fashion now is to pay equal attention to private space. In the most sophisticated designs, a gradient of spaces is often proposed, starting with private spaces contiguous to the dwelling unit, going on to semiprivate spaces, under the control of immediate neighbors, and ending with public spaces, available to the surrounding community. (Alexander's selection in Part Five discusses an example of such a design scheme.)

Schwartz's essay shows that designing in terms of both community and privacy is based on sound sociological theory. He makes the point that privacy has important positive functions in personality development and that the chance to withdraw from the group also makes the individual more effective when he returns to active participation in group life. His selection discusses numerous examples from the research literature to indicate that when privacy disappears the maintenance of harmonious social relations

Reprinted from Barry Schwartz, "The Social Psychology of Privacy," *American Journal of Sociology* 73 (May 1968): 741–752. Reprinted by permission of the University of Chicago Press.

among peers is threatened, and that it is also essential for the preservation of authority and efficiency in social structures that are organized on hierarchical principles. However, the special relevance of Schwartz's discussion to this volume lies in his conviction that the physical environment plays an important mediating role in satisfying the dual and sometimes opposing demands of individuals and groups for both community and privacy. Schwartz describes the different kinds of environmental barriers that are developed in social situations, the functions of particular types of doors and windows as screening or transmission devices, and the elaborate ways in which institutions formulate social rules and conventions to govern the use of walls and barriers in private and public situations.

☐

Patterns of coming and staying together imply counterpatterns of withdrawal and disaffiliation which, as modalities of action, are worthy of analysis in their own right.[1] Simmel makes the identical point in his essay, "Brücke und Tür":

> Usually we only perceive as bound that which we have first isolated in some way. If things are to be joined they must first be separated. Practically as well as logically it would be nonsense to speak of binding that which is not separate in its own sense. . . . Directly as well as symbolically, bodily as well as spiritually, we are continually separating our bonds and binding our separations.[2]

Simmel, however, ignores the question of how separation subserves integration—of how men are bound by taking leave of one another as well as by their coming together. One sociologically relevant approach to this problem is through the analysis of privacy, which is a highly institutionalized mode of withdrawal.

The Group-Preserving Functions of Privacy

Withdrawal into privacy is often a means of making life with an unbearable (or sporadically unbearable) person possible. If the distraction and relief of privacy were not available in such a case, the relationship would have to be terminated if conflict were to be avoided. Excessive contact is the condition under which Freud's principle of ambivalence most clearly exercises itself, when intimacy is most likely to produce open hostility as well as affection.[3] Issue must therefore be taken with Homans' proposition, "Persons who interact frequently with one another tend to like one another" (providing the relationship is not obligatory).[4] The statement holds generally, but misses the essential point that there is a threshold beyond which interaction is unen-

153

durable for both parties. It is because people frequently take leave of one another that the interaction-liking proposition maintains itself.

Guarantees of privacy, that is, rules as to who may and who may not observe or reveal information about whom, must be established in any stable social system. If these assurances do not prevail—if there is normlessness with respect to privacy—every withdrawal from visibility may be accompanied by a measure of espionage, for without rules to the contrary persons are naturally given to intrude upon invisibility. "Secrecy sets barriers between men," writes Simmel, "but at the same time offers the seductive temptations to break through the barriers." [5] Such an inclination is embodied in the spy, the Peeping Tom, the eavesdropper, and the like, who have become its symbols.

"Surveillance" is the term which is generally applied to institutionalized intrusions into privacy. And social systems are characterizable in terms of the tension that exists between surveillant and anti-surveillant modes. Much of our literature on the anti-utopia, for example, George Orwell's 1984, which depicts the dis-eases of excessive surveillance, is directed against the former mode. But dangers of internal disorder reside in unconditional guarantees of invisibility against which many administrative arms of justice have aligned themselves. On the other hand, surveillance may itself create the disorder which it seeks to prevent. Where there are few structural provisions for privacy, social withdrawal is equivalent to "hiding." For Simmel, "This is the crudest and, externally, most radical manner of concealment." [6] Where privacy is prohibited, man can only imagine separateness as an act of stealth.[7]

Since some provisions for taking leave of one another and for removing oneself from social observation are built into every establishment, an individual withdrawal into privacy and the allowance of such a withdrawal by other parties reflects and maintains the code that both sides adhere to. Leave taking, then, contains as many ritualistic demands as the act of coming together. Durkheim, like Homans, is not altogether correct in his insistence that the periodic gatherings of the group are its main sources of unity.[8] After a certain point the presence of others becomes irritating and leave taking, which is a mutual agreement to part company, is no less a binding agent than the ritual of meeting. In both cases individual needs (for gregariousness and isolation) are expressed and fulfilled in collectively endorsed manners. The dissociation ritual presupposes (and sustains) the social relation. Rules governing privacy, then, if accepted by all parties, constitute a common bond providing for periodic suspensions of interaction.

If privacy presupposes the existence of established social relations its employment may be considered as an index of solidarity. Weak social relationships, or relationships in the formative stage, cannot endure the strain of dissociation. By contrast, members of a stable social structure feel that it is not endangered by the maintenance of interpersonal boundaries. This point is of course well reflected in the Frostian dictum, "Good fences make good neighbors."

Privacy Helps Maintain Status Divisions

It is also well known that privacy both reflects and helps to maintain the status divisions of a group. In the armed forces, for example, the non-commissioned officer may reside in the same building as the dormitoried enlisted man but he will maintain a separate room. The officer of higher rank will live apart from the non-commissioned, but on the same base, often in an apartment building; but officers of highest status are more likely to have private quarters away from the military establishment.

In organizational life the privacy of the upper rank is insured structurally; it is necessary to proceed through the lieutenant stratum if the top level is to be reached. In contrast, the lower ranks, enjoying less control over those who may have access to them, find their privacy more easily invaded. Even in domestic life persons of the lower stratum lack "the butler" by means of whom the rich exercise tight control over their accessibility to others.

Privacy is an object of exchange. It is bought and sold in hospitals, transportation facilities, hotels, theaters, and, most conspicuously, in public restrooms where a dime will purchase a toilet, and a quarter, a toilet, sink and mirror. In some public lavatories a free toilet is provided—without a door.

Privacy has always been a luxury. Essayist Phyllis McGinley writes:

> The poor might have to huddle together in cities for need's sake, and the frontiersman cling to his neighbor for the sake of protection. But in each civilization, as it advanced, those who could afford it chose the luxury of a withdrawing place. Egyptians planned vine-hung gardens, the Greeks had their porticos and seaside villas, the Romans put enclosures around their patios. . . . Privacy was considered as worth striving for as hallmarked silver or linen sheets for one's bed.[9]

In this same respect Goffman comments upon the lack of front and back region differentiation in contemporary lower-class residences.[10]

The ability to invade privacy is also reflective of status. The physician's high social rank, for instance, derives perhaps not only from his technical skill but also from his authority to ignore barriers of privacy.

155

However, this prerogative is not limited to those of high status. We must not forget the "non-person" who lacks the ability to challenge the selfhood of his superiors. Goffman cites Mrs. Frances Trollope:

> I had indeed frequent opportunities of observing this habitual indifference to the presence of their slaves. They talk to them, of their condition, of their faculties, of their conduct exactly as if they were incapable of hearing. . . . A young lady displaying modesty before white gentlemen was found lacing her stays with the most perfect composure before a Negro footman.[11]

In general society the assumption of the social invisibility of another is looked upon as indecency, that is, as a failure to erect a barrier of privacy between self and other, under prescribed conditions.

The general rule that is deducible from all of this is that outside of the kinship group an extreme rank is conferred upon those for whom privacy shields are voluntarily removed. The prestige afforded the physician is exaggerated in order to protect the self from the shame which ordinarily accompanies a revelation of the body to a stranger, particularly if he is of the opposite sex. Likewise, the de-statusing of the servant is necessary if he is to be utilized for purposes of bathing, dressing, etc.

Persons of either high or low rank who have access to the private concerns of their clients are subject to definite obligations regarding both the manner in which secret knowledge is to be obtained and, most importantly, the way in which it is treated once it has been obtained. Explicit or implicit guarantees of confidentiality neutralize the transfer of power which would otherwise accompany the bestowal of private information. Both the possession of an extreme rank and the assurance of confidentiality thus legitimize the "need to know" and the intrusions which it makes possible.

Privacy and Deviation

Up to this point we have tried to indicate privacy's stabilizing effect upon two dimensions of social order. Withdrawal subserves horizontal order by providing a release from social relations when they have become sufficiently intense as to be irritating. Privacy is also a scarce social commodity; as such, its possession reflects and clarifies status divisions, thus dramatizing (and thereby stabilizing) the vertical order. But we must recognize that privacy also opens up opportunities for such forms of deviance as might undermine its stabilizing effects. However, privacy admits of *invisible* transgression and therefore serves to maintain intact those rules which would be subverted by the public disobedience that might occur in its absence.

Moore and Tumin, in their discussion of the function of ignorance, stated: "All social groups . . . require some quotient of ignorance to preserve esprit de corps." [12] And Goffman has made it clear that every establishment provides "involvement shields" for its members wherein "role releases" may take place, particularly deviant ones.[13] As Merton puts it:

> Resistance to full visibility of one's behavior appears, rather, to result from structural properties of group life. Some measure of leeway in conforming to role expectations is presupposed in all groups. To have to meet the strict requirements of a role at all times, without some degree of deviation, is to experience insufficient allowances for individual differences in capacity and training and for situational exigencies which make strict conformity extremely difficult. This is one of the sources of what has been elsewhere noted in this book as socially patterned, or even institutionalized, evasions of institutional rules.[14]

Thus, each group has its own "band of institutionalized evasion" which expands and contracts as conditions change. Rose L. Coser, in this connection, has considered observability in terms of the social status of the observer. She indicates that persons of high rank tend to voluntarily deprive themselves of visibility by signaling their intrusion with a prior announcement.[15] The deviation band, then, is normally condoned by both the upper and lower strata.

Moore and Tumin stress the importance of preventing deviation from being known to the group as a whole.[16] No doubt, a publication of all of the sins, crimes, and errors that take place in a social unit would jeopardize its stability. The preoccupation of the press with sensational deviations from norms might be considered from this point of view. Similarly, the more one person involves himself with another on an emotional basis the more both will need private facilities to conceal nasty habits and self-defaming information from each other. If the child, for instance, became suddenly aware of all the non-public performances of his father, and if the latter were aware of all the perversions that are privately enacted by his offspring, a father-son relationship characterized by mutual admiration would be impossible. This same point is illustrated in well-adjusted marriages which depend not only upon mutually acceptable role playing but also upon the ability of both parties to conceal "indecent" performances. This presupposes a modicum of physical distance between husband and wife. Simmel, in addition, adds that a complete abandon of one's self-information to another "paralyzes the vitality of relations and lets their continuation really appear pointless." [17]

Privacy enables secret consumption. We observe, for example, the adolescent practices of smoking or drinking in their locked rooms. Similarly, "women may leave *Saturday Evening Post* on their living room table but keep a copy of *True Romance* ('something the cleaning woman must have left around') concealed in their bedroom." [18] However, some modes of secret consumption have come into the public light. The erotic "girlie magazines," for example, no longer need be employed privately by the middle-class male since the advent of the *Playboy* magazine. As some activities emerge from secrecy others go underground. Thus, the person who nowadays finds pleasure in the Bible will most likely partake of it in private rather than in a public place or conveyance. These new proprieties are perhaps specific instances of a general rule set down by Simmel, that

> *what is originally open becomes secret, and what was originally concealed throws off its mystery. Thus we might arrive at the paradoxical idea that, under otherwise like circumstances, human associations require a definite ratio of secrecy which merely changes its objects; letting go of one it seizes another, and in the course of this exchange it keeps its quantum unvaried.* [19]

Incidentally, just as the person must employ proper language for the public situations in which he finds himself, he is required to maintain an appropriate body language as well. Differing postures must be assumed in his public encounters. But public postures do not exhaust the many positions of which the human body is capable. Anyone who has maintained a single position over a long period of time knows that the body demands consistent postural variation if it is to remain comfortable and capable of good role performance. Privacy enables the person to enact a variety of non-public postures and thus prepares him physically for public life.

It should be stressed that the absence of visibility does not guarantee privacy. The hypertrophied super-ego certainly makes impossible the use of solitude for deviant objectives. The person who is constantly in view of an internalized father, mother, or God leads a different kind of private life than those possessed by a less demanding conscience. This reveals an interesting paradox. Privacy surely provides for some measure of autonomy, of freedom from public expectation; but as Durkheim so persistently reminded us, the consequences of leaving the general normative order are moral instability and social rootlessness. (It is for this reason that secret societies compensate for the moral anarchy inherent in pure autonomy by means of ritual.[20]) Is it then possible that through privacy the ego escapes the dominion of the public order only to subordinate itself to a new authority: the super-ego? In some measure this is certainly the case, but one may also venture the suggestion that the super-ego, like the social structure whose demands it incorporates, has its own "band of institutionalized evasion." The super-ego cannot be totally unyielding, for if every deviation of the ego called into play its punitive reaction the consequences for the self would be most severe.

Privacy and Establishments

It was earlier noted that rules or guarantees of privacy subserve horizontal and vertical order. Such rules are embodied in the physical structure of social establishments. Lindesmith and Strauss, for instance, have noted that proprieties concerning interpersonal contact and withdrawal are institutionalized in the architecture of buildings by means of a series of concentric circles. Specific regulations permit or forbid entry into the various parts of this structure, with a particular view to protecting the sacred "inner circle." [21] A more specific instance of the physical institutionalization of norms is found in the case of the bathroom, whose variation in size and design is limited by the requirement that body cleansing and elimination be performed privately.[22] This norm is reinforced by the architectural arrangements in which it is incorporated. The fact that the bathroom is only built for one literally guarantees that the performances which it accommodates will be solos. However, this normative-physical restriction admits of more complicated, secondary proprieties. Bossard and Boll write:

> The fact that the middle-class family rises almost together, and has few bathrooms, has resulted in a problem for it, which has been resolved by a very narrowly prescribed ritual for many of them—a bathroom ritual. They have developed set rules and regulations which define who goes first (according to who must leave the house first), how long one may stay in, what are the penalties for overtime, and under what conditions there may be a certain overlapping of personnel.[23]

The very physical arrangement of social establishments thus opens and shuts off certain possibilities for interaction and withdrawal and creates a background of sometimes complex ritual in support of a foreground of necessary proprieties. Needless to say, the form taken by such ritual is always subject to modification by architectural means.

Charles Madge also urges the architect to take explicit account in his designs of the ambivalences of social life. Men, for example, are given to both withdrawal and self-display. This duality, notes Madge, requires an "intermediate area" in housing projects, such as a backyard or garden which separates the home or inner circle from the "common green." [24] But it is one thing to so divide our physical living space as to insure ourselves of interactional options; it is another to regulate the interactional patterns that the division of space imposes upon us. The latter task is most efficiently met by the door.

Doors. McGinley has referred to the door as a human event of significance equal to the discovery of fire.[25] The door must surely have had its origin among those whose sense of selfhood had already developed to the extent that they could feel the oppression of others and experience the need for protection against their presence. Continued use of the door very probably heightened that feeling of separateness to which it owed its creation. Doors, therefore, not only stimulate one's sense of self-integrity, they are required precisely because one has such a sense.

The very act of placing a barrier between oneself and others is self-defining, for withdrawal entails a separation from a role and, tacitly, from an identity imposed upon oneself by others via that role. Therefore, to waive the protection of the door is to forsake that sense of individuality which it guarantees. As Simmel points out, some measure of de-selfing is characteristic of everything social.[26]

I would like now to discuss various kinds of doors, including horizontal sliding doors (drawers) and transparent doors (windows). I shall also treat of walls, as relatively impermeable interpersonal barriers, in contrast to doors, which are selectively permeable.

Doors provide boundaries between ourselves (i.e., our property, behavior, and appearance) and others. Violations of such boundaries imply a violation of selfhood. Trespassing or housebreaking, for example, is unbearable for some not only because of the property damage that might result but also because they represent proof that the self has lost control of its audience; it can no longer regulate who may and who may not have access to the property and information that index its depths.[27] The victim of a Peeping Tom is thus outraged not only at having been observed naked but also for having lost control of the number and type of people who may possess information about her body. To prove this we note that no nakedness need be observed to make Peeping Tomism intolerable.

"Alone, the visual feeling of the window," writes Simmel, "goes almost exclusively from inward to outward: it is there for looking out, not for seeing in." [28] This interdiction insures that the inhabitants of an establishment may have the outside world at their visual disposal, and at the same time it provides for control over their accessibility to this world. But, whereas the shade or curtain may be employed to regulate accessibility between the private and public spheres of action, situational proprieties are depended upon for protection in public. One such norm is that of "civil inattention" which has been elaborated by Goffman.[29]

Unlike the window, "the door with an in and out announces an entire distinction of intention."[30] There must be very clear rules as to who may open what doors at what times and under what conditions. The front and back doors are normally the only doors that any member of a family may enter at any time and under any circumstances. A parent may enter a child's room at any time and may inspect and replenish drawers, but visiting friends may not. But the parent must learn that some private doors (drawers) may not be opened (although they may be to friends); if they are, new receptacles for ego-indexes will be found, for example, the area between mattress and spring. The child, however, must never inspect the contents of the drawers of his parents nor enter their room at night. Thus the right of intrusion is seen to be an essential element of authority, whose legitimacy is affected by the degree to which it is exercised. Correspondingly, authority is dependent upon immunity against intrusion. Cooley notes that "authority, especially if it covers intrinsic personal weakness, has always a tendency to surround itself with forms and artificial mystery, whose object is to prevent familiar contact and so give the imagination a chance to idealize . . . self-concealment serves, among other purposes, that of preserving a sort of ascendancy over the unsophisticated."[31] In this same connection, Riesman writes:

> As compared with the one room house of the peasant or the "long house" of many primitive tribes, he (the inner directed child) grows up within walls that are physical symbols of the privacy of parental dominance. Walls separate parents from children, offices from home, and make it hard if not impossible for the child to criticize the parents' injunctions by an "undress" view of the parents or of other parents. What the parents say becomes more real in many cases than what they do. . . .[32]

Moreover, it is possible to map personal relations in terms of mutual expectations regarding intrusion. The invasion of various degrees of privacy may be a duty, a privilege, or a transgression, depending upon the nature of the interpersonal bond. And, clearly, expectations regarding such impositions may not be mutually agreed to.

Parental obligations concerning the care of a child override the child's rights to seclusion and place him in a position of social nakedness wherein he has no control over his appearance to others. However, to be subject to limitless intrusion is to exist in a state of dishonor, as implied in the rule against "coming too close." This point is made in Simmel's discussion of "discretion" as a quality which the person-in-private has a right to demand of another who is in a position to invade his seclusion.[33] Compromises between child and parent are therefore necessary and generally employed by the manipulation of the door. For example, the bedroom door may be kept half open while the child sleeps, its position symbolic of the parents' respect for the youngster's selfhood. Furthermore, a general temporal pattern might emerge if a large number of cases were examined. During infancy the door to self is generally fully open;[34] it closes perhaps halfway as a recognition of self development during childhood, it shuts but is left ajar at pre-puberty, and closes entirely—and perhaps even locks—at the pubertal and adolescent stages when meditation, grooming, and body examination become imperative. Parents at this time are often fully denied the spectatorship to which they may feel entitled and are kept at a distance by means of the privacy that a locked door insures.

There are also certain situations wherein husband and wife must remain separate from one another. A spouse, for example, must generally knock before entering a bathroom if the other is occupying it. This is a token of deference not to nudity but to the right of the other party to determine the way he or she wishes to present the self to the other. This rule insures that the self and its appearance will remain a controllable factor, independent of the whims of others, and it contributes to self-consciousness as well. This is seen most clearly in total institutions like the armed forces where open rows of toilets are used first with some measure of mortification and later with a complete absence of consciousness of self. In such doorless worlds we find a blurring of the distinction between "front and back regions," between those quarters where the self is put on and taken off and those in which it is presented.[35] In conventional society those who confuse these two areas are charged with vulgarity.

In contrast to the door, the wall symbolizes "separation" rather than "separateness" and denies the possibility of the encounter and withdrawal of social exchange. It strips away that element of freedom which is so clearly embodied in the door. "It is essential," notes Simmel, "that a person be able to set boundaries for himself, but freely, so that he can raise the boundaries again and remove himself from them."[36] In privacy, continues Simmel, "A piece of space is bound with himself and he is separated from the entire world."[37] But in enforced isolation man is bound *to* space. While the door separates outside from inside, the wall annihilates the outside. The door closes out: the wall encloses. Yet doors are converted into walls routinely, as is seen in the popular practice of "sending a child to his room" for misdeeds and the like. In this sense, many homes contain private dungeons or, rather, provisions for transforming the child's room into a cell—which forces upon us the distinction between formal and informal imprisonment.

Privacy is not dependent upon the availability of lockable doors. Goffman, for example, discusses "free places" in the institution where inmates may, free of surveillance, "be one's own man . . . in marked contrast to the sense of uneasiness prevailing on some wards."[38] In addition there is "personal territory" established by each inmate: for one a particular corner; for another a place near a window, etc. "In some wards, a few patients would carry their blankets around with them during the day and, in an act thought to be highly regressive, each would curl up on the floor with his blanket completely covering him; within the covered space each had some margin of control."[39] Thus do men withdraw from others to be at one with themselves and to create a world over which they reign with more complete authority, recalling Simmel's observation that "the person who erects a refuge demonstrates, like the first pathfinder, the typically human hegemony over nature, as he cuts a particle of space from continuity and eternity."[40]

In summary, islands of privacy exist in all establishments and throughout even the most intimate household. These islands are protected by an intricate set of rules. When these rules are violated secret places are sought after, discovered, and employed as facilities for secret action. These places and their permeability constitute one type of map, as it were, of interpersonal relationships and reveal the nature of the selves participating in them.

Privacy, Property and Self. Implied in any reference to a private place is its contents, personal property. One perhaps more often than not withdraws into privacy in order to observe and manipulate his property in some way, property which includes, of course, body and non-body objects.

There are two types of objects: those which may be observed by the public (and which may be termed personal objects) and those which are not available to public view (private property). Private property, as we are using the term, may be further delineated in terms of those intimate others who may have access to it in terms of visibility or use. Some private objectifications of self may be observed by family members, but some may be observed by *no one except the self*. There is no doubt that these latter objects have a very special meaning for identity; some of these are sacred and must not be contaminated by exposing them to observation by others; some are profane, and exposure will produce shame, but both are special and represent an essential aspect of self and, from the possessor's point of view, must not be tampered with.

It is because persons invest so much of their selves in private and personal things that total institutions require separation of self and material objects. When individualism must be minimized private ownership is always a vice worthy of constant surveillance. In such situations the acquisition and storage of personal things persist in the form of the "stash," which might be anything from a long sock to the cuff of one's pants.[41]

It follows that those who have direct or indirect access to the belongings of others or to articles which have been employed by them in private ways enjoy a certain amount of power which, if judiciously employed, may serve their interests well. Hughes observes:

> It is by the garbage that the janitor judges, and, as it were, gets power over the tenants who high-hat him. Janitors know about hidden love affairs by bits of torn-up letter paper; of impending financial disaster or of financial four-flushing by the presence of many unopened letters in the waste. Or they may stall off demands for immediate service by an unreasonable woman of whom they know from the garbage that she, as the janitors put it, "has the rag on." The garbage gives the janitor the makings of a kind of magical power over that pretentious villain, the tenant. I say a kind of magical power, for there appears to be no thought of betraying any individual and thus turning his knowledge into overt power.[42]

But, certainly, power need not be exercised to be effective. The mere knowledge that another "knows" invokes in the treatment of that other a certain amount of humility and deference.

Deprivatization

We have attempted to show that the possibility of withdrawal into well-equipped worlds which are inaccessible to others is that which makes intense group affiliations bearable. But we have also seen that men are not always successful in protecting their invisibility. Accidental leakages of information as well as the diverse modes of espionage threaten the information control that privacy is intended to maintain. But information control also consists of purposeful information leakage and even of the renunciation of secrecy. Just as men demand respite from public encounter they need periodically to escape themselves, for a privacy which lacks frequent remissions is maddening. The over-privatized man is he who is relieved of public demand only to become a burden to himself: He becomes his own audience to performances which are bound for tedium. Self-entertainment is thus a most exhausting business, requiring the simultaneous performance of two roles: actor and spectator. Both tire quickly of one another. When privacy thereby exhausts itself new and public audiences (and audienceships) are sought.

Moreover, we are led to relinquish our private information and activities by the expediencies and reciprocities routinely called for in daily life. We all know, for example, that in order to employ others as resources it is necessary to reveal to them something of ourselves, at least that part of ourselves which for some reason needs reinforcement. When this occurs (providing support is forthcoming), two things happen. First, we achieve some degree of gratification; second, and most important, our alter (or resource) reveals to us information which was heretofore withheld, for self-revelation is imbued with reciprocal power: It calls out in others something similar to that which we give of ourselves. There is both mutual revelation and mutual gratification. It is easy to see that when stress or need is prolonged this process may become institutionalized: Intimacy is then no longer an alternative; it is enforced, and private activity becomes clandestine and punishable. The deprivatization process approaches completion when we are not only penalized for our withdrawals but feel guilty about them. A housewife who had probably undergone the deprivatization process confided to Whyte: "I've promised myself to make it up to them. I was feeling bad that day and just plain didn't make the effort to ask them in for coffee. I don't blame them, really, for reacting the way they did. I'll make it up to them somehow." [43]

But loss of privacy among conventional folk is free of many of the pains of social nakedness which are suffered by inmates and by others undergoing total surveillance. The civilian voluntarily subjects himself to publicity and is relatively free of the contamination of unwanted contacts. His unmaskings are selective and subject to careful forethought. The intruder is chosen rather than suffered; indeed, his resourcefulness depends upon his ability to "know" his client-neighbor.

165

Therefore, in civil life, we find valid rationalization for our self-revelations. The demand that we "be sociable" is too compelling and too rewarding to be ignored by any of us.

But a substantial self-sacrifice is made by those who actually believe themselves to be what they present to public view. An awareness of the masquerades and deceptions that are part of good role performance is necessary to recall ourselves to our *own* selfhood and to our opposition to that of others. We must indeed deceive others to be true to ourselves. In this particular sense privacy prevents the ego from identifying itself too closely with or losing itself in (public) roles. Daily life is therefore sparked by a constant tension between sincerity and guile, between self-release and self-containment, between the impulse to embrace that which is public and the drive to escape the discomfort of group demands. Accordingly, our identities are maintained by our ability to hold back as well as to affiliate. Thus Goffman writes:

> *When we closely observe what goes on in a social role, a spate of sociable interaction, a social establishment—or in any other unit of social organization—embracement of the unit is not all that we see. We always find the individual employing methods to keep some distance, some elbow room, between himself and that with which others assume he should be identified.*
>
> *Our sense of being a person can come from being drawn into a wider social unit; our sense of selfhood can arise through the little ways in which we resist the pull. Our status is backed by the solid buildings of the world, while our sense of personal identity often resides in the cracks.*[44]

For Goffman, privacy is one of "the little ways in which we resist the pull" of group commitments and reinforce our selfhood.

NOTES

1. The initiation of a social contact generally entails a withdrawal from a preceding one. Therefore, men may withdraw into new social circles as well as into seclusion. In this particular sense it would be most exact to employ the term "contact-withdrawal," as opposed to a single term for engagement and another for disengagement. However, this distinction does not apply to movements into privacy.
2. Georg Simmel, "Brücke und Tür," in *Brücke und Tür* (Stuttgart: K. F. Koehler, 1957), p. 1.
3. Sigmund Freud, *Group Psychology and the Analysis of the Ego* (New York: Bantam Books, Inc., 1960), pp. 41–42.
4. George C. Homans, *The Human Group* (New York: Harcourt, Brace & Co., 1950), p. 111.
5. Georg Simmel, "The Secret and the Secret Society," in Kurt Wolff, ed., *The Sociology of Georg Simmel* (New York: The Free Press, 1964), p. 334.
6. *Ibid.*, p. 364.
7. *Ibid.*
8. Émile Durkheim, *The Elementary Forms of the Religious Life* (Glencoe, Ill.: The Free Press, 1947), pp. 214–219.

9. Phyllis McGinley, "A Lost Privilege," in *Province of the Heart* (New York: Viking Press, 1959), p. 56.

10. Erving Goffman, *The Presentation of Self in Everyday Life* (Edinburgh: University of Edinburgh, 1958), p. 123.

11. *Ibid.*, p. 95.

12. Wilbur E. Moore and Melvin M. Tumin, "Some Social Functions of Ignorance," *American Sociological Review*, XIV (December, 1949), 792. See also Barney Glaser and Anselm Strauss, "Awareness Contexts and Social Interaction," *American Sociological Review*, XXIX (October, 1964), 669–679, in which social interaction is discussed in terms of "what each interactant in a situation knows about the identity of the other and his own identity in the eyes of the other" (p. 670). A change in "awareness context" accompanies acquisitions of knowledge, provisions of false knowledge, concealment of information, etc.

13. The "involvement shield" and Everett C. Hughes' concept of "role release" are elaborated in Erving Goffman's *Behavior in Public Places* (New York: The Free Press, 1963), pp. 38–39.

14. Robert K. Merton, *Social Theory and Social Structure* (New York: The Free Press, 1964), p. 343.

15. Rose L. Coser, "Insulation from Observability and Types of Social Conformity," *American Sociological Review*, XXVI (February, 1961), 28–39.

16. Moore and Tumin, *op. cit.*, p. 793.

17. Simmel, "The Secret and the Secret Society," *op. cit.*, p. 329.

18. Goffman, *The Presentation of Self in Everyday Life, op. cit.*, p. 26. Needless to say, many instances of the employment of privacy for "secret production" could be given.

19. Simmel, "The Secret and the Secret Society," *op. cit.*, pp. 335–336.

20. *Ibid.*, pp. 360–361.

21. Alfred R. Lindesmith and Anselm L. Strauss, *Social Psychology* (New York: Henry Holt & Co., 1956), p. 435. However, in an interesting statement, McGinley announces the death of the very idea of the "inner circle": "It isn't considered sporting to object to being a goldfish. On the same public plan we build our dwelling places. Where, in many a modern house, can one hide? (And every being, cat, dog, parakeet, or man, wants a hermitage now and then.) We discard partitions and put up dividers. Utility rooms take the place of parlors. Picture windows look not onto seas or mountains or even shrubberies but into the picture windows of the neighbors. Hedges come down, gardens go unwalled; and we have nearly forgotten that the inventor of that door which first shut against intrusion was as much mankind's benefactor as he who discovered fire. I suspect that, in a majority of the bungalows sprouting across the country like toadstools after a rain, the only apartment left for a citadel is the bathroom" (*op. cit.*, pp. 55–56).

In contrast, Edward T. Hall observes: "Public and private buildings in Germany often have double doors for soundproofing, as do many hotel rooms. In addition, the door is taken very seriously by Germans. Those Germans who come to America feel that our doors are flimsy and light. The meanings of the open door and the closed door are quite different in the two countries. In offices, Americans keep doors open; Germans keep doors closed. In Germany, the closed door does not mean that the man behind it wants to be alone or undisturbed, or that he is doing something he doesn't want someone else to see. It's simply that Germans think that open doors are sloppy and disorderly. To close the door preserves the integrity of the room and provides a protective boundary between people. Otherwise, they get too involved with each other. One of my German subjects commented, 'If our family hadn't had doors, we would have had to change our way of life. Without doors we would have had many, many more fights. . . . When you can't talk, you retreat behind a door. . . . If there hadn't been doors, I would always have been within reach of my mother' " (*The Hidden Dimension* [Garden City: Doubleday & Co., 1966], p. 127.) For a discussion of the norms regulating privacy among the English, French, Arab, and Japanese, see pp. 129–153.

22. Alexander Kira, *The Bathroom* (New York: Bantam Books, Inc., 1967),

THE SOCIAL PSYCHOLOGY OF PRIVACY

pp. 178–184. The requirement of complete privacy for personal hygiene is only a recent phenomenon (see pp. 1–8).

23. J. H. S. Bossard and E. S. Boll, *Ritual in Family Living* (Philadelphia: University of Pennsylvania Press, 1950), pp. 113–114 (cited by Kira, *op. cit.,* pp. 177–178).

24. Charles Madge, "Private and Public Places," *Human Relations,* III (1950), 187–199. F. S. Chapin (in "Some Housing Factors Related to Mental Hygiene," *Journal of Social Issues,* VII [1951], 165) emphasizes that the need for relief from irritating public contact must be consciously and carefully met by the architect. On the other hand, Kira writes: "There are problems which cannot be resolved by architects and industrial designers alone, however; they also pose a challenge to the social scientists and to the medical and public health professions. This is an area in which the stakes are enormous and in which little or no direct work has been done." (*Op. cit.,* p. 192.)

25. See n. 21.

26. Simmel, "The Secret and the Secret Society," *op. cit.,* p. 373.

27. The law recognizes the psychological effect of such criminal acts and provides additional penal sanction for them. Wolfgang and Sellin report that "the chain store is more outraged by theft from a warehouse, where the offender has no business, than from the store where his presence is legal during store hours." Moreover, "the victim of a house burglary is usually very disturbed by the fact that the offender had the effrontery to enter the house illegally. . . . For these and similar reasons, breaking and entering as well as burglary carry more severe sanctions in the law" (Marvin E. Wolfgang and Thorsten Sellin, *The Measurement of Delinquency* [New York: John Wiley & Sons, 1964], pp. 219–220).

28. Simmel, "Brücke und Tür," *op. cit.,* p. 5.

29. Goffman, *Behavior in Public Places, op. cit.,* pp. 83–88.

30. Simmel, "Brücke und Tür," *op. cit.,* p. 4.

31. Charles Horton Cooley, *Human Nature and the Social Order* (New York: Schocken Books, Inc., 1964), p. 351.

32. David Riesman, *The Lonely Crowd* (Garden City: Doubleday & Co., 1953), p. 61. Another characteriologist, William H. Whyte, suggests that "doors inside houses . . . marked the birth of the middle class" (*The Organization Man* [Garden City, N.Y.: Doubleday & Co., 1956], p. 389).

33. Simmel, "The Secret and the Secret Society," *op. cit.,* pp. 320–324. Similarly, Erving Goffman writes: "There is an inescapable opposition between showing a desire to include an individual and showing respect for his privacy. As an implication of this dilemma, we must see that social intercourse involves a constant dialectic between presentational rituals and avoidance rituals. A peculiar tension must be maintained, for these opposing requirements of conduct must somehow be held apart from one another and yet realized together in the same interaction; the gestures which carry an actor to a recipient must also signify that things will not be carried too far" ("The Nature of Deference and Demeanor," *American Anthropologist,* LVIII [June, 1956], 488).

34. The absence of ability among infants and children to regulate the appearance and disappearance of their audience does not mean that privacy or separateness is not an important feature of their development; the privacy need is simply expressed differently. The infant, for example, can sometimes remove himself from the field of stimulation by going to sleep or wriggling away from the adult who holds him. This is probably why pathology resulting from overcontact is less likely than that due to undercontact, for the former is far more easily regulated by the infant than the latter. At a later stage of development, the infant learns that he can hold back and let go in reference not only to sphincters but to facial expressions and general dispositions as well. He comes to view himself as a causal agent as he inherits the power of voluntary reserve. When the child is locomoting he first confronts privacy imposed against him by others and begins to define himself in terms of where he may and may not go. On the other hand, his ambulatory ability gives him enormous control over his audience, a power in which he delights by "hiding." Espionage is practiced as well and suspected in others—whereby the condition of

shame begins to acquire meaning for the child. These incomplete comments suffice to illustrate the point that the privacy impulse is not at all inactive in infancy and childhood. They further suggest that each stage of development has its own mode of privacy, which may be defined in terms of the ego's relationship to those from whom privacy is sought and the manner in which withdrawal is accomplished.

35. Goffman, *The Presentation of Self in Everyday Life, op. cit.*, pp. 66–86.

36. Simmel, "Brücke und Tür," *op. cit.*, p. 4.

37. *Ibid.*, p. 3.

38. Erving Goffman, "The Underlife of a Public Institution," in *Asylums* (Garden City, N.Y.: Doubleday & Co., 1961), p. 231.

39. *Ibid.*, p. 246. For more on norms regulating territorial conduct in face-to-face encounters, see Nancy Felipe and Robert Sommer, "Invasions of Personal Space," *Social Problems*, XIV (May, 1966), 206–214; and Robert Sommer, "Sociofugal Space," *American Journal of Sociology*, LXXII (May, 1967), 654–660.

40. Simmel, "Brücke und Tür," *op. cit.*, p. 3.

41. Goffman, *Asylums, op. cit.*, pp. 248–254.

42. Everett C. Hughes, *Men and Their Work* (Glencoe, Ill.: The Free Press, 1958), p. 51.

43. Whyte, *op. cit.*, p. 390.

44. Goffman, *Asylums, op. cit.*, pp. 319–320.

11

Social Theory in Architectural Design

MAURICE BROADY

Despite the findings of behavioral science research, which indicate that design factors do not by themselves determine patterns of social interaction or produce social cohesion, many architects and planners continue to ignore the complexity of the relationship between spatial organization and group life. They believe instead in the doctrine of architectural determinism, or, to put it crudely, that the architect's decisions about the placement of buildings determine the social relationships of the occupants. Why does this doctrine persist? What alternative theory or conceptual orientation more in accord with behavioral science research should be substituted for it? What can architects do to increase the chances that the social consequences they have in mind will in fact be realized?

These are some of the questions that Broady discusses in his selection. He believes that the continued advocacy of the doctrine of architectural determinism is indicative of the intellectual blindness that leads members of every profession, whether law, architecture, or medicine, to believe that their function is socially critical. Because architects *hope* that certain social outcomes will result from their designs, they tend to expect that these outcomes will happen. They also tend to assume that the lay public will be as discriminating in judging the visual elements of a building as trained architects are and will give to purely architectural features the same weight they give to utilitarian qualities.

To the doctrine of architectural determinism, Broady opposes the theoretical distinction originally promulgated by Herbert Gans between the potential and the effective environment. The physical form is only a potential environment that provides clues for social behavior. The effective environment, the totality of the significant variables influencing behavior, includes not only the physical environment but also the social structure and cultural attributes of the people who use it.

Architects should find ways to apply this insight in their own work. If the use of the environment is heavily influenced by the people who will inhabit it, regardless of what the architect may intend, then it is incumbent on the designer to consult his prospective users before he develops a design.

Reprinted from Maurice Broady, "Social Theory in Architectural Design," *Arena*, The Architectural Association Journal, London, 81, no. 898 (January 1966): 149–154, by permission of the editor.

Broady also believes that every design scheme should be accompanied by a social and administrative program, which would help the implementation of the plans for the physical environment. To facilitate the future development of such collaborative undertakings, Broady calls for more rigorous instruction in the social sciences in schools of architecture and for the formation of joint architect-sociologist design and planning teams.

☐

One does not have to talk with architects and town-planners for very long to discover that they are interested in social theory. There are, of course, the aesthetes pure and simple—the people I used to meet in the Liverpool School in the early fifties, whose fifth-year schemes were likely to be designs of swish villas for equally swish colleagues on the Riviera. But most of the designers I meet now are better described as "social consciences." They are idealists—even radicals. They share a sense of social purpose. They want to improve society and they believe that their work as architects or planners can help them to do so. They are, accordingly, interested in sociology. They have read their Geddes and their Mumford and now know all about the mums of Bethnal Green and the sidewalks in Greenwich Village. They talk a lot about "survey before plan"; they have even consorted (not perhaps very profitably) with the odd sociologist like myself.

For my part, I greatly enjoy these encounters with people who are convinced of the importance of their work and bubbling over with the desire to create new and better environments. It is a change from the atmosphere of a university where creativity may often be inhibited and vision narrowed by the demands of scholarship. I would not wish in any way to weaken this ardor and idealism. And yet, at times, one stands aghast at the naivety, the sheer lack of intellectual discipline which often marks the enthusiastic designer's confrontation with social theory. Perhaps one ought not to worry about all this hot air: for it may not be taken seriously even by its exponents. Indeed, it sometimes seems to be used not so much to guide design as to bolster morale and to add a patina of words to ideas intuitively conceived. In the end, however, one *must* be concerned. For phoney social theory is likely to produce phoney expectations and spurious designs. It may equally hinder effective collaboration between social scientists and designers and inhibit the development of more valid ideas about the relationship between architectural design and social structure. That is why a largely critical article (which this will be) is not as negative as

171

might at first be supposed. For one of the best ways to begin to elaborate new ideas is to criticize the inadequacies of current theory.

At least three types of architectural theorizing can be found. There is, first of all, straight waffle:

> *The vertical segregation of traffic as an urban system (meaning?) offers us potentially one effective component (why effective if only potentially offered?) in such a* shaping-strategy *(what?) not simply because in organisational terms (meaning again?), for example, cars can get to the right place without even having to cross pedestrian lines on the same plane, but because the very independence of each layer offers a* potential for generating a new urban syntax *(cool!) in as much as it allows for independent development of each level, etc.*[1]

I suppose this simply means that the vertical segregation of traffic and pedestrians enables cars to move without bumping into people and allows traffic and pedestrian areas to be developed independently of each other: which is a good deal less significant a point than the original form of expression would lead one to imagine.

The second type of theorizing involves grafting a spurious social theory onto a useful and sensible technical solution. This is evident in a review of Denys Lasdun's cluster-blocks in Bethnal Green which states:

> *The cluster concept offers a viable alternative on the visual side by creating tower accents without visually destroying the existing grain; on the human side it shows promise in possessing domestic scale in the component parts of those towers and maintaining something like the pre-existing sociological grouping of the street that gave the original urban grain to the district.*

To which Edmund Cooney has tartly commented that

> *the sociological thinking has been grafted onto an aesthetic dogma, and it has been assumed, without observation, that the graft has taken successfully and is bearing fruit. It might have been less confusing simply to explain that if housing policy required 64 households to be accommodated on such a small site then they would have to live in some form of high tower or slab, in which case a cluster block would look better than anything else.*[2]

I myself first came across this unnecessary grafting of social ideas a number of years ago when a well-known architect was explaining the principle of vertical segregation of pedestrians and traffic. He had made an extremely good technical case for this idea; and he concluded —in no flippant manner—by arguing, on completely redundant social grounds, that this design would be entirely consonant with the *Zeitgeist* of the second half of the century (or something) since it would enable pedestrians to enjoy the sight of myriads of brightly colored cars flashing along below them and thus to be more fully part of the exciting flux of an automobile era. The *exact* detail of expression may well have escaped me in this example: but no one who has heard enthusiastic architects in their romantic vein will doubt its plausibility. Nor can one doubt that the function of these various kinds of utterance is not to clarify social understanding so much as to cheer their authors up and to show what remarkable chaps they really are. This kind of thinking may be necessary for the designer's morale and thus have *something* useful to contribute to his profession. But it is much more likely to confuse understanding and jeopardize clear thinking.

Architectural Determinism

Architects, however, are apt to subscribe to a much more funda-mental and pervasive kind of theorizing which may be labelled "architectural determinism." It is more often found implicit in archi-tects' thinking than in any clearly argued form: and it is probably the more dangerous for that. How influential it is, is difficult to say. But the fact that it has been vigorously defended in at least four archi-tectural schools in which I have recently had occasion to criticize it and that it has also been the subject of critical comment by other sociolo-gists on both sides of the Atlantic supports the view that it is fairly widely held among architects and town-planners.[3] Indeed, earlier this year, Gabriel Epstein made the point in a discussion on university design that plans ought not to be produced "in the sense in which architects were trained to think . . . not in the *determined* way of architects."[4] Nor is it difficult to catch examples. There was, for instance, the group-architect at Cumbernauld who asked my advice on whether it would be socially more desirable to place three point-blocks in triangle rather than in line. Then there was the planner at Basingstoke who assured me that the most satisfied and well-settled residents in the four estates which we were studying in the town would be found in the one that was outstanding in lay-out and design. Quite the reverse was in fact the case—24 per cent of the residents of that estate expressed themselves dissatisfied as compared with only 11 per cent in the three other estates.[5] And the Cumbernauld architect was rather taken aback when I said that I doubted whether it would make any real difference socially which way he placed his point-blocks!

That these expectations were both wrong is less interesting than the fact that they were held. For they indicate very clearly the assumptions which derive from an implicitly held theory of architectural determinism. The theory has been expressed as follows: "The architect who builds a house or designs a site plan, who decides where the roads will and will not go, and who decides which directions the houses will face and how close together they will be, also is, to a large extent, deciding the pattern of social life among the people who will live in these houses."[6] It asserts that architectural design has a direct and determinate effect on the way people behave. It implies a one-way process in which the physical environment is the independent, and human behavior the dependent variable. It suggests that those human beings for whom architects and planners create their designs are simply moulded by the environment which is provided for them. It is of a kind with the other varieties of popular determinism—such as the view that national character is determined by climate—which save the layman the trouble and worry of observing accurately and thinking clearly.

The Neighborhood Unit Theory

The classic case of architectural determinism is the neighborhood unit theory. Here again, a dubious social theory was grafted onto a reasonable technical solution. The idea, as it was first elaborated by Clarence Perry in the 1920s, was essentially a means of relating physical amenities systematically to population, with particular regard to the safety and convenience of pedestrians and especially children. As Peter Mann has pointed out, Perry's *social* claims for the neighborhood unit were "very careful and extremely modest."[7] Much the same could be said of the Dudley Report[8] in which the idea received semi-official endorsement when it was published in 1944; while the report prepared in 1943 by the National Council of Social Service on *The Size and Social Structure of a Town* similarly argued that "Though physical planning and administrative measures *cannot by themselves change social relationships*, they can, if wisely and positively conceived, encourage and facilitate the growth of that spirit of fellowship without which true community life is impossible."[9] As so often happens, however, the qualifications embodied in this statement were in practice largely ignored. To the theory of how to allocate amenities in housing areas, which the neighborhood unit idea originally was, there was added after the war a crude social theory which asserted that the neighborhood plan, and the way in which amenities were allocated within it, *would* foster a sense of belonging and community spirit among the residents of each neighborhood.

174

One of the major puzzles in the history of recent planning theory is why this idea should have been so enthusiastically received in the years immediately after the war.[10] (Why, indeed, despite all the criticism to which it has been subjected, does it still find such ardent defenders not only in this country but in the States and on the Continent, too?) I think the answer is that it was really ideological: that it was accepted not because it could be shown to be valid, but because it was *hoped* that it would be so. You have only to think of the circumstances in which it was accepted to appreciate why this should have been the case. The new town idea had been buttressed by the criticisms which had been levelled at the inter-war housing estates. These estates had been criticized not only because they were ugly, badly designed and lacking even the basic social amenities, but also because the people who lived in them were said to miss the friendliness, neighborliness and the sense of belonging to a definite community which, despite bad housing and a poor physical environment, they had enjoyed in the slum districts from which they had been moved. How then, could the good housing of the new estates be combined with the friendliness of the slums? That was the sort of problem with which socially conscious, idealistic planners, architects, social workers and administrators were concerned in the 1930s.

In the answer which they found, the assumptions of architectural determinism stand out clearly. What was it about the slum street that made it so friendly? Obviously, they said, its amenities: its pubs and church halls and, above all, the dear little corner shops where Ma could get "tick" to bide her over till wage night and meet her friends for a chat. The answer for the new towns, then, was to provide the same kind of amenities (especially the little corner shops) and, *eureka!* people would be as friendly and neighborly in their new surroundings as they had been in the old. Of course, people do meet each other and chat in pubs and corner shops. But not all pubs and corner shops engender the neighborliness of the slum street. For what is much more important in explaining that neighborliness are the *social* facts, first, that the people who lived in the slums had often lived in the same street for several generations and thus had long-standing contacts with their neighbors and kin; and second, that people who suffer economic hardship are prone to band together for mutual help and protection. It is true that neighborliness is induced by environmental factors. Of these, however, the most relevant are social and economic rather than physical. But it can be readily understood why planners (and others who wished to do something to make life better for their fellow-men)

175

should have been so ready to suppose that the prime factor in the growth of "community spirit" was the design of the *physical* environment which it was uniquely in their power to modify.

Inadequacies of Current Theory

There is no reason to expect that idealistic young architects graduating in the 1960s will think any differently. The disposition which I am criticizing has its roots deep in the intellectual bias of the architectural profession. We are all inclined to see the whole world through our own professional spectacles, and thus to see it distortedly. The lawyer, dealing daily as he is with divorces and separations, often seems to suppose that the family is held together only by the constraint of the law. Once admit a modification of the divorce laws, he seems to be saying, and fornication will be rampant and we shall all be running off with our neighbors' wives. The physicist is apt to suppose that the world could be run much better if only scientists were in charge; the psychologist, that the assumptions about rat behavior that are helpful in the lab are equally valid as general principles of human conduct. By the same token, the designer may easily come to believe that his work will achieve the social objectives which not only his client, but he himself, wishes to promote.

Nor does the architect's training help him to understand, except in a very superficial way, the approach of the social scientist to the kind of problems he is interested in. Sociologists, it is true, are invited to give short courses of lectures in many architectural schools. But they are usually expected to contribute on such a narrow, vocationally oriented tack that it is difficult for them to communicate so that it sinks in what social theory is all about, how it is established and by what criteria it should be evaluated. Architectural students, therefore, tend to get a general notion of how social surveys are conducted but —even if they are told—they usually fail to appreciate that a survey forms only part of a sociological *argument* and that it is in order to provide particular kinds of evidence for such arguments that surveys are undertaken. In my opinion, it is this imbalance between a rigorous training in visual and a superficial training in social scientific thinking that makes it possible for our students to accept a deterministic answer to the complex problem of how social organization and architectural design interact, and which thus contributes to that extreme, at times even obsessive anxiety about the effects that their work is likely to have on other people's lives which one so often notices in

176

them. A further result of this imbalance is that students tend to collect lots of factual information only to be at a loss what to do with it all once they have got it and frequently fail to control their intuitive designer's approach with coherent and systematic thinking.[11]

The superficiality of architects' social theory can be shown quite as clearly in the detail of planning practice. In one planning scheme in which I was recently involved, the problem was being considered how shops should be allocated in residential areas. Two divergent views were advanced. On the one hand, it was proposed that, in order to maximize convenience, suites of shops should be located so that no resident was more than a quarter of a mile from one of them. This would have meant building one suite of 6,000 square feet for every 3,000 people. The alternative view held that the over-riding criterion in allocating shops was "to establish focal points that will foster a sense of community within the area served"; and this, it was argued, would be more effectively achieved by building one suite of 9,000 square feet for every 5,000 people.

This second view is a typical expression of the neighborhood unit idea that amenities should be sited so as to foster a sense of community. But the idea that such a minor difference of size as that between 3,000 and 5,000 people would have any material influence upon something so nebulous as a sense of community is sheer speculation masquerading as sociological truth. Neither figure can be said to be more valid than the other in this connection. If it is argued that the experience of Hemel Hempstead, for instance, indicates that a unit of 5,000 people is best, then similarly impressionistic evidence, of no more but no less validity, can be adduced from Crawley to show that there, in even larger neighborhoods which range in size from 5,500 to 7,000 residents, the sense of community is so strong that it has inhibited the development of identity with the town as a whole. Furthermore, even if differences *could* be shown in the degree of community feeling in neighborhoods of different sizes, it would still remain open to doubt whether such differences were caused, or even directly influenced by the size of the neighborhood or the way in which amenities were disposed within them. Accordingly, this kind of "sociological" argument seems designed to support a proposition which if it were valid, would be so for reasons quite different from this.

At first glance, the convenience argument seems much more plausible. It does not depend upon the singularly narrow definition of social welfare that is involved in regarding the development of community feeling as the primary criterion in allocating shops, and it at least seeks

177

to achieve some tangible benefit for the consumer. Yet it is curious how narrow and conventional was the designer's view of what benefits the consumer might wish to have maximized. Convenience, after all, is only one aspect of economy: it is a measure of the economy of time and distance. But there is also economy of the purse. The housewife surely wants shops that are both convenient and cheap; and if the convenience of having shops within one quarter of a mile of everybody meant that only one grocer could make a living in each suite of shops, this might encourage, even if it did not oblige him to charge monopoly prices which could probably be avoided if convenience were marginally reduced, by increasing the radius served by the shops, in order to have two grocer's shops in competition with each other. Thus, the fact that the planner was thinking primarily in terms of *physical* distance prevented him from thinking realistically about shopping provision by taking into account all the social requirements which shops need to meet. In such simple but significant ways does inadequate social theory hinder sound thinking about design problems.

The Counter-Argument

But to return to the basic issue of the effect of architectural design on social organization. Surely, it will be argued, buildings and lay-outs *do* influence social behavior? There is certainly some evidence to support this view. In the end, one is likely to develop social contacts with people one meets and whom one meets within a residential area *is* affected by its lay-out. A number of studies of planned communities both here and in America have certainly shown the significance of proximity in the formation of social relationships.[12] Their conclusions are summed up by Irving Rosow in the phrase: "People select their friends primarily from those who live nearby and those whom their house faces." [13] Even the location of a kitchen door can matter! If it is at the side of the house, contacts are more likely to be made with the side-neighbor; if at the back of the house, with the party-neighbor.[14]

These data, however, valid though they are, have been used to support the belief that "the tenants' entire social life may hang on the smallest whim of the greenest draftsman. . . ." [15] But this kind of conclusion is hardly justified. In the first place, the relationship between proximity and friendship is obviously not absolute, for friendships *are* made with people who live down the street as well as in adjacent houses and in districts far away as well as near at hand. Even though Kuper's study of a Coventry estate showed that more intensive interaction between neighbors takes place in cul-de-sacs than in long terraces of houses, there is also evidence that, in older areas of terraced-housing, street groups may be even more cohesive and active.[16] The second point is that, while design features may facilitate neighborly intercourse, they cannot be said to influence its quality. Those who subscribe to architectural determinism always seem to suppose that the influence of design will be beneficial. But people may be rancorous as well as friendly, and, as several studies of neighboring families have shown, they may equally well wish to defend themselves against their neighbors as to welcome every opportunity to meet them.[17] How they will react to their physical environment depends on so much more than physical design; and if propinquity provides the occasion for contact between neighbors, how that contact develops depends chiefly upon social factors.

The Basingstoke example which was quoted earlier illustrates the point very clearly. The reason why the residents of the best-designed estate were the least satisfied was that their satisfaction depended only marginally upon architectural design. Broadly speaking, the working-class residents of the other estates had moved in order to get better housing. They, therefore, were well satisfied to have a house of their own, away from nagging in-laws and rapacious London landlords. The middle-class residents of the well-designed estate, on the other hand, had mostly had a decent enough house before moving to Basingstoke, and had moved chiefly to get a better job. For them, the fact that they were living in a reasonably well-designed house in the best laid-out estate in the town was inadequate compensation for their general disappointment with the social life of Basingstoke itself.

Two other examples will suffice to clinch the point. In one university a few years ago, the attempt was made to encourage staff and students to meet together informally by installing a coffee-lounge between the senior and junior common rooms, especially furnished with comfortable chairs and thick carpets. This has not worked. Nor, without supporting social and possibly administrative arrangements, could it possibly have done so. For it is quite unrealistic to suppose that the provision of a coffee-lounge could change a pattern of social segregation which rests upon substantial differences of function and responsibility, not to mention of age and status, and which the whole pattern of academic organization tends to emphasize.

Conversely, social intercourse, if deeply enough rooted, may continue in the teeth of architectural disincentives. The Institute of Community Studies, for instance, in a study of tenant reaction to four contrasting types of housing in the East End of London found that the people who felt most cut off from their neighbors and who considered that the layout of the building made it particularly difficult to keep in touch with other tenants were the residents of Denys Lasdun's cluster-block, but that these same tenants were nevertheless much more sociable than the residents of the other types of building. The reason had to do with their social background. For most of them had previously lived in one of the most gregarious tenements in the district and they simply carried on these social activities, such as baby-sitting for one another, visiting and going shopping together, which over time had become part of their way of life.[18]

In the light of such evidence, therefore, even if it be admitted that architectural design may influence, it cannot be said to determine social behavior. Indeed, there is much to be said for the view that it has, at most, only a marginal effect on social activity. Among other evidence, it is particularly interesting to note that whenever architects are discussing their own domestic affairs this is the view which they invariably appear to adopt. In the discussions that have been going on about the future of the AA School, it is, I suggest, significant that the discussion has been much less concerned with the present fabric and its many inadequacies than with the constitution of the School in these new circumstances—with how it is to be organized as a *social* institution. By the same token, the RIBA report on *The Architect and his Office* was equally unconcerned with the physical aspects of architectural offices but focussed again upon the way in which those offices were organized. If architects pay so little attention to architecture when their own professional activities are at issue, it is surely odd that they should be so excessively concerned with it when *other* people's affairs are concerned and so persuaded that architectural design can have the great effect upon them which they are inclined to ignore for themselves!

Towards a More Viable Social Theory

Clearly, then, as social theory, architectural determinism will not do. So where do we go from here? The answer is that we must now begin to develop a more realistic understanding of the relations between architectural design and human behavior: one, that is to say, which reflects what actually happens rather than what we hope might happen. I say "begin" advisedly, because in this country, at least, we have barely started to consider the problem systematically. All I can do here, therefore, is to make some very general remarks about some of the considerations that need to be taken into account.

These days, architects and planners are concerned not simply with buildings but with environments. As Hugh Wilson put it in his recent inaugural address: "If it (planning) is concerned *with the total environment,* with the creation of towns of quality and character *and with the well-being of people,* then I claim to be a planner." [19] The assumption which I have been criticizing is that environment is created uniquely by buildings and physical design. The first step in correcting this theory is to introduce the useful distinction, put forward by Herbert Gans, between a potential and an effective environment.[20] The point of this distinction is clear enough. The physical form is only a potential environment since it simply provides possibilities or clues for social behavior. The effective—or total—environment is the product of those physical patterns plus the behavior of the people who use them, and that will vary according to their social background and their way of life: to what sociologists, in their technical language, call social structure and culture.

This distinction entails two simple but important points which now need to be made clear. Designers often fail to realize how much difference it makes to their view of the world that they respond to buildings and townscapes with eyes more discriminating and intellects more sensitive to design than those of the average layman. Their failure to appreciate the point leads them to make the fallacious assumption that the users of buildings will react to them as they do themselves. There is substantial evidence to justify our being very skeptical of this belief. Vere Hole, for example, found that tenants in a Scottish housing estate which she was studying noticed and complained about practical things, such as the lack of made-up footpaths, but failed to remark upon the unsightly colliery slag-heaps or the monotonous appearance of their houses. Indeed, in another estate, they even failed to distinguish consciously between an older and a more modern style of housing.[21] A similar conclusion came out of a study of a Glasgow redevelopment scheme in which the authors were surprised to find how comparatively insensitive the tenants were to questions of design.[22] Nearer home, reactions to the Smithsons' "Economist" building ranged from the sophisticated comments of architects to the negative responses of members of "The Economist" staff, of whom Tom Houston reports that he "asked several of our people but failed to get an answer to the question: Does this place stimulate or not?" [23]

A similar disparity must also be noted between commonsense assumptions about the way human beings react to environmental stimuli and how they actually do react. The psychology of design is singularly ill-developed; but what we *do* know about it suggests that we should be equally cautious about commonsense, layman's psychology. For example, it has always been assumed that people can judge accurately how much daylight there actually is in a room. An investigation by Brian Wells of the Department of Building Science at Liverpool University, however, has shown that "the strength of beliefs about daylighting and view were *independent of physical context* . . . and that people tended to overestimate the proportion of daylight that they had to work by at increasing distances from the windows." [24] Any theory of the relationship between design and human behavior, therefore, needs to take full account of the empirical evidence adduced by social scientists which calls commonsense ideas so clearly in question.

The second point which we must go on to make is that human beings are a good deal more autonomous and adaptable than a deterministic theory would lead one to suppose. Architects, indeed, especially those who use prefabricated and standardized dwellings, for example, have been criticized for "stamping people to a common mould." The answer to this sort of criticism is simply to go and look at the interiors of those standardized rooms—better still, at the interior designs on the even more standardized cupboards in army barrack-rooms—to appreciate how little individuality is inhibited by standardization.

Furthermore, people may well be more adjustable than is often supposed. Cullingworth, for instance, found that, although 54 per cent of the residents of the Worsley overspill estate had not wished to leave Salford, by the time they had lived in Worsley for a few years, only 17 per cent of them wished to return to the city.[25] Similarly, while any movement of population inevitably causes some personal disturbance which people dislike, all the evidence shows that, for most people, this is a temporary phase and that they settle equally well in the new area as in the old.[26]

A further demonstration of the point came from an inquiry into the tenants' reaction to moving into the first precinct of the Hutchesontown-Gorbals redevelopment scheme in Glasgow. The scheme comprised flats and maisonettes. Allocation to the houses was made by ballot, so that it was a matter of chance which kind of dwelling each tenant got. When the tenants were asked about their preferences, it was discovered that the flat-dwellers preferred the flats and the maisonette-dwellers the maisonettes and that each group of tenants justified its preference by criticizing aspects of the other type of dwelling which did not trouble the people who actually lived in them.[27]

Conclusions

Two main conclusions follow from all this. First, architectural design, like music to a film, is complementary to human activity; it does not shape it. Architecture, therefore, has no kind of magic by which men can be redeemed or society transformed. Its prime social function is to facilitate people's doing what they wish, or are obliged to do. The architect achieves this by designing a physical structure that is able to meet known and predictable activities as conveniently and economically as possible. However, human behavior is like runny jelly—not formless, but wobbly and changeable; and since he cannot predict its changes, the designer also has to allow as best he can for such new demands as may come to be made of his buildings. More positively, perhaps, it is open to him to provide cues in the potential environment which he is creating which might serve as foci for these new activities or suggest them. He may even be able, as Mackintosh did for the modern movement, to set forth in design ideas and suggestions which may then directly influence a society's aesthetic and, through that, its whole *Weltanschauung*. But even this is far from architectural determinism: and the first conclusion, I believe, is that architects should be more modest and realistic about their ability to change the world through design.

The second conclusion is that architecture should be considered more carefully in relation to other factors that contribute to the total environment. This point applies particularly to town-planning. It seems to me that this is the *leitmotiv* of Jane Jacobs' critique of American planning practice.[28] For the main point of her book is that, instead of razing great areas of American cities to the ground and injecting "cataclysmic money" into massive and deadening rebuilding projects, planners should think about what might be done to encourage the process of rehabilitation which is undertaken, in places like Boston's North End, by the people of the district in the teeth of unsympathetic planning departments and credit-houses. It is similarly expressed in the report which I recently prepared for the Basingstoke development committee on the social aspects of town development, which began by proposing social unity and social vitality as the main social objectives of such a scheme and went on to suggest ways in which the pattern of

183

social administration and the people themselves who would be moving into the town, *as well as* physical design, could jointly contribute to the achievement of those objectives.[29]

The adoption of this view-point leads, I believe, to a reappraisal of the sociologists' role in the design process. At present, I suspect, sociology is regarded simply as a method of inquiry, as tantamount to "doing a survey." The sociologist, then, is thought of *à la* Geddes, as the specialist fact-finder who provides some of the specifications of a "mass" demand to which large municipal building projects must be tailored. That this is too limited a view comes out very clearly when different groups of consumers take different views about the design of the same kind of building. Brian Wells, for instance, discovered that office-managers preferred large, open office spaces while supervisors and clerks preferred smaller spaces; and that both groups could produce good organizational reasons to support their preferences. If a social survey were all that were required, then the sociologist's task would end there. But, as Wells points out, he must go on to examine what consequences large and small office-areas have for social attitudes and behavior and to relate this analysis to the functions for which the office, as a social organization, is set up. In this sense, Wells concludes, "organizational and management problems will become part of the architectural and design problem."[30] Social theory is concerned precisely with these questions of social organization; and sociologists and social psychologists have at their disposal an increasingly sophisticated theory as well as the methods for analyzing organizational structures. They may thus be able to contribute more fully to the elucidation of design briefs.[31] Their contribution, however, would be the more valuable if it were based upon a clearer understanding of how physical design, people and patterns of administration interact to produce whatever we might mean by "total" or "effective" environments. If it is agreed that determinism is a most inadequate make-shift for such an understanding, then the somewhat critical tenor of this paper may perhaps be accepted as a positive step towards the development of a more fruitful and creative partnership than presently obtains between architecture and the social sciences.

NOTES

1. From an article in *Architectural Design*, 1963: my emphases and comments.
2. E. Cooney, *New Homes and Social Patterns*, Institute of Community Studies (mimeoed draft), p. 80.

3. See H. J. Gans, "Planning and Social Life"; I. Rosow, "The Social Effects of the Physical Environment," both in *Journal of the American Institute of Planners*, May 1961; M. Abrams, "Planning and Environment," *Journal of the Town Planning Institute*, May 1962; P. Willmott and E. Cooney, "Community Planning and Sociological Research: A Problem of Collaboration," *Journal of the American Institute of Planners*, May 1963 (also published in *Architectural Association Journal*, February, 1962).

4. *Architectural Association Journal*, January 1965, p. 167; my italics.

5. "The Social Implications of a Town Development Scheme," Southampton, 1962 (mimeo), p. 7.

6. L. Festinger, S. Schachter and K. Back, *Social Pressures in Informal Groups*, New York, 1950, p. 160.

7. P. H. Mann, *An Approach to Urban Sociology*, London, 1965, p. 172.

8. "Site Planning and Layout in Relation to Housing," in *Design of Dwellings*, London, 1944.

9. *The Size and Social Structure of a Town*, London, 1943.

10. For an alternative view, see N. Dennis, "The Popularity of the Neighbourhood Community Idea," *The Sociological Review*, December, 1958.

11. As Hugh Wilson commented in his inaugural address earlier in the year: "We all know those extensive publications of useless facts." *Architectural Association Journal*, February, 1965, p. 198.

12. For a useful bibliography and review of these studies, consult the articles already cited by H. J. Gans and I. Rosow, in *Journal of the American Institute of Planners*, May 1961.

13. I. Rosow, *op. cit.*, p. 131.

14. L. Kuper, "Blueprint for Living Together," in *Living in Towns*, London, 1953 and V. Hole, "Social Effects of Planned Rehousing," *The Town Planning Review*, July 1959, p. 168.

15. C. Bauer, quoted in I. Rosow, *op. cit.*

16. See, for example, M. Broady, "The Organization of Coronation Street Parties," *The Sociological Review*, December, 1956.

17. *Neighbourhood and Community*, Liverpool, 1954; J. M. Mogey, *Family and Neighbourhood*, Oxford, 1956.

18. P. Willmott and E. Cooney, *op. cit.*, pp. 125–126.

19. H. Wilson, *op. cit.*, p. 197: my italics.

20. H. J. Gans, "Some Notes on Physical Environment, Human Behaviour and their Relationships," quoted in M. Abrams, *op. cit.*, p. 122.

21. V. Hole, *op. cit.*, p. 169.

22. "The Design and Use of Central Area Dwellings," *Housing Review*, January–February, 1961.

23. *Architectural Association Journal*, February, 1965, p. 207.

24. "Subjective Responses to the Lighting Installation in a Modern Office Building and their Design Implications," *Building Science*, 1965, p. 66: my italics.

25. J. B. Cullingworth, "Social Implications of Overspill: the Worsley Social Survey," *The Sociological Review*, July 1960, pp. 80, 93.

26. M. Broady, "Social Adjustment in New Communities," *Royal Society of Health Congress*, 1962.

27. *Housing Review*, *op. cit.*

28. J. Jacobs, *The Death and Life of Great American Cities*, London, 1964.

29. M. Broady, "The Sociological Aspects of a Town Development Scheme," Basingstoke Town Development Joint Committee, 1964 (mimeo).

30. B. Wells, "A Psychological Study with Office Design Implications," *The Architects Journal Information Library*, 1964, p. 881.

31. Cf. Boris Ford's statement "I think we would genuinely have to go on to say that you architects are as ill-equipped to think sociologically as we academics have proved ourselves to be"; and Nicholas Malleson's plea for the social scientist as the "third party in the transaction between the brief-making academic and the architect holding the brief": in "University Planning," *Architectural Association Journal*, January 1965, pp. 160, 168.

PART THREE
Environmental Influences on Health and Well-Being

12

The Housing Environment
and Family Life

DANIEL M. WILNER, ROSABELLE PRICE WALKLEY,
THOMAS C. PINKERTON, AND MATTHEW TAYBACK

The oldest tradition of scientific investigation of the social effects of architecture and the planned environment deals with their effect upon health. As we stated earlier, Vitruvius was aware of this aspect of building, but empirical studies of the influence of housing and of work environments on disease and mortality first became widespread in the early nineteenth century. The stimuli for these studies were the increases in epidemic diseases and death rates that accompanied the rapid urbanization of European and American cities. These investigations provided the intellectual underpinnings for housing reform movements and for legislation to improve factory conditions on both sides of the Atlantic. Scientific work has continued unabated now for well over a century and a half, extending beyond physical health to include consideration of mental health and symptoms of social pathology, such as delinquency, crime, family disorganization, and divorce.

Several issues have emerged from this work around which current research tends to focus. One is the degree to which the negative or positive influence of housing on health is the result of the impact of the physical environment per se and the degree to which it can be attributed to the social characteristics of the people who live in good or bad housing. A second is the delineation in precise terms of those aspects of architecture and the environment that are principally responsible for the influence that the physical environment can exert on illness and social pathology. A third is the clarification of the kinds of behavior or illness that are most likely to be affected by the quality of the environment.

Information pertaining to all of these issues was collected for the study reported in the following selection. The selection itself is the summary and concluding chapter of a monograph written by Wilner and his associates describing a study they conducted in Baltimore during the 1950s. In their research the authors examined the effect that rehousing of a low-income Negro population from a slum area to a new, nearby public housing project had on the health of the individuals involved. The health of this test group

Reprinted from Daniel M. Wilner, Rosabelle Price Walkley,
Thomas C. Pinkerton, and Matthew Tayback, "Summary and
Conclusions," in *The Housing Environment and Family Life*
(Baltimore: The Johns Hopkins Press, 1962), pp. 241–252.

of about 300 families was compared with the health of a control group of about the same size who remained in the slum area. Data were collected and interviews conducted over a 6-year period.

Wilner and his colleagues discovered that the health of the test group improved in many respects. This result has been interpreted to mean that when housing conditions are highly inadequate, the physical environment itself can have a deleterious effect upon health, and that when a group that formerly lived in such conditions moves to better housing its illness rates will diminish. Because this study dealt with a group living in an unusually poor environment, its implications for the influence of more favorable environmental conditions is not clear. However, most epidemiologists and other specialists working in the field of environmental health have concluded that except in such cases of extreme environmental inadequacy, social factors have at least as much influence as physical factors upon the health of the population.

Wilner and his colleagues measured a vast array of housing characteristics for both the test and control populations. They examined housing structure; the type and condition of available facilities, including bathrooms, kitchens, water supply, and heating; and the quality of maintenance of the dwelling unit; they also made various measures of density, including number of people per floor area, persons per room, and persons per sleeping room. In general, they found that density was the most powerful factor for explaining variations in the health of the two groups.

For the most part, housing studies have shown that the environment has a greater impact on behavior within the dwelling unit and on attitudes toward the home environment itself than it does on behavior outside the home or on attitudes relating to problems and situations outside the home, such as attitudes toward work or school. The Baltimore study confirms this generalization, except for the interesting finding that the school performance of the children in the test group was superior to the performance of the children who remained behind in the slum.

□

This selection provides the summary and conclusions for three principal components of a study of the effects of housing on physical and mental health. The study was carried out at The Johns Hopkins University in the years 1954–1960 and involved measurement of approximately 1000 families (5000 persons) over a 3-year period of time (1955–1958).

The instigation to undertake the research arose from three principal considerations. First, is the scholarly general interest in the effects of man's physical environment on behavior, an environment which in our epoch is, of course, largely of man's own devising. Secondly, in a more pragmatic vein, is the belief and conviction among social planners and officials in public agencies that improved housing leads to an improve-

ment in health and the amelioration of social ills. A third consideration to some extent bridges the first two. This is the need to gain experience in the conduct of the sort of systematic research on complex
social variables that may lead to relatively unequivocal assessment of
effects.

A review of representative research revealed some demonstration of
the relationship between housing and health, the direction of the relationship in most cases being: the better the housing, the better the
health, and the fewer the social maladjustments. However, in many instances, an equally plausible relationship could very likely be demonstrated between health and many correlates of housing quality, such as
education, income, or general cultural level. In other words, because of
the research design principally employed—the cross-sectional study—
it has been difficult to rule out the effects of non-housing factors.

In an effort to provide more conclusive findings, a nearly classical
study design was adopted in the present research. It involved two
samples, each surveyed 11 times during the study: a test group originally living in the slum but subsequently moving to a new public
housing project; a control sample matched to the test families on many
characteristics and slated to *remain* in the slum. The housing development to which the test families moved consisted architecturally of
both high-rise and low-rise buildings.

Both groups were surveyed initially *before* the test sample moved to
good housing. Subsequently, a total of 10 "after" surveys were conducted with each family in the home. Detailed assessment was made of
housing quality, physical morbidity, and social psychological adjustment. In addition, the performance of every child attending public
school was assessed from school records.

Originally, the test group consisted of approximately 400 families
(2000 persons); the control group of 600 families (3000 persons). Two
problems arose which made necessary some adjustment of the two
samples before the final analysis of the data began. The first problem
was attrition in the samples over time. Such losses were not unexpected,
and, in fact, unusually time-consuming measures were used to keep
them to a minimum. In the course of the ten waves of morbidity and
adjustment surveys in the "after" period of the study, the sample loss
was approximately 1.3 per cent per wave, or about 13 per cent of the
originally constituted matched groups.

The second problem was totally unexpected. It was found that control families were, in the passage of time, not only moving about in the
city at the rate of approximately 10 per cent per wave, but also that

much of the movement was to improved housing—both public and private. This development undoubtedly was due to the increasing availability of adequate housing in the period 1955–1958, while the study was being conducted.

In order to adhere to the experimental conditions required by the study design, the original samples were adjusted to take losses and moves into account. There resulted two reduced effective samples, well-matched on a number of demographic, initial health and initial adjustment characteristics: a test group of 300 families (1341 persons), all in good housing after the initial move, and 300 control families (1349 persons), who, despite some improvement in housing during the study, were in poorer housing on the average, than the test families. Both samples consisted of low-income Negro families. All subsequent findings were based on these adjusted samples.

Physical Health

At the outset of the study, consideration of the ways in which the housing quality of test and control groups would differ led to a number of hypotheses and expectations regarding the role of housing in disease. Among important housing items considered were density and crowding, hot water and facilities for cleanliness, toilet, sharing of facilities, screening, rodent infestation, food storage and refrigeration. It was anticipated, for example, that variation in the quality of these factors would affect introduction of infective organisms into the dwelling unit and their subsequent transmission among family members either by airborne or contact means.

Beginning with initial over-all comparability on morbidity matters, it was expected that, as a consequence of subsequent differences in housing quality, test rates of the incidence of illness would be lower than control rates. The prediction of lower test incidence included both serious and less severe episodes of illness. There was, in addition, the expectation that rates of disability would be lower in the test group than among controls. Finally, it was expected that certain categories of disease might be particularly affected by the housing differences: acute respiratory infections, the communicable diseases of childhood, tuberculosis and syphilis, digestive complaints, and inflammatory and noninflammatory diseases of the skin. The incidence of accidents in and about the home was expected to be influenced by housing dimensions such as space, maintenance and repair. It was thought, also, that the generally "harder" living in the slum might contribute to a higher

192

rate of exacerbation of chronic conditions in the control than in the test population.

MORBIDITY

The morbidity data provided findings which, in general, confirmed the hypotheses for persons under 35 years of age, and especially for children, but there was little confirmation of the hypotheses for persons of age 35–59.

Persons under 35 Years of Age: Episodes of Illness and Disability. For persons under 35 years of age, general confirmation of the hypotheses was observed in the last 2 years of the study for serious episodes, for less severe episodes, and for total days of disability.[1] Several subgroups, distinguished by age and sex, varied in degree of confirmation of the general directional trend.

Males under 20 years of age as a group appeared to show the greatest effects, the magnitude of the test-control differences appearing larger for them than for girls, both in rates of episodes and days of disability. While all of the more refined age groups contributed to the general findings for persons under 20, the 5–9 year-old group, for both sexes, showed most consistently lower test than control rates of illness and of disability.

Among young adults ages 20–34, females showed far greater and more consistent effects than did males. Test rates among the females in this age group were lower than control rates in episodes of any severity as well as in days of disability.

Persons under 35 Years of Age: Types of Illness. Expectations regarding the categories of disease that would be most affected by housing quality were only partially borne out. Among *children* (under 20 years of age), the findings indicated that in the final 2 years of the study, test rates were regularly lower than control rates in three illness categories: infective and parasitic conditions (mainly the communicable diseases of childhood), digestive conditions, and accidents.[2] The findings with respect to accidents are especially important and clear. Accidents were one-third lower in the housing project as contrasted with the slum. The data showed general confirmation of this fact among all age and sex groups under 20. In at least 1 of the 2 years, test rates were also lower than control rates in respiratory conditions, and allergic and metabolic episodes.

Among *adults* (20–34 years of age), hypotheses regarding communicable diseases, such as respiratory and digestive conditions, were in general not borne out. However, slightly lower test than control rates of episodes were distributed over a wide range of conditions, including some that were predominantly chronic in nature, such as allergic, endocrine and metabolic diseases, mental disorders, and circulatory conditions.

Persons under 20 Years of Age: Morbidity in the "Interim" Period. The data for children during the "interim" period, approximately 5 months following the resettlement of test families into their new quarters, was of considerable epidemiologic interest. The findings showed during this period that test rates of illness and disability were *higher* than control rates for almost every age-sex category in the group under 20 years of age. Further examination of "interim" period data by classification of disease revealed that the higher test rates were entirely accounted for by three categories of conditions: infective and parasitic, respiratory, and digestive, all of which have communicability as a principal feature. The most likely explanation was that the test children, newly assembled into the housing project, were strangers to one another in more than just a social sense, and lacked group immunity to common communicable diseases. A similar phenomenon has been observed in the rise of infectious disease in other newly assembled groups, for example, new recruits in the armed services.

Persons 35–59 Years of Age. In contrast to the morbidity data for persons under 35, the findings for persons 35–59 years of age showed general nonconfirmation of the study hypotheses in the "after" period. In the final 2 years, test rates were higher than control rates, among males, for serious episodes of illness and days of disability; among females, for both serious and less severe episodes and for days of disability. The test-control differences, while not statistically significant, were of considerable magnitude. Investigation of the reasons for this unexpected direction of differences revealed the existence of a small but disproportionate number—more among tests than controls—of persons with a relatively large number of episodes in the "interim" period, and with a history of chronic illness at Wave 1. Adjusting the data to take this inequality into account resulted, for males, in lower test than control disability rates in the final year of the study, and for females, resulted in lower test than control episode and disability rates in the last two years.

MORTALITY

It was found, unexpectedly, that 10 control deaths in contrast to 2 test deaths occurred in the "after" period of the study. The 2 test deaths

194

were among children under 6 years of age. Of the control deaths, 5 were likewise very young children, and 5 were among persons 60 years of age and older.

Among the older persons, the finding of 5 control deaths compared to no test deaths was of interest in itself, although the numbers were too small to be anything but suggestive of the relationship of housing to mortality. One consequence of the control deaths among the older persons in the study was the necessity for removing the cohort of persons 60 years of age and older from the morbidity analysis. The 20 test and 20 control persons who originally constituted this age group had the highest rates of episodes of illness and disability of any of the age categories in the study. To analyze the morbidity of this cohort would therefore have involved estimating the illness rates of the controls who had died, and it was felt that this could not be done properly.

FREEDOM FROM ILLNESS

Wave-by-wave data as a per cent of all persons in the test and control samples showed only small differences between the two groups in the proportions of individuals who experienced *no* illness. At most, there was a modest directional trend in which tests were more likely than controls to be free of illness in nine out of the ten "after" waves. Test persons of all ages tended to be freer of illness than control persons, more so for males than for females.

CHILDBEARING EXPERIENCE

The general childbearing experience of females in the study was described in terms of the outcomes of pregnancy and the morbidity of the mother. The data reported were for Waves 3–11, this time period being designated in order to insure that pregnancies of the test women began after the move into the project, and, therefore, that the prenatal experience took place under good housing circumstances.

The findings revealed little to suggest that differential housing affected, in any significant way, the outcomes of pregnancies. There was similarity between the test and control mothers as to the number of pregnancies that occurred and the ages of the women at outcome. There appeared to be a slight excess of perinatal mortality among the test outcomes, but there was evidence of somewhat greater incidence of prematurity among the control live births. Little difference occurred between the two groups in the incidence of either minor or more serious complaints during the pregnancies. A slightly smaller proportion of

195

the test than of the control pregnancies were *free* of episodes of illness related to childbearing, the test-control difference being equally distributed among major and minor complaints.

Social Psychological Adjustment

Test-control differences in the quality of housing were expected to play a role not only in physical health but also in matters of social psychological adjustment. Of the specific elements that distinguished test from control housing, it was expected that a few factors, such as space in the dwelling unit, would influence both morbidity and social adjustment. However, several elements of housing quality that were thought to affect social attitudes and behavior differed from those believed to influence morbidity. Among these were aspects of the larger housing environment such as architecture and community facilities, as well as the esthetic qualities of the dwelling unit.

It was also apparent that there was a difference between social-psychological adjustment and physical health or illness, in connection with their dimensional aspects. Whereas morbidity may be considered as consisting primarily of a unitary dimension, measured by episodes of illness and days of disability, attitudes and behavior in social settings, on the other hand, were thought of as multidimensional, consisting of a number of relatively discrete components. Six major social psychological content areas were therefore delineated, and measures were devised for each area which were felt to be suitable for testing the relationship to housing quality.

For each major area, hypotheses were formulated regarding the differences that would be likely to emerge between the test and control groups over time, following the move of the test families to good housing. Various housing elements, individually or in combination, were singled out as likely to be related to the subject matter of the particular adjustment area. Since some of the content areas more clearly involved interchange with the physical environment while others were more deeply rooted in the self, the degree to which confirmation of the hypotheses was expected varied according to the area. Thus, the areas, in their anticipated order of confirmation of housing connectedness, were: reactions to housing and space, relations with neighbors, personal and family relations, attitudes and behavior toward neighborhood and community, social self-concept and aspirations, and psychological state.

The basic social adjustment findings indicated that a majority of the

196

items in each area showed at least a directional trend confirming the expectations specified for the area. However, in most of the areas, by no means all of the test-control differences confirming the hypotheses reached statistically acceptable levels of confidence. The anticipated order in which the areas would confirm the hypotheses was in general borne out, the one major exception being personal and family relations. The status of each area is indicated in the following brief review of the original expectations and the subsequent findings.

REACTIONS TO HOUSING AND SPACE

It was expected that, due to the alteration in numerous physical aspects of their housing, test women would be more likely than controls to express "positive" reactions to specific aspects of the housing environment, and would in other ways indicate awareness of the improvement in their living circumstances.

The data showed marked confirmation of the expectations. A larger proportion of test than control women liked their apartments, commented favorably on the safety of their children's play places, felt they were getting their money's worth for the amount of the rental, indicated an increased likelihood for personal privacy, and reported less friction and dissension directly related to space.

RELATIONS WITH NEIGHBORS

Closer and more amicable relations with neighbors were expected to occur among test than among control families as a consequence of differences in their physical environments. Some of the factors in the housing project that were considered conducive to the formation of these relationships by the test group were: a dwelling architecture providing many opportunities for daily contact, a dwelling unit possessing some esthetic qualities and sufficient room space, and the existence of facilities used in common and under non-competitive circumstances.

The hypotheses of this content area were in general confirmed. Notably, the rehoused families, in contrast to the controls, underwent a marked increase in neighborly interaction of a mutually supportive variety, such as helping out with household activities, with children, and in time of illness. This heightened interaction was not viewed as infringing on privacy. The test women were more likely than controls to report both pleasant *and* unpleasant experiences with nearby women, but they were also more apt to have formed new, close friendships in the immediate neighborhood.

197

PERSONAL AND FAMILY RELATIONS

Housing-related factors, such as greater space, and general practical and esthetic improvement of the dwelling unit were expected to be conducive to better personal relations within the test families, as manifested by an increase in mutually shared activities (in connection with both routine tasks and leisure-time pursuits), greater feelings of warmth and compatibility, and lessened friction among family members.

The data for this area showed directional trends confirming the hypotheses only in connection with common family activities and the mothers' reactions to, and discipline of, children. Other aspects of intra-familial activities, cooperation, and affect revealed findings that were mixed or counter to the hypotheses.

ATTITUDES AND BEHAVIOR TOWARD NEIGHBORHOOD AND COMMUNITY

The project and the slum neighborhoods were viewed as differing from one another with respect to general physical characteristics, availability and accessibility of community facilities, characteristics of the inhabitants, and quality of the individual dwelling unit. It was expected that these factors would give rise to differences between the test and control groups in feelings of allegiance to, and interest in, the neighborhood, extent of participation in community and neighborhood activities, and in other indicators of good citizenship.

The findings revealed that test-control differences in the expected direction emerged in a number of matters related to the immediate neighborhood. Test respondents showed more pride in their immediate neighborhoods than did control respondents, reported more activities devoted to keeping up the neighborhood, and gave far more favorable views regarding its adequacy as a place to live and to raise children. Other topics which pertained more to the "broader" neighborhood or community, such as satisfaction with proximity to various facilities, interest in "larger issues," and evaluation of Baltimore as a place to live, showed either no systematic test-control differences or only a slight advantage for the test group.

SOCIAL SELF-CONCEPT AND ASPIRATIONS

Although change in perceived social status is customarily associated with altered occupation and income, it was anticipated that an alteration in housing quality, alone, and without attendant increment in income, might give rise to upgrading of self-perceived class affiliation,

198

particularly for members of a socially and economically deprived group like the test families. This in turn led to the supposition that having achieved as self-concept the image of persons "on the way up," the test families might also acquire heightened aspirations: for themselves, in connection with such matters as home ownership or better jobs; for their children, in connection with schooling, future jobs, and other benefits.

In general, the findings revealed partial confirmation of the hypotheses. Test respondents, more than controls, were likely to indicate felt improvement in their position in life, and to report themselves as rising in the world. However, the expectation that heightened aspirations would accompany this perceived betterment was, with a few exceptions, generally not borne out.

PSYCHOLOGICAL STATE

It was expected that the move from a generally depressed and deprived environment to good housing might result, for the test women, in some psychological alterations. These changes were viewed as probably involving intermediary processes rather than being directly relatable to the more tangible, physical elements of housing quality improvement.

Findings for the series of ten psychosocial scales consisting of variables pertaining to the *self*, revealed directional trends confirming expectations on all the scales. Those topics dealing with general morale (Optimism-Pessimism, Satisfaction with Personal State of Affairs, and Potency) were more likely than the scales involving stressful, inner feeling states (Mood, Control of Temper, and Nervousness) to show test-control differences confirming the hypotheses.

School Performance of Children

Consideration of several direct and indirect outcomes of differences in test-control housing quality suggested the possibility of differential scholastic achievement of the test and control children. The housing variable expected to be most directly related to school performance was that of dwelling unit density which, being lower for the test children, was expected to provide greater opportunity to study and to do homework unhampered by interruptions from other family members. In addition, there was the possible advantage accruing to test children related to some other expected effects of good housing: better morale, increased parental aspirations for the education of children, and activi-

199

ties related to their aspirations. Finally, it was anticipated that illness rates, expected to be lower among test than control children, might also play a role in school performance.

To test these hypotheses, a total of 486 test and 510 control school-age children were identified in September, 1956. Approximately 150 in each group were excluded in the interest of maintaining uniformity of school records and in view of the unavailability of data on intitial comparability. After follow-up losses, the records of 293 test and 287 control children attending Baltimore city public schools were examined for evidence relevant to school performance. Age, sex, and grade distributions showed a generally fair degree of comparability between the two groups of children, with test children tending to be slightly in excess in age 10 and under, and grade 5 and under.

Three types of tests were administered to Baltimore public school children: intelligence (Kuhlmann-Anderson and Otis), arithmetic achievement (Metropolitan and Stanford), and reading achievement (Iowa, Metropolitan, and Stanford). The data showed that these tests were administered fairly equally to test and control children, slight differences in pattern of administration being related to the age and grade differences.

Mean scores of the test and control children on the intelligence and achievement measurements were similar in the "before" period, thus indicating close initial comparability of the groups. *In the "after" period, mean test scores (adjusted for grade level of children tested) were also closely similar. Thus, the hypotheses regarding housing and one measure of school performance were not borne out.*

Examination of records of promotions showed that, in a 1-year "before" period, test and control children were comparable in the proportions experiencing normal promotions from grade to grade. *In a 2-year "after" period, test children were considerably more likely to be promoted at a normal pace, control children being held back more often for one or more semesters. In connection with record of promotions, then, study hypotheses were confirmed.*

Efforts to reconcile the findings regarding test performance and promotions suggest several possibilities. One is that promotion standards varied systematically in schools attended by test children in comparison with those attended by control children. There is no evidence in the data to indicate such differential standards. In fact, many test and control children attended the same schools. Where they attended different schools, it is worth noting that "test" and "control" schools were under the same general school administration.

200

Another possible reason for the test-control promotion difference is suggested by the data on daily attendance at school. Corresponding to morbidity differences already described, mean daily attendances of test children was considerably higher than that of control children.

Improved housing quality may thus play an indirect role in school performance of children in a way not completely anticipated by the original hypotheses, by lessening illness and in turn making possible more regular attendance at school. School promotion, while undoubtedly affected by intelligence and intellectual achievement as in more general school samples, is evidently also related in a significant way to regularity of school attendance. The data suggest a modest but specific illustration of the interweaving of environmental, physical, and social variables.

NOTES

1. Serious episodes were those that involved either medical attention or had one or more days of attendant disability; less severe episodes were without either medical attention or disability.

2. Disease classifications derived from the *Manual* of the *International Statistical Classification of Diseases, Injuries, and Causes of Death*, World Health Organization Geneva, 1949.

13

Medical Consequences of
Environmental Home Noises

LEE E. FARR

The previous selection by Wilner and his colleagues illustrates the fact that when housing conditions are well below a society's standards, the negative influence on health can be substantial. It would be dangerous, however, to conclude that such findings imply that if housing conditions conformed to current standards, the occupants would necessarily be healthy. For the fact of the matter is that most of the environmental standards developed in our society and incorporated into building codes and design conventions have been oriented to too narrow a conception of the way in which the physical environment and health interact.

The validity of this observation seems to be confirmed in the following selection by Farr. Farr's subject is the effect on health of noise within the home, and more particularly, the process through which unwanted and intrusive sound works its deleterious effect on the psychological and physiological functioning of the human organism. He points out that most discussions of urban and domestic noise have been concerned with the negative consequences of very loud sounds, which can cause hearing impairment, and that building standards have been shaped in order to prevent noise levels that cause direct damage to hearing acuity. However, Farr notes that even noise levels that are acceptable in terms of these standards typically cause nervous tension, anxiety, psychosomatic illness, and, indeed, exacerbate the effects of specific infectious diseases. The reason that these effects have been ignored in setting standards is that epidemiologists and physicians have failed to note that the critical factor in noise is that it is unwanted sound, in other words, that there is an important subjective and social element in people's response to sound, which must be taken into account if the full range of its effects on health are to be understood. Thus quieter sounds made by a neighbor are more annoying than louder sounds made by oneself. With urban densities increasing in our society, the psychological and social processes in the response to noise are likely to become more important relative to the purely biological or somatic impacts. Farr concludes therefore that present American standards for permissible domestic noise are too lenient and recommends collaborative research among architects, physicians,

Reprinted from Lee E. Farr, "Medical Consequences of Environmental Home Noises," *Journal of the American Medical Association* 202, no. 3 (October 16, 1967): 171–174.

and behavioral scientists, as well as collaborative efforts to change building codes.

□

Noise, or "unwanted and intrusive sound," as a pollutant of personal home environment is a matter of wide public interest. This concern has arisen from a combination of only a few factors. First is the increase in city populations indoctrinated with ideas of home automation. Second is the efficiency with which mechanical devices for household and individual use have been adapted from more costly commercial models. Third, there has been a period of extraordinary prosperity for the great majority of people in the United States which, in turn, has generated a financial capability previously undreamed of for each household and which now permits each abode to have several of the devices increasingly considered not as luxuries but as necessities of modern living. Fourth, the advertising and the general mood of the past few years has, in part, dictated a selection of devices based upon advertising impact rather than on personal need for these so-called laborsaving devices. The general mores of today's society have reinforced advertising appeals by making status symbols of these domestic units. On such a basis, possession is emphasized over performance. Fifth, and finally, an ever-increasing fraction of the ever-increasing number of city dwellers are living in the composite structures known as apartments.

Urbanization, population explosions, technology, and prosperity have thus set the stage for another phase of man's ever-broadening battle to control his surroundings sufficiently to prevent his environment from damaging him. In this instance, home sounds can threaten the health and well-being of one's emotional state.

Crowded conditions in cities have led to less space per home, with gradual abandonment of single dwellings for multiple, because of cost and convenience factors. In apartment dwellings a wall, frequently a very thin one, separates one from his fellows, and no sound-absorbent band of space, plants, earth, or trees serves to diminish sound transmittal from one household to the next.

Exposure to noise is upsetting emotionally and frequently may lead to outbursts of fury or threats, neither of which satisfies and each of which leaves frustration as a legacy. While sound can be generated at levels potentially hazardous to hearing by mechanical devices very frequently found in the home, exposure is not steady enough or sufficiently prolonged to cause hearing impairment—though Rosen's ob-

TABLE 13-1
Intensity of Sounds Common in the Home *

Appliances Being Operated	Apartment A (db)	Apartment B (db)
Living Room†		
Quiet	50	50
Vacuum Cleaner (nozzle engaged on carpet)	72	72
Vacuum Cleaner (nozzle free)	81	73‡
Hi-Fi (loud but not vibrant)	80	75
Television (average volume)	—	68
Kitchen §		
Quiet	56	56
Stove Vent Fan	84‖	68‡
Stove Vent Fan and Dishwasher	88	71‡
Stove Vent Fan, Dishwasher, and Garbage Disposal	91	84‡
Garbage Disposal Empty	—	72
Garbage Disposal with Ice Cubes	—	78
Dishwasher Only	—	69
Bedroom		
Quiet	53	50
Air Conditioner (central system)	—	55
Air Conditioner and Air Filter Fan Unit	—	57
Bathroom		
Quiet	—	53
Ventilating Fan	—	63
Ventilating Fan and Toilet	—	72

*Measurements were made with a sound level meter (C scale). The apartments were in different buildings with different floor plans.

†Measurements were made 6 feet from the vacuum cleaner, 16 feet from the hi-fi, and 8 feet from the television.

§Measurements were from the center of the kitchen.

‡Newer models.

‖Lower and steady sound productions. When hard materials such as bones were introduced into the disposal unit, the sound level rose to above 100 db.

servations on the African tribe living in a quiet environment whose members retain youthful hearing acuity into the older ages gives one pause.[1,2] Measurement of the intensity of some of these sounds reveals intensities sufficient to impair hearing if the exposure were for eight hours per day for the usual working week (Table 13-1). However, when one examines the impact of homemade sounds on man, it is his emotional status rather than his hearing acuity that is in the greater danger.

Both aspects of sound problems must be mentioned—presence and absence. Absence of certain components of sound in a heterogeneous environment may also be pointed to as capable of causing a type of trauma that should be mentioned. Absence of sound perception may follow absence of a given sound and be absolute, or it may appear to exist as a result of a loss of hearing acuity. This is well-documented for the older-age groups. The real or apparent absence of certain sound elements commonly perceived in the background spectra may result in a sense of uneasiness readily interpreted as annoyance. Through inability to effect proper selection and discrimination within certain sound spectra because of hearing acuity loss, a similar annoyance can develop. The effect can be of the same type and degree as that which ensues from sound intrusion. Gaps in sound spectra may have much the same psychological attributes as does noise.

During the last 30 years, much attention has been given to effects of various sound intensities upon the hearing acuity of workers. Maximum permissible levels of sound intensity for factories and offices have been established by regulation. In relation to home environment, until very recently there has been no evidence that design and operational criteria for any single unit in the home need be examined other than for performance or for salability. No attention whatever was given to its operational sound intensity.

In this same 30 years, only one paper on the subject is recorded in the literature, and it touches only obliquely on the necessity and desirability for control of sound in the home. It was written in 1938 by McCord et al., who stated:

> It follows as a natural consequence that occupants of buildings, living in artificial atmosphere and thus not dependent on open windows and doors, will in some measure be protected against extraneous noise arising from traffic, nearby buildings, or low flying aircraft.
> The multiple and insidious ill effects of noise constitute an inadequately recognized, baneful influence on lives of millions of persons throughout the country, especially those who live in urban areas. Noise deafness constitutes the most serious and tangible of the ill noise effects (echoseoses), but there is in addition a host of scarcely measurable injuries made evident by neurosis, loss of sleep, excessive fatigue, emotional disturbances and the like that jeopardise the complete well-being of most persons, and in which noise may well play a part.[3]

In December 1963, Farr read a paper at the Scientific Assembly of the American Medical Association calling attention to the mechanical devices in the home as sources of noise which could be of significance in health impairment.[4] In the last three years, industry has been extremely progressive in changing design to provide increased performance at less intense sound levels for many devices used in the home (Table 13–1). Industry now uses quietness as a selling quality—a market-tested attribute which shows the need for such attention.

It must be reaffirmed that we are not concerned with noise as an agent in the home which induces hearing loss but rather with the attitudes of household members toward the inescapable sounds of household operation today and with the effects of those attitudes upon the person's health.

Sound as Noise

Noise was defined earlier in this paper as unwanted sound, and it must be emphasized that high sound intensity *is not* a requisite component. Noise thus defined, becomes a highly personal subjective reaction to, and interpretation of, sound perceived. While noise as a quality must not be confused with loudness, in general, a loud, sharp sound will have all of the attributes of noise, since it is usually, particularly if unexpected, intrusive by virtue of its intensity and has a high annoyance value. It seems reasonable that under most circumstances sounds of high intensity are less easily ignored, day or night, than are sounds of low intensity.

We are thus dealing largely with what Kryter called the annoyance value of sound.[5] This he characterized under five qualities: (1) unexpectedness, (2) interference, (3) inappropriateness, (4) intermittency, and (5) reverberation. To Kryter's listing one additional and very important quality should be added—the origin of sound. Self-generated sound commands a very high tolerance in the individual generating it, yet it may have two or more of Kryter's annoyance values of sound. But sound generated by another person or an impersonal sound, such as a sonic boom, has a very high annoyance value, for external sound generally seems to amplify each of the qualities responsible for annoyance.

Age is another factor which may result in sound becoming annoying and irritating, for at advanced ages most people have a loss in hearing acuity. The gradual loss of hearing with advancing age increases the likelihood of extraneous sounds causing interference in communication with greater frequency and at lower intensities of the extraneous sound. Inability to discriminate effectively between some sounds of approximately equal intensities may lead to social embarrassment, which in turn leads to changes in patterns of behavior in efforts to mitigate the degree of interference. These behavioral changes are assumed to temper the source of embarrassment to the person who suffers from the loss of hearing acuity.

In some instances, such a changed pattern appears also to have been incorporated into "status symbols of success." During the era when the older patterns of executive privileges were established, it was undoubtedly true that the executive was an older person. The older executive may compensate, in part, for his loss of hearing acuity by reducing background noise. For example, the pattern of office privileges and amenities by which the executive has a quiet noise-controlled office may reflect the very simple fact that the executive, usually being older, may have lost some of his hearing acuity. If this be so, his ability to select and discriminate among a variety of sounds may have been reduced. This fact is then noted in establishment of a new criterion for executive behavior. This same type of behavior and status pattern is carried over into the executive's home where certain noise control mechanisms are effected, usually by distance rather than specific noise suppression or sound absorbing measures.

The ability to discriminate among sounds and select at will the desired sounds from a complex of heterogeneous sounds as a background or to reject the undesired sounds is in part a function of hearing acuity. When heterogeneous background noise becomes significant, as at a cocktail party in full progress, the problem of discrimination and selection of conversational sound from an adjacent person speaking may require a major effort in an older person. The inability to clearly distinguish what is said then can result in a rejection of participation in such gatherings by this individual, despite the fact that invitations to such affairs within some circles are a measure of success. The high and complex noise level in the background in the instance cited may be traumatic to an individual, because it transcends his speech interference level.

This suggestive pattern of executive behavior has been interfered with by the explosive advance of technology which has catapulted young men into executive positions, and now we are increasingly seeing executives sitting at open desks or at least in glass-walled cubicles.

The converse picture of this loss of discriminating ability is epitomized by a teen-ager studying in front of the television or radio set at or near full volume. This same teen-ager, if a telephone call be anticipated, will hear with astonishing perception the ring of a distant telephone and immediately sort this sound pattern out of a varied mixture of high-intensity environmental sounds. Perhaps this high level of discriminatory ability explains, in part, the tolerance of teen-agers to a background of complex sounds of high intensity.

The differences noted above in ability to discriminate among various sounds in a complex background of sound may help to explain why certain sound backgrounds may be annoying to some and a matter of indifference to others. However, sounds of such intensity as are made by many household devices in present-day living quarters are well capable of generating sounds in excess of that necessary to transcend the speech interference level and of interfering with other types of sound communications as well.

Sound in the Home

While acoustical engineers and architects of this country have been aware of the deterioration of sound environment in the home, their major concern and effort have been directed toward control of noise in places of employment to protect the health of employees. Factories, offices, and many public gathering places have been engineered acoustically at but a small cost increment, with a readily observed return in increased industrial efficiency and improvement in industrial health. Home designers, meanwhile, seem to have concentrated upon appearance, with little thought of quality control of sound, and upon style, which could be merchandised as a status symbol.[6] The ultimate result has been inadvertently to turn kitchens into miniature transient simulators of old-fashioned boiler factories by introducing a variety of sound-producing mechanical devices useful in the performance of kitchen tasks. The ventilating fan over the stove, the dishwasher, the garbage disposal unit, the blender, all make significant contributions to sound, which the steel cabinets or hard plastic covered surfaces reflect, augment, and cause to reverberate. From a basic sound intensity level of 56 db, these may produce an increment to over 100 db in an ordinary kitchen (Table 13-1). A tired, taut person will certainly not leave a kitchen pleasantly relaxed; nor do the roars, squeaks, whirrs, and whines issuing from it lead to quiet contemplation of pleasant meals by those who are waiting.

Further, the sound intensity is of such loudness that for many apartment dwellers conversation in the living room is virtually impossible while some of these devices are in operation. In a large living room tested, a standard vacuum cleaner raised the sound level from 50 to 73 db when the nozzle was fully engaged on the rug, but when this was lifted, the intensity rose to 81 db. The occupants of this household consider their hi-fi record player to be very loud at 80 db. In each case, the instruments were placed in a position simulating that of the user's ear and about 6 feet from the sound source.[4]

Neither have the bedrooms or bathrooms escaped this blight of noise. Bedroom air conditioners, bathroom ventilating fans, and poorly designed plumbing all make their contribution to this melee of sound.

Effects on Illness

The effects of noise in exacerbating disease may be seen in a specific infectious disease, such as tetanus. In other disease states such as anxieties, duodenal ulcer, and other kindred so-called tension ills, the additive deleterious effect of noise is real and immediate. Any disease which may be associated with an emotional charge requires as part of the therapy a calm, relaxed, quiet environment. This is particularly true of disturbed emotional states. The frequency of the latter has brought the attention of psychiatrists to this problem, but it has usually been noted only in passing, although its significance was appreciated as the following quote from Denzel attests:

We know that noise interferes with rest and relaxation and especially with sleep. While sleep, the complete withdrawal from the world around us, is an obvious necessity for physical and emotional health, less complete withdrawal into the quiet of our homes may also be necessary if we want to retain individual integrity . . . It appears rational and feasible to take positive steps to reduce the sound level of our modern environment if enough people feel the need to do so.[7]

It has already been noted that loudness is not a necessary quality of noise. The cacophony resulting from several radios and televisions tuned to low intensities, but to a variety of programs, can lead to a most annoying experience for the involuntary listener and may be just as destructive of sleep as a loud shot. Increasingly, thought has been given to temperature and humidity control within the home, as well as light, color, and ventilation. It is time that man realizes that his home can be designed to acoustic criteria, resulting in a pleasant environment for him and medically conducive to a state of well-being—permitting him to daily relax, refresh, restore, and reinvigorate himself for the tasks, chores, and strains of life.

Studies on Sound Control

While physicians and psychologists have not been unmindful of the desirability of maintaining sound control in homes, they have done little experimental work on the problem. This stems directly from the complexity inherent in making objective measurements of effects resulting from subjective interpretation. Sound must jar the mood to become noise, and if it does so, then noise results whether the sound be a classical rendition of Bach or a soft off-key hum of a contented individual doing personal chores.

The trauma of noise may bring to the surface a scarcely submerged tension and result in an emotional outburst, or it may provoke symptomatology manifesting itself as a well-recognized medical syndrome. The control of pathways which lead to these diverse expressions is not known. Perhaps with telemetry now becoming a practical means of study, it may be possible to design adequate, meaningful experiments dealing with this problem.

Because of a lack of medical clarity in estimating the significance of noise as an agent of disease, some have sought to control the bane of noise by advocating legislative enactments setting forth specific criteria of construction materials and designs to provide acoustic control in buildings to be used as homes.[8] It is true that often government is looked to as a source of authority which, if properly exercised, can banish many problems involving numbers of people, but there is also some disillusionment with this source as an efficacious agent for control of one's immediate environment. It is clear that the definitive control of a person's immediate environment must be exercised by that individual both to promote health and well-being and to avoid or mitigate illness. Further, it is seen that especially in setting the standards of acoustic criteria for personal needs, no wide area exists for specific exercise of community police powers or extension of community health services. The questions to be resolved are essentially personal, though some broad limits may be set for guidance.

With a basic design which takes into account existing ambient sound patterns, it is possible to construct private quarters in which acoustical properties can be emphasized by choice of furnishings to augment or minimize sound effects just as these are used to accentuate light or color. The physician must join with the acoustical engineer, the architect, and the decorator to establish general acoustical standards of personal environment. Once these standards are agreed upon they can be readily attained by selecting construction materials for their special qualities of absorbance and reflectance. If necessary, these can be created to meet the need, for with the new plastic materials, surface qualities and hardness can be varied at will.

NOTES

1. Rosen, S., et al: Presbycusis Study of a Relatively Noise Free Population in the Sudan, *Ann Otol* 71:727–744 (Sept) 1962.

2. Rosen, S.: Hearing Studies in Selected and Rural Populations: Series 2, *Trans NY Acad Sci* 29:9 (Nov) 1966.

3. McCord, C. P.; Teal, E. E.; and Witheridge, W. N.: Noise and Its Effect on Human Beings: Noise Control as By-Product of Air Conditioning, *JAMA* 110:1553–1560 (May 7) 1938.

4. Farr, L. E.: The Trauma of Everyday Noise, read before the Scientific Assembly of the American Medical Association, Portland, Ore, Dec 3, 1963; abstracted, *JAMA* 187: 36–37 (Jan. 25) 1964.

5. Kryter, K. D.: The Effects of Noise on Man, *J. Speech Hearing Dis [Monogr]* 1:17 (Sept) 1950.

6. Farr, L. E.: "The Increasing Medical Significance of Environmental Domestic Noise," in *Texas Conference on Our Environmental Crisis*, Austin, Tex: University of Texas Press, 1966, pp. 210–219.

7. Denzel, H. A.: Noise and Health, *Science* 143:992 (March 6) 1964.

8. Kupferman, T.: H. R. Bill 14602, *Congressional Record* April 21, 1966, pp 8339–8361.

14

Effects of Esthetic Surroundings:
I. Initial Short-Term Effects of
Three Esthetic Conditions upon Perceiving
"Energy" and "Well-Being" in Faces[1]

ABRAHAM H. MASLOW AND NORBETT L. MINTZ

Architects have long been interested in studies that investigated the effects on behavior of such relatively simple properties of the perceived environment as color, light levels, the presence or absence of daylight, and the like, because of their obvious implications for design. However, the design tradition is also concerned with the effects stemming from the esthetic properties of buildings. The esthetic environment differs from the perceived environment in being more complex. Perceptions of beauty and ugliness, of course, also depend upon the senses, but they involve to a greater degree the cognitive capacities of the organism and are heavily influenced by cultural experience.

Despite the considerable discussion among designers, design critics, and philosophers of esthetics about the effects of "beautiful" environments on people, there has been very little empirical research into the question. One of the few examples of such research is reported in the following selection by Maslow and Mintz. The authors asked three groups of college undergraduates to evaluate the degree of energy and well-being displayed in photographs of human faces. One group sat in a "beautiful" room, the second group in an "ugly" room, and the third in an "average" room. The three rooms were decorated and furnished by the authors and Mrs. Maslow.

The group in the beautiful room consistently rated the photographs higher in energy and well-being than did the groups in the average or ugly rooms. To make sure that the differences in the ratings associated with each setting could really be attributed to the esthetic properties of the rooms and not to the attitudes of the examiners, and to find out if the differences endured or were simply an initial adaptive response, the examiners themselves were treated as subjects, although they did not know it. According to Mintz the response patterns of the examiners, who worked in the rooms over a 3-week period, were similar to those of the subjects they tested. Observations of the

Reprinted from Abraham H. Maslow and Norbett L. Mintz, "Effects of Esthetic Surroundings: I. Initial Short-Term Effects of Three Esthetic Conditions upon Perceiving 'Energy' and 'Well-Being' in Faces," *Journal of Psychology* 41 (1956): 247–254.

examiners' behavior indicated that in the ugly room they reacted with boredom, fatigue, and hostility; in the beautiful room they reacted with pleasure, felt comfortable, and had a desire to continue their activity. Indeed, the response to the different esthetic surroundings became more pronounced with time.

This selection also implies that judgments of beauty and ugliness are not totally idiosyncratic, but rather are shared among groups of people. Furthermore, the selection demonstrates that these shared judgments of esthetic quality do affect the way people react psychologically to activities going on around them. However, there is a danger that the architect may over-interpret these findings when he comes to utilize them in dealing with practical design issues. For example, it is not clear from the Maslow and Mintz study how widely standards of esthetic judgment are shared in the population as a whole. Their respondents were all college undergraduates. Would low-income groups have responded to the three rooms in the same way? Would a trained architect have agreed with the authors, Mrs. Maslow, and the undergraduates as to what constitutes a beautiful room? One rather suspects that a hidden cultural dimension was affecting both the standards that defined beauty and ugliness and the reactions to the different settings.

□

The Problem

Esthetically sensitive individuals together with city planners, art educators, and related workers have long been intuitively aware of the effects of esthetic surroundings. Yet as far as we know there have been no experimental studies published on the effects of beautiful and ugly environments upon people. Surveys of the experimental esthetics (1,3), color (12), and art (5) literature show research to be centered on "formal" properties of rhythm, style, color, line, etc., color preference and personality studies, color-concept matching experiments, and projective technique and art therapy work. We have found research on the effects of music (9,16,17) and color (2,4,6,7,10,11,13,14,15,18) to be focused on the behavioral consequences of different melodic styles or hues *per se*, but not on music or color as part of the complex esthetic environment. The present experiment was undertaken as an initial step in studying the effects of beauty and ugliness upon people. It tested the short-term effects of three visual-esthetic conditions: "beautiful," "average," and "ugly" rooms.

Method

Three rooms were used. The "beautiful" room (BR) impressed people as "attractive," "pretty," "comfortable," "pleasant." It was 11' × 14' × 10' and had two large windows, beige-colored walls, an indirect overhead light, and furnishings to give the impression of an attractive, comfortable study. Furnishings included a soft armchair, a mahogany desk and chair combination, two straight-backed chairs, a small table, a wooden bookcase, a large Navajo rug, drapes for the windows, paintings on the walls, and some sculpture and art objects on the desk and table. These were all chosen to harmonize as pleasantly as possible with the beige walls.[2] The "ugly" room (UR) evoked comments of "horrible," "disgusting," "ugly," "repulsive." It was 7' × 12' × 10' and had two half-windows, battleship-gray walls, an overhead bulb with a dirty, torn, ill-fitting lampshade, and "furnishings" to give the impression of a janitor's storeroom in disheveled condition. There were two straight-backed chairs, a small table, tin cans for ashtrays, and dirty, torn window shades. Near the bare walls on three sides were such things as pails, brooms, mops, cardboard boxes, dirty-looking trash cans, a bedspring and uncovered mattress, and assorted refuse. The room was neither swept nor dusted and the ashtrays were not emptied. The "average" room (AR) was a professor's office 15' × 17' × 10', with three windows, battleship-gray walls, and an indirect overhead light. Furnishings included two mahogany desk and chair combinations, two straight-backed chairs, a metal bookcase, window shades, a metal filing cabinet, and a cot with a pleasant-looking green bedspread. It gave the appearance of a clean, neat, "worked-in" office in no way outstanding enough to elicit any comments. To help restrict room differences to the visual mode, the experiment was done in the evening when the building was quiet; the S's chair in the three rooms was of the same type; the rooms were well-lit (though UR had direct, harsh light); and the windows were always open, preventing the dust and dirt in UR from developing a musty odor.

A six-point, two dimension rating scale was used to test the effects of the conditions upon an S's judgment of ten negative-print photographs of faces. The dimensions to be rated were "energy" and "well-being" for each photograph. The rating scale thus had ten judgments per dimension, each judgment with a weight of from 1–6. Summing the dimensions separately would give two total scores, each having a possible range of from 10–60. These totals were averaged, giving an average "energy" and "well-being" score for each S. This average score could likewise range between 10 and 60. The ten photographs were arranged alternately male and female, with two dummy extras [3] preceding and following this series. Duplicate series were used for the three rooms.

As each S was met by the interviewer (NLM), he was told approximately the following: "We are conducting an experiment on facial stereotypy. You are familiar with Shakespeare's Cassius who had a lean and hungry look; this is an example of facial stereotypy. There cannot be any right or wrong answers as we are interested in the *impressions* faces give you." At this point Kohler's expressive-line figures (8, p. 225) were demonstrated. "In just the same way as these lines appeared to have particular concept characteristics, we think faces will have certain trait characteristics. You are going to see negative prints like this sample. By negative printing, and dressing the people in this unusual fashion, we minimized hairline, clothing, and expression and emphasized bone structure and shape. We want you to give your impressions of these faces, similar to the way you gave impressions of the lines previously." The BR and UR Ss were sent to their respective rooms to be tested by a naive examiner who also thought the experiment was on facial stereotypy. The interviewer brought the AR Ss to their room and tested them. This elaborate prelude served two purposes. It insured the naivete of the Ss and examiners (just one S guessed the purpose, and then only when thinking about the test a few days later), and it helped to reduce tension.

A test of visual-esthetic environment should emphasize spontaneity and informality or else task orientation or test anxiety may reduce the effects. This was demonstrated in a pilot study of similar design to this one, which failed to show significant differences between conditions in part due to the Ss anxiety and task orientation; they hardly looked away from the test material.[4] Therefore, as each S entered the room the examiner was called out on some pretext. The S was left in the room for two minutes, allowing him to "soak" in the visual field. When the examiner returned he engaged the S in a rambling discussion of "fatigue/energy" and "displeasure/well-being" with the intention of getting the S to name the moods just discussed. By allowing the S to choose his own concepts instead of being given our concepts for the dimensions, we felt there was greater likelihood of achieving a common semantic process among the Ss. Assuming the S chose "weary/zestful" and "irritable/content," the examiner then continued: "Now I would like you to tell me if this first face looks slightly, rather, or

215

very weary, or slightly, rather, or very zestful. Then do the same for irritable/content." This was done for each of the ten faces plus the four dummy extras. The S was encouraged to give any other impressions, and task-interrupting, idle conversation initiated by the examiner kept the atmosphere informal. The scores were marked on a scoresheet by the examiner. The S was in the room with the examiner at least 10 minutes additional to the time spent in the room alone.

Twenty-six male and sixteen female undergraduate Brandeis University students volunteered for this experiment. They were recruited at large and simply told that we wanted them for "a study in faces and traits." Sixteen were for the BR group, sixteen for the UR group, and ten for the AR group. There were an even number of males and females in BR and UR, only males in AR. A naive male and a naive female were hired to examine the BR and UR Ss; one of the authors (NLM) examined the AR group.

The following controls were used with the BR and UR groups. Each experimenter tested eight Ss in the BR group and eight in the UR group, four of which were of one sex and four of the other. Half of the Ss in each group were asked to rate "energy" first and half to rate "well-being" first. After these groups were tested, the AR group was added to give additional information. Analysis of the BR and UR groups indicated these controls would be unnecessary, so all AR Ss were males, tested by a male examiner, and asked to rate "energy" first.[5]

Our hypotheses were that scores obtained in the "beautiful" room would be higher (more "energy" and "well-being") than those in either the "average" or "ugly" rooms, and that scores in the "ugly" room would be lower (less "energy" and "well-being") than those in either the "average" or "beautiful" rooms.

Results

Table 14–1 gives the results of an analysis of variance on the differences in scores obtained in the three rooms. The scores for the three rooms were significantly different, as shown by the F ratio. Since the variances were not significantly heterogenous, the F indicates a significant difference in the means. Table 14–2 shows these differences. The average ratings for "energy" and "well-being" in BR were significantly higher (beyond the .001 level) than ratings in UR, and significantly higher (beyond the .05 level) than ratings in AR. The average ratings in AR were higher, but not significantly so, than ratings in UR.

TABLE 14-1

Differences in Scores Obtained for Three Room Conditions
Based on an Average Score for Each of 42 Ss

Source of Variation	df	Variance Estimate	F	p
Between Rooms	2	153.25	6.49	.01
Within Rooms	39	23.63		
Total	41			

Since an average score below 35 would indicate the S generally rated the ten faces as "fatigued" and "displeased," while one above 35 would indicate the S rated the faces as having "energy" and "well-being," Table 14-2 indicates a second result.[6] It can be seen that the mean for the UR group is within the "fatigued" and "displeased" range; the mean for AR at the upper limit of the "fatigued" and "displeased" range; and the mean for the BR group within the "energy" and "well-being" range.

Discussion

We may summarize the results as follows. The Ss in our "beautiful" room gave significantly higher ratings (more "energy" and "well-being") than Ss in either the "average" or "ugly" rooms. Also, while the mean for the scores in the "beautiful" room fell in the "energy" and "well-being" range, the means for the other two groups fell in the "fatigued" and "displeased" range, indicating a qualitative difference in the group scores. We can be rather confident that the difference between the

TABLE 14-2

Differences between the Means of Scores in Three Room Conditions

Room	Mean	Compared to Room	Mean Difference	t*	p†
UR	31.81	AR	2.19	1.12	.30
AR	34.00	BR	3.99	2.04	.05
BR	37.99	UR	6.18	3.54	.001

*The within rooms variance estimate of Table 14-1 was used as the estimate of the standard error of the difference.

†Since the standard error was based on 39 df, the t was entered as a CR in the normal probability table.

scores obtained in BR and UR is reliable. While the scores in AR are significantly lower than those in BR and somewhat higher than those in UR (results which are in the expected order), we cannot be as confident of where, between BR and UR, the AR group is placed. Recognizing the situational nature of our definitions of beauty, average and ugly, there still are interesting implications if our research would continue to find the effects of "average" surroundings to lie closer to those of "ugly" than to those of "beauty," rather than finding that effects of "average" lie midway between the two, or closer to "beauty." This, of course, would have immediate relevance for professors and their offices.

While many questions remain to be answered by research now in progress, certain points may be noted at the present time. We may begin by excluding the possibility that differences between groups resulted from suggestion or a "role-playing" attitude assumed by the examiners or the Ss. Indirect interviewing of the examiners after each day's testing, and each S after being tested, assured us that the examiners and Ss continued to be unaware of the experimental purpose. The controls for noise, odor, time of day, type of seating, examiners, etc., make us rather confident that the potent factor lay in the visual-esthetic qualities of the three rooms.

Regarding the effects obtained, a number of problems come to mind, some of which will be treated in the second section of this selection. Were these merely short-term effects; would the Ss adapt to the rooms with time and negate the initial differences obtained? How many individuals in each group were affected by the conditions? Were the Ss affected by the rooms *per se*? The possibility also exists that the results could have been obtained via the effect of conditions upon the examiners. This, of course, would not change the major implication of the findings; it would shift the emphasis from the rooms having a short-term effect directly upon the Ss to their having a long-term effect upon the examiners, which sufficiently affected the interpersonal relations between examiner and S so as to cause differences in group scores irrespective of which examiner was present.

In considering what may be the "potent" visual-esthetic aspects of the rooms, we may tentatively exclude as crucial in themselves the differences between room sizes, and neatness, orderliness, or cleanliness. Although UR was the smallest, AR was the largest; although UR was dirty and messy, AR was clean and neat. Both UR and AR had gray walls and cold colors in contrast to beige walls and warm colors in BR. While this may be important for understanding the difference between BR and AR scores, by itself it would not explain the possibly genuine difference between AR and UR scores. At present the most reasonable conclusion appears to be that all of these aspects were operating to produce three esthetically different-appearing rooms, which in the case of "beautiful" and "ugly" resulted in clear differences between Ss ratings of the "energy" and "well-being" of faces.

Summary of Section One

An experiment was conducted as an initial step in studying the effects of esthetic surroundings upon people. Three visual-esthetic conditions were used: "beautiful," "average," and "ugly" rooms. In each room, subjects unaware of the experimental purpose were asked to rate the "fatigue/energy" and "displeasure/well-being" of ten negative-print photographs of faces. The results were: (1) the group in the "beautiful" room gave significantly higher ratings (more "energy" and "well-being") than groups in either the "average" or "ugly" rooms; (2) the "average" room group had somewhat higher ratings than the "ugly" room group; (3) the mean score for ratings in the "beautiful" room fell in the "energy" and "well-being" range, while the mean for the ratings in the other two rooms fell within the "fatigued" and "displeased" range. Discussion pointed out that: (1) suggestion, "role-playing," or variables other than visual-esthetic ones did not account for the differences obtained; (2) there seems at present to be no single visual-esthetic quality that can account for the differences among all three groups; (3) the effects may possibly have been obtained by the rooms' affecting the subject-examiner relationship.

Effects of Esthetic Surroundings:
II. Prolonged and Repeated Experience in
a "Beautiful" and an "Ugly" Room[7]

NORBETT L. MINTZ

The Problem

The first section of this selection reported that when Ss spent 10–15 minutes rating a series of face-photographs, Ss tested in a "beautiful" room rated the faces as having significantly more "energy" and "well-being" than Ss tested in either an "average" or an "ugly" room. In discussing these results, one question was, "Were these merely short-term effects; would the Ss adapt to the rooms with time and negate the initial differences obtained?" The differences might simply reflect either activity appropriate to a "laboratory" situation, or initial adjustments to the room conditions. If this were so, then Ss having prolonged or repeated experience in less "experimental" circumstances either would show no effects at all, or effects that would rapidly diminish with time. This section utilizes material obtained from the examiners of the previous section that pertains to this problem.

Method

The Brandeis undergraduates who were the male and female examiners referred to in the previous section were also the "subjects" of this study. They were told that they were to be examiners in an experiment "on facial stereotypy." The examiners thus did not know that they were testing the effects of esthetic surroundings, and were *unaware that*

Reprinted from Norbett L. Mintz, "Effects of Esthetic Surroundings: II. Prolonged and Repeated Experience in a 'Beautiful' and an 'Ugly' Room," *Journal of Psychology* 41(1956): 459–466.

they were to be "subjects" themselves. Therefore, the examiners' behavior can show what happens when people are not acting as Ss in an "experiment."

The examiners each spent six sessions (two per week) testing a total of thirty-two Ss. They tested Ss concurrently; while one examiner tested someone in the "B" room, the other examiner was testing another S in the "U" room. (In the previous section these were referred to as BR and UR respectively.) The first week had two sessions, on successive days, and each was an hour long; the second week had two sessions, separated by one day, and each was two hours long; the third week had two sessions, on successive days, and each was an hour long. The examiners spent the whole of one session in the same room; they would switch rooms on alternate sessions. Each examiner thus spent three sessions in the "B" room and three sessions in the "U" room.

Two measures plus observational notes form the basis of this report. The first measure was the same six-point, two-dimension rating scale used to test the effects of conditions upon Ss of the first section. The dimensions rated were "energy/fatigue" and "displeasure/well-being" for a series of ten negative print face-photographs. Each face was rated as being very, rather, or slightly "fatigued," or slightly, rather, or very "energetic"; likewise for the dimension "displeasure/well-being." Each judgment had a weight of from 1–6; a total score was computed by summing the 10 rating-weights for each dimension and averaging the two sums. This average, which could range from 10–60, then represented a score of "energy" *and* "well-being." Before the formal part of the experiment began, the writer tested each examiner (as if they were Ss) for 15 minutes in one of the two rooms followed by a 15-minute retest with duplicate photographs in the other room. This "practice" period served both to show the examiners the procedure, and to obtain data from these examiners that would be comparable to data obtained from the 32 Ss they would test. The examiners also administered the rating scale to themselves at the end of each session. Each examiner thus had three self-tests in the "B" room and three in the "U" room. This procedure enabled weekly checks on any effects. The purpose given for these retests was, "to establish the reliability of the tests."

The effects of conditions upon the examiners' general interest in and enjoyment of the testing situation might be inferred from a comparison of testing-times for the thirty-two pairs of test situations. Since the

TABLE 14-3
Rating Scale Total Scores for the "B" Room and the "U" Room

Rooms*	Examiners as *Ss* "Practice" Periods		Prolonged Sessions, Examiners Testing *Ss*					
			First Week		Second Week		Third Week	
	"B"	"U"	"B"	"U"	"B"	"U"	"B"	"U"
"Sheila"	39.0	36.5	35.0	33.5	37.0	33.0	36.0	33.5
"Sid"	38.5	35.0	36.0	34.0	38.0	32.0	36.0	32.5
Means	38.75	35.75	35.50	33.75	37.50	32.50	36.00	33.00
Differences	3.00		1.75		5.00		3.00	

*"Sheila" was in the "B" room for the first "practice" period and the "U" room for the second; "Sid" was in the "U" room for the first "practice" period and the "B" room for the second. "Sheila" was in the "U" room for the first session of each week and the "B" room for the second; "Sid" was in the "B" room for the first session and the "U" room for the second.

examiners tested *Ss* concurrently and since the test procedure and the time each pair of *Ss* entered the rooms was identical for both examiners, the number of times an examiner in the "U" room finished before an examiner in the "B" room can provide a second measure of the effects. Besides recording testing-times, the writer took observational notes whenever possible.

The data will be examined as follows: In these more natural circumstances, will any effects be found? Will any effects that are found *rapidly decrease* after initial adjustments (*i.e.* after the first week)?

Results of Rating Scale

Table 14-3 shows that there were differences between scores for both the 15-minute "practice" periods and the prolonged sessions. The two examiners had higher scores (more "energy" and "well-being") in the "B" room. An analysis of variance for two subjects with repeated mea-

TABLE 14-4
Analysis of Variance for Scores in Prolonged "B" and "U" Room Sessions

Source	df	Mean Square	F	p
Sessions	5	7.5	18.75	<.01
Examiners	1	.1	—	
E X S	5	.4		
Total	11			

TABLE 14-5

Mean Difference between "B" and "U" Sessions of the Same Week

First Week			Second Week			Third Week		
$\bar{X}\Delta$	t^*	p	$\bar{X}\Delta$	t^*	p	$\bar{X}\Delta$	t^*	p
1.75	2.74	$<.05$	5.00	7.81	$<.001$	3.00	4.76	$<.01$

*Based upon the E X S mean square, with 5 df, of Table 14-4.

sures was computed to test these differences between prolonged sessions. The results are presented in Table 14-4. The overall F test for the difference between sessions was significant well beyond the .01 level of confidence. The difference between examiners was negligible. Table 14–5 presents the analysis of the mean difference in scores obtained between a "B" room and "U" room session of the same week. Scores were significantly higher in the "B" room for *each* of the three weeks of prolonged sessions. Table 14–5 also shows that the mean difference in scores for the first week was the *smallest* obtained during the 3 weeks, while that for the *second* week was the largest. Thus, the effects did *not* decrease after the first week.

Results of Testing-Time Comparisons

Table 14–6 tabulates which examiner finished testing first for each of the thirty-two pairs of test situations. When "Sheila" was in the "U" room and "Sid" was in the "B" room, "Sheila" finished before "Sid" a total of thirteen times, compared with twice when she was in the "B" room and "Sid" was in the "U" room. When "Sid" was in the "U" room and "Sheila" was in the "B" room, "Sid" finished before "Sheila" a total of fourteen times, compared with three times when he was in the "B" room and "Sheila" was in the "U" room. The total combined sum shows that the examiner in the "U" room finished testing before the examiner in the "B" room twenty-seven times out of the thirty-two situations; this difference was significant beyond the .001 level of confidence. The combined sums in Table 14–6 show that the examiner in the "U" room finished before the examiner in the "B" room seven out of eight times the first week, thirteen out of sixteen times the second week, and again seven out of eight times the third week. Thus, once again the effects did *not* decrease after the first week.

223

TABLE 14-6
Number of Times an Examiner Ends
First in the "B" Room and in the "U" Room

Weeks	One		Two		Three		Totals		
Testing Rooms	"B"	"U"	"B"	"U"	"B"	"U"	"B"	"U"	p
"Sheila" First	0	3	2	7	0	3	2	13	.02
"Sid" First	1	4	1	6	1	4	3	14	.01
Combined Sums	1	7	3	13	1	7	5	27	.001

Observational Notes

The following are the notes taken by the writer. It must be emphasized that they are *selective* notes; that is, the writer recorded only those comments and behavior that appeared relevant.

"Sheila"—During the 15-minute "practice" period in the "B" room, she handled and admired an ashtray and remarked enthusiastically upon a piece of sculpture. She commented, "The rug on the floor doesn't quite match the rest of the decor." When taken to the "U" room for the second 15-minute period, she remarked, while rating a picture, "They all look more *blah* (fatigued) in here." As she was led to the "U" room for the first testing session, she exclaimed, "I have to start in here? After testing two *Ss* she asked the writer, "Can't we change rooms, now, or something to break up the monotony? I'm falling asleep in there." On the second session of the first week "Sheila" tested four *Ss* in the "B" room; when told she is through for that day she said, "Only four subjects? I was just getting warmed up."

"Sheila" spent the first 2-hour session of the second week in the "U" room. After the first hour, while the examiners had a 5-minute break, she smiled, stretched, and said (to "Sid"), "The dungeon is all yours." She assumed that they were to switch after 1 hour. When she was told this was not the case, she asked, "You mean I've got to spend the next hour in there too?" She was told that she must test four more *Ss* in the "U" room. When the next *S* arrived, "Sheila" led him down the corridor in the direction of the "U" room. The corridor is a dead end, at the end of which, on the left wall, is the door opening into the "U" room. However, instead of opening this left-wall door, she turned to the *right* wall and opened the only other door at the end of that corridor, mistakingly leading her *S* into the women's toilet! Has the rat in his T maze ever performed a more classical avoidance response?

After testing this S in the correct room, "Sheila" approached the writer and told him she was tired and was developing a headache. "Could we quit early?" She was told that this "would ruin the experimental design." She unhappily returned to the "U" room. The writer found that while waiting for this next S, "Sheila" had fallen asleep.

The second 2-hour session "Sheila" knew she was to spend in the "B" room. As she met the writer, she remarked, "A 2-hour session today? Good; I really feel like working tonight." This mood was sustained throughout that session. The first session of the third week she again was in the "U" room. Throughout this session she waited in the corridor for her Ss; previously she had waited for her next S in whichever room she was testing. At the end of this session she asked, "Tomorrow is the last day (of the experiment)? How nice; I'll end testing upstairs (the "B" room)."

"Sid"—During the 15-minute "practice" period in the "U" room "Sid" remarked, as he entered the room, "Ugh, what the hell did they do, empty the whole building's junk in here?" When taken to the "B" room for the second 15-minute period, he asked, "Is this M's office? Pretty nice. He really makes things comfortable for himself." At the end of the first session, which he spent in the "B" room, he said, "I was really beginning to feel like a wheel in here, sitting in a swivel chair and making like a psychologist. It's a lot of fun." When he was told, at the start of the second session, that he was to test in the downstairs ("U") room, (the rooms were simply called the "upstairs" and the "downstairs" room throughout the experiment) "Sid" remarked, "I knew I couldn't be in 'heaven' forever." After testing one S he approached the writer and said, "I think it's pretty stupid to use this room for an experiment." He was reminded that we were replicating a previous experiment and "must do it exactly the same." At the end of the second session he said, in a question-assertion manner, "Next week I return upstairs, eh?"

The first 2-hour session of the second week "Sid" was in the "B" room. He gave a pleased smile when the writer told "Sheila" that they would not switch rooms after the break. The second 2-hour session he spent in the "U" room. At the break he was generally aggressive in his conversation. He complained about having to add up the scoresheets (a procedure initiated the *first* session of the second week), and in a half-jocular, half-aggressive manner told the writer, "I think I'll just let you add them up from now on." When "Sheila" asked for a match, "Sid" looked in his shirt pockets, found a pack of cigarettes, but no matches. After the break, as he led his next S toward the "U" room, he took a cigarette from his shirt pocket and lit it from matches he suddenly found in his pants pocket. At the end of that session, he asked, "Next week I go back upstairs?" The last session of the third week, "Sid" commented as he entered the "U" room, "Well, this is the last time I'll have to see this hole." [8]

Discussion

The results of the rating scale, the testing-time comparisons, and the observational notes all demonstrated the significant effects of esthetic surroundings. Furthermore, these effects were not limited to initial adjustments. In fact, there were indications on the rating scale and in the observational notes that the 2-hour sessions of the second week *exaggerated* the effects.

May we infer that if the groups previously reported had prolonged experience in these conditions, they too would have continued to show differences in effects? It may be remembered that the 15-minute "practice" periods obtained data from the examiners comparable to data of the previous report. Therefore, the scores of the *initial* 15-minute "practice" period that "Sheila" spent in the "B" room and that "Sid" spent in the "U" room may be compared to the means reported previously for the "B" room and "U" room groups. The means for the groups were 37.99 and 31.81 respectively, with a standard deviation of 4.8. "Sheila" had an initial "B" score of 39.0 and "Sid" had an initial "U" score of 35.0 (see Table 14–3). Although their scores were slightly higher, they were well within one standard deviation for the respective group means; in other words, their scores were not significantly different from scores obtained in similar conditions from unselected college students.

Since the examiners did not have atypical results, it might be expected that the "B" room group would have continued to show higher scores. If bias was introduced by the choice of examiners, it possibly was reflected in the observational notes. That is, other examiners might not have had such gross behavioral changes, or might not have been as free in expressing their feelings.

In the first section, Maslow and Mintz also asked, "Were the *Ss* affected by the rooms *per se*? . . . the results could have been obtained via the effect of conditions upon the examiners." In like manner it may be asked, "Were the effects upon the examiners brought about by the rooms *per se*?" It is conceivable, for example, that the examiner in the "U" room finished testing first simply because his S "hurried" the procedure along. However, there is ample evidence from the behavioral notes to indicate that the results were not solely determined by the Ss being tested. There probably was a complex relationship whereby the esthetic conditions affected the Ss and the examiners, and the Ss and examiners in turn affected each other.

Summary and Conclusions of Section Two

The present section investigated whether the effects of esthetic surroundings reported in the first section simply reflect either "laboratory" activity or initial adjustments to the room conditions. During a period of 3 weeks, two examiners, *unaware* that they were "subjects" for this study, each spent prolonged sessions testing Ss in a "beautiful" room and in an "ugly" room. On a rating scale, the examiners had short-term effects similar to those reported previously; furthermore, during the entire 3 weeks of prolonged sessions the ratings continued to be significantly higher in the "B" room. The testing-time comparisons showed that an examiner in the "U" room usually finished testing more quickly than an examiner in the "B" room. Observational notes showed that in the "U" room the examiners had such reactions as monotony, fatigue, headache, sleep, discontent, irritability, hostility, and avoidance of the room; while in the "B" room they had feelings of comfort, pleasure, enjoyment, importance, energy, and a desire to continue their activity. It is concluded that visual-esthetic surroundings (as represented by the "B" room and "U" room) can have significant effects upon persons exposed to them. These effects are not limited either to "laboratory" situations or to initial adjustments, but can be found under naturalistic circumstances of considerable duration.

NOTES

1. This research was supported by Brandeis University. We wish to express our thanks to R. Held and R. B. Morant for their helpful discussion and assistance, and J. Glick for his photography work. The second section of this selection will present the more complex data obtained from Ss moving into a second esthetic condition.

2. We wish to thank B. Maslow for her assistance in this.

3. Used for purposes to be discussed in the second section of this selection.

4. The pilot study was conducted by B. Maslow and A. H. Maslow.

5. A four-way classification analysis of variance was done on BR and UR for rooms, experimenters, sexes, and rating order. The scores for rooms were significantly different, but those for experimenters, sexes, and rating order were not, nor did the four variables interact significantly.

6. A *rho* based on the 42 *Ss* for the separate dimension totals ("fatigue/energy" and "displeasure/well-being") showed the dimensions to have a positive correlation of .79, significant beyond the .001 level.

7. The writer extends his appreciation to the Maslows for inspiring this research, to R. M. Held, J. B. Klee, and R. B. Morant for helpful discussion, and especially to "Sheila" and "Sid" for their cooperation. A Brandeis University research fellowship provided the necessary leisure time.

8. On completing this study, the writer told the examiners the real purpose of the experiment. They evidenced surprise at the whole procedure. Especially impressive was their reaction to the notes; *they were not aware that their activities were in such close relationship to the room conditions,* though they both realized that they did not prefer to test in the downstairs ("U") room.

REFERENCES

1. Chandler, A. R. & Barnhart, E. N. *A bibliography of psychological and experimental esthetics, 1864–1937.* Berkeley: U. of California Press, 1938.

2. Deutsch, F. Psycho-physical reactions of the vascular system to influences of light and to impressions gained through light. *Folia Clinica Orientalia,* 1937, Vol. I, Facs. 3 & 4.

3. Drought, R. A. A survey of studies in experimental esthetics. *J. of Educa. Research,* 1929, *20,* 97–102.

4. Ehrenwald, N. Referred to by Ellinger, F. *The biologic fundamentals of radiation therapy.* New York: Elsevier Pub. Co., 1941.

5. Faulkner, R. A survey of recent research in art and art education. In G. M. Whipple, ed., *Art in American life and education, fortieth yearbook, NSSE.* Chicago: U. of Chicago Press, 1941, pp. 369–377.

6. Goldstein, K. Some experimental observations concerning the influence of colors on the function of the organism. *Occup. Ther.,* 1942, *21,* 147–151.

7. Goldstein, K. & Rosenthal, O. Zum Problem der Wirkung der Farben auf den Organismus. *Schweiz. Arch. Neurol. Psychiat.,* 1930, *26,* 3–26.

8. Kohler, W. *Gestalt psychology.* New York: Liveright, 1929.

9. Mitchell, S. D. & Zanker, A. The use of music in group therapy. *J. of Mental Sci.,* 1948, *94,* 737–738.

10. Mitra, S. C. & Datta, A. The influence of color on the estimation of area. *Indian J. Psychol.,* 1939, *14,* 91–94.

11. Mogensen, M. F. & English, H. B. The apparent warmth of colors. *Amer. J. Psychol.,* 1926, *37,* 427–428.

12. Norman, R. D. & Scott, W. A. Color and affect: a review and semantic evaluation. *J. Gen. Psychol.,* 1952, *46,* 185–223.

13. Pierce, D. H. & Weinland, J. D. The effect of color on workmen. *Person. J.,* 1934, *13,* 34–38.

14. Prescott, D. B. Psychological analysis of light and color. *Occup. Ther.,* 1942, *21,* 135–146.

15. Pressey, S. L. The influence of color upon mental and motor efficiency. *Amer. J. Psychol.,* 1921, *32,* 326–356.

16. Rubin, H. E. & Katz, E. Aurotone films for the treatment of psychotic depressions in an army general hospital. *J. Clin. Psychol.,* 1946, 333–340.

17. Schullien, D. M. & Schoen, M. *Music and medicine.* New York: H. Schuman, 1948.

18. Wallis, W. A. The influence of color on apparent size. *J. Gen. Psychol.,* 1935, *13,* 193–199.

15

Grieving for a Lost Home

MARC FRIED

The importance of paying attention to the cultural background of users when trying to understand the effects of the environment on health and well-being cannot be stressed often enough. Farr's selection on home noises points out that even environments that meet established building codes can have deleterious effects because of the way in which the response to noise is mediated through psychological processes and cultural values. Oddly enough, the reverse of this point also seems to be true: environments that are officially regarded as unhealthful and injurious to well-being sometimes have a salutary influence on users, again because of the associations and social experiences the inhabitants have built up over time with the supposedly dangerous or unpleasant environment.

The latter theme is the fundamental concern of the following selection by Fried. Fried interviewed families displaced from the West End of Boston who were forced to find housing in other parts of the city or in the surrounding metropolitan region when the buildings in which they had lived for many years were torn down. The buildings were demolished because, according to the official physical criteria of the urban renewal agency, they were slums in a blighted area: there were too few bathrooms, they did not allow sufficient daylight into the interior, and many of them were poorly maintained. Although the housing undoubtedly was "blighted" in the technical sense defined by these standards, it was part of a social environment that was highly satisfactory to the residents and possessed many characteristics, such as social cohesion, established friendship networks, and a sense of community, that the residents were unable to reproduce in the settings to which they moved. The loss of familiar associations turned out to have a serious negative effect on many of the former West End population, which showed up in the form of poorer mental health. Fried discusses these effects in terms of the "grief reaction," a feeling of depression comparable to the loss one feels after the death of a loved one.

Fried's selection is particularly apposite to the concerns of this volume, because, in addition to demonstrating the importance of the cultural context for plotting the effect of the environment on health, he explains the grief reaction by referring to the sense of spatial identity, or sense of place, a favorite concept of architects and designers when they discuss the signifi-

Reprinted from Marc Fried, "Grieving for a Lost Home," in *The Urban Condition*, Leonard J. Duhl, ed. (New York: Basic Books, 1963), pp. 151–171. © 1963 by Basic Books, Inc., Publishers.

cance of the built environment for behavior and attitudes. He asserts that the sense of spatial identity is fundamental to human functioning, describes its social and psychological components, discusses the way in which the loss of this sense was revealed in many of his interviews, and makes several practical suggestions about how to conduct urban renewal programs so that the sense of place is not totally destroyed in the process of relocation.

□

Introduction

For some time we have known that the forced dislocation from an urban slum is a highly disruptive and disturbing experience. This is implicit in the strong, positive attachments to the former slum residential area—in the case of this study the West End of Boston—and in the continued attachment to the area among those who left before any imminent danger of eviction. Since we were observing people in the midst of a crisis, we were all too ready to modify our impressions and to conclude that these were likely to be transitory reactions. But the post-relocation experiences of a great many people have borne out their most pessimistic pre-relocation expectations. There are wide variations in the success of post-relocation adjustment and considerable variability in the depth and quality of the loss experience. But for the majority it seems quite precise to speak of their reactions as expressions of *grief*. These are manifest in the feelings of painful loss, the continued longing, the general depressive tone, frequent symptoms of psychological or social or somatic distress, the active work required in adapting to the altered situation, the sense of helplessness, the occasional expressions of both direct and displaced anger, and tendencies to idealize the lost place. (1)

At their most extreme, these reactions of grief are intense, deeply felt, and, at times, overwhelming. In response to a series of questions concerning the feelings of sadness and depression which people experienced *after* moving, many replies were unambiguous: "I felt as though I had lost everything," "I felt like my heart was taken out of me," "I felt like taking the gaspipe," "I lost all the friends I knew," "I always felt I had to go home to the West End and even now I feel like crying when I pass by," "Something of me went with the West End," "I felt cheated," "What's the use of thinking about it," "I threw up a lot," "I had a nervous breakdown." Certainly, some people were overjoyed with the change and many felt no sense of loss. Among 250 women, however,

26 per cent report that they still feel sad or depressed two years later, and another 20 per cent report a long period (six months to two years) of sadness or depression. Altogether, therefore, at least 46 per cent give evidence of a fairly severe grief reaction or worse. And among 316 men, the data show only a slightly smaller percentage (38 per cent) with long-term grief reactions. The true proportion of depressive reactions is undoubtedly higher since many women and men who report no feelings of sadness or depression indicate clearly depressive responses to other questions.

In answer to another question, "How did you feel when you saw or heard that the building you had lived in was torn down?" a similar finding emerges. As in the previous instance, the responses are often quite extreme and most frequently quite pathetic. They range from those who replied: "I was glad because the building had rats," to moderate responses such as "the building was bad but I felt sorry," and "I didn't want to see it go," to the most frequent group comprising such reactions as "it was like a piece being taken from me," "I felt terrible," "I used to stare at the spot where the building stood," "I was sick to my stomach." This question in particular, by its evocative quality, seemed to stir up sad memories even among many people who denied any feeling of sadness or depression. The difference from the previous result is indicated by the fact that 54 per cent of the women and 46 per cent of the men report severely depressed or disturbed reactions; 19 per cent of the women and about 31 per cent of the men report satisfaction or indifference; and 27 per cent of the women and 23 per cent of the men report moderately depressed or ambivalent feelings. Thus it is clear that, for the majority of those who were displaced from the West End, leaving their residential area involved a moderate or extreme sense of loss and an accompanying affective reaction of grief.

While these figures go beyond any expectation which we had or which is clearly implied in other studies, the realization that relocation was a crisis with potential danger to mental health for many people was one of the motivating factors for this investigation.[1] In studying the impact of relocation on the lives of a working-class population through a comparison of pre-relocation and post-relocation interview data, a number of issues arise concerning the psychology of urban living which have received little systematic attention. Yet, if we are to understand the effects of relocation and the significance of the loss of a residential environment, it is essential that we have a deeper appreciation of the psychological implications of both physical and social aspects of residential experience. Thus we are led to formulations which deal with the functions and meanings of the residential area in the lives of working class people.

The Nature of the Loss in Relocation: The Spatial Factor

Any severe loss may represent a disruption in one's relationship to the past, to the present, and to the future. Losses generally bring about fragmentation of routines, of relationships, and of expectations, and frequently imply an alteration in the world of physically available objects and spatially oriented action. It is a disruption in that sense of continuity which is ordinarily a taken-for-granted framework for functioning in a universe which has temporal, social, and spatial dimensions. From this point of view, the loss of an important place represents a change in a potentially significant component of the experience of continuity.

But why should the loss of a place, even a very important place, be so critical for the individual's sense of continuity; and why should grief at such loss be so widespread a phenomenon? In order to clarify this, it is necessary to consider the meaning which this area, the West End of Boston, had for the lives of its inhabitants. In an earlier paper we tried to assess this, and came to conclusions which corroborate, although they go further, the results from the few related studies.

In studying the reasons for satisfaction that the majority of slum residents experience, two major components have emerged. On the one hand, the residential area is the region in which a vast and interlocking set of social networks is localized. And, on the other, the physical area has considerable meaning as an extension of home, in which various parts are delineated and structured on the basis of a sense of belonging. These two components provide the context in which the residential area may so easily be invested with considerable, multiply-determined meaning. . . . The greatest proportion of this working-class group . . . shows a fairly common experience and usage of the residential area . . . dominated by a conception of the local area beyond the dwelling unit as an integral part of home. This view of an area as home and the significance of local people and local places are so profoundly at variance with typical middle-class orientations that it is difficult to appreciate the intensity of meaning, the basic sense of identity involved in living in the particular area (2).

Nor is the intense investment of a residential area, both as an important physical space and as the locus for meaningful interpersonal ties, limited to the West End (3). What is common to a host of studies is the evidence for the integrity of the urban, working-class, slum community as a social and spatial unit. It is the sense of belonging someplace, in a particular place which is quite familiar and easily delineated, in a wide area in which one feels "at home." This is the core of meaning of the local area. And this applies for many people who have few close relationships within the area. Even familiar and expectable streets and houses, faces at the window and people walking by, personal greetings and impersonal sounds may serve to designate the concrete foci of a sense of belonging somewhere and may provide special kinds of inter-personal and social meaning to a region one defines as "home."

It would be impossible to understand the reactions both to disloca-tion and to relocation and, particularly, the depth and frequency of grief responses without taking account of working-class orientations to residential areas. One of our primary theses is that the strength of the grief reaction to the loss of the West End is largely a function of prior orientations to the area. Thus, we certainly expect to find that the greater a person's pre-relocation commitment to the area, the more likely he is to react with marked grief. This prediction is confirmed again and again by the data.[2,3] For the women, among those who had said they liked living in the West End *very much* during the pre-location interviews, 73 per cent evidence a severe post-relocation grief reaction; among those who had less extreme but positive feelings about living in the West End, 53 per cent show a similar order of grief; and among those who were ambivalent or negative about the West End, only 34 per cent show a severe grief reaction. Or, considering a more specific feature of our formulation, the pre-relocation view of the West End as "home" shows an even stronger relationship to the depth of post-relocation grief. Among those women who said they had no real home, only 20 per cent give evidence of severe grief; among those who claimed some other area as their real home, 34 per cent fall into the severe grief category; but among the women for whom the *West End* was the real home, 68 per cent report severe grief reactions. Although the data for the men are less complete, the results are substantially similar. It is also quite understandable that the length of West End residence should bear a strong relationship to the loss reaction, although it is less powerful than some of the other findings and almost certainly it is not the critical component.

More directly relevant to our emphasis on the importance of places, it is quite striking that the greater the area of the West End which was known, the more likely there is to be a severe grief response. Among the women who said they knew only their own block during the pre-relocation interview, only 13 percent report marked grief; at the other extreme, among those who knew most of the West End, 64 per cent have a marked grief reaction. This relationship is maintained when a wide range of interrelated variables is held constant. Only in one instance, when there is a generally negative orientation to the West End, does more extensive knowledge of the area lead to a somewhat smaller proportion of severe grief responses. Thus, the wider an individual's familiarity with the local area, the greater his commitment to the locality. This wider familiarity evidently signifies a greater sense of the wholeness and integrity of the entire West End and, we would suggest, a more expanded sense of being "at home" throughout the entire local region. It is striking, too, that while familiarity with, use of, and comfort in the spatial regions of the residential area are closely related to extensiveness of personal contact, the spatial patterns have independent significance and represent an additional basis for a feeling of commitment to that larger, local region which is "home."

The Sense of Spatial Identity

In stressing the importance of places and access to local facilities, we wish only to redress the almost total neglect of spatial dimensions in dealing with human behavior. We certainly do not mean thereby to give too little emphasis to the fundamental importance of interpersonal relationships and social organization in defining the meaning of the area. Nor do we wish to underestimate the significance of cultural orientations and social organization in defining the character and importance of spatial dimensions. However, the crisis of loss of a residential area brings to the fore the importance of the local spatial region and alerts us to the greater generality of spatial conceptions as determinants of behavior. In fact, we might say that a *sense of spatial identity* is fundamental to human functioning. It represents a phenomenal or ideational integration of important experiences concerning environmental arrangements and contacts in relation to the individual's conception of his own body in space.[4] It is based on spatial memories, spatial imagery, the spatial framework of current activity, and the implicit spatial components of ideals and aspirations.

It appears to us also that these feelings of being at home and of belonging are, in the working class, integrally tied to a *specific* place. We would not expect similar effects or, at least, effects of similar proportion in a middle-class area. Generally speaking, an integrated sense of spatial identity in the middle class is not as contingent on the external stability of place or as dependent on the localization of social patterns, interpersonal relationships, and daily routines. In these data, in fact, there is a marked relationship between class status and depth of grief; the higher

234

the status, by any of several indices, the smaller the proportions of severe grief. It is primarily in the working class, and largely because of the importance of external stability, that dislocation from a familiar residential area has so great an effect on fragmenting the sense of spatial identity.

External stability is also extremely important in interpersonal patterns within the working class. And dislocation and relocation involve a fragmentation of the external bases for interpersonal relationships and group networks. Thus, relocation undermines the established interpersonal relationships and group ties of the people involved and, in effect, destroys the sense of group identity of a great many individuals. "Group identity," a concept originally formulated by Erik Erikson, refers to the individual's sense of belonging, of being a part of larger human and social entities. It may include belonging to organizations or interpersonal networks with which a person is directly involved; and it may refer to "membership" in social groups with whom an individual has little overt contact, whether it be a family, a social class, an ethnic collectivity, a profession, or a group of people sharing a common ideology. What is common to these various patterns of group identity is that they represent an integrated sense of shared human qualities, of some sense of communality with other people which is essential for meaningful social functioning. Since, most notably in the working class, effective relationships with others are dependent upon a continuing sense of common group identity, the experience of loss and disruption of these affiliations is intense and frequently irrevocable. On the grounds, therefore, of both spatial and interpersonal orientations and commitments, dislocation from the residential area represents a particularly marked disruption in the sense of continuity for the majority of this group.

The Nature of the Loss in Relocation: Social and Personal Factors

Previously we said that by emphasizing the spatial dimension of the orientation to the West End, we did not mean to diminish the importance of social patterns in the experience of the local area and their effects on post-relocation loss reactions. Nor do we wish to neglect personality factors involved in the widespread grief reactions. It is quite clear that pre-relocation social relationships and intrapsychic dispositions *do* affect the depth of grief in response to leaving the West End. The strongest of these patterns is based on the association between depth of grief and pre-relocation feelings about neighbors. Among those women who had very positive feelings about their neighbors, 76 per cent show severe grief reactions; among those who were positive but less extreme, 56 per cent show severe grief; and among those who were relatively negative, 38 per cent have marked grief responses. Similarly, among the women whose five closest friends lived in the West End, 67 per cent show marked grief; among those whose friends were mostly in the West End or equally distributed inside and outside the area, 55 per cent have severe grief reactions; and among those whose friends were mostly or all outside, 44 per cent show severe grief.

The fact that these differences, although great, are not as consistently powerful as the differences relating to spatial use patterns does not necessarily imply the *greater* importance of spatial factors. If we hold the effect of spatial variables constant and examine the relationship between depth of grief and the interpersonal variables, it becomes apparent that the effect of interpersonal contacts on depth of grief is consistent regardless of differences in spatial orientation; and, likewise, the effect of spatial orientations on depth of grief is consistent regardless of differences in interpersonal relationships. Thus, each set of factors contributes independently to the depth of grief in spite of some degree of internal relationship. In short, we suggest that *either* spatial identity or group identity may be a critical focus of loss of continuity and thereby lead to severe grief; but if *both* bases for the sense of continuity are localized *within the residential area* the disruption of continuity is greater, and the proportions of marked grief correspondingly higher.

It is noteworthy that, apart from local interpersonal and social relationships and local spatial orientations and use (and variables which are closely related to these), there are few other social or personal factors in the pre-relocation situation which are related to depth of grief. These negative findings are of particular importance in emphasizing that not all the variables which influence the grief reaction to dislocation are of equal importance. It should be added that a predisposition to depression markedly accentuates the depth of grief in response to the loss of one's residential area. But it is also clear that prior depressive orientations do not account for the entire relationship. The effects of the general depressive orientation and of the social, interpersonal, and spatial relationships within the West End are essentially additive; both sets of factors contribute markedly to the final result. Thus, among the women with a severe depressive orientation, an extremely large proportion (81 per cent) of those who regarded the West End as their real home show marked grief. But among the women without a

236

depressive orientation, only a moderate proportion (58 per cent) of those who similarly viewed the West End as home show severe grief. On the other hand, when the West End is not seen as the person's real home, an increasing severity of general depressive orientation does *not* lead to an increased proportion of severe grief reactions.

The Nature of the Loss in Relocation: Case Analyses

The dependence of the sense of continuity on external resources in the working class, particularly on the availability and local presence of familiar places which have the character of "home," and of familiar people whose patterns of behavior and response are relatively predictable, does not account for all of the reaction of grief to dislocation. In addition to these factors, which may be accentuated by depressive predispositions, it is quite evident that the realities of *post*-relocation experience are bound to affect the perpetuation, quality, and depth of grief. And, in fact, our data show that there is a strong association between positive or negative experiences in the post-relocation situation and the proportions who show severe grief. But this issue is complicated by two factors: (1) the extent to which potentially meaningful post-relocation circumstances can be a satisfying experience is *affected* by the degree and tenaciousness of previous commitments to the West End, and (2) the post-relocation "reality" is, in part, *selected* by the people who move and thus is a function of many personality factors, including the ability to anticipate needs, demands, and environmental opportunities.

In trying to understand the effects of pre-relocation orientations and post-relocation experiences of grief, we must bear in mind that the grief reactions we have described and analyzed are based on responses given approximately two years after relocation. Most people manage to achieve some adaptation to their experiences of loss and grief, and learn to deal with new situations and new experiences on their own terms. A wide variety of adaptive methods can be employed to salvage fragments of the sense of continuity, or to try to re-establish it on new grounds. Nonetheless, it is the tenaciousness of the imagery and affect of grief, despite these efforts at dealing with the altered reality, which is so strikingly similar to mourning for a lost person.

In coping with the sense of loss, some families tried to remain physically close to the area they knew, even though most of their close interpersonal relationships remain disrupted; and by this method, they appear often to have modified their feelings of grief. Other families try to move among relatives and maintain a sense of continuity through some degree of constancy in the external bases for their group identity. Yet others respond to the loss of place and people by accentuating the importance of those role relationships which remain. Thus, a number of women report increased closeness to their husbands, which they often explicitly relate to the decrease in the availability of other social relationships for both partners and which, in turn, modifies the severity of grief. In order to clarify some of the complexities of pre-relocation orientations and of post-relocation adjustments most concretely, a review of several cases may prove to be instructive.

It is evident that a very strong positive pre-relocation orientation to the West End is relatively infrequently associated with a complete absence of grief; and that, likewise, a negative pre-relocation orientation to the area is infrequently associated with a strong grief response. The two types which are numerically dominant are, in terms of rational expectations, consistent: those with strong positive feelings about the West End and severe grief; and those with negative feelings about the West End and minimal or moderate grief. The two "deviant" types, by the same token, are both numerically smaller and inconsistent: those with strong positive pre-relocation orientations and little grief; and those with negative pre-relocation orientations and severe grief. A closer examination of those "deviant" cases with strong pre-relocation commitment to the West End and minimal post-relocation grief often reveals either important reservations in their prior involvement with the West End or, more frequently, the denial or rejection of feelings of grief rather than their total absence. And the association of minimal pre-location commitment to the West End with a severe grief response often proves on closer examination to be a function of a deep involvement in the West End which is modified by markedly ambivalent statements; or, more generally, the grief reaction itself is quite modest and tenuous or is even a pseudo-grief which masks the primacy of dissatisfaction with the current area.

Grief Patterns: Case Examples

In turning to case analysis, we shall concentrate on the specific factors which operate in families of all four types, those representing the two dominant and those representing the two deviant patterns.

1. The Figella family exemplifies the association of strong positive pre-relocation attachments to the West End and a severe grief reaction. This is the most frequent of all the patterns and, although the

238

Figella family is only one "type" among those who show this pattern, they are prototypical of a familiar West End constellation.

Both Mr. and Mrs. Figella are second-generation Americans who were born and brought up in the West End. In her pre-location interview, Mrs. Figella described her feelings about living in the West End unambiguously: "It's a wonderful place, the people are friendly." She "loves everything about it" and anticipates missing her relatives above all. She is satisfied with her dwelling: "It's comfortable, clean and warm." And the marriage appears to be deeply satisfying for both husband and wife. They share many household activities and have a warm family life with their three children.

Both Mr. and Mrs. Figella feel that their lives have changed a great deal since relocation. They are clearly referring, however, to the pattern and conditions of their relationships with other people. Their home life has changed little except that Mr. Figella is home more. He continues to work at the same job as a manual laborer with a modest but sufficient income. While they have many economic insecurities, the relocation has not produced any serious financial difficulty for them.

In relocating, the Figella family bought a house. Both husband and wife are quite satisfied with the physical arrangements but, all in all, they are dissatisfied with the move. When asked what she dislikes about her present dwelling, Mrs. Figella replied simply and pathetically: "It's in Arlington and I want to be in the West End." Both Mr. and Mrs. Figella are outgoing, friendly people with a very wide circle of social contacts. Although they still see their relatives often, they both feel isolated from them and they regret the loss of their friends. As Mr. Figella puts it: "I come home from work and that's it. I just plant myself in the house."

The Figella family is, in many respects, typical of a well-adjusted working-class family. They have relatively few ambitions for themselves or for their children. They continue in close contact with many people; but they no longer have the same extensiveness of mutual cooperation in household activities, they cannot "drop in" as casually as before, they do not have the sense of being surrounded by a familiar area and familiar people. Thus, while their objective situation is not dramatically altered, the changes do involve important elements of stability and continuity in their lives. They manifest the importance of externally available resources for an integral sense of spatial and group identity. However, they have always maintained a very close marital relationship, and their family provides a substantial basis for a sense of continuity. They can evidently cope with difficulties on the strength of their many internal and external resources. Nonetheless, they have suffered from the move, and find it extremely difficult to reorganize their lives completely in adapting to a new geographical situation and new patterns of social affiliation. Their grief for a lost home seems to be one form of maintaining continuity on the basis of memories. While it prevents a more wholehearted adjustment to their altered lives, such adjustments would imply forsaking the remaining fragments of a continuity which was central to their conceptions of themselves and of the world.

2. There are many similarities between the Figella family and the Giuliano family. But Mrs. Giuliano shows relatively little pre-relocation commitment to the West End and little post-relocation grief. Mr. Giuliano was somewhat more deeply involved in the West End and, although satisfied with the change, feels that relocation was "like having the rug pulled out from under you." Mr. and Mrs. Giuliano are also second-generation Americans, of similar background to the Figellas'. But Mrs. Giuliano only moved to the West End at her marriage. Mrs. Giuliano had many objections to the area: "For me it is too congested. I never did care for it . . . too many barrooms, on every corner, too many families in one building. . . . The sidewalks are too narrow and the kids can't play outside." But she does expect to miss the stores and many favorite places. Her housing ambitions go beyond West End standards and she wants more space inside and outside. She had no blood relatives in the West End but was close to her husband's family and had friends nearby.

Mr. Giuliano was born in the West End and he had many relatives in the area. He has a relatively high status manual job but only a modest income. His wife does not complain about this although she is only moderately satisfied with the marriage. In part she objected to the fact that they went out so little and that he spent too much time on the corner with his friends. His social networks in the West End were more extensive and involved than were Mrs. Giuliano's. And he missed the West End more than she did after the relocation. But even Mr. Giuliano says that, all in all, he is satisfied with the change.

Mrs. Giuliano feels the change is "wonderful." She missed her friends but got over it. And a few of Mr. Giuliano's hanging group live close by so they can continue to hang together. Both are satisfied with the house they bought although Mrs. Giuliano's ambitions have now gone beyond this. The post-relocation situation has led to an improved marital relationship: Mr. Giuliano is home more and they go out more together.

Mr. and Mrs. Giuliano exemplify a pattern which seems most likely to be associated with a beneficial experience from relocation. Unlike Mr. and Mrs. Figella, who completely accept their working-class status and are embedded in the social and cultural patterns of the working class, Mr. and Mrs. Giuliano show many evidences of social mobility. Mr. Giuliano's present job is, properly speaking, outside the working-class category because of its relatively high status and he himself does not "work with his hands." And Mrs. Giuliano's housing ambitions, preferences in social relationships, orientation to the class structure, and attitudes toward a variety of matters from shopping to child rearing are indications of a readiness to achieve middle-class status. Mr. Giuliano is prepared for and Mrs. Giuliano clearly desires "discontinuity" with some of the central bases for their former identity. Their present situation is, in fact, a transitional one which allows them to reintegrate their lives at a new and higher status level without too precipitate a change. And their marital relationship seems sufficiently meaningful to provide a significant core of continuity in the process of change in their patterns of social and cultural experience. The lack of grief in this case is quite understandable and appropriate to their patterns of social orientation and expectation.

3. Yet another pattern is introduced by the Borowski family, who had an intense pre-location commitment to the West End and relatively little post-relocation grief. The Borowskis are both second-generation and have four children.

Mrs. Borowski was brought up in the West End but her husband has lived there only since the marriage (fifteen years before). Her feelings about living in the West End were clear: "I love it—it's the only home I've ever known." She had reservations about the dirt in the area but loved the people, the places, and the convenience and maintained an extremely wide circle of friends. They had some relatives nearby but were primarily oriented towards friends, both within and outside the West End. Mr. Borowski, a highly skilled manual worker with a moderately high income, was as deeply attached to the West End as his wife.

Mr. Borowski missed the West End very much but was quite satisfied with their new situation and could anticipate feeling thoroughly at home in the new neighborhood. Mrs. Borowski proclaims that "home is where you hang your hat; it's up to you to make the adjustments." But she also says, "If I knew the people were coming back to the West End, I would pick up this little house and put it back on my corner." She claims she was not sad after relocation but, when asked how she felt when the building she lived in was torn down, a strangely morbid association is aroused: "It's just like a plant . . . when you tear up its roots, it dies! I didn't die but I felt kind of bad. It was home. . . . Don't look back, try to go ahead."

Despite evidences of underlying grief, both Mr. and Mrs. Borowski have already adjusted to the change with remarkable alacrity. They bought a one-family house and have many friends in the new area. They do not feel as close to their new neighbors as they did to their West End friends, and they still maintain extensive contact with the latter. They are comfortable and happy in their new surroundings and maintain the close, warm, and mutually appreciative marital relationship they formerly had.

Mr. and Mrs. Borowski, and particularly Mrs. Borowski, reveal a sense of loss which is largely submerged beneath active efforts to deal with the present. It was possible for them to do this both because of personality factors (that is, the ability to deny the intense affective meaning of the change and to detach themselves from highly "cathected" objects with relative ease) and because of prior social patterns and orientations. Not only is Mr. Borowski, by occupation, among the highest group of working-class status, but this family has been "transitional" for some time. Remaining in the West End was clearly a matter of preference for them. They could have moved out quite easily on the basis of income and many of their friends were scattered throughout metropolitan Boston. But while they are less self-consciously mobile than the Giulianos, they had already shifted to many patterns more typical of the middle class before leaving the West End. These ranged from their joint weekly shopping expeditions to their recreational patterns, which included such sports as boating and such regular plans as yearly vacations. They experienced a disruption in continuity by virtue of their former spatial and group identity. But the bases for maintaining this identity had undergone many changes over the years; and they had already established a feeling for places and people, for a potential redefinition of "home" which was less contingent on the immediate and local availability of familiar spaces and familiar friends. Despite their preparedness for the move by virtue of cultural orientation, social experience, and personal disposition, the change

242

was a considerable wrench for them. But, to the extent that they can be categorized as "over-adjusters," the residue of their lives in the West End is primarily a matter of painful memories which are only occasionally reawakened.

4. The alternate deviant pattern, minimal pre-relocation commitment associated with severe post-relocation grief, is manifested by Mr. and Mrs. Pagliuca. As in the previous case, this classification applies more fully to Mrs. Pagliuca, since Mr. Pagliuca appears to have had stronger ties to the West End. Mr. Pagliuca is a second-generation American but Mrs. Pagliuca is first-generation from an urban European background. For both of them, however, there is some evidence that the sadness and regret about the loss of the West End should perhaps be designated as pseudo-grief.

Mrs. Pagliuca had a difficult time in the West End. But she also had a difficult time before that. She moved into the West End when she got married. And she complains bitterly about her marriage, her husband's relatives, West Enders in general. She says of the West End: "I don't like it. The people . . . the buildings are full of rats. There are no places to play for the children." She liked the apartment but complained about the lady downstairs, the dirt, the repairs required, and the coldness during the winter. She also complains a great deal about lack of money. Her husband's wages are not too low but he seems to have periods of unemployment and often drinks his money away.

Mr. Pagliuca was attached to some of his friends and the bars in the West End. But he didn't like his housing situation there. And his reaction tends to be one of bitterness ("a rotten deal") rather than of sadness. Both Mr. and Mrs. Pagliuca are quite satisfied with their post-relocation apartment but are thoroughly dissatisfied with the area. They have had considerable difficulty with neighbors: ". . . I don't like this; people are mean here; my children get blamed for anything and everything; and there's no transportation near here." She now idealizes the West End and claims that she misses everything about it.

Mr. Pagliuca is an unskilled manual laborer. Financial problems create a constant focus for difficulty and arguments. But both Mr. and Mrs. Pagliuca appear more satisfied with one another than before relocation. They have four children, some of whom are in legal difficulty. There is also some evidence of past cruelty toward the children, at least on Mrs. Pagliuca's part.

It is evident from this summary that the Pagliuca family is deviant in a social as well as in a statistical sense. They show few signs of adjusting to the move or, for that matter, of any basic potential for successful adjustment to further moves (which they are now planning). It may be that families with such initial difficulties, with such a tenuous basis for maintaining a sense of continuity under any circumstances, suffer most acutely from disruption of these minimal ties. The Pagliuca family has few inner resources and, having lost the minimal external resources signified by a gross sense of belonging, of being tolerated if not accepted, they appear to be hopelessly at sea. Although we refer to their grief as "pseudo-grief" on the basis of the shift from pre-relocation to post-relocation statements, there is a sense in which it is quite real. Within the post-relocation interviews their responses are quite consistent; and a review of all the data suggests that, although their ties were quite modest, their current difficulties have revealed the importance of these meager involvements and the problems of re-establishing anew an equivalent basis for identity formation. Thus, even for Mr. and Mrs. Pagliuca, we can speak of the disruption in the sense of continuity, although this continuity was based on a very fragile experience of minimal comfort, with familiar places and relatively tolerant people. Their grief reaction, pseudo or real, may further influence (and be influenced by) dissatisfactions with any new residential situation. The fact that it is based on an idealized past accentuates rather than minimizes its effect on current expectations and behavior.

Conclusions

Grieving for a lost home is evidently a widespread and serious social phenomenon following in the wake of urban dislocation. It is likely to increase social and psychological "pathology" in a limited number of instances; and it is also likely to create new opportunities for some, and to increase the rate of social mobility for others. For the greatest number, dislocation is unlikely to have either effect but does lead to intense personal suffering despite moderately successful adaptation to the total situation of relocation. Under these circumstances, it becomes most critical that we face the realities of the effects of relocation on working-class residents of slums and, on the basis of knowledge and understanding, that we learn to deal more effectively with the problems engendered.

In evaluating these data on the effect of pre-location experiences on

244

post-relocation reactions of grief, we have arrived at a number of conclusions:

1. The affective reaction to the loss of the West End can be quite precisely described as a grief response showing most of the characteristics of grief and mourning for a lost person.

2. One of the important components of the grief reaction is the fragmentation of the sense of spatial identity. This is manifest, not only in the pre-location experience of the spatial area as an expanded "home," but in the varying degrees of grief following relocation, arising from variations in the pre-relocation orientation to and use of local spatial regions.

3. Another component, of equal importance, is the dependence of the sense of group identity on stable, social networks. Dislocation necessarily led to the fragmentation of this group identity which was based, to such a large extent, on the external availability and overt contact with familiar groups of people.

4. Associated with these "cognitive" components, described as the sense of spatial identity and the sense of group identity, are strong affective qualities. We have not tried to delineate them but they appear to fall into the realm of a feeling of security in and commitment to the external spatial and group patterns which are the tangible, visible aspects of these identity components. However, a predisposition to depressive reactions also markedly affects the depth of grief reaction.

5. Theoretically, we can speak of spatial and group identity as critical foci of the sense of continuity. This sense of continuity is not *necessarily* contingent on the external stability of place, people, and security or support. But for the working class these concrete, external resources and the experience of stability, availability, and familiarity which they provide are essential for a meaningful sense of continuity. Thus, dislocation and the loss of the residential area represent a fragmentation of some of the essential components of the sense of continuity in the working class.

It is in the light of these observations and conclusions that we must consider problems of social planning which are associated with the changes induced by physical planning for relocation. Urban planning cannot be limited to "bricks and mortar." While these data tell us little about the importance of housing or the aspects of housing which are important, they indicate that considerations of a non-housing nature are critical. There is evidence, for example, that the frequency of the

245

grief response is not affected by such housing factors as increase or decrease in apartment size or home ownership. But physical factors may be of great importance when related to the subjective signifi- cance of different spatial and physical arrangements, or to their capac- ity for gratifying different socio-cultural groups. For the present, we can only stress the importance of local areas as *spatial and social* arrangements which are central to the lives of working-class people. And, in view of the enormous importance of such local areas, we are led to consider the convergence of familiar people and familiar places as a focal consideration in formulating planning decisions.

We can learn to deal with these problems only through research, through exploratory and imaginative service programs, and through a more careful consideration of the place of residential stability in sal- vaging the precarious thread of continuity. The outcomes of crises are always manifold and, just as there is an increase in strain and diffi- culty, so also there is an increase in opportunities for adapting at a more satisfying level of functioning. The judicious use of minimal resources of counseling and assistance may permit many working- class people to reorganize and integrate a meaningful sense of spatial and group identity under the challenge of social change. Only a rela- tively small group of those whose functioning has always been mar- ginal and who cannot cope with the added strain of adjusting to wholly new problems are likely to require major forms of intervention.

In general, our results would imply the necessity for providing increased opportunities for maintaining a sense of continuity for those people, mainly from the working class, whose residential areas are being renewed. This may involve several factors: (1) diminishing the amount of drastic redevelopment and the consequent mass demo- lition of property and mass dislocation from homes; (2) providing more frequently for people to move within their former residential areas during and after the renewal; and (3) when dislocation and relocation are unavoidable, planning the relocation possibilities in order to provide new areas which can be assimilated to old objectives. A closer examination of slum areas may even provide some concrete information regarding specific physical variables, the physical and spatial arrangements typical of slum areas and slum housing, which offer considerable gratification to the residents. These may often be translated into effective modern architectural and areal design. And, in conjunction with planning decisions which take more careful account of the human consequences of urban physical change, it is possible to utilize social, psychological, and psychiatric services. The use of highly skilled resources, including opportunities for the education of professional and even lay personnel in largely unfamiliar problems and methods, can minimize some of the more destructive and widespread effects of relocation; and, for some families, can offer constructive experiences in dealing with new adaptational possibilities. The problem is large. But only by assuring the integrity of some of the external bases for the sense of continuity in the working class, and by maximizing the opportunities for meaningful adaptation, can we accomplish planned urban change without serious hazard to human welfare.

NOTES

1. This is implicit in the prior work on "crisis" and situational predicaments by Dr. Erich Lindemann under whose initiative the current work was undertaken and carried out.

2. The analysis involves a comparison of information from interviews administered *before* relocation with a depth of grief index derived from follow-up interviews approximately two years *after* relocation. The pre-relocation interviews were administered to a randomly selected sample of 473 women from households in this area at the time the land was taken by the city. The post-relocation interviews were completed with 92 per cent of the women who had given pre-relocation interviews and with 87 per cent of the men from those households in which there was a husband in the household. Primary emphasis will be given to the results with the women since we do not have as full a range of pre-relocation information for the men. However, since a split schedule was used for the post-relocation interviews, the depth of grief index is available for only 259 women.

3. Dr. Jason Aronson was largely responsible for developing the series of questions on grief. The opening question of the series was: Many people have told us that just after they moved they felt sad or depressed. Did you feel this way? This was followed by the three specific questions on which the index was based: (1) Would you describe how you felt? (2) How long did these feelings last? (3) How did you feel when you saw or heard that the building you had lived in was torn down? Each person was given a score from 1 to 4 on the basis of the coded responses to these questions and the scores were summated. For purposes of analysis, we divided the final scores into three groups: minimal grief, moderate grief, and severe or marked grief. The phrasing of these questions appears to dispose the respondent to give a "grief" response. In fact, however, there is a tendency to reject the idea of "sadness" among many people who show other evidence of a grief response. In cross-tabulating the "grief" scores with a series of questions in which there is no suggestion of sadness, unhappiness, or dissatisfaction, it is clear that the grief index is the more severe criterion. Those who are classified in the severe grief category almost invariably show severe grief reactions by any of the other criteria; but many who are categorized as "minimal grief" on the index fall into the extremes of unhappiness or dissatisfaction on the other items.

4. Erik Erikson includes spatial components in discussing the sense of ego identity and his work has influenced the discussion of spatial variables (4). In distinguishing the sense of spatial identity from the sense of ego identity, I am suggesting that variations in spatial identity do not correspond exactly to variations in ego identity. By separating these concepts, it becomes possible to study their interrelationships empirically.

REFERENCES

1. Abraham, K., "Notes on the Psycho-analytical Investigation and Treatment of Manic-Depressive Insanity and Allied Conditions" (1911), and "A Short Study of the Development of the Libido, Viewed in the Light of Mental Disorders" (1924), in *Selected Papers of Karl Abraham*, Vol. I, New York: Basic Books, 1953; Bibring, E., "The Mechanisms of Depression," in *Affective Disorders*, P. Greenacre, ed., New York: International Univ. Press, 1953; Bowlby, J., "Processes of Mourning," *Int. J. Psychoanal.*, 42:317–340, 1961; Freud, S., "Mourning and Melancholia" (1917), in *Collected Papers*, Vol. III, New York: Basic Books, 1959; Hoggart, R., *The Uses of Literacy: Changing Patterns in English Mass Culture*, New York: Oxford Univ. Press, 1957; Klein, M., "Mourning and Its Relations to Manic-Depressive States," *Int. J. Psychoanal.*, 21:125–153, 1940; Lindemann, E., "Symptomatology and Management of Acute Grief," *Am. J. Psychiat.*, 101:141–148, 1944; Marris, P., *Widows and Their Families*, London: Routledge and Kegan Paul, 1958; Rochlin, G., "The Dread of Abandonment," in *The Psychoanalytic Study of the Child*, Vol. XVI, New York: International Univ. Press, 1961; Volkart, E. H., with S. T. Michael, "Bereavement and Mental Health," in *Explorations in Social Psychiatry*, A. H. Leighton, J. A. Clausen, and R. N. Wilson, eds., New York: Basic Books, 1957.

2. Fried, M., and Gleicher, P., "Some Sources of Residential Satisfaction in an Urban Slum," *J. Amer. Inst. Planners*, 27:305–315, 1961.

3. Gans, H., *The Urban Villagers*, New York: The Free Press, 1963; Gans, H., "The Human Implications of Current Redevelopment and Relocation Planning," *J. Amer. Inst. Planners*, 25:15–25, 1959; Hoggart, R., *op. cit.*; Hole, V., "Social Effects of Planned Rehousing," *Town Planning Rev.*, 30:161–173, 1959; Marris, P., *Family and Social Change in an African City*, Evanston, Ill.: Northwestern Univ. Press, 1962; Mogey, J. M., *Family and Neighbourhood*, New York: Oxford Univ. Press, 1956; Seeley, J., "The Slum: Its Nature, Use, and Users," *J. Amer. Inst. Planners*, 25:7–14, 1959; Vereker, C., and Mays, J. B., *Urban Redevelopment and Social Change*, New York: Lounz, 1960; Young, M., and Willmott, P., *Family and Kinship in East London*, Glencoe, Ill.: The Free Press, 1957.

4. Erikson, E., "Ego Development and Historical Change," in *The Psychoanalytic Study of the Child*, Vol. II, New York: International Univ. Press, 1946; "The Problem of Ego Identity," *J. Amer. Psychoanal. Assoc.*, 4:56–121, 1956.

16

Health Consequences of
Population Density and Crowding

JOHN CASSEL

No discussion of the effects of the environment on health can be considered complete without paying some attention to the phenomenon of overcrowding. The assumption that overcrowding produces negative effects underlies many proposals in favor of lower density settlement patterns, population control, and designing buildings to ensure privacy. The subject of overcrowding is also important because of all the many environmental variables whose association with health have been repeatedly studied over the last century, it has been the fact of high urban density that has been most often shown to be related to poor health and social pathology.

Cassel's selection is especially important because it argues that the relationship between overcrowding and illness and social pathology is not nearly as simple or unidirectional as the current excitement over the phenomenon of the "behavioral sink" among rats and mice has led people to believe. He summarizes the major bodies of evidence that have offered support to the view that overcrowding is bad for health and indicates that the evidence is not substantial. In many studies the more densely settled urbanized populations evidenced superior health to the lower density rural populations. Furthermore, Cassel points out that it is often isolated population groups that show a greater susceptibility to chronic and epidemic diseases. There is even some evidence that suggests that overcrowding can not only be neutral, but actually beneficial to health.

On the basis of the present evidence, Cassel proposes a model for identifying the critical factors other than population density that determine the response of the human organism and of human groups to overcrowding. His fundamental thesis is that to the degree that population density is associated with poor health, the negative association comes about because density

Reprinted from John Cassel, "Health Consequences of Population Density and Crowding," in *The Consequences of Population Change and Their Implications for National and International Policies.* Forthcoming from The Johns Hopkins Press.

249

increases the salience of the social environment as a determinant of the organism's reaction to potentially infectious stimuli. The effects of the physical environment on health, therefore, cannot be predicted without knowledge of the social experiences and characteristics of people living at different density levels. Two social factors are singled out and given special weight in Cassel's scheme: the hierarchical status structure of the urban community and social group and the individual's location within the hierarchy; and the degree of social integration and social cohesion within the group or community. Cassel argues that individuals higher up in the status hierarchy, regardless of the density levels under which they live, are less likely to suffer from bad health. He also believes that people who live in more cohesive communities are healthier. By applying this model, Cassel is led toward the conclusion that many of the negative effects on health associated with urban densities are not caused by the densities but rather by the rapidity of urban growth and the relatively limited experience of many recent urban migrants in learning how to adapt to the stresses imposed by city life.

☐

The view that crowding and increased population density are deleterious as far as health is concerned, is so widespread and generally accepted as to have become almost a medical axiom. Furthermore, it is currently believed that the harmful effects of crowding are not merely confined to increasing the spread of infectious diseases but also increase the risk of non-infectious disease. These views can perhaps be best illustrated by two quotations from a standard text on epidemiology, which with minor variations can be found in all textbooks dealing with the subject.

> *It has long been recognized that crowded communities provide a more fertile ground for the spread of infection than more scattered communities.* (1) *... The deleterious effects of crowding are not, however, confined to matters concerned with the spread of infection, but are also seen in increased mortality from all causes, both infectious and non-infectious.* (2)

The evidence supporting this point of view is derived largely from four sources:

A. The higher death and morbidity rates that traditionally have been reported from the more densely populated urban centers.

B. The dramatic increase in death rates, primarily due to infectious diseases that have followed industrialization and urbanism.

C. The higher rates of various diseases reported under crowded conditions such as military training camps, nurseries, etc.

250

D. Animal studies, which have shown that as the number of animals housed together increases, with other factors such as diet, temperature and sanitation kept constant, maternal and infant mortality rates rise, the incidence of atherosclerosis increases, and the resistance to insults such as drugs, micro-organisms, and x-rays is reduced.

A careful review of recent data, however, indicates some important inconsistencies in the relationship between crowding and health status which throw some doubt on this generally accepted formulation, particularly on the processes through which crowding may influence health. It would appear from these data that the relationship between crowding and health status is a far more complex phenomenon than was originally envisaged, and that while under certain circumstances crowding is clearly associated with poor health states, under other circumstances it may be neutral or even beneficial. The data casting some doubt on this relationship will be briefly reviewed under the same categories that have provided the evidence used to support the notion that crowding inevitably leads to deleterious health consequences.

URBAN-RURAL DEATH AND MORBIDITY RATES

As is shown in Figure 16–1, death rates for all causes in the United States were indeed higher in urban areas than in rural prior to 1950. By 1960, however, the ratio had become reversed, rural rates being higher than urban, and since 1960 the ratio of rural to urban deaths has been steadily increasing. Thus, paradoxically, even though cities have been increasing in size since 1940, death rates have fallen more rapidly in these crowded circumstances than in the more sparsely populated rural areas. Part of this phenomenon may be due to the improved medical care and sanitation in the cities and part to the migration of younger people to the cities leaving an older, more susceptible population behind in the rural areas. These processes, it could be argued, might overwhelm or obscure the effects of crowding. That these can only be partial explanations for this reversal in the rural-urban health ratios is evident from the data shown in Table 16–1. While the rural excess in both incidence and mortality rates from typhoid fever, for example, may well be due to differences in sanitation, and the more effective immunization programs in cities account for the lower urban rates of diphtheria and pertussis, the rural excess in the incidence of scarlet fever can hardly be due to either of these processes as we do not as yet possess any means to

251

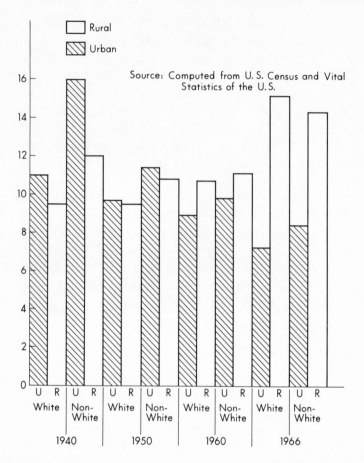

Figure 16–1 Death Rates—All Causes, U.S. (by Place of Residence 1940, 1950, 1960, and 1966). Computed From U.S. Census and Vital Statistics of the U.S.

prevent the occurrence of streptococcal infections. Similarly, as far as the migration hypothesis is concerned, this could not explain the excess mortality rates in rural children both black and white, male and female.

Data from other parts of the world tend to confirm this seeming paradox. Dubos (3), for example, reports that despite the fact that Hong Kong and Holland are among the most crowded areas in the world, they enjoy one of the highest levels of physical and mental health in the world. The data from Britain in 1961 on the age standardized mortality ratios for all causes of death is even more convincing (4). (See the table on p. 254.)

252

TABLE 16-1

Selected Urban-Rural Differences in Health Status, U.S. 1959-1961

	Incidence		Mortality	
	Metropolitan Counties	Non-Metropolitan Counties	Metropolitan Counties	Non-Metropolitan Counties
Childhood Mortality Rates Per 100,000 Population—All Causes (Ages 5-14 years)[1]				
White Male			48.6	59.7
White Female			32.3	37.6
Non-White Male			67.5	82.3
Non-White Female			45.5	60.9
Typhoid Fever[2]	3.3	7.0	0.1	0.1
Diphtheria[2]	3.2	7.1	0.2	0.6
Pertussis[2]	111.1	141.1	0.4	1.6
Scarlet Fever and Streptococcal Sore Throat[2]	1579	2374	0.5	1.1
Influenza[2]			13.5	41.9

[1] SOURCE: Shapiro, Sam et al., *Infant, Perinatal, Maternal, and Childhood Mortality in the United States*, Vital and Statistical Monographs APHA, Harvard University Press, 1968.

[2] SOURCE: Dauer, Carl C. et al., *Infectious Diseases*, Vital and Statistical Monographs APHA, Harvard University Press, 1968.

	Males	Females
Urban areas population 100,000 +	101	98
Urban areas population 50,000-99,999	91	90
Urban areas population under 50,000	104	105
Rural areas	91	98

THE RISE IN DEATH RATES THAT FOLLOWED
INDUSTRIALIZATION AND URBANISM

Tuberculosis has been used as an example par excellence of a disease which following industrialization, and the accompanying crowding, showed a marked increase in rates. What is not so well recognized, however, is that in all countries for which data is available, tuberculosis rates having risen for 75–100 years following industrialization, started to fall spontaneously, and have continued to fall in the face of ever increasing population density. Improvements in medical care and anti-tuberculosis programs cannot account for this reversal in trends, at least initially. The fall in Britain and the U.S., for example, started in 1850 and 1900 respectively (5); that is, 50 to 100 years before any useful anti-tuberculosis drugs were discovered and several decades before any organized anti-tuberculosis programs were initiated.

Furthermore, in some relatively recent studies it has been found that, contrary to prevailing theory, tuberculosis does not necessarily occur under crowded conditions but under some circumstances at least occurs more frequently in people who are socially isolated. In a careful study conducted in Britain, for example, all the families living in a city were x-rayed to determine the prevalence of tuberculosis in relationship to an index of crowding derived from dividing the number of people in a household by the number of rooms in that house (6). While a strong social class gradient in the prevalence of tuberculosis was discovered within each social class, no relationship between the crowding index and tuberculosis prevalence was found. In fact, those lodgers who were living alone in the houses had a tuberculosis rate some three to four times higher than family members even though the lodgers were, by definition, living in uncrowded conditions. Similar results were found in a study in the U.S.A. (7) in which it was found that tuberculosis was occurring most frequently in people living alone in a single room and not in those living under the most crowded conditions.

254

THE HIGHER RATES OF DISEASE (PARTICULARLY INFECTIOUS
DISEASE) REPORTED UNDER CROWDED CONDITIONS
SUCH AS MILITARY TRAINING CAMPS, ETC.

While there can be little doubt that outbreaks of disease, particularly acute upper respiratory disease, are more common under the crowded conditions of military training camps, for example, than under less crowded conditions, there is considerable doubt that such outbreaks can be ascribed solely to the physical fact of increased crowding.

In recent years, for example, intensive study of outbreaks of upper respiratory infection in recruits in military training camps have indicated that the agent responsible is usually the adenovirus IV. The orthodox explanation for such outbreaks holds that they result from the herding together of large numbers of susceptible young men with a few infected individuals and that the crowded conditions facilitate the spread of the agent. Such an explanation, however, fails to account for some of the known facts. For example, the same agent, the adenovirus IV, is widespread in civilian populations, but even under conditions of crowding such as occur in colleges and schools has never been implicated in an outbreak of upper respiratory infection. Furthermore, the permanent staff of the military installations, even though living under the same crowded conditions as the recruits, are not involved in such outbreaks. Finally, when immunization experiments against adenovirus IV have been conducted under appropriate double blind conditions, the immunized companies, while displaying a reduction in the number of cases ascribed to adenovirus IV, have experienced just as much upper respiratory illness as have the control companies, but now due to a different agent—adenovirus VII. Studies conducted by my colleagues on Marine recruits in Parris Island, South Carolina (8), on the patterning of such outbreaks, provide further evidence against the orthodox explanation. The basic training program lasts for 8 weeks. As can be seen from Figure 16-2, the number of upper respiratory infections increases from the first through the fourth week, decreases in the fifth and sixth weeks, and begins to increase again in the seventh and eighth weeks. As far as can be determined, there are no differences in crowding during these 8 weeks, and furthermore, as shown in Figure 16-3, sick calls from all causes including musculo-skeletal, skin infections, trauma, and all other causes display an identical pattern. Not only is this regularity observed for all platoons, but there are systematic differences in the rate of infection

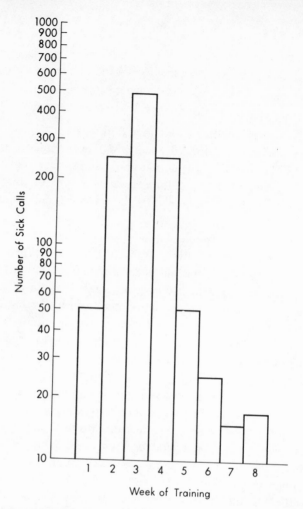

Figure 16–2 Recruit Sick Calls—Respiratory or Gastro–Intestinal Infection (by Week of Training: Parris Island, April–August 1967).

between platoons (living under identical conditions), some exhibiting a markedly higher rate for their entire 8 weeks than others.

As indicated later in this selection, such data do not necessarily refute the role of crowding in changing susceptibility to disease, but they do provide clues which may necessitate a change in our thinking concerning the processes through which crowding can influence health and the circumstances under which this occurs.

ANIMAL STUDIES

Even the animal data which at first sight appear so convincing need to be re-examined both in terms of their consistency and in terms of

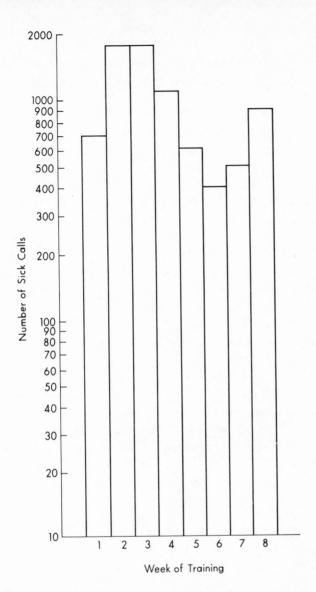

Figure 16–3 Recruit Sick Calls—All Causes (by Week of Training: Parris Island, April–August 1967).

the extrapolation that can be made to human populations. Alexander Kessler at the Rockefeller University, for example, has indicated that under extreme conditions of crowding in mice no increase in pathology was noted once the population had achieved its maximum density and no further population growth was occurring. Under these circumstances asocial behavior was common but physical pathology no more frequent than in the control group living under uncrowded conditions.

257

During the phase of rapid population growth, however, which preceded this plateau, disease was much more frequent than in the control group (9).

It is apparent, therefore, even from these fragmentary illustrative data that population density and/or crowding does not inevitably lead to poorer health status. For the remainder of this selection I intend to examine some of the reasons that may account for these conflicting data and to suggest the need to reformulate some of our conceptual models if the effects of such phenomena are to be better understood in the future.

Part of the reason for the discrepancies in the data presented above lies in the well recognized fact that many studies have used different and often inadequate indicators of crowding. The indicators used have frequently been unable to distinguish between a high population density in some arbitrary delineated areas of land and increased social interaction. Secondly, crowding under certain circumstances may be associated with certain factors which themselves can influence health (poverty, poor nutrition, poor housing, etc.) but under other circumstances may be associated with different factors. The relationship of crowding to disease states, therefore, may be a reflection of these other factors rather than the crowding per se.

Perhaps of greater importance than the inadequacy of the indicators or the presence of "contaminating" factors has been the failure of most investigators to identify explicitly the processes through which increased social interaction can lead to disease. The orthodox model which, implicitly at least, is espoused by the majority of authorities holds that crowding increases the risk for disease mainly through an increased opportunity for the spread of infection. Newer data and re-examination of older data is making this view increasingly untenable. It obviously cannot account for the increase in non-infectious disease, which occurs under conditions of crowding, but even for infectious diseases there is a growing body of opinion which indicates that such a view is at best only a partial explanation for any effects crowding may have. Dubos, the pioneer micro-biologist, has perhaps stated this view most clearly:

The sciences concerned with microbial diseases have developed almost exclusively from the study of acute or semi-acute infections caused by virulent micro-organisms acquired through exposure to an exogenous source of infection. In contrast, the microbial diseases most common in our communities today arise from the activities of micro-organisms that are ubiquitous in the environment, exist in the body without causing obvious harm under ordinary circumstances, and exert pathological stress. In such a type of

258

microbial disease the event of infection is of less importance than the hidden manifestation of the smoldering infectious process and than the physiological disturbances that convert latent infection into overt symptoms and pathology. (10)

According to Dubos, then, microbial disease is not necessarily acquired through exposure to a new micro-organism. In a large number of cases disease occurs through factors which disturb the balance between the ubiquitous organisms and the host that is harboring them. It may well be that under conditions of crowding this balance may be disturbed, but this disturbance is then not a function of the physical crowding but of other processes. The studies reported above on upper respiratory infections in Marine recruits woud tend to support this point of view, suggesting that a large proportion of the recruits are harboring viruses when entering into their military training, and that something about the military environment, particularly something about the environment of their own platoon or company, leads to the type of physiological stress to which Dubos refers that converts latent infection into overt symptoms and pathology. As is discussed below, it would appear that these factors that produce the physiological stress are unlikely to occur in the absence of crowding but are not themselves due necessarily to the physical presence of many infected individuals.

In addition to being guided by what now may be considered an inappropriate set of hypotheses, most research into the health consequences of crowding has failed to take into account the adaptability of living organisms. The current views are, to a large extent, based upon data which has examined health conditions under varying degrees of crowding at one point in time. It is less common to find studies in which the reactions of individuals to crowded conditions have been studied with the passage of time. Those few studies that have been conducted would indicate that organisms have the power to adapt to a wide range of conditions, including crowding, provided that the changes which they called upon to adapt to occur reasonably slowly, and would suggest then that many of the deleterious effects of crowding will occur only, or maximally, in those individuals who are newcomers to the crowded scene. Such a formulation may explain Kessler's findings in his long-term studies of crowding among mice, which, as has been indicated, are in contradiction to other animal studies which have examined the effects of crowding on first generation animals only.

Toward a Reformulation of the Conceptual Model

As is evidenced in the preceding section of this selection, it is our opinion that a considerable amount of the confusion concerning the health consequences of crowding resides in the lack of utility of the network of hypotheses that have been utilized to determine research strategy and interpret research results. Stated in its most simplistic form the hypothesis implicit in most of existing research holds that crowding is "bad" simply because it increases the opportunity for interpersonal contact and thus facilitates the inter-change of external disease agents. That this model does not explain many of the known phenomena and is generally an inadequate guide for the development of research strategy is illustrated in some of the data presented previously. If, then, the relationships between crowding and human health are to be elucidated in a more satisfactory manner a more appropriate set of hypotheses needs to be elaborated.

As has been indicated, animal experiments have quite convincingly demonstrated some of the short-term health consequences of increased population density. While these findings cannot necessarily be extrapolated directly to man, and will, we believe, have to be modified by taking into account the adaptability of biological organisms before drawing long-term conclusions, some of the underlying concepts that have been discovered in such studies may have extreme utility in developing new sets of hypotheses for studies in man. Welch (11), for example, in studying the effects of increased population size on mice, noted that as the size of the population increases, physiological changes occur in the animal such as enhancement of the adrenocortical and adrenal medullary secretions. He has postulated that increased population size leads to increased social interaction, and among gregarious animals such increased social interaction enhances emotional involvement and elicits central activation necessary for sensory fixation and recognition even in emotionally neutral encounters. Thus, he postulates that *every such stimulus* contributes to the level of activation of brainstem reticular formation and major endocrine systems. Thus, Welch's studies seem to indicate that one of the effects of increased population size and density is *to increase the importance of the social environment as a determinant of physiological response to various stimuli*, including disease-producing agents to which the population is subjected. This seems to me to be an extraordinarily important possibility. It would suggest that the effect of any disease-producing agent, be this a micro-organism, a toxin, or some other physico-chemical element, cannot be assessed in the absence of knowledge concerning the size and nature of the group within which the exposed population interacts, and that the larger the interacting group the more important will these group phenomena be in modifying the responses to such factors. Such a formulation receives at least circumstantial support from the studies on the level of blood pressure that have been conducted over the last 30 years in every continent in the world (12–37). These studies have indicated that, with few exceptions, populations living in small, cohesive societies tend to have low blood pressures which do not differ in the young and the aged. In a number of these studies, groups who have left such societies and who have had contact with Western urban culture, were also studied and found to have higher levels of blood pressure and to exhibit the familiar relationships between age and blood pressure found in studies of Western populations.

This formulation, useful as it may be as a general proposition, requires further specification and modification if it is to determine future research strategy. Specifically, it seems important to recognize that the influences of increases in population size are going to vary for different categories of individuals. The first such category is constituted by hierarchical position within the group. Welch (11) and Mason (38) have shown, in animal experiments, that those animals occupying subordinate positions within any group tend to respond in a far more extreme fashion to standardized stimuli than do those in dominant positions. These responses include changes in endocrine secretions as well as manifestations of disease and pathology. To the best of my knowledge, no human studies have been conducted to test whether this particular phenomenon applies in humans, but there seems no a priori reason to suspect that it does not. The second category that needs to be taken into consideration, and one in which there is both human as well as animal evidence, revolves around the degree to which the exposed populations have or have not been prepared by previous experience for the demands and expectations of the new situations. In other words, the general formulation needs to be modified by invoking the concept of the adaptability of the biological organisms. As has already been indicated, Kessler's work indicated that those cohorts of mice born and reared in a situation of extreme population density, did not display the same reactions as did their progenitors to whom this was a newer and less familiar set of experiences. As applied to humans, the extraordinary regularity with which various diseases have waxed and then waned as populations have become exposed and presumably adapted to urban living and the accompanying industrialization could well be taken as evidence supporting this point of view. The rise and fall of tuberculosis following industrialization, for example, has already been mentioned. As tuberculosis began to decline, it was replaced as a central health problem, in both Britain and the United States, by major malnutrition syndromes. In Britain, rickets was the scourge; in the United States, pellagra. These disorders, in turn, reached a peak and declined for reasons that are only partly understood and were themselves replaced by some of the diseases of early childhood. These, too, waxed and then waned largely, but not entirely, under the influence of the improvements in the sanitary environment and through the introduction of immunization programs, to be replaced between the World Wars by an extraordinary increase in the rate of duodenal ulcer, particularly in young men. This phenomenon, while more marked in Britain, occurred in the United States as well, and in both countries, for totally unknown reasons, the rates have declined in a dramatic fashion. Duodenal ulcer has now been replaced by our modern epidemics of coronary heart disease, hypertension, cancer, arthritis, diabetes, mental disorders, and the like. There is some evidence now that some of these disorders have reached a peak and at least in some segments of the population are declining. Death rates for hypertensive heart disease, for example, apparently have been declining in the United States since about 1940 to 1950, that is, before the introduction of anti-hypertensive drugs (39). Furthermore, there is some evidence in both Britain and the United States that the social class distribution of many of the "modern" diseases is changing. While 30 years ago coronary heart disease, for example, was more prevalent in Britain among the upper social classes, today there is almost no class difference. This change has occurred coincidentally with the increased length of exposure of the upper social classes to urban twentieth-century ways of living and with the more recent involvement in these ways of living of many of the lower social classes who have been the migrants from rural to urban situations.

Some more direct evidence for this formulation also exists. Hinkle and his co-workers (40) found marked differences in disease prevalence in a group of managers who had completed college as opposed to those doing the same job for the same pay in the same company but who had not completed college prior to coming to the industry. Those who had completed college were, with few exceptions, fourth generation Americans; sons of managers, proprietors, and white-collar workers and had grown up in families in middle to high income groups in good neighborhoods. In contrast, the group who had not completed college were hired as skilled craftsmen and later advanced to managerial status. They were sons and grandsons of immigrants, their fathers were skilled or unskilled laborers with an average of grammar school education or less, and they had grown up in families of low income in modest to sub-standard neighborhoods. This latter group (presumably the less well prepared group for the demands and expectations of managerial status) shared a significantly greater number of illnesses of all sorts than did the former group. The findings of a study by Cassel and Tyroler (41) lead to similar conclusions. They studied two groups of rural mountaineers; one of which was composed of individuals who were the first of their family ever to engage in industrial work, while the second comprised workers in the same factory, drawn from the same mountain coves, of the same age, and doing the same work for the same wages as the first group, but differing from the first group in that they were children of previous workers in this factory. This study was undertaken to test the hypothesis that the second group, that is the sons of previous factory workers, by virtue of their prior familial experience, would be better prepared for the expectations and demands of industrial living than would the first group, and would thus exhibit fewer signs of ill health. Health status was measured by responses to the Cornell Medical Index and by various indices of sick absenteeism. As predicted, the sons of previous factory workers had lower Cornell Medical Index scores (fewer symptoms) and lower rates of sick absenteeism after the initial few years of service, at each age than had the "first generation" workers. Perhaps even more convincing was the study conducted by Haenszel and his associates (42) on death rates from lung cancer in the U.S. These investigators discovered that death rates from lung cancer, when controlled for degree of cigarette smoking, were considerably higher in the farm-born who had migrated to cities than they were in lifetime urban dwellers. The study initially had been designed in an attempt to quantify the importance of length of exposure to atmospheric pollution of the cities, but despite the lifetime of exposure, urban livers had apparently "adapted" better to the effects of such atmospheric pollution than had the migrants.

A further concept that has to be taken into account in developing a useful formulation is the strong possibility that, under certain circumstances, group membership can exert a protective influence on the individual. Holmes (7) in his studies on tuberculosis in Seattle, for example, has shown that the disease occurs most frequently in "marginal" people; that is, in those individuals deprived of meaningful social contact. He found higher rates of tuberculosis in those ethnic groups who were distinct minorities in the neighborhoods in which they lived, in people living alone in one room, in those who had had multiple occupational and residential moves, and who were more often single or divorced than was true of the general population. Similar findings have been found in respect to schizophrenia, accidents, suicide, and other respiratory diseases (43–47). One of the concomitants of increasing population density, particularly when associated with increasing urbanization, is the atomization of those groups which in rural folk societies provide emotional support and thus presumably some degree of protection for the individual. While, in the course of time, new types of groups develop to fulfill some of the functions originally played by the family and kin group, it is often difficult, particularly for the newcomer to such scenes, to become effectively integrated into such groups.

Finally, given the importance of the social environment under conditions of increasing population density and crowding, the question of specificity has to be raised. Is it to be anticipated that the social processes (both positive and negative) inherent in group membership and position within the group, particularly under conditions of populations newly experiencing growth and crowding, are likely to result in specific disease syndromes or merely to increase general susceptibility to illness? This question is the subject of considerable controversy at the moment, and both points of view have been hotly argued. In a penetrating review on the subject, Thurlow (48) indicates that the argument centers around the question of whether certain stimuli, particularly those of a social and psychological nature, operate in a non-specific fashion increasing general susceptibility to all illnesses, or whether such stimuli merely increase the predilection for illness reporting and illness behavior. A further point of view holds that the non-specific effect of social processes is but a reflection of our ignorance and that with further study more specific "agents" will be discovered for which these social processes can be visualized as "vehicles." These agents, it is held, will be related to some specific disease entity. Most of these arguments are based upon the supposition that social and emotional processes are the direct initiators of disease conditions through the activation of inappropriate neuro-endocrine arousal mechanisms. While this may undoubtedly be a useful formulation, the animal work quoted above would seem to indicate that a more likely role of the social factors is to increase the susceptibility of the organism to other disease-producing agents, that is, to act in an indirect fashion in the etiology of any disease syndrome or pattern. This formulation then would clearly indicate that the health consequences of such social processes are likely to be non-specific. The manifestations of specific disease syndromes thus will be dependent not upon the nature of the social processes but upon the presence or absence of other disease-producing agents of a biological or a physico-chemical nature, as well as the constitution, both genetic and experiential of the individuals exposed to such situations. Thus it would not seem unreasonable to postulate that individuals deprived of meaningful group membership, exposed to ambiguous and conflicting demands for which they have had no previous experience, and frustrated insofar as their goals and aspirations are concerned, who are exposed to the tubercle bacillus, may well be victims of tuberculosis. Similar individuals, not so exposed to the tubercle bacillus but who from childhood have lived on a high saturated fatty acid diet, who tend to be sedentary and heavy cigarette smokers, may well be victims of myocardial infarction. The point being made is that if the circumstances under which population density and crowding are deleterious to health are to be elucidated, it would seem important that we recognize the limitations of the existing classificatory schemes used to identify disease entities. These schemes, to a large extent, have been developed because of their usefulness for therapeutic purposes, and the possibility needs to be raised that they may not be the best methods for classifying disease outcome for purposes of identifying the factors responsible for genesis.

Conclusions

On the basis of these findings and the theories that emerge from them a number of predictions or "working hypotheses" concerning the health consequences of future population growth and crowding can tentatively be advanced.

It can be anticipated that in most developing countries rapid population growth, particularly if associated with a deterioration in housing and nutritional status will, in all likelihood, be accompanied initially by increased death and disease rates. This increased health burden will be greatest on those segments of the population who have had least previous experience with living in crowded conditions. Over a period of some decades the diseases responsible for these high death and morbidity rates will probably decline, and while this will result in an improvement in the overall disease rates, "new" diseases will replace the old, requiring a major change in the nature and format of the health services. While the diseases responsible for the initial rise in rates are likely to be acute infectious diseases and diseases associated with under and malnutrition, the later diseases are more likely to be chronic long-term disorders. Even though the rate for these disorders will be lower than for the acute diseases, the disability resulting from them will pose as great a strain on the national economy as did the high rates of the earlier diseases.

The more rapid the rate of population growth and the more it is accompanied by disruption of important social groups, the more dramatic will these effects be. The rate of population growth and the ensuing crowding will largely determine the ability of the population to adapt successfully to the new situation, and the degree to which new types of social groups can develop to fulfill the function originally played by the family and kin group will in large part determine how deleterious such changes are.

While the changing disease patterns described above are likely to occur in all developing countries undergoing rapid population growth, the *specific* diseases constituting this pattern are likely to vary. The particular diseases which will be most prevalent will depend not so much on the degree and rate of crowding as on the constitution (both genetic and experiential) of the population and the nature of physical and biological agents to which the population is, or has been, exposed.

Finally, if the harmful effects on health of crowding are to be prevented and an orderly and healthful rate of population growth to be planned, the processes through which crowding is related to health need to be understood better than they are today. As indicated in this selection the relatively simplistic notion that crowding exerts its deleterious effects solely through facilitating the inter-personal spread of disease agents is no longer adequate to explain the known phenomena. A more appropriate formulation would seem feasible if we recognize that increased population density increases the importance of the social environment as a determinant of physiological response to various stimuli, including potentially disease-producing agents; that within this social environment the quality of social interactions and position within the group seem to be important factors; and that adaptation to these social changes can and does occur given time, but that the newcomers to the situation will always be the segment of the population at highest risk.

REFERENCES

1. Taylor, Ian and John Knowleden, *Principles of Epidemiology*, Little, Brown, and Co., Boston, 1957, p. 199.
2. *Ibid.*, p. 199.

3. Dubos, René, "The Human Environment in Technological Societies." *The Rockefeller Review*, July–August, 1968.

4. From The Registrar General's Decennial Supplement England and Wales 1961, Area Mortality Tables, H. M. S. O., London, 1967.

5. Grigg, E. R. N., "The Arcana of Tuberculosis." *Am. Rev. TB.*, 78, 1958, 151–172, 426–453, 583–603.

6. Brett, G. Z. and B. Benjamin, "Housing and Tuberculosis in a Mass Radiography Survey." *British Journal of Preventive and Social Medicine*, Vol. 11, No. 1, January, 1957, p. 7.

7. Holmes, Thomas H., "Multidiscipline Studies of Tuberculosis." In *Personality Stress and Tuberculosis*, Phineas J. Sparer ed., International Univ. Press, N.Y., 1956.

8. Stewart, G. T. and A. W. Voors, "Determinants of Sickness in Marine Recruits." *American Journal of Epidemiology*, Vol. 89, No. 3, May 14, 1968, pp. 254–263.

9. Kessler, Alexander, Doctoral Dissertation, "Interplay between Social Ecology and Physiology, Genetics, and Population Dynamics."

10. Dubos, René, *Man Adapting*. Yale University Press, New Haven, 1965, pp. 164–165.

11. Welch, Bruce L., "Psychophysiological Response to the Mean Level of Environmental Stimulation: A Theory of Environmental Integration." In *Symposium on Medical Aspects of Stress in the Military Climate*, Walter Reed Army Institute of Research, April, 1964.

12. Scotch, Norman A. and H. Jack Geiger, "The Epidemiology of Essential Hypertension II. Psychologic and Sociocultural Factors in Etiology." *J. Chron. Dis.*, 16, 1963, 1183–1213.

13. Kilborn, L. G., "A Note on the Blood Pressure of Primitive Races with Special Reference to the Maio of Kiweichaw." *Chinese J. Physiol.*, 11, 1937, 135.

14. Krakower, A., "Blood Pressure of Chinese Living in Eastern Canada." *Am. Heart J.*, 9, 1933, 376.

15. Kean, B. H., "Blood Pressure Studies on West Indians and Panamanians Living on Isthmus of Panama." *Arch. Int. Med.*, 68, 1941, 466.

16. Saunders, G. M., "Blood Pressure in Yucatans." *Am. J. Med. Sci.*, 185, 1933, 843.

17. Kean, B. H., "Blood Pressure of the Cuna Indians." *Am. J. Trop. Med.*, 24, 1944 (Suppl), 341.

18. Levine, V. E., "The Blood Pressure of Eskimos." *Fed. Proc.*, 1, 1942, 121.

19. Alexander, F., "A Medical Survey of the Aleutian Islands." *New England J. Med.*, 240, 1949, 1035.

20. Fulmer, H. S. and R. W. Roberts, "Coronary Heart Disease Among the Navajo Indians." *Ann. Int. Med.*, 59, 1963, 740–764.

21. Fleming, H. C., "Medical Observations on the Zuni Indians." *Contribution to Museum of American Indians*, Heye Foundation, 7, No. 2, New York, 1924.

22. Kaminer, B. and W. P. Lutz, "Blood Pressure in Bushmen of the Kalahari Desert." *Circulation*, 22, 1960, 289.

23. Donninson, C. P., "Blood Pressure in the African Native." *Lancet*, 1, 1929, 56.

24. Mann, G. V., *et al.*, "Cardiovascular Disease in the Masai." *J. Atherosclerosis Res.*, 4, 1964, 289.

25. Abrahams, D. G., C. A. Able, and G. Bernart, "Systemic Blood Pressure in a Rural West African Community." *W. Afr. Med. J.*, 9, 1960, 45.

26. Scotch, N. A., "A Preliminary Report on the Relation of Sociocultural Factors to Hypertension Among the Zulu." *Ann. New York Acad. Sci.*, 86, 1960, 1000.

27. Scotch, N. A., "Sociocultural Factors in the Epidemiology of Zulu Hypertension." *Am. J. Pub. Health*, 52, 1963, 1205–1213.

28. Bibile, S. W., *et al.*, "Variation with Age and Sex of Blood Pressure and Pulse Rate for Ceylonese Subjects." *Ceylon J. Med. Sci.*, 6, 1949, 80.

29. Padmayati, S. and S. Gupta, "Blood Pressure Studies in Rural and Urban Groups in Delhi." *Circulation*, 19, 1959, 395.

30. Lowell, R. R. H., I. Maddocks, and G. W. Rogerson, "The Casual Arterial Pressure of Fejians and Indians in Fiji." *Australasian Annals of Med.*, *9*, 1960, 4.

31. Murphy, W., "Some Observations on Blood Pressures in the Humid Tropics." *N. Zealand Med. J.*, *54*, 1955, 64.

32. Murril, R. I., "A Blood Pressure Study of the Natives of Ponape Island." *Human Biology*, *21*, 1949, 47.

33. Maddocks, I., "Possible Absence of Hypertension in Two Complete Pacific Island Populations." *Lancet*, *2*, 1961, 396.

34. Whyte, W. M., "Body Fat and Blood Pressure of Natives of New Guinea: Reflections on Essential Hypertension." *Australasian Annals Med.*, *7*, 1958, 36.

35. Cruz-Coke, R., R. Etcheverry, and R. Nagel, "Influence of Migration on Blood Pressure of Easter Islanders." *Lancet*, *1*, 1964, 697–699.

36. Hoobler, S. W., G. Tejada, M. Guzman, *et al.*, "Influence of Nutrition and 'Acculturation' on the Blood Pressure Levels and Changes with Age in the Highland Guatamalan Indian." *Circulation*, *32*, 1965, 4.

37. Lowenstein, F. W., "Blood Pressure in Relation to Age and Sex in the Tropics and Subtropics: A Review of the Literature and an Investigation in Two Tribes of Brazil Indians." *Lancet*, *1*, 1961, 389.

38. Mason, John W., "Psychoendocrine Approaches in Stress Research." *Medical Aspects of Stress in the Military Climate*, U.S. Government Printing Office, Washington, 1965.

39. Paffenberger, Ralph S., Jr., Robert N. Milling, Norman D. Poe, *et al.*, "Trends in Death Rates from Hypertensive Disease in Memphis, Tennessee 1920–1960." *J. Chron. Dis.*, *19*, 1966, 847–856.

40. Christenson, William N. and Lawrence E. Hinkle, Jr., "Differences in Illness and Prognostic Signs in Two Groups of Young Men." *J.A.M.A.*, *177*, 1961, 247–253.

41. Cassel, John and H. A. Tyroler, "Epidemiological Studies of Culture Change I. Health Status and Recency of Industrialization." *Arch. Envir. Health*, *3*, 1961, 25.

42. Haenszel, William, Donald B. Loveland, and Monroe G. Sirken, "Lung-Cancer Mortality as Related to Residence and Smoking Histories." *J. Nat. Cancer Inst.*, *28*, 1962, 947–1001.

43. Dunham, H. Warren, "Social Structures and Mental Disorders: Competing Hypotheses of Explanation." *Milbank Mem. Fund Quart.*, *39*, 1961, 259–310.

44. Mishler, Elliot G. and Norman A. Scotch, "Sociocultural Factors in the Epidemiology of Schizophrenia: A Review." *Psychiatry*, *26*, 1963, 315–351.

45. Tillman, W. A. and G. E. Hobbs, "Social Background of Accident Free and Accident Repeaters." *Am. J. Psychiat.*, *106*, 1949, 321.

46. Durkheim, Emile, *Suicide*. The Free Press, Glencoe, Ill., 1957.

47. Holmes, Thomas H., Personal Communication.

48. Thurlow, H. John, "General Susceptibility to Illness: A Selective Review." *Canadian Med. Ass. J.*, *97*, 1967, 1–8.

PART FOUR
The Social Meaning of Architecture

17

Images of Urban Areas:
Their Structure
and Psychological Foundations

DERK DE JONGE

It is evident from the intensity with which people react to architecture that an examination of the utilitarian features of architecture and the influence of these features on social interaction or health does not by any means exhaust the range of architectural properties relevant to man and society. The kind of joy, agony, frustration, pleasure, and ideological commitment that so often characterizes the human reaction to the environment would hardly develop if a building were only a bundle of heat, light, and humidity conditions; a communications network; or an implied level of population density. A building is also a specific three-dimensional form, a set of decorative elements including color and materials, and an interior space possessing particular qualities of enclosure. Those who hold strong views about architecture, and the number who do is far greater than the number of architects and design professionals, usually are reacting to these features of a building as well as to its operational virtues or disadvantages.

The architectural tradition, of course, has long emphasized the formal, stylistic, esthetic, and architectonic dimensions of buildings, and most architectural criticism has explored the origins and significance of these design qualities. Until recently the discussion of the ontological status of the non-utilitarian features of architecture, their source in the nature of man, and the processes through which they work their effect on society has been conducted without much assistance from the social sciences. The selection by de Jonge, and the others in Part Four, are illustrative of the emerging sociological, anthropological, and psychological literature that attempts to relate behavioral studies to some of these classical interests of designers.

De Jonge's principal concern is with what one might call the "reality" of urban form and the relevance of urban form to behavior in space. Is there a procedure for describing an environment in such a way that independent observers will agree about its visual organization? Will urban settlements that are eligible or imageable be easier for city residents to navigate?

Reprinted from Derk de Jonge, "Images of Urban Areas: Their Structure and Psychological Foundations," *Journal of the American Institute of Planners* 28, no. 4 (November 1962): 266–276. Reprinted by permission of the Journal of the American Institute of Planners.

De Jonge is interested in the problem of form independent of judgments of its beauty; also, an important part of his goal was to test the usefulness of the conceptual model for describing the properties of urban form first developed by Kevin Lynch. This kind of research is important because it confronts the accusation often leveled against the design tradition that judgments about the formal coherence of the environment are highly subjective and do not correspond to a reality that can be understood by the public.

The study reported by de Jonge was conducted in Holland. He examined urban form in the central areas of Amsterdam, Rotterdam, and the Hague, as well as in two neighborhoods in Delft. Following Lynch, the degree of order and regularity in the form of each settlement was first analyzed in terms of five design features: paths, nodes, landmarks, districts, and edges. Two groups of people were then asked about their perceptions of the environment: about twenty urban design and planning professionals, who were selected to represent the judgments of trained experts on design matters, and a sample of about 100 lay people, mostly wives of skilled workers and white collar employees. Information about their perceptions was obtained by asking the respondents to draw a map of the area. They were also interviewed to determine their spatial orientation and to learn how easy they found it to move through the area.

According to de Jonge, there was a high degree of consensus in the perceptions and judgments of the design professionals and the public. In general the imageability of urban form, as represented by the map drawings, was stronger where the street plan had a regular pattern, and where, as in central Amsterdam, there was a single dominant path or route running through the settlement and outstanding landmarks. In areas in which, according to the method of analysis developed by Lynch, the basic form was not highly legible, more attention was given in the maps to isolated landmarks. De Jonge also suggests that spatial orientation was easier in the more imageable settlements and in the neighborhoods in which the environment was not visually monotonous.

□

The ideal of city planning is the arrangement of human artifacts in urban space to ensure optimum conditions for the development of social life and human happiness. We can achieve this object only to a limited extent, as we do not have sufficient knowledge of the means to attain this goal. But we may assume that one of the conditions for an effective use of urban space is that residents and visitors should be able to find their way about with ease, or at least without a great effort.

A fascinating study of the images of a city that exist in people's minds, and which enable them to orient themselves in urban areas has been made by Kevin Lynch.[1] He has found that people consistently use and organize sensory clues from the environment, relying on a selection of impressions to simplify the over-all structure. One urban environment lends itself better to this process than another. A city is most likely to evoke a strong image in any given observer if it can be apprehended as a pattern of high continuity, with a number of distinctive parts clearly interconnected. Lynch has called this quality "imageability."

In order to test the idea of imageability, he made analyses of the central areas of Boston, Jersey City, and Los Angeles. A systematic field reconnaissance of each area, made by a trained observer, was compared with the images of a small sample of residents. In a lengthy interview, each informant was requested to give descriptions, indicate locations, and make sketches of the area in question. He was also asked to perform a number of imaginary trips. Lynch found there were distinct differences in the imageability of the three cities studied and that the images were generally composed of five kinds of elements: path, nodes, landmarks, districts, and edges. If a city is to have a satisfying form, these elements must be patterned together in a legible structure. Paths may form a network (a grid, for example) in which repetition makes relationships sufficiently regular and predictable. It is also necessary that the parts have "identity"—that is, those qualities by which one object can be distinguished from another and recognized as a separate entity.

The work of Lynch has rightly been called "one of the most important contributions to large-scale design theory." [2] It has further been pointed out that the sample of informants was too small and too specialized to allow generalization of the findings. This will be possible only after further systematic empirical study, for which the methods and concepts contributed by Lynch's pioneer research can serve as starting-points.

The Scope of This Inquiry

The following account describes an attempt to make a contribution in this field. The purpose of this piece of research was to find answers to the following questions:

a. Can the research methods and techniques developed by Lynch be used, in a simplified form, for studies that are less elaborate, but that can cover a wider variety of urban areas and of informants?

b. If this is so, are the conclusions formulated by Lynch about the formation and nature of city images confirmed by such studies, and can any further relations be established between "urban form" and "city image"?

c. At what level can the results be generalized?

This investigation was made at the Housing and City Planning Research Section in the Department of Architecture of the Technical University of Delft (Holland).

In the first phase of the inquiry some twenty staff members of the Department of Architecture in Delft were interviewed to see what their images were of the central areas of Amsterdam, Rotterdam, The Hague, Utrecht, Leyden, and Delft. The structures of these cities are entirely different from those of the American cities studied by Lynch; further, there are also considerable variations in pattern from one Dutch city to another. The character of these central areas has been determined largely by topographic and historic factors. In Rotterdam, however, there was extensive reconstruction on more modern lines after the large-scale destruction during the last war.

In the second phase the investigation was extended to about one hundred people, selected at random, living in a number of urban residential neighborhoods in South Holland. In each area twenty to forty people, predominantly wives of skilled workers and white-collar employees, were interviewed. For most of the areas studied, the images of a number of laymen were compared with those of the professional city planners working in Delft; in some cases, further comparisons were made with maps drawn by professionals in other fields. For the downtown areas, a systematic comparison of the cities was made both for each individual informant and for all the informants together.

The main questions asked were:

1. *To what extent are you familiar with this area?*

2. *Will you draw a rough map of the area such as you imagine it for yourself? Can you also indicate the boundaries of the area?*

3. *What are, in your opinion, the most striking elements and buildings in this area?*

4. *Are there any places, here or elsewhere, where you find orientation difficult?*

In recording the statements of the informants, attention was given to the order of the elements in the sketch maps, remarks as to ease or difficulty in orientation, and the relation of the imaged area to the surrounding parts of the city. Each interview took about a quarter of an hour to half an hour.

The planners were asked to approach the subject in a non-technical way—to think of the everyday use they make of the area, rather than of their professional views. Under these conditions, their reactions did not differ significantly from those of other people of the same educational level. Many housewives, however, found it difficult, if not impossible, to draw sketch maps of their neighborhood. In these cases, the interview was focused on routes and problems of orientation, without direct reference to maps.

In the registration and presentation of the map images a technique was adopted that is somewhat different from the one used by Lynch. In comparing the map images of his subjects and of trained observers, Lynch transferred elements from sketch maps to accurate base maps. Thus the objective structure of urban space (represented on his base maps) as well as the subjective perception of this structure entered into the picture. To a certain extent, subjective and objective data were mixed on every map.

As a social scientist, I have first of all aimed at studying the relations between objective data (rendered on accurate maps and recorded by means of aerial photos) and subjective images (appearing in the form of sketch maps). I have kept the two kinds of maps apart, so that they are given in "pure" form. Thus, any resemblance between an accurate map (or aerial photo) and the image map will be inherent in them, and not a result of the method of recording or presentation. The sketch maps chosen for illustration here are typical ones, showing features which appear on most of the sketches of a particular area.

Results

The reactions of the informants showed a high degree of uniformity and consistency so far as the main points of image formation and image structure were concerned. In general, the quality of the sketch maps produced paralleled orientation in the field. Where most people had difficulties in sketching a rough map of an area, orientation was also difficult, for casual visitors if not for residents. Where people generally found it easy to draw a sketch map that was both simple and adequate, orientation was also easy, provided that the identity of the separate elements of the area was clear enough.

On the whole the methods and techniques described by Lynch were found to be useful instruments for the investigation of people's images of urban areas. This is also true if they are simplified for use in extensive investigations, including the comparison of several urban areas and their respective images. So the question formulated under (a) can be answered in the affirmative. Additional data must be presented in order to answer the questions posed under (b) and (c). In doing this I shall focus on the most interesting areas: Amsterdam, Rotterdam, The Hague, and three residential neighborhoods.

Amsterdam

Objective Structure. Three key elements in the structure of the old town are closely related to the river: the Mint Square, the Dam, and the Central Station. The Mint Square, with its notable Mint Tower, is located where the river first enters the ancient city. Where the mouth of the Amstel used to be, the Central Station has been built on an artificial island in the estuary. Midway between the Mint Square and the Central Station is the Dam, a great square that marks the site of the original dam on the river, and is now the location of the Royal Palace. As a public meeting place for important occasions, the Dam has a national and civic importance comparable to that of Trafalgar Square in London. Two parallel streets connect the Mint Square to the Central Station, passing through the Dam at mid-point. One is a major traffic route, called Damrak on one side of the Dam, Rokin on the other. The other route is a narrow shopping street called Nieuwendijk north of the Dam and Kalverstraat to the south.

Around this old linear core, the city laid out a major extension in the seventeenth century. Its dominant element consists of three major concentric canals, which, together with a number of radial streets and canals, form a spider web pattern. The major canals are further distinguished by rows of impressive homes built by prosperous merchants in the seventeenth century. A large number of the one-time patricians' homes are now used as offices, but there are still many artists and bohemians whose ideal is to live in an old house along one of the fine old canals. The present-day central shopping area of Amsterdam is situated partly within the old linear city and partly along some of the radial streets intersecting the belt of canals.

General Characteristics of the Image. As Lynch had conjectured, the map structure of Amsterdam produces a very strong image. Every informant indicates as the central path the main route along the river bank from the Central Station via the Dam Square to the Mint. This route is visualized as an axis placed in the middle of a series of concentric semi-circles, representing the major canals. The shopping streets (Nieuwendijk and Kalverstraat) form a secondary element accompanying the main route, although in fact this narrow path, with its attractive shop windows, is the route that most people take when they walk. The Central Station Square, the Dam Square, and the Mint are seen as

Figure 17-1   Photograph and Sketch Maps of Amsterdam.

A. Amstel River   D. Central Station (just above edge)
B. Mint Square   E. Damrak
C. Dam   F. Rokin

(Air photo by K.L.M. Aerocarto N.V.—archief Topografische Dienst.)

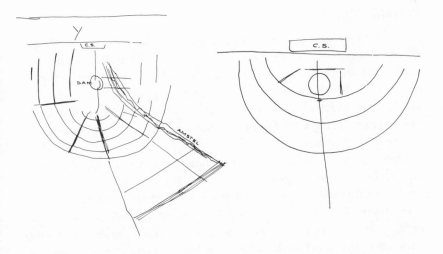

nodes marked by unique landmarks (the railroad station, the Royal Palace and the Mint Tower respectively).

Irregularities in the actual plan are smoothed out in the image. The central main route is seen as a straight line, although in reality there are some bends. The semi-circles of the image are more abstract than the spiderweb of the actual plan. This simplified pattern is accurate enough for general orientation. Since the main structure of the city is essentially regular, minor irregularities are not troublesome.

It should be noted that the bends in the major canals can be seen from any point along them. This feature gives a sense of direction, since the city center is on the inner side of the curve. The spiderweb structure also gives great prominence to the most central spaces: the Central Station and the Dam, either of which can be regarded as the center of the semi-circle. Further, the series of canals makes the whole central area of Amsterdam stand out clearly from the surrounding nineteenth-century neighborhoods.

The strong predominance of the main elements in the spatial structure should also be noted: informants give comparatively little attention to separate buildings. At the same time, many elements have a clear identity, so that there is no tedious repetition. The main difficulty for strangers seems to be in distinguishing the three major canals from one another. According to the police, people sometimes think their parked car has been stolen because they have returned to the wrong canal.

Rotterdam

Objective Structure. The ancient city took the form of a triangle, situated on a bend in the river Meuse (Maas). What is now the wide Coolsingel artery was once a canal at the western boundary of the old city. Gradually the central business and shopping district has been shifting westward—a process accelerated by the postwar reconstruction that was necessary after the devastation of much of the center by the bombardment of 1940.

Those elements of the city whose function is most central are now largely located near the Coolsingel, and the Central Station is even farther to the west. Thus the situation is quite different from that in Amsterdam. The triangle of the old city is intersected by an elevated railway. The Central Station is near a second traffic artery, the Weena, which runs at a right angle to the Coolsingel. The two arteries come together at the Hofplein traffic circle.

278

Figure 17–2   Photograph and Sketch Map of Central Rotterdam.

A. Hofplein Traffic Circle   D. Weena
B. Coolsingel   E. Central Station
C. Lijnbaan Shopping Mall

(Air photo by K.L.M. Aerocarto N.V.—archief Topografische Dienst.)

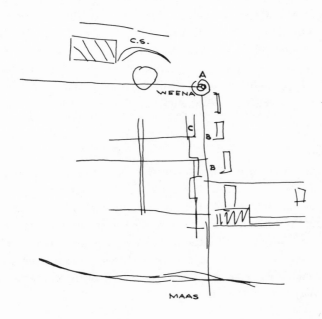

Hardly any old houses or other buildings that were worthwhile from an aesthetic or historic point of view have survived the blitz and the reconstruction. The Coolsingel is characterized by a great number of big, modern buildings (including Breuer's Bijenkorf Department Store) along this wide artery. A new shopping mall, the Lijnbaan, runs partly parallel and partly at right angles to the Coolsingel. Large scale building activities are constantly going on in the center of Rotterdam, such as the construction of new buildings and a tunnel works for the new subway.

The Image. Those informants who have the clearest image visualize this central area as an L-shaped configuration of the Weena and Coolsingel–plus–Lijnbaan. The link between these two parts of the L is the Hofplein node, with its characteristic form and its fountains. The Coolsingel is the major path mentioned by about 90 per cent of the informants. The Lijnbaan is indicated on the sketch maps by approximately the same number. Eighty per cent draw the Central Station, 70 per cent indicate the Weena as a major path, and 60 per cent show the Hofplein node.

Most informants have no clear picture of the boundaries between the central area and surrounding parts of the city. Thus in five sketches the elevated railway is indicated as the edge of the central area, while in five others it is there, but not as a boundary line. There is also a lack of clarity in the relation of the central area to other elements, such as the harbor and the district on the other side of the elevated railroad.

Individual buildings and other objects are mentioned to a greater extent than in Amsterdam. This may be due in part to the fact that buildings are more widely separated in Rotterdam, so that each of them is seen more clearly at some distance. But the fact that the over-all image of Rotterdam is weaker than that of Amsterdam may also explain why more attention is given to elements.

The Hague

Objective Structure. The plan of the central area developed largely in the Middle Ages. Here is the ancient Binnenhof (Earl's Court) in which the Parliament buildings and a number of ministries are located. Adjoining the Binnenhof are some squares and a large rectangular lake. West of the Binnenhof lies the main shopping area. Within this chessboard structure there are a number of irregularities, such as discontinuities in paths near the lake, and a curious bend in the Hofweg (Court Way) round the Binnenhof.

Figure 17–3   Photograph and Sketch Map of Earl's Court and Surroundings, The Hague.

A. Earl's Court (Binnenhof)   D. Grote Marktstraat
B. Lake   E. Lange Voorhoot
C. Hofweg

(Air photo by K.L.M. Aerocarto N.V.—archief Topografische Dienst.)

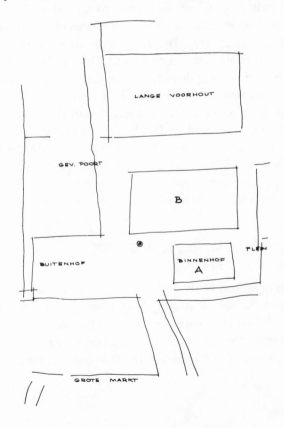

It should be noted that the general spatial structure of The Hague, a roughly rectangular grid parallel to the North Sea coast line, is different from that of most cities in the west of the Netherlands. The Hague traditionally lacked independent status, and the city has never been strongly fortified. In most other Dutch cities, fortifications have promoted a more concentric structure. According to an old saying, The Hague is "the finest village of Europe," and this phrase is still used jocularly to distinguish The Hague from Amsterdam and Rotterdam.

The Image. The method of composing most sketch maps of The Hague differs fundamentally from the methods used for the other two cities. In Amsterdam and Rotterdam, the paths and nodes that are important for transportation tend to be the primary elements of the pattern. In The Hague the dominant element is the Court with the adjoining lake. These two objects are taken as the starting-point for the majority of the sketch maps, and then other nearby elements are placed in relation to them. In doing this, many people move outward in a spiral; but on the whole they do not go very far.

The old canals (*singels*) round the eighteenth-century city do not play any part in the images recorded. They seem to disappear into the chessboard pattern of which they form part. It should also be noted that in the field these canals are not at all conspicuous elements. On the other hand, the bend in the Hofweg path is sketched by eighteen out of nineteen informants drawing this route. This can be explained by the fact that here is a striking departure from the general structure, clearly visible at a point just before the central open space.

In The Hague there is no wide, straight, and clearly dominant path as in Amsterdam or Rotterdam. Hardly any landmarks can be seen from a distance. Yet, the number of separate elements and buildings that are mentioned, in addition to the main ones, is quite large.

Most people are very vague as to the extent of the city's central area, and almost none have definite ideas of its boundaries.

Comparison of the Images of Amsterdam, Rotterdam, and The Hague

From a comparison of these three cities it is apparent that Amsterdam produces the strongest and clearest image. This is because here we have an urban area with a unique spatial structure standing out from its environs as the result of a deliberate aesthetic creation. In Rotterdam some clarity is achieved by wide major paths and big buildings placed in large spaces, but there is less unity of structure than in Amsterdam. (See Table 17–1.)

Although the center of Amsterdam has many fine and interesting buildings and places, more separate elements are mentioned for Rotterdam, and still more for The Hague. Apparently people tend to concentrate more on details when the total structure is less clear.

For both Rotterdam and The Hague, about one-third of the informants state that they find the pattern (if any) more difficult to comprehend than that of Amsterdam, in spite of the fact that the majority live farther from Amsterdam than from the other two cities. In general the map image of The Hague is vaguer and less unified than that of Rotterdam. Almost no one has been able to relate the central area of The Hague to the over-all grid of this city in his sketch.

Amsterdam is loved by many people, both residents and strangers. There are many reasons for this love, but one among them may be the beautiful structure of the central area, with both a clear over-all pattern and many identifiable parts.

Two Residential Neighborhoods in Delft

Objective Structure. A comparative study was made of two residential neighborhoods built in Delft in recent years. One of them, the Bomenbuurt, has a very simple structure. It numbers about 635 dwellings on an area of 300 × 350 meters. There is a mixed development of rowhouses and apartment buildings of two or three stories. Generally, rowhouses have been built on one side of a street and an apartment block on the other. All the dwellings have concrete outer walls, and all have been built according to a new, non-traditional method.

The street pattern is a rectangular grid, with one diagonal line leading from the edge of the neighborhood to a community building and a small square with a few shops. Near this square there are also a number of semi-detached houses. This is a comparatively small area with a regular street plan, showing irregularity only near the core.

The Voordijkhoornsepolder is about twice as large (about 850 × 325 meters), and numbers some 1200 dwellings: one-family houses, apartments, maisonettes, and seven high-rise blocks, three of which had been completed when the study was made.

The street pattern is roughly rectangular, with a number of small deviations from the right angle and the straight line. A broad road, the van Foreestweg, divides the neighborhood into two halves. On this road are

TABLE 17-1

City Elements Included on Sketch Maps	Number of Informants Identifying Each Element
Amsterdam: *Total Number of Informants, 25*	
PATHS:	
Main Path, Central Station to Mint	22
Drawn as a Straight Line	15
Semi-Circle of Canals	20
Other Paths, Secondary	17
NODES:	
Central Station Square	18
Dam Square	17
Mint Circut	9
Other Nodes	10
Rotterdam: *Total Number of Informants, 22*	
PATHS:	
Coolsingel	19
Coolsingel plus Lijnbaan	18
Weena	15
Other Paths	24
NODES:	
Station Square	17
Hofplein	13
BUILDINGS:	
Town Hall	10
Wholesale Trade Building	6
Bijenkorf Department Store	6
Exchange	6
OTHER ELEMENTS:	7
The Hague: *Total Number of Informants, 25*	
PATHS:	
Hofweg	19
Bend Indicated in Sketch	18
Grote Markstraat	15
Spui	12
Kneuterdijk	11
Poten	9
OTHER ELEMENTS:	
Lake near Earl's Court	21
Earl's Court	19
Outer Court	15
All Others, Combined	60

some twenty-five shops, a small canal, and a sizeable square. There are some supermarkets that are used also by people from the adjacent parts of Delft. One large, central, green area is situated on both sides of the square, and within the neighborhood there are four other green spaces, with apartment blocks and houses around them. Thus each street is situated in a characteristic way in relation to the edge of the neighborhood, the center of the neighborhood, or one of the squares.

The Image. The interviews showed that in the Bomenbuurt visitors, and even some absent-minded residents, often took the wrong street in consequence of the great uniformity in layout and architecture. This was especially true of the central streets when approached from the north. From the southern entrance—the diagonal line along the shops—it was much easier to find the right street. When coming from the North, some people even relied on minor details, such as the window curtains of the apartments or houses. A succession of more than three similar elements seems to impede spontaneous recognition and consequent choice of the right street.

Thus, in the most monotonous part of the Bomenbuurt there was regularity of structure, but lack of identity of the parts. Informants also had a number of complaints about the uniform appearance of the housing blocks and the "ugly" appearance of the concrete outer walls.

In the Voordijkhoornsepolder the situation was quite different. As each street and each housing block had its own distinctive orientation and architecture, identity was established more or less automatically by residents and visitors. Here there were many fewer complaints of monotonous blocks or streets. Variety among the elements was greatly increased by the different types of dwellings and by the presence of open spaces of various dimensions.

This comparison demonstrates that present-day planning can avoid monotony even in modern housing developments, and create a pattern that makes orientation easy.

The Leeuwendaal Neighborhood

As an example of a difficult area to be oriented properly in, several informants mentioned the Leeuwendaal neighborhood in Rijswijk (a suburb of The Hague). This area was rebuilt about the turn of the century, and the street plan reveals *Art Nouveau* influences. The streets run mostly in gentle curves, the interrelations of which (if any) cannot be comprehended in the field.

Interviews with some thirty residents showed that many casual visitors lose their way, and that even people who have lived here for decades find it difficult to draw an adequate sketch map. The one reproduced here shows an attempt that failed. The curves of the longest streets that are basic to the total pattern were not imaged adequately; thus it became impossible to link them up correctly with other streets.

Most inhabitants were able to find their way in the area not because they comprehended the total pattern (which was too complicated for them to remember), but because they knew each path separately. Those who only visited the area occasionally knew just a few isolated routes, which is what one tends to do in an area where orientation is difficult.

Conclusions

The following conclusions can be drawn: Formation of a map image is easiest where there is a street plan with a regular pattern, and a single dominant path, characteristic nodes, and unique landmarks. Where the general pattern is not clear, a greater amount of attention is given to isolated landmarks, individual paths, and visual details.

People tend to imagine patterns that are almost regular as perfectly regular. There is a stereotyping of the perception and recollection of spatial relations. Circles, semi-circles, and right angles are very easy to imagine, while quarter-circles and minor bends tend to create difficulties in orientation and map image formation.

Orientation is difficult in areas with an irregular street pattern, consisting of paths with curves that are not clearly connected with each other in a readable configuration. However, difficulties may also arise where the structure is quite clear but the elements are too uniform to be distinguished from each other. It seems that identity is especially difficult to establish where there are more than three elements of the same appearance.

We have seen that there is some dislike for neighborhoods that are too monotonous. At the same time, an area where visitors have trouble orienting themselves may be popular with residents on account of its quaint and exclusive character or because of other attractive qualities. This view is further supported by the fact that there are in Holland a number of expensive villa parks with complicated road patterns (Wassenaar, Bloemendaal, and Zeist) that have long been popular with people in upper-income brackets.

On the whole, Lynch's conclusions about image formation and image structure are further confirmed by this material; and it has been shown how these principles work in a number of different urban areas.

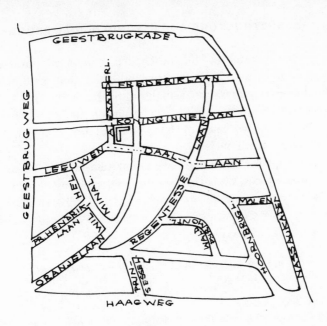

Figure 17–4   Leeuwendaal Neighborhood. (Sketch map appears below.)

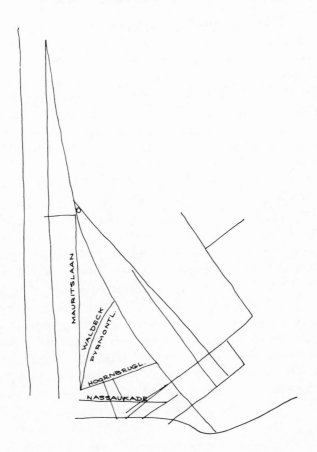

The fact that research in Holland has led to much the same conclusions as those of Lynch's is in itself an indication that his findings are not limited to the comparatively small sample he used. Further indications of the validity of the above conclusions on map image formation are to be found in two kinds of data: 1) orientation maps, and 2) the "laws" of Gestalt psychology.

1. Simple maps for rapid and easy orientation in given areas are issued by tourist offices, transit companies, and such institutions. In this connection, Lynch mentions the pocket map of subway lines of the London Transport Corporation. This map has also been commented upon by Arnheim, who says:

(It) gives the needed information with the utmost clarity and at the same time delights the eye through the harmony of its design. This is achieved by renouncing all geographic detail except for the pertinent topological properties—that is, sequence of stops and interconnections. All roads are reduced to straight lines; all angles to the two simplest: ninety degrees and forty-five degrees. The map leaves out and distorts a great deal, and just because of this it is the best possible picture of what it wants to show.[3]

Arnheim has also noted that more than three or four similar elements are "visually undistinguished."

The orientation maps show the same kind of selection of details and simplification of pattern as the sketch maps drawn by our informants. In addition, landmarks are often indicated on these maps in the form of small drawings showing the objects in perspective. Although most readers will remember such maps from their own experience, I add for purposes of illustration two maps of the island of Dordrecht. One is an ordinary topographical map; the other an orientation map issued by the municipal ferry service, which runs three ferries to the surrounding islands. This map shows the locations of the ferries, and of bridges, main roads, and railroads. The path structure has been simplified and landmarks are indicated in perspective.

2. A basic problem for Gestalt psychology has been to identify factors that organize the visual field into independent units. Many experiments have been made with figures composed of points and lines, in which subjects were asked to indicate what configurations they recognized. A number of conditions were thus found to play an important, if not exclusive, part in producing visual form: proximity, similarity, closed form, "good contour," common movement, and experience.[4] The perception of separate elements as one visual form is further promoted by such characteristics as regularity, symmetry, inclusiveness, harmony, maximal simplicity, and conciseness.

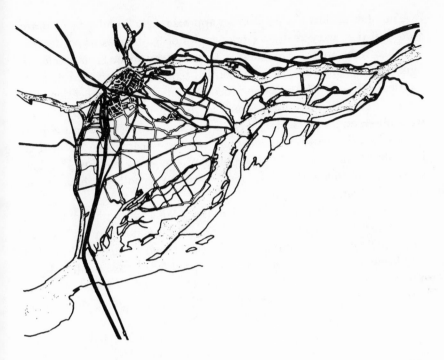

Figure 17–5 Maps of the Island of Dordrecht. (Orientation map, prepared by municipal ferry service, appears below.)

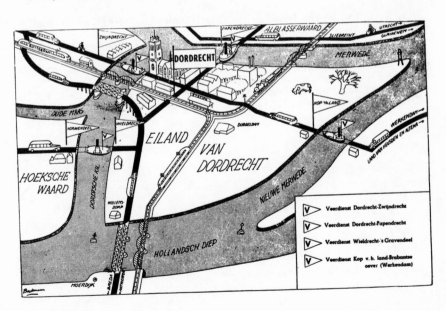

A number of dots arranged in an approximately circular fashion are seen as if they were really a circle, angles of 87 degrees or 93 degrees look like right angles. Drawings with gaps tend to be seen as closed, figures which are not quite symmetrical tend to be perceived as symmetrical. Thus, much the same process of selection, simplification, and predilection for "pure" forms (such as the right angle and the circle) were observed in the Gestalt experiments as were observed in the map images of urban areas studied here. So our research can be said to have shown that people's perceptions of the main pattern of urban space tend to follow the same "laws" Gestalt psychologists have found in their laboratory experiments.

We may therefore conclude that the results with regard to map images can be generalized, at any rate for literate man in Western society. Of course it still remains to be seen to what extent and in what way insight into image structure can be used to increase the liveability of cities and towns. This problem cannot be solved by social scientists alone; it calls for study by designers and social psychologists working jointly to investigate this important aspect of design.

NOTES

1. Kevin Lynch, *The Image of the City* (Cambridge, Mass.: The Technology Press and Harvard University Press, 1960).

2. David A. Crane, Review in *Journal of the American Institute of Planners*, 27 (May, 1961), 152.

3. Rudolph Arnheim, *Art and Visual Perception: A Psychology of the Creative Eye* (Berkeley: University of California Press, 1954), p. 123.

4. David Katz, *Gestalt Psychology, its Nature and Significance*, trans. Robert Tyson (London: Methuen, 1951), pp. 24–28 and 40–41.

18

Furniture Arrangement as a Symbol of Judicial Roles

JOHN N. HAZARD

In the previous selection, de Jonge discusses the degree of consensus in descriptions by the public of the form of urban areas and touches on the role of imageability in helping urban dwellers orient themselves while moving through urban space. The implication of this approach is that form acquires its social importance because of the way in which it is tied to the perceptual apparatus of the human organism. However, it is important to realize that form also acquires significance through its links to the cognitive faculties, which endow buildings with social meaning. Through its connection with the psychic structure of the organism, with the needs of the human personality for order and communication, and with the influence on personality of cultural experience, architecture is capable of serving as a symbol that can represent, reflect, and express values, group norms, and ideological beliefs. The passionate reactions to buildings of clients, designers, and users are apparently founded on this symbolic capacity of architecture rather than on its geometric or esthetic properties. It is not the building itself, therefore, but what the building seems to stand for that typically matters to people. Architects, of course, try to capitalize on architectural symbolism and claim proudly that their design constitutes a "statement"; designers like to say that architecture is a language, or that plans and forms can be "read" for their social meaning.

The symbolic content of architectural form is well illustrated in Hazard's discussion of what can be learned about the judicial systems of various nations simply by examining the furniture arrangements in their courtrooms. Among the formal properties he comments on are the respective locations of judges, juries, press, defendants, and prosecutors; the height of the chairs in which they are seated; and the spatial distance separating the actors in the courtroom. Hazard advises legal scholars that these architectural data offer an important clue to such questions in comparative law as the relative importance in a society of common and civil law traditions, the rights of the accused, and the nature of the hierarchical relationship between state authority and the populace.

Reprinted from John N. Hazard, "Furniture Arrangement as a Symbol of Judicial Roles," *ETC.: A Review of General Semantics* 19, no. 2 (July 1962): 181–188. Reprinted by permission of the International Society for General Semantics.

In view of the fact that Hazard is discussing those aspects of architectural form that were discussed in Part Two under the heading of Spatial Organization and Social Interaction, it should be emphasized that his selection does not deal with the actual behavioral effects of courtroom design or with the social or legal rationale for furniture arrangements. For example, each of the different arrangements presumably developed in an effort to dispense justice more equitably, but Hazard's selection does not attempt to evaluate the corresponding legal systems in terms of their fairness. Instead, he argues that the spatial organization of a courtroom is a sign system through which a society tries to communicate its ideal model of the relationship between judges, prosecutors, juries, and others involved in judicial proceedings. The aspect of form being considered here, in other words, is very similar to the concept so popular with architects of the building's "intention," the kind of social outcome it is supposed to achieve. However, just as in the case of the architect's intention, the determination of the quality of justice that is dispensed in a particular society with a particular form of courtroom remains an empirical question that must await further research.

□

Walk into an empty courtroom and look around. The furniture arrangement will tell you at a glance who has what authority. In nearly every country, judges now look down on their courtrooms from a raised platform, and when the bench is collegial, the presiding judge has a chair whose back protrudes several inches above the rest. This is so even in the Soviet Union where the judge has been elevated above his 1917 role when he was wise friend and conciliator to his village. Today, he sits with his colleagues even in the lowest court upon a platform rather than around a table with the parties. His dignity is enhanced not only by his elevated chair but by the attendant's cry, "All stand," as he and the lay assessors file into the room to take their places. Only a robe is missing to command respect. And in the People's Republic of Poland, after the "October" of 1956, even the robe was redraped on judicial shoulders, with its purple piping in traditional designation of the majesty of the law. The portrait of power was further enhanced at that time by encircling his neck with a great gold seal and chain of office in traditional Polish fashion.

The judge's commanding seat catches first attention, but the eye soon wanders to the other furniture. In a British or American courtroom, the jury box stands out to the right of the enclosure behind the "bar." Between it and the judge's bench on a raised platform somewhat lower than that of the judge stands the chair waiting for the witness, facing outward into the room so that all can hear, including the press for whom a gallery or at least a bench is often reserved to give meaning to the concept of "publicity" characteristic of the common law concept of "due process."

Compare the assize court in the canton of Geneva, and you will find the jury, but in a different place. It is in no box separated from the judge, but arranged on two rows of chairs to the judge's left behind the great semi-circular bench that extends the width of the room. One scarcely needs to be told that the judge retires with the jury in this Swiss canton, and that he shares with the jurymen the decision on guilt and punishment. At the eastern end of Europe there is no jury box at all, for the Soviet legal procedure relies on two lay assessors in every type of case, both criminal and civil, to share with the judge the decision on matters both of fact and law. This is so in all of the Eastern European states that have adopted the Soviet legal system, and has been accepted even in Communist China.

Witness stands in continental Europe traditionally face in toward the judge rather than out toward the courtroom. The assembled public sees only the back of the witness's head when he testifies and hears little of what he says unless he raises his voice. In Geneva the press is aided because the press bench is placed along the right hand wall below the great semi-circular bench of judge and jury but forward of the public's seats. Reporters may hear and see everything and perform their critical democratic function of informing the wider public of what transpires. In the Eastern European courtrooms there are no special press galleries, unless the defendant happens to be an American U-2 pilot and the affair a cause célèbre. Soviet concepts of "due process" require no participation of a press independent of the state and prepared to sound the tocsin if injustice is done. If the press is present, it is because the court has a case with a public message which the judges believe the public should hear.

The prosecutor's seat is placed in a wide variety of positions in various legal systems. In the American courtroom the casual visitor will note no chair that can be quickly identified as one of special dignity. The district, state's or United States' attorney, as he is likely to be called, will sit in a chair placed on the other side of the center aisle from the chair of the defense counsel and inside the "bar." This chair has no ornate carved seal on its back, but is whatever standard model the janitor chooses to set at the table. Both prosecutor and defense counsels are placed on the same level, without benefit of elevation above the courtroom's floor, and the prosecutor is not farther forward or on the side to provide his voice with a more effective sounding board than that of his opponent.

This location of equality with that of the defense is suited to the prosecutor's standing in a legal system that reveres the adversary procedure under which the prosecutor is in theory as well as in fact a state's attorney charged with presenting the strongest possible case for the state and expecting to be countered with the strongest possible case for the defense so that there are created conditions like that of an ancient tournament. The judge becomes under this system the arbiter to assure conformity to the procedural rules that have evolved over centuries to constitute the rules of fair play, and the jurymen will decide the issues on the basis of those facts the judge permits them to hear. The humble location of the state's attorney's chair indicates to the jury that his word is no more weighty than that of counsel for the defense.

Consider the contrast offered by Geneva. The prosecutor in the assize court sits at the left end of the great semicircular bench at the middle of which sits the judge in frock coat, flanked by his jury at the other end. The prosecutor's seat places him well above the level of the chairs of the counsel for defense, the accused, and the witness stand, all of which are on the main floor. He carries by virtue of his location a certain majesty, not wholly distinguishable from the majesty of the judge. He is above the battle, and the procedural codes place a special responsibility upon him accordingly. He is required to be impartial, to be more than a state's attorney. In some countries, as in France, he is technically an arm of the magistracy.

The nonpartisan position of the prosecutor adheres even in the Soviet Union, where the procedural codes require the prosecutor to act in protection of legality even against a judgment in his favor by the court but too severe in its sentence. Look at the Cour Correctionelle in Paris' Palais de Justice, and you will find "Le Parquet" on a raised platform to the left of the judge's bench, less elevated and somewhat in front of the judges but quite unrelated to the position given the "avocat" who must plead for the defense. The continental prosecutor has such an unfamiliar position to the Anglo-American attorney, that it has often been suggested that he be called by his title in his own language to avoid confusion caused by a term that has other connotations for the common-law-trained mind.

While placing a special burden upon the prosecutor and treating him as more than an attorney for the state than is usual in Western Europe, the Soviet procedural codes espouse the adversary proceeding while retaining elements of the inquisitorial procedure of Western Europe as well. Thus, the Soviet prosecutor's chair is on the main floor at the same level as defense counsel, but it is usually placed at a desk on the left side of the room permitting the prosecutor to put his back to the wall and face the witness and the parties without rising. This seat puts him at an advantage over the defense counsel, and his dignity is further enhanced by a special uniform of office. This might create in the accused's mind an image of greater dignity than the judges, for they wear the clothes of the average Soviet man of the street.

The prosecutor's special position in continental Europe once created a struggle over furniture arrangement in the People's Republic of Poland that illustrates the problem with exceptional clarity. Before the Gomulka reforms of 1956, attempting to overcome some of the extreme Soviet influences upon communist Poland, the prosecutor sat at the left end of the same bench as the judges, and to the untutored defendant, he must have looked like a fourth judge, albeit seated around the corner from the other three. This made for too much dignity in the eyes of the reformers of 1956, and they hit upon a solution of some novelty. They brought in the carpenters to cut a narrow slit in the table at the prosecutor's end, so that today the Polish prosecutor sits at the same level as the judges above the rest of the room, but his table is physically distinct from that of the judges. He is almost but not quite as authoritative as the men and women charged with reaching the decision. His status is clearer than before, but he still has special dignity. He wears a black robe like a judge, except that his is piped with red in preservation of the traditional color of the medieval inquisitor for the Church, from whom his office is descended.

The Polish defense attorney, since the reform, also wears the black robe of his office, as does the barrister of the English court, but he has no specially designed wig as does his English counterpart to mark his position and difference from the judge and Crown's attorney each with his distinctive wig. The defense attorney's mark in Poland is the green piping that runs along the hem of his garment giving his robe a bit of color down the front.

Bitter conflict over the location of the prosecutor's chair has raged in Germany since the war. Perhaps under the impact of common law thinking, there has been a demand in some German states for a change in the prosecutor's place from the exalted traditional seat at the end of the bench with the judges to a position on the main floor no more prestigious than that of defense counsel. This movement has had its effect in one state as has the demand that the witness' chair face out toward the courtroom rather than in toward the judges' bench.

295

Next, there will be in many European criminal courts one more chair that would not appear in the American or English courtroom at all. This is the chair reserved for the attorney of the "civil plaintiff." Having no differing standards of proof for civil and criminal cases, the continental jurists have no difficulty in deciding the rights of the victim to damages at the same time as they determine the guilt of the accused. In consequence, the victim, or his survivor in the event of his death, is in the courtroom not solely as a witness, but as a party, and his attorney may rise to question witnesses or plead arguments if he believes that the prosecutor is failing in his duty.

Last, but not inconsequential among the participants in the trial, is the court secretary, for on him falls the task of preparing the record without which no appellate system can have validity, unless the appellate judges are authorized to recall witnesses and retry the case. The American courtroom is characterized by the early entrance of the court stenographer with his silent stenotype machine. He takes his place just under the judge's nose at a table placed where everything from the bench, the witness stand, and the tables for state's attorney and defense can be heard. He is expected to record every word spoken by any participant, and to reproduce it during the night in neatly typed pages made available to all concerned on payment of costs. His chair and his silent machine with endless strips of stenographic paper symbolize the determination of American courts to record everything.

Contrast Geneva or Cambridge, England. The court secretary will be sitting below the judge with a heavy desk typewriter. He will sit motionless while the testimony proceeds, but when the witness finishes, he cocks an ear to the bench without turning around and types swiftly and noisily what His Honor dictates as the substance of the testimony. Then he will strip his machine and place the page before the witness who has remained in place to affix his signature in verification. No English court wants to be burdened with a record of hundreds of pages of all that has been said, for this seems to the British to be cumbersome, wordy and confusing.

In the Soviet courtroom the secretary presents a sharp contrast. Usually a young woman, the secretary sits at the end of the bench in the People's Court with foolscap, ink pot, and pen to record what she can catch and thinks important without benefit of dictation by a judge, except in the unusual and complicated instance. It is no wonder that the U.S.S.R. Supreme Court has had to remand a case for retrial in some instances because of the inadequacy of the record for appellate purposes.

296

When considering the making of court records it is well to consider the bench to which the British assize judge mounts in majestic scarlet robe and wig following the blaring of trumpets from the courthouse steps as his carriage rumbles up from his temporary lodgings. That bench is completely clean of papers. There is no record of prior proceedings. The judge begins his hearing with a *tabula rasa*. Not so on the continent. Every judge who mounts the bench on the other side of the English Channel will have before him several volumes of "dossier" awaiting verification at the trial. In these volumes stands another symbol of a basic difference between the procedures of the common and civil law.

Civil law systems, including the Soviet, provide for preliminary review of the case, not as a grand jury would hear a United States attorney in New York, merely to determine whether there is likelihood of adequate evidence to proceed to trial, but to determine to the best of the preliminary investigator's opinion whether conviction can be expected to occur. The continental preliminary investigator is a magistrate charged with a special function like that of the judge's at the trial, to determine "objective truth," to create within his own mind a sense of "intimate conviction" of guilt. In consequence a continental trial in most countries, even in the words of some distinguished continental experts, is a verification of the work of the preliminary investigator, or the *juge d'instruction,* as he may be called.

By procedural codes the trial judges, where the "instruction" has occurred, must verify in open court by rehearing the witnesses and looking at the material evidence anew everything on which a finding of guilt is to be rested. In fact, there are times when to a common-law-trained mind, the judges violate "due process," for they permit reading of the testimony at the preliminary investigation when a witness who has testified before cannot return for reasons that seem like nothing more than inconvenience. In France, the trial judge will even read the preliminary record of testimony of a defendant who refuses to speak at the trial.

Perhaps in the light of the situation it is not facetious to suggest that while comparative law scholars are currently concerned with exhaustive examination of what is meant by the rule of law in various legal systems, a comparison of furniture arrangement in the courtroom merits a chapter in their study.[1]

NOTE

1. A first attempt to move in this direction has appeared in Sybille Bedford's *The Faces of Justice: A Traveller's Report* (New York, 1961).

19

Fear and the House-as-Haven in the Lower Class

LEE RAINWATER

The literature on architectural symbolism conventionally distinguishes three levels of symbolic meaning: syntactical meaning, or the meaning that an element of form or style acquires by virtue of its location in a chain of form or style elements; semantic meaning, or the meaning it acquires because of the norm, idea, or attitude that it represents or designates; and pragmatic meaning, or the meaning that is to be understood in relation to the architect, client, or social group that invents or interprets the building's form or style.

Rainwater's selection can be looked upon as an attempt to explore the semantic and pragmatic meanings of housing in American society. The research on which it is based consists of 2,500 depth interviews with working-class people living in many different communities. Those interviewed were asked how they felt about their present homes, what plans they had for changing their housing, and what the relation of these plans was to their personal and familial goals.

With regard to the semantic meaning of housing, Rainwater's major point is that symbolic attitudes toward the house are very different for slum dwellers, members of the traditional working class, and families in the modern working class who are on their way upward into the middle class. The primary aim of the slum dwellers is to find a house or apartment that will provide safe shelter, in other words, adequate room for sleeping, relaxing, and eating, and a haven from noise, odors, dirt, and interpersonal violence and abuse. Families from the traditional working class can apparently count on their house being relatively safe, and what they seek in housing is a reasonably comfortable dwelling unit and neighborhood, nicely maintained and stocked with conveniences that ease the burden of domestic work on the mother. Only in the advanced working class and in the middle class does one find a more elaborate conception of the house as a private domain that offers opportunities for recreation and expressive self-fulfillment and a stage for the display of affluence.

In terms of the pragmatic meaning of housing, two facts seem clear. First, the different meanings assigned to housing by slum dwellers, traditional

Reprinted from Lee Rainwater, "Fear and the House-as-Haven in the Lower Class," *Journal of the American Institute of Planners* 32, no. 1 (January 1966): 23–31. Reprinted by permission of the Journal of the American Institute of Planners.

working-class people, and members of the middle class reflect their previous experience with the environment. Slum dwellers, for example, are emphatic in their concern that the house serve as a haven because they inhabit a world in which homicide, burglary, and social pathology are commonplace. Members of the other social classes have correspondingly more favorable experiences that establish the context for the meanings that they assign to the house. Second, it seems that underlying the different meanings assigned to the house is a hierarchy of human needs that the dwelling unit is able to satisfy. At the bottom of the hierarchy are the basic biological needs for air, light, warmth, and protection against molestation. At the next level upward are the needs for greater efficiency and comfort, induced by the requirement that family members should be able to function at work or school. When the satisfaction of these needs is assured, then the house can begin to acquire its significance as a place for display and the attainment of pleasure.

The varying meanings of the house for different social groups have implications for design. At the very least, they suggest that architects, most of whom are drawn from the middle class, should not try to impose design features significant to themselves on lower- and working-class users without making certain they are also responding to the simpler meaning of housing to people whose first priority is the achievement of a safe and healthy environment.

□

Men live in a world which presents them with many threats to their security as well as with opportunities for gratification of their needs. The cultures that men create represent ways of adapting to these threats to security as well as maximizing the opportunities for certain kinds of gratifications. Housing as an element of material culture has as its prime purpose the provision of shelter, which is protection from potentially damaging or unpleasant trauma or other stimuli. The most primitive level of evaluation of housing, therefore, has to do with the question of how adequately it shelters the individuals who abide in it from threats in their environment. Because the house is a refuge from noxious elements in the outside world, it serves people as a locale where they can regroup their energies for interaction with that outside world. There is in our culture a long history of the development of the house as a place of safety from both nonhuman and human threats, a history which culminates in guaranteeing the house, a man's castle, against unreasonable search and seizure. The house becomes the place of maximum exercise of individual autonomy, minimum conformity to the formal and complex rules of public demeanor. The house acquires a sacred character from its complex intertwining with the self and from the symbolic character it has as a representation of the family.[1]

300

These conceptions of the house are readily generalized to the area around it, to the neighborhood. The fact is most readily perceived in the romanticized views people have about suburban living.[2] The suburb, just as the village or the farm homestead, can be conceptualized as one large protecting and gratifying home. But the same can also be said of the city neighborhood, at least as a potentiality and as a wish, tenuously held in some situations, firmly established in others.[3] Indeed, the physical barriers between inside and outside are not maintained when people talk of their attitudes and desires with respect to housing. Rather, they talk of the outside as an inevitable extension of the inside and of the inside as deeply affected by what goes on immediately outside.

When, as in the middle class, the battle to make the home a safe place has long been won, the home then has more central to its definition other functions which have to do with self-expression and self-realization. There is an elaboration of both the material culture within the home and of interpersonal relationships in the form of more complex rituals of behavior and more variegated kinds of interaction. Studies of the relationship between social class status and both numbers of friends and acquaintances as well as kinds of entertaining in the home indicate that as social status increases the home becomes a locale for a wider range of interactions. Whether the ritualized behavior be the informality of the lower middle class family room, or the formality of the upper middle class cocktail party and buffet, the requisite housing standards of the middle class reflect a more complex and varied set of demands on the physical structure and its equipment.

The poverty and cultural milieu of the lower class make the prime concern that of the home as a place of security, and the accomplishment of this goal is generally a very tenuous and incomplete one. (I use the term "lower class" here to refer to the bottom 15 to 20 percent of the population in terms of social status. This is the group characterized by unskilled occupations, a high frequency of unstable work histories, slum dwellings, and the like. I refer to the group of more stable blue-collar workers which in status stands just above this lower class as the "working class" to avoid the awkwardness of terms like "lower-lower" and "upper-lower" class.) In the established working class there is generally a somewhat greater degree of confidence in the house as providing shelter and security, although the hangovers of concern with a threatening lower class environment often are still operating in the ways working class people think about housing.[4]

In Table 19-1, I have summarized the main differences in three

TABLE 19-1
Variations in Housing Standards within the Lower and Working Classes

		Most Pressing Needs in Housing	
Focus of Housing Standard	Core Consumer Group	Inside the House	Outside Environs
Shelter	Slum Dwellers	Enough Room; Absence of Noxious or Dangerous Elements	Absence of External Threats Availability of Minimum Community Services
Expressive Elaboration	Traditional Working Class	Creating a Pleasant, Cozy Home with Major Conveniences	Availability of a Satisfying Peer Group Society and a "Respectable Enough" Neighborhood
All-American Affluence	Modern Working Class	Elaboration of the Above along the Line of a More Complex Material Culture	Construction of the All-American Leisure Style in Terms of "Outdoor Living"; "Good" Community Services

orientations toward housing standards that are characteristic of three different consumer groups within the lower and working classes. I will elaborate below on the attitudes of the first group, the slum dwellers, whose primary focus in housing standards seems to be on the house as a shelter from both external and internal threat.

Attitudes toward Housing

As context for this, however, let us look briefly at some of the characteristics of two working class groups. These observations come from a series of studies of the working class carried out by Social Research, Inc. over the past ten years. The studies have involved some 2,000 open-ended conversational interviews with working class men and women dealing with various life style areas from child rearing to religion, food habits to furniture preferences. In all of this work, the importance of the home and its location has appeared as a constant theme. These studies, while not based on nationally representative samples, have been carried out in such a way as to represent the geographical range of the country, including such cities as Seattle, Camden, Louisville, Chicago, Atlanta, as well as a balanced distribution of central city and suburban dwellers, apartment renters, and home owners. In these studies, one central focus concerned the feelings working class people have about their present homes, their plans for changes in housing, their attitudes toward their neighborhoods, and the relation of these to personal and familial goals. In addition, because the interviews were open-ended and conversational, much information of relevance to housing appeared in the context of other discussions because of the importance of housing to so many other areas of living.[5] In our studies and in those of Herbert Gans and others of Boston's West End, we find one type of working class life style where families are content with much about their housing—even though it is "below standard" in the eyes of housing professionals—if the housing does provide security against the most blatant of threats.[6] This traditional working class is likely to want to economize on housing in order to have money available to pursue other interests and needs. There will be efforts at the maintenance of the house or apartment, but not much interest in improvement of housing level. Instead there is an effort to create a pleasant and cozy home, where housework can be carried out conveniently. Thus, families in this group tend to acquire a good many of the major appliances, to center their social life in the kitchen, to be relatively unconcerned with adding taste in furnishings to comfort. With respect to the immediate outside world the main emphasis is on a concern with the availability of a satisfying peer group life, with having neighbors who are similar, and with maintaining an easy access back and forth among people who are very well known. There is also a concern that the neighborhood be respectable enough—with respectability defined mainly in the negative, by the absence of "crumbs and bums." An emphasis on comfort and contentment ties together meanings having to do with both the inside and the outside.

Out of the increasing prosperity of the working class has grown a different orientation toward housing on the part of the second group which we can characterize as modern instead of traditional. Here there is a great emphasis on owning one's home rather than enriching a landlord. Along with the acquisition of a home and yard goes an elaboration of the inside of the house in such a way as not only to further develop the idea of a pleasant and cozy home, but also to add new elements with emphasis on having a nicely decorated living room or family room, a home which more closely approximates a standard of all-American affluence. Similarly there is a greater emphasis on maintenance of the yard outside and on the use of the yard as a place where both adults and children can relax and enjoy themselves. With this can come also the development of a more intense pattern of neighborhood socializing. In these suburbs the demand grows for good community services as opposed to simply adequate ones, so that there tends to be greater involvement in the schools than is the case with traditional working class men and women. One of the dominant themes of the modern working class life style is that of having arrived in the mainstream of American life, of no longer being simply "poor-but-honest" workers. It is in the service of this goal that we find these elaborations in the meaning of the house and its environs.

In both working class groups, as the interior of the home more closely approximates notions of a decent standard, we find a decline in concerns expressed by inhabitants with sources of threat from within and a shift toward concerns about a threatening outside world—a desire to make the neighborhood secure against the incursions of lower class people who might rob or perpetrate violence of one kind or another.

As we shift our focus from the stable working class to the lower class, the currently popular poor, we find a very different picture. In addition to the large and growing literature, I will draw on data from three studies of this group with which I have been involved. Two studies deal with family attitudes and family planning behavior on the part of lower class, in contrast to working class couples. In these studies, based on some 450 intensive conversational interviews with men and women living in Chicago, Cincinnati, and Oklahoma City housing was not a subject of direct inquiry. Nevertheless we gained considerable insight into the ways lower class people think about their physical and social environment, and their anxieties, goals, and coping mechanisms that operate in connection with their housing arrangements.[7]

The third study, currently on-going, involves a five year investigation of social and community problems in the Pruitt-Igoe Project of St. Louis. This public housing project consists of 33 11-story buildings near downtown St. Louis. The project was opened in 1954, has 2,762 apartments, of which only some 2,000 are currently occupied, and has as tenants a very high proportion (over 50 percent) of female-headed households on one kind or another of public assistance. Though originally integrated, the project is now all Negro. The project community is plagued by petty crimes, vandalism, much destruction of the physical plant, and a very bad reputation in both the Negro and white communities.[8] For the past two years a staff of ten research assistants has been carrying out participant observation and conversational interviewing among project residents. In order to obtain a comparative focus on problems of living in public housing, we have also interviewed in projects in Chicago (Stateway Gardens), New York (St. Nicholas), and San Francisco (Yerba Buena Plaza and Westside Courts). Many of the concrete examples which follow come from these interviews, since in the course of observation and interviewing with project tenants we have had the opportunity to learn a great deal about both their experiences in the projects and about the private slum housing in which they previously lived. While our interviews in St. Louis provide us with insight into what it is like to live in one of the most disorganized public housing communities in the United States, the interviews in the other cities provide the contrast of much more average public housing experiences.[9] Similarly, the retrospective accounts that respondents in different cities give of their previous private housing experience provides a wide sampling in the slum communities of four different cities.

In the lower class we find a great many very real threats to security, although these threats often do seem to be somewhat exaggerated by lower class women. The threatening world of the lower class comes to be absorbed into a world view which generalizes the belief that the environment is threatening more than it is rewarding—that rewards reflect the infrequent working of good luck and that danger is endemic.[10] Any close acquaintance with the ongoing life of lower class people impresses one with their anxious alienation from the larger world, from the middle class to be sure, but from the majority of their peers as well. Lower class people often seem isolated and to have but tenuous participation in a community of known and valued peers. They are ever aware of the presence of strangers who tend to be seen as potentially dangerous. While they do seek to create a gratifying peer group society, these groups tend to be unstable and readily fragmented. Even the heavy reliance on relatives as the core of a personal community does not do away with the dangers which others may bring. As Walter Miller has perceptively noted, "trouble" is one of the major focal concerns in the lower class world view.[11] A home to which one could retreat from such an insecure world would be of great value, but our data indicate that for lower class people such a home is not easy to come by. In part, this is due to the fact that one's own family members themselves often make trouble or bring it into the home, but even more important it is because it seems very difficult to create a home and an immediate environment that actually does shut out danger.[12]

Dangers in the Environment

From our data it is possible to abstract a great many dangers that have some relation to housing and its location. The location or the immediate environment is as important as the house itself, since lower class people are aware that life inside is much affected by the life just outside.

In Table 19–2, I have summarized the main kinds of danger which seem to be related to housing one way or another. It is apparent that these dangers have two immediate sources, human and nonhuman, and that the consequences that are feared from these sources usually represent a complex amalgam of physical, interpersonal, and mortal damage to the individual and his family. Let us look first at the various sources of danger and then at the overlapping consequences feared from these dangers.

There is nothing unfamiliar about the nonhuman sources of danger. They represent a sad catalogue of threats apparent in any journalist's account of slum living.[13] That we become used to the catalogue, however, should not obscure the fact that these dangers are very real to many lower class families. Rats and other vermin are ever present companions in most big city slums. From the sense of relief which residents in public housing often experience on this score, it is ap-

TABLE 19-2

A Taxonomy of Dangers in the Lower Class Home and Environs:
Each of These Can Involve Physical, Interpersonal, and Moral Consequences

	Source of Danger	
Nonhuman		*Human*
Rats and Other Vermin		Violence to Self and Possessions
Poisons		Assault
Fire and Burning		Fighting and Beating
Freezing and Cold		Rape
Poor Plumbing		Objects Thrown or Dropped
Dangerous Electrical Wiring		Stealing
Trash (broken glass, cans, etc.)		Verbal Hostility, Shaming, Exploitation
Insufficiently Protected Heights		Own Family
Other Aspects of Poorly Designed		Neighbors
or Deteriorated Structures		Caretakers
(e.g. thin walls)		Outsiders
Cost of Dwelling		Attractive Alternatives that Wean
		Oneself or Valued Others Away
		from a Stable Life

parent that slum dwellers are not indifferent to the presence of rats in their homes. Poisons may be a danger, sometimes from lead-base paints used on surfaces which slum toddlers may chew. Fires in slum areas are not uncommon, and even in a supposedly well designed public housing project children may repeatedly burn themselves on uncovered steampipe risers. In slums where the tenant supplies his own heating there is always the possibility of a very cold apartment because of no money, or, indeed, of freezing to death (as we were told by one respondent whose friend fell into an alcoholic sleep without turning on the heater). Insufficiently protected heights, as in one public housing project, may lead to deaths when children fall out windows or adults fall down elevator shafts. Thin walls in the apartment may expose a family to more of its neighbor's goings-on than comfortable to hear. Finally, the very cost of the dwelling itself can represent a danger in that it leaves too little money for other things needed to keep body and soul together.

That lower class people grow up in a world like this and live in it does not mean that they are indifferent to it—nor that its toll is only that of possible physical damage in injury, illness, incapacity, or death. Because these potentialities and events are interpreted and take on symbolic significance, and because lower class people make some efforts to cope with them, inevitably there are also effects on their interpersonal relationships and on their moral conceptions of themselves and their worlds.

The most obvious human source of danger has to do with violence directed by others against oneself and one's possessions. Lower class people are concerned with being assaulted, being damaged, being drawn into fights, being beaten, being raped. In public housing projects in particular, it is always possible for juveniles to throw or drop things from windows which can hurt or kill, and if this pattern takes hold it is a constant source of potential danger. Similarly, people may rob anywhere—apartment, laundry room, corridor.

Aside from this kind of direct violence, there is the more pervasive ever-present potentiality for symbolic violence to the self and that which is identified with the self—by verbal hostility, the shaming and exploitation expressed by the others who make up one's world. A source of such violence, shaming, or exploitation may be within one's own family—from children, spouse, siblings, parents—and often is. It seems very likely that crowding tends to encourage such symbolic violence to the self but certainly crowding is not the only factor since we also find this kind of threat in uncrowded public housing quar-

307

ters.[14] Most real and immediate to lower class people, however, seems to be the potentiality for symbolic destructiveness by their neighbors. Lower class people seem ever on guard toward their neighbors, even ones with whom they become well-acquainted and would count as their friends. This suspiciousness is directed often at juveniles and young adults whom older people tend to regard as almost uncontrollable. It is important to note that while one may and does engage in this kind of behavior oneself, this is no guarantee that the individual does not fear and condemn the behavior when engaged in by others. For example, one woman whose family was evicted from a public housing project because her children were troublemakers thought, before she knew that her family was included among the twenty families thus evicted, that the evictions were a good thing because there were too many people around who cause trouble.

Symbolic violence on the part of caretakers (all those whose occupations bring them into contact with lower class people as purveyors of some private or public service) seems also endemic in slum and public housing areas. Students of the interactions between caretakers and their lower class clients have suggested that there is a great deal of punitiveness and shaming commonly expressed by the caretakers in an effort to control and direct the activities of their clients.[15]

The defense of the client is generally one of avoidance, or sullenness and feigned stupidity, when contact cannot be avoided. As David Caplovitz has shown so well, lower class people are subjected to considerable exploitation by the commercial services with which they deal, and exploitation for money, sexual favors, and sadistic impulses is not unknown on the part of public servants either.[16]

Finally, outsiders present in two ways the dangers of symbolic violence as well as of physical violence. Using the anonymity of geographical mobility, outsiders may come into slum areas to con and exploit for their own ends and, by virtue of the attitudes they maintain toward slum dwellers or public housing residents, they may demean and derogate them. Here we would have to include also the mass media which can and do behave in irresponsibly punitive ways toward people who live in lower class areas, a fact most dramatically illustrated in the customary treatment of the Pruitt-Igoe Project in St. Louis. From the point of view of the residents, the unusual interest shown in their world by a research team can also fit into this pattern.

Finally, the lower class person's world contains many attractive alternatives to the pursuit of a stable life. He can fear for himself that he will be caught up in these attractive alternatives and thus damage his life chances, and he may fear even more that those whom he values, particularly in his family, will be seduced away from him. Thus, wives fear their husbands will be attracted to the life outside the family, husbands fear the same of their wives, and parents always fear that their children will somehow turn out badly. Again, the fact that you may yourself be involved in such seductive pursuits does not lessen the fear that these valued others will be won away while your back is turned. In short, both the push and the pull of the human world in which lower class people live can be seen as a source of danger.

Having looked at the sources of danger, let us look at the consequences which lower class people fear from these dangers. The physical consequences are fairly obvious in connection with the nonhuman threats and the threats of violence from others. They are real and they are ever present: One can become the victim of injury, incapacitation, illness, and death from both nonhuman and human sources. Even the physical consequences of the symbolic violence of hostility, shaming, and exploitation, to say nothing of seduction, can be great if they lead one to retaliate in a physical way and in turn be damaged. Similarly there are physical consequences to being caught up in alternatives such as participation in alcohol and drug subcultures.

There are three interrelated interpersonal consequences of living in a world characterized by these human and nonhuman sources of danger. The first relates to the need to form satisfying interpersonal relationships, the second to the need to exercise responsibility as a family member, and the third to the need to formulate an explanation for the unpleasant state of affairs in your world.

The consequences which endanger the need to maintain satisfying interpersonal relations flow primarily from the human sources of danger. That is, to the extent that the world seems made up of dangerous others, at a very basic level the choice of friends carries risks. There is always the possibility that a friend may turn out to be an enemy or that his friends will. The result is a generalized watchfulness and touchiness in interpersonal relationships. Because other individuals represent not only themselves but also their families, the matter is further complicated since interactions with, let us say, neighbors' children, can have repercussions on the relationship with the neighbor. Because there are human agents behind most of the nonhuman dangers, one's relationships with others—family members, neighbors, caretakers—are subject to potential disruptions because of those others' involvement in creating trash, throwing objects, causing fires, or carrying on within thin walls.

With respect to the exercise of responsibility, we find that parents feel they must bring their children safely through childhood in a world which both poses great physical and moral dangers, and which seeks constantly to seduce them into a way of life which the parent wishes them to avoid. Thus, childrearing becomes an anxious and uncertain process. Two of the most common results are a pervasive repressiveness in child discipline and training, and, when that seems to fail or is no longer possible, a fatalistic abdication of efforts to protect the children. From the child's point of view, because his parents are not able to protect him from many unpleasantnesses and even from himself, he loses faith in them and comes to regard them as persons of relatively little consequence.

The third area of effect on interpersonal relations has to do with the search for causes of the prevalence of threat and violence in their world. We have suggested that to lower class people the major causes stem from the nature of their own peers. Thus, a great deal of blaming others goes on and reinforces the process of isolation, suspiciousness, and touchiness about blame and shaming. Similarly, landlords and tenants tend to develop patterns of mutual recrimination and blaming, making it very difficult for them to cooperate with each other in doing something about either the human or nonhuman sources of difficulty.

Finally, the consequences for conceptions of the moral order of one's world, of one's self, and of others, are very great. Although lower class people may not adhere in action to many middle class values about neatness, cleanliness, order, and proper decorum, it is apparent that they are often aware of their deviance, wishing that their world could be a nicer place, physically and socially. The presence of nonhuman threats conveys in devastating terms a sense that they live in an immoral and uncontrolled world. The physical evidence of trash, poor plumbing and the stink that goes with it, rats and other vermin, deepens their feeling of being moral outcasts. Their physical world is telling them they are inferior and bad just as effectively perhaps as do their human interactions. Their inability to control the depredation of rats, hot steam pipes, balky stoves, and poorly fused electrical circuits tells them that they are failures as autonomous individuals. The physical and social disorder of their world presents a constant temptation to give up or retaliate in kind. And when lower class people try to do something about some of these dangers, they are generally exposed in

310

their interactions with caretakers and outsiders to further moral punitiveness by being told that their troubles are their own fault.

Implications for Housing Design

It would be asking too much to insist that design per se can solve or even seriously mitigate these threats. On the other hand, it is obvious that almost all the nonhuman threats can be pretty well done away with where the resources are available to design decent housing for lower class people. No matter what criticisms are made of public housing projects, there is no doubt that the structures themselves are infinitely preferable to slum housing. In our interviews in public housing projects we have found very few people who complain about design aspects of the insides of their apartments. Though they may not see their apartments as perfect, there is a dramatic drop in anxiety about nonhuman threats within. Similarly, reasonable foresight in the design of other elements can eliminate the threat of falling from windows or into elevator shafts, and can provide adequate outside toilet facilities for children at play. Money and a reasonable exercise of architectural skill go a long way toward providing lower class families with the really safe place of retreat from the outside world that they desire.

There is no such straightforward design solution to the potentiality of human threat. However, to the extent that lower class people do have a place they can go that is not so dangerous as the typical slum dwelling, there is at least the gain of a haven. Thus, at the cost perhaps of increased isolation, lower class people in public housing sometimes place a great deal of value on privacy and on living a quiet life behind the locked doors of their apartments. When the apartment itself seems safe it allows the family to begin to elaborate a home to maximize coziness, comfortable enclosure, and lack of exposure. Where, as in St. Louis, the laundry rooms seem unsafe places, tenants tend to prefer to do their laundry in their homes, sacrificing the possibility of neighborly interactions to gain a greater sense of security of person and property.

Once the home can be seen as a relatively safe place, lower class men and women express a desire to push out the boundaries of safety further into the larger world. There is the constantly expressed desire for a little bit of outside space that is one's own or at least semiprivate. Buildings that have galleries are much preferred by their tenants to those that have no such immediate access to the outside. Where, as in the New York public housing project we studied, it was possible to lock the outside doors of the buildings at night, tenants felt more secure.

A measured degree of publicness within buildings can also contribute to a greater sense of security. In buildings where there are several families whose doors open onto a common hallway there is a greater sense of the availability of help should trouble come than there is in buildings where only two or three apartments open onto a small hallway in a stairwell. While tenants do not necessarily develop close neighborly relations when more neighbors are available, they can develop a sense of making common cause in dealing with common problems. And they feel less at the mercy of gangs or individuals intent on doing them harm.

As with the most immediate outside, lower class people express the desire to have their immediate neighborhood or the housing project grounds a more controlled and safe place. In public housing projects, for example, tenants want project police who function efficiently and quickly; they would like some play areas supervised so that children are not allowed to prey on each other; they want to be able to move about freely themselves and at the same time discourage outsiders who might come to exploit.

A real complication is that the very control which these desires imply can seem a threat to the lower class resident. To the extent that caretakers seem to demand and damn more than they help, this cure to the problem of human threat seems worse than the disease. The crux of the caretaking task in connection with lower class people is to provide and encourage security and order within the lower class world without at the same time extracting from it a heavy price in self-esteem, dignity, and autonomy.

NOTES

AUTHOR'S NOTE: This selection is based in part on research aided by a grant from the National Institute of Mental Health, Grant No: MH-09189 "Social and Community Problems in Public Housing Areas." Many of the ideas presented stem from discussions with the senior members of the Pruitt-Igoe Research Staff—Alvin W. Gouldner, David J. Pittman, and Jules Henry—and with the research associates and research assistants on the project.

1. Lord Raglan, *The Temple and the House* (London: Routledge & Kegan Paul Limited, 1964).

2. Bennett M. Berger, *Working-Class Suburb* (Berkeley: University of California Press, 1960) and Herbert Gans, "Effect of the Move From the City to Suburb," in Leonard J. Duhl, ed., *The Urban Condition* (New York: Basic Books, 1963).

3. Anselm L. Strauss, *Images of the American City* (New York: The Free Press, 1961).

4. In this paper I am pulling together observations from a number of different studies. What I have to say about working class attitudes toward housing comes primarily from studies of working class life style carried out in collaboration with Richard Coleman, Gerald Handel, W. Lloyd Warner, and Burleigh Gardner. What I have to say about lower class life comes from two more recent studies dealing with family life and family planning in the lower class and a study currently in progress of social life in a large public housing project in St. Louis (being conducted in collaboration with Alvin W. Gouldner and David J. Pittman).

5. These studies are reported in the following unpublished Social Research, Inc. reports: *Prosperity and Changing Working Class Life Style* (1960) and *Urban Working Class Identity and World View* (1965). The following publications are based on this series of studies: Lee Rainwater, Richard P. Coleman, and Gerald Handel, *Workingman's Wife: Her Personality, World and Life Style* (New York: Oceana Publications, 1959); Gerald Handel and Lee Rainwater, "Persistence and Change in Working Class Life Style," and Lee Rainwater and Gerald Handel, "Changing Family Roles in the Working Class," both in Arthur B. Shostak and William Gomberg, *Blue-Collar World* (New York: Prentice-Hall, 1964).

6. Marc Fried, "Grieving for a Lost Home," and Edward J. Ryan, "Personal Identity in an Urban Slum," in Leonard J. Duhl, ed., *The Urban Condition* (New York: Basic Books, 1963); and Herbert Gans, *Urban Villagers* (New York: The Free Press, 1962).

7. Lee Rainwater, *And the Poor Get Children* (Chicago: Quadrangle Books, 1960), and Lee Rainwater, *Family Design: Marital Sexuality, Family Size and Family Planning* (Chicago: Aldine Publishing Company, 1964).

8. Nicholas J. Demerath, "St. Louis Public Housing Study Sets Off Community Development to Meet Social Needs," *Journal of Housing*, XIX (October, 1962).

9. See, D. M. Wilner, *et al.*, *The Housing Environment and Family Life* (Baltimore: The Johns Hopkins Press, 1962).

10. Allison Davis, *Social Class Influences on Learning* (Cambridge: Harvard University Press, 1948).

11. Walter Miller, "Lower Class Culture as a Generating Milieu of Gang Delinquency," in Marvin E. Wolfgang, Leonard Savitz, and Norman Johnson, eds., *The Sociology of Crime and Delinquency* (New York: John Wiley & Sons, 1962).

12. Alvin W. Schorr, *Slums and Social Insecurity* (Washington, D.C.: Department of Health, Education and Welfare, 1963).

13. Michael Harrington, *The Other America* (New York: Macmillan Co., 1962).

14. Edward S. Deevey, "The Hare and the Haruspex: A Cautionary Tale," in Eric and Mary Josephson, *Man Alone* (New York: Dell Publishing Company, 1962).

15. A. B. Hollinghead and L. H. Rogler, "Attitudes Toward Slums and Private Housing in Puerto Rico," in Leonard J. Duhl, *The Urban Condition* (New York: Basic Books, 1963).

16. David Caplovitz, *The Poor Pay More* (New York: The Free Press, 1963).

20

Pecuniary Canons of Taste

THORSTEIN VEBLEN

If we accept the concept of a hierarchy of human needs to which architecture responds, then it is evident, as Rainwater argues in the previous selection, that the particular significance that a building assumes in the psychic life of its occupants is determined partly by whether the building does or does not satisfy the need for shelter. In the case of housing, for example, if the basic needs are not met, then the house is regarded simply as a haven; if the environment is safe, then the house can begin to assume a more complex significance in the lives of its users.

In the following selection, taken from his *The Theory of the Leisure Class,* Veblen offers a theory to explain the meaning of architecture and of objects in the more affluent sectors of society. At these upper reaches of the class system, it is obvious that an explanation cannot be deduced from information about the frustration of elementary biological needs, since the members of the leisure class are generally not deprived in this sense. When they do suffer from a lack of commodiousness, as sometimes happens to the wealthy who would rather sacrifice modern conveniences than forego the symbolic pleasures of their villas and rundown town houses, the choice is deliberate.

Veblen's method for explaining the symbolic content of architecture is to examine the properties or features of architectural style that seem to be most highly valued in the leisure class and that mold what he calls its "canon of taste." In the present selection this method is illustrated in a discussion of lawns, yards, and parks, which, as Veblen says, "appeal so unaffectedly to the taste of Western peoples." He argues that lawns and greenswards in public grounds have very little practical use for a society no longer dependent upon grazing. Indeed, Veblen argues, it is this very characteristic of "reputable futility" that is the clue to why lawns are valued: their care is so costly of time and money and their maintenance so often a frustrating task that the possession of a lawn testifies indubitably to the capacity of its owner to indulge in wasteful expenditure. Through the operation of the principle of "pecuniary emulation" even those classes in the population that cannot afford to waste energy and resources in the ownership and maintenance of a lawn, nevertheless strive to possess one. In this way standards of architectural

Reprinted from Thorstein Veblen, "Pecuniary Canons of Taste," *The Theory of the Leisure Class* (New York: Modern Library, 1934), pp. 130–139; 149–159. Reprinted by permission of the Viking Press, Inc.

design, which are set at the top of the social order, percolate downward and become also the canons of taste of the middle and lower classes.

Although Veblen believed that the motivation that underlay the development of established taste was that the style chosen should evidence the capacity for waste, he apparently also believed it was possible to distinguish the intrinsic beauty of an object or building from the component of beauty attributed to it by virtue of its service as an object of "invidious comparison." In fact, he looked upon his book and its method as a means for liberating him and his readers from the esthetic misperceptions induced by the common human desire to engage in "pecuniary emulation." He was, for example, a rebel against Victorian ideas of beauty, and preferred styles of architecture and domestic art that were close to what later came to be known as the machine or industrial esthetic. Thus, in the following selection one finds Veblen declaiming against the "endless variety of fronts presented by the better class of tenements and apartment houses" and instead taking the position that "the dead walls and sides and back of these structures are commonly the best features of the buildings."

☐

Any valuable object in order to appeal to our sense of beauty must conform to the requirements of beauty and of expensiveness both. But this is not all. Beyond this the canon of expensiveness also affects our tastes in such a way as to inextricably blend the marks of expensiveness, in our appreciation, with the beautiful features of the object, and to subsume the resultant effect under the head of an appreciation of beauty simply. The marks of expensiveness come to be accepted as beautiful features of the expensive articles. They are pleasing as being marks of honorific costliness, and the pleasure which they afford on this score blends with that afforded by the beautiful form and color of the object; so that we often declare that an article of apparel, for instance, is "perfectly lovely," when pretty much all that an analysis of the aesthetic value of the article would leave ground for is the declaration that it is pecuniarily honorific.

This blending and confusion of the elements of expensiveness and of beauty is, perhaps, best exemplified in articles of dress and of household furniture. The code of reputability in matters of dress decides what shapes, colors, materials, and general effects in human apparel are for the time to be accepted as suitable; and departures from the code are offensive to our taste, supposedly as being departures from aesthetic truth. The approval with which we look upon fashionable attire is by no means to be accounted pure make-believe. We readily, and for the most part with utter sincerity, find those things pleasing that are in vogue. Shaggy dress stuffs and pronounced color effects, for

315

instance, offend us at times when the vogue is goods of a high, glossy finish and neutral colors. A fancy bonnet of this year's model unquestionably appeals to our sensibilities to-day much more forcibly than an equally fancy bonnet of the model of last year; although when viewed in the perspective of a quarter of a century, it would, I apprehend, be a matter of the utmost difficulty to award the palm for intrinsic beauty to the one rather than to the other of these structures. So, again, it may be remarked that, considered simply in their physical juxtaposition with the human form, the high gloss of a gentleman's hat or of a patent-leather shoe has no more of intrinsic beauty than a similarly high gloss on a threadbare sleeve; and yet there is no question but that all well-bred people (in the Occidental civilized communities) instinctively and unaffectedly cleave to the one as a phenomenon of great beauty, and eschew the other as offensive to every sense to which it can appeal. It is extremely doubtful if any one could be induced to wear such a contrivance as the high hat of civilized society, except for some urgent reason based on other than aesthetic grounds.

By further habituation to an appreciative perception of the marks of expensiveness in goods, and by habitually identifying beauty with reputability, it comes about that a beautiful article which is not expensive is accounted not beautiful. In this way it has happened, for instance, that some beautiful flowers pass conventionally for offensive weeds; others that can be cultivated with relative ease are accepted and admired by the lower middle class, who can afford no more expensive luxuries of this kind; but these varieties are rejected as vulgar by those people who are better able to pay for expensive flowers and who are educated to a higher schedule of pecuniary beauty in the florist's products; while still other flowers, of no greater intrinsic beauty than these, are cultivated at great cost and call out much admiration from flower-lovers whose tastes have been matured under the critical guidance of a polite environment.

The same variation in matters of taste, from one class of society to another, is visible also as regards many other kinds of consumable goods, as, for example, is the case with furniture, houses, parks, and gardens. This diversity of views as to what is beautiful in these various classes of goods is not a diversity of the norm according to which the unsophisticated sense of the beautiful works. It is not a constitutional difference of endowments in the aesthetic respect, but rather a difference in the code of reputability which specifies what objects properly lie within the scope of honorific consumption for the class to which the critic belongs. It is a difference in the traditions of propriety with respect to the kinds of things which may, without derogation to the consumer, be consumed under the head of objects of taste and art. With a certain allowance for variations to be accounted for on other grounds, these traditions are determined, more or less rigidly, by the pecuniary plane of life of the class.

Everyday life affords many curious illustrations of the way in which the code of pecuniary beauty in articles of use varies from class to class, as well as of the way in which the conventional sense of beauty departs in its deliverances from the sense untutored by the requirements of pecuniary repute. Such a fact is the lawn, or the close-cropped yard or park, which appeals so unaffectedly to the taste of the Western peoples. It appears especially to appeal to the tastes of the well-to-do classes in those communities in which the dolicho-blond element predominates in an appreciable degree. The lawn unquestionably has an element of sensuous beauty, simply as an object of apperception, and as such no doubt it appeals pretty directly to the eye of nearly all races and all classes; but it is, perhaps, more unquestionably beautiful to the eye of the dolicho-blond than to most other varieties of men. This higher appreciation of a stretch of greensward in this ethnic element than in the other elements of the population, goes along with certain other features of the dolicho-blond temperament that indicate that this racial element had once been for a long time a pastoral people inhabiting a region with a humid climate. The close-cropped lawn is beautiful in the eyes of a people whose inherited bent it is to readily find pleasure in contemplating a well-preserved pasture or grazing land.

For the aesthetic purpose the lawn is a cow pasture; and in some cases to-day—where the expensiveness of the attendant circumstances bars out any imputation of thrift—the idyl of the dolicho-blond is rehabilitated in the introduction of a cow into a lawn or private ground. In such cases the cow made use of is commonly of an expensive breed. The vulgar suggestion of thrift, which is nearly inseparable from the cow, is a standing objection to the decorative use of this animal. So that in all cases, except where luxurious surroundings negative this suggestion, the use of the cow as an object of taste must be avoided. Where the predilection for some grazing animal to fill out the suggestion of the pasture is too strong to be suppressed, the cow's place is often given to some more or less inadequate substitute, such as deer, antelopes, or some such exotic beast. These substitutes, though less beautiful to the pastoral eye of Western man than the cow, are in such cases preferred because of their superior expensiveness or futility, and their consequent repute. They are not vulgarly lucrative either in fact or in suggestion.

Public parks of course fall in the same category with the lawn; they too, at their best, are imitations of the pasture. Such a park is of course best kept by grazing, and the cattle on the grass are themselves no mean addition to the beauty of the thing, as need scarcely be insisted on with any one who has once seen a well-kept pasture. But it is worth noting, as an expression of the pecuniary element in popular taste, that such a method of keeping public grounds is seldom resorted to. The best that is done by skilled workmen under the supervision of a trained keeper is a more or less close imitation of a pasture, but the result invariably falls somewhat short of the artistic effect of grazing. But to the average popular apprehension a herd of cattle so pointedly suggests thrift and usefulness that their presence in the public pleasure ground would be intolerably cheap. This method of keeping grounds is comparatively inexpensive, therefore it is indecorous.

Of the same general bearing is another feature of public grounds. There is a studious exhibition of expensiveness coupled with a make-believe of simplicity and crude serviceability. Private grounds also show the same physiognomy wherever they are in the management or ownership of persons whose tastes have been formed under middle-class habits of life or under the upper-class traditions of no later a date than the childhood of the generation that is now passing. Grounds which conform to the instructed tastes of the latter-day upper class do not show these features in so marked a degree. The reason for this difference in tastes between the past and the incoming generation of the well-bred lies in the changing economic situation. A similar difference is perceptible in other respects, as well as in the accepted ideals of pleasure grounds. In this country as in most others, until the last half century but a very small proportion of the population were possessed of such wealth as would exempt them from thrift. Owing to imperfect means of communication, this small fraction were scattered and out of effective touch with one another. There was therefore no basis for a growth of taste in disregard of expensiveness. The revolt of the well-bred taste against vulgar thrift was unchecked. Wherever the un-sophisticated sense of beauty might show itself sporadically in an approval of inexpensive or thrifty surroundings, it would lack the "social confirmation" which nothing but a considerable body of like-minded people can give. There was, therefore, no effective upper-class opinion that would overlook evidences of possible inexpensiveness in the man-

agement of grounds; and there was consequently no appreciable divergence between the leisure-class and the lower middle-class ideal in the
physiognomy of pleasure grounds. Both classes equally constructed
their ideals with the fear of pecuniary disrepute before their eyes.

To-day a divergence in ideals is beginning to be apparent. The portion
of the leisure class that has been consistently exempt from work and
from pecuniary cares for a generation or more is now large enough to
form and sustain an opinion in matters of taste. Increased mobility of
the members has also added to the facility with which a "social confirmation" can be attained within the class. Within this select class the
exemption from thrift is a matter so commonplace as to have lost much
of its utility as a basis of pecuniary decency. Therefore the latter-day
upper-class canons of taste do not so consistently insist on an unremit-
ting demonstration of expensiveness and a strict exclusion of the appearance of thrift. So, a predilection for the rustic and the "natural" in
parks and grounds makes its appearance on these higher social and intellectual levels. This predilection is in large part an outcropping of the
instinct of workmanship; and it works out its results with varying degrees of consistency. It is seldom altogether unaffected, and at times it
shades off into something not widely different from that make-believe
of rusticity which has been referred to above.

A weakness for crudely serviceable contrivances that pointedly suggest immediate and wasteless use is present even in the middle-class
tastes; but it is there kept well in hand under the unbroken dominance
of the canon of reputable futility. Consequently it works out in a
variety of ways and means for shamming serviceability—in such contrivances as rustic fences, bridges, bowers, pavilions, and the like decorative features. An expression of this affectation of serviceability, at
what is perhaps its widest divergence from the first promptings of the
sense of economic beauty, is afforded by the cast-iron rustic fence and
trellis or by a circuitous drive laid across level ground.

The select leisure class has outgrown the use of these pseudo-service-
able variants of pecuniary beauty, at least at some points. But the taste
of the more recent accessions to the leisure class proper and of the
middle and lower classes still requires a pecuniary beauty to supplement the aesthetic beauty, even in those objects which are primarily admired for the beauty that belongs to them as natural growths.

The popular taste in these matters is to be seen in the prevalent high
appreciation of topiary work and of the conventional flower-beds of
public grounds. Perhaps as happy an illustration as may be had of this
dominance of pecuniary beauty over aesthetic beauty in middle-class

tastes is seen in the reconstruction of the grounds lately occupied by the Columbian Exposition. The evidence goes to show that the requirement of reputable expensiveness is still present in good vigor even where all ostensibly lavish display is avoided. The artistic effects actually wrought in this work of reconstruction diverge somewhat widely from the effect to which the same ground would have lent itself in hands not guided by pecuniary canons of taste. And even the better class of the city's population view the progress of the work with an unreserved approval which suggests that there is in this case little if any discrepancy between the tastes of the upper and the lower or middle classes of the city. The sense of beauty in the population of this representative city of the advanced pecuniary culture is very chary of any departure from its great cultural principle of conspicuous waste.

The love of nature, perhaps itself borrowed from a higher-class code of taste, sometimes expresses itself in unexpected ways under the guidance of this canon of pecuniary beauty, and leads to results that may seem incongruous to an unreflecting beholder. The well-accepted practice of planting trees in the treeless areas of this country, for instance, has been carried over as an item of honorific expenditure into the heavily wooded areas; so that it is by no means unusual for a village or a farmer in the wooded country to clear the land of its native trees and immediately replant saplings of certain introduced varieties about the farmyard or along the streets. In this way a forest growth of oak, elm, beech, butternut, hemlock, basswood, and birch is cleared off to give room for saplings of soft maple, cottonwood, and brittle willow. It is felt that the inexpensiveness of leaving the forest trees standing would derogate from the dignity that should invest an article which is intended to serve a decorative and honorific end.

● ● ●

The connection here indicated between the aesthetic value and the invidious pecuniary value of things is of course not present in the consciousness of the valuer. So far as a person, in forming a judgment of taste, takes thought and reflects that the object of beauty under consideration is wasteful and reputable, and therefore may legitimately be accounted beautiful; so far the judgment is not a *bona fide* judgment of taste and does not come up for consideration in this connection. The connection which is here insisted on between the reputability and the apprehended beauty of objects lies through the effect which the fact of reputability has upon the valuer's habits of thought. He is in the habit of forming judgments of value of various kinds—economic, moral, aesthetic, or reputable—concerning the objects with which he has to do, and his attitude of commendation towards a given object on any other ground will affect the degree of his appreciation of the object when he comes to value it for the aesthetic purpose. This is more particularly true as regards valuation on grounds so closely related to the aesthetic ground as that of reputability. The valuation for the aesthetic purpose and for the purpose of repute are not held apart as distinctly as might be. Confusion is especially apt to arise between these two kinds of valuation, because the value of objects for repute is not habitually distinguished in speech by the use of a special descriptive term. The result is that the terms in familiar use to designate categories or elements of beauty are applied to cover this unnamed element of pecuniary merit, and the corresponding confusion of ideas follows by easy consequence. The demands of reputability in this way coalesce in the popular apprehension with the demands of the sense of beauty, and beauty which is not accompanied by the accredited marks of good repute is not accepted. But the requirements of pecuniary reputability and those of beauty in the naïve sense do not in any appreciable degree coincide. The elimination from our surroundings of the pecuniarily unfit, therefore, results in a more or less thorough elimination of that considerable range of elements of beauty which do not happen to conform to the pecuniary requirement.

The underlying norms of taste are of very ancient growth, probably far antedating the advent of the pecuniary institutions that are here under discussion. Consequently, by force of the past selective adaptation of men's habits of thought, it happens that the requirements of beauty, simply, are for the most part best satisfied by inexpensive contrivances and structures which in a straightforward manner suggest both the office which they are to perform and the method of serving their end.

It may be in place to recall the modern psychological position. Beauty of form seems to be a question of facility of apperception. The proposition could perhaps safely be made broader than this. If abstraction is made from association, suggestion, and "expression," classed as elements of beauty, then beauty in any perceived object means that the mind readily unfolds its apperceptive activity in the directions which the object in question affords. But the directions in which activity readily unfolds or expresses itself are the directions to which long and close habituation has made the mind prone. So far as concerns the essential elements of beauty, this habituation is an habituation so close

321

and long as to have induced not only a proclivity to the apperceptive form in question, but an adaptation of physiological structure and function as well. So far as the economic interest enters into the constitution of beauty, it enters as a suggestion or expression of adequacy to a purpose, a manifest and readily inferable subservience to the life process. This expression of economic facility or economic serviceability in any object—what may be called the economic beauty of the object—is best served by neat and unambiguous suggestion of its office and its efficiency for the material ends of life.

On this ground, among objects of use the simple and unadorned article is aesthetically the best. But since the pecuniary canon of reputability rejects the inexpensive in articles appropriated to individual consumption, the satisfaction of our craving for beautiful things must be sought by way of compromise. The canons of beauty must be circumvented by some contrivance which will give evidence of a reputably wasteful expenditure, at the same time that it meets the demands of our critical sense of the useful and the beautiful, or at least meets the demand of some habit which has come to do duty in place of that sense. Such an auxiliary sense of taste is the sense of novelty; and this latter is helped out in its surrogateship by the curiosity with which men view ingenious and puzzling contrivances. Hence it comes that most objects alleged to be beautiful, and doing duty as such, show considerable ingenuity of design and are calculated to puzzle the beholder —to bewilder him with irrelevant suggestions and hints of the improbable—at the same time that they give evidence of an expenditure of labor in excess of what would give them their fullest efficiency for their ostensible economic end.

This may be shown by an illustration taken from outside the range of our everyday habits and everyday contact, and so outside the range of our bias. Such are the remarkable feather mantles of Hawaii, or the well-known carved handles of the ceremonial adzes of several Polynesian islands. These are undeniably beautiful, both in the sense that they offer a pleasing composition of form, lines, and color, and in the sense that they evince great skill and ingenuity in design and construction. At the same time the articles are manifestly ill fitted to serve any other economic purpose. But it is not always that the evolution of ingenious and puzzling contrivances under the guidance of the canon of wasted effort works out so happy a result. The result is quite as often a virtually complete suppression of all elements that would bear scrutiny as expressions of beauty, or of serviceability, and the substitution of evidences of misspent ingenuity and labor, backed by a conspicuous ineptitude; until many of the objects with which we surround ourselves in everyday life, and even many articles of everyday dress and ornament, are such as would not be tolerated except under the stress of prescriptive tradition. Illustrations of this substitution of ingenuity and expense in place of beauty and serviceability are to be seen, for instance, in domestic architecture, in domestic art or fancy work, in various articles of apparel, especially of feminine and priestly apparel.

The canon of beauty requires expression of the generic. The "novelty" due to the demands of conspicuous waste traverses this canon of beauty, in that it results in making the physiognomy of our objects of taste a congeries of idiosyncrasies; and the idiosyncrasies are, moreover, under the selective surveillance of the canon of expensiveness.

This process of selective adaptation of designs to the end of conspicuous waste, and the substitution of pecuniary beauty for aesthetic beauty, has been especially effective in the development of architecture. It would be extremely difficult to find a modern civilized residence or public building which can claim anything better than relative inoffensiveness in the eyes of any one who will dissociate the elements of beauty from those of honorific waste. The endless variety of fronts presented by the better class of tenements and apartment houses in our cities is an endless variety of architectural distress and of suggestions of expensive discomfort. Considered as objects of beauty, the dead walls of the sides and back of these structures, left untouched by the hands of the artist, are commonly the best feature of the building.

What has been said of the influence of the law of conspicuous waste upon the canons of taste will hold true, with but a slight change of terms, of its influence upon our notions of the serviceability of goods for other ends than the aesthetic one. Goods are produced and consumed as a means to the fuller unfolding of human life; and their utility consists, in the first instance, in their efficiency as means to this end. The end is, in the first instance, the fullness of life of the individual, taken in absolute terms. But the human proclivity to emulation has seized upon the consumption of goods as a means to an invidious comparison, and has thereby invested consumable goods with a secondary utility as evidence of relative ability to pay. This indirect or secondary use of consumable goods lends a honorific character to consumption, and presently also to the goods which best serve this emulative end of consumption. The consumption of expensive goods is meritorious, and the goods which contain an appreciable element of cost in excess of what goes to give them serviceability for their ostensible mechanical purpose are honorific. The marks of superfluous costliness in the goods are therefore marks of worth—of high efficiency for the indirect, invidious end to be served by their consumption; and conversely, goods are humilific, and therefore unattractive, if they show too thrifty an adaptation to the mechanical end sought and do not include a margin of expensiveness on which to rest a complacent invidious comparison. This indirect utility gives much of their value to the "better" grades of goods. In order to appeal to the cultivated sense of utility, an article must contain a modicum of this indirect utility.

While men may have set out with disapproving an inexpensive manner of living because it indicated inability to spend much, and so indicated a lack of pecuniary success, they end by falling into the habit of disapproving cheap things as being intrinsically dishonorable or unworthy because they are cheap. As time has gone on, each succeeding generation has received this tradition of meritorious expenditure from the generation before it, and has in its turn further elaborated and fortified the traditional canon of pecuniary reputability in goods consumed; until we have finally reached such a degree of conviction as to the unworthiness of all inexpensive things, that we have no longer any misgivings in formulating the maxim, "cheap and nasty." So thoroughly has this habit of approving the expensive and disapproving the inexpensive been ingrained into our thinking that we instinctively insist upon at least some measure of wasteful expensiveness in all our consumption, even in the case of goods which are consumed in strict privacy and without the slightest thought of display. We all feel, sincerely and without misgiving, that we are the more lifted up in spirit for having, even in the privacy of our own household, eaten our daily meal by the help of hand-wrought silver utensils, from hand-painted china (often of dubious artistic value) laid on high-priced table linen. Any retrogression from the standard of living which we are accustomed to regard as worthy in this respect is felt to be a grievous violation of our human dignity. So, also, for the last dozen years candles have been a more pleasing source of light at dinner than any other. Candle-light is now softer, less distressing to well-bred eyes, than oil, gas, or electric light. The same could not have been said thirty years ago, when candles were, or recently had been, the cheapest available light for domestic use. Nor are candles even now found to give an acceptable or effective light for any other than a ceremonial illumination.

A political sage still living has summed up the conclusion of this whole matter in the dictum: "A cheap coat makes a cheap man," and there is probably no one who does not feel the convincing force of the maxim.

The habit of looking for the marks of superfluous expensiveness in goods, and of requiring that all goods should afford some utility of the indirect or invidious sort, leads to a change in the standards by which the utility of goods is gauged. The honorific element and the element of brute efficiency are not held apart in the consumer's appreciation of commodities, and the two together go to make up the unanalyzed aggregate serviceability of the goods. Under the resulting standard of serviceability, no article will pass muster on the strength of material sufficiency alone. In order to [have] completeness and full acceptability to the consumer it must also show the honorific element. It results that the producers of articles of consumption direct their efforts to the production of goods that shall meet this demand for the honorific element. They will do this with all the more alacrity and effect, since they are themselves under the dominance of the same standard of worth in goods, and would be sincerely grieved at the sight of goods which lack the proper honorific finish. Hence it has come about that there are to-day no goods supplied in any trade which do not contain the honorific element in greater or less degree. Any consumer who might, Diogenes-like, insist on the elimination of all honorific or wasteful elements from his consumption, would be unable to supply his most trivial wants in the modern market. Indeed, even if he resorted to supplying his wants directly by his own efforts, he would find it difficult if not impossible to divest himself of the current habits of thought on this head; so that he could scarcely compass a supply of the necessaries of life for a day's consumption without instinctively and by oversight incorporating in his home-made product something of this honorific, quasi-decorative element of wasted labor.

It is notorious that in their selection of serviceable goods in the retail market, purchasers are guided more by the finish and workmanship of the goods than by any marks of substantial serviceability. Goods, in order to sell, must have some appreciable amount of labor spent in giving them the marks of decent expensiveness, in addition to what goes to give them efficiency for the material use which they are to serve. This habit of making obvious costliness a canon of serviceability of course acts to enhance the aggregate cost of articles of consumption. It puts us on our guard against cheapness by identifying merit in some degree with cost. There is ordinarily a consistent effort on the part of the consumer to obtain goods of the required serviceability at as advantageous a bargain as may be; but the conventional requirement of obvious costliness, as a voucher and a constituent of the serviceability of the goods, leads him to reject as under grade such goods as do not contain a large element of conspicuous waste.

It is to be added that a large share of those features of consumable goods which figure in popular apprehension as marks of serviceability, and to which reference is here had as elements of conspicuous waste, commend themselves to the consumer also on other grounds than that of expensiveness alone. They usually give evidence of skill and effective workmanship, even if they do not contribute to the substantial serviceability of the goods; and it is no doubt largely on some such ground that any particular mark of honorific serviceability first comes into vogue and afterward maintains its footing as a normal constituent element of the worth of an article. A display of efficient workmanship is pleasing simply as such, even where its remoter, for the time unconsidered outcome is futile. There is a gratification of the artistic sense in the contemplation of skilful work. But it is also to be added that no such evidence of skilful workmanship, or of ingenious and effective adaptation of means to end, will, in the long run, enjoy the approbation of the modern civilized consumer unless it has the sanction of the canon of conspicuous waste.

21

Place, Symbol, and Utilitarian Function in War Memorials

BERNARD BARBER

It should be clear from the selections presented in Part Four that an important dimension of the built environment is the weight of social meaning that architecture carries. Architecture as we know it is highly dependent upon the symbol-making and symbol-understanding capacities of man. But does this symbolic dimension of architecture perform any function in society that could not be performed equally well, or better, by other modes of communication, such as literature or music?

The following analysis by Barber of the underlying intellectual issues in the post–World War II disputes over the location and design of war memorials offers a basis for answering these questions. Barber's discussion is based on a content analysis of the popular literature dealing with war memorial design, which was apparently abundant in the mid and late 1940s. He argues that physical objects, and ceremonial architecture in particular, serve two special functions in the cultural life of man. In the first place, buildings concretize beliefs by providing a physical focus to which sentiments can be attached. Barber is referring here to the idea often advanced by sociologists of religion, namely that most people are unable to sustain a commitment to abstract concepts, ideologies, and beliefs unless such ideas and norms are embodied in an objective presence that can be seen and touched. Secondly, ceremonial architecture localizes sentiments by creating a place in which groups with shared feelings can gather to express and reaffirm them. This notion, too, is borrowed from the sociology of religion, which has pointed out the fragility of ideas of the sacred. Religious ideas, ideas of God, concepts of national loyalty, and sentiments of reverence for the dead are hard for people to sustain in isolation. Individuals who cherish such ideas need the emotional support of others, which they can find when they join together in the ceremonies that typically occur (or take "place") in churches, public plazas, or at the sites of war memorials.

Like many sociologists who think in the tradition of the sociology of religion and functional anthropology, Barber reifies the concept of "the social order." He is arguing not only that individuals who wish to memorialize the dead need the visual and emotional support that architecture provides;

Reprinted from Bernard Barber, "Place, Symbol, and Utilitarian Function in War Memorials," *Social Forces* 28 (October 1949): 64–68.

he is also saying that "society" needs ceremonial places and environments because, in order for the social order to be cohesive, integrative values must be continuously reaffirmed. As evidence in support of this position, Barber cites cases in which the design of war memorials that emphasized utilitarian or esthetic purposes were abandoned when these designs were revealed to be incompatible symbolically with the values of American society.

□

In the recent years just preceding and following the end of World War II, popular American journals have contained numerous reports of recommendations and plans for memorials to those who participated and died in that war. Practically all of the discussion has been cast in polemical, either-or terms. The main line of battle, often openly drawn, has been between the larger army of those who favor "living memorials," that is, memorials with some present utilitarian function, and the smaller or at least less articulate group of those who resent the intrusion of secular purposes into sacred spheres.[1] This literature and the social activities it represents afford a convenient opportunity for a re-examination and elaboration of the theory of social symbolism. Perhaps a sociological analysis of the relations among physical place, social symbol, and utilitarian function in war memorials will add to our knowledge as well as facilitate practical planning in this area.

The essential purpose of a war memorial, although not necessarily the only one, is to express the attitudes and values of a community toward those persons and deeds that are memorialized. These sentiments can be and have been expressed in a large number of different ways both in different periods of history and contemporaneously in any given society. Misunderstanding results from the failure to appreciate this fact, that it is the sentiments and values which give significance to the form chosen to embody them. The memorial is a symbol of the feelings of the social group.

Physical objects and places are almost always required for the localization of the memorial symbol.[2] Memorial places and objects are the locations at which the sentiments represented may be appropriately and publicly expressed by individuals, alone or in groups. The coming together of a group at the memorial place both confirms the legitimacy of the sentiments expressed and reinforces their strength in those who gather together to express them. Ceremonies, ritual, and attitudes of "high seriousness" are the vehicles of this expression and reinforcement.[3] It should be pointed out, parenthetically, that such ceremonies and attitudes occur at all physical places connected with the fundamental values of the society, for example, in such places as houses of parliament, important battlefields, and, of course, churches.[4]

Most war memorials implicitly recognize this social function of physical place, but many provide for it inadequately. A few ignore it altogether. Thus, certain war memorials, such as a college scholarship fund, which do not provide for the ceremonial coming together of those who feel the sentiments which inspire them to create this symbol, operate at a disadvantage. However, this is not necessarily a mortal disadvantage, because the sentiments involved may be neither originally strong nor persistent over a period of time. But where the sentiments are originally powerful and where they persist, some kind of spatial localization of the memorial symbol is necessary for their expression.

This is not to say that any and all physical places are appropriate for the expression of values which a community may wish to memorialize. There are conditions for the compatibility of place and sentiment.[5] Although it requires further empirical refinement and grounding, Durkheim's distinction between the "sacred" and the "profane" is still useful in this connection. The "sacred" is that toward which men feel respect; what is "profane" is properly carried on in a utilitarian context.[6] Some part of the physical place of all war memorials is required to be sacred in this sense.[7] These qualities, of sacredness and profaneness, are not, of course, given in the nature of physical space as such. They are projected upon space only by social values and their concomitant sentiments. For this reason, any physical space can be made sacred by the appropriate attitudes.

Just because they do take their meaning from the expression of sentiments, social symbols like war memorials are not endlessly rigid and stable. Their significance has to be continually defined and affirmed by manifestation of the relevant sentiments. When these are not forthcoming, symbols lose their meaning. There are a large number of memorials from previous wars which have lost their meaning for the present generation. Memorials lose their meaning more quickly still, perhaps, when inappropriate sentiments are expressed toward them. It has been pointed out very often that there is a delicate balance between the sacred and the profane, that there is a contagiousness about them by which they infect each other with their own significance. If some war memorials, expressing sacred sentiments, are contaminated by profane and secular sentiments by virtue of their very physical location, those war memorials are unsuited to their essential purpose. For example, there is some opposition to students' activities centers as war memorials in colleges for this reason. Older college graduates tend to feel that it is impossible, not merely difficult, to house sacred war memorials and profane daily activities in the same building.[8] The point can be seen most clearly if we consider certain activities which are irreducibly secular in our society and thus wholly inappropriate in collocation with the values embodied in war memorials. For example, despite their obvious public utility, public toilets have *never* been suggested as appropriate places for war memorials. The mere imaginative juxtaposition of such notions even in the present scientific context, let alone one of proposed action, causes embarrassed feelings and nervous laughter.

We can now state the several functions of memorials and their relations to one another and to physical place more inclusively and more systematically. Any physical place or object, and thus any war memorial, can have at least three different types of function. First, it may, as we have already said, have symbolic functions—to express certain social values and sentiments, and also to strengthen them. This function for the present generation, as against the past one which is memorialized, is too often not appreciated by those who have been planning war memorials. Second, it may have esthetic functions—to appeal to our socially-conditioned standards of taste and beauty. And, third, it may have utilitarian functions—to serve as an instrument for the achievement of certain proximate social purposes and limited ends. A war memorial will have, by definition, the symbolic functions. It will almost certainly have esthetic functions, since societies tend to endow all physical place of which they are at all aware with some esthetic significance. But it may or may not have utilitarian functions. A war memorial may be just a plaque or a monument, free-standing, for example like the Cenotaph in London or the Tomb of the Unknown Soldier in Arlington Cemetery.

Until the quite recent historical past in Western Society, in the construction of war memorials, emphasis was chiefly on their symbolic and esthetic functions. A trend of attention toward utilitarian functions began in the late nineteenth century. In the United States, this trend has culminated after this last war in a great cry for "living memorials." [9] Among the types of living war memorials already existing and proposed are the following: a community building, a civic center, a city hall, a museum, a library, an auditorium, a municipal theater, a park, a playground, a swimming pool, a bandstand, a community forest, a boulevard, a bridge, a "boulevard of light," and an arboretum.[10] Undoubtedly a complete explanation for this change of emphasis must be discovered in the larger transformation of social processes in our society.[11] But some partial sources may be suggested. First of all, the desire for useful memorials is an expression of the hostility to "waste" in our society, especially as this was supposed to have been exemplified in the more grandiose of past attentions wholly to the symbolic and esthetic functions of monuments. Secondly, there are those among the advocates of "living memorials" who have unwarrantedly inferred from the obsolescence of some *particular* monument the *general* unimportance of the symbolic functions of war memorials. And most important of all, this change of emphasis is the result of a culturally induced rationalistic blindness to the importance of the symbolic functions of war memorials, or, in any case, to the necessary limits of the utilitarian functions.[12]

We can now perhaps give a general answer to the question of whether any given community must choose either a "dead" monument or a living memorial. We can say that a war memorial may be a mixture of the symbolic, the utilitarian, and the esthetic, but only when the necessary conditions under which these three functions can be related to one another have been complied with. What are some of these necessary conditions?

In the matter of the relation between the symbolic and the esthetic, obviously the esthetic aspect of the memorial place or object must not offend those who want their sentiments symbolized. For example, a memorial which was built in a Japanese architectural style, however esthetically noble that style intrinsically, would not be appropriate as a memorial to those who died in a war against the Japanese. Nor should the esthetic emphasis in a war memorial ever be made primary, as in a building or monument which was beautiful for the sake of beauty itself. Under this canon, good taste in war memorials requires "dignity" rather than "beauty."

The relation between the symbolic and the utilitarian is of more immediate practical concern. As we have already pointed out, certain purposes are so irreducibly utilitarian in terms of the cultural definitions that they inevitably clash with the sacred sentiments of war memorials. Other utilitarian functions have a varying appropriateness for the deeds memorialized. Let us consider the basis of this variable suitability in connection with a war memorial for college undergraduates. Those utilitarian activities contributing to the most important values of undergraduate life are considered appropriate for a war memorial, e.g., college chapels, scholarships, and libraries. Into an intermediate range of appropriateness fall such other student memorials as extra-curricular activities centers and athletic facilities. These represent desirable but subordinate values in college life. Least suitable, perhaps not appropriate at all, indeed, would be war memorials built around a student "dance palace" or a student beer hall. Dancing and drinking beer are normal activities for most undergraduates, but they are peripheral to the values of college life and therefore least appropriate as vehicles for the expression of sacred sentiments. We may state the relation of symbolic and utilitarian functions in its most general form, thus: The compatibility of utilitarian activities and symbolic functions in a war memorial is determined by the degree to which the utilitarian activities are expressive of the same set of values as the activities which are being memorialized. As utilitarian activities diverge from such expression, they must be placed lower on the rough continuum of symbolic appropriateness.[13]

We may note other examples of this principle in non-war memorials. Thus, the Walter Reed Hospital is especially appropriate as a memorial to Dr. Walter Reed of the United States Army, who gave his life in the service of the values to which the hospital is devoted. Endowed chairs in universities are especially noble tributes to scholars who have spent their lives in university teaching and research. Famous athletes are fittingly remembered in athletic facilities, as in the Hobey Baker hockey rink at Princeton University. The book-collecting and cultural interests of Harry Elkins Widener are appropriately memorialized in the university library at Harvard. By contrast, a library would be a grotesque memorial for some chieftain of an urban political machine, however much his admirers might wish to have his deeds recalled.

When the symbolic and utilitarian functions of war memorials are compatible with reference to a common system of values, the memorial serves to strengthen these values and thereby contributes to the solidarity of the society. In the case of an incompatibility, however, the inconsistent values embodied in the war memorial are dysfunctional for the integration of the group. Thus, if the activities of "dance palaces" are as important as national patriotism, that is, if this is implied by some war memorial which places them together so that they seem to be merged, then the actual values of the society, which do not hold the former to be compatible with the latter, are being called into question. The consequence is a reduction in the integration of the group.

These, then, are some of the general relations between the different functions of war memorials. Obviously no single highly concrete statement can be made about their application in all societies or all sub-communities of a single society. Since the symbolic functions of war memorials take their significance from the cultural values of a society,

332

and since, further, the compatibility of the symbolic, the esthetic, and the utilitarian functions also derives from these values, any particular war memorial can only be considered appropriate or not in terms of the values of a particular society or particular sub-community of that society. Keeping these general relations in view, each particular group must choose a suitable memorial for itself. Since values vary among societies, appropriate war memorials will always, as they have done in the past and still do, take different concrete forms. Owing to the difficulty of suitably combining the several possible component functions, excellent war memorials can only be constructed by the most careful consideration of these functions and their relations in the atmosphere of a particular set of social values.

NOTES

1. See, for example, the following typical materials: Various issues of the journal, *The American City,* especially all issues of 1945 and 1946. This magazine was the rallying center for those favoring the "living memorial." Joseph Hudnut, "The Monument Does Not Remember," *The Atlantic Monthly* (September 1945) is the most sophisticated and noblest attempt to justify the "living memorial." Lincoln Rothschild, "What 'Lives' in a War Memorial?" *The Saturday Review of Literature* (June 1, 1946) argues for the artistic and symbolic memorial. Margaret Cresson, "Memorials Symbolic of the Spirit of Man," *The New York Times Magazine Section* (July 22, 1945), is "a statement of the case for beauty" in war memorials.

2. For a study of the temporalized concentration of localized memorial activities, see W. Lloyd Warner's study of Memorial Day, "The American Town," in W. F. Ogburn, ed., *American Society in Wartime* (Chicago: The University of Chicago Press, 1943), esp. pp. 51–62.

3. The classic statement of the relation between social symbol, physical space, and the values of a society remains that of E. Durkheim, *The Elementary Forms of the Religious Life,* trans. by J. W. Swain (Glencoe, Illinois: The Free Press, 1948), pp. 230–231. An excellent empirical study of the way in which physical space becomes a symbol of the values of a society may be found in W. Firey, *Land Use in Central Boston* (Cambridge: Harvard University Press, 1947), esp. chaps. III and IV.

4. The tendency of visitors to these places to speak in whispers or in subdued voices can be taken as a crude operational index of these attitudes of respect.

5. There are also conditions of minimum accessibility of physical place to the society dedicating the war memorial. These conditions are neglected, for example, by those who propose memorial forests. In our urban society, a memorial forest is not likely to be accessible enough to any but a very small community. See *The American City* (February 1946).

6. Durkheim, *op. cit.,* pp. 37–38, 206ff. See also, Talcott Parsons, *The Structure of Social Action* (New York: McGraw-Hill Book Co., 1937), esp. pp. 411ff. Cresson, *op. cit.,* quotes Mumford: "A memorial is a religious act of dedication. . . ."; and also Fletcher Steele: "A monument to commemorate an ideal . . . should be set apart from the humdrum affairs of life lest its chief function be forgotten."

7. "Within the structure there should be . . . a hallowed chamber of dignity and beauty wherein the pilgrim or the passer-by may pause for meditation and

dedication to the end that 'from these honored dead we take increased devotion to that cause for which they gave the last full measure of devotion.'" Letter to the Editor, *Harvard Alumni Bulletin* (April 26, 1947).

8. "I am not only against a utilitarian memorial, I think it is an imposition—a horrible commercial exploitation of the affection that mothers and fathers have for their boys. The memorial must be a reminder. . . ." Letter to the Editor, *Harvard Alumni Bulletin* (April 26, 1947).

9. For evidence of this trend, see *The American City* (February 1945), p. 64, and (July 1945), p. 5. In July it was reported that a survey of plans of communities for war memorials found that four-fifths of them wanted "living memorials" of various kinds, with dedicatory plaques.

10. *The American City* (February 1946).

11. A similar account would be necessary for the recent glorification in war memorials of the common soldier as against previous idolization of the General on Horseback.

12. An example of such rationalistic bias: "Unless one feels the past war to have been frivolous and all human labor ineffectual, how can one favor the commemoration of the war by expending human labor on a frivolous structure of stone and metal which affects nothing?" Letter to the Editor, *Harvard Alumni Bulletin* (December 13, 1947). The rationalistic bias is probably the inclusive basis of all these partial sources.

13. Some of those who favor the utilitarian memorial see this point. For example, Dean Hudnut, *op. cit.*, says: "I am not for Memorial Convention Halls or Memorial Baseball Fields or Memorial Waterworks . . . there are degrees in dignity. There are buildings which lift the communal life out of the narrow business of getting and spending."

PART FIVE

The Application
of Behavioral Science
to Design

22

The Questions Architects Ask [1]

ROBERT GUTMAN

Although there has been a tendency in American architectural circles to emphasize the "art" of architecture and to regard an alliance between architecture and the sciences as a threat to the design tradition, the fact is that architecture has always been responsive to developments in science. One need only recall the influence of developments in mathematics on Renaissance architecture, the role that the engineering sciences played in the Gothic revival of the nineteenth century, or the significance of advances in environmental control technology to the modern movement in architecture during this century. In each of these periods, developments in basic and applied science influenced the form and esthetic of building and the theory of architectural design, and also transformed the architectural profession's concept of the procedures that should be followed in formulating design schemes, or what is known among architects as the design process.

The kind of alliance that developed in the past between architecture and the natural and mathematical sciences is now developing between architecture, planning, and the behavioral sciences. This development shows up in the extensive care that many architects now give to determining user needs before beginning to work on designs, in the efforts to include sociologists and psychologists as members of the design-building team, and in the growing tendency, both in America and in England, to allow building forms to express behavioral science concepts about the nature of man and society. These developments, and other examples of behavioral science influence on architecture and urban design, are illustrated in the selections included in Part Five.

The following selection is intended to provide a context for interpreting the new "behavioral architecture." It discusses some of the reasons why architects have suddenly found it necessary to familiarize themselves with sociological and psychological knowledge, emphasizing in particular the role played by the emergence of new building types that require a much more thorough and systematic inquiry into user needs than was customary in past centuries. It also deals with the different aspects of user behavior—institutional and personal goals, the organization as a means for achieving goals, and space as a facility for allowing the means to operate—that are relevant to building design and discusses the competence of sociologists to

Reprinted from Robert Gutman, "The Questions Architects Ask," *Transactions of the Bartlett Society,* Bartlett School of Architecture, University College, London 4 (1965–1966): 49–82.

provide data and advice relating to these aspects. The third part of the selection describes the design process and some of the issues that arise when the architect asks the sociologist to help him convert information about the user into a three-dimensional design solution.

Although the selection was written shortly after I first began conducting research into architecture and teaching sociology to architecture students, it was obvious even then that architects and sociologists were often finding their initial contacts disappointing and frustrating. Much of the selection, therefore, is devoted to describing, from a sociologist's point of view, the nature of architectural design, the organization of the design process, and the many important differences between the social role of the architect as practitioner and decision maker and the scholarly, academic, and scientific role of the behavioral scientist. The final part of the selection analyzes these role differences as sources of misunderstanding between the disciplines and sketches a strategy for enabling architects and sociologists to develop more effective forms of cooperation in the future.

☐

Introduction

For the last eight months I have had the good fortune to be involved with the world of architects and architecture. During this period I have been stationed at architecture schools, for the first half of the current academic year at Princeton, and since February at the Bartlett. I have taken advantage of this informal association with two important centers of architectural education to listen to lectures and sit in on seminars dealing with a variety of subjects that make up the curriculum of these schools. I have had a chance to visit and observe the work of the studio classes, and from time to time, at the invitation of my hosts, I have been asked to participate as a critic or examiner in review sessions and juries. From my base in the schools, I also have gone out to architectural offices, to talk with architects about their work. Between times I have tried to familiarize myself with the written literature that embodies the architectural tradition, to keep up with the architectural press, and also, of course, to visit buildings, sometimes in the company of the architects who designed them. It goes without saying that these experiences have been stimulating and exciting and I am extremely grateful to my hosts for having given me these opportunities, which will, I hope, be made available to many more sociologists in the future.[2]

My general purpose this past year has been to familiarize myself with what an anthropologist might call the culture of architecture, to learn how the architect works and is trained, in the hope of being able to suggest ways in which sociology can contribute to the problems that today face the profession and the schools. Architecture is beset by a sense of crisis, probably for very good reasons, and so it will come as no surprise to you to learn that the problems I was told about are numerous; there are intellectual problems having to do with the theory and method that guide design, there are organizational problems involving the way the profession finances, arranges and carries out its work, and there are communication problems reflecting the relation of architects to other members of the building team, and to the public.

In view of the magnitude and importance of some of these issues it may seem selfish of me to talk about the subject I have chosen to discuss with you, but it is one with respect to which I can claim some competence, since it is a problem involving my own discipline. I wish to discuss the difficulties that have arisen in the relations between architecture and sociology, as these difficulties have been revealed to me in interviews with practising architects, and in observations of the work of design teams in school studios and in offices. I also have discussed these problems with other sociologists besides myself who have had a chance to collaborate and associate with architects. The problems that have been reported to me resemble other difficulties faced by the architect at present. As happens in his relationship with the engineer or the contractor, the architect is found complaining that the sociologist doesn't tell him what he wants to know and that the sociologist doesn't do what the architect wants him to do. And the sociologist, just like the builder or the engineer, is usually found muttering that the architect doesn't present his requests for information clearly, is not certain about what he wants done, or is asking for impossible things.

I had better admit right at the outset that as a member of one of the parties in the relationship between architecture and sociology, it is hard for me to pose as an objective observer and commentator on the problems of this relationship, but I will try to present a fair view of the issues nevertheless. This isn't easy, but perhaps I can help my case by stating now, at the beginning, that the complaints registered by both sides strike me as grossly oversimplified. Both positions arise from a failure to comprehend the nature of the architect's task and the role of sociology as this task and this role have been defined traditionally.

Why Architects Turn to Sociology

It has been encouraging to me to discover the enormous interest of the architectural profession in sociology. In many schools in England and in the States, students are expected to take at least one course of lectures in sociology, with particular attention to the topics of the city and metropolis, family institutions, bureaucracy, the organization of the professions, and small group behavior. There has even been some experimentation with using sociologists in the design studio as specialist consultants and critics, particularly in relation to problems of urban design and housing. The program of the Bartlett is, of course, outstanding in demanding that the student pass a general examination in social science subjects; and the Bartlett his probably proceeded further than any other school in involving social scientists in studio work.

The use of sociology now is hardly limited to the schools. Town planning architects often consult sociologists in the States especially in connection with urban renewal schemes; and real estate developers of large suburban complexes, such as Reston, Va., and Columbia, Md., have sought the advice of sociologists in formulating their site plans and making provision for community facilities. Although there is perhaps less use of sociology by architects in private practice in the U.K., sociology and the findings of sociological research have been extremely influential in the determination of design standards for public authority housing and for hospitals and other health facilities that are established and administered by the central government. Indeed, one of the most impressive features of the English architectural scene to the American visitor is the presence of professional sociologists on the staffs of the research and development groups in the ministries.

The interest of the architect in sociology arises from the simple but important fact that a building cannot be conceived apart from the human activities it serves to facilitate and encourage. This is what architectural critics and aestheticians have had in mind when they have called architecture the most social of the fine arts. Buildings are objects of use in addition to being objects of pleasure, which offer delight to their beholder. Architecture is so essentially a social art that no architect can talk about his medium or about his schemes without reference to how they will be used by people; and a good deal of the conscious intention behind any design, as well as various decisions about its elements, are expressed in terms of its consequences for social behavior. This social nature has been characteristic of the architectural medium since buildings were first planned and designed and there has never been an architect who was not, in some sense, a student and critic of society. Is it any wonder therefore that once a science was developed whose specific task it is to understand the structure and function of society and to set out the principles that govern group behavior, the architect should turn to this discipline and to people who are learned in it for expert advice and guidance?

340

The current rage for sociology is not fully explained, however, by recognizing the natural ambition of the architect to substitute professional, scientific expertise for the informal, casual interpretation of human purposes and motives which has always been intrinsic to the architectural tradition. It also reflects the emphasis now current in the profession on making buildings that are responsive to the specific and unique needs of their users. It indicates, too, the recognition by architects that modern, complex building types which demand high and efficient levels of services and which shelter groups that undergo rapid changes in organization can be designed only by means of thorough and comprehensive briefs. The emphasis on designing and fabricating buildings that respond to the needs of users is probably stronger in Great Britain, with its tradition of ethical architecture extending back into the last century, than it is in the States. The attention now being paid to sociology cannot, therefore, be held responsible for the widespread discussion of user requirements, even though the interest in sociology may be the contemporary expression of this concern. But I think it can be argued that the interest in commodious built environments now being displayed by architects in America is the direct consequence of the criticisms that many sociologists have made of building schemes. In the States, during the 1930s, it was sociology that launched the attack on simple notions about the influence, say, of the housing environment on behavior. This has resulted in a public housing movement that now is concerned principally with the amenities provided in buildings rather than with building form.[3] The contrast is interesting: British architects are interested in sociology because they have always been fairly good amateur sociologists; American architects have begun to use sociology because the sociologists have been among the leading critics of architecture.

In both countries the interest expressed in sociology has been intensified by the confused state of architectural theory and design methods. Architectural theory is the set of principles that guide the architect in making decisions about the complex problems that arise in translating the requirements of the brief into the design of a building. One can argue over whether theory is necessary for architectural practice—its very emergence can be read as a sign that the traditions of the craft are breaking down. But leaving this issue aside, the current despair over the state of theory is said to arise because the principles of the modern movement did not establish the appropriate priorities among the variety of design elements that are part of any design scheme. It is claimed, say, that recent theory was too occupied with the symbolic and aesthetic

341

functions of the structural system or skin of a building and ignored the function of the building envelope and structure in providing a commodious, workable environment. The criticism is sufficiently well entrenched so that even architects who by personality, experience or intellectual style are disposed to accept theories that emphasize technology or form see themselves on the defensive. They attempt to buttress their design theory by arguing that it is confirmed by the principles and observations of Gestalt psychology; or that it can be "explained" in the language of set theory and finite mathematics. I don't think that it would be right to give sociology the credit for this intellectual revolution; it probably is more accurate to say that the difficulty in which the advocates of a principled architecture now find themselves and the development of sociology are two cultural phenomena, both of which stem from the break down in established intellectual absolutes, the rise of pragmatic philosophy and the general emergence of a scientific ethos as the dominant ideology of Western culture.

Design method is the series of mental procedures that architects adopt in applying their favorite principles to the design problem. Here, too, the scientific ethos has done damage and fewer and fewer architects are willing to defend their application of principles on the grounds of intuition alone. Some of them wish to abandon intuition entirely as a basis for decision-making; others continue to use it because they regard no other method as relevant to the architect's task, but are ambitious to understand what intuition is and how it works; still other architects recognize a place for intuition but wish to narrow the range of decisions within which intuition still must operate. My impression is that one could probably rank architects along a continuum, with those who cling to a belief in the importance of intuition at one end and the proponents of a scientific approach to design located at the other extreme. Architects who are likely to base their design method on intuition will also turn out to be those architects who accept a theory emphasizing the formal dimensions of a building; whereas the advocates of scientific design methods believe that it is important to design building primarily in terms of user requirements. It is the "scientific" architects who are most likely to adopt sociology, in the hope that full knowledge of the user, his needs and his social activities will enable the architect to deduce the design of a building. This view is an extreme one, and to my mind, it is also absurd, because it ignores the essential nature of the problem of building design. A more moderate viewpoint among the "scientific" architects is that design must remain

342

an achievement of the individual architect, requiring the intervention of his creative talents, but sociology can be used to evaluate the proposed scheme in terms of its suitability to user needs.

I said earlier that it is difficult to find an architect who is not a student and critic of society; I would extend this notion further, and add that most architects are also reformers. Indeed, one of the facts that first struck me when I began my encounter with the architectural profession was that architecture is today one of the few fields that keeps alive the utopian tradition of social thought. Many architects hold to a vision of some future social organization that comes closer to achieving goals of justice, humaneness and order than the society we live in now. They regard every building they design as an opportunity for bringing this utopian state into existence. In exploiting this opportunity, architecture in the past has looked to historical studies. Architectural historiography is today under serious intellectual attack on the grounds of having focused its concern on the externalities of building. This criticism is undoubtedly warranted, but in making it, design educators have tended to ignore the stream in art history that not only advocated a particular style of building but that also, by implication, proposed a social vision in the direction of which architecture was or should be moving. Recent examples of this way of using historical studies are Wittkower's book on renaissance architecture and the essays of Colin Rowe.[4] Both Rowe and Wittkower espouse a formal theory of building. They link this view of the design problem with a belief in the possibility of a humane social order founded on reason in which architecture will instruct man by means of its intellectual content rather than its emotional appeal. Most students in the schools do not read these essays now, but the need of the architect to find an intellectual ally who will offer theoretical and philosophical support for his natural determination to change society through building lingers. The survival of this need also helps to explain the current interest in sociology. Sociology, as many an architect defines the discipline, is a field that can not only help him to understand how people behave but also add to his stock of knowledge about how they ought to behave.

Sociology in the Briefing Process

Before discussing the content of the questions that architects tend to address to sociologists, I would like to make two general comments about the situations in which these questions are raised. In the first place, my observations suggest that sociologists are consulted about architectural issues more often by design educators working with students on hypothetical problems in studio classes than by practitioners concerned with actual design and building projects. There are probably numerous reasons for this pattern: the use of sociology is still in an experimental phase, and the schools are a more appropriate setting for experimentation than the world of practice; architects and sociologists are more easily available to each other within the context of a university; the use of consultants is expensive in practice, but collaboration between architects and sociologists within the university can be justified in terms of the academic tradition of interdisciplinary co-operation; design educators and academic sociologists are more disposed and also have more time to overcome the communication barrier that exists between the two fields than are practitioners and independent sociological consultants.

My second general comment is that the expertise of the sociologist is not thought to be relevant to all phases of the building process to the same degree, at least judging by observations of how sociologists have been used by architects and design educators.

We can divide the building process into four stages: the briefing stage, during which the demands of the client and user are presented and articulated to the architect and other members of the building team; the design stage, during which the brief is translated into the design scheme; the building stage, during which the design scheme is transformed into the object we call the building; and the use stage, during which the building is inhabited.

In all of these stages problems arise about which it is conceivable that the knowledge and expertise of the sociologist could be employed and indeed have been sought, but it is interesting that the questions addressed by architects to sociologists deal principally with the briefing and design phases. In so far as questions are raised about the building stage, they have in most instances come to the sociologists from other members of the building team, particularly representatives of the construction industry itself. Questions dealing with the user stage are most often raised by client users, including the ministries and local authorities in this country and large industrial firms in the United States. The fact that persons and groups other than architects are usually the ones to raise questions for sociologists about the problems of a building during the construction and use phases is surely not without significance: it indicates either that architects tend to regard their task as completed once the brief and design schemes have been completed or that the architect himself is regarded as the problem that requires study and treatment.

When the architect turns to the sociologist during the briefing stage, he usually wants three things from him.

1. The architect wants guidance in understanding the purposes and objectives of the client or user. In some situations, he wants guidance because the client has given him almost exclusive responsibility for developing the brief. Before he is able to formulate the schedule of accommodations, the architect wants to feel confident that he knows what the client is aiming to do with his organization, what, say, his ultimate objective is in running a university or building a house. If the architect has been presented with a pretty adequate brief, he wants the sociologist to help him decide whether the objectives stated by the client are valid. Since clients, either in their briefs, or in their talks with architects, usually mention a number of objectives, the architect hopes that the sociologist will help him to select those that deserve greater emphasis. Running right through the encounter with the sociologist in this stage of briefing is the ambition of the architect I mentioned earlier: the ambition to employ the building project as a means for improving the quality of social life. In pursuing this ambition, the contemporary architect often has doubts about the propriety of this ambition. Even if he suppresses his doubt, he still is confused about how to translate general goals of order, justice, and democracy into the particular objectives that can be attained through building schemes. This confusion is less prevalent when the building is a house, a school, a church, or some other building type for which there are many precedents in the architectural tradition. However, almost all architects are baffled by the prospect of translating their general notions about social purpose into a brief dealing with a relatively new, complex building type such as a university for 10,000 or 20,000 students, an air terminal, or a teaching hospital with research functions.

2. Architects also look to sociologists for expert advice to help them decide whether the present or proposed social organization of the client represents a reasonable means for achieving the objectives that are articulated or implicit in the brief. As a result of the critical attitude that seems to be built into the architectural tradition, many of the better architects suspect that clients and users do not arrange their activities in the manner most likely to achieve objectives efficiently and in a humane way. Once more, in the case of established building types, such as private houses, architects are fairly confident of their compe-

tence to judge the reasonableness of the client's round of activities; and this is one reason, I suspect, why so many of the important planning and space innovations associated with the modern movement in architecture, such as the open plan of Wright or Le Corbusier's Domino, were explored originally in the designs of large and luxurious private dwellings. The architect's self-confidence diminishes, however, in direct relation to the size and complexity of the project and is particularly fragile when the brief is for a large factory or a new kind of mass transport system.

3. My interviews suggest that outside of the school studio the majority of architects still rely upon their own knowledge, information and skill in evaluating the client's objectives and his social organization. To the degree that sociologists have contributed to the development of real briefs in practice, it has most often been with respect to formulating the schedule of accommodations; that is, the sociologists have often been assigned the task of estimating the spaces required for the client's activities.

The problems that arise when the sociologist is consulted about these three issues during the briefing process can be illustrated by the experience of architects and sociologists concerned with university building. The development of university briefs is a good example to choose because it represents one of those new building types I said are particularly likely to find the architect confused and uncertain about the objectives and demands of the client and user. Furthermore, the newer universities, both in Great Britain and in the States, are committed to the belief that traditional conceptions of university education are archaic and irrelevant to the problems that modern societies now are facing. The ferment in higher education arises from the sense that the universities are not producing individuals with the skills needed to operate the organizations of society and are not creating ways of action and group life that are responsive to the demands of a technologically advanced society.

I have spoken with architects for several of the universities involved in major building projects here and in America and they are agreed that the task of developing university briefs was difficult but also fascinating and exciting. It was difficult because no one involved in the client's organization—not the vice-chancellor or president, not the building committee, the department head, or professor—no one was able to articulate his objectives except in the most vague terms. Was it the aim of the university to improve the quality of undergraduate teaching or was it to increase the volume and competence of scientific research; did the university acknowledge its responsibility to break down the barriers of the established class structure; did the university want to emphasize the virtues of humanistic culture or did it wish to forward the advance of the scientific, technological ethos? Architects who asked questions of this kind—and their ability to do so is an example of the sophisticated kind of utopian thinking that is so often characteristic of architects—often got an indeterminate response. These briefs required the expenditure of a good deal of office and staff time, particularly the time of the project director; the pleasant feature was that it gave the architect a good deal of leeway in proposing objectives and organizational solutions himself. It was fascinating because the architect could feel that he was engaging in genuine innovation, blazing a new trail not only architectonically but also in terms of social organization.

A few of the university architects I talked with had used sociologists to help them in thinking about the purposes of a university or to assist them in determining the objectives that clients and users intended the university to serve. They claim to have found the sociologists helpful in devising the interview schedules and other research instruments by means of which clients and potential users were interrogated; but they report that they were generally disappointed that the sociologists were not more adept in guiding them toward the articulation of university purposes and goals. According to the architects, the sociologists who had been selected as consultants did not know much more about the general issues involved in university planning than the architect himself and often were not very imaginative in proposing objectives.

I am not surprised by these responses. We must keep in mind several characteristics of contemporary sociology that make it difficult for many sociologists to respond to the architect's queries in a positive way. In the first place, we must realize that sociology regards itself as a discipline, divided into various sub-fields of specialized knowledge. All sociologists are trained to have a familiarity with the general principles that regulate group behavior and social organization, but not every sociologist is familiar to the same degree with the norms, values, structures and behavior patterns of the particular groups and institutions out of which a modern society is organized. There are sociologists who know a great deal about the family and its problems, others who are specialists in the organization of religious institutions, others who are expert in industrial organizations, and there are a few sociologists who have conducted research and are acquainted with planning problems in higher education. If the architect has had the misfortune to consult

347

a sociologist who knows a lot about the problems of families, naturally he isn't going to get the best advice in preparing a brief for a university, even though the family sociologist might be useful to him in designing a dwelling unit. The dissatisfaction is therefore similar to that expressed by a man with a kidney ailment who has mistakenly consulted an ophthalmologist.

Secondly, we must consider a more fundamental difficulty, more serious because it is likely to inhibit the relationship of sociology and architecture even if the right specialist has been chosen. Sociology for some time now, ever since the second world war in the United States, and within the last decade in England, has become a scientific discipline that is extremely self-conscious about the distinction between values and facts. Most sociologists tend to believe that the methods their discipline has adopted enable them to describe the way in which people behave with some degree of accuracy and also to foretell the consequences for behavior of particular value choices; but sociologists, on the whole, do not believe their methods are capable of determining which one among a particular range of possible values should be selected. However, it is expert and informed advice about which values and objectives to choose for clients and users that architects so often desire from sociologists; or if they do not expect the sociologist to propose objectives to them, at least they want the sociologist to tell them which of the values the client already holds are worthwhile and deserve to be selected as implicit objectives of building. Presented with these demands by the architect, the sociologist responds by criticizing the architect for his apparent assumption that determinations of values can be objective. This is one reason, I think, why architects so often accuse sociologists of being destructive rather than constructive allies during the briefing process.

In my interviews with university architects I also tried to get them to talk about their experiences in understanding and evaluating the organizations proposed or developed by the client for attaining the objectives of higher education. In general, I discovered that architects felt much easier about this phase of the briefing process than they did when dealing with the objectives alone. The social organization of a client's work has a certain concreteness which makes it more accessible to the architectural imagination than concepts dealing with goals and purposes; clients, too, the architects report, were able to be more intelligent and articulate when discussing the way a research laboratory worked, or how residential activities should relate to eating and to study. There was a substantial backlog of experience around which to construct this portion of the brief: the architects were themselves products of schools of higher education, the clients had spent many years working in different kinds of university situations, and many universities embodying at least some of the goals of the client had been built in the past. However, the more self-critical architects recognized that the availability of this experience and the existence of buildings could be a danger, too, in so far as they led both clients and architects to think in terms of established precedents instead of encouraging them to explore new and original ways of achieving the purposes of a university.

In view of their doubts about planning a new campus on the basis of established building, combined with the desire to be truly innovative, some of the architects I interviewed consulted sociologists or read reports of social research studies dealing with university activities. These studies relate to such diverse facilities as dining halls, research laboratories, residence halls, and classrooms. The architects consulted these sources because they wanted further information about the advantages and disadvantages, say, of planning a common eating facility for all students or providing many eating spaces for smaller numbers of undergraduates; about whether to have undergraduates and graduates eat together or separately; about whether to provide common facilities for faculty and students. They sought further understanding of the preferences of students for one-, two- or three-bedroom units, for assigned work spaces in laboratories, for classrooms giving access to the outside or rooms completely insulated from the natural environment, and so on.

Architects who spoke with sociologists about these questions ran into some of the same difficulties encountered by the architects who sought the advice of sociologists for understanding the objectives of higher education. A frequent complaint is that the sociologist consulted did not have much more expertise on these questions than the architect, or the client himself. Again, here, I think part of the problem was that the architects did not pick the right sociologist. It astonishes me, frankly, that architects are not more aware of the need to consult sociological specialists, and I wonder why this awareness is not more widespread. Is it because the architect regards himself as someone who can design any type of building, and therefore he assumes that other disciplines and professions should be able to exhibit the same degree of generalized skill? If so, it seems to me the architect fails to realize that his own profession has become highly specialized, with some firms and offices devoting themselves primarily to hospital design, others to town planning, others to factory building, and still others to housing. It may be, of course, that the sociologist is at fault; perhaps he does not take advantage of the opportunities offered to him to make clear to the architect the complex division of labor that has developed in the discipline.

As I said, picking the right sociologist is part of the problem, but there is also a more profound issue involved here. Architects who express their disappointment also have in mind the indubitable fact about sociologists that they are much better at describing the activities and organization that already exist in universities than they are at proposing new organizations, or at forecasting the consequences of new organizations proposed by the architect. A typical situation is that in which the architect says to the sociologist: "I gather from what you tell me that students don't like those large impersonal universities made up of undergraduate colleges of 10,000 or 15,000 students. They lead, you tell me, to a sense of isolation, loneliness, apathy and all those other reactions that are said to be responsible for the student revolt at a place like Berkeley. Well, then, can you propose to me a better way for organizing collegiate life?" Many sociologists fail the architect at this point in their collaboration, in part because they are, as I said, not skillful at suggesting new solutions, in part because even when they can conceive of organizational alternatives, they are reluctant to stick their necks out and make forecasts when data to support their interpretation are lacking.

I happen to believe that this incapacity is an unfortunate weakness of contemporary sociology, but I think it is important for the architect and sociologist to understand its basis. It arises from the commitment of sociology to the scientific method. Sociology, as I said earlier, is devoted to the development of principles that will help to describe group behavior in general. Every historical event is the result, however, not only of the operation of principles that are generally applicable, but of specific determinants that work in combination with these principles. In the study of already existing groups or in the investigations of historical episodes these specific determinants can usually be discerned *ex post facto*; but for events still to occur, it is virtually impossible to anticipate the full range of specific determinants that will operate to modify the impact of the general principles. Trained as he is to be as certain as possible of the factors that impinge on an event, the sociologist is incapacitated for the task of estimating outcomes when these factors are, by the nature of the case, not yet ascertainable. However, if he is to be helpful to the architect in providing the information the architect really wants, the sociologist must learn to relax these strictures. I will say more about this later on.

350

Let me report an odd finding here which may be of interest to you. I have run into a few situations, and I have discussed similar situations with one other social scientist, in which the sociologist undertook to make the leap into the future demanded of him by the architect, only to find himself rebuffed. These situations occurred over the drawing boards in an office in which I, and my colleague, were consulted by the architects about design problems, once about a town center for a new suburban community, another time about a housing project in a central city, a third time about the plan for a new psychiatric hospital. We were asked to propose new organizational solutions for achieving the objectives of these building types; and since we were bent over the drawing board, naturally these proposals could not be expressed without revealing immediately their implications for spatial organization, without, that is, our talking about them in the language of form. In all three cases, our proposals were met with cold stares by the architects involved and as one of the architects later reported to a friend of mine: "That damn sociologist thinks he's a designer!" But surely this is what sociologists will indeed become if they begin finally to respond to the questions of the architect.

Architects who have consulted social research studies in dealing with the organizational aspects of universities say of these studies that they were hard to find, that their results are often diffuse and contradictory, and that they would like to find available a compendium or manual that summarizes the findings and relates them to problems of university design. It certainly is true that a greater effort should be made to inform architects about the available sources and to collate them, but I think it will be less easy to resolve the confused interpretations to which these studies easily can give rise. The contradictions, after all, emerge because each study, even when it was concerned with establishing generalized knowledge, nevertheless dealt with a particular historical event.

Incidentally, for the record, I perhaps ought to make it clear that the university architects whose comments I have reported were working in England and dealing with new university campuses in which the brief was very informal. This seems to be a common situation in this country, in spite of the program of the architecture development group of the University Grants Committee. These problems are handled quite differently in the United States now, especially in the large state systems, such as the University of California, with its master plan providing for the establishment of twenty-four campuses by the year 2000, compared to the nine campuses already built or in the construction stage. California and other state systems have major administrative units concerned exclusively with planning the organization of each campus; the existence of these offices undoubtedly transforms the way in which the social sciences contribute to the briefing process.

As I said, of the three fundamental issues raised in briefing, sociologists have enjoyed their principal opportunity to demonstrate the relevance of their expertise by helping to develop the schedule of accommodations. This seems to have been the case with regard to the formulation of university briefs, too. The architects I talked with, even when they did not consult sociologists or social research studies in determining objectives and appropriate university activities, did make use of sociology for ascertaining the floor area for student rooms, the furniture and other equipment that should be installed in these rooms, the kinds of wall surfaces to construct, the size and number of places for refectory dining, the floor plan for student rooms, and an almost endless number of details involving spatial requirements and the provision of amenities.

The architects I met were no more enthusiastic about the contribution of sociologists to the resolution of their problems in this stage of briefing than they were about their role in the other stages. Their specific criticisms, however, were different. It was in this context, for example, that they raised the traditional complaint about social research, that it tells a good deal about what people want but does not offer sufficient guidance about the weight that should be given to these desires. The architects said that the sociological surveys they had sponsored might tell them how much space students now were using in existing dormitories, how satisfied or dissatisfied students were with this space, but little about how much space students ought to have. They complained too that the sociologists were not able to translate their information about student activities and organization into the spatial organization these activities required. Faced with these deficiencies in sociological research, it is obvious that the architects proceeded much as they have in the past when faced with the problem of developing a schedule of accommodations, except perhaps with a better sense of the possibilities for modification and criticism. Instead of developing wholly new schedules on the basis of sociology, ergonomics or anthropometrics, they examined previous university residence halls, took into account the design standards established by the UGC, corrected them on the basis of taste, experience and the available budget, and formulated their design scheme accordingly.

I can well understand the disappointment of the architects I spoke to; if anything, I am surprised that it was not more keen. For the fact of the matter is that even though there are sociologists, say, who know a great deal about higher education, its goals and organizations, there are extremely few individuals within any sociological specialty who have given thought to, or who have conducted research about, the way in which these goals and organizations can be facilitated and served through building. How should a building be defined in order to make this phenomenon most accessible to sociological inquiry? What are the social functions that buildings perform in a society? Which elements of a building are of primary significance for particular kinds of social activities? At what point along the continuum over which any behavior pattern extends is the building likely to become a significant determinant of the pattern? How wide a range of behavior within any single behavior pattern is compatible with a particular spatial organization? These are not questions that many sociologists have thought about or discussed, and therefore little in the way of a "conventional wisdom" is available.

In reporting the dissatisfaction of the private university architects with the sociologist's contribution to the schedule of accommodations, we ought not to overlook the fact that many of the research and development groups in the central government ministries in Britain seem to be quite pleased with the role of the sociologist in this phase of briefing. I am not sure of the reason behind this more favorable response but I suspect it has something to do with the manner in which the sociologist makes his contribution to the work of these groups. He acts as a gentle critic to architects who are accustomed to reviewing the components of schedules of accommodation and it may well be that gentle criticism, administered in the right setting, is more valuable than the answers that can only be obtained through the development of the complex intellectual apparatus of systematic social research.

Sociology and the Design Process

I said earlier that the interest of architects in sociology has been concentrated on its possible contribution to the development of the brief and to the formulation of the design scheme. In reviewing the questions architects ask, it has struck me, too, that questions raised with respect to designs have a different character from those asked with regard to briefs. For example, architects naturally, and quite legitimately, anticipate that their design schemes will have certain social consequences. But they rarely invite the sociologist to comment on the validity or propriety of these consequences; instead they only ask his opinion about whether the design scheme is likely to *result in* the intended consequence.

Let me give an example. About a year ago an architectural firm in the United States asked me to help with the design of a major privately developed housing scheme to involve 15,000 housing units with an expected population of 60,000 residents. When I arrived at the office, I first was shown an elaborate series of slides, drawings and models to acquaint me with the scheme, the same presentation, incidentally, that previously had been shown to the leaders of the city in which the speculative builder was hoping to install this complex. The chief architect, his staff, and I then spent several hours discussing the drawings and models in more detail while they peppered me with questions about the likelihood that the particular scheme would result in the formation of what the team called "community spirit among the residents." I was happy to give my opinion about the virtues and deficiencies of the scheme in terms of this criterion, but as the discussion proceeded, I injected questions of my own in an effort to get a better, more rounded idea of the site, the social and political structure of the existing city, its social problems, the general social objectives of the team, and the ambitions of the developer. The more I found out about this city and its problems, the harder it was for me to keep my mind focused on the questions being addressed to me, because it soon became obvious that the designers, who had been ingenious, resourceful and sophisticated in imagining a variety of alternative design solutions to their problem as stated, had never once subjected their objective—the production of community spirit—to critical examination. Yet it was in fact questionable whether this was the appropriate objective for new housing in this particular city: it was a city with a Negro population of almost 40 per cent, with one of the highest unemployment rates in the whole United States; the average per capita income in the city, for both whites and Negroes, was one of the lowest of any city in the State; the public physical plant, including schools, public transportation, and hospitals, was in bad condition, and the statistics indicated a long-run trend of deterioration. Civic morale was low, and evidence of political corruption was high. The intensification of what the designers called "community spirit" in their proposed enclave could only result in its further reduction in the city as a whole, since the developers in fact were asking the city to endow their project with special resources, in excess of those being provided in the older parts of the city. Furthermore, the production of community spirit could only be achieved through a series of design elements and amenities that would turn the attention of the residents inward on to themselves away from the problems of the city as a total community. I stated some of these probable consequences to the architects; as good, decent, liberal Americans they recognized the point immediately, although they admitted they never had before doubted the validity of their single objective, nor, they confessed, was this the kind of issue about which they expected advice from the sociologist. We then spent another few hours reviewing objectives that the design scheme conceivably could try to implement in addition to the original objective of "community spirit"; and then went back over some of the design elements to consider how they would enhance or inhibit the achievement of these objectives. I think that by the time I left for the airport we had achieved a certain meeting of minds. However, all of us were very aware that to plan a housing development that met the needs of the total community might result in a scheme that would be uneconomical for the developer and that therefore could be achieved only with additional subsidies from the city and federal governments. The issues are still being discussed among the parties and it will be some time before a resolution will be determined.

Cases of the sort I have described are legion in the experience of social scientists who have worked with planners, architects and private developers in the United States. I cite it to illustrate in capsule form the simple fact that once the process of building has reached the design stage the interest of the architect in understanding social objectives which he displays so forcefully during briefing tends to be relaxed, and intellectual energy is concentrated instead on finding the most efficient means in terms of design elements for achieving social objectives that are assumed *a priori* to be valid. To put it in another way, I would say that during the briefing stage there is a great willingness to consult others, including the client and the sociologist, about ends and means; once the design stage is reached, the architect chooses the ends, and asks the help of others in evaluating the means.

I would like, in the presence of this audience, to be able to say that my experience here in England is inconsistent with the generalization I have just made, but unfortunately it has confirmed it. Indeed, what is especially striking is that many of the same criteria are used by architects here as in the States to justify design schemes, including the objective of developing community spirit. Apparently, throughout Western democratic society there is a strong feeling that we have lost many of the social virtues that were present in the rural and pre-industrial village; architects regard it as their responsibility, and believe that it is

within their competence to redevelop these virtues. Frankly, this finding surprises me. As I said earlier on, the architectural tradition in
Great Britain is distinguished by its concern for the public interest; and
design education is notable, in contrast to the education of architects in
the States, for teaching students to be concerned with the needs of
users and the social consequences of building. Therefore, one is led to
look for the source of the critical deficiency of the designer not in the
social role of the architect in a particular culture but rather in the universal nature of the architectural enterprise. What is it about this enterprise that leads the architect, who often is open-minded to the possibility of design alternatives, to be set in his determination to evaluate
these alternatives in terms of their contribution to the attainment of a
previously chosen, single objective?

Many features of the design task are probably relevant here. The
architect is pressed for time; especially if he has been industrious in
compiling the brief, he must get on with the job of designing and building and he cannot afford to re-examine social objectives all along the
way. His training is not one that encourages him to devote as much
energy to the consideration of objectives as he devotes to the development of a design scheme; in most schools the student is rewarded for
design performance rather than for analytical skill. Regardless of the
rewards, the curriculum of the schools does not give him the background in analytical philosophy, in social thought or in politics that
conceivably could improve his sophistication in weighing the desired
social consequences of designs. To the extent that these concerns are
emphasized at all, the emphasis is all stated in the context of improving briefing competence. The tradition for briefing is so vague anyway
that when dealing with briefs the architect is open for guidance and
advice from any quarter. When he begins to design, however, the tradition comes to his rescue. What if the tradition is imprecise in the way
in which it relates the vocabulary and language of form to the categories of social thought, at least a tradition is available. I am always
struck by how architectural students and practitioners will talk as if they
know what people want or should have; seldom in their training, except perhaps here at the Bartlett, is this informal language of user
needs and user behavior ever subjected to critical scrutiny. The self-
confidence of the architect is often shaky and febrile in the composition
of the brief and in the encounter with the client, but it rises to a
plateau of authority when he is at the drawing board, back at the office, alone or with his peers.

The demands imposed by the design phase of any building project

are so stringent that it may, indeed, present almost insuperable difficulties to the critic who still wants to reconsider the social objectives
implicit in the design during this phase. Many of the more radical educators and practitioners now recognize this fact, and this is one reason,
I think, why so much attention is given to getting the social objectives
and activities of the user crystal clear during the briefing process. This
is all to the good, but there are problems still to be mentioned even
here. In the first place, as we all know, it is impossible in practice to
separate the briefing process from the design process. Much of what is
unclear about the client's requirements is revealed only well after the
sketches, the working drawings and the specifications are produced.
Secondly, how is the sociologist to react when he is consulted only after
the design process is well under way and he then discovers that, from
his point of view, the brief has been prepared inadequately? Should he
suppress his awareness and not point out to the architect the serious
social consequences that may follow from the architect's failure to consider a broader range of design objectives? Some architects seem to be
asking the sociologist to forget about these issues and to attend only to
the questions that the architect poses within the confines of his established frame of reference. It would be judicious, however, for the architect to recognize that the sociologist's commitment to the canons of his
discipline are as firm and compelling as those of the architect to his
ethical code, and a new strategy must be developed to persuade both
parties in the relationship to overcome the constraints imposed by the
principles that govern their professional and scholarly lives.

I have said that when the architect becomes involved in the design
stage the scope of the questions he addresses to the sociologist is narrowed. He asks the sociologist to evaluate the social and behavioral
consequences of alternative building plans that he, the architect, proposes. I would like for the moment to ignore the sociologist's disposition to urge upon the architect the re-examination of the objectives implicit in his proposed scheme and to consider, instead, the problems
that emerge when the architect and the sociologist agree about the
validity and propriety of the chosen objective.

One problem that emerges is that the architect asks the sociologist
to estimate the probable social consequences of a proposed scheme
without allowing the sociologist to consider a variety of other alternatives for achieving the same objective. In a situation in which the
agreed objective is to produce a sense of belonging in a housing project,
the architect will ask the sociologist to weigh the advantages of two
different schemes for producing this feeling of "rootedness." One

357

scheme will be described as a building having a linear shape; and the other scheme will be described as a group of buildings arranged around a courtyard. "Which of these two," the architect will say, "is more likely to give the residents a feeling of responsibility for the community?" The response of the sociologist to this kind of query is a mixture of bafflement and disdain. A wealth of sociological research has already shown that the shape of buildings and site plans is a relatively insignificant determinant of social interaction, compared, say, to the positive effect that follows from the provision of such amenities as a nursery school for the area, or a community hall. Even more important as a factor contributing to the emergence of community spirit than either the shape of the building or the amenities it contains is whether the building is owned by the residents or only rented. If it is owned, they have an economic stake in maintaining it, and through the act of maintaining it they are brought together with other owners into what one might call a community.

A second difficulty emerges when the architect responds to this kind of criticism from the sociologist by saying, quite legitimately, that he, the architect, is still faced with the question of deciding whether the building should be of linear shape or arranged around a courtyard. "Do you mean to tell me," the architect says, "that there is nothing the sociologist can offer in the way of advice about which of these two is better for the inhabitants?" The sociologist can offer advice but it is usually with respect to effects that don't interest the architect who asks the question.[5] Every aspect of a building certainly does have consequences, but not all aspects of buildings are relevant to a particular consequence. Thus, in the example mentioned, it probably is wrong to assume that a relevant criterion for evaluating the form of a building is whether or not it contributes to community spirit, for the simple reason that building form is not something that is capable of determining a complex social interaction of this kind immediately and directly. If the architect is interested in influencing community spirit he is better advised to pay attention to the amenities he provides in the building and the pattern of ownership. If he continues to require objective social criteria for evaluating building form then he must consider other possible effects, such as the consequence of efficient or inefficient land use. In this respect, he will discover, as Martin and March have recently pointed out, that building form is important.[6] Courtyard buildings, they show, apart from whatever other virtues or deficiencies they may possess, can be justified on the grounds that they constitute an economical means for utilizing urban land.

I have been chided so often by thoughtful and intelligent architects for making these or similar comments that I had better take a few moments to clarify what I am not saying as well as what I do intend to imply. First of all, let me point out that the formal alternatives I referred to in the comparison of the courtyard to the linear building were both high blocks with eight storeys, in one case distributed around a large open green space, in the other situated and set along a street. The courtyard, in other words, offered by one alternative was not the intimate inner space of a French *hôtel*. I am perfectly willing to recognize the probability that buildings that differ significantly in scale are going to constitute significantly different kinds of living environments.

Even were the comparison between two buildings of different scale, I still would be inclined to argue that given the architect's intention to create a residential group exhibiting community spirit, it is more important to pay atttention to the amenities in the area and the pattern of ownership than to issues of building form. Not that building form does not matter or does not make a difference, but, I would argue, it makes a difference only initially, in the first few weeks or months after the residents move in and over the long run, after residents have lived there for a generation. But I don't think that the planners of contemporary housing developments are concerned with the initial response or the generational reaction: they want to produce communities that will work well over the next five or ten years. Human communities with this particular planning trajectory are best achieved, if they can be planned at all, by concentrating attention on community facilities and ownership patterns.

I think the irritation architects display when this view of the matter is presented is directly related to the fact that building form exerts a lasting impact only gradually; as I put it, rather arbitrarily, over the period of a generation or more. Building forms are capable of expressing an intention; and if the designer of the building is what we call a good designer, the form he designs will express that intention. But the fact of the matter is that the designer's intention is not immediately obvious to most people, although it may be clear to the designer and to the *cogniscenti* who are familiar with the language through which architecture tries to communicate its intention. The populace of a democratic society can, however, eventually come to understand the architect's intention but it will take a very long time. They can understand it if they use the building often enough; or they can understand it if they are taught how to use it in the way the architect intended; or they can understand it if the architect's vision of society which is intended by the form of his building catches on and is reproduced in the form of other new building in the society; or if his vision is consistent with the intention of buildings already established in the society and is thus reinforced by the forms generally visible and present in the built environment. In other words, the architect can be didactic, he can instruct, but like most of the messages put forth by the good teacher, some lessons can be learned easily and others are too subtle to be understood until long after the students have left the school, or the teacher has resigned, or the teacher is dead, or the students are dead, or the building itself perishes.

Still another difficulty that typically arises when the architect approaches the sociologist for advice about the social consequences of particular design proposals must be mentioned. I have in mind here numerous occasions on which I have been asked to evaluate specific elements in schemes that, I thought, should not have been specific to begin with, but should rather have consisted of generalized solutions. Perhaps two examples will serve to illustrate what I mean. An architectural firm in the United States was preparing as part of an urban renewal plan the design for a large housing project in a section of Chicago noted for its high juvenile delinquency rate. The basic elements of the scheme were groups of row houses surrounding on three sides a large central green space, the space to be used as a common area for children's play, recreation and informal community activities, such as picnics, fairs, etc. I was asked to comment on a number of features of the scheme, including whether it was advisable to fence off the open end of the green space, providing a private locked gate which could be opened only by a key belonging to the residents. The architect was confused about what to propose. He felt that if the space were open, the area could easily become a "turf" for the gangs of the surrounding neighborhood; if it were closed, the fence might discourage visiting among the residents of different groups within the project. A closed space, he suspected, would also confirm their fears that the area was located in a hazardous section of the city, and thus would discourage the sale or rental of the dwelling units. I agreed with the view that the fence could be interpreted in the way the architect suggested but I said that it was almost impossible to anticipate the contribution of these interpretations to the overall satisfaction of users with the proposed scheme. "Why not," I said to the architect, "design the housing and green area in such a way that the residents could later decide for themselves whether they wanted to put up a fence, or take the fence down if one were put up. Or establish fences in some of the groups and have no fences in others to begin with." The architect, I discovered, was unwilling to accept this flexible arrangement and insisted upon reaching some conclusion ahead of time about the proper or improper way to build the fence into the scheme.

A second example that casts light upon the same issue is this one. A group of architects responsible for the design of university residence halls for a campus of a new college within a large American state university were uncertain about the proportion of one-, two- and three-bedroom units they should provide. They asked me whether there was any guidance I could give them on the basis of the social research done on housing that would help them to make a decision on this matter. It so happens, as you know, that this is one of the best researched areas within the general field of user requirements in university building; but, as I commented earlier, there is little agreement among the conclusions of these studies.[7] A larger proportion of the students in colleges in the Eastern states seem to prefer communal units; in the West there is a greater preference for single units. Private college students prefer large units, state university students, smaller units. Apart from generalizations of this sort, however, it is really impossible on the basis of these studies to recommend in more precise terms the proportions in which large and small, single or communal, units should be incorporated into a new campus. I recommended that the buildings should be designed so that the units could be altered in size depending upon the university's experience with their students in the halls. I am sorry to say I was not able to convince the architects of the reasonableness of my suggestion and they have gone ahead to plan a fixed proportion of units of different size.

I find these cases very interesting. They exemplify what I regard as the unwarranted ambition of many architects to find specific solutions in building designs even when these specific solutions are incompatible with the pattern of user behavior or client needs relevant to the building type being considered. I am aware, of course, that the entire question of indeterminate building, building of generalized spaces, endless building, etc., is a controversial subject in the design studio these days, and that there are serious and important issues involved in deciding what should be fixed and what indeterminate in any building, and in assessing the problems for which indeterminate solutions are applicable. Nevertheless, it is clear that the significance of the issue being debated has made little impact so far on the practical work of the architectural profession. The possibility of variable or flexible solutions interests me, too, because it shifts part of the burden for dealing with the contradictions of the findings of sociological research back on to the shoulders of the architect. Thus, it can be argued that the inconsistency of sociological findings is not only an indication of the necessary historicity of all studies of past behavior but also a sign that not all future behavior of building users is determinable through social research. The population of students who use residence halls is likely to be different from one year to another; and the same students are often likely to change their desired requirements for space from one year to another. Buildings and architectural designs should somehow be able to accommodate this characteristic of building users.

Sources of Misunderstanding

Throughout this selection I have discussed not only the questions architects address to sociologists but also the attitudes these questions generate in architects and sociologists. The attitudes are generally a mixture of disappointment, irritation, and sometimes of horror, on both sides. Architects, the sociologists seem to be saying, don't ask the correct questions at the right time; and the sociologists, according to the architects, don't tell us what we really want to know. At various places I have suggested some of the reasons that may help to account for the poor relationship, the misunderstanding, which now seems to prevail. I want to conclude now by reducing these reasons to their fundamental sources. There are three sources I want to discuss: (A) The requirements of design; (B) The nature of building and groups; and (C) The social roles of architects and sociologists.

A. The building the architect is responsible for designing must, as Vitruvius implied, meet standards of firmness, commodity and delight: it must stand up as a work of structural engineering, it must meet the needs of its users in a reasonably satisfactory fashion, and it should conform to established or original standards of beauty or aesthetic integrity. More recently, the architectural tradition has pointed to this same trichotomy of building by saying that the architect must be skillful in developing the technology, the program and the form of the building. If we recognize building as made up of these three dimensions, it might be said that the dilemma of architecture's relationship to sociology emerges from the fact that the architect must be concerned with all three dimensions during the design process, whereas sociology relates to only one of them, namely, the program.

Because sociology only deals with one of the elements that the architect must respond to and that he must manipulate in the design of the built environment, information about the objectives of users and about the activities the building must shelter cannot conceivably by itself be used to dictate a design solution. Most architects, of course, recognize this point: I don't think that the architectural tradition, for example, has ever seriously argued that a design method could be formulated in terms of the program, any more than architects really believe that structure, technology or form alone can be used to prescribe the design scheme, in spite of the pretence within the Modern Movement to argue sometimes as if this were possible. What those architects have meant who have stressed in the past, or argue today, that form or technology is the means to solving design problems is rather that the language of form or the vocabulary of technology provides a medium for grasping the totality of the architectural problem; or that the pursuit of one of these elements should be given priority in organizing the remaining elements.

I regret to say that sociologists are often not aware of the threefold nature of building design and this is often the reason why they evidence so much difficulty in responding positively to the questions stated by architects. They do not realize, in other words, that while the architect is asking questions about the program, he is trying to balance the sociologist's answers with what he knows about the demands imposed on the design scheme by the elements of form and technology. Nor does the sociologist realize that the content of the question posed by the architect, or the way in which it is stated, is often determined by the previous experience of the architect in grappling with the formal and technological elements of the building. I frankly do not know what attitude to take toward this situation: in part, I would think it demands that the sociologist somehow become conversant with the technological and formal elements that have determined the statement of the problem by the time it is presented to him; at the same time, I have sometimes felt that the architect has given more weight to these demands than they deserve and that more fruitful collaboration between the fields could have been developed had the sociologist been consulted earlier during the design process.

I think the nature of building design has an additional implication for the sociologist's response to the architect—what I am going to say may seem patronizing, but it certainly is not stated with this intention. I think that there is a sense in which the sociologist takes the architect's questions too seriously. Just because a building is more than the solution to the problem represented by the program, it cannot hope to satisfy the demands of the program fully. There is no design that works

363

equally well for builders, engineers, clients, and users; there is no building that can hope to serve the needs of all its potential users to the same degree; there is no building that can achieve a maximum effect as form, as technique, and as user environment. The good designer knows this, or if he doesn't, he certainly should. Therefore, the good designer who turns to the sociologist really wants approximate answers rather than precise ones. He wants to know whether one proposed feature of a particular scheme will be better or worse than some other proposal: he does not demand that it should be the best of all possible alternatives. Since he has to juggle so many features and dimensions of building simultaneously, the responsible designer just wants to make sure that he is not too far off in the solution he is proposing to deal with a particular problem.

Sociologists may find it hard to understand this mood in which the architect addresses them, and even if they do understand, it often is difficult for the sociologist to respond on these terms. Sociology prides itself today on being a scientific discipline that investigates problems systematically and that aims to provide systematic answers. It is hard for the sociologist to relinquish the methods of work that these standards impose on him, just as the architect apparently finds it difficult to do the opposite, namely to abandon his impulse to find design solutions in favor of a careful, analytical examination of a problem. Yet I have found that the sociologists who have been most successful in their dealing with architects are those who are willing to adopt a somewhat more casual attitude toward their own discipline. When presented with a problem, they don't as sociologists so often tend to do, propose a research project; instead, they try in a responsible way to give the architect their best judgment about the issue, based on their accumulated experience in conducting research, teaching, and reviewing the research of others.

B. The subject matter of sociology is social groups, society and human activities; the subject of architecture is building. There are fundamental distinctions between the essential nature of these phenomena, building and society. Buildings are physical objects but societies and groups are social and cultural facts. One important difference between physical objects and social facts is that physical objects can be sensed directly through the eye and by touching them; values, norms, statuses, classes, and social roles are ascertainable indirectly, only by inferring their existence from the behavior patterns that they regulate and determine. I think that many of the difficulties that develop between architects and sociologists arise from these differences in the way in which one learns about the nature of objects and social facts. For example, physical objects have form; inescapably they are sculptural phenomena. Anyone who works with them regularly in a professional capacity, as the architect does, becomes sensitive to variations in form and to the capacity of forms to communicate significant information. Sociologists don't spend their time considering objects as part of their occupational routine. I think this is one important reason why sociologists often do not understand the architect's emphasis on formal and aesthetic considerations in building, or why they are puzzled when the architect poses questions about the social consequences of formal differences. It works the other way, too, I would guess. For the reason that he is necessarily busy dealing with the world of form, the architect tends to anthropomorphize forms, to endow them with life, and to search out their possible social significance. The architect finds it difficult to accept the fact that phenomena with such potent tactile qualities do not have an important immediate influence on many patterns of social action. The sociologist, on the other hand, devotes himself full time to inferential activities; since values, norms, statuses and classes cannot be perceived by the eye, he develops a capacity to guess at their existence even though they are not immediately apparent. It is not at all difficult for him to believe that the important determinants of human action are not available to touch or to look at; and he is frankly suspicious of anyone who, in his view, is so simple-minded as to equate what is visible with what is influential.

The differences between the nature of building and the nature of social groups is of greater fundamental significance than is implied by only pointing to the intellectual styles they engender in architects and sociologists respectively. Buildings behave differently than people do. Buildings are generally fixed in space, whereas groups can and do move about easily. The simplest illustration of this difference is that the same family in the course of a generation can occupy several different dwelling places, but only rarely is a building transferred from one location to another. Social groups are reorganized more easily and can shift their elements more speedily than is possible for the units that make up a building. For example, compare the high turnover rate in the staff of industrial work groups with the difficulties encountered in renovating a Victorian factory. Furthermore, groups can be enormously resourceful in finding new means for achieving established goals. But a building has no sensorium. It cannot by itself learn its shortcomings, communicate this knowledge to part of itself, and then reform itself in order to maintain its capacity under new external conditions to achieve its original purpose.

These differences in the natural capacity of buildings and social groups impose serious limitations on the power of buildings to influence social action. A building is not capable of outwitting a recalcitrant or unsympathetic user. The user can leave it and maintain his established mode of behavior intact. The inhabitant can alter the building, making it respond to his needs, and the building cannot fight back. If the facilities provided by the building somehow manage to frustrate a user in attaining or maintaining a way of life, this is only temporary; the user can find new means, independent of the building, for achieving the same objective. This is very odd, because again judging by looks alone, buildings should be more powerful than people. They are heavier, can withstand more physical assault, and are usually bigger. But men have capacities for survival that buildings don't have and this makes all the difference. So long as buildings are different from groups in these respects—and even the ambition of the architects of indeterminism to make buildings grow, change, and generally behave like people is unlikely to transform their fundamental nature—it will continue to be difficult to forecast the effect that buildings will have on society.

C. The act of designing necessarily demands information about other matters than user requirements, but nevertheless all of us would recognize that a conscientious concern for the program is an essential ingredient of good design. The nature of buildings, on the one hand, and of human beings and groups, on the other, however, suggest that our understanding of the program and how the building can be used to fulfill it will always remain imprecise. The information and the theory that the designer must use thus will always fall short of meeting the standards of exactness and certainty that some designers desire and that most sociologists recognize as essential for the further progress of their own discipline.

As a sociologist, given my background and training, I find it amazing and wonderful that architects are willing and able to design buildings given the fragmentary character of the knowledge in terms of which they must proceed. I have asked myself how it is possible for them to do it. The answer I give to this question is itself sociological. Architects are able to be good designers because our society has thrown up the culture of architecture and created a social role in which the individual who adopts this culture and fulfills its demands is rewarded. If the individual who is an architect manages to design buildings that work reasonably well, that stand up and are pleasant to the eye he gets paid a regular salary, he can become a member of a chartered society, and he earns the respect of colleagues and the admiration of the nation. If he should prove incapable of proposing a building that meets these standards, if he balks at the fact that he is being asked to commit himself to a plan without sufficient knowledge on which to base that plan, then he doesn't get a job as an architect, he doesn't get the respect of his colleagues, and he cannot put the initials ARIBA or AIA after his name. To put it in another way, we can say that the social role, "architect," and the culture, "architecture," are organized in a way that is particularly appropriate for encouraging individuals to assume the responsibility of making design decisions.

The culture and role structure of sociology and the sociologist are very different. Architects seem not to realize, for instance, that sociology is the name of a particular scholarly discipline and sociologists traditionally have been members of learned societies rather than professional associations. Academic rewards do not go to the sociologist who plans or builds a society on the basis of fragmentary knowledge about human needs, social structure and technology, but to the sociologist who studies an important social problem in a new way, or who develops a theory that explains a variety of apparently unrelated facts. Many sociologists are members of the teaching profession, but this is something else; in their role as sociologists they are researchers, students and analysts. Judgments about their competence as sociologists are made privately, by other sociologists rather than, as is so often the case in architecture, by clients, users and tourists who are not expert in the subject of building. Sociologists are not compelled to serve social purposes immediately or to provide solutions to problems on short notice.

I am aware, of course, that the distinction I have introduced is exaggerated and idealized, and no longer describes adequately the condition either of sociology or architecture. In fact, at the urging of the other professions, including architecture, sociology is gradually being forced to assume the kind of responsibilities traditionally associated only with the professions. And architecture, in order to merit its admission into the British university structure and to demonstrate its relation to modern scientific philosophies, is becoming more like a discipline. Still these changes are developing only gradually, and I don't think it is seriously proposed that architecture will ever be anything other than a highly skilled and subtle craft, no matter how sophisti-

367

cated it becomes as a profession, or that sociology will ever abandon its status as a learned, scholarly enterprise. In admitting this fact about their essential nature, however, sociologists must continue to explore the possibility that sociology would be a better and more competent discipline if some sociologists at least had the experience of applying their information in the context of professional problems; and if they from time to time assumed the burden of decision making that goes along with being a professional person. Just as architects must strive to make architecture a more perfect craft by having some of their colleagues devote themselves to social research.

But do we really believe these commands? Statements of the kind I just offered are often espoused on suitable ritual occasions, such as this one, when architects, educators and social scientists meet together. If we do honestly believe them we must consider much more carefully than we have up to now how the curriculum of architectural schools should be revised; and how faculties and departments of sociology can begin to acquaint postgraduate and research students with the culture and dilemmas of architecture. What kind of sociology should architecture schools teach? Who should teach it for them? What kind of architecture should be taught to sociology students? Who should teach it to them? In what ways should we restructure the context in which architects now make use of sociology? How can we ensure that research on buildings conducted by sociologists will make maximum use of the experience, knowledge and wisdom of the architect? How, in other words, are we to produce a true social architecture and a genuine architectural sociology? These are the questions that architects and sociologists should ask.

NOTES

1. I wish to thank the Rutgers University Research Council and the Russell Sage Foundation for the support that made it possible for me to undertake the research on which this selection is based.

2. I am especially grateful for the hospitality extended to me in the U.S.A. by Professor Robert Geddes, Dean, School of Architecture, Princeton University; and in England for the help given me by Professor Lord Llewelyn-Davies (Professor of Architecture), Mr. John Madge (Director of the Sociological Research Unit) and Mr. Peter Cowan (Director of the Joint Unit for Planning Research), all of University College, London.

3. Alvin Schorr, *Slums and Social Insecurity*, U.S. Department of Health, Education and Welfare, Social Security, Administration, Division of Statistics, Research Report No. 1, Washington 25, D.C., 1963.

4. Rudolf Wittkower, *Architectural Principles in the Age of Humanism*, London: Tiranti Ltd., 1962.

Colin Rowe, especially, "The Mathematics of the Ideal Villa," *Architectural Review*, March 1947, pages 101–104; and "Mannerism and Modern Architecture," *Architectural Review*, May 1950, pages 289–298.

5. Social research dealing with the influence of the built environment on social action is discussed in my paper, "Site Planning and Social Behavior" in Joachim Wohlwill and Robert Kates, eds., "Man's Response to His Environment," *Journal of Social Issues*, October 1966.

6. Sir Leslie Martin and Lionel March, "Land Use and Built Forms," *Cambridge Research*, April 1966, pages 8–14.

7. Sim Van der Ryn, *et al.*, *The Ecology of Student Housing: A Case Study in Environmental Analysis and Design*, Berkeley, Calif.: University Students Cooperative Association, no date.

23

The Room, A Student's Personal Environment

SIM VAN DER RYN AND MURRAY SILVERSTEIN

It could easily be inferred from the tone of many of the selections in this book that although there is a growing awareness of the relevance of the behavioral sciences to architecture, little has as yet been done to apply the concepts and research techniques of these sciences to actual design projects. However, the situation is otherwise; both in this country and in Europe one can point to a variety of program documents, design proposals, and in some cases, finished building projects, that have utilized sociology and psychology as collaborative disciplines.

The following selection by Van der Ryn and Silverstein deals with a dormitory program and design proposal. Presented with the problem of formulating basic program information and generating building specifications for student housing for the University of California, these two architects decided that, before beginning to work on the program, they would study how space in existing dormitories was being used and try to determine the degree and sources of satisfaction or dissatisfaction among the occupants. Their data consisted of observations of the pattern of space use, activity logs which indicated the students' schedules and the kinds of activities that took place in the dormitories or elsewhere on campus, and interviews to identify the attitudes of students toward existing facilities.

One of the most interesting features of the inquiry is that Van der Ryn and Silverstein made practical use of many of the behavioral science concepts discussed earlier in this volume, such as personal space, territoriality, and privacy. These concepts helped them anticipate the possible sources of tension and strain in the existing dormitories, and the questions included in the interviews and the types of behavior observed were focused around these concepts. These concepts also served as dominating ideas to guide the spatial organization and the choice of materials incorporated in the design schemes. In this sense, it may be appropriate to regard the building specifications included in the text as early examples of what may well be an emerging trend in contemporary architecture, namely an architecture whose form

Reprinted from Sim Van der Ryn and Murray Silverstein, *Dorms at Berkeley: An Environmental Analysis*, Center for Planning and Development Research (Berkeley, University of California Press, 1967), pp. 31–34; 36; 38; 70; 72–75.

and style can be traced to a behavioral science view of human nature and man's principal social needs.

The selection reprinted here deals only with the room environment. In the larger work on dormitory design from which the selection is taken, the authors also discuss their findings and proposals as they relate to common rooms, lounges, food facilities, and other amenities appropriate to student housing.

☐

Our activity logs and interviews indicate that students spend one-third of their waking hours in their rooms. The total time spent in the room is greater than that spent anywhere else. The design of the individual student room and its immediate surroundings is the key planning element in college housing.

The Berkeley high-rise dorms are a good example of the most prevalent plan in student housing over the past twenty years: a multi-story building, each floor with a central corridor lined on both sides with identical two-student-to-a-room quarters. It was this plan that David Reisman and Christopher Jencks had in mind when they wrote, "At an average cost of roughly $4,000 per student, the typical student residence joins two students, two beds, two bureaus, two desks, two straight chairs, and two hundred square feet of floor in an effort to produce enlightenment." [1] Creating conditions where students can achieve privacy and solitude has yet to be achieved by most housing planners. The literature of student housing is rich with phrases such as "experience in group living," "social adjustment," etc. Such rhetoric may be a justification for the fact that typical dormitory plans do not resolve the prime student need for *individual* living. Sociologist Marvin Trow, in a keynote speech to a workshop discussing life in the residence halls, stressed that one of the three functions he saw as essential for dorms was, "the opportunity to be alone, to think, to read, to work, or to just be alone." [2]

The concept of "personal space realm" or "personal territory," which has been understood by students of animal behavior for some time, [3] and studied more recently by anthropologists and social psychologists, [4] provides a clue to the nature of student irritation with the room. Whether it is expressed by the song bird who warbles in defense of her nest, or by the urban gang defending its "turf," both men and animals exhibit the need for a personal territory. The student wants to establish a unique home territory that is fixed in space and that is the locus of those activities most important to him. The room is the focal point of private and semi-private activities. For students it is "home" territory.

When personal space characteristics are not available, problems result. Control over personal space is of special importance in a large, urban university like the Berkeley campus; the new student, overwhelmed by the size and impersonal nature of the campus, needs some kind of place to identify with and hang his hat in. There is some evidence that in circumstances that require the individual to adapt to drastically altered cultural settings, "home" and its amenities assume ever greater importance than when the social and physical environment is familiar.

The room is one place where an individual, at-home feeling ought to be available for the student, since most other areas in the residence hall housing must be shared with others. Lounges and date rooms serve 200 students. The recreation rooms are "about as homey as a Greyhound depot," as one student put it.[5] The bathroom, which in the family home is one haven for privacy, serves about 25 students on each floor. One girl who moved out of the dorm said of apartment life, "where else could you sit in the bathtub for hours and read the *Tropic of Cancer?*"[6]—certainly not in the dormitory.

Perhaps the greatest single deterrent to adequate privacy is sharing less than 200 square feet of space with someone else for 35 weeks. Clashes between incompatible roommates appear commonplace, and probably affect a student's approach to his work. Over half of the students we interviewed simply told us, "I can't stand my roommate." Sleep, study, and intimacy are activities which require personal territory, while other needs may be met by degrees of common space.

Even when two roommates are compatible, there are irritations inherent in sharing private space. One girl said, "You don't have privacy in a dorm when you have a roommate"; another, "It's impossible to be able to be by yourself in the dorms; you go to campus if you want this." No one has measured the psychic stress or the effect on student well-being or academic performance caused by the strain of living in close quarters. We have, however, documented some of the ways students adapt to the double occupancy situation. The most obvious adaptation is that one roommate is forced out of the room. Students often have incompatible schedules. Spot checks and analysis of activity log data indicate that both students seldom are studying together in the room at the same time. Thus the supposed economies of two-to-a-room occupancy planning tend to shift the burden of pro-

372

viding places for study, solitude, and relaxation to other facilities on campus.

The individual room is most responsive to differing schedules. A realistic look at schedule determinants would show a rich set of variations. Some university work can only be done at a particular place and time (certain libraries, for example); some work, while it is due at a special time, is left to each individual to complete as his time permits; other types of study demand peculiar conditions and special environments, while some are dependent on nothing more than a place to sit with good light; exam schedules vary from class to class, and exam preparation time will differ correspondingly. Every student has a slightly different schedule imposed on him from campus, and this schedule effectively structures much of his time. Furthermore, each student has a personal or idiosyncratic schedule. Of course the personal schedule will often respond to the campus schedule—if a student contracts for a class at 8:00 a.m., he presumably will give up his habit of sleeping in—but personal schedules should not be overlooked. With increased emphasis on individual work and independent research, college housing must be designed to tolerate eccentric schedules.

Henry Wriston, a college president for many years, sums it up this way:

> If I had been able to find money enough, every dormitory I had anything to do with would have been made up of single rooms—no doubles, much less suites for three or four. Single rooms constitute no danger that undergraduates will not learn how to live with other people. Their lives are much too gregarious; even if they have one room where privacy is possible, they will still have enough group experience to avoid becoming anti-social.[7]

Along with shared living space, noise is a great enemy of privacy. Loud noises carry along the corridor and through adjacent rooms. Complaints about noise were numerous in the group interviews and in unsolicited comments written on the student logs. Rooms next to lounges, across from the elevator, laundry or bathroom suffer from lack of sufficient wall insulation and sealing around doors. Rooms at the ends of the hall are reputed to be quieter, and the residents experience fewer interruptions. Slamming doors, conversations, radios, and hi-fi's are common problems at night. One student observed that "because of the 'community living,' there seems to be a constant low-volume noise. This can be very irritating at times."

Another source of irritation is the awareness that one might disturb others. "It would be nicer if the rooms were soundproof. For instance, when I practice ballet or play my guitar, there is always someone complaining that they are trying to study."

Girl students are particularly sensitive to the feeling of being watched while in their rooms. In a letter to the *Daily Cal*, one girl wrote, "The men from the neighborhood dorm have no need for social events and mixers for they have already met us with binoculars and telescopes." [8] It may be that there are various thresholds of visual invasion. The residence halls at Berkeley seem to fall short here, as more than once they have given rise to comments that dorm life is like "living in a crowded fish bowl." [9]

Another related source of irritation comes from wanting to protect one's possessions. There have been a number of cases of thefts of clothing and other equipment. Most often such losses are the result of leaving rooms unlocked during dinner. During one dispute about maid service, a student charged that he had found a maid looking through his belongings. It turned out that she had briefly glanced at a newspaper he had left open on his desk.[10] A trivial incident perhaps, but indicative of conditions which can destroy the feeling of security in one's personal environment.

Inflexibility of room equipment and regulations pertaining to its use are a major source of student discomfort. Two issues that are cited continually are wall surface decoration and built-in furniture. One girl who had moved from the dorm to an apartment put it quite clearly: "We've got space. . . . I can hang things up if I want to, and rearrange the furniture . . . everything!" [11]

When new students move into the dorm, they are, of course, eager to hang prints and clippings, even paint the walls. The University responds by prohibiting "tacking, taping or otherwise marring the wall finish." It is the Housing Administrators' point of view that, while students come and go, the building remains and must be kept up at reasonable expense. As a result, decorating is confined to a small 12″ x 24″ cork-board, placed behind the door. (However, many students ignore the rule; hence, unannounced inspections are necessary.) This is typical of student housing on many campuses. One student explained how to cope with the situation: "I put a lot of posters, etc. on my ceiling to decorate the place a little . . . the bulletin board, the little thing it is, is located behind the door, so when the door is open— it covers the bulletin board completely! Hanging stuff from those stupid hooks at the ceiling corners is ridiculous."

Psychiatric observations suggest that the rooms for women are seen as extensions of their physical persons.[12] It becomes as important to

374

dress the room as to dress oneself. One girl remarked during Spring 1964 that she planned to leave because, "the dorms are just too much like home, having everything done for you." [13]

Rules which prohibit room decoration, while motivated in part by the desire to maintain a clean and uniform front, are dictated by administrative decisions to avoid damage to wall finishes. While much effort has gone into promulgating rules, little seems to have gone into finding innovative solutions to the problem. Student rooms should be designed so that residents can make non-permanent changes. One approach is to line permanent wall elements with a surface that can be decorated and replaced periodically at a cost not exceeding routine painting and maintenance.

With regard to the inflexibility of room arrangement and equipment, the program for the design competition for these dormitories was quite specific:

Bedrooms: *Each bedroom shall have a floor area of 182 square feet net. The bedrooms shall have no built-in furniture or fixed equipment of plumbing fixtures. Items of moveable furniture (the design of which is not part of this program) with their respective dimensions are as follows:*

2 beds each 6'-8" x 3'-0"
2 wardrobe units each 2'-0" x 5'-0"
2 chests of drawers each 21-12" x 28" x 45" high
2 desks each 26½" x 41½" x 30" high
2 chairs

It is desired that each student have the maximum opportunity to arrange this furniture as he pleases. The owner, through experience, has found that room dimensions of 14' of exterior wall by 13' in depth have provided such maximum opportunity. These room dimensions are strongly recommended.[14]

The assumption about moveable furniture appears to be well-founded. We discovered that a great variety of furniture arrangements were created by students, although many of these arrangements fell into identical patterns. It appears that roommates rearrange furniture as often as once every ten weeks.

Two out of three of the women's arrangements were represented by one plan, in which desks faced away from each other and towards the wall and beds were placed against the wall with the head at the corner. Men's room arrangements tended to be more asymmetrical and represented a wider variation of arrangements. The fixed relationships in the room (closet, window, mirror, wall lamps and door) eliminated many arrangement possibilities. However, we conclude that in the double occupancy situation, roommates try to create their own territory; they try to escape each other's field of vision; they seek spatial isolation while sleeping.

The desire for personal territory is expressed in room arrangement in a number of ways. An analysis of room arrangement patterns shows that 94 per cent of the sample group arranged furniture completely on one side of a hypothetical line that splits the room into two equal halves, in spite of the fact that many other arrangements are possible. The inference we draw from this is that the desire to create personal territory is stronger than the desire to share space with a roommate. Another finding concerns the desire of students to study without being observed by their roommates. In the majority of rooms, students re-arranged desks so that when they are at their desks their angle of vision excludes one another from view. It is likely that when students share a room, they prefer not to be observed by one another.

In the Berkeley dorm, moveable furniture *alone* does not provide the degree of flexibility or convenience that students would prefer. Our interviews and questionnaires revealed a seemingly endless list of specific complaints about features of the room design, which we will not recount here. Our hunch is that many of these complaints were generated by basic social and psychological dysfunctions of double occupancy.

Equipment that must, by its nature, be fixed should be placed conveniently; one student notes that "it would be nice if the phone were located differently, so that people coming in the door don't run into you while you're talking on the phone." Another student added, "under the present conditions it is impossible to open the door when someone is standing at the [book] shelves." Inadequate space is another source of complaints; "I need room for the phonograph, it bothers the person next door when next to the wall."

A woman student noted that "the rooms are too small for any convenient arrangement giving both occupants sufficient privacy, typing or studying late for example." Another woman student added a short, unsolicited essay on the same subject at the end of our questionnaire:

> *There simply isn't enough space in this room. My phonograph sticks out into the middle of the room, and I had to turn my dresser sideways to make room for a guitar. Also we would appreciate having curtains that could be opened without our having to stand on the beds and pull them. A light in the middle of the room instead of one small one over the back mirror would be a big improvement; so would moveable mirrors. It would also be nice if the phone was located differently, so that people coming in the door don't run into you while you're talking on the phone. The location of the light*

switch is also inconvenient—it makes the use of one bookshelf impossible. We also feel that a different type of window sill would be a great improvement if possible; the metal sills now make it impossible to sit on your bed and lean against the window. Therefore, we are almost forced to have just one room arrangement. . . . Other than that, the rooms are fine, other than the fact that if we wish to adjust the heat we have to either crawl under our desks or move our beds, depending on the room arrangement. Thank you for giving us the chance to air our complaints.

The trend in student housing is away from moveable furniture and towards built-in furnishings. This is unfortunate because built-in systems further limit the potential for variety and the ability of students to shape their room space to meet personal needs. It is clear that just as there is no ideal student, there is no ideal fixed room arrangement; what is important is that students make a place their home by asserting their own preferences and changing it. Periodic furniture rearrangement may also be a way of letting off steam, trying to achieve variety in an otherwise monotonous environment, and expressing frustration with difficult social conditions. It may be that if the room and its surfaces lent themselves to other forms of personalization, the need to have moveable furniture might not be as great.

However, many administrators have substantial reasons for holding other views. Although moveable furniture may be financed through Federal College housing loan programs, some lenders follow the practice of considering only built-ins as part of the real estate package. Secondly, free standing furniture pieces are commonly of heavier construction and use more material than built-in systems (which can use walls for structural support), and thus are often more expensive. It is claimed that it is more efficient for maids to clean around the built-in equipment which is wall-hung and has no dust-collecting floors beneath it. Built-in equipment gives the room a neater appearance than free-standing furniture, and damage due to moving furniture around is minimized.

While these views are reasonable, they ignore the realities of student living as we have seen them. Many precedents for college housing administration and planning are derived from hotel management. Yet the student room is not a hotel room for a transient, it is the student's home for at least 200 days. Thus a fixed furniture arrangement which may be fine for the casual guest becomes an irritant to a resident over a period of time. The wish of a hotel keeper to show off a neatly arranged room to the public is reasonable, but the dorm is not a hotel. We question whether routine cleaning is not better left to residents

377

rather than outside help. Finally, with respect to furniture, resistance to wear in relation to first cost has usually been the prime criterion. Tolerance and recovery from wear are equally important criteria. It may be appropriate in some instances to deliberately choose inexpensive furniture with a short use life. Pieces can be replaced periodically, over the life of the building, at no higher annual cost than expensive highly resistant furnishings.

Administrators, of course are not unaware of these points. Their professional journals show them to be continually interested in the products of modern materials research. Chester Winter, writing in *College and University Business*, emphasizes the importance of a personal and personally determined student room environment. He states that

> . . . *students were genuinely concerned with regimentation. . . . The opportunity, though limited, to move furnishings as an expression of the student's personal living habits appeared to be very important. . . . Furnishings and decor deserve special attention. The details of the finishing touches largely set the tone of the room and make the difference between a homelike atmosphere and the stilted, barren character typical of much college housing.*[15]

Finally, the results of a survey at St. Olaf's College correspond to our Berkeley findings:

> . . . *after a certain point is reached, the effort to find a perfectly efficient size and arrangement for a dormitory room is not fruitful . . . the rooms in Ellingson Hall in St. Olaf were planned to provide what is generally agreed to be a lucid, logical and efficient space for two students. In them there is one arrangement of furniture which exploits this potential to its fullest. In an inspection of forty-one rooms two weeks after school began in September, 1962, however, only six were found to be remaining in the original efficient arrangement. In the others the furniture had been rearranged in an almost baffling variety of ways. This sort of thing could be found in any dormitory where rooms are all identical to each other. The obvious conclusion is that "functional" efficiency is not a very important thing in the mind of the student. . . . One way for him to assert uniqueness is to arrange his room differently from that of his neighbors . . . and he does this at the expense of efficiency, which his vitality can compensate for, and sometimes at the expense of any at all.*[16]

The old Las Casitas housing on the Santa Barbara campus of the University of California is reported to have been heavily favored by students over accommodations of better physical quality. The housing officer on the campus suggests that the reason for this popularity was that students could do what they wanted to their rooms. Similar results are reported for the rather cramped trailer units used at Santa Cruz for temporary housing.

The editor of the *Daily Californian*, in an editorial on the students' apparent preference for apartments, states that "people will put up with a lot when on their own as compared to being at home or in a dorm." [17]

• • •

Our evaluation at Berkeley and additional surveys of student housing conditions across the country lead us to some conclusions about student housing needs and how they may be met through design. Following are user needs and performance specifications for (1) room furnishings and personal space arrangement and (2) the room itself.

• • •

Furniture and Equipment

USER NEEDS:

1. Students want to rearrange their furniture from time to time.

2. Bed is a popular study location.

3. Desks must permit comfortable study involving two or three books, typewriter, and papers.

4. Desk chair must permit free shifting, tilting, leg stretching, etc., comfortably; when students cannot make such adaptations they are likely to have less productive study sessions.

5. Students occasionally try to visually "break-up" their room-space. Moveable closets provide a needed barrier.

6. Students want to extensively "personalize" their rooms; this involves tacking, painting, hanging, etc., on wall surfaces.

7. Because student residents come and go, housing administrators want to periodically return rooms to original conditions at minimum cost.

SPECIFICATIONS:

1. All components are moveable (e.g., all furnishings may be rearranged by two freshman girls).

2. The bed unit can be either free standing or hung from the wall (at student's discretion), bed unit includes adjustable backrest, integral lighting fixture, swing-away night table.

3. Desk unit has minimum dimensions:

45" long   24–30" wide   28–30" high

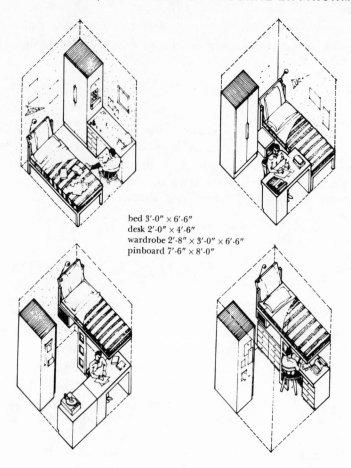

bed 3'-0" × 6'-6"
desk 2'-0" × 4'-6"
wardrobe 2'-8" × 3'-0" × 6'-6"
pinboard 7'-6" × 8'-0"

Figure 23–1   Typical Unit Furnishing Arrangements in 7' × 6" by 7' × 6" Space.

There is adequate clear-space beneath desk for stretching and crossing legs; desk unit includes soft-covered tilt-back chair (doubles as an easy chair).

4. The closet unit is free-standing and moveable; it may contain drawers and double as a dresser; optional free-standing bureau (compatible with desk height for added surface). Some minimum dimensions for closet unit:

Full length hanging space: 60" high   20–30" wide
½ length hanging space: 30" high   16" wide
24" closet depth

The external surface of closet (back, sides, front) is usable as tackboard surface.

380

5. Wall surface panels provided for painting, hanging, etc.; panels are moveable and are dimensioned 7′6″ x 4 or 7′6″ x 8; panels may be installed and replaced without complicated tools.

Room

USER NEEDS:

1. For the most part students want single rooms; a few, usually incoming freshmen, will prefer double rooms; some students will accept roommates to reduce costs.

2. Some students will want to change from double to single accommodations as they progress through school.

3. In general, students want choice in the cost of their accommodations; they want to choose from a variety of living conditions; various amenities, single or double, etc., according to their pocketbook needs.

4. Student residents will want to put up an occasional visitor; off-campus commuters may want to rent sleep and study space for one or two days/week only.

5. Even when sharing a room students want a personal space (capable of containing all their furnishings and equipment) that is visually separate from their roommate.

6. Students prefer privacy in bathrooms; for the most part they resist "gang bathrooms."

7. Students want to have visitors in their quarters without inconvenience to others.

8. Acoustical privacy is an essential students require of their rooms; double doors with buffer space is a sure way of providing this kind of privacy.

9. Students may want to come and go in their private space without running into others from their shared living space.

10. Total space per student should not, for economic feasibility, exceed 250 square feet or $5000.

Specifications:

1. All rooms are of three types:
   a) strictly single rooms   b) optional, single or double rooms
   c) strictly double rooms
   (Note: types b and c can accommodate visitors, e.g., commuters needing an occasional sleep/study space.)

381

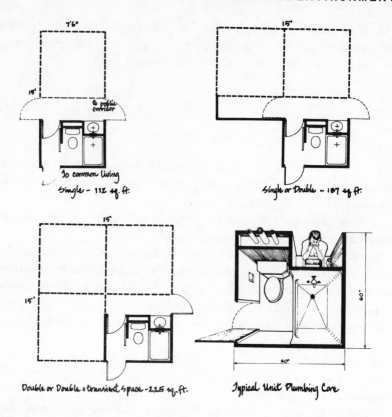

1. Single Occupancy—112 Square Feet

2. Single or Double Occupancy—187 Square Feet

3. Double Occupancy (with guest space)—225 Square Feet

4. Typical Unit Plumbing Core

Figure 23–2 Typical Unit Plans.

2. All rooms are based on a 7′6″ module; each module capable of containing complete personal territory for one student; bed, storage, and desk in a visually protected space.

3. Each room has its own bathroom core.

4. Each room has two entrances:

   a) one entrance directly onto public passageway;

   b) one entrance to common living space shared by several other rooms.

5. Each entrance has two doors separated by a usable acoustic buffer space.

6. Each room receives natural light from at least one window; the window is at eye level for a person both sitting and standing.

NOTES

1. Jencks, Christopher and David Reisman, "Patterns of Residential Education: A Case Study of Harvard," in Nevitt Sanford, ed., *The American College* (New York: John Wiley and Sons, 1964), p. 732. Average cost in 1967 is closer to $6000 per student.

2. Trow, Martin, "Reflections on the Residence Hall Program," unpublished speech given at Residence Hall Workshop, Berkeley, October 1961.

3. See works by John B. Calhoun, Robert Ardrey, H. Hediger, H. Tinbergen, C. R. Carpenter, K. Lorentz.

4. See works by Edward T. Hall, Robert Sommer, Humphrey Osmond.

5. *Daily Californian*, October 20, 1961.

6. *Daily Californian*, November 10, 1961.

7. Wriston, Henry, *Academic Procession* (New York: Columbia University Press, 1955), p. 192, quoted in Trow, *op. cit.*

8. *Daily Californian*, February 17, 1964.

9. *Daily Californian*, February 6, 1964.

10. *Daily Californian*, March 1, 1965.

11. Friedlander, Neal and Alan T. Osborne, "Apartments for Women," *Comment*, University of Pennsylvania, Philadelphia, Pa., Fall 1965, p. 8.

12. See Theodore Reik, *Of Love and Lust: On the Psychoanalysis of Romantic and Sexual Emotions*, or Jurgen Ruesch and Weldon Kees, *Non-Verbal Communication* (Berkeley: University of California Press, 1956).

13. *Oakland Tribune*, February 6, 1964.

14. Program for the competition for dormitories written by John Lyon Reid.

15. Winter, Chester N., "Full-Scale Model Gives Room a Trial Run," *College and University Business*, Vol. 37, No. 6, December 1964, pp. 47–49.

16. University Facilities Research Center and Educational Facilities Laboratories, *High Rise or Low Rise? A Study of Decision Factors in Residence Hall Planning*, New York, November 1964, p. 44.

17. *Daily Californian*, March 13, 1964.

24

Old People's Flatlets at Stevenage

MINISTRY OF HOUSING AND LOCAL GOVERNMENT

Architectural design has been described as a process of successive approximation in which the architect proposes a series of tentative hypotheses stating a reasonable fit between the shifting needs of building users and the environments they plan to inhabit. If this view of the design process is valid, then the behavioral sciences must be involved in a continuing collaborative relationship during the design process. In practice, this means that in addition to helping develop basic program information, sociologists and psychologists should also have a hand in translating the program into a design scheme and in evaluating completed projects. The aim of this form of collaboration should be to use the information about user response turned up in the building evaluation as a basis for improving the quality of future design.

This total approach to cooperation between architecture and the behavioral sciences has been tried with some success in England, particularly by the research and development groups in the national ministries responsible for building. Teams made up of architects, sociologists, cost estimators (the British call them quantity surveyors), and engineers work together in the same office. They assess existing environments, use this information in the formulation of programs (in British usage, briefs), collaborate on the design of the project, assess the design once it is built, and then use this information for the subsequent round of design and construction.

The following selection reports on such a combined effort made by the Ministry of Housing and Local Government to develop a scheme for old people's housing in the new town of Stevenage, outside London. The Ministry had been concerned with housing for the aged since the 1950s, when it first published general recommendations for architectural standards for such housing. In 1962 it issued reports of two studies (made in 1960 and 1961) that had assessed user response to some of the existing old people's housing in England, and on the basis of these inquiries developed a new set of standards and design recommendations. The Stevenage housing, which made use of these studies, was built in 1962, and the Stevenage report, from which the selection reprinted here is taken, is a reassessment of the standards and basic schemes that emerged from the 1960 and 1961 studies.

Reprinted from Ministry of Housing and Local Government
Design Bulletin 11—*Old People's Flatlets at Stevenage* (London:
HMSO, 1966), pp. 3–6. Reprinted by permission of the
Controller of Her Britannic Majesty's Stationery Office.

384

Two features of the assessment studies are especially worthy of note. One is the wide range of user needs and requirements that were included in the project brief and evaluated in the finished units. These requirements include elements relating to basic biological needs, such as sanitary facilities, heating, ventilation, lighting, and sleeping accommodations, as well as elements relating to social needs, such as the design of common rooms and the provision of facilities for social life. The second is the deliberate effort on the part of the research and development group to incorporate the design of social conveniences into the physical design. For example, the initial assessment studies of 1960 and 1961 indicated the importance of providing a warden in old people's housing and of making sure the warden would be available to deal with the emergencies that continually plague the elderly. Accommodation for a warden, usually a woman and often a woman whose husband is responsible for the physical maintenance of the building, was included in both the basic project brief and the recommended design schemes. This amenity seems to have worked out quite well in meeting the needs of the old people, although the warden herself could have used more privacy.

□

Introduction

1. For some years the Ministry of Housing and Local Government has urged local authorities to build more dwellings of all kinds for old people and to provide grouped flatlets, with full-time resident wardens, for those old people who may sometimes need a helping hand. The Ministry's recommendations on the design of grouped flatlets were published in 1958 and 1960.[1]

2. During 1960 and 1961 the Ministry carried out more detailed studies of the problems of old age. The results of these studies were published as two of the Ministry's series of design bulletins.[2] In particular, Design Bulletin 2, which will be often referred to in this bulletin, embodied a survey of the first six blocks of flatlets for old people constructed by local authorities in this country.

3. The intention of these studies was that they should be put to practical effect, and the Ministry had decided to undertake, as a development project, the design and construction of a grouped flatlets scheme. The Stevenage Development Corporation, who were at the time about to make further provision for old people, agreed to be the client authority for the development project. The Ministry's architects thus acted in effect as private architects to the Corporation.

4. The Corporation's Architects' Department collaborated with the Ministry and advised on the project. Their quantity surveyors, with

their detailed knowledge of local conditions, were responsible for general cost advice and undertook the preparation of the cost plan and analyses and of the bills of quantities. The Corporation's landscape architect carried out the design of the landscaping.

5. The development team within the Ministry consisted of architects, an administrator, a sociologist and a housing manager. The advice in *Flatlets for old people* and *More flatlets for old people* was taken as a starting point, but it was implicit in the terms of reference for the project that the detailed suggestions in those two handbooks would be modified where necessary to take account of the team's surveys and investigations.

6. The ever-lengthening time needed to carry out building contracts, the scarcity of site labor and increasing shortages of technical staff highlighted the need for the development of a component system of construction. Although this was not part of the original brief, it was undertaken as part of the project. A nominated contractor was appointed to collaborate during the design period.

7. The project included a social appraisal made after the flatlets, now called Ross Court, had been occupied for 18 months. The summary which follows juxtaposes in parallel columns the findings of Design Bulletin 2 and the other preliminary studies, the requirements of the project brief, and the evaluation of the project brief in the appraisal survey. This makes it possible to see, in outline, what the user requirements were, how far they were planned for and what lessons are to be learnt from them.

8. At the same time, sweeping conclusions should not be drawn from either the project or the appraisal. Design Bulletin 2 was compiled from only six local authority flatlet schemes and the number of elderly residents interviewed was ninety-nine. The appraisal discussed here is based on interviews with only twenty. Thus the requirements in the project brief and the findings of the appraisal survey reflect the views of a minute sample of elderly people. And no two schemes of this type are exactly similar in site, cost, methods of selecting tenants, etc.

9. However, many of the lessons to be drawn from the Stevenage project, such as elderly people's extreme sensitiveness to draughts and their sturdy refusal to do just what they were expected to do in such matters as placing their beds, are probably of general application. Since 1960, when the study embodied in Design Bulletin 2 was carried out, many more local authorities have embarked on flatlet schemes

386

and will have encountered similar problems to those which faced the Development Group's architects. But others, who are contemplating schemes, may find the account of the Stevenage project and the lessons to be learnt from it of value.

The Surveys

SURVEY FOR USER REQUIREMENTS

10. At the outset, in 1960, the sociologist carried out a survey of the first six blocks of flatlets built by local authorities in different parts of the country. Information was gathered by observation and by interviews with housing managers, wardens and tenants. The results of the survey are published as Design Bulletin 2.

11. In addition, visits were made to accommodation of all types, from self-contained dwellings to welfare homes. The views of managements and designers, as well as those of old people themselves, were heard, and the quantity, size and arrangement of furniture were studied. The information was recorded and used during the planning stage.

12. Little information about the physical dimensions of old people was available. As this design information was urgently needed a small pilot study of these dimensions was commissioned. The results are set out in Design Bulletin 1.

APPRAISAL SURVEY

13. In the winter of 1963–1964, when the flatlets had been occupied for some 18 months, as many tenants as were willing were interviewed by a team of sociologists and architects. Two married couples out of four were interviewed, and sixteen people out of twenty living on their own. The sociologists used a prepared questionnaire, and the architects drew sketches of the furniture arrangement and recorded the amount of furniture in each flat.

The Summary

14. The following paragraphs contain a summary of the findings of the studies for user requirements; the project brief which emerged from them; and the evaluation of the project's design in the appraisal survey.

387

Study Findings	*Project Brief*	*Evaluation*
15. Warden The success of any flatlets scheme for old people depended largely on the qualities of the warden. The wardens visited had widely different backgrounds, from nursing to housekeeping. Most were kindly and understanding with sympathy for the difficulties of old age, and willing to be helpful in most situations.	The scheme to be planned with accommodation for one warden, looking after twenty people living alone in bed-sitting rooms and four couples in one-bedroom flats.	
The warden's duties are described in detail in Design Bulletin 2 (pages 2–3). In general, they exercised inconspicuous supervision, gave good-neighborly day-to-day assistance to the tenants, helped them in emergencies and acted as the link with the management.	The accommodation of the warden to allow easy access to the tenants.	This was achieved, but the warden should have been given more privacy.
The contact between warden and tenants was easier where covered and heated circulation space was provided between the flatlets and the warden's house.	Link warden's house and the flatlets with heated corridor.	Successful.
16. Number of Tenants	Twenty people living alone and four married couples.	The total number appeared satisfactory, but there were too few men living alone to be company for each other.
17. One-Person Bed-Sitting Rooms Minimum-sized rooms of 140 sq. ft. caused some dissatisfaction, but rooms of 170–180 sq. ft. satisfied almost all tenants.	Bed-sitting rooms to be at least 170 sq. ft.	The bed-sitting room of 166 sq. ft. proved adequate in size, but was designed too specifically for a preconceived quantity and arrangement of furniture. Bulkier furniture than was expected sometimes obscured low windows.

388

Study Findings	Project Brief	Evaluation
		A design suited to a greater variety of furniture arrangement would have been preferable.
It was evident that a bed recess gave a more convenient arrangement of furniture, but there were complaints about ventilation and the absence of a window in the recess.	A well-ventilated bed recess with a window and an interesting view to be provided.	Ventilation and lighting of the bed recess were found satisfactory, although the position of the windows did not allow air movement across the bed recess. Often the head of the bed was placed out of reach of the light switch and bell pull, and study is needed of other ways of placing these so that they can be used from different positions. An optional curtain to draw across the bed recess would have been appreciated. The considerable demand for separate bedrooms should be borne in mind in future schemes.
Sound reduction between corridor and flatlet was inadequate where front doors from the corridor opened directly into the bed-sitting room.	A lobby should be provided between corridor and bed-sitting room.	The only disturbing noise heard from the corridor was doors banging. Door fittings to prevent this are needed.

18. Storage Provision for linen and brooms was often inadequate.	All dwellings to be fitted with hanging space for clothes and with linen and broom cupboards.	Adequate, but a shelf needed in the broom cupboard. In general, more shelving would have been appreciated.

19. Kitchens Cupboard kitchens in bed-sitting rooms were generally criticized for lack of storage and food preparation space, and for the difficulty of eliminating cooking smells.	Separate kitchens required.	The separate kitchens were found satisfactory, but storage capacity was often insufficient and the food cupboard was too near the hot water cylinder.

389

Study Findings	Project Brief	Evaluation
Top shelves were sometimes beyond the reach of tenants, working tops at unsuitable heights, and sinks too wide for comfortable reach to the taps.	Anthropometric data to be used to determine optimum heights and widths for fittings and sinks.	No person in normal health had any difficulty in reaching any shelves.

20. Shared Sanitary Facilities

In flatlets, only half the tenants used the bath. This was usually due to physical disability rather than to any objection to sharing. Some tenants with skin disorders were worried about the possibility of passing them on.	Baths to be shared in the ratio of one to four persons. A variety of arrangements and aids to be provided for different physical disabilities. The shower to be designed for easy use.	The number of baths was ample, and sharing did not lead to any difficulties. The aids were useful, but in a small scheme of this kind not so many different ones were needed. The shower was used by a handicapped man, but otherwise not liked or used at all.
In flatlets where handbasins were not provided, only one-fifth of the tenants used those provided in the shared bathrooms and w.c.s: they preferred to use their own kitchen sinks.	Each flatlet to have a handbasin.	This was generally used.
Although there were few objections to sharing a w.c., it was clear this was inconvenient to some tenants, particularly at night, and encouraged the use of pots.	Each flatlet to have a w.c. (The Development Corporation felt that in any case the housing standards of the New Town demanded this.)	The individual w.c. was much preferred to more space in the flatlet. The internal w.c. compartment, though occasionally criticized, was satisfactory.

21. Common Room and Social Life

Wardens explained that, though most old people enjoyed watching television, it had limited the use of the common room for other social activities and caused some arguments over program selection.	The common room to have two separate spaces, one for television viewing, the other for other social activities.	In practice, one large subdivisible room would have been more useful than the two rooms.
It was observed that in flatlet blocks the corridor was used as a social meeting place.	Informal sitting spaces to be provided in the corridor.	These spaces were well-sited and well-justified.

390

Study Findings	Project Brief	Evaluation
Most guest rooms in flatlet schemes were large, and none had been used for accommodating visitors.	Only minimum provision to be made for guests.	In fact, no provision was made for guests, as the idea of using the small common room also as a guest room could not be carried out because it was a through room. The tenants of the flatlets expressed no wish for guest rooms, but they usually had relatives living near who could presumably put up guests. The warden, however, would have appreciated a spare room for guests.
A common room in the center of the building with a view of life going on was more popular than a secluded one. Planning the warden's flat next to the common room encouraged the warden to help things along from her kitchen when necessary.	The common room to overlook the center of interest, and to adjoin the warden's accommodation.	The common room was well placed in the center of the flatlets, but it was unnecessarily disturbing to have it as a corridor from the front door to one wing of the flatlets.

22. Call-Bell

Most flatlets were provided with a warning bell system connected to the warden's home, but some indicator boards did not identify the flat which needed help. Very few schemes made provision for someone to deputize when the warden left the building.	Devise efficient call-bell system enabling a tenant to deputize for the warden.	The warden would have liked the call-bell to sound in her bedroom or her garden, by a switch-over. And a supplementary indicator outside rooms could have been provided. The deputizing system worked well.

23. Heating

Central heating was the service most highly valued in the flatlets studied. Tenants had many problems with open fires, which are described in Design Bulletin 1, page 4.	Provide the kind of central heating best suited to the physiological needs of old people.	The off-peak electric floor-warming system was chosen to ensure warmth throughout without stuffiness and to avoid the effects of dust-laden air on sufferers from respiratory complaints. (As the first floor is timber, under floor heating could not be used there.)

391

Study Findings	Project Brief	Evaluation
		It succeeded in this, but as operated initially did not yield sufficient heat in a very cold winter. Even so, it was too much at night for many tenants. Owing to the cold it was used to provide a higher temperature than originally calculated, and this, together with a structural defect, resulted in the running costs being higher than originally estimated. Costs were reduced in the second year, but were still high. At first the level of heating was uneven through the week but this has been adjusted.
24. Communal Food Stores In centrally heated flatlets there were problems of keeping food cool.	Investigate the provision of communal refrigerators.	Provision of communal refrigerators has been justified, although the milk is not delivered directly to them. However, the refrigerators should be on the same floor level as the flats.
25. Laundry Survey suggested that about one-third of the tenants were able to do all their own washing, about a quarter were not doing any at all, and the remainder were washing small items at home and sending the larger wash to the laundry. The scheme where the highest percentage of old people did all their own washing was well equipped with washing and drying machines. Where constant advice and assistance was given by the warden, all the old people used the machines; in schemes	Investigate provision of suitable washing machines, and outdoor and indoor drying facilities.	One type of washing machine installed proved easy to operate, but the other type did not and is being replaced. Their provision was justified by their use, but more outdoor drying facilities are needed.

392

Study Findings	Project Brief	Evaluation

where explanation and encouragement were not given, the complexity of the machines tended to discourage the old people from using them. There were very few complaints about drying arrangements when both indoor and outdoor facilities were provided within easy distance of the flats.

26. Floor Preference

Study Findings	Project Brief	Evaluation
Most of the tenants interviewed lived on the ground floor and only a few would have preferred to live any higher. The preference of some tenants for the first floor is discussed in Design Bulletin 2, page 10; with increasing age and disability this preference naturally decreased.	Most of the accommodation to be provided at ground level.	No one was dissatisfied with his floor level, and there was ample room on the ground floor for all who could not manage stairs easily.

NOTES

1. Ministry of Housing and Local Government. *Flatlets for old people.* HMSO 1958 (2s. 6d) and *More flatlets for old people.* HMSO 1960 (2s.).

2. Ministry of Housing and Local Government. Design bulletins: 1. *Some aspects of designing for old people.* HMSO 1962 (2s. 6d.) and 2. *Grouped flatlets for old people: a sociological study.* HMSO 1962 (5s.).

25

Typology and Design Method

ALAN COLQUHOUN

The use of the behavioral sciences in architecture is often based on the assumption that the architect, by relying on the techniques and concepts of the behavioral sciences, will be able to circumvent some of the traditional difficulties of arriving at design solutions. One such difficulty, present in every design situation, is that of closing the gap between the information contained in a building program and the final organization of three-dimensional space that constitutes the constructed artifact. Many architects and designers who use the behavioral sciences in their work often seem to be arguing that their solutions can be derived more or less directly from the program, or if this is not possible, that the gap can be closed and the solutions obtained from the interaction of the program's content with the architect's intuitive, creative ability.

In the following selection Colquhoun argues against this doctrine. He is concerned with the application of the biological and engineering sciences to design, what he calls biotechnical determinism, but his position is equally relevant to architectural solutions based upon sociological or psychological data. His argument is that both the belief in a scientifically determined architecture and the belief in an architecture based on the combination of science and intuition rest on false premises. With regard to the former doctrine Colquhoun cites the autobiographical statements of several architects who have tried to use objective data and mathematical techniques in their own work. These statements make it quite clear that the designer is always faced with making voluntary decisions and that these decisions are based on intentions and purposes that exist prior to the development of the program. In other words, Colquhoun is contending that architects or planners who claim, in the manner of evolutionary theorists, that their solutions follow from their data in a teleologically determined manner, simply do not understand the mental processes they experience during the process of design.

Colquhoun's argument against the significance of free intuition is based upon anthropological findings, in particular the structuralist theories of Lévi-Strauss. According to Lévi-Strauss the images and representations that develop in a society are not simply derived from objective facts—there is, Lévi-Strauss argues, no discernible biological basis for explaining the variety of kinship systems that emerge in different societies or the preferences

Reprinted from Alan Colquhoun, "Typology and Design Method," in *Arena*, The Architectural Association Journal, London (June 1967): 11–14, by permission of the editor.

people exhibit for particular kinship forms. Instead, kinship systems are arbitrary systems of social interrelationships whose sources can be found in the histories and rule systems of particular cultures. Although these rules exhibit certain regularities, the regularities exist at the level of culture and cannot be reduced to biological or technical principles. Colquhoun cites the conclusions of Lévi-Strauss to support his assertion that the freedom of the individual imagination is a fiction, a fiction built into modern architectural thinking. In his view it derives from the expressionist phase in modern architecture, which was so popular in Europe during the 1920s and is still pervasive in American design circles. This may explain why it is that the behavioral science approach has been more popular among those American architects who identify themselves with the modern movement than it is among those still committed to conventional styles of building.

Given the fact that design solutions cannot be based entirely on scientific knowledge about people's needs and behavior or on the fusion of this knowledge with the designer's creative ability, Colquhoun turns to the much maligned tradition of "building typologies" as a source of design solutions. Building typologies, in his use of the term, are sociospatial organizational schemata, which through time have yielded forms appropriate for sheltering human activities. Since, given the nature of architectural phenomena, reliance on these typologies is, in Colquhoun's view, inevitable, designers would be better off to admit their influence. Only to the degree that the importance of typologies is made manifest, and their influence made the subject of discussion and evaluation, can one hope to achieve a rational architecture, that is an architecture that is neither deterministic or intuitive, but one that makes the most appropriate use of both scientific knowledge and the individual designer's creative ability. Colquhoun is astute enough to recognize the possibility that his theory will be taken to justify a conservative stance toward building and the rejection of advances in the use of scientific knowledge and innovations in building form, but he obviously believes that an intelligent use of his approach can avoid these pitfalls.

□

During the last few years a great deal of attention has been given to the problem of design methodology, and to the process of design as a branch of the wider process of problem solving.

Many people believe—not without reason—that the intuitive methods of design traditionally used by architects are incapable of dealing with the complexity of the problems to be solved, and that without sharper tools of analysis and classification, the designer tends to fall back on previous examples for the solution of new problems—on type solutions.

One of the designers and educators who has been consistently preoccupied by this problem is Tomas Maldonado. At a recent seminar at Princeton University, Maldonado admitted that, in cases where it was not possible to classify every observable activity in an architectural program, it might be necessary to use a typology of architectural forms in order to arrive at a solution. But he added that these forms were like a cancer in the body of the solution, and that as our techniques of classification become more systematic it should be possible to eliminate them altogether.

Now, it is my belief that beneath the apparently practical and hard-headed aspect of these ideas lies an aesthetic doctrine. It will be the purpose of this selection to show this to be the case, and, further, to try and show that it is untenable without considerable modification.

One of the most frequent arguments used against typological procedures in architecture has been that they are a vestige of an age of craft. It is held that the use of models by craftsmen became less necessary as the development of scientific techniques enabled man to discover the general laws underlying the technical solutions of the pre-industrial age.

The vicissitudes of the words "art" and "science" certainly indicate that there is a valid distinction to be drawn between artefacts that are the result of the application of the laws of physical science and those that are the result of mimesis and intuition. Before the rise of modern science, tradition, habit and imitation were the methods by which all artefacts were made, whether these artefacts were mainly utilitarian or mainly religious. The word "art" was used to describe the skill necessary to produce all such artefacts. With the development of modern science, the word "art" was progressively restricted to the case of artefacts that did not depend on the general laws of physical science, but continued to be based on tradition and the ideal of the final form of the work as a fixed ideal.

But this distinction ignores the extent to which artefacts have not only a "use" value in the crudest sense, but also an "exchange" value.

The craftsman had an image of the object in his mind's eye when starting to make it. Whether this object was a cult image (say a sculpture) or a kitchen utensil, it was an object of cultural exchange, and it formed part of a system of communications within society. Its "message" value was precisely the image of the final form which the craftsman held in his mind's eye as he was making it and to which his artefact corresponded as nearly as possible. In spite of the development of the scientific method we must still attribute such social or iconic values to the products of technology, and recognize that they play an essential role in the generation and development of the physical tools of our environment. It is easy to see that the class of artefacts that continue to be made according to the traditional methods (for example paintings or musical compositions) have a predominantly iconic purpose, but such a purpose is not so often recognized in the creation of the environment as a whole. This fact is concealed from us because the intentions of the design process are "hidden" in the overt details of performance specification.

The idolization of "primitive" man, and the fundamentalist attitude which this generates, have also discouraged the acceptance of such iconic values. There has been a tendency since the eighteenth century to look on the age of primitive man as a golden age in which man lived close to nature. For many years, for instance, the primitive hut or one of its derivatives has been taken as the starting point for architectural evolution, and has been the subject of first-year design programs, and it would not be an exaggeration to say that frequently a direct line of descent is presumed to exist from the noble savage, through the utilitarian crafts to modern science and technology. In so far as it is based on the idea of the noble savage, this idea is quite baseless. The cosmological systems of primitive man were very intellectual and very artificial. To take only kinship systems, the following quotation from the French anthropologist Claude Lévi-Strauss will make the point clear: "Certainly," he says, "the biological family is present and persists in human society. But what gives to kinship its character as a social fact is not what it must conserve of nature; it is the essential step by which it separates itself from nature. A system of kinship does not consist of objective blood ties; it exists only in the consciousness of men; it is an arbitrary system of representations, not the spontaneous development of a situation of fact." [1]

There seems to be a close parallel between such systems and the way modern man still approaches the world. And what was true of primitive man in all the ramifications of his practical and emotional life—namely the need to *represent* the phenomenal world in such a way that it becomes a coherent and logical system—persists in our own organizations, and more particularly in our attitude towards the man-made objects of our environment. An example of the way this applies to contemporary man is in the creation of what are called sociospatial schemata. Our sense of place and relationship in, say, an urban environment, or in a building, are not dependent on any objective fact that is measurable; they are phenomenal. The purpose of the aesthetic organization of our environment is to capitalize on this subjective schematization, and make it socially available. The resulting organization does not correspond in a one-to-one relationship with the objective facts, but is an artificial construct which *represents* these facts in a socially recognizable way. It follows that the representational systems which are developed are, in a real sense, independent of the quantifiable facts of the environment, and this is particularly true if the environment is changing very rapidly.

No system of representation, no meta-language, however, is totally independent of the facts which constitute the objective world. The modern movement in architecture was an attempt to modify the representational systems which had been inherited from the pre-industrial past, and which no longer seemed operable within the context of a rapidly changing technology. One of the main doctrines at the root of this transformation was based essentially on a return to nature, deriving from the romantic movement, but ostensibly changed from a desire to imitate the surface of natural forms or to operate at a craft level, to a belief in the ability of science to reveal the essence of nature's mode of operation.

Underlying this doctrine was an implied belief in bio-technical determination. And it is from this theory that the current belief in the supreme importance of scientific methods of analysis and classification derives. The essence of the functional doctrine of the modern movement was not that beauty or order or meaning was unnecessary, but that it could no longer be found in the deliberate search for final forms. The path by which the artefact affected the observer aesthetically was seen as short-circuiting the process of formalization. Form was merely the result of a logical process by which the operational needs and the operational techniques were brought together. Ultimately these would fuse in a kind of biological extension of life, and function and technology would become totally transparent. The theory of Buckminster Fuller is an extreme example of this doctrine.

The relation of this notion to Spencerian evolutionary theory is very striking. According to this theory the purpose of prolonging life and the species must be attributed to the process as a whole, but at no particular moment in the process is it possible to see this purpose as a conscious one. The process is therefore unconscious and teleological. In the same way, the bio-technical determinism of the modern movement was teleological because it saw the aesthetic of architectural form as something which was achieved without the conscious interference of the designer, but something which none the less was postulated as his ultimate purpose.

It is clear that this doctrine contradicts any theory which would give priority to an intentional iconic form, and it attempts to absorb

398

the process by which man tries to make a representation of the world of phenomena back into a process of unconscious evolution. To what extent has it been successful, and to what extent can it be shown to be possible?

It seems evident, in the first place, that the theory begs the whole question of the iconic significance of forms. Those in the field of design who were—and are—preaching pure technology and so-called objective design method as a sufficient and necessary means of producing environmental devices, persistently attribute iconic power to the creations of technology, which they worship to a degree inconceivable in a scientist. I said earlier that it was in the power of all artefacts to become icons, no matter whether or not they were specifically created for this purpose. Perhaps I might mention certain objects of the nineteenth-century world of technology which had power of this kind —steamships and locomotives, to give only two examples. Even though these objects were made ostensibly with utilitarian purposes in mind, they quickly became *gestalt* entities, which were difficult to disassemble in the mind's eye into their component parts. The same is true of later technical devices such as cars and airplanes. The fact that these objects have been imbued with aesthetic unity and have become carriers of so much meaning indicates that a process of selection and isolation has taken place which is quite redundant from the point of view of their particular functions. We must therefore look upon the aesthetic and iconic qualities of artefacts as being due, not so much to an inherent property, but to a sort of availability or redundancy in them in relation to human feeling.

The literature of modern architecture is full of statements which indicate that after all the known operational needs have been satisfied, there is still a wide area of choice in the final configuration. I should like to quote two designers who have used mathematical methods to arrive at architectural solutions. The first is Yona Friedmann, who uses these methods to arrive at a hierarchy of organization in the program. In a recent lecture, in which he was describing methods of computing the relative positions of functions within a three-dimensional city grid, Friedmann acknowledged that the designer is always after computation, faced with a choice of alternatives, all of which are equally good from an operational point of view.

The second is Yannis Xenakis, who, in designing the Philips Pavilion while he was in the office of Le Corbusier, used mathematical procedures to determine the form of the enclosing structure. In the book which Philips published to describe this building, Xenakis says that calculation provided the characteristic form of the structure, but that after this logic no longer operated; and the compositional arrangement had to be decided on the basis of intuition.

From these statements it would appear that a purely teleological doctrine of technico-aesthetic forms is not tenable. At whatever stage in the design process it may occur, it seems that the designer is always faced with making voluntary decisions, and that the configurations which he arrives at must be the result of an *intention,* and not merely the result of a deterministic process. The following statement of Le Corbusier tends to reinforce this point of view. "My intellect," he says, "does not accept the adoption of the modules of Vignola in the matter of building. I claim that harmony exists between the objects one is dealing with. The chapel at Ronchamp perhaps shows that architecture is not an affair of columns but an affair of plastic events. Plastic events are not regulated by scholastic or academic formulae, they are free and innumerable."

Although this statement is a defense of functionalism against the academic imitation of past forms and the determinism it denies is academic rather than scientific, it none-the-less stresses the release that follows from functional considerations, rather than their power of determining the solution.

One of the most uninhibited statements of this kind comes from Moholy-Nagy. In his description of the design course at the Institute of Design in Chicago, he makes the following defense of the free operation of intuition. "The training," he says, "is directed towards imagination and inventiveness, a basic condition for the ever-changing industrial scene, for technology in flux. The last step in this technique is the emphasis on integration through the conscious search for relationships. The intuitive working methods of genius give a clue to this process. The unique ability of the genius can be approximated by everybody if one of its essential features be apprehended: the flashlike act of connecting elements not obviously belonging together. If the same methodology were used generally in all fields we could have *the* key to the age—seeing everything in relationship.[2]

We can now begin to build up a picture of the general body of doctrine embedded in the modern movement. It consists of a tension of two apparently contradictory ideas—biotechnical determinism on the one hand, and free expression on the other. What seems to have happened is that, in the act of giving a new validity to the demands of function as an extension of nature's mode of operation, it has left a vacuum where previously there was a body of traditional practice. The

400

whole field of aesthetics, with its ideological foundations and its belief in ideal beauty, has been swept aside. All that is left in its place is permissive expression, the total freedom of the genius which, if we but knew it, resides in us all. What appears on the surface as a hard, rational discipline of design, turns out rather paradoxically to be a mystical belief in the intuitional process.

I would like now to turn back to the statement by Maldonado which I mentioned at the beginning of this selection. He said that so long as our classification techniques were unable to establish all the parameters of a problem, it might be necessary to use a typology of forms to fill the gap. From the examples of the statements made by modern designers it would seem that it is indeed never possible to state all the parameters of a problem. Truly quantifiable criteria always leave a choice for the designer to make. In modern architectural theory this choice has been generally conceived of as based on intuition working in a cultural vacuum. In mentioning typology, Maldonado is suggesting something quite new, and something which has been rejected again and again by modern theorists. He is suggesting that the area of pure intuition must be based on a knowledge of past solutions to related problems, and that creation is a process of adapting forms derived either from past needs or on past aesthetic ideologies to the needs of the present. Although he regards this as a provisional solution—"a cancer in the body of the solution"—he none the less recognizes that this is the actual procedure which designers follow.

I suggest that this is true, and moreover that it is true in all fields of design and not only that of architecture. I have referred to the argument that the more rigorously the general physical or mathematical laws are applied to the solution of design problems the less it is necessary to have a mental picture of the final form. But, although we may postulate an ideal state in which these laws correspond exactly to the objective world, in fact this is not the case. Laws are not found in nature. They are constructs of the human mind; they are models which are valid so long as events do not prove them to be wrong. They are models, as it were, at one remove from pictorial models. Not only this. Technology is frequently faced with different problems which are not logically consistent. All the problems of aircraft configuration, for example, could not be solved unless there was give and take in the application of physical laws. The position of the power unit is a variable, so is the configuration of the wings and tailplane. The position of one affects the shape of the other. The application of general laws is a necessary ingredient of the form. But it is not a sufficient one for

401

determining the actual configuration. And in a world of pure technology this area of free choice is invariably dealt with by adapting previous solutions.

In the world of architecture this problem becomes even more crucial because general laws of physics and the empirical facts are even less capable of fixing a final configuration than in the case of an airplane or a bridge. Recourse to some kind of typological model is even more necessary in this case.

It may be argued that, in spite of the fact that there is an area of free choice beyond that of operation, this freedom lies in the details (where, for instance, personal "taste" might legitimately operate). This could probably be shown to be true of such technically complex objects as airplanes, where the topological relationships are largely determined by the application of physical laws. But it does not seem to apply to architecture. On the contrary, because of the comparatively simple environmental pressures that operate on buildings, the topological relationships are hardly at all determined by physical laws. In the case of Philips Pavilion, for example, it was not only the acoustic requirements which established the basic configuration, but also the need for a building which would convey a certain impression of vertigo and fantasy. It is in the details of plan or equipment that these laws become stringent, and not in the general arrangement. Where the designer decides to be governed by operational factors, he works in terms of a thoroughly nineteenth-century rationalism, for example in the case of the office buildings of Mies and SOM, where purely pragmatic planning and cost considerations converge on a received neoclassic aesthetic to create simple cubes, regular frames and cores. It is interesting that in most of the projects where form determinants are held to be technical or operational in an avant-garde sense, rationalism and cost are discarded for forms of a fantastic or expressionist kind. Frequently, as in the case of "Archigram," forms are borrowed from other disciplines, such as space engineering or pop art. Valid as these iconographic procedures may be—and before dismissing them one would have to investigate them in relation to the work of Le Corbusier and the Russian constructivists which borrowed the forms of ships and engineering structures—they can hardly be compatible with a doctrine of determinism, if we are to regard this as a *modus operandi,* rather than a remote and utopian ideal.

The exclusion by modern architectural theory of typologies, and its belief in the freedom of the intuition, can at any rate be partially explained by the more general theory of expression which was current

402

at the turn of the century. This theory can be seen most clearly in the work and theories of certain painters—notably Kandinsky, both in his paintings and in his book *Point and Time to Plane*, which outlines the theory on which his paintings are based. Expressionist theory rejected all historical manifestations of art, just as modern architectural theory rejected all historical forms of architecture. To it these manifestations were an ossification of technical and cultural attitudes whose *raison d'être* had ceased to exist. The theory was based on the belief that shapes have physiognomic or expressive content which communicates itself to us directly. This view has been subjected to a great deal of criticism, and one of its most convincing refutations occurs in E. H. Gombrich's book *Meditations on a Hobby Horse*. Gombrich demonstrates that an arrangement of forms such as is found in a painting by Kandinsky is in fact very low in content, unless we attribute to these forms some system of conventional meanings not inherent in the forms themselves. His thesis is that physiognomic forms are ambiguous, though not wholly without expressive value, and that they can only be interpreted within a particular cultural ambience. One of the ways he illustrates this is by reference to the supposed affective qualities of colors. Gombrich points out in the now famous example of traffic signals, that we are dealing with a conventional and not a physiognomic meaning, and maintains that it would be equally logical to reverse the meaning system, so that red indicated action and forward movement, and green inaction, quietness and caution.[3]

Expressionist theory probably had a very strong influence on the modern movement in architecture. Its application to architecture would be even more obvious than to painting, because of the absence, in architecture, of any forms which are overtly representational. Architecture has always, with music, been considered an abstract art, so that the theory of physiognomic forms could be applied to it without having to overcome the hurdle of anecdote representation, as in painting. But if the objections to expressionist theory are valid, then they apply to architecture as much as to painting.

If, as Gombrich suggests, forms by themselves are relatively empty of meaning, it follows that the forms which we intuit will, in the unconscious mind, tend to attract to themselves certain associations of meaning. This could mean not only that we are *not* free from the forms of the past, and from the availability of these forms as typological models, but that, if we assume we are free, we have lost control over a very active sector of our imagination, and of our power to communicate with others.

It would seem that we ought to try to establish a value system which takes account of the forms and solutions of the past, if we are to gain control over concepts which will obtrude themselves into the creative process, whether we like it or not.

There is, in fact, a close relationship between the pure functionalist or teleological theory that I have described, and expressionism, as defined by Professor Gombrich. By insisting on the use of analytical and inductive methods of design, functionalism leaves a vacuum in the form making process. This it fills with its own reductionist aesthetic— the aesthetic that claims that "intuition," with no historical dimension, can arrive spontaneously at forms which are the equivalent of fundamental operations. This procedure postulates a kind of onomatopoeic relationship between forms and their content. In the case of a bio-technico/determinist theory the content is the set of relevant functions—functions which themselves are a reduction of all the socially meaningful operations within a building—and it is assumed that the functional complex is translated into forms whose iconographical significance is nothing more than the rational structure of the functional complex itself. The existent facts of the objective functional situation are the equivalent of the existent facts of the subjective emotional situation, in the case of expression theory. But traditionally, in the work of art, the existent facts, whether subjective or objective, are less significant than the values we attribute to these facts or to the system of representation which embodies these values. The work of art, in this respect, resembles language. A language which was simply the expression of emotions would be a series of single-word exclamations; in fact language is a complex system of representation in which the basic emotions are structured into an intellectually coherent system. It would be impossible to conceive of constructing a language *a priori.* The ability to construct such a language would have to presuppose the language itself.[4] Similarly a plastic system of representation such as architecture has to presuppose the existence of a given system of representation. In neither case can the problem of formal representation be reduced to some pre-existent essence outside the formal system itself, of which the form is merely a reflection. In both cases it is necessary to postulate a conventional system embodied in typological solution/problem complexes.

My purpose in stressing this fact is not to advocate a reversion to an architecture which accepts tradition unthinkingly. This would imply that there was a fixed and immutable relation between forms and meaning. The characteristic of our age is change, and it is precisely because this is so that it is necessary to investigate the part which modifications of type solutions play in relation to problems and solutions which are without precedent in any received tradition.

I have tried to show that a reductionist theory according to which the problem/solution process can be reduced to some sort of essence is untenable. One might postulate that the process of change is carried out, not by a process of reduction, but rather by a process of exclusion, and it would seem that the history of the modern movement in all the arts lends support to this idea. If we look at the allied fields of painting and music, we can see that, in the work of a Kandinsky or a Schoenberg, traditional formal devices were not completely abandoned, but were transformed and given a new emphasis by the exclusion of ideologically repulsive iconic elements. In the case of Kandinsky it is the representational element which is excluded; in the case of Schoenberg it is the diatonic system of harmony.

The value of what I have called the process of exclusion is to enable us to see the potentiality of forms as if for the first time, and with naivety. This is the justification for the radical change in the iconic system of representation, and it is a process which we have to adopt if we are to keep and renew our awareness of the meanings which can be carried by forms. The bare bones of our culture—a culture with its own characteristic technology—must become visible to us. For this to happen, a certain scientific detachment towards our problems is essential, and with it the application of the mathematical tools proper to our culture. But these tools are unable to give us a ready-made solution to our problems. They only provide the framework, the context within which we operate.

NOTES

1. Claude Lévi-Strauss. *Structural Anthropology.* Basic Books, New York, 1963.
2. L. Moholy-Nagy. *Vision in Motion.* Paul Theobald, Chicago, 1947.
3. It is interesting that, since his book came out, the Chinese have in fact reversed the meanings of their traffic signals.
4. For the study of language as a system of symbolic representation see Cassirer, *Philosophy of Symbolic Forms.* Yale University Press, 1957. For a discussion of language in relation to literature (metalanguage) see Roland Barthes, *Essais Critiques.* Editions du Seuil, Paris, 1964.

26

The City as a Mechanism for Sustaining Human Contact

CHRISTOPHER ALEXANDER

In the previous selection Colquhoun argues that to believe that design solutions can be derived from scientific data alone runs the danger of misrepresenting the nature of architectural phenomena and the process through which buildings in fact get designed. From the point of view of the behavioral sciences the current interest in applying the findings of these disciplines to design runs another risk. It would appear from the way in which architects and planners tend to make use of sociology and psychology, that they do not allow these disciplines to deal with the full range of building and design issues to which they are potentially relevant.

Probably the most striking instance of this underutilization is the tendency of many architectural users of sociology or psychology either to assume that the behavioral scientist is proficient only in providing technical assistance in gathering data about user requirements, which the architect or client will then use for his own purposes, or, at the other extreme, to assume that the sociologist or psychologist is in all situations an ideologically committed representative of the neglected, and in many cases impoverished, user, and should therefore be employed in the design process as the users' spokesman. Both of these views are caricatures. In practice, most sociologists would argue that their competence to serve as technical assistants for identifying user requirements is limited, primarily because the discipline has only recently become interested in group activities in space. And many certainly eschew the role of serving as political representative for one group or class in society, even though the organization of our society today has made many people conclude that it is the poor and the blacks whose opinions and preferences are most easily overlooked in the design and building process, and who must therefore receive extra attention and support.

A more reasonable view of the potential contribution of the behavioral sciences is to regard them as concerned with the examination of the ends and purposes implicit in programs and design schemes and the evaluation of these ends, not just in terms of the needs of the user population, but from

This is an abridged version of Christopher Alexander's article,
"The City as a Mechanism for Sustaining Human Contact,"
which appeared in *Environment for Man*, edited by William R.
Ewald (Bloomington: Indiana University Press, 1967), pp. 60–102.
© 1967 by Indiana University Press. Reprinted by permission
of the publisher.

the perspective of the needs of the community as a whole. The behavioral sciences should also be regarded as capable of dealing with the full range of means, both physical and social, on which architectural solutions depend if their intentions are to be fulfilled. Used in this way the behavioral sciences are not, as they are sometimes accused of being, antithetical to the utopian tradition in architecture. Rather they offer the possibility of establishing fundamental reforms of the social and physical order on a more rational basis.

It is his sensitivity to the possibility of using behavioral research to deal with both the ends and means of design that makes Alexander's selection interesting. Its subject is the problem of loneliness, anomie, and alienation in the contemporary urban environment; the author, consistent with good sociological practice, redefines this problem as the absence of human contact. Alexander summons a substantial body of empirical research to show that the lack of human contact is the cause of many individual and social pathologies, such as psychosis and juvenile delinquency. He also discusses the evidence for the view that anomie is largely the consequence of the highly fragmented social and physical organization of urban society.

In the final portion of his selection, Alexander proposes a design scheme for reducing the amount of loneliness in the city. This scheme is an amalgam of twelve separate design elements, each of which is derived from a rational analysis of the lack of good fit between social needs and existing urban environments. The rational analysis is based on the behavioral research reported in the earlier portions of his selection. It uses a model that assumes that social pathology is the consequence of need frustration, and explains the frustration of needs in terms of the absence of compatibility between buildings and urban forms and basic psychological or group process requirements. Each of the twelve design elements proposed is justified in terms of the likelihood that it will eliminate or minimize the poor fit, thus hopefully reducing the need frustration, and, in turn, again hopefully, leading to the reduction of neurosis and anomie. The solution considered as a totality is reminiscent of many solutions developed by avant garde architects in this country and in Europe over the last 50 years: high-density housing; self-designed dwelling units; multilevel streets, corridors, and parks; abundant private and semiprivate spaces; and separate pedestrian and high-speed vehicular traffic flow systems.

Students of the relationship of architecture to behavior will be made uncomfortable by Alexander's ambition to control or influence activity patterns by providing just the right fit between the physical environment and human needs; the degree of indeterminacy in the interaction between man and the environment is a major issue which demands further investigation. From the point of view of many sociologists and architects it may be preferable for architects to design spaces with very general qualities and characteristics, on the assumption either that the users will know best how to accommodate their needs to the spaces after occupancy, or that a wide range of human activities can use similar spatial organizations. It is also somewhat disturbing to find that Alexander makes no recommendations for the social and administrative programs that might be required if his model of urban form is to achieve the desired aims. Both these shortcomings illustrate what one might call the tragedy of architecture today, namely that when he is forced to consider his designs in terms of their social consequences, even an architect with a sophisticated grasp of the behavioral sciences and committed to rational analysis tends to fall back on the assumption of architectural determinism. The note that Alexander has written for this abridged version of his original article indicates that he has become aware of this difficulty and that he looks upon his selection as a more general proposal than a literal interpretation of his model of urban form would suggest.

□

Author's Note: I wrote this article five years ago, and I see its shortcomings very clearly now. I believe that the two central insights, concerning the need to strengthen children's primary groups, and the need to make informal dropping-in more common among adults, are still correct.

However, I should like to make it clear that the configuration of houses that I proposed to accommodate these two needs is no more than a diagram, and as I now realize—a very exaggerated diagram. In 1965 I was anxious to show that physical design could be drawn directly from social problems— and this led me to make a much more literal diagram than I should make today. The two central needs are real needs—but they can be used to shape a far more subtle, and more humane, kind of housing than I showed in my diagram.

People come to cities for contact, yet almost all the people who live in cities suffer from endless inner loneliness. They have thousands of contacts, but the contacts are empty and unsatisfying. *What physical organization must an urban area have, to function as a mechanism for sustaining deeper contacts?*

Before we can answer this question, we must first define exactly what we mean by "contact" and we must try to understand just what it is about existing cities that prevents the deepest contacts from maturing. This selection therefore has four parts: In the first part I shall define the most basic, and most urgently needed kind of contact, *intimate contact*. In the second part I shall present evidence that strongly suggests that the social pathologies associated with urban areas—delinquency and mental disorder—follow inevitably from the lack of intimate contact. In the third part I shall describe the interplay of phenomena that causes the lack of intimate contact in urban areas today. These phenomena are facets of a single complex syndrome: *the autonomy-withdrawal syndrome*. I shall try to show that this syndrome is an inevitable by-product of urbanization, and that society can only re-create intimate contacts among its members if they overcome this syndrome. In the fourth part I shall show that in order to overcome the autonomy-withdrawal syndrome a city's housing must have twelve specific geometric characteristics, and I shall describe an arrangement of houses that has these characteristics.

408

Intimate Contact

Modern urban society has more contact and communication in it than any other society in human history. As metropolitan areas grow, society will become even more differentiated, and the number and variety of contacts will increase even more. But as the total number of the individual's contacts increases, his contacts with any one person become shorter, less frequent, and less deep. In the end, from a human point of view, they become altogether trivial. It is not surprising that in just those urban centers where the greatest expansion of human contacts has taken place, men have begun to feel their alienation and aloneness more sharply than in any pre-industrialized society. People who live in cities may think they have lots of friends, but the word friend has changed its meaning.

Intimate contact, by which we mean that close contact between two individuals in which they reveal themselves in all their weakness, without fear, is very rare. It is a relationship in which the barriers that normally surround the self are down. It is the relationship that characterizes the best marriages, and all true friendships. We often call it love. It is hard to give an operational definition of this kind of intimate contact, but we can make it reasonably concrete by naming two essential preconditions without which it can't mature.

These conditions are: (1) The people concerned must see each other very often, almost every day, though not necessarily for very long at a time. If people don't meet almost every day—even if they meet once a week, say—they never get around to showing themselves; there are too many other things to talk about. (2) They must see each other under informal conditions. Many people meet every day at work. But here the specific role relationship provides clear rules about the kinds of things they talk about, and also defines the bounds of the relationship. The same thing is true if they meet under "social" circumstances, where the rules of what is proper make deep contact impossible.[1]

It may help to keep in mind an even more concrete criterion of intimacy. If two people are in intimate contact, then we can be sure that they sometimes talk about the ultimate meaning of one another's lives; and if two people do sometimes talk about the ultimate meaning of their lives, then we are fairly safe in calling their contact an intimate contact.

By this definition, it is clear that most so-called "friendly" contacts are not intimate. Indeed, it is obvious that the most common "friendly" occasions provide no opportunity for this kind of contact to mature. Let us therefore begin by asking what social mechanism is required to make contacts intimate.

In pre-industrial society, intimate contacts were sustained by primary groups. "A primary group is a small group of people characterized by intimate face to face association and cooperation." [2] The three most universal primary groups are the family, the neighborhood group of elders, and the children's playgroup. These three primary groups have existed in virtually every human society, and they have been primary in forming the social nature and ideals of the individual. It is clear that the contacts that these primary groups created do meet the two conditions I have named. The members of a primary group meet often—almost daily; and they meet under unspecialized conditions, where behavior is not prescribed by role, so that they meet as individuals, man to man.

Because primary groups have, so far, always been the vehicles for intimate contact, and because intimacy is so important, many anthropologists and sociologists have taken the view that man cannot live without primary groups.[3] Many architects and planners have therefore tried to recreate the local primary group artificially, by means of the neighborhood idea. They have hoped that if people would live in small physical groups, round modern village greens, the social groups would follow the same patterns, and these artificial groups would then once more provide the intimate contact that is in such short supply in urban areas today.[4] But this idea of recreating primary groups by artificial means is unrealistic and reactionary: it fails to recognize the truth about the open society. The open society is no longer centered around place-based groups, and the very slight acquaintances that do form round an artificial neighborhood are once again trivial; they are not based on genuine desire.[5] Though these pseudo-groups may serve certain ancillary purposes (neighbors may look after one another's houses while they are away) there is no possible hope that they could sustain truly intimate contact, as I have defined it.

The only vestige of the adult primary groups that still remains is the nuclear family. The family still functions as a mechanism for sustaining intimate contact. But where the extended family of pre-industrial society contained many adults, and gave them many opportunities for intimate contact, the modern nuclear family contains only two adults. This means that each of these adults has at most *one* intimate contact within his family. (Although the contact between parent and child is,

410

in a colloquial sense, an intimate one, it is not the kind of contact that I am discussing here; it is essentially one-sided; there can be no mutual revealing of the self between adults and children.) Furthermore, one-third of all households in urban areas contain only one adult (either unmarried, widowed, or divorced).[6] These adults have *no* intimate contacts at all, at home.

Modern urban social structure is chiefly based on secondary contacts—contacts in which people are related by a single role relationship: buyer and seller, disc jockey and fan, lawyer and client.[7] Not surprisingly, the people who find themselves in this dismal condition try madly to make friends. It is not hard to see that this is an inevitable consequence of urbanization and mobility. In a society where people move about a lot, the individuals who are moving must learn to strike up acquaintances quickly since they often find themselves in situations where they don't know anybody. By the same token, since deep-seated, old, associations are uncommon, people rush to join new associations and affiliations, to fill the gap they feel. But the very life stuff of social organization is missing.

People may not be ready to admit that most of their contacts are trivial, but they admit it by implication in their widespread nostalgia for college days, and for army days. At college men and women had an experience that many of them never have again: they had many intimate friends; intimate contact was commonplace. The same is true of army days. However grisly war may be, it is a fact that the vast majority of men never forget their army days. They remember the close comradeship, the feelings of mutual dependence, and they regret that later life never quite recreates this wonderful experience.

All the recent studies of dissatisfaction when slum dwellers are forced to move say essentially the same.[8] These people are moving from a traditional place-based society into the larger urban society where place-based community means nothing. When they make the move they lose their intimate contacts. This is not because the places they go to are badly designed in some obvious sense that could be easily improved. Nor is it because they are temporarily uprooted, and have only to wait for the roots of community to grow again. The awful fact is that modern urban society as a whole has found no way of sustaining intimate contacts.

Some people believe that this view is nothing but nostalgia for an imaginary past and that what looks like alienation is really just the pain of parting from traditional society, and the birth pang of a new society.[9] I do not believe it. I believe that intimate contacts are essential for human survival, and, indeed, that each person requires not one, but several intimate contacts at any given time. I believe that the primary groups which sustained intimate contact were an essential functional part of traditional social systems and that since they are now obsolete, it is essential that we invent new social mechanisms able to sustain the intimate contacts that we need.

Expressed in formal terms, this belief becomes a fundamental hypothesis about man and society: *An individual can only be healthy and happy when his life contains three or four intimate contacts. A society can only be a healthy one if each of its individual members has three or four intimate contacts at every stage of his existence.*[10]

Every society known to man, except our own, has provided conditions that allow people to sustain three or four intimate contacts. If the hypothesis is correct, the very roots of our society are threatened. Let us therefore examine the evidence for the hypothesis.

Evidence

Unfortuately, the only available evidence is very indirect. Individual health is hard to define; social health is even harder. We have no indices for low-grade misery or sickness; we have no indices for fading social vitality. In the same way, the relative intimacy of different contacts is hard to define and has never explicitly been studied. The evidence we really need, showing a correlation between the intimacy of people's contacts, and the general health and happiness of their individual and social lives, does not exist.

In a strictly scientific sense, it is therefore only possible to examine an extreme version of the hypothesis: namely, that *extreme* lack of contact causes *extreme* and well-defined social pathologies like schizophrenia and delinquency. Several large-scale studies do support this extreme form of hypothesis.

Faris and Dunham studied the distribution of mental disorders in Chicago in the 1930s. They found that paranoid and hebephrenic schizophrenias have their highest rates of incidence among hotel residents and lodgers, and among the people who live in the rooming house districts of the city. They are highest, in other words, among those people who are most alone.[11]

Faris and Dunham also found that the incidence of schizophrenia among whites was highest among those whites living in predominantly

412

Negro areas, and that the incidence for Negroes was highest among those Negroes living in predominantly non-Negro areas.[12] Here again, the incidence is highest among those who are isolated.

Alexander Leighton and his collaborators, in their Nova Scotia study, found that people in a disintegrated society, that is, people with no personal contacts of any sort, have substantially higher rates of psycho-physiological, psychoneurotic, and sociopathic disorders, than people who live in a closely knit traditional community.[13]

Langner and Michael, studying the incidence of mental disorders in Manhattan, found that people who report having less than four friends have a substantially higher chance of mental disorder than those who report having more than four friends.[14] They also show that member-ship in formal organizations and clubs, and contact with neighbors, have relatively slight effect on mental health—thus supporting the idea that the contacts must be intimate before they do much good.[15]

Many minor studies support the same conclusion. Most important are the studies reporting the widely known correlations between age and mental health, and between marital status and mental health. Various studies have shown that the highest incidence of mental dis-orders, for males and females, occurs above age 65, and, indeed, that the highest of all occurs above 75.[16] Other studies have shown that the incidence rates for single, separated, widowed, and divorced per-sons are higher than the rates for married persons. Rates per thousand, for single persons, are about one-and-a-half times as high as the rates for married persons, while rates for divorced and widowed persons are between two and three times as high.[17]

Of course, the disorders among old people may be partly organic, but there is no getting away from the fact that old people are almost always more lonely than the young and that it is usually hard for them to sustain substantial contacts with other people. In the same way, although the disorders among divorced and single people could actu-ally be the source of their isolation, not the cause of it, the fact that the rate is equally high for widowers and widows makes this unlikely.

So far we have discussed only cases of adult isolation. It is very likely that the effects of social isolation on children are even more acute, but here the published evidence is thinner.

The most dramatic available results come from Harlow's work on monkeys. Harlow has shown that monkeys isolated from other infant monkeys during the first 6 months of life are incapable of normal social, sexual, or play relations with other monkeys in their later lives.[18]

413

Although monkeys can be raised successfully without a mother, provided they have other infant monkeys to play with, they cannot be raised successfully by a mother alone, without other infant monkeys, even if the mother is entirely normal.[19]

In Harlow's experiments, the first 6 months of life were critical. The first 6 months of a rhesus monkey's life correspond to the first three years of a child's life. Although there is no formal evidence to show that lack of contact during these first 3 years damages human children—and as far as I know, it has never been studied—there is very strong evidence for the effect of isolation between the ages of 4 and 10.

The most telling study is that by Herman Lantz.[20] Lantz questioned a random sample of 1,000 men in the United States Army who had been referred to a mental hygiene clinic because of emotional difficulties. Army psychiatrists classified each of the men as normal or as suffering from mild psychoneurosis, severe psychoneurosis, or psychosis. Lantz then put each man into one of three categories: those who reported having five friends or more at any typical moment when they were between four and ten years old, those who reported an average of about two friends, and those who reported no friends at that time. The results are astounding: Among men who had five friends or more as children, 61.5 per cent had mild cases, while 27.8 per cent had severe cases. Among men with no childhood friends, only 5 per cent had mild cases, and 85 per cent had severe cases.

It is almost certain then, that lack of contact, when it is extreme, has extreme effects on people. There is a considerable body of literature beyond that which I have quoted.[21] Even so, the evidence is sparse. We cannot be sure the effect is causal, and we have found evidence only for those relatively extreme cases that can be unambiguously counted. From a strictly scientific point of view, it is clearly necessary to undertake a special, extensive study, to test the hypothesis in the exact form that I have stated it.

However, just because the scientific literature doesn't happen to contain the relevant evidence, doesn't mean that we don't know whether the hypothesis is true or not. From our own lives we know that intimate contact is essential to life, and that the whole meaning of life shows itself only in the process of our intimate contacts.[22] The way of life we lead today makes it impossible for us to be as close to our friends as we really want to be. The feeling of alienation, and the modern sense of the "meaninglessness" of life, are direct expressions of the loss of intimate contact.

414

The Autonomy-Withdrawal Syndrome

As far as we can judge, then, people need three or four intimate contacts at every moment of their lives. It is therefore clear that every human society must provide social mechanisms that sustain these intimate contacts in order to survive as a society. Yet as we know, the historic mechanisms that once performed this function for our own society are breaking down.

I shall now try to show that we are not merely faced with the collapse of one or two social mechanisms, but rather with a massive syndrome, a huge net of cause and effect in which the breakdown of primary groups, the breakdown of intimacy itself, the growth of individualism, and the withdrawal from the stress of urbanized society, are all interwoven. I shall call this syndrome the *autonomy-withdrawal syndrome*.

In pre-industrial societies the two institutions that sustained intimate contacts between adults were the extended family and the local neighborhood community. These two primary groups have almost entirely disappeared, and the modern metropolis is a collection of many scattered households, each one small. In the future, individual households will probably be even smaller and the average size of urban areas even larger.[23] We must therefore ask how, in a society of scattered, mobile individuals, these individuals can maintain intimate contact with one another.

The first answer that comes to mind is this: since friendships in modern society are mostly based on some community of interest, we should expect the institutions that create such friendships—work place, golf club, ski resort, precinct headquarters—to provide the necessary meeting ground. It sounds good, but it doesn't work. Though people do meet each other in such groups, the meetings are too infrequent and the situation too clearly prescribed. People achieve neither the frequency, nor the informality, that intimacy requires. Further, *people can only reach the true intimacy and mutual trust required for self-revelation when they are in private.*

Frequent, private, almost daily meetings between individuals, under conditions of extreme informality, unencumbered by role prescriptions or social rules, will only take place if people visit one another in their homes. It is true that occasional meetings in public places may also be very intimate, but the regular, constant, meetings that are required to build up the possibility of intimacy cannot happen in public places.

415

In a society of scattered mobile individuals people will therefore only be able to maintain intimate contacts with one another if they are in the habit of constant informal visiting or "dropping-in."

In modern American society dropping-in is thought of as a peculiar European custom. Yet in fact, dropping-in is a normal part of life in every pre-industrial society. In part it has to be because there are no telephones in pre-industrial society. But dropping-in is not merely the pre-industrial version of what we do by phone. The very notion of friendship demands that people be almost totally exposed to one another. To be friends they must have nothing to hide; and for this reason, informal dropping-in is a natural, and essential, part of friendship. This is so fundamental that we may even treat it as a definition of true friendship.

Why is dropping-in so rare in mobile urban society? The first reason, of course, is still mechanical. Two people will not sustain a pattern of daily dropping-in unless they live within a few minutes of each other, ten minutes at the most. Although the car has enormously enlarged the number of people within ten minutes' distance of any given household, most of the people in the metropolis are still outside this distance. Potential friends see each other very rarely—at most once or twice a month for dinner—and when they do meet, it is after careful invitation, worked out in advance. These kinds of evening contact have neither the frequency, nor the informality, that intimacy requires.

However, distance alone, though it is a serious obstacle, does not fully explain the loss of intimacy. There is another reason for it, far more devastating, and far more profound: when people get home, they want to get away from all the stress outside. People do not want to be perpetually exposed; they often want to be withdrawn. But withdrawal soon becomes a habit. People reach a point where they are permanently withdrawn, they lose the habit of showing themselves to others as they really are, and they become unable and unwilling to let other people into their own world.

At this stage people don't like others dropping in on them, because they don't want to be caught when they aren't ready—the housewife who doesn't like anyone coming around except when she has carefully straightened up her house, the family which doesn't like to mix its friends and has them to visit one couple at a time in case the couples shouldn't get along. Afraid of showing themselves as they really are, such people never reach a truly intimate degree of contact with others.

This fear is partly caused by stress. The man who lives in modern urban society is exposed to innumerable stresses: danger, noise, too many strangers, too much information, and above all, the need to make decisions about the complexities of personal life without the help of traditional mores. These stresses are often too much to bear, so he withdraws from them. Even when they are in public, people behave as though the other people who surround them are not there. A woman cheerfully wears curlers in the street because, although she is curling her hair for people who are real to her, the people who surround her don't exist; she has shut them out.

In its extreme form, this withdrawal turns into schizophrenia: that total withdrawal into the self, which takes place when the outside world is so confusing, or so hard to deal with, that the organism finally cannot cope with it and turns away.[24] Schizophrenics are completely individualistic; the world they live in is their own world; they do not perceive themselves as dependent on the outside world in any way, nor do they perceive any interaction between themselves and the outside world. Nor indeed, do they enter into any interaction with the world outside.[25]

The stress of urban life has not yet had this extreme and catastrophic effect on many people. Nevertheless, what is nowadays considered "normal" urban behavior is strikingly like schizophrenia: it is also marked by extreme withdrawal from stress, and this withdrawal has also led to an unrealistic belief in the self-sufficiency of individuals.

Any objective observer comparing urban life with rural or pre-industrial life must be struck by the extreme individualism of the people who live in cities.[26] Though this individualism has often been criticized by non-Americans as a peculiarity of American culture, I believe this view mistaken. Individualism of an extreme kind is an inevitable by-product of urbanization—it occurs as part of the withdrawal from stress—and is very different from healthy democratic respect for the individual's rights.[27]

An obvious expression of this individualism is the huge amount of space that people need around them in the United States. Edward Hall has suggested that each person carries an inviolable "bubble" of personal space around with him and that the size of the bubble varies according to the intimacy of the situation.[28] He has also shown that the size of bubble required varies from culture to culture. Apparently people need a larger bubble in the United States, for any given situation, than in any other country; this is clearly associated with the fear of bodily contact, and with the fact that people view themselves as isolated atoms. This isolation of the individual is also expressed clearly by the love of private property in the United States, and the wealth of laws and institutions that keep people's private property inviolate.

Another form of extreme individualism, which threatens the development of intimate contacts, is the exaggerated accent on the nuclear family. In modern urban society it is assumed that the needs for intimate contact that any one individual has can be completely met in marriage. This concentration of all our emotional eggs in one basket has gone so far that true intimacy between any friends except man and wife is regarded with extreme suspicion.

It is true that this exaggerated arrogant view of the individual's strength is a withdrawal from stress. But it could never have happened if it weren't for the fact that urbanization makes individuals autonomous. The extreme differentiation of society in an urban area means that literally any service can be bought, by anyone. In material terms, any individual is able to survive alone.

Of course these isolated, apparently autonomous, individuals are in fact highly dependent on society—but only through the medium of money. A man in a less differentiated rural economy is constantly reminded of his dependence on society, and of the fact that his very being is totally intertwined with the being of the social order, and the being of his fellows. The individual who is technically autonomous, whose dependencies are all expressed in money terms, can easily make the mistake of thinking that he, or he and his family, are self-sufficient.

Now, naturally, people who believe that they are self-sufficient create a world that reinforces individualism and withdrawal. In central cities this is reflected in the concept of apartments. Though collected together at high densities, these apartments are in fact, like the people themselves, totally turned inward. High density makes it necessary to insulate each apartment from the world outside; the actual dwelling is remote from the street; it is virtually impossible to drop in on someone who lives in an apartment block. Not surprisingly, recent studies report that people who live in apartments feel more isolated than people who live in any other kind of dwelling.[29]

But autonomy and withdrawal, and the pathological belief in individual families as self-sufficient units, can be seen most vividly in the physical pattern of suburban tract development. The houses stand alone—a collection of isolated, disconnected islands. There is no communal land, and no sign of any functional connection between different houses. If it seems far-fetched to call this aspect of the suburb pathological, let us examine the results of a study made in Vienna in

418

1956. The city planning department gave a questionnaire to a random sample of 4,000 Viennese to find out what their housing preferences were. Most of them, when asked whether they would rather live in apartments or in single family houses, said they preferred apartments, because they wanted to be near the center, where everything was happening.[30]

A Viennese psychiatrist then gave the same questionnaire to 100 neurotic patients in his clinic. He found that a much higher proportion of these patients wanted to live in one-family houses, that they wanted larger houses relative to the size of their families, that they wanted more space per person, and that more of them wanted their houses to be situated in woods and trees. In other words, they wanted the suburban dream. As he says, "The neurotic patients are marked by a strong desire to shun reality and to isolate themselves." [31]

Most people who move to suburbs are not sick in any literal sense. The four main reasons people give for moving to the suburbs are: (1) Open space for children, because children can't play safely in central urban areas.[32] (2) More space inside the house than they can afford in the central city.[33] (3) Wanting to own a house of their own.[34] Ownership protects the owner from the uncertainties of tenancy and from reliance on others, and creates the illusion that the owner and his family have a world of their own, where nobody can touch them. (4) More grass and trees.[35]

Each of these is a withdrawal from stress. The withdrawal is understandable, but the suburb formed by this withdrawal undermines the formation of intimate contacts in a devastating way. It virtually destroys the children's playgroup.

As we saw earlier, the intimate contacts in pre-industrial society were maintained by three primary groups: the extended family, the neighborhood group, and the children's playgroup. The first two, those that maintain intimate contacts between adults, are obsolete—and need to be replaced. But the third primary group—the children's playgroup—is not obsolete at all. Little children, unlike adults, do choose their friends from the children next door. It is perfectly possible for children's playgroups to exist in modern society just as they always have; and indeed, it is essential. The children's playgroup sets the whole style of life for later years. Children brought up in extensive playgroups will be emotionally prepared for intimate contacts in later life; children brought up without playgroups will be prone to individualism and withdrawal.

On the face of it, the suburb ought to be a very good place for children's playgroups—it has open space and safety. Yet, paradoxically, this children's paradise is not a paradise at all for little children.

If you drive through a subdivision, watching children play, you will see that children who are old enough to have school friends do have local playgroups of a sort. But if you look carefully, you see the smallest children squatting forlornly outside their houses—occasionally playing with an older brother or sister and occasionally in groups of two or three, but most often alone. Compare this with the situation in a primitive village, or in a crowded urban slum: there the little children are out on the street fending for themselves as soon as they can walk; heaps of children are playing and falling and rolling over one another.

Why are suburban playgroups small? There are several reasons. First of all, suburban density is low and little children can't walk very far. Even if every house has children in it, the number of two- and three-year olds that a given two-year-old can reach is very small. Secondly, even though the suburb is safer than the central city, the streets still aren't entirely safe. Mothers keep their two- and three-year-olds off the street, inside the individual yards, where they can keep an eye on them. This cuts the children's freedom to meet other children. Further, many suburbs have no common land at all in them, not even sidewalks. There isn't any natural place where children go to find each other; they have to go and look for each other in one another's houses. For a child this is a much more formidable enterprise than simply running out to see who's on the street. It also makes the children hard to find and keeps the size of groups down, especially since many parents won't allow large groups of children in the house. And finally, when children play in one another's yards, parents can control the playmates they consider suitable.

It is small wonder that children who grow up in these conditions learn to be self-reliant in the pathological sense I have described. As they become adults they are even less able to live lives with intimate contacts than their parents; they seek even more exaggerated forms of individualism and withdrawal. As adults who suffer from withdrawal they create a world that creates children who are even more prone to suffer from withdrawal, and more prone to create such worlds. This closes the cycle of the syndrome, and makes it self-perpetuating.

The autonomy-withdrawal syndrome is not a unique American phenomenon. It is true that it is, so far, more acute in the United States than in any other country; but this is merely because urbanization is more advanced in the United States than anywhere else. As massive urbanization spreads, the syndrome will spread with it. I believe this syndrome is the greatest threat to social human nature that we face in this century. We have already seen that it can create misery and madness. But in the long run its effects are far more devastating. An individual human organism becomes a self only in the process of intimate contacts with other selves. Unless we overcome the syndrome, the loss of intimate contacts may break down human nature altogether.

Solution

How can cities help to overcome the syndrome? If the city is to be a mechanism for sustaining intimate human contact, what geometric pattern does the mechanism need?

Of course, no amount of geometric pattern in the environment can overcome the syndrome by itself. The syndrome is a social and psychological problem of massive dimensions; it will only be solved when people decide to change their way of life. But the physical environment needs changing too. People can only change their way of life if the environment supports their efforts.

There are two fundamentally different approaches to the problem. On the one hand we may decide that intimate contact can only be sustained properly by primary groups; we shall then try to create new kinds of primary groups that might work in our society. On the other hand we may decide that adult primary groups are gone forever, and that it is unrealistic to try to re-create them in any form whatever in modern society; in this case we must try a more radical approach, and create a social mechanism that is able to sustain informal, daily contact between people without the support of a primary group.

It may be that the first of these approaches is the more hopeful one. This is what T-groups try to do, it is the idea behind the groups of families that Aldous Huxley describes in *Island*, and above all, it is the idea behind group work. If work can be reorganized, so that people band together in small work groups of about a dozen, and each group is directed toward a single concentrated socially valuable objective, then the dedication and effort that develop in the group are capable of creating great intimacy, which goes far beyond the working day.

However, so far none of these methods has met with any great success. So far the forces that are breaking primary groups apart have been stronger than the efforts to build artificial primary groups. In this selection I shall therefore assume that more radical steps will have to be taken: that although children's playgroups can be saved, adult primary groups are doomed, and that adults will have to sustain their intimate contacts in a new way, by frequent casual visiting. I shall now describe the reorganization of the housing pattern that is required by this approach.

At present, people have two main kinds of housing open to them: either they live in apartments or they live in single family houses. Neither helps them overcome the autonomy-withdrawal syndrome. I shall now try to show that, in order for them to overcome the syndrome, the houses in a city must have twelve specific geometric characteristics, and that these twelve characteristics, when taken together define a housing pattern different from any available today.

1. Every dwelling must be immediately next to a vehicular through street. If there are any multi-story buildings with dwellings in them—like apartments—then there must be vehicular through streets at every level where there are entrances to dwellings.

In the modern city, many houses, and almost all apartments, are some distance off the street. Yet people live so far apart they have to move around by car or motor bike. Informal dropping-in will only work properly if all dwellings are directly on the street, so that people in the dwelling can be seen from a passing car.

It may be said that this is unnecessary since people who want to visit one another informally can telephone ahead and ring the doorbell when they get there. This argument is superficial. People will only make a regular habit of informal visiting if they can be certain they are really wanted when they get there. A phone call in advance does not convey enough information to make this possible, and this will be true even with TV-telephones. But if you go and knock on someone's door and it turns out to be a bad moment, your visit is already too far advanced for you to withdraw gracefully.

It is therefore essential to see the people you intend to visit inside their home, from your car. You wave to them; you sound the horn; you shout a few words. By then you have had a chance to assess the situation, and they have had a chance to react. If it is the right moment for a visit, they will invite you in. If it is not, you talk for a few moments, without leaving your car—and you can then drive on, without

422

embarrassment to either side. It is therefore essential that the house be directly on a through street, and that some part of the house be transparent and directly visible from passing cars.

2. Each dwelling must contain a transparent communal room with the following properties: on one side the room is directly adjacent to the street, on the opposite side the room is directly adjacent to a private open air court or garden. Since the room is transparent, its interior, seen against the garden, and the garden itself, are both visible from the street.

The part of the house that is visible must be indoors so that it can be used year round, and since it is indoors it must have windows both on the street side and on the far side, so that people inside can be seen from the street. The room must be designed in such a way that people will go there whenever they are feeling sociable and likely to welcome a casual visitor. But if the room is merely facing the street, people won't want to sit there; the street is far less pleasant than it used to be. The transparent room, though visible from the street, must therefore be oriented toward a private court or garden, with a view beyond. Under these circumstances it will be a natural place for people to go for family meals, to read the paper, to have a drink, to gossip. In warm seasons they may also sit in the court beyond, where they will still be visible from the street.

3. The transparent communal room must be surrounded by freestanding, self-contained pavilions, each functioning as a bed-living unit, so arranged that each person in the family, or any number of people who wish to be undisturbed, can retire to one of these pavilions and be totally private.

If the communal room is visible from the street, and open to passing friends, then the private rooms must be far more private than they are today, so that their privacy is not infected by the openness of the communal room. Each of these private rooms must be a more or less self-contained pavilion, where people can be entirely undisturbed—

423

either alone, or in twos, or in a group. People who live in such a house must learn to distinguish deliberately between being accessible and being inaccessible. When they want to be accessible, they go to the communal room; when they want to be inaccessible, they go to one of the private pavilions.

4. The street immediately outside the dwelling must be no more than about 1,000 feet long, and connected to a major traffic artery at each end.

The house must be so placed that people can drive past it easily, without having to go too far out of their way. This means that the house must be on a street that is reasonably short, and connected at each end to a traffic artery that plays a major part in the overall traffic system.

5. There must be a continuous piece of common land, accessible and visible from every dwelling.

Suburban yards are far too private. They only allow small groups to form, they make it hard for children to find each other, and they allow parents to regulate the other yards their own children may visit. In order to give children the chance to meet freely in groups, there must be common land where they can go to find each other.

In some of the older and denser suburbs, the wide sidewalks provide such common land. However, most suburban tract developments have very narrow sidewalks, or no sidewalks at all, and anyway most middle-class parents consider even the sidewalk dangerous, or rule it out on the grounds that "well brought up children don't play in the street." Most important of all, even in the suburbs parents still feel very protective about the smallest children. They will only allow these children to play freely on common land if they are convinced the children will be completely safe while playing there.

This means, first of all, that the access to the common land must be direct from every house; it must not be necessary to cross streets or other public thoroughfares to get there. Second, the common land must be visible from the house itself so that parents can, if they want to, watch their children playing there. Third, the common land must be so placed that a child cannot get to any vehicular street without going through a house. Finally, the common land must be disassociated from the street, and clearly meant for play, so that it has no connotation of "playing in the street." If all these conditions are met, parents will allow the little children—even toddlers—to roam freely on and off the common land, and playgroups have a good chance of forming.

6. This common land must be separated from the streets by houses, so that a child on the common land has to go through a house to get to the street, for reasons given under 5.

7. The common land, though continuous, must be broken into many small "places," not much larger than outdoor "rooms," each surfaced with a wide variety of ground surfaces, especially "soft" surfaces like earth, mud, sand, and grass.

This condition must be met to make sure the children really like the common land and don't end up preferring their own yards, or other places. Little children do not enjoy playing in great big open areas. They seek small corners and opportunities for secrecy, and they seek plastic materials—water, earth, and mud.[36]

8. Each house must be within 100-yards walk of 27 other houses.

Let us assume that there are two children per household (the modal figure for suburban households) and that these children are evenly distributed in age from 0 to 18. Roughly speaking, a given preschool child who is x years old, will play with children between $x-1$ and $x+1$ years old. In order for playgroups to form, each child must be able to reach at least five children in this age range. It can be shown that for each child to have a 95 per cent chance of reaching five such potential playmates, he must be in reach of 27 households.[37]

If we assume that preschool children are not able, or allowed, to go more than about 100 yards in search of playmates, this means that each house must be within 100 yards of 27 other houses. To achieve this density in a conventional suburban layout, house lots would have to be less than 40 feet wide, about half the width and twice the density they are today.

9. Overall residential densities throughout the metropolitan area must be as high as possible.

There is a second reason why residential densities must be higher than they are today. Informal daily dropping-in will not take place between two households that are more than about 10 minutes apart. Since average door-to-door speeds in urban areas are about 15 m.p.h., 10 minutes is about 2½ miles, thus putting each person in reach of about 20 square miles, or about 100,000 people at current metropolitan densities. This is a tiny fraction of the population of a metropolitan area—a twentieth of a small one, a hundredth of a large one. Since we have started out with the axiom that a person's best friends may live anywhere in the metropolitan area, this means that people are within dropping-in distance of no more than a twentieth of their potentially closest friends.

Obviously vehicle speeds and streets can be improved. But it seems unlikely that average door-to-door speeds will more than double in this century. This means that people in the largest metropolitan areas will still be within informal distance of less than one-twentieth of the population. While transportation must be improved, it is clear that overall mean densities must *also* be raised as far as they can be.

Many planners believe that high density is bad for man. This is based on the fact that high density is often correlated with the incidence of crime, delinquency, ill health, and insanity. If this belief were justified, any attempt to increase the density of population would obviously be ill advised. However, though the belief has a long history, the evidence available today does not support it.

There seems little doubt that overcrowding—too little living space per person—does cause damage. Calhoun has shown this dramatically for rats; [38] Loring, Chombard de Lauwe, and Lander have shown that it is true for humans.[39] It is clear that people who are now forced to live in crowded conditions either need more income or need ways of reducing the square foot costs of living space. But this does not imply that the density of population per square mile should be reduced. Even dwellings that are individually very large can still be arranged at high population densities without overcrowding.

426

It is true that there is often a positive correlation between high population density and various indices of social disorder like crime, delinquency, ill health, and insanity rates.[40] However, it seems almost certain that these effects are caused by intervening variables and are not directly caused by density. There are places—Boston's North End and Hong Kong, for example—which have exceptionally high densities, and exceptionally low indices of social disorder.[41] Unless we assume that Italian-Americans and Chinese are organically different from other people, this means that density, as such, cannot be the source of trouble in the cases where a correlation does exist.

The following hypothesis fully explains all the observed correlations: those social disorders apparently caused by density, are in fact caused by low income (combined with poor education) and by social isolation. People who are poor, and badly educated, tend to live in high density areas. People who are socially isolated also tend to live in high density areas. Both variables are associated with high indices of social disorder. Although some published studies of density have controlled for one or the other of these variables, no study has controlled them both. Lander has shown that the correlation between *overcrowding* and delinquency, when controlled for these two variables, vanishes altogether.[42] Schmitt has published a table showing that the correlations persist when income-education is controlled, but also showing a strong negative correlation between household size and social disorder (larger households are less prone to social disorders), which suggests strongly that social isolation may be responsible for the persistent correlation.[43] The fact that there are very few social disorders in Boston's North End and in Hong Kong is clearly due to the existence of close knit extended families—the lack of social isolation. I predict that the partial correlation between density and social disorder, when controlled for income-education *and* for social isolation, will disappear altogether.

This hypothesis explains all the available data. Although it is untested, there is no published evidence that contradicts it. As far as we can tell, the high density called for by the need for contact is perfectly safe.

10. The entire exterior surface of the residential area must be an undulating hillside, covered with grass and flowers and trees; the houses are set immediately under the surface of this hillside.

427

We cannot expect people to live at high densities just because they have certain social benefits. The low density of suburban tracts has been created by demands far more important to consumers than the point of view I have presented. Unless these demands can be satisfied equally well at higher densities, there is not the slightest hope that overall densities will ever be increased.

The pattern of density in an urban region is created by the conflict between two basic tendencies: the desire for land and the desire for easy access to central areas. For a given income, each person can choose less land at the center, or more land further from the center. When a population of individuals tries to resolve this conflict for itself, a characteristic pattern of density comes into being: density declines exponentially with distance from the center according to the equation: $d_r = d_o e^{-br}$.[44] This relation holds for cities all over the world.[45] What is even more surprising, the relation is almost entirely fixed by absolute population, and by the age of the city. This means that in a free market, neither the overall mean density of a city, nor the densities at different distances from the center, can be controlled by planning action.

They can, however, be controlled indirectly. If we can make land more useful, so that a person can get a given level of satisfaction from a smaller piece of land than he needs to get that satisfaction now, then the desire for access will balance differently against the desire for land, and densities will increase.

Land is valuable for two basic reasons. First of all, it is the prime building surface. Secondly, it provides open space. The first is replaceable. The second is not. It is easy to create artificial building surfaces at many levels. But the area of open space cannot be increased beyond the area of the land. Yet this basic natural resource is almost entirely wasted in urban areas today. Fifty per cent is wasted on roads and parking lots, and 15 per cent is wasted on roofs; none of these need it. The 25 per cent of open space left over is chopped up and useless.

If a city were built so as to conserve this resource, with all roofs covered with grass and trees, and all roads roofed over, so that the total exterior surface of the city was a parkland of grass and flowers and bushes and trees, people could have the same amenities they have today, at far higher densities. To make it work, the surface would have to undulate like a range of rolling hills, so that windows in the hillsides can get daylight to the houses under the surface.

How much useful open land does a family in a suburban tract command? At a gross density of 5,000 persons per square mile, each family has a lot of about 70 feet by 100 feet, 7,000 square feet in all; 2,000 square feet go to the house and another 1,000 square feet to the driveway, leaving about 4,000 square feet of open land, or about 1,000 square feet per person. If the entire exterior surface of the city were artificial open land, it would be possible to house 25,000 people per square mile, and still give them the same 1,000 square feet of open land per person.

11. Each house must be on an individual load-bearing pad, which doesn't touch any other pad, and which may be clearly visualized as a piece of private property. The pad has its own open space, and allows the owner to build and modify his house as he wishes.

So that people can get the same feeling of ownership and the same opportunity to build what they want and the same private open space they get in the suburbs, the houses under the hillside must be built on individual artificial lots. To avoid the half-hearted feeling of ownership that condominium apartments offer, each lot must be totally separate from the other lots, and so made that the owner can build what he wants to on his own lot. Each lot is an individual load-bearing pad, large enough to hold a 2,000 square foot house with a private garden.

CENTER ⟶

12. The hills vary in height and slope according to their location in the urban region. They are highest and steepest near commercial centers, and low and flat near the periphery.

Since density will still vary with distance from urban centers, even if the land-access equation changes, the hills must vary in height and slope. The highest and steepest hills, whose density is greatest, will be near the urban centers, the low flat hills at the periphery.

It now remains to find a single concrete configuration of dwellings, in which all of these twelve relations are simultaneously present. The drawings that follow show such a configuration.

The residential area of the city is a continuous series of rolling linear hills. The hills are about 700 feet long, connected at each end to major traffic arteries. They change in height and slope according to their dis-

429

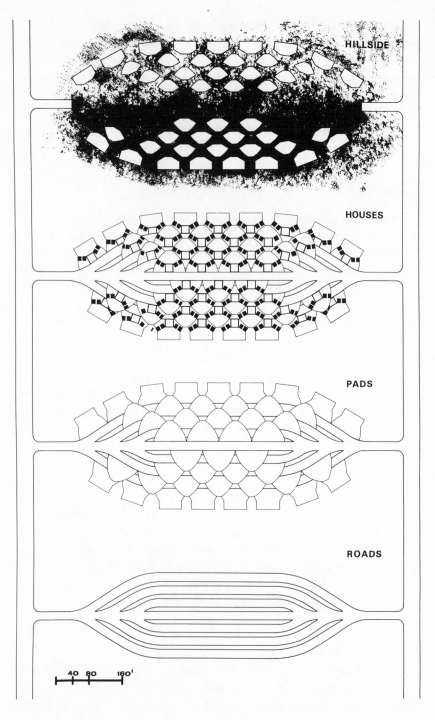

HILLSIDE

HOUSES

PADS

ROADS

40 80   160'

Figure 26–11   Four Hills in Plan, with Different Amounts Cut Away.

tance from the major urban centers. The outer surface of these hills is publicly owned common land, covered by grass and trees and bushes and flowers. Each house is built on a pad immediately under the surface of the hill. The outer half of this pad is a private, fenced garden, which connects directly with the outer surface of the hill. Daylight for the house comes from the garden. The common part of the hill, which surrounds the private gardens, is broken down to form a series of small places, connected by slopes and stairs. Each house is served by a street inside the hill, at its own level. The house is immediately next to its street. Each house has two basic components: a communal room, and a number of private pavilions. The communal room, which is next to the street, between the street and the garden, is open to the street, and transparent, so that the garden is visible through it, and so that people inside this room are visible against the light. The private pavilions are arranged around this communal room, under the roof provided by the hillside above.

This configuration contains all twelve relations specified. Although it can be varied in many details without damaging any of the twelve relations, I do not believe it is possible to find a configuration that differs fundamentally from the one I have described, and still contains all of the twelve. However, I should not like this configuration to be thought of as a building. Many problems still need to be worked out before it can be built. The configuration must be thought of simply as a partial specification of what a city has to be to function as a mechanism for sustaining human contact.

Let me once more repeat the central argument. It is inevitable that urban concentrations create stress. Our first reaction to this urban stress is to move away from it; to turn our backs on it; to try to escape it. This is very natural. Yet the remedy is worse than the disease. The ills of urban life which are commonly attributed to density and stress, are in fact not produced by the original stress itself, but by our own actions in turning away from that stress. If urban society is to survive, we must overcome this over-reaction. If people do not expose themselves, if they do not dare to make themselves vulnerable, life will become more and more intolerable, and we shall see more and more of the signs of dissociation which are already far too evident. The pattern of twelve relations that I have presented has only this one objective. It brings people out of hiding, and lets them expose themselves to the larger fabric of the city and to society and to their friends. In such a city there is some chance of breaking down the autonomy-withdrawal syndrome. In our own cities there is no chance at all.

431

NOTES

1. Of course, people do occasionally have intimate contact with one another, even when these two conditions are not fulfilled. This happens between old friends who now live 3,000 miles apart and see each other every few years for a day or two. But even in these cases, there must have been some period in the past when the two conditions *were* satisfied.

2. C. H. Cooley, *Social Organization* (Glencoe, Ill.: 1956), pp. 23–31.

3. See, e.g., Edward A. Shils, "The Study of Primary Groups," in Lerner and Lasswell, *The Policy Sciences* (Stanford: 1951), pp. 44–69; W. I. Thomas, *Social Behavior and Personality*, ed. E. H. Volkart (New York: 1951); George Homans, *The Human Group* (New York: 1950); Ralph Linton, *The Study of Man* (New York: 1963), p. 230.

4. For instance, Clarence Stein, *Towards New Towns for America* (Chicago: 1951).

5. Melvin M. Webber, "The Urban Place and the Nonplace Urban Realm," in Webber *et al.*, *Explorations into Urban Structure* (Philadelphia: 1964), pp. 79–153; Ikumi Hoshin, "Apartment Life in Japan," *Marriage and Family Living* 26 (1964), pp. 312–317; Rudolf Heberle, "The Normative Element in Neighborhood Relations," *Pacific Sociological Review* 3, no. 1 (Spring 1960), pp. 3–11.

6. Ruth Glass and F. G. Davidson, "Household Structure and Housing Needs," *Population Studies* 4 (1951), pp. 395–420; S. P. Brown, *Population Studies* 4 (1951), pp. 380–394. This is also the same as saying that one-fifth of all adults in urban areas are either single, separated, widowed, or divorced. See U. S. Census, Vol. 1, *General U.S. Statistics* (1960), Table 176.

7. Emile Durkheim, *The Division of Labor in Society*, trans. by George Simpson (Glencoe, Ill.: 1949); Cooley, *op. cit.*; Louis Wirth, "Urbanism as a Way of Life," *American Journal of Sociology* 40 (1938), pp. 1–24; James M. Beshers, *Urban Social Structure* (New York: 1962); Janet Abu-Lughod, *The City is Dead, Long Live the City* (Berkeley: 1966).

8. H. Gans, *The Urban Villagers* (New York: 1962); Michael Young and Peter Willmott, *Family and Kinship in East London* (London: 1957); M. Fried and P. Gleicher, "Some Sources of Residential Satisfaction in an Urban Slum," *AIP Journal* (1961), pp. 305–315.

9. Abu-Lughod, *op. cit.*

10. The numbers three and four have no special significance. I have chosen the range three to four, simply because one or two are too few, and more than about five too many to sustain at the level of intimacy I have defined.

11. R. E. L. Faris and H. H. Dunham, *Mental Disorders in Urban Areas* (Chicago: 1939), pp. 82–109.

12. *Ibid.*, pp. 54–57.

13. Alexander Leighton, *My Name is Legion*, The Stirling County Study, Vol. I (New York: 1959); Charles C. Hughes, Marc-Adelard Tremblay, Robert N. Rapoport, and Alexander Leighton, *People of Cove and Woodlot*, The Stirling County Study, Vol. II (New York: 1960); Dorothea Leighton *et. al.*, *The Character of Danger*, The Stirling County Study, Vol. III (New York: 1963). See esp. Vol. II, pp. 267 and 297, Vol. III, p. 338.

14. T. S. Langner and S. T. Michael, *Life Stress and Mental Health* (New York: 1963), p. 285.

15. *Ibid.*, pp. 286–289.

16. Neil A. Dayton, *New Facts on Mental Disorders* (Springfield, Ill.: 1940), p. 464; C. Landis and J. D. Page, *Modern Society and Mental Disease* (New York: 1938), p. 163; Benjamin Malzberg, *Social and Biological Aspects of Mental Diseases* (Utica: 1940), p. 70; Benjamin Malzberg, "Statistical Analysis of Ages of First Admission to Hospitals for Mental Disease in New York State," *Psychiatric Quarterly* 23 (1949), p. 344; H. F. Dorn, "The Incidence and Future Expectancy

of Mental Disease," *U.S. Public Health Reports* 53 (1938), pp. 1991–2004; E. M. Furbush, "Social Facts Relative to Patients with Mental Disease," *Mental Hygiene* 5 (1921), p. 597.

17. Malzberg, *op. cit.* (1940), p. 116; Landis and Page, *op. cit.*, p. 69; L. M. Adler, "The Relationship of Marital Status to Incidence of and Recovery from Mental Illness," *Social Forces* 32 (1953), p. 186; Neil A. Dayton, "Marriage and Mental Disease," *New England Journal of Medicine* 215 (1936), p. 154; F. J. Gaudet and R. I. Watson, "Relation Between Insanity and Marital Conditions," *Journal of Abnormal Psychology* 30 (1935), p. 368.

18. Harry F. Harlow and Margaret K. Harlow, "The Effect of Rearing Conditions on Behavior," *Bull. Menninger Clinic* 26 (1962), pp. 213–224.

19. Harry F. Harlow and Margaret K. Harlow, "Social Deprivation in Monkeys," *Scientific American* 207, no. 5 (1962), pp. 136–146.

20. Herman R. Lantz, "Number of Childhood Friends as Reported in the Life Histories of a Psychiatrically Diagnosed Group of 1000," *Marriage and Family Living* (1956), pp. 107–108. See also Anna Freud and Sophie Dann, "An Experiment in Group Upbringing," *Readings in Child Behavior and Development*, ed. Celia Stendler (New York: 1964), pp. 122–140.

21. R. E. L. Faris, "Cultural Isolation and the Schizophrenic Personality," *American Journal of Sociology* 40 (September 1934), pp. 155–169; R. E. L. Faris, *Social Psychology* (New York: 1952), pp. 338–362; R. E. L. Faris, *Social Disorganization* (New York: 1948), ch. 8; Paul Halmos, *Solitude and Privacy* (New York: 1952), pp. 88–92; Carle C. Zimmermann and Lucius F. Cervantes, S. J., *Successful American Families* (New York: 1960); R. Helanko, "The Yard Group in the Socialization of Turku Girls," *Acta Sociologica* 4, no. 1 (1959), pp. 38–55; D. Kimball, "Boy Scouting as a Factor in Personality Development," Ph.D. thesis, Dept. of Education, University of California, Berkeley, 1949; Melvin L. Kohn and John A. Clausen, "Social Isolation and Schizophrenia," *American Sociological Review* 20 (1955), pp. 265–273; Dietrich C. Reitzes, "The Effect of Social Environment on Former Felons," *Journal of Criminal Law, Criminology and Police Science* 46 (1955), pp. 226–231; E. Gartly Jaco, "The Social Isolation Hypothesis and Schizophrenia," *American Sociological Review* 19 (1954), pp. 567–577; Aldous Huxley, *Island* (New York: 1963), pp. 89–90; Arthur T. Jersild and Mary D. Fite, "The Influence of Nursery School Experience on Children's Social Adjustments," *Child Development Monographs* 25 (1939); Helena Malley, "Growth in Social Behavior and Mental Activity After Six Months in Nursey School," *Child Development* 6 (1935), pp. 303–309; Louis P. Thorpe, *Child Psychology and Development* (New York: 1955); K. M. B. Bridges, *Social and Emotional Development of the Pre-School Child* (London: 1931); W. R. Thompson and R. Melzack, "Early Environment," *Scientific American* 194 (1956), pp. 38–42.

22. This is, in effect, the same as the classic thesis of Cooley and George Herbert Mead, which says that the individual self appears only as a result of interaction with others, and that it is liable to disintegrate when these interactions are not available. Mead, *Mind, Self and Society* (Chicago: 1934); Cooley, *op. cit.*

23. Glass and Davidson, *op. cit.*, p. 400.

24. "The person who is diagnosed as suffering from schizophrenia perceives himself as bombarded by a multiplicity of personal and family problems he is not able to handle." L. H. Rogler and A. B. Hollingshead. *Trapped: Families and Schizophrenia* (New York: 1965).

25. Robert Sommer and Humphrey Osmond, "The Schizophrenic No-Society," *Psychiatry* 25 (1962), pp. 244–255.

26. Durkheim, *op. cit.*, pp. 283–303.

27. J. G. Miller, "Input Overload and Psychopathology," *American Journal of Psychiatry* 116 (1960), pp. 695–704; Richard Meier, *A Communications Theory of Urban Growth* (Cambridge, Mass.: 1960).

28. E. T. Hall, *The Hidden Dimension* (Garden City: 1966).

29. Ministry of Housing, *Families Living at High Density* (London: 1966), pp. 29–33; John Madge, "Privacy and Social Interaction," *Transactions of the Bartlett Society* 3 (1964–1965), p. 139.

433

30. Leopold Rosenmayr, Wohnverhältnisse und Nachbarschaftsbeziehungen, Der Aufbau, Monograph No. 8 (Vienna: 1956), pp. 39–91.

31. Hans Strotzka, Spannungen und Lösungsversuche in Städtischer Umgebung, Der Aufbau, Monograph No. 8 (Vienna: 1956), pp. 93–108.

32. Nelson Foote, Janet Abu-Lughod, Mary Mix Foley, and Louis Winnick, Housing Choices and Housing Constraints (New York: 1960), pp. 107 and 392.

33. Ibid., pp. 223–263 and Peter H. Rossi, Why Families Move (Glencoe, Ill.: 1955).

34. Ibid., pp. 187–193 and Irving Rosow, "Homeownership Motives," American Sociological Review 13 (1948), pp. 751–756.

35. Center for Urban Studies, "Tall Flats in Pimlico," Aspects of Change (London: 1964), ch. 8; Santa Clara County Study, unpublished, 1966.

36. L. E. White, "The Outdoor Play of Children Living in Flats," Living in Towns, ed. Leo Kuper (London: 1953), pp. 235–264.

37. The problem may be stated as follows: In an infinite population of children, one-sixth are the right age and five-sixths are the wrong age. A group of r children is chosen at random. The probability, $P_{r,k}$ that these r children contain exactly k right-age children is given by the hypergeometric distribution. The probability that r has five or more right-age children in it is $1 - \sum_{k=0}^{4} P_{r,k}$.

If we now ask what is the least r that makes $1 - \sum_{0}^{4} P_{r,k} > .95$,

r turns out to be fifty-four, requiring twenty-seven households.

38. J. B. Calhoun, "Population Density and Social Pathology," Scientific American 206 (1962), pp. 139–146.

39. William C. Loring, "Housing Characteristics and Social Disorganization," Social Problems (January 1956); Paul Chombard de Lauwe, Famille et Habitation (Paris: 1959); B. Lander, Towards an Understanding of Juvenile Delinquency (New York: 1954).

40. Robert C. Schmitt, "Delinquency and Crime in Honolulu," Sociology and Social Research 41 (March–April 1957), pp. 274–276 and "Population Densities and Mental Disorders in Honolulu," Hawaii Medical Journal 16 (March–April 1957), pp. 396–397.

41. Jane Jacobs, The Death and Life of Great American Cities (New York: 1961), pp. 10 and 206; Robert C. Schmitt, "Implications of Density in Hong Kong," AIP Journal 29 (1963), pp. 210–217.

42. Lander, op. cit., p. 46.

43. Robert C. Schmitt, "Density, Health and Social Disorganization," AIP Journal 32 (1966), pp. 38–40.

44. Brian J. L. Berry, James W. Simmons, and Robert J. Tennant, "Urban Population Densities: Structure and Change," Geographical Review 53 (1963), pp. 389–405; John Q. Steward and William Warntz, "Physics of Population Distribution," Journal of Regional Science, Vol. 1 (1958), pp. 99–123.

45. Colin Clark, "Urban Population Densities," Journal of the Royal Statistical Society, Series A, 114 (1951), Part 4, pp. 490–496; Berry, op. cit.

Annotated Bibliography

ROBERT GUTMAN AND BARBARA WESTERGAARD

I. Behavioral Constraints on Building Design

1. BASIC APPROACHES TO THE BEHAVIORAL STUDY OF ARCHITECTURE

DuBos, René. *Man Adapting*. New Haven: Yale University Press, 1965. An exploration of "some of the biological and social implications of man's response to his total environment." States of health or disease are seen as the results of the organism's success or failure in its attempts to respond adaptively to environmental challenge.

Frankl, Paul. *Principles of Architectural History*, translated and edited by James F. O'Gorman. Cambridge: The M.I.T. Press, 1968. First published in German in 1914, this history of architectural principles is distinguished by its unusually systematic approach, by its method of treating several architectural properties simultaneously, and, above all, by its specific interest in the functional properties of architecture.

Gutman, Robert. "Site Planning and Social Behavior." *Journal of Social Issues* 22, no. 4 (October 1966): 103–115. A summary of research that has tried to answer the question, "How does the spatial arrangement of dwelling units influence the residents of a site?" The empirical evidence that site plans influence individual behavior or collective social action is not very strong, but the author suggests that the studies have not investigated a wide enough variety of site plans, and have ignored many of the behavioral mechanisms through which social organization and architecture are connected.

Proshansky, Harold M., Ittelson, William H., Rivlin, Leanne G., eds. *Environmental Psychology: Man and His Physical Setting*. New York: Holt, Rinehart and Winston, 1970. A collection of readings intended to define and establish the substantive and conceptual boundaries of the field of environmental psychology. As a new but rapidly growing field that is highly interdisciplinary, its literature is consequently widely dispersed, and the collection is intended to be useful to both students and practitioners.

435

RAPOPORT, AMOS. *House Form and Culture*. Englewood Cliffs, N.J.: Prentice Hall, 1969. A comprehensive attempt using behavioral science material to provide a conceptual framework for looking at a wide variety of house forms and types and the forces that affect them. On the basis of an examination of the primitive and vernacular architecture of many countries, the author concludes that given the various constraints of climate, technology, and the like, house form depends finally on people's views of the ideal life.

SELLS, S. B. and BERRY, C. A., eds. *Human Factors in Jet and Space Travel*. New York: Ronald, 1961. A collection of articles dealing with some of the problems involved in maintaining individuals in hostile and unusual environments. Included are discussions of the effects of such environments on perception, physical functioning, performance of skilled tasks, and group behavior.

2. ANATOMICAL AND PHYSIOLOGICAL FACTORS IN DESIGN

DREYFUSS, HENRY. *The Measure of Man,* 2nd ed. New York: Whitney Library of Design, 1967. Includes anthropometric data charts, life-size figure charts, a space standards check list, and a bibliography listing sources of anthropometric data. Written from the point of view of an industrial designer.

GOROMOSOV, M. S. *The Physiological Basis of Health Standards for Dwellings*. Public Health Papers no. 3, Geneva: WHO, 1968. Physiological aspects of home comfort and health, with discussion of thermal comfort, air circulation, illumination, noise, and the characteristics of new materials. The bibliography includes many Russian items.

LE CORBUSIER [JEANNERET-GRIS, CHARLES ÉDOUARD]. *The Modulor; A Harmonious Measure to the Human Scale Universally Applicable to Architecture and Mechanics*, translated by Peter de Francia and Anna Bostock. Cambridge, Mass.: Harvard University Press, 1954; *Modulor 2, 1955*, translated by Peter de Francia and Anna Bostock. Cambridge, Mass.: Harvard University Press, 1958. A description by Le Corbusier of the development and uses of the modulor, a measuring tool "based on the human body and on mathematics." He argues that the modulor, because it is a measure based on man, should be used as a basic design tool, and describes his use of it for many projects, including the Unité d'Habitation at Marseilles and his plans for the U.N. buildings. The second volume includes the reactions and corrections of architects and other users of the modulor.

436

MORGAN, CLIFFORD T. *et al., Human Engineering Guide to Equipment Design.* New York: McGraw-Hill, 1963. Intended as a handbook of design principles. Chapters include discussions of man-machine systems, visual and auditory presentation of information, speech communication, man-machine dynamics, the design of controls, the layout of workplaces, the arrangement of groups of men and machines, designing for ease of maintenance, and the effects of the environment on human performance. There is also a chapter of anthropometric data.

RAMSEY, CHARLES G. and SLEEPER, HAROLD R. *Architectural Graphic Standards.* New York: John Wiley & Sons, 5th ed., 1963. A handbook for architects, engineers, decorators, builders, draftsmen, and students. Drawings and specifications are presented that provide information on such items as construction with different materials; details such as stairs, fireplaces, and doors; and space standards for homes and schools.

3. CULTURAL VARIATIONS IN ENVIRONMENTAL STANDARDS

AMERICAN PUBLIC HEALTH ASSOCIATION, COMMITTEE ON THE HYGIENE OF HOUSING. *Planning the Neighborhood.* Chicago: Public Administration Service, 1960. A reprint, with an expanded bibliography, of a 1948 manual of environmental standards on the neighborhood scale, including discussions of the physical setting in which homes should be located and the basic health criteria that should guide the planning of the residential neighborhood.

DORE, RONALD PHILIP. *City Life in Japan: A Study of a Tokyo Ward.* Berkeley: University of California Press, 1958. A neighborhood study of one section of Tokyo, consisting of about 300 households, made during a period of social change. Chapter 4, "Houses and Apartment Blocks," describes housing standards and conditions and illustrates the capacity of those in other cultures to live under much more crowded conditions than are considered acceptable in the United States.

FITCH, JAMES M. AND BRANCH, DANIEL P. "Primitive Architecture and Climate." *Scientific American* 203, no. 6 (1960): 134–144. A study of the high performance of primitive architecture designed for extreme climatic conditions and usually with meager resources. American designers tend to ignore the physical environment and overestimate their technical competence, often producing buildings with poorer performance.

SONNENFELD, JOSEPH. "Variable Values in Space and Landscape: An

Inquiry into the Nature of Environmental Necessity." *Journal of Social Issues* 22, no. 4 (1966): 71–82. The kind of landscape that people prefer varies with culture, sex, age, personality, occupation, and environmental experience. The author argues that man could adapt to much less space than he now has, since people accept what they have grown up with.

TAUT, BRUNO. *Houses and People of Japan*. London: John Gifford Ltd., 1938. A thorough but highly personal study of housing design in another culture. The author's attempt to explain Japanese residential architecture is in part historical and sociological, but primarily he sees housing design in Japan as a response to climate.

WEBBER, MELVIN M. "Culture, Territory, and the Elastic Mile." In Regional Studies Association *Papers and Proceedings* 13 (1964): 59–69. The author states that space perception is culturally specific. He speculates on the space-related behavior of intellectuals, summarizes some empirical findings on working class behavior in relation to space, and offers suggestions for research into space-related behavior.

4. THE CONCEPT OF PERSONAL SPACE

CONDER, P. J. "Individual Distance." *Ibis* 91 (1949): 649–655. A description, based largely on the author's observations but with references to the literature, of individual distance as it occurs among birds. The relation of individual distance to territory is clarified.

LITTLE, KENNETH B. "Personal Space." *Journal of Experimental Social Psychology* 1 (August 1965): 237–247. Includes a summary of the literature on personal space and a report of the results of a study done by the author. The author's study attempted to assess the effect that degree of acquaintance would have on interaction distance in different settings.

SIMMEL, GEORG. "Discretion." In *The Sociology of Georg Simmel*, translated and edited by Kurt H. Wolff. Glencoe, Ill.: The Free Press, 1950, pp. 320–324. An early statement of the concept that was to become known as "personal space." Simmel discusses the sphere that surrounds each personality and the distance that separates great men from others.

SOMMER, ROBERT. *Personal Space, the Behavioral Basis of Design*. Englewood Cliffs, N.J.: Prentice-Hall, 1969. A plea for basing building design on the concerns of those who will use the building. The author describes some of his empirical work on the concept of per-

438

sonal space and discusses the use of space in mental hospitals, schools, taverns, and college dormitories.

WOHLWILL, JOACHIM F. "The Emerging Discipline of Environmental Psychology." *American Psychologist* 25, no. 4 (April 1970): 303–312. A discussion of the relationship between the field of psychology and the general increase in interest in the physical environment. Until recently, psychologists have not concerned themselves with the physical environment but have concentrated instead on social and interpersonal influences. The author reviews the work being done, the potential benefits to both psychology and the field of environmental management, and some of the institutional problems of doing research in this area.

5. THE PHENOMENON OF TERRITORIALITY

BOURLIÈRE, F. *The Natural History of Mammals.* New York: Alfred A. Knopf, 1954. Chapter 3, "Home, Territory, and Home Range," discusses the concept of territory, and cites evidence for the lack of territory among some animals. Apparently territory is not as important for mammals as it is for birds.

CARPENTER, C. R. "Territoriality: A Review of Concepts and Problems." In *Behavior and Evolution,* edited by A. Roe and G. G. Simpson. New Haven: Yale University Press, 1958, pp. 224–250. Also in C. R. Carpenter. *Naturalistic Behavior of Nonhuman Primates.* University Park, Pa.: Penn State University Press, 1964, pp. 407–429. Bibliographical article, which reviews the development of the concept of territoriality historically and discusses its varying nature for different animals and its evolutionary and behavioral significance.

LIPMAN, ALAN. "Territoriality: A Useful Architectural Concept?" *RIBA Journal* 77, no. 2 (February 1970): 68–70. An attempt, based on past studies and the author's experience with old people's homes, to define the concept of territory, a term borrowed from animal studies, so that it can be meaningful and useful to architects and designers.

STEA, DAVID. "Space, Territory and Human Movements." *Landscape* 15, no. 1 (Autumn 1965): 13–16. A discussion of the way in which territories are affected or shaped by the designed environment; if the environment changes, the territory may too. Conversely, changes in behavior may produce territorial changes. Illustrated with examples from real and hypothetical business offices.

SUTTLES, GERALD D. *The Social Order of the Slum; Ethnicity and Ter-*

ritory in the Inner City. Chicago: University of Chicago Press, 1968. An intensive participant-observer study of a mixed ethnic community on the near West Side of Chicago. Negroes, Italians, Puerto Ricans, and Mexicans live in different sections of the area, and the importance of territory to the ordering of the social structure is stressed.

6. STUDIES AND DISCUSSIONS OF SENSORY STIMULATION

BROWNFIELD, CHARLES A. *Isolation: Clinical and Experimental Approaches.* New York: Random House, 1965. A semipopular review of the subject and literature of isolation with an extensive bibliography. The point is made that changing and varied stimulation are necessary to the organized functioning of the human organism.

HEBB, D. O. *Organization of Behavior.* New York: John Wiley & Sons, 1949. Psychology text that is in large part responsible for psychologists' increased interest in the importance of the physical environment. Introduced work on sensory deprivation into the mainstream of psychology.

HERON, W. "The Pathology of Boredom." *Scientific American* 196, no. 1 (1957): 52–56. A description of the famous McGill University experiments, under Hebb's leadership, which first showed the cognitive, perceptual, and emotional impairment that result from prolonged exposure to a completely monotonous environment.

RAPOPORT, A. AND KANTOR, R. E. "Complexity and Ambiguity in Environmental Design." *Journal of the American Institute of Planners* 33 (1967): 210–221. The authors base their argument that there is a need to provide more interesting visual fields on the psychological literature. Ambiguity (that is visual nuance allowing alternative reactions to the same building) is suggested as a way to achieve the desired complexity.

SOLOMON, PHILIP, *et al.*, eds. *Sensory Deprivation.* Cambridge, Mass.: Harvard University Press, 1961. Papers from a symposium, covering perceptual, cognitive, and motor effects of sensory deprivation, including the effect on adults of childhood sensory deprivation.

VENTURI, ROBERT. *Complexity and Contradiction in Architecture.* New York: Museum of Modern Art, 1966. An architect's attempt to present both a theory of architectural criticism and an apologia for his own work. Venturi stresses the importance of complexity and contradiction, and believes that esthetic simplicity is the result of inward complexity and that richness of meaning is more important than clarity of meaning.

440

II. Spatial Organization and Social Interaction

7. SPATIAL ORGANIZATION AS A BEHAVIOR DETERMINANT

ALEXANDER, CHRISTOPHER. "A City is Not a Tree," *Architectural Forum* 122, Part I (April 1965): 58–62 and Part II (May 1965): 58–61. To reduce confusion and ambiguity, people tend to organize situations into nonoverlapping units. This habit of mind, when it occurs among planners and designers, is responsible for producing unsuccessful planned cities, since natural cities are made up of overlapping units.

BARKER, R. G. "On the Nature of the Environment." *Journal of Social Issues* 19 (1963): 17–38. A Kurt Lewin memorial address, urging that psychologists study behavior in its natural setting and showing how both the relation of the individual to his actual social and physical environment and the effect of that environment on the individual can be handled scientifically.

CAPLOW, THEODORE, *et al. The Urban Ambience.* Totowa, N.J.: Bedminster, 1964. An empirical study of twenty-five neighborhoods in San Juan, Puerto Rico, which led both to refinements in the theory of the neighborhood and to practical information for the San Juan city planners. Included are sociometric charts of interaction networks for each neighborhood, and analyses of the relationship between the intensity and extensity of interaction, of the conditions that determine residential satisfaction and stability, and of the bases on which neighbors choose each other for interaction.

GULLAHORN, J. T. "Distance and Friendship as Factors in the Gross Interaction Matrix." *Sociometry* 15, nos. 1–2 (1952): 123–134. A study of the social organization of clerical workers: even where work did not require cooperation, the gross interaction rate was largely determined by distance.

OLSSON, GUNNAR. *Distance and Human Interaction: A Review and Bibliography.* Regional Science Research Institute Bibliography Series, no. 2. Philadelphia: The Institute, 1965. A review of the literature and a bibliography of the role of distance in human interaction. Special attention is paid to the spatial patterns of location theories, migration and diffusion models, and gravity and potential models.

STRODTBECK, F. L. AND HOOK, L. H. "The Social Dimensions of a Twelve-Man Jury Table." *Sociometry* 24, no. 4 (1961): 397–415. A sociometric study of the influence of spatial position on small group

441

interaction. Participation is probably determined more by visual accessibility than by actual distance.

8. THE SOCIAL CONTEXT OF ENVIRONMENTAL PLANNING

FESTINGER, LEON, SCHACTER, STANLEY, AND BACK, KURT. *Social Pressures in Informal Groups.* New York: Harper and Brothers, 1950. The classic study of the effect of propinquity on interaction. The authors studied interaction and communication in a married students housing project and found that group cohesion was largely determined by the ease of interaction (measured in terms of both physical nearness and the position of the house within the court).

GANS, HERBERT J. "Planning and Social Life, Friendship and Neighbor Relations in Suburban Communities." *Journal of the American Institute of Planners* 27 (May 1961): 134–140; also in *People and Plans.* New York: Basic Books, 1968, pp. 152–165. Propinquity may influence interaction, particularly in a new community, but friendship depends more on homogeneity of interests, background, and the like. The site planner should not try to impose a particular pattern of social relationships, but should rather introduce sufficient diversity in house types and siting to make sure the residents can choose their own patterns of social relationships.

KUPER, LEO, ed. *Living in Towns.* London: Cresset, 1953. A collection of research papers in urban sociology. Two-thirds of the book is taken up with a report of the editor's sociological field study of two low-income neighborhoods in Coventry, one an old neighborhood and the other a new public development, from which he concludes that planned environments do not in themselves directly influence behavior.

LITWAK, EUGENE. "Voluntary Associations and Neighborhood Cohesion." *American Sociological Review* 26 (April 1961): 258–271. An attempt to consider some of the large-scale organizational factors that influence community cohesion. The author believes that voluntary associations help integrate individuals into local groups, and thus large corporations by encouraging local community participation increase local cohesion.

MERTON, ROBERT K. "The Social Psychology of Housing." In *Current Trends in Social Psychology,* edited by W. Dennis. Pittsburgh: University of Pittsburgh Press, 1948, pp. 163–217. A general discussion of the use of social psychology in the field of housing and a report on studies carried out in three housing developments. In one of

442

these studies it was found that propinquity was a strong determinant of interaction.

Webber, Melvin M. "Order in Diversity: Community without Propinquity." In *Cities and Space,* edited by Lowdon Wingo, Jr. Baltimore: Johns Hopkins Press, 1963, pp. 23–54. The argument is made that the city derives from cultural, not spatial, factors. Its essence is specialization, which leads to interdependence and interaction; urban order therefore lies not in spatial, mappable patterns, but in complex social organization.

Wilner, Daniel M., Walkley, Rosabelle Price, and Cook, Stuart W. *Human Relations in Interracial Housing.* Minneapolis: University of Minnesota Press, 1955. A study of four housing projects to determine whether the interaction coming from proximity in integrated projects led to increased harmony between races or increased antagonism. Opportunities for contact plus a favorable social climate produced the most improvement in relations.

9. CULTURAL VARIATIONS IN SPATIAL RELATIONSHIPS

Erikson, Erik H. "Inner and Outer Space: Reflections on Womanhood." *Daedalus* 93, no. 2 (Spring 1964): 582–606. Although the article is intended as an analysis of the fundamental nature of women, there is discussion of what Erikson sees as basic differences in the attitudes of men and women toward space.

Hall, Edward Twitchell. *The Hidden Dimension.* Garden City, N.Y.: Doubleday, 1966. The major book-length discussion of "proxemics," or man's use of space as a specialized elaboration of culture. Cultural differences in attitudes toward personal space are described. Particular attention is paid to the stress that results from overcrowding.

Hallowell, A. Irving. "Cultural Factors in Spatial Orientation." In *Culture and Experience.* Philadelphia: University of Pennsylvania Press, 1955, pp. 184–202. A discussion of cultural variability in spatial orientation with a detailed description of the spatial orientation of the Saulteaux.

Rosengren, W. R. and DeVault, S. "The Sociology of Time and Space in an Obstetrical Hospital." In *The Hospital in Modern Society,* edited by E. Freidson. New York: The Free Press, 1963, pp. 261–292. People's interactions are not adequately defined by their status and roles; the interactions also depend on the physical setting. In the interstitial areas of the hospital (hallways, corridors) behavior

443

was less stereotyped and more informal social organizations prevailed.

WATSON, MICHAEL AND GRAVES, THEODORE. "An Analysis of Proxemic Behavior." *American Anthropologist* 68, no. 4 (August, 1966): 971–985. An empirical study, using Arab and American students at the University of Colorado as subjects. The authors collected proxemic data and tested Hall's notation and the validity of his impressions of Arab-American differences. They did indeed find that Arab interaction distance is less than American.

10. COMMUNITY AND PRIVACY

ALEXANDER, CHRISTOPHER AND CHERMAYEFF, SERGE. *Community and Privacy*. Garden City, N.Y.: Doubleday, 1963. Urban areas must be designed so that everyone has the opportunity to be private and yet retain the advantages of living in a community. A list of categories for solving the problem of fitting private housing into an urban pattern is developed and several cluster plans are evaluated in terms of these categories.

HALMOS, PAUL. *Solitude and Privacy: A Study of Social Isolation; Its Causes and Therapy*. London: Routledge & Kegan Paul, 1952. An inquiry into the problem of social isolation based on extensive reading in psychological and other literatures and on the author's empirical study. Society, as it is presently organized, frustrates man's attempts to achieve a satisfactory group life, but without the proper balance between community and privacy, neurosis results.

MADGE, CHARLES. "Private and Public Spaces." *Human Relations* 3, no. 2 (1950): 187–199. A discussion of one type of social decision—the subdivision of living spaces, both public and private. The problem is to balance the need for privacy against the dangers of withdrawal, and the author considers the social and psychological consequences of too much and too little privacy.

MADGE, JOHN. "Privacy and Social Interaction." *Transactions of the Bartlett Society* 3 (1964–1965): 123–141, Bartlett School of Architecture, University College, London. A review of some of the psychological and sociological reasons for the need for privacy, with some design suggestions for achieving it. The author argues that the home must make allowance for both privacy and social interaction, particularly since most people's jobs today require that they remain accessible to others at all times.

SIMMEL, ARNOLD. "Privacy." *International Encyclopedia of the Social Sciences*, Vol. 12. New York: Macmillan and The Free Press, 1968, pp. 480–487. Comments on changing ideas about the right to privacy, a discussion of the determinants and indicators of privacy, a functional analysis of privacy, and a discussion of the law of privacy.

SIMMEL, GEORG. "Secrecy" and "The Secret Society." In *The Sociology of Georg Simmel*, translated and edited by Kurt H. Wolff. Glencoe, Ill.: The Free Press, 1950, pp. 330–376. A classic discussion of the role of secrecy (and privacy) in social life, both for the individual and for the group.

WESTIN, ALAN F. *Privacy and Freedom*. New York: Atheneum, 1967. Drawing on the sociological and psychological literature, the author presents a thorough discussion of the function of privacy for the individual and the group, including the nation. There is an extensive bibliography.

11. CRITIQUES OF ARCHITECTURAL DETERMINISM

BROADY, MAURICE. *Planning for People*. London: National Council of Social Service, 1968. A collection of essays in which the author attempts to integrate social planning with land-use and economic planning. He offers positive advice to planners in an effort to counter his rejection of architectural determinism.

GANS, HERBERT J. *The Levittowners*. New York: Pantheon, 1967. A report of the two years the author spent in Levittown, N.J., in the attempt to find out how a new community comes into being, how people change when they leave the city, and what their lives and politics are like in suburbia. The author found that the nature of the community depended upon the nature of those who moved there, that most suburbanites were happy, and that life in the suburbs was not the competitive wasteland pictured in the suburban myth.

GANS, HERBERT J. "The Potential Environment and the Effective Environment." In *People and Plans*. New York: Basic Books, 1968, pp. 4–11. The physical environment is relevant to behavior insofar as it affects the social system of those who will use it. However, what the urban designer plans is only a potential environment; the way in which it is used makes it into an effective environment. Planned facilities should take this distinction into account.

KELLER, SUZANNE. *The Urban Neighborhood*. New York: Random House, 1968. A thorough review of the different meanings of the concept of neighborhood and of the evidence for the effect of physical planning on neighborhoods. The author is generally pessimistic about the role the physical planner can play in encouraging the development of a sense of neighborhood.

MICHELSON, WILLIAM H. *Man and His Urban Environment.* Reading, Mass.: Addison Wesley, 1970. A sociological approach to the question of how much and how the physical form of the city shapes the lives of its inhabitants. A synthesis of past research relating life style, stage in the life cycle, social class, values, and pathology to the urban environment.

WILLMOTT, P. AND COONEY, E. "Community Planning and Sociological Research: A Problem of Collaboration." *Journal of the American Institute of Planners* 29, no. 2 (May 1963): 123–126. A general discussion of the difficulties of coordinating architectural practice and sociological research, plus a brief description of a study designed to see if sociological research on physical planning could be useful. Although people reported differences in sociability, privacy, and isolation with buildings of different types, the difficulty of weighing, for example, the benefits of privacy against the costs of isolation remains.

III. Environmental Influences on Health and Well-Being

12. HOUSING AND PHYSICAL HEALTH

LEVINE, SOL AND SCOTCH, NORMAN A., eds. *Social Stress.* Chicago: Aldine, 1970. A collection of essays reviewing the sources of social stress (family, work, class, degree of urbanization) and the consequences to the individual (including physical and mental illness and social pathology). Theoretical models and problems of research methodology are also discussed.

LORING, WILLIAM C. "Housing Characteristics and Social Disorganization." *Social Problems* 3, no. 3 (1956): 160–168. Description of a pilot study by the housing authority of metropolitan Boston to discover just what aspects of density and bad housing have a causal effect on health and social disorganization. The conclusion is that the number of social roles played by people per given amount of space determines whether or not housing will be harmful.

MARTIN, A. E. "Environment, Housing and Health." *Urban Studies* 4, no. 1 (February 1967): 1–21. A history of the relation between housing and health and a discussion of the research methods that could show the influence of housing and environment on mortality and health. The British literature is reviewed, and methodological problems, which are considerable in this area, are discussed.

POND, M. ALLEN. "The Influence of Housing on Health." *Marriage and*

446

Family Living 19, no. 2 (May 1957): 154–159. A short, clear summary of the relationship of housing to health including sections on communicable diseases, chronic diseases, mental illness, accidents, and overcrowding. The characteristics of healthful housing are reviewed, and a plea is made for more research.

SCHORR, ALVIN LOUIS. *Slums and Social Insecurity*. Washington, D.C.: Government Printing Office, 1963. Also London: Nelson, 1964. A thorough review of the interrelation between bad housing and poverty and of the need for coordination between physical and social planning. Housing affects one's perception of oneself, contributes to or relieves stress, and affects health.

SELYE, HANS. *The Stress of Life*. New York: McGraw-Hill, 1956. Includes a history of the concept of stress and a description of the body mechanisms involved. The discussion of the medical aspects of stress includes material on diseases of adaptation, that is, diseases caused by failures in the stress-fighting mechanisms (*e.g.* digestive disorders, heart failures).

13. ACOUSTICAL AND VISUAL FACTORS IN HEALTH AND WELL-BEING

BLACK, JOHN W. "The Effect of Room Characteristics upon Vocal Intensity and Rate." *Journal of the Acoustical Society of America* 22 (March 1950): 174–176. Rate and intensity of reading are affected by reverberation time and the size of a room, not by its shape. The rate is slower in larger and less reverberant rooms, the vocal intensity is greater in smaller and less reverberant rooms, and intensity increases as reverberation decreases.

GLASS, DAVID C., SINGER, JEROME E., AND FRIEDMAN, LUCY N. "Psychic Cost of Adaptation to an Environmental Stressor." *Journal of Personality and Social Psychology* 12, no. 3 (July 1969): 200–210. Description of two experiments that led to the conclusion that unpredictable noises lower a person's tolerance for frustration and his performance efficiency. The effect is greater the louder the noise but is smaller if the person thinks he is controlling the noise. Predictable noises do not have this effect.

HOPKINSON, R. G., PETHERBRIDGE, P., AND LONGMORE, J. *Daylighting*. London: Heinemann, 1966. Handbook for students and practitioners based largely on research done at the Building Research Station in England. The approach is essentially psychophysical, that is, the emphasis is on *good* lighting, not on quantitative standards. The final chapter gives examples of designing for daylight to illustrate the use of the techniques.

MANNING, PETER, ed. *Office Design: A Study of Environment.* Liverpool University, Pilkington Research Unit, 1965. A study of the design and performance of office buildings and office spaces and people's attitudes toward their offices. An attempt is made to present a picture of the total environment of the office, rather than separating the requirements for heating from the requirements for lighting, and so on.

RODDA, MICHAEL. *Noise and Society.* Edinburgh and London: Oliver & Boyd, 1967. An attempt to make present knowledge about noise available to laymen. The major problem for most people is not a loss of hearing acuity but annoyance and possibly lower efficiency. The worst noise sources are domestic equipment, advertising, automobiles, and airplanes; airplanes are likely to prove most troublesome in the future.

WELLS, B. W. P. "Subjective Responses to the Lighting Installation in a Modern Office Building and their Design Implications." *Building Science* 1 (1965): 57–68. Examines conditions under which subjective needs and comfort are met, not the levels of illumination physiologically necessary for clerical work. People think they need daylight and a view from a window; actually they tend to think they have more daylight than they in fact do; therefore buildings could be deeper without lowering office workers' comfort.

14. THE BEHAVIORAL EFFECTS OF ESTHETIC CONDITIONS

BERLYNE, D. E. *Conflict, Arousal and Curiosity.* New York: McGraw-Hill, 1960. A psychological study primarily concerned with the motivation of perceptual and intellectual activities, which includes material on the role of sensory deprivation as an influence on the formation of esthetic judgment.

BIRREN, FABER. *Light, Color, and Environment.* New York: Van Nostrand Reinhold, 1969. Contains a summary of research on the effect of color on plants and animals, historical material on the use of color, and a discussion of the psychological and emotional effects of color. Practical suggestions are given for the use of color in offices, industrial plants, hospitals, and schools.

DEWEY, JOHN. *Art As Experience.* New York: Capricorn, 1959. An attempt to understand art and its role in civilization in terms of the continuity between esthetic experience and the normal processes of living. An argument against the separation of works of art and everyday life.

448

PARR, A. E. "Psychological Aspects of Urbanology." *Journal of Social Issues* 22, no. 4 (1966): 39–45. A discussion of the psychological effect of visual monotony and enclosure, qualities the author believes are typical of today's cities.

SEGALL, MARSHALL H., CAMPBELL, DONALD T., AND HERSKOVITS, MELVILLE J. *The Influence of Culture on Visual Perception*. New York: Bobbs-Merrill, 1966. A report of a research project designed to determine the role that culturally determined experience plays in visual perceptions. The research demonstrated that there are cross-cultural differences in the perception of illusory line drawings, based on different habits of visual inference learned by people in different visual environments.

15. THE BUILT ENVIRONMENT AND MENTAL HEALTH

FARIS, ROBERT E. L. AND DUNHAM, H. WARREN. *Mental Disorders in Urban Areas; an Ecological Study of Schizophrenia and Other Psychoses*. Chicago: University of Chicago Press, 1939. A pioneer study in the social aspects of mental disorder. Social isolation was found to produce mental breakdown, but different types of mental illness were found in different areas of the city or in specific types of communities. The basic data are from Chicago, but there is comparative data from Providence.

GUTMAN, ROBERT. "Population Mobility in the American Middle Class." In *The Urban Condition*, edited by Leonard J. Duhl. New York: Basic Books, 1963, pp. 172–183. A discussion of the movement of population to the suburbs—both old established suburbs and new developments—and an attempt to answer three questions: How do suburban settlements react to middle-class whites after they've moved in, how do the migrants respond to the settlements, and what is the impact of mobility on the migrants themselves?

HARE, E. H. AND SHAW, G. K. *Mental Health on a New Housing Estate*. London: Oxford University Press, 1965. A comparative study of health in two districts in Croyden, one a new housing estate and the other an older neighborhood. Mental health in the two populations was roughly the same, suggesting that either the lack of amenities on the new estate did not lead to problems or that it was compensated for by other factors.

KANTOR, MILDRED B., ed. *Mobility and Mental Health*. Springfield, Ill.: Charles C Thomas, 1965. Proceedings of a conference on community mental health. Part I contains previously unpublished research deal-

449

ing with mobility and mental health by workers in psychiatry, epidemiology, sociology, psychology, and demography; part II contains discussion papers and a summary prepared after the conference.

PLANT, J. S., "Some Psychiatric Aspects of Crowded Living Conditions." *American Journal of Psychiatry* 86 (March 1930): 849–860. A discussion, based on clinical evidence, of the effects of crowded living conditions, particularly on children. The author suggests that it is difficult for children raised in crowded conditions to develop a strong sense of individuality.

SROLE, LEO, *et al. Mental Health in the Metropolis* 1. The Midtown Manhattan Study. New York: McGraw-Hill, 1962. LANGER, T. S. AND MICHAEL, S. T., *Life Stress and Mental Health* 2. The Midtown Manhattan Study. New York: The Free Press, 1963. A large-scale empirical study, made in midtown Manhattan, of the relationship between mental disorder and the sociocultural environment. Volume 1 deals with the relationship of demographic factors to mental disorder; volume 2 with the relationship of stressful experiences, lack of close friends, and mental worries to mental disorder.

16. THE SOCIAL CONSEQUENCES OF OVERCROWDING

CALHOUN, JOHN B. "Population Density and Social Pathology." *Scientific American* 206 (February 1962): 139–146. Rats conditioned to eat in company develop a tendency to congregate in one place, leading to what is called a "behavioral sink." The article describes the disruption of nesting, sexual, aggressive, and feeding behavior caused by the overcrowding.

CHOMBART DE LAUWE, PAUL. *Famille et Habitation.* Paris: Editions du Centre National de la Recherche Scientific, 1959. A thorough empirical study of three postwar French housing estates, including one by Le Corbusier. The architects' decisions seem to have been based more on government regulations than on users' needs, and the resultant overcrowding, bad soundproofing, and lack of amenities produced family strains, particularly for the children.

CHRISTIAN, J. J. "Endocrine Adaptive Mechanisms and the Physiological Regulation of Population Growth." In *Physiological Mammalogy,* edited by William V. Meyer and Richard G. Van Gelder. Vol. 1, Mammalian Populations. New York: Academic Press, 1963, pp. 189–353. Purely behavioral or social interaction acting through the central nervous system produces an endocrine response, which is described in the first section. The second section reviews the physiology of endocrine adaptation in different mammalian populations,

450

including descriptions of lab populations of fixed and growing size and reports of natural populations.

GRAHAM, HUGH DAVID AND GURR, TED ROBERT, eds. *Violence in America; Historical and Comparative Perspectives*. Washington, D.C.: U.S. Government Printing Office, 1969, 2 vols. A staff report to the National Commission on the Causes and Prevention of Violence, the book attempts a descriptive and analytical history of violence in the United States and Western Europe. Chapter 21 deals with the connection between overcrowding and aggression.

SCHMITT, ROBERT C. "Implications of Density in Hong Kong." *Journal of the American Institute of Planners* 29 (1963): 210–217. Hong Kong has one of the highest overall density rates in the world without high rates of death, disease, or social disorganization. This is partly a result of Chinese tradition, partly because the refugees are accustomed to worse conditions, and partly a result of the fact that there are not many cars.

WINSBOROUGH, H. H. "The Social Consequences of High Population Density." *Law and Contemporary Problems* 30, no. 1 (Winter 1965): 120–126. An attempt to help the city planner by disentangling (with confusing results) the effects of density on health from the effects of other, associated variables.

IV. The Social Meaning of Architecture

17. ENVIRONMENTAL PERCEPTION

GREGORY, R. L. *Eye and Brain*. New York: McGraw-Hill, 1966. A clearly written examination of the physiological and psychological problems involved in seeing: how is information from the eyes coded into neural terms, into the language of the brain, and reconstituted into the experience of surrounding objects?

HOWARD, I. P. AND TEMPLETON, W. B. *Human Spatial Orientation*. London: John Wiley & Sons, 1966. A thorough discussion of those aspects of human behavior that are determined by the angular position of the body or head with respect to any stable, external reference system. The development of orientation in children is also discussed. There is an extensive bibliography.

LOWENTHAL, DAVID, ed. *Environmental Perception and Behavior*. University of Chicago, Department of Geography, Research Paper no. 109, 1967. A collection of essays, of uneven quality, dealing with people's attitudes toward the environment, particularly the subjec-

451

tive, often unconscious, and culturally dominated forces that play a major role in determining how people see the environment and how they act in it.

LYNCH, KEVIN. *The Image of the City*. Cambridge, Mass.: The Technology Press and Harvard University Press, 1960. A seminal work dealing with the mental image of the city held by its citizens, particularly the clarity or legibility of that image. A good environmental image produces a sense of emotional security, and the argument is made that we should build our cities to encourage, not discourage, our tendencies to organize our environment.

PIAGET, JEAN AND INHELDER, BÄRBEL. *The Child's Conception of Space*, translated by F. G. Langdon and J. L. Lunzer. New York: W. W. Norton, 1967. A study of the development of the child's conception of representational (not perceptual) space. The child starts with certain primitive topological relationships such as proximity and separation, order and enclosure, which are necessary to his subsequent grasp of Euclidean notions.

RAPOPORT, AMOS AND HAWKES, RON. "The Perception of Urban Complexity." *Journal of the American Institute of Planners* 36, no. 2 (March 1970): 106–111. Complexity, defined in terms of the maximum rate of usable information received and processed by the individual, is a desirable quality for an urban environment. The significance of information provided by any object or event depends not just on the object but also on the individual's culture, personal experience, learning, and current emotional and motivational states.

THIEL, PHILIP. "A Sequence-Experience Notation for Architectural and Urban Spaces." *Town Planning Review* 32, no. 1 (April 1961): 33–52. An attempt to develop a system of graphic notation to represent the perception of architectural and urban spaces. Since architecture must be experienced in time, the planner, to understand his material, needs a tool analogous to dance notation.

18. THEORY OF ARCHITECTURAL SYMBOLISM

CHOAY, FRANÇOISE. *The Modern City: Planning in the Nineteenth Century*. New York: George Braziller, 1969. A history of nineteenth-century urban planning that makes use of semiological theory to account for the chaotic condition of twentieth-century urban forms. The author believes that twentieth-century urban planning is still heavily influenced by nineteenth-century modes of thought.

CONSTANTINE, MILDRED AND JACOBSON, EGBERT. *Sign Language*. New

York: Reinhold, 1961. They show, mainly by pictures, how signs can contribute to the total effect of a building or cityscape. "Properly understood, placed and designed, all of our signs can become a new kind of heraldry, enriching the structures and the landscape."

GOODMAN, PAUL. "Seating Arrangements: An Elementary Lecture in Functional Planning." In *Utopian Essays and Practical Proposals.* New York: Vintage Books, 1951, pp. 156–181. Current seating arrangements in, for example, houses of parliament, reflect cultural attitudes; future seating arrangements could be planned in terms of what one wishes to accomplish rather than by convention.

JENCKS, CHARLES AND BAIRD, GEORGE, eds. *Meaning in Architecture.* New York: George Braziller, 1969. A crude and not always successful attempt to apply the principles of semiology to the understanding of architecture. The book includes alongside each article a running commentary by the editors and other contributors with an occasional rejoinder by the author.

WOHL, R. RICHARD AND STRAUSS, ANSELM L. "Symbolic Representation and the Urban Milieu." *American Journal of Sociology* 63, no. 5 (March 1958): 523–532. Cities are so complex that people must represent them by devices that simplify and evoke images and sentiments. The article describes the manner and means whereby city people organize their perceptions of the environment to achieve social perspective on urban life.

19. THE RELATION OF ARCHITECTURE TO PERSONALITY DYNAMICS

BACHELARD, GASTON. *The Poetics of Space.* New York: Orion Press, 1964. A study by a French phenomenologist of many aspects of attitudes toward space. Of particular interest are the chapters on the house, in which Bachelard examines the special qualities of the image of the house.

BALINT, MICHAEL. "Friendly Expanses—Horrid Empty Spaces." *International Journal of Psychoanalysis* 36, part 4/5 (1955): 225–241. People can be divided into two groups in terms of their attitudes toward space: those who enjoy a temporary loss of security and those who hold on to firm ground. For the first the world consists of friendly expanses dotted more or less densely with dangerous and unpredictable objects; for the second the world consists of objects separated by horrid empty spaces.

BROWER, SIDNEY N. "Territoriality, The Exterior Spaces, The Signs We Learn to Read." *Landscape* 15, no. 1 (Autumn 1965): 9–12. Four different kinds of territory are distinguished, according to the degree of restriction of admission and controls over action within the territory. It is important that the design communicate clearly what kind of territory is involved.

FLÜGEL, J. C. *The Psychology of Clothes.* London: Hogarth, 1930. An analysis by a prominent psychoanalyst of the functions served by clothes other than mere protection. The method of analysis could be used for a similar study of the functions served by architecture.

GOLDFINGER, ERNO. "The Elements of Enclosed Space" and "Urbanism and Spatial Order." *Architectural Review* (November 1941): 129–131, (December 1941): 163–166, (January 1942): 5–9. A series of three articles which focus particularly on the implications arising from the fact that buildings (and cities) enclose space. What makes up the sensation of space and the ways in which high-speed travel has changed our urban perceptions are also discussed.

HARTMAN, CHESTER W. "Social Values and Housing Orientations." *Journal of Social Issues* 19, no. 2 (April 1963): 113–131. One cannot judge residents' attitudes toward housing simply on the basis of its physical condition. In Boston's West End 80 per cent of those in an area condemned by the housing authority as a slum liked their housing; the objective quality of the apartment mattered only to those who were not attached to the neighborhood.

RUESCH, JURGEN AND KEES, WELDON. *Nonverbal Communication.* Berkeley and Los Angeles: University of California Press, 1956. An attempt to analyze what we mean when we discuss the "atmosphere" of a house or a section of a city. Includes discussion of what is being expressed by the arrangement of furniture in a house or merchandise in a shop window.

SEARLES, HAROLD F. *The Nonhuman Environment.* New York: International Universities Press, 1960. The author, a psychiatrist dealing primarily with schizophrenic patients, believes that the nonhuman environment, far from being of little or no importance to the development of personality, is one of the most important ingredients of human psychological existence. Each individual has a strong sense of relatedness to his nonhuman environment, which he ignores at his psychological peril.

20. ARCHITECTURAL PROPERTIES AND SOCIAL STATUS

CHAPMAN, DENNIS. *The Home and Social Status.* London: Routledge & Kegan Paul, 1955. An empirical study of the interaction of family and social status; differences in social status were found to be re-

454

flected in differences in the pattern of use of the home, in material, cultural, and esthetic equipment, and in location.

FORM, WILLIAM H. AND STONE, GREGORY P. "Urbanism, Anonymity, and Status Symbolism." *American Journal of Sociology* 62 (March 1957): 504–514. Status symbolism is important to urban sociology, because in the city, unlike the small town, the individual must deal with so many other individuals that there is no time for the kind of social contact that enables status to be bestowed in terms of rights and duties. The authors examine the variation in the symbolism used by different socioeconomic groups to bestow status on anonymous others.

MACK, RAYMOND W. "Ecological Patterns in an Industrial Shop." *Social Forces* 32, no. 4 (May 1954): 351–356. A case study applying ecological analysis to an industrial situation. A man's residential location within certain physical boundaries was taken as a status symbol and became a datum in defining his social relations, in this example extending from residence to work.

SEELEY, JOHN R., SIM, R. ALEXANDER, AND LOOSLEY, ELIZABETH W. "Shelter." In *Crestwood Heights, A Study of the Culture of Suburban Life.* New York: Basic Books, 1956, pp. 42–62. A chapter from a study of a middle-class Canadian suburb, in which the special role of the house is discussed. Particularly relevant is the discussion of the psychocultural functions of the house: the house as property, the house as stage, the house as home.

WERTHMAN, CARL, MANDEL, JERRY S., AND DIENSTFREY, TED. *Planning and the Purchase Decision.* University of California at Berkeley, Institute of Urban and Regional Development, Center for Planning and Development Research, Preprint no. 10 (July 1965). A study to find out what people who bought into planned communities thought they were buying and why. The class image of the community and the investment potential of a home were found to be important and intertwined considerations. Furthermore, the choice of a home also involves a choice of social identity.

21. THE SOCIAL FUNCTION OF ARCHITECTURAL SYMBOLISM

DURKHEIM, ÉMILE. *The Elementary Forms of the Religious Life,* translated by Joseph Ward Swain. New York: Macmillan, n. d. Durkheim's classic study of comparative religion, which includes discussion of the social role of religious beliefs and practices.

ELIADE, MIRCEA. *Images and Symbols,* translated by Philip Mairet. New York: Sheed & Ward, 1969. Includes a discussion of the universal nature of the idea of the city as sacred because it lies at the center of the universe. The idea of the city as the place where the cosmic mountain, with roots in the earth and the summit on heaven, is to be found is also discussed, and examples from a wide range of cultures are used as illustration.

FIREY, WALTER. "Sentiment and Symbolism as Ecological Variables." *American Sociological Review* 10, no. 2 (April 1945): 140–148. Space is not only an impediment but also a symbol. Locational activities are not just economizing agents but bear sentiments that influence the process of location. An argument against economic ecology, illustrated with examples from Boston.

GUTMAN, ROBERT. "Library Architecture and People." In *The Library Building Consultant Role and Responsibility*, edited by Ernest R. De Prospo, Jr. New Brunswick, N.J.: Rutgers University Press, 1969, pp. 11–29. An analysis of library buildings in terms of five properties considered significant for the relation of buildings to society and behavior: ambiance, amenity, communication net, symbol, and architectonic space. Many of the difficulties that arise in the relationship between library architects and library planners can be traced to the failure to admit that symbolism is an inescapable element in building design.

V. The Application of Behavioral Science to Design

22. PROBLEMS OF APPLYING THE BEHAVIORAL SCIENCES
    IN THE DESIGN PROCESS

GUTMAN, ROBERT. "What Architectural Schools Expect from Sociology." *AIA Journal* 49, no. 3 (March 1968): 70–77. A review of the kinds of sociology courses typically taken by architectural students in the United States and Britain, and the kinds of questions architectural students tend to expect sociologists to be able to answer. Some of the reasons why the interaction between architectural students and sociologists is not always successful are also discussed.

HIGGIN, GURTH AND JESSOP, NEIL. *Communications in the Building Industry*. London: Tavistock Publications, 1965. A report of a study of the building industry made by a specialist in operations research and a social psychologist with recommendations for research projects that would help the industry. The difficulties in communication faced by the industry are seen as consequences of the fact that the resource controllers are technically interdependent and organizationally independent.

LIPMAN, ALAN. "The Architectural Belief System and Social Behaviour." *British Journal of Sociology* 20, no. 2 (June 1969): 190–204. An examination of the way in which the architect's belief that he can influence social behavior helps him resolve some of the difficulties in his working situation. Because he sees himself as satisfying profound needs, it is not so upsetting that he makes money from his clients, nor that there is a gulf between his esthetic ideas and those of the public.

NORBERG-SCHULZ, CHRISTIAN. *Intentions in Architecture.* Oslo: Universitetsforlaget, 1966. An attempt to assimilate sociological and psychological concepts into the tradition of architectural criticism. The book presents a theory that would encompass both the study of building tasks and the finished building, and then uses it to analyze the state of contemporary architecture.

SOMMER, ROBERT. "Can Behavioural Studies be Useful as Well as Ornamental?" *Transactions of the Bartlett Society* 5 (1966–1967): 47–65, Bartlett School of Architecture, University College, London. A discussion of the difficulties faced by designers trying to incorporate social science findings in their work. Unless these findings are translated into a form that shows how they affect design, they may be only of interest, not of use.

23. BEHAVIORAL APPROACHES TO DESIGN SOLUTIONS

BROLIN, BRENT C. AND ZEISEL, JOHN. "Mass Housing: Social Research and Design." *Architectural Forum* 129, no. 1 (July–August 1968): 66–71. An attempt to apply social science principles to the design of mass housing. The authors believe that architects should not impose their ideas of proper social organization on other people. Using Gans' observations on the Italian-Americans in Boston's West End, the authors suggest ways in which housing could be designed to support the group's existing way of life.

GOOD, LAWRENCE R., SIEGEL, SAUL M., AND BAY, ALFRED PAUL, eds. *Therapy by Design.* Springfield, Ill.: Charles C Thomas, 1965. Part I is a report of a project carried out at the Topeka State Hospital in which the influence of architecture on mental patients was studied. Part II contains the proceedings of a conference of social scientists and architects called to discuss the project.

HOLE, W. V. AND ATTENBURROW, J. J. *Houses and People: A Review of*

User Studies at the Building Research Station. London: HMSO, 1966. A review of British research showing people's reactions to planning and facilities in existing mass housing. Meant as a guide to design, the book considers family activity patterns and their effect upon room use and suggests likely future trends in user needs.

LANGDON, F. J. *Modern Offices: A User Survey.* Ministry of Technology, Building Research Station, National Building Studies, Research Paper no. 41. London: HMSO, 1966. A report of a survey on attitudes toward offices. The physical environment was found to be much less important to satisfaction than the intrinsic characteristics of the job, but this did not mean that it was totally unimportant.

RAVEN, JOHN. "Sociological Evidence on the House." *Architectural Review* 142, no. 845 (July 1967): 68–72, and 142, no. 847 (September 1967): 236–240. A review in two parts of the empirical sociological evidence on housing, both British and American. The first article deals with space within the dwelling, the second with what people expect of their home environment and the influence it exerts on them.

STOKE, STUART M. *et al. Student Reactions to Study Facilities.* Amherst, Mass.: 1960. A report of a study made at four New England colleges as part of the planning for a new college. The spaces used by students to study and their reactions to these spaces were investigated. There was a clear preference for small spaces, and most studying was done in the student's room.

24. ENVIRONMENTAL ASSESSMENT

"BUILDING APPRAISAL: ST. MICHAEL'S ACADEMY, KILWINNING." *Architects' Journal* 151, no. 1 (January 7, 1970): 9–50. A study by the Building Performance Research Unit, an interdisciplinary team at the University of Strathclyde, of a school in Scotland. The team is trying to develop techniques of appraisal in use and appraisal in design so that it will be possible to predict how a building will work.

"HOUSING RESEARCH AND DEVELOPMENT." *Architectural Design* 36 (August 1966): 379–402. A report on the work of the British Ministry of Housing and Local Government Research and Development Group. An explanation is given of the methods they use for preparing briefs, designing projects, and evaluating finished projects, and examples are shown of some of the projects they have undertaken.

MICHIGAN, UNIVERSITY OF, SCHOOL ENVIRONMENTS RESEARCH PROJECT. *The Effect of Windowless Classrooms on Elementary School Children.* Ann Arbor: Architectural Research Laboratory, Department of Architecture, University of Michigan, 1965. A report of a case study of the effect of windowless classrooms on primary school children. Windowless rooms decreased outside distractions and increased available wall space and apparently had little effect on learning ability.

RAE, JOHN. "Heathrow." *Architects' Journal* 151, no. 20 (May 20, 1970): 1243–1262 and 151, no. 21 (May 27, 1970): 1323–1338. An evaluation study of an airport terminal. The article compares the actual use of the building with the architects' intentions and examines the relationship of the planning concepts to the finished building.

TRITES, DAVID K. "Radial Nursing Units Prove Best in Controlled Study." *Modern Hospital* 112, no. 4 (April 1969): 94–99. A description of a hospital deliberately constructed in order to test alternative floor plans. The follow-up study questioned patients, nurses, doctors, administrators, and visitors, and found a clear preference for a radial design, a preference substantiated by some of the objective measurements made in the study.

WHITE, R. B. *Qualitative Studies of Buildings.* Ministry of Technology, Building Research Station, National Building Studies, Special Report no. 39. London: HMSO, 1966. A study of the long-term durability and functional performance of the De La Warr Pavilion in Bexhill-on-Sea and the Gilbey Building in London in relation to their owners' and designers' intentions.

25. PROBLEMS OF SCIENTIFIC DESIGN METHODOLOGY

FRAMPTON, KENNETH. "The Visionary vs the Utilitarian." *Architectural Design* 38 (March 1968): 134–136. An analysis and comparison of the Palais des Nations competition designs of Hannes Meyer and Le Corbusier. The complex relationship between utility and iconography is discussed, and the point is made that a building that is "automatically determined" from the program may in fact turn out to be less utilitarian than one built according to an esthetic founded on utopian idealism.

JONES, J. CHRISTOPHER AND THORNLEY, D. G., eds. *Conference on Design Methods.* Oxford: Pergamon, 1963. A collection of papers presented at a conference on systematic and intuitive methods in engineering, industrial design, architecture, and communications. The conference brought together people from different fields in an attempt to establish systematic methods of problem solving, particularly with respect to design, and to consider how design could best be taught.

RYKWERT, JOSEPH. "The Sitting Position, A Question of Method." In

Meaning in Architecture, edited by Charles Jencks and George Baird. New York: George Braziller, 1969, pp. 233–243. The author's argument that the whole of the environment is a tissue of symbolic forms is illustrated by a discussion of the chair. The dependence of comfort on social convention severely limits the usefulness of ergonomics to design.

STUDER, RAYMOND G. "The Dynamics of Behavior-Contingent Physical Systems." In *Design Methods in Architecture*, edited by G. Broadbent and A. Ward. New York: Wittenborn, 1969, pp. 55–70. An elaborate model for locating the important junctures at which human behavior and the physical environment interact. The relevance of the model to solving design problems is discussed and a strong stand is taken in favor of working with behaviorally oriented definitions of human needs and social organization rather than relying on typological solutions to design problems.

SUMMERSON, JOHN. "The Case for a Theory of Modern Architecture." *RIBA Journal* 64 (1957): 307–311. An extremely influential article among contemporary designers. The author argues that modern architecture is distinguished by a new concern for the program, in particular for the qualitative aspects of the program. Designers are no longer content to work from a list of quantitative requirements.

26. FUTURE ROLES OF THE BEHAVIORAL SCIENCES
  IN THE DESIGN PROCESS

ALEXANDER, CHRISTOPHER. *Notes on the Synthesis of Form.* Cambridge, Mass.: Harvard University Press, 1964. Design problems have become so complex that a way must be found to break them up into smaller problems that can be understood. Part I contains an account of the nature of design problems and Part II a method of representing design problems so that they can be broken up into solvable units; the appendix shows how the method works in practice.

DEASY, C. M. AND BOLLING, R. D. *Actions, Objectives and Concerns.* Los Angeles, 1969. (Available through Educational Facilities Laboratory, New York, N. Y.) An experiment in the use of behavioral science techniques for architectural objectives. Before preparing the program for a student union building at California State College in Los Angeles, the architects, with the help of a social psychologist and the college building coordinator, made a study of actual and desired student activity patterns.

GANS, HERBERT J. "Social Planning: A New Role for Sociology." In *Neighborhood, City, and Metropolis,* edited by Robert Gutman and

David Popenoe. New York: Random House, 1970, pp. 920–932. There is a need for sociologists to become more involved in city planning. They should work at developing theoretical schemes to guide planning, at improving the methods for deciding on social goals, at formulating programs for achieving these goals, and at conducting research to evaluate action programs.

MOORE, GARY T., ed. *Emerging Methods in Environmental Design and Planning.* Cambridge, Mass.: The M.I.T. Press, 1970. Proceedings from the first international conference of the Design Methods Group. The conference was concerned with finding new methods for solving the problems of the physical environment. The subjects covered include building layout models, problem structuring, computer aided design, evaluation systems, and applications of systems engineering. There is also considerable theoretical discussion.

PERIN, CONSTANCE. *With Man in Mind. An Interdisciplinary Prospectus for Environmental Design.* Cambridge, Mass.: The M.I.T. Press, 1970. An attempt to bridge the gap between what we do when we design and change the environment and what people really want from the environment. The author puts forth the concept of the "behavioral circuit" as a framework for bridging the gap and also suggests concrete proposals that can be carried out now, in particular by social scientists and building users, to make the environment more responsive to people's desires.

Index

adaptation, to environmental stimulation, 89–91

aesthetics, *see* esthetics

aged, housing for the: social conveniences, incorporation of, 395; sound, reaction of aged to, 206; user requirements, 385, 387–393; warden, accommodations for, 385, 388

air conditioning, living standards and, 45

Alberti, Leon Battista: geometry of design based on dimensions of human figure, 17; height of steps, 40

alienation, urban areas and, 408–434 *passim*

Amsterdam (Holland): city image, 276, 278, 281–283; structure, 276, 277

anatomy: architecture and, 17 (*see also* anthropometrics); of urination, 19–20

animals: habitat, determination of, 99; overcrowding, effects of, 250, 256–258, 260, 261; social isolation, effects of, 413–414; spatial behavior, 62, 63

anthropology, esthetic standards and, 8

anthropometrics, physical design and, 17, 33, 34, 35–41

apartments, *see* housing

architectural determinism, 170, 173–174, 179, 180, 182

architecture (*see also* design): ceremonial, *see* ceremonial architecture; complexity, 3; criticality, 35; group membership and, 120–134; impact on man, 9; incongruity, 87, 88; mathematical applications, 88, 399–400; social importance of, 125–127; sociology of, *see* sociology; theory of, 341–343; "third environment," architecture as, 3, 9

Ardrey, Robert: territorial defenses, 82

Arnheim, Rudolph, 288

Aronson, Jason, 247

Australia: stair standards, 41; temperature standards, 43, 45

autonomy-withdrawal syndrome, 408, 415–421, 422

Back, Kurt, 128

bathroom (*see also* urination facilities): cleanliness, 45; privacy, 159, 162

beauty, pecuniary standards of, 315–326

bedroom: student dormitories, 378

beds, size of, 37

behavioral sciences, *see* psychology; sociology

Beranek, Leo L.: standards for noise control, 42

Berlyne, D. E.: dimensions of stimulation, 87, 88

biological survival, institutional structure and, 98–99

biology (*see also* anatomy): as constraint on design, 17

biotechnical determinism, 394, 398, 400, 404

THE FIVE AGES OF MAN

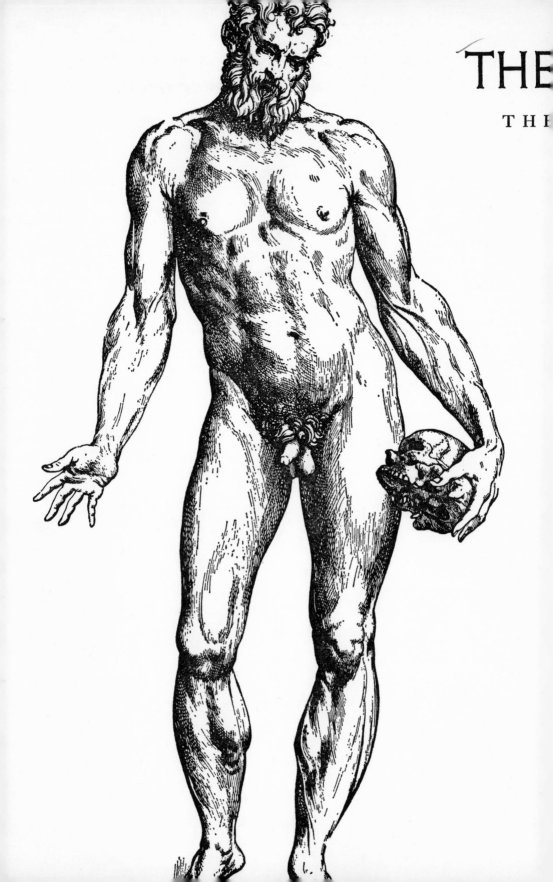

FIVE AGES OF MAN

PSYCHOLOGY OF HUMAN HISTORY

BY GERALD HEARD

The Julian Press, Inc., Publishers
New York

Published by *The Julian Press, Inc.*
119 Fifth Avenue, New York 3
© *Copyright 1963 by Gerald Heard*
Library of Congress catalog card number: 63-22142
Design: MARSHALL LEE

My thanks to
JAY MICHAEL BARRIE
for his help as collaborator and editor,
and to
THE BOLLINGEN FOUNDATION
whose grant made this work possible.

BOOKS BY GERALD HEARD

The Source of Civilization

The Ascent of Humanity
 (awarded The Henrietta Hertz Prize by The British Academy)

The Social Substance of Religion

Pain, Sex and Time

The Third Morality

Man the Master

Is God in History?

Is God Evident?

The Human Venture

Contents

III THE DEVELOPMENT OF INITIATIONS OR PSYCHOPHYSICAL RELIGIOUS EXERCISES [*The five mysteries*]

Epilogue: THE PSYCHOPHYSICAL FUTURE OF MAN [*Evolution resumed*] 283

Appendixes

THE FIVE AGES OF MAN

Introduction

The most vital question that confronts humanity today is a three-fold one. Can man, who has so catastrophically changed his power over his environment, change his own nature? Has he ever done so? If he has, how has he done it? Whether or not we can have any hope of answering this triple question depends on whether or not, in looking at history, we can discern any over-all pattern or process of development.

Alfred North Whitehead, together with many other philosophers and historians of science, has called the one hundred years from 1600 to 1700 the Century of Invention. These were the three generations during which the basic insights were made in regard to the Sciences. But it is a strange fact that although in that formative period history, too, was looked on as being a process that could only be understood as a science, later historians have refused so to regard it.

Hugo Grotius (1583–1645) was the founder of International Law. In 1604 he wrote, although he did not publish it, his *De Jure Praedae*. It was the first sketch of his classic *De Jure Belli* which, including *Jus Pacis*, was written in 1625. This book has often been said to have founded a new science, the science of International Law extracted from consideration of the actual process of history. As Mark Patterson has said, "the law in war" was but a small part of the whole of Grotius' study of those principles which hold men together; principles to which man's basic nature compels him to return, however often he may behave aberrantly.

Giovanni Vico (1668–1744) develops and enriches these insights into the structure of history and into the cohesive forces that shape its process. By the end of the eighteenth century (and using the cold scientism of Francis Bacon to remove the orthodox prejudices from Grotius' thinking) he could perceive the anthropological basis underlying law. Therefore, as the eighteenth century opened he was able (from his universal law, *de universi juris uno principio et fine uno*) to arrive at his classic contribution to a philosophy of history, *Principii d'una Scienza Nuova*.

From the fragmentary evidence yielded by the Jewish canonical books and Greek literature, he recognized that man had gone through at least three great stages. Primitive tribes have an almost instinctive power to hold together: a power of coconsciousness or group-suggestibility (I have called it hypnocratic; see Part III, Chapter 2, footnote *c*). This stage is succeeded by the heroic which, in turn, is followed by the humane epoch. Strangely enough (and, it may be, out of subconscious caution) Vico neglects the ascetic epoch.

However, we can see that this is not only a schema of history, an outline of a significant process. This is also an interpretation of history in psychological terms. It shows that there can be a historia[a] of man, just as there can be a natural history, a science of the other creatures. But man's history is not to be understood in terms of instinct any more than it is to be understood in terms of economics. Though for the first epoch of his history man was raised

[a] This is the word that Aristotle uses for a science.

by an *unconscious* drive, that drive finally lifted him into intentional development in his effort to satisfy an inborn wish to understand. His story is not the result of his reaction to blind forces that work either from within or without. Man's story is specifically the winning of an increasing awareness, purpose, intention, and objective. In short, man's history is the record of how he has gained in the intensification of consciousness, of self-understanding. It is a psychological story. For the spiral evolution of the psyche is the theme of the human venture. It is the clue to man's varied and successive behaviors, to the interpretation of his activities. It is the key to the explanation of his conflicts and his constructs, his orders and revolts, his catastrophies and recoveries, his breakdowns and resumptions.

Intensified special studies of history, and indeed the increasing restriction of history to a study in itself that is confined to documents, made historians neglect Vico's magnificent map. Goethe, visiting Naples, was shown the master's work. But the great concept fell barren on that polished mind that was divided into the two facets of natural science and poetry. Gibbon, who can span and compose fifteen hundred years, could only confirm the prejudices of rationalistic taste and mechanistic science: human history is divided between brutal or superstitious ignorance and critical, sophisticated knowledge. There were no alternatives other than the reign of reason or "the triumph of barbarism and religion."

Soon the historian was relieved of the task of having to handle predocumentary data—by the archaeologist. And when with Boucher de Perthes' discoveries of the Old Stone Age tools (and after a hard struggle that was thoroughly discreditable to the guardians of history) there was disclosed a further and vaster past lying back of the archaeological ages, this awkward revelation was handed to the paleontologist. Then this latest research began to show that here might lie the only basic datum line of history, that in this amazing evidence (again, it was passionately resented by "the custodians of the past"), which had been brought to light by the discovery of the great paleolithic cave frescoes and bas reliefs, might be mirrored a different, pre-self-conscious type of mind and level of consciousness. But again, the historian refused to shoulder the obligation. To the anthropologist was left the fascinating and informative task of correlating the surviving stone age cultures[b] of Australia with the dawn cultures of Ice Age Europe, and so catch glimpses of the vast process whereby man's mind, as it contracted focus, achieved increasing objectivity.

Now, therefore, the historian is self-confined to his own ever narrower documentation. Naturally, such voluntary myopia denies any general pattern. A tapestry cannot be understood by studying its threads with a magnifying glass. Exchange the glass for a microscope and the higher magnification will only render the design less perceptible. We need a lens with a wider angle, not a more intense focus, if we are to perceive an aeonic process. As it was pointed out by James Anthony Froude, the capable and popular nineteenth-century Oxford historian, it was this very lack of extent and span, not a lack of detail and particulars, that prevented his generation of students of the past from perceiving its vast pattern— a lack which he did not hold was irremediable.

Sir Flinders Petrie was the founding father of predocumentary (or nondocumentary) history, a chronology of culture deduced from a series of artifacts. He had an almost unsurpassed knowledge of Egyptian history, and at the beginning of the twentieth century he did indicate (in his *Revolutions of Civilization*) that he had detected a process of alternating cycles of order, arrest, revolt, and restored order throughout the millennia of the Nile culture-course and social heredity.

Max Weber, as a Comtist Positivist and influenced by Herbert Spencer, with truly German eruditional pertinacity collected a vast mass of documentation to establish his thesis that the whole process of history brings man to a complete and final rationalism, in the name of which he dismisses religion and metaphysics as irrationalisms. In spite of his immense learning he (like Sir James Frazer with his vast but fruitless *Golden Bough*) uses it only to establish this utterly inadequate thesis: All religion is magic and magic is

[b] "Prehorticultural," to use W. D. Strong's still economic serial classification. See also Carleton S. Coon (15).

merely man's first, fumbling, mistaken effort to make science. All metaphysic is also man's false view of things seen through the superstition-clouded minds of the past, and now corrected for good by the critical self-conscious mind of modern man, who at last is able to see things as they are, have always been, and will be.

Even Breasted, like Petrie, could not make use of his great insight: the recognition that a new kind of person had appeared almost in one century (the three generations required for a new challenge to be made and a new question to be put, a new answer to be offered and that new answer to be put into practice). Breasted called it "the rise of conscience" (after which we all become individually responsible egos). He did not recognize this phase as a midterm in the condensation of consciousness; that it lay between the phase of the simple-minded, unreflective hero and that of the fully isolated consciousness of the modern Renaissance man who believes only in the critical, skeptical reason.

And even Karl Jaspers, in his *Ursprung und Ziel der Geschichte,* though he does recognize this the ascetic phase and its importance (for this doctrine of secession from the going concern is found extending in three lifetimes from Shantung, the peninsula pointing northeast to the Upper China Sea, to Calabria, the peninsula that reaches down into the Western Mediterranean) nevertheless calls it "the axis of time in human history." He can view it only as a fulcrum up to which mankind rises and then, like a child crawling up a teeter-totter, having passed the pivot can now come easily down to ground again. He does not recognize any more than Breasted that the mind after having reached this middle phase of self-consciousness condensed even further, and then, and then only, has begun again to re-expand.

Eric Voegelin (88), in his huge, still unfinished study of history, gives us the philosophy that will rule his work. In the first volumes, and most succinctly in his *New Science of Politics, An Introduction* (88), he takes his stand on that neo-Catholicism which, in one comprehensive excommunication, dismisses all concepts of development, improvement, and resumed epigenesis as heresy, as gnosticism. And he calls on, as allies, such antipathetic figures as Richard (called

contemporaneously "the Judicious") Hooker, the Elizabethan Anglican Divine, and Thomas Hobbes, the designer of the monster
state-master Leviathan, the power elite focused in one man, the
absolute autocrat.

Indeed, this continued refusal to look at the huge design now
exposed to our view is so unreasonable that we are bound to suspect an unconscious prejudice. An unfriendly reception was given
by most professional historians to Arnold Toynbee's attractive and
inspiring study of history. Also that compendious historian refused
to start his interpretation with the basic platform of human history.
He traced only those mesas, benches, and buttes of cultures that
rise from that common peneplain. He started at the archaeological
level of history, not at its paleontological base. These two facts seem
to me to be evidence of a deep unwillingness to face the possibility
of a psychological interpretation of history in which the clue to
man's historia is the evolution of his consciousness.

As it is in the case of the long rejected results of research into
extrasensory perception, this appears to be due to a rare concatena-
tion of forces usually so opposed to each other that, when they
combine to deny something, the public is convinced that what they
deny needs no further examination; it cannot but be false. The
theologians of the Western World have claimed that one of the
reasons for the superiority of their religion was that it was historical.
But at least since the dismissal of the Alexandrine Fathers (especially Origen, A.D. 185–254) they have been hostile to any information, whether astronomical or biological, which might suggest
that their view of the process of history was too narrow because their
concept of the developmental emergence of man was too local and
brief. "Ours, the one true religion and therefore the one historical
religion," they said, "is being endangered by irresponsible research."
For the greater part of the last one hundred years this slogan
allowed the theologians to prevent new historical knowledge from
being incorporated into the basis for a growing morality.

On the other hand, the biologists were just as anxious to prevent the public being offered any picture that was less out of date
than that of the theologians. Smarting from the reception given

to the evolutionary hypothesis of man's ascent, they certainly had strong negative motivation to collect and stress all the evidence that might indicate the meaninglessness of creation.

Nevertheless, although most biologists have clung to the belief that almost throughout its course the evolutionary process has been completely blind and fortuitous, and although this belief has been accepted by historians as showing that man's story must be as incoherent and pointless as Nature's, some influential biologists have themselves not accepted this deduction. Probably no biologist has been more influential in informing and directing American public opinion on evolution than G. G. Simpson. In his most popular and probably most telling presentation of the present majority view of evolution, *The Meaning of Evolution* (79), he states categorically that man was never intended; he is simply a fluke, the blind consequences of a totally unconscious randoming. Yet in concluding this work Professor Simpson goes on to assert that no one must say man is pure freak or simple brute. On the contrary, he is incomparable, the intensest appearance of a power form whose essence can only be described by his unique characteristics, by his traits that are found in no other creature. So in him there arises "a new form of evolution." Further, this new form can largely overrule the old. This new evolution is social heredity, the ascent and blending of ideas (information, correlation, and supposition). Thus man can psychically, purposively evolve because of his capacity to choose and to give all manner of answers to outer challenges. And these answers spring far less from built-in reactions than from a capacity to recognize that the situation has altered and that the new here-and-now is the challenge, not old circumstances and the familiar associations. Though design, we are told by Simpson, was never present in life before, with man and his process it is. Here then is biological authorization for regarding history as significant growth, purposive evolution.

Meanwhile, though the historian as a rule still seems anxiously desirous of denying any process in the history of this unique creature that strives toward goals, the anthropologist is certain now that sequence can be detected. And though it is still described in economic terms (as perhaps it must be first rendered because of our lack of psychological insight into or direct evidence of the psychological changes, the successive alterations in consciousness, which attended the material cultural developments) yet this sequence, even as we have it now in bare outline, can hardly fail to be recognized by any open mind as being symptomatic of an alteration and evolution of ideas.

In studying the progressive shapes and uses of man's gear we see the coagulation of material into patterned, functional forms and objects as the stimuli of the outer world were focused, by an intensifying consciousness, into a ray of ever more powerful intention. W. D. Strong has given six steps of mankind's ascent from the wandering food-gatherer up to what he calls the imperial epochs. Starting man at the food-gatherer state, he has, of course, in this first phase of necessity included in one basic aeon the six or more epochs of the Paleolithic. His stage two is incipient horticulture. At stage three the designation has been altered from one that describes development of food production to one that describes a political-social process, the formation of local civilizations. The fourth heading is to describe the flowering of such separate cultural units. Stage five is the time when such units, as they spread, began to coalesce. Stage six is when these coalescences are compulsorily structured into the larger coercive units of empires.

J. H. Steward (82) has indicated that this sequence is shown just as much across the centers of culture-origins in the entire Eurasian land mass as throughout the Americas. Gordon Childe has shown that different rates of development, and the confusion caused by the collision of cultures at different levels, still makes difficult the correlation of at least the cultural growth stages of Europe and the Near East.

When, however, in the study of vertebrate evolution the paleontologist finds himself with a section of the fossil record confused or lacking, he has discovered that owing to the recapitulatory growth process of the fetus in the womb it is possible from embryology to fill in these lacunae. And so it can now be done with the cultural evolution of man and the evolution of consciousness that precipitates those cultural sequences. As Stanley Hall, Cyril Burt, Stanley Hall's outstanding student Arnold Gesell, and many other child psychologists have established, the individual infant, child, and adolescent are recapitulating, in their individual growth phases, the past epochs of mankind's psychosocial evolution. This is, of course, an extension into human history and cultural evolution of the biological principle that has helped in elucidating biological evolution: the principle that ontogeny, the history of the individual's developmental growth, is an epitome of phylogeny, the history of the race's development.

So the individual infant, being in the preindividualized, symbiotic field-relationship with its mother, permits us to understand the pre-critical, pre-self-conscious mind of primitive man. In turn, the child, being in the protoindividualistic stage that protestingly struggles for independence from the closed circle of infancy's symbiosis, is recapitulating the Heroic Age that smashed the pristine culture and having destroyed the hypnocracies (the suggestion-imposed consent of the governed) had, when tired of loot, to impose the military dictatorships.[c] These two correlations of what may be called the individual's psycho-ontogeny and the race's psycho-phylogeny are now, we see, recognized by the child psychologists. They permit us to do two things. First, they make it possible for us to help the young with their growth, to help them not to stand in their own light. Secondly, if we realize that the young are now epitomizing history it is possible for us to understand the past, to recognize the process and avoid its mistakes (which were tragic enough to have been desperate but vital enough to have been survived), to have hope of the future and co-operative capacity with the present.

The third correlation of man's history with the individual's third stage is emerging only today. However, Gesell (30) and his collaborator have in their *Youth: The Years from Ten to Sixteen* now carried on into its third stage the elucidation of the individual's growth. So to the stages of inherent development of the infant and the child they have added that of youth. Applying the particu-

[c] See Appendix A, "The Hyrid Psyche."

lar quality of character that is found to emerge at this third stage of the individual's growth (human psycho-ontogeny), we can see that it is a recapitulation of the age which in history succeeded the Heroic, protoindividualistic epoch. This third stage of man is the Ascetic.

We can, from our knowledge of the inherency of the individual's psychophysical growth process now, recognize the psychosocial forces that brought man from protoindividualism to midindividualism. We can have still further insight (as we did with infancy and childhood) into our past and also perceive that its formative and directive force was fundamentally psychological, not economic or political. History can not only be elucidated (that is, recognized as having a patterned direction) but also we can recognize the nature of the drive in it as being the growth of consciousness, the intensified awareness of intention.

But if the preindividualistic, preheroic epoch of man is today recapitulated by the infant, the protoindividualistic epoch recapitulated by the child, and the midindividualistic by the adolescent—what then? Neither the race nor the individual has closed its development with the adolescent, midindividualistic epoch. The individual goes on into first maturity and human society went on into the Humanic epoch that succeeded the Ascetic. Both are marked by correlative psychological symptoms of development, increasing self-consciousness, intensification of individualism.

We can, then, answer the first part of our threefold question. Man can hope to change himself constructively because there is a power of unexpended growth in him. He does grow in consciousness, learn from experience, and make sense of an increasing area of awareness. But when that is allowed (as the findings of modern psychoanthropology and of the growth psychology of Gesell and others compel us to allow) we have to face the second part of the question. Let us grant that there is an intense growth vitality in man, which has made it possible for him to survive the shattering of his primal society by the Heroic explosion and, in turn, the failure of nerve and secession of the Ascetic shrinkage. But does not the evidence show that with every epoch there is an intensification of individualism and so a steady loss of cohesion, of loyalty, and of any sense of any purpose beyond personal and indeed sensory satisfaction?

Two facts contradict this foreboding. When the Ascetic epoch passed into the Humanic this meant, and was caused by, a rapid intensification of consciousness. Mankind suffered terribly: for example, from the fiendishly cruel methods of the Inquisition as, increasingly through the fourteenth century, the Church tried to extirpate all heretics and, during the fifteenth and sixteenth centuries, from the ghastly Wars of Religion that at last ended with the Peace of Westphalia in 1648. Nevertheless, and this is the first contradictory fact, although there was great shock no Dark Age of breakdown ensued between these two epochs. The second fact (as we shall see in Chapter 4 of Part I) is that as man found himself rapidly subjected to an intensification of self-consciousness he did, as a historical fact, undertake specfic psychological training to counter this contraction. However, these countermeasures were reactionary not progressive. They were of the nature of a parachute, to break a fall rather than, like a helicopter, to bear upward the person who was plummeting earthward under the pull of gravitation. Nevertheless, time was gained, catastrophe was postponed, the loss of loyalty was delayed, shock and disintegration were extended so as to become a sustained strain, a protracted tension, a tautening *angst,* not a paralyzing dismay.

This, then, will deal with the third part of our question. If man *can* change his nature and if he has done so, then how has he done it? As a hypothesis, I have attempted a correlation between four aspects of man's history, each of which divides into five parts. The first aspect is that of the race's history. I see it as five epochs during which, through the contraction of consciousness, man becomes first a creature of a spoken tradition; secondly, a being of protest against that stifling tradition; thirdly, a person of self-blame; fourthly, an individual of objectivity; and fifthly, an individual who is objectively aware of his subjectivity.

The second fivefold aspect is that of the five age-stages through which each individual passes to complete his life span today: (i) infancy, (ii) childhood, (iii) adolescence, (iv) first maturity, and (v) second maturity (the veterine).

The third aspect is the delineation of the five dominant symptoms of mental morbidity that mark and indicate the specific disintegration-stress and collapse-states both of each of the historic epochs and of each of the age-stages of the individual life. These are (i) the trauma of birth, the extreme resultant of which is womb-recessionalism; (ii) paranoia;[d] (iii) schizophrenia; (iv) manic-depressive insanity, and (v) involutional melancholy. The allotment of each one of these five types of insanity to one of the five historical social and individual breakdowns will be dealt with in Part II. There we shall deal with the question at some length and try to show that although there are two of these insanities which may, through arrested development of the individual, appear outside its age-group, each particular type of mental illness does belong to a specific mental age-group.

The fourth fivefold aspect is an account of those five methods and therapies whereby, with increasing purposiveness and self-consciousness, man has remedied the five psychophysical morbidities that threaten not only his personal sanity but his society's survival. This fourth fivefold aspect of history is complementary to the other three because here we can trace the steps in which man did devise, in the beginning almost unawarely, those five successive therapeutic psychophysical methods whereby he could remedy both his individual psychoses and also the psychosocial disasters of his successive societies.

(i) The rite of burial and resurrection, called the mystery of Earth, recovers the individual from (*a*) the trauma of birth and the inability to develop beyond infantile reactions and a suckling, tethered emotional life and (*b*) that blind desire for an unmoving, infallible, completely and comprehensively authoritarian society and tradition.

(ii) Next, the rite of immersion and catharsis, called the mystery of water, recovers the individual from (*a*) the paranoid overreaction against society, the nor-adrenaline violence (28) of the

[d] See Part I, Chapter 5, footnote *b*.

child who, in its uninstructed and unguided demand for liberty and the right for approved independence, verges toward dementia praecox and (*b*) from that desire to join, and in the end lead, a free-lance delinquent gang that as freebooters preys on a society for which it has nothing but contempt.

(iii) Then there comes the rite of breathing and auditory suggestion, which is called the mystery of air. This aimed at releasing the psyche from fixation at an adolescent level, from an arrest at self-contempt and self-despairing when, facing the unlimited demands of society and the newly confronted unruliness of its own nature, it becomes schizoid. Those who have newly reached puberty must be restored from a disgust with the psychophysique, a loathing that is a hypertrophied development, an unbalanced reaction to self-knowledge and self-criticism that emerged and emerges at that age (individually and racially). The young, then, have to be taught by a psychophysical training (*a*) to tolerate themselves and understand, without disgust or indulgence, their new equipment and (*b*) to serve without servility or contempt a society wherein the administrators are not men of superhuman self-denial.

(iv) Next there is the still further tonicity given by intensified use of infrared radiation. This is called the mystery of fire and it is employed to cure the manic-depressive, alternating psychosis to which those in first maturity are subject. This discipline is directed at reducing and healing this exaggerated reaction by rebalancing the individual so that by a new knowledge of the extent of his nature and its unfamiliar capacities, of which he is ignorant, he may (*a*) be led beyond his premature trust in his individualism and discover his paraconscious nature and (*b*) he may be able to conceive of a society beyond the economic and political structure of today's international anarchy and ideological deadlock.

(v) Finally, by what was called the mystery of aether, or the finer fire, those in second maturity may be educted by a psychophysical method or praxis through which (*a*) there is removed for the individual the death phobia and (*b*) he is given an experience of the essential part he can and must play in constructing that fivefold society which, till now, has not existed and for lack of which social pattern there is, in our society today, neither any place for those veterine in second maturity (therefore they are the prey of their specific and most stubborn mental complaint, involutional melancholy) nor any design whereby death may be significantly incorporated into the life cycle.

Briefly, then, this is the thesis of this book: man can train himself, and he has done so with increasing understanding. Although at first this training was implicit in a rite that worked without being consciously comprehended and, next, it was esoteric and a mystery understood only by psychophysical pioneers, today it can become explicitly exoteric, rendered in contemporary terms and applied with scientific exactitude and as a therapeutic education. Such an education can fully develop both an entire person and a complete society. It can produce a constituent able to accept and fulfill his whole personal process and also be the conscious, willing, and developmental unit of a civilization that is creatively run by a common consent and coterminous with a nonviolent mankind.

I

THE PSYCHOLOGICAL STORY OF SOCIAL MAN

1 The preindividual
[*Coconscious man*]

In the introduction we have presented the basis of a faith in the future of mankind. We have given the reasons for believing that, through those exercises, technics, praxes, and education whereby conduct, character, and consciousness can now be developed to total capacity, man's behavior may at last be commensurate with his powers.

Now, and first, we must present the outline of human phylogeny. And once this is clear, we may view history as an increasingly accelerated and coordinated process whereby the two sides of man's nature (individual man and social man, man with self-consciousness and man with a preterconsciousness, critical man and creative man) have been kept in reciprocal play until they are perfectly balanced. But this is not all. We may also find in the individual development, in specific human ontogeny, in the process stages of each person's lifetime sequences, the recapitulation and, finally, the extrapolation of man's story and destiny.

Here lies the only real cure for our present discouragement with ourselves. The first discoveries that man had a past, that his present was mainly ruled by that past, that that rulership was largely a mortmain, a dead hand, a husk of prejudices, tabus, misapprehensions, irrational fears, and cowardly dislikes led to dismay. Most historians felt, during those brief times when momentary order permitted an educated leisure in which to study the past, that we clung precariously to a raft of reason (or rather to a quaking sargasso coil of floating sea-wrack) which, between storms, permitted the creamy scum of culture to gather on the surface of a deep that would soon again be churned by the blasts of barbarian violence.

This crude idea that mankind's story begins with barbarism, achieves occasional civilization, and relapses periodically into the barbarian magma out of which it cooled, was, of course, an application to history of the Indian ascetic Sankhya dualistic philosophy of a cosmos perpetually oscillating between *prakriti* and *purusha,* matter and energy, form and flux.

Vico, the seventeenth- and eighteenth-century Neapolitan historian (1668–1744) had perceived, with extraordinary insight aided by studies of epic literature and hints from the Sumerian fragments embedded in the Hebrew Pentateuch, that beside and behind the saga and epic ages lay another epoch that was as different from barbarism as barbarism was alien to civilization. Vico's insight, however, had to wait until this century to become convincing and to wean historians from their taste for melodrama, for self-pitying tragedy. Now, such discoveries as those made by Arthur Evans of the Minoan culture (which was millennially previous to and far more lasting than its successor, the Hellenic, classical Greece) together with those made about the Sumerian and Indus cultures and the Shang Dynasty in China have made historians realize that there was a protohistory, when man lived in a cultured society compacted largely by coconscious suggestion: a suggestion hypnotically so powerful that I have called this form of government a hypnocracy.

And anthropology was able to add confirmation to this discovery. In Central Australia, and later in Papua, tribes were found living a balanced life which, though at the price of the inhibition of experiment and adventure, avoided the self-willed violence of the epic barbarian. The discovery of these still surviving, food-gathering cultures helped, still further, in the understanding of the prehistoric ages brought to light by the slow studies of flint implements (for example, by Boucher de Perthe's studies of the Chellean flints on the Somme terraces) and the latest studies of the eidetic imagery of the fresco artists in the Dordogne caves (l'Abbé Breuil). Here, there can be no doubt, there was not only another type of culture, there was another quality of consciousness. Beside the unreflective, boastful violence of the barbarian and the critical constructiveness of the civilized man there was also at least (and back of them both, it is reasonable to surmise) a third type of mind that was precritical but creative, preindividual but considerate.

In short, today we find ourselves to be the first generation able to walk on the floor of history. We are the first civilization that can, at last, see the foundation on which all mankind's cultural development has been reared, that can understand the basic and balanced adjustments to landscape-environment, to fellowship-community that were made by our superanimal ancestor—that speechful, tool-extending and depending, fire-fencing and focusing creature, protoman.

And this fuller, more complete knowledge of our story has produced two further insights. The first is one of the main supports of our hope for and faith in the future of man. This is the fact that the story has accelerated so intensely. Today, our generation can add an epoch to the saga of mankind by the way that each one of us lives out his individual span. The second insight is complementary to the first. The history of man is not to be understood as being a survival by violence: drum and trumpet history. Man is man (the supreme animal) because of his teachability, his openness of mind. And this is not only a firm part of his biological structure; it is built up in his entire development. Nor, again, can man be understood (and his story explained) by saying that he is an accident of economy, that all his culture has risen from his physical necessities. It is true that his art and his science have aided his physical survival, but only because he has been fascinated by form and because his curiosity has forced him to pursue knowledge of his environment. Human history, if we are to understand it, is psychological history. Man's works and his instruments are the silt lines of his mind's currents, the tide-marks of his consciousness. At first it is as slow as the rivulets that ooze from the melting fringes of the glaciers, but it carries, in solution, the rich alluvium of the ice-ground rock. That is to say, the primal community's fluidity-of-response, its capacity to understand its environment and to react to it with a modifying conduct is equaled, and kept within social bounds, by the fact that all its percepts are automatically censored by concepts. In other words, means and meaning are kept in creative play because all individual apprehensions of the outer world are, as it were, seen through the condensing lens made by the apprehensions of the entire tribe. Only those things that make sense can be noticed and remembered. Anomalies do not register—at least not as exceptions that might disturb the rule (36, 39). And, if the Abbeyvillian food-hunting, food-gathering Paleolithic dates from 450,000 B.C. and if the first agricultural society begins at about 10,000 B.C., this means that man's gradual change in consciousness continued for something like 440,000 years.

So, in the first vast epoch of man's history his religic capacity, his ability to make sense, kept pace with his scanning power, his ability to grasp new facts about his environment. This capacity for making sense was both compositional and censorial. In other words, although man, at this point, rejected data too odd to even up with ordinary experience or to fit in with antecedent probability, the anomaly was not treated with horror, disgust, or contempt. These are later reactions, and they summon such strong resistance because the data can no longer be denied. At the start, the mind of man was like the subhuman, mammal consciousness: it recorded, memorably, only what had been repeated to it often enough. Just as through the night hours the photographic plate that is put into the telescope camera in order to record a star that is invisible to the naked eye gradually soaks up sufficient photons to retain an image, so some natural event brought persistently enough to his attention at last made an enduring impression on the mind of early man. And since man is not only the most curious of the mammals but also the one most inclined to communicate, and because his mind at this point was not wholly inelastic, this gave him sufficient time to bring his new discoveries to the attention of others and agree with them on an explanation.

However, the elasticity of wonder is a child factor and always stands in danger of being lost. As tradition grows by its successful incorporation of data, an incorporation increasingly expressed in the rigid form of words rather than in the comparatively free medium of responsive behavior, tradition grows self-assured and stiff. The more successful the solutions prove to be the more they tend to become comprehensively final answers. Provisional responses, apt for the occasion, fossilize into repressive dogmas. Those who have had the most experience, those heartwood *robur* veterans (as the Romans later called such seasoned sergeants) who, because they have survived more dangers and are therefore less inclined to panic, and whose stubbornness makes them invaluable when the younger are alarmed and retreat, have the large vice of their rigid virtue. In a moving world they mistrust movement. They will not give ground, but neither will they open ranks and advance.

On the other hand, the younger members of the tribe, because they are young, tend to grow in curiosity—curiosity that is whetted by each new success of the tribe in extending its exploration farther afield and, thereby, bringing itself up against more and more anomalies. But the failure of the old to give the young an expanded explanation (to set, compose, and frame the newfound data) makes for either subservience or secret doubt. The extension of the lifespan into old age (owing to easier economic conditions) must already have meant, as it means so gravely today, an overwhelming disbalance of the social values in the direction of fear, suspicion, arrest, and reaction. On these grounds alone, the sum of human enterprise and happiness must have been steadily diminished, unless some method was known whereby voluntary death might be brought on among those who had finished their usefulness. Plenty of cases are now known, from the Eskimo to the pygmies of the central forest of Africa, who when conditions are too severe for the tribe to preserve the ailing and costly old, do abandon them.

However, the fissure of the primal mind was postponed and the pressures contained longer, which made the ultimate burst catastrophic when it did come.

This delay seems to have been due, at least in part, to the growth of language, which was also largely responsible for the hardening of the rite into the dogmatic spell. After the first choruses of coencouragement (more phatic than informative) speech became increasingly instructive but was still used mainly for emotional purposes. However, because of its great success as a descriptive-informative instrument the word tends to become definatory. The definatory term, sooner or later, becomes definitive, terminal, final. Language, because it became descriptive of separate objects, could not deal with succession (97). Mathematics, with its calculus, is needed for that. So there can be little doubt that the first sense of the-power-holding-things-together, of the-way-things-go (Tao), of the growth process, is pananimistic. It not only *is* everywhere, it is equally, pervasively diffused through one's self and it dilates one's entire physique.

But with words came distinctions, and with distinctions came further specific, localized, and concentrated attentions. The surge of life in the whole body becomes concentrated in the genitals. The lingam and the yoni become the almost obsessional foci of emotion and, indeed, sensation.

Meanwhile, woman comes to be regarded as the specific aspect of fertility. This is due, in large part, to the fact that she advances more slowly toward the exclusiveness of individualism. Physically, she remains less specialized in muscle and skeleton than the male and her part in the reproductive function involves more of her physique and her psyche. Therefore, reproduction now becomes typified as the abundant power of parturition. In the middle Paleolithic figurines that have been found, we see depicted female physiques that are dilated into ample containers and yielders of plentiful, easy births. They are as faceless and almost as distended as the queen termite.

From such beginnings we can then trace the path of what we find to be fully emerged when the Paleolithic is over and the Neolithic has begun. At this point, with his management of an annual agriculture, man has become aware of time. Now religion has become gynolatrous: that is, the woman's figure is now the object of excitational adoration. The general sensing that all adults are reproductively charged has concentrated into one specific object of desire and the definite worship of fecundity forms. The dawning capacity to reason led, of necessity, to crude, overdeveloped notions of purpose and cause. There could be only one purpose and reason for a process. The panesthetic psychophysical rapture became increasingly to be regarded solely as a surge for reproduction. Therefore, rites had to be devised to canalize this tide and to prevent its natural diffusedness. *Pari passu,* such an attempt to confine the excitation to one purpose led to the feeling that the power must be confined to the one male organ that served the female's purpose. Hence, gynolatry (worship of woman) inevitably leads to phallolatry (phallic worship).

Then, as the rites become more formalized they become divided into two: (*a*) the food rites for increasing luck in the hunt and, later on, increase among the kept animals[a] and (*b*) the sex rites for increasing human fecundity. To define is always to disturb what was, originally, an unquestioning awareness. To give reasons is equally likely to make those who are given such explanations watch to see whether or not the reason proves to be correct and, if it does not, to suggest another. The hunting magic must have failed often. The sex magic, both by its concentration on the reproductive act and by its tabu against any variation in the theme, must have raised as many questions and caused even more serious breaches of the rules. Departures from the hunting magic might go unnoticed because these deviations would take place out in the wild open. But deviations from the reproductive magic could not long escape inquisition in the close purlieus of the cave.

We shall see in Part III that in tribes which preserved their

[a] Miss G. R. Levy (53) points out that even in Paleolithic cave drawings there are pictures of penned cattle.

cohesion, which did not explode in rebel protest but continued intact (such as the Arunta in mid-Australia), there has been a method of keeping at least the leaders in touch with their own dawn or birth consciousness. While in at least one culture (the Indus), which rose to and retained civilization for at least a millennium without being disintegrated by rebellion, there was a method of reducing the fever of revolt. These cases where a ritual was devised that really gave a regressional experience, and relieved—at least among the ruling caste—the mounting pressure of protesting frustration, are certainly rare.

However, such instances are valuable to us because they show that explosive cataclysm, violent psychic mutational revolt, is not invariably necessary. It is true that the Australian tribes have anchylosed, to use the phrase of Moret and Davy in *From Tribe to Empire*, (63). They have become hypercomplex, rigid social structures, ruled wholly by their routine-obsessed elders and in which there is no place for growth. And apparently the Indus culture perished from an inanition that may be basically similar (67). Yet each of these cultures had its specific psychophysical method for giving the burgeoning consciousness the capacity to continue some growth, without having to repress and become severed from a past that is now repugnant because it has been wrongly lived through. So, as it will be suggested later, each culture did make some contribution to the problem of educating the total mind.

But in the vast majority of cases the tribe's pattern of culture, under the pressure of the crystallizing consciousness of its constituents, became definitional and explanatory. And this produced the conviction that every custom and habit must be pruned to fit the utilitarian purpose that the one-track reasoning mind now regarded as being the whole purpose of the behavior. And where this took place the process of constriction continued. Finally, all movement, all variety became impossible. Any experiment and, at last, any alternative explanation became blasphemy. There was nothing left for the growing mind but death or revolt.[b] And as the growing seed bursts the pod, so the pioneers broke their way out and the emptied husk of their society finally collapsed.

[b] See Chapter 2, Part I, on the rise of the hero.

Still, although the process whereby the protoindividual, heroic, self-assertive man emerged and rent the old coconscious social structure was cataclysmic, it was slow and diffident. Reformations were repeatedly followed by counterreformations. The old Life religion, the worship of the Yoni and the Lingam, made repeated come-backs. We can trace its stubborn return in Hebraism, for instance, where we see the desert-minded prophets worshiping a sky god and butchering, time and again, the priesthood that worshiped the tree phallus. Elijah massacres them in his day. They are back in the Temple again in time for Hosea to denounce their libidinous rites—rites which, in accordance with the religious custom of the time, involve his wife who goes up to the national shrine to be fertilized by the holy men, the priesthood who represented the fertility god. Hezekiah and again Jehoshaphat carry out bloody purges. But until the destruction of the Temple by Nebuchadnezzar and the carrying away of the people into Mesopotamia, the worship of fertility continued. This we know from the prophets' denunciations of the latest kings.

Nevertheless, growth is of the nature of the mind of man. Consciousness evolves just as does the brain, the structure that consciousness precipitates. Though the fertility rites continued and gave some outlet to deep racial drives otherwise repressed, the forms were increasingly inadequate. It may be that they could help men not to become wholly sundered from their racial past. But they could not help men to make contemporary answers to a world that was seen, increasingly, in the light of reason and subject to the discipline and censorship of experience and sometimes of experiment. The rites, themselves infected by reason, rationalized their procedures. Therefore, instead of being regarded as psychophysical exercises for altering conduct, character, and consciousness, for reducing egotism by giving a direct sense of belonging to the general life, the rite became magic for giving the individual egotist his personal desires and so confirming his obsession with his private selfishness.

The process of consciousness growth was, therefore, with the rebels. A damaged birth is better than a still one. The heroic outburst was so frustrant and so violent that it obliterated, rather than recovered, resuscitated, and made explicit the procedures that once had given not only solidarity to the tribe but also a comprehension of its environment. Nevertheless, man went on. And so by anguish, endured as agony, he attained at least enough understanding that even when the prestige-image of the hero proved to be inadequate it could be replaced, in the minds of men, by the ideal figure of the ascetic. In the following chapter, therefore, we trace the rise and fall of the hero: the coconscious tribe's successor.

2

The protoindividual
[Heroic, self-assertive man]

We must regard the hero as being an inevitable development of consciousness. The critical faculty had to grow and, since the coconscious tribe had become negative to all invention and hostile to the capacity for asking questions, it had to grow because of an increasing sense of separateness. Objectivity and detachment could only arise from rejection. Spontaneous revulsion gave the position and status necessary for perspective and proportion. Thus, the heroic epoch is such an inevitable reaction to the rigidifying of the coconscious tradition that we find it (together with its characteristic, the saga-epic literature) in all the giant cultures. It was so emphatic, so aggressive that until this century there was no general recognition, among historians, of the preheroic, priest-kingly, coconscious, or hypnocratic culture that lay behind it, from which the hero was ejected and which the hero in turn destroyed. Such a belt of Cimmerian darkness, dividing us from the mild saturnine kings and queens, seemed to be only disaster. No wonder that Hesiod, living under one of the later deluges (that of the Dorian "iron-bearing Kings"), joined and gave classic expression to the chorus that lamented a previous Age of Gold, an aeon of Peace. The sad poets, "praisers of previous ages," in the clash of arms and under the pressure of despots, could not conceive the suffocating tyranny of "custom that lies upon him as a weight heavy as frost and deep almost as life." Nor could he imagine that Man, left alone, can honestly cry, "Better dwell in the midst of alarms than reign in this horrible place." As Professor Spearman, the London University psychologist, has remarked, "We only know two basic things about the central nervous system of man:—one, that it likes the same stimulant, and the other, that it doesn't." Boredom is the subtle misery with which life nags man into adventure. No doubt the timid would have sacrificed curiosity to security —as they still do today. But there is natural selection in human history, as in all life. The vital welcome risk.

Whether or not man's history, his psychosocial evolution, the development of his social heredity could have been a gradual process, without spastic mutations, without the cyclic spiral of revolt, destruction, reimposition, and again revolt, we cannot say. It does not seem to have been possible in the past, though it is not impossible now, as this essay hopes to indicate. For up until now man does not seem to have been able to understand, consciously, and to cooperate, deliberately, with the life process that not only has brought him to his superanimal station but is still driving him on to higher achievement, greater powers, and greater comprehension.

The "nothing fails like success" principle suggests that the capacity for comprehension ends in being content with the achieved reaction. This is the weakness of an efficiency that is achieved by specialized response: the more finished it becomes, the less conscious it is of its partiality. The vast achievement of coconscious man—a balanced tradition of technics and psychics—made the powerful become complacent, turned obedience into subservience, and made the entire group lethargic. If man was to progress he must again raise questions, seek adventure, give hostages to fortune, offer challenges.

In Part II we shall see how deeply this pattern is etched into our individual characters. Self-consciousness must arise in each and as the group, naturally, does not welcome this, the individual protects his unwelcomed sense of separateness with the husk of egotism. Man's second phase, the Heroic Age, therefore seems chaotic, purposeless, anarchic. Closer examination, however, has shown that it certainly is not. For although man may strangulate off his surface, objective, personal intelligence from his deep racial mind, he never succeeds in separating himself completely from this profound continuum of consciousness. We have proof of that in the reaction of the hero hordes to the original culture. They not only wish to attack it for loot. They are filled with a righteous disgust at its two distinctive communicatory convictions: the pervasiveness of eroticism (the constant interest in glamor, the constant awareness of longing for tactile closeness) and the pervasiveness of magic (the constant interest in spells, in psychological methods of getting one's way, the constant awareness of longing for communion with the nonhuman and the unseen). The hero, because of his sense of separateness, dreads and shuns the seductive caress. He keeps others at arm's length, and when he closes with someone else it is to subdue that one, either by duel or rape. Yet when he has conquered and crushed he is often seized with remorse. Especially when he has killed, the sense that his own fate is common with that of the victim, whom he has sent only a little ahead of himself into the shades, shakes him with grief.

Thus, the Heroic Epoch is psychologically (and therefore socially) unstable. The rules that it could not but observe seemed, to the protoindividual egotist, to be irrational and, indeed, to endanger a man's safety. Why should an individual spare an enemy or feel any compunction at the death of a rival? David Hume's childish remark, "There is no reason why I should prefer the pricking of my own finger to the death of a hundred human beings," is preanthropological. But it is a natural enough attitude for the first egotist, the hero. And yet, providentially, this self-assertive creature could not act on his inadequate reasoning, which was false in its mistaken premise that each individual is really separate. For, firstly, he is always seeking for praise and fearing shame.[a] These are psyche states that indicate the power of a common field of consciousness. True, this rudimentary individualist still projects his inner conflict in rage against all who thwart him. But if his passion becomes complete delusional paranoia, then, when in moments of lucidity he sees that he has lost face, the hero has no way out but to commit suicide.[b] So suicide is always at hand, especially in the heroic phase that produced Bushido and the Samurai in Japan. And in its grotesque form of hara-kiri we see that although the Japanese hero begins with boastful exhibitionism of his physical equipment, in the end he is driven to complete contempt for the body. This drive, naturally, is from his repressed nature.

Inevitably, therefore, this shame will turn into guilt, this wounded self-love will lead to self-destructive humiliation. Probably no Heroic Age lasts longer than half a dozen generations. It is too self-degenerative. Of course, there are attempts, more or less convulsive, to revive this outlived pattern of prestige.[c] And from the point of view of epochs these attempted throwbacks are as significant as the Gothic revival, Palladian architecture, or existentialism. In spite of all their arrogance, cruelty, and destructiveness they are mere reactions, histrionics, fancy dress, adopted, and temporarily dangerous, because the Humanist house had been left empty, swept, and garnished; the scientific machine had stood ready without a driver in the seat.

The hero, then, becomes increasingly pessimistic, a prey to his own suppressed preterconscious. Gloom becomes his standard feel-

[a] E. R. Dodds (19) has called the Greek phase of the Heroic Age "the shame culture." See his *The Greeks and the Irrational*.

[b] Ajax, when he finds that he has slaughtered a flock of sheep thinking that they were men-at-arms, kills himself because he is mocked.

[c] For example, the Shintoistic Menji revival that was started in Japan in the sixties, the melodramatics of a Mussolini, and the Wagnerian operatics of a Hitler.

ing tone. And like all paranoics, he attempts to burn this melancholy out of his nature by bouts of homicidal rage. For when he rests he can foresee for himself (after that bodily death which he knows is hurrying inevitably toward him) only a ghostly life. To him, to whom his body is everything and to whom physical action is the sum of experience, this prospect is frightful in its certain futility. "Better be a poor man's slave than King among the dead." In these words Homer's Achilles, the paragon of heroes, estimates the common, unavoidable doom of hero and slave alike. Naturally, therefore, rage is the immediate reaction. For, to quote Homer, the primal authority on the heroic predicament, "anger rises in a man's mind like smoke and is sweeter in his mouth than honey." The nor-adrenaline (see later, Chapter 2, Part II) not only gets rid of misgiving, in the blaze of animal courage, but it releases so much sugar-for-energy that the palate is flooded with sweetness.

But, inevitably, there follows the let-down of depletion and despair. Hence, after rage on the field, after drinking delight of battle, there follows drunkenness in the evening. Finally, alcohol, which is a depressant and not a stimulant, makes for maudlin self-pity. Then to this depressant drug the hero had to add a further narcotic. When grief became intolerable the Achaeans took "a banisher of sorrow," which is the meaning of the word *nepenthe*. Apparently, the Homeric heroes employed this drug regularly. Once thought to be opium, it now seems more probable that it was one of those rare alkaloid-yielding plants that give powerful sedation.[d]

The Indian hero, we know, had his soma. This was also a rare plant from the Persian Highlands and seems to have become extinct. And from the descriptions in the Vedas it seems that it

[d] R. N. and G. S. Chopra (14), two authoritative writers on Indian hemp, say that Herodotus tells of hemp apparently being used, as an excitant, by the Scythians: the heroic tribal culture that in the first millennium drove the Cimmerians out from the lands north of the Black Sea. Messrs. Chopra think, therefore, that the Greek *nepenthe* (brought from Thebes in Egypt) must also have been hemp. It is clear, however, that the effects were completely different: nepenthe produced sedation and hemp produced excitement.

was, in contrast to *nepenthe,* highly elational. "I have drunk soma and become a god" is the classical description of its effect. We also know that soma was so inspirational that the god Indra, chief of the Aryan deities, was equated with it, as later Dionysus was identified with wine. But also—and in this way it differed from *nepenthe*—soma was highly toxic. Instead of an alteration in consciousness it often produced death in those who took it.

But besides the intoxicants and the anodynes, we can detect a specific method of ordeal and initiation that those who, during the Heroic Age, emerged into the problem of protoindividualism might undergo if they so desired. And it was the specific praxis whereby that particular psychopathic illness of the Heroic phase, hyperrajasic fury (paranoic frenzy), might be cured. As the coconscious phase had its particular ritual for enabling the postulant to rid himself of the trauma of birth (a trauma that, because it produced regressive fear, may well have been the basic psychological cause of the coconscious primal society's failure to evolve) so the Heroic Age, it would seem, had its therapy of antiwrath. Although we shall study this therapy at length in Part III, Chapter 2, we may suggest here that it was the Heroic Age's specific way of restoring, to those who carried on the succession of seership, that freedom from anger, and indeed all sense of separateness, without which extrasensory insight and precognition are impossible.

At any rate, we have seen that nepenthe was the drug which, when alcohol would not staunch grief, staved off despair. However, a third vegetable drug (moly) is mentioned in the *Odyssey.* It is given to Ulysses by Hermes, who is a pre-Olympian god of the underworld: that is, the subconscious. And as Indra seems to have been identified with soma and Dionysus with the vine, so it is possible that Hermes was similarly identified with the power of moly. Moly was a defender from magic. That is, it made its taker immune to hypnotic illusion and it rendered him invisible to his enemies. This would then appear to be an increase of detachment, which enabled the person to remain free from the power of outer suggestion; the provocations of enemies no longer roused him or entangled him. And because he is inwardly unperturbed, no longer producing (through adrenal excitement) "the odor of anger," he can easily disguise himself and be overlooked, as, for example, Ulysses (whom some authorities believe to be the human manifestation of Hermes) fooled the suitors by escaping their detection.

The reduction of rage and fear by biochemicals will be considered further in the second and third parts of this essay. At this point, in dealing with the hero and his problem of nor-adrenaline rage, we need only note that psychotherapeutic sedatives and detensioners were used by the heroes themselves. Their *vates* and seers may have used a hydrotherapy, the particulars of which will be discussed in Chapter 2 of Part III. However, it is worth noticing that, according to Homer, the supreme seer of the epic period is Teiresias who, as mentioned later, is the only one permitted to retain his memory and intelligence after death, who throughout his earthly life retains an hermaphrodite nature, and who is blind from the age of seven years.

To summarize then (and viewing the Heroic Age as the second great psychosomatic phase in man's development): after his break away from and destructive revenge on the ancient traditional society in which he had found himself imprisoned, the hero discovered that he could not live merely as an adventurer. For just being free to follow one's impulses meant a life of violence with increasing relapses into suicidal melancholy. He could not live without values. He found that he had to have standards, patterns of prestige, because his nature demanded, peremptorily, that he must be admired, that he must not be shamed. He had to exercise restraint when it was in his power to satisfy, to the full, his passion for revenge or for spoil.[e] He still had to respect the rules of human commonalty even though they appeared to be mere negative tabus. It was a terrible offense against heaven to strike a herald, an unarmed arbiter who could and often would interpose between two brawling fighters and order them to desist. Ajax Telemon, the

[e] For example, when Achilles gives the body of Hector back to Priam, and again, when he has killed a kinglet he does not take the golden armor but, out of *aidos* (a kind of intuitive sense of decency), he buries his victim in it under a cairn mound.

Little, after having (at the sack of Troy) burst into Athena's Temple and murdered Pholoxena, who had taken refuge at the altar, was drowned on his way back to his Greek homeland. However, this did not, in the opinion of the brawling world of that day, expiate so monstrous a violation of the unseen moral majesty of Heaven and of the rights of a suppliant who sought that intangible protection. So for centuries the home town of Ajax had to send (and did send, summer after summer) a working band of youths to cultivate the land where Troy had stood. And this obligation was followed right down to the time of the Roman Empire in the reign of the Emperor Augustus.

Definite standards were taught in the epic literature. The sagas had their norms of seemliness. These were not lofty but neither were they mere aspirations. The hero was taught to believe (and did believe) in a world whose invisibility did not render it only an ineffective ideal. On the contrary, the intangibility of the spiritual force gave it power to judge and to strike from an intimate vantage point against which concealment, armor, or circumspection were no defense.

The hero, like the devils of St. James, believed and trembled. The gods had to be reckoned with constantly. And such a concept of deity had so much of an egotist's fearfulness projected onto it that the divine rules were fraught, to the point of confusion, with splenetic tabus. Teiresias, the seer, is supposed to have been struck blind by Athena for no other reason than that he had inadvertently glimpsed the goddess while she was bathing. And, according to legend, Acteon, the hunter, was turned into a stag by Artemis, for the same involuntary offense, and killed by his own hounds. Nevertheless, at the same time the deep preterconscious still projected, from behind the repressive mask of egotism, the profound racial knowledge that all life is basically one, and that it advances through sensitive trust, not through brutal suspicion.

The Homeric epics have been called the Bible of the Greeks. And the phrase is a stimulating half-truth if we consider those parts of the Hebrew Scriptures that also deal with the same epoch, the Heroic Age. Epics and sagas are the standard-setters, the prestige-pattern-makers of the protoindividualistic society. *The Book of the Wars of Jahweh,* referred to in Genesis, much of Genesis itself (with its picture of pastoralist sheiks maneuvering across the grasslands from wells to springs, seeking water for their flocks), the Book of Judges, Samuel, and I Kings still show, even under the gloss of later editing, the kind of hard-hitting fighter who was "a man after Jahweh's heart." The Sanskrit Mahabarata and Ramayana, even under their glosses, show the same epic standards. The instruction is not by rule and precept. Right behavior is not conveyed by generalizations, still less by legal definition of offenses and penalties. It is conveyed by inspiring illustrative accounts of the fine person in action. Nor did the Epic poets lightly condone the blunders of their heroes. Some authorities have thought that Homer actually came from the race that was conquered by the Achaean Greeks he immortalized. And most readers of the *Iliad* would certainly agree with the insight of Simone Weil: that it is an Epic of Violence. It stands on the brink of despair and is held back from the abyss only by the magic cord of beauty—beauty which often, in a brutal age when pity is dismissed as weakness and truth as a fantasy, still constrains men to consider once more the bright enigma of a world that is entrancing though agonizing. And the Western epic (though it does avoid the final answer of *vanitas vanitatum*), turning from despair, refusing to feel that man is hopelessly at bay, points to the tunnel of tragedy as being the only way on through the rock face of nature's hard indifference.

However, in the East, the epic became allegorized instead of tragic. As the protoindividualistic, heroic epoch passed into the ascetic the pattern of prestige changed. It was no longer the man who was absorbed in outer "mighty acts of labor." It became the man who has turned within to do battle with inner conflicts and to achieve conquests by detachment and abandonment. Correspondingly, the epic, with increasing diminishment of disguise, becomes a parable-vehicle for ascetic instruction. The classic example of this change in ideals and education is, of course, the Bhagavad-Gita.

But in the West, the problem of dawning self-consciousness found still another statement, though not an answer, in the *Odyssey.*

The *Iliad* is a summing up. Its counsel is "courage through en-durance." But the *Odyssey* opens a new chapter. The protoindivid-ual finds himself inevitably asking, "Is not all morality only a mixture of mistakes compacted into a shrewd device to frighten persons into sacrificing themselves for the sake of the tribe and the timid elders that control it? Could not a truly lively man, a man of many wiles, slip out from under this noose and wander from exploit to exploit through this fantastically entertaining world?" This epic closes neither with noble, tragic death (as the *Iliad* does) nor with the hero living happy-ever-after with his bride (as does the Ramayana). The genius-composer of the *Odyssey* was enough of a realist to know that this is not a magic world. But at the same time he was sufficiently speculative to realize that we do not know its bounds and that in such a world, therefore, curiosity is, of all the passions, the most staunchless, the most invincible. Ulysses re-turns to Ithaca to liquidate the suitors, to salute his ancient father, mature wife, and adult son and then, having settled these minute affairs of a past responsibility, to go off on a new exploration. The accident of an incompetently delayed return turned into the oppor-tunity of seeking the outer world for its own sake. If the *Iliad* prophecies the oncoming of tragedy and suspects that the gray morning of asceticism was to follow the Heroic Age's red sunrise, the *Odyssey* foretells that beyond the chill first hours of day (the Ascetic Epoch) there will come the noontide of the Humanic Epoch when man, feeling self-sufficient, will investigate the universe without fear of its wrath or hope of its favor. And further, the story of Ulysses hints that even Humanism will not prove sufficient nor be the final station of the human mind.

For this primal explorer is not content to sail every unknown sea and pass every horizon. Unlike and outreaching the Renaissance mind, he also visits the underworld, the world of the subconscious. And there, with the aid of the spirit of Teiresias, the master seer, he strives to understand his own nature and destiny by attempting to look not merely beyond spatial limits but beyond time. By going in and down (ordeal-initiation), this archetypal, transitional man, who is no longer a hero and yet is still not an ascetic, attempts by a mystery experience to understand completely.

The seeming irrelevance of the manifold refuses, however, to compose into a totality under his objective curiosity. For he is determined to be the onlooker and he leaves himself out of the picture. So it cannot become a composition of enlightening power but only an unstinted collection of curiosities. Consequently, Ulysses foresees not his assumption but his death, which the unknown author of the *Odyssey* rightly describes as a peaceful killing: a death that comes to him at the unwitting hands of a natural son whom he begot from Circe, the supernatural witch. And, further, it is this Circe who, when he left her, guided him to the underworld where Teiresias shows him his fate.

So from the literature of Heroicism, we can see the standards and education of the protoindividual, the first self-assertive man. Roughly speaking, one third of that instruction is cautionary, minatory. It warns: be careful, be wary, don't let the hot fit, which is a fine starter, take you too far. There is an unknown quantity that is up to something in the world out there, and while you are getting your way take care that your fishing lines don't foul its extensive nets. Another third of the teaching is admonitory: don't lose face and remember that though you may, for a moment, stun people with your successful violence, the shock at your excess will turn into censure. However just you may feel your anger to be, you must not act with disregard for the standards of the unangered onlookers. Besides, your own cold fit will condemn you.

And this leads to the third instruction. Your wish is not merely to be uncensured but to be praised, to "live in men's mouths" as the noble man, the majestic pattern of prestige, the man who, because of his courage, munificence, and magnanimity is honored forever.

The Heroic Age was a necessary phase in the human development: a development that has gone on as a spiral process, an oscillation between outer knowledge and inner comprehension, since the end of the preindividual, primal culture. But this protoindividualistic culture was explosive. It was driven out from the land-locked harborage of the tribal estuary that had become a sandbar-blocked, stagnant lake with no more access to the outer ocean. These huddled squadrons, lifted by line squalls of protest, found themselves to be startled navigators, borne over the bar and out onto the high seas. There they found no other port in some island of the blest; only the vast waters welcomed them into a new freedom. And for many this was too much. Unable to manage the gale in their canvas and the waves on their thwarts, they foundered in the storm of passion that was let loose and sank into paranoia. They became incapable of understanding any but their personal demand for expression. But in the main they rode out the storm with the aid of a sea anchor, that long submarine cable and sack that holds in the bucking ship and keeps its prow facing the storm. Such a sea anchor was the modifying morality which, the sagas and epics show us, was being worked out as a means of educating the boastful hero until (when he does not turn into the Ulyssean navigator) he becomes hammered and tempered into the pattern of chivalry, the honorable knight, the guardian of the weak.

However, the knight (the word means "servant") is not and cannot be the full pattern of prestige. He wishes to obey. A man of action, he defers to the one who has the conviction of command. If he wishes to investigate, the soldier does not research into the mind and its motives; he explores nature and its shape. Guardianship preserves, it does not develop, it does not progress. The knight and his descendant the gentleman are then maintenance men and innovation is not natural to them. Therefore, they are collateral cadet lines of the human ascent. They cannot have that individual insight which is the symptom of being possessed by the new and oncoming field of mankind's consciousness.

So the drill-sergeant mind, with its military parade discipline and uniform, is not the nucleus of mankind's next phase. The solid phalanxes of impacted automata that swept away the last relics of the single man-to-man fighting of the Heroic Age are not the formative pattern of the social structure that was to replace Heroism. The successor to the hero (as the unresolved contractive intensity of individualism increases) is not a military type.

But who gives the orders? Who answers the hero's unspoken question: "Where is not merely moral authority for the obedient but inspiration for the pioneer; not only vision for the explorer but disciplinary sanction for the original and the creative?" "Who guards the guardian?" asked Roman law. It is a question that cannot be answered without first finding a reply to this riddle: "How can we guard just for the sake of preserving those who are too timid to move and who desire only immobile security? What is the goal for which we act as preservatives? If we are making reservations and protectorates, are these to arrest growth or to promote it? If they are to promote growth, then growth toward what goal? Who has the vision to perceive it clearly and convincingly?"

It was these galling questions that made even the noble hero inadequate. Greater discipline was demanded but how was it to be achieved and what aim could make it worthwhile? What insight could make the strain of postponement endurable? Man's education had reached a new challenge-level. He was to be taken out of Junior High Heroism as he had previously been taken out of the kindergarten and child grades of the coconscious. He was to pass into the Senior High of a new seriousness and, it must be added, a new self-consciousness and personal concern. He was to enter the mid-Individualistic Age, that specific epoch known as the Ascetic, the phase in which man is no longer implicitly, unquestioningly, unconsciously obedient, nor, on the other hand, frankly self-assertive. Now for the first time, man, with a new intensity of self-awareness, will blame himself.

3

The midindividual
[Ascetic, self-accusing man]

It is clear that about the eighth century B.C. a change was going on in man's consciousness. "The rise of conscience" is a datum line in the history of the human psyche and it is placed at somewhat different dates by students of different cultures. Breastead would put it far earlier than the eighth century B.C. in Egypt. And this may well have been so, because of the unique forcing-and-arresting conditions of the Nile Valley. However, most psychoanthropological students of the Hebraic culture would probably not quarrel with the eighth century B.C. datum line. For the protoprophets of sexual exclusiveness and social responsibility (Hosea and Amos) appear at this time. Hellenic thought seems to have reached a crisis in this same century. The rise of reflective philosophy in India, indicated by the most thoughtful Upanishads, seems to be about 750 B.C.

Arthur Waley, the sinologist, has said that about 1200 B.C. a change did come over the Chinese ritual, which until then had been mainly magical and compurgative. The emergence of conscience that culminated with Confucius (550–478 B.C.) may well lie between this change in ritual (1200 B.C.) and the rise of the explicit reasonableness and recognition of self-conscious individualism that we find in the Confucian *Analects*.

This sixth to fifth century B.C. period may be regarded as a time during which there was a rapid precipitation of self-awareness, for, as Rhys Davis (the Pali authority) and other scholars have pointed out, Confucianism, Buddhism, and Pythagorianism are contemporary. Leading up to these precipitations was a period pregnant with considerable spiritual travail. In India, we know that the Heroic culture of the invading Aryans had, until the eighth century B.C., practiced mainly a luck religion of *do ut des* (I give in order that you may give): that is, give the gods (who are simple projections of oneself) what one likes oneself and they will do likewise. Such crude religion has to modify under actual experience. The Hellenic-Aryans (the Achaeans) became tragic while the Indian Aryans became ascetic.

In Egypt and China, we may remark, the ascetic did not appear until centuries after his appearance in India. In their own ways, both Egypt and China succeeded in encysting themselves in the cocoon of their particular, complacent social success. Conscience was limited to social obligation. Neither of them produced its own psychic pressures for neither of them permitted the Heroic phase to go far enough. Nipped in the bud by the counterdevelopment of a semimilitarized priest-king—half general and half magician— the hero could not grow to those intensities of interior conflict that produce tragedy or asceticism.[a] Foreign religions (Indian Buddhism for China and Levantine Christianity for Egypt) were needed to make these self-enclosed lands confront the individual enigma.

In India, with its acute interest in states of consciousness, the hero was under particular stress. First, we see him striving to keep himself with enough aggressive initiative to remain in control of a situation in which climatic enervation, the mirage in the desert, the fecundity of tropical life, and an equally rich jungle of mystic

[a] See Appendix A.

thought made the hard certainties of courage, will, and ambition swim before his eyes. This struggle to hold his supremacy led to Tapas: those increasingly strenuous exercises whereby at first the hero-king literally attempted to sweat it out. One such common exertion was for the ruler to sit naked under the noonday sun and surrounded by blazing fires. Such violent efforts may have caused the focus of consciousness to shift. It may also have suggested the procedure of the ordeal by fire (with which this work deals in Part III, Chapter 4).

These grueling treatments of the body could naturally and very easily slip from the wish to become tough into the desire to torture oneself, from the aim of adapting an instrument into the aim of escaping from a trap by prising back its bars. It is difficult to trace the actual rise of asceticism and its intensification into mortification. The mount which at first is to be tamed by being whipped is now to have its will broken. The carnal nature is to be beaten to death. Previous psychological frontiers, like submerged beach-lines, leave little trace; spiritual faultings and dislocations can seldom be dated. The word "asceticism" comes from the Greek word *askesis*, which was their term for athletic training. And these first *tapas* or exertions seem to have been just that. But the human psyche was no longer at boastful ease with itself. Self-consciousness, which was at first displayful fun, was modulating, with experience, into its minor key.

In the West, tragedy was interposed between the epic and the manual of self-discipline, the codified rule of the mortificatory order. For the epic is not an art form that was made to express a personal problem, a psychological issue. It is to show a complex of action and to illustrate the mighty deeds of great leaders. The hero is still sure of himself and of the crowd's admiration. Self-assertive man is still the pattern of prestige. True, the *Iliad* crystallizes out around the wrath of Achilles. But the hero's anger is the thread around which action precipitates. And the heroes, even in their rages, are examples of the chief heroic virtue, courage. However, in tragedy we find the hero no longer opposing men, and gods who are mainly but men writ large; he is caught in the toils of nonhuman forces against which arms are helpless. Nature seems to turn on him and he is attacked below the waterline of his self-conscious courage. A spiritual world is forcing itself on his attention. He is beginning to lose his nerve. He is having to ask for a new defense, another discipline, which the training manuals of the monastic orders will produce.

But, as we have said, tragedy, in the West, created an interlude between the high warrior and the low penitent. An issue that involves the mind-body of man (and must therefore be worked out psychosomatically) is laid out, arranged, and confined in a strictly limited area: the stage. Man's advance toward his next crisis, his progression from heroism to asceticism, is now postponed by the threefold device of the drama. In the first place, the flood-pressure of the new conflict, the conflict now known to be an inner one, is diverted for a space by being run into the artificial flood channel or sump hole of the theater. The personal issue is now projected onto another person, a hero.

Secondly, it is talked about rather than acted out. Aeschylus, the father-member of the great trinity of Greek tragic art, employs nothing but conversation on the stage. Although he is an innovator in raising monologue to dialogue, words now rule. This strange screen and filter has been put between the onlooker and the deed.

Thirdly, the crisis is projected backward in time. This is the story of a legendary person and the problem need not be regarded as instant. It not only happened long ago but (and this makes it far less immediate) it befell men different from the democratic, equalitarian Greeks. Tragedy, Aristotle saw and said, had to be about heroes, nobles, outstanding men. So the "so sorry for the big guy beaten down" is mixed with a *sotto voce* "serves the arrogant fellow right." When Aeschylus chooses a contemporary figure around which to write a tragedy, it is Xerxes the Great King, a dim image that is impersonally mythical to the small, bright, sharply defining Greek minds. And the Persian is seen (it is significant that the play is not called *Xerxes* but *The Persians*) as a titan force, only half human, who is punished not for attacking the independent Hellenes but for his Luciferian pride, the insane *hubris* against divine nature shown by his attempt to chain the Hellespont with a bridge of boats.

Another cushion-against-shock was playing with Time by alteration of actual tempo. The dramatic unities insisted that the whole play, with all its acts, should refer only to the incidents of a single day. These rigid rules ran through the entire history of the Greek tragedy. Sophocles, the master second person of the Attic stage, greatly increased the flexibility of the play. Euripides, the third person, humanized even more both story and language. But the close and confining rules were not lifted. The stage is the crucible of art-convention in which the anarchic passions are to be held and considered, as, through a quartz eyehole, a furnace-minder may watch iron being melted. Hence, every thing, every action and incident that could not be reduced in this receptacle was utterly out of bounds and so, it being impossible to deal with them on the scene, they were called obscene.

So we now see that tragedy is a phase. It cannot last because it is a projection of a crisis, and it is of the nature of a crisis to pass, either into death or birth. Tragedy was necessary because it permitted man (while he was undergoing a rapid alteration of awareness, a contraction of consciousness) to speak out his immediate problem under projected parabolic terms. Using the symbols of a dying pattern of prestige—the hero and his peers, the Great King and the apparently world-wide, time-long majesty that made him superhuman or the Titan Prometheus who defied Zeus—it was possible for the ordinary man to think obliquely of his own problems and not wholly repress the fermenting questions asked by the transitional psyche: "Is the Universe alien from me? What are the limits of human power? Is it possible, if not to be happy, at least to be unafraid?" Tragedy has never been able to answer these questions. All it has been able to do is to give a projection of the conflict through an art form, the play. This device of the dramatist gives some detachment, some ironic temper to an audience and, for a few hours, persuades it that it is looking on at another's suffering—which, as the French cynically say, we always have the power to bear.

But *de te fabula*: the story, although disguised, was about the onlooker himself. And he knew that the catharsis of being purged of pity for another and of fear of a dead hero's predicament was only a palliative.

In the original play, the primal comedy, there had been the real metarsis. It was not catharsis (the purging of the emotions), nor yet anarsis, the raising of the spirit to that level where *patheia* (defeating, demoralizing pain) becomes *agonia* (a wrestling with the antagonist until agony touches ecstasy). In the communal revel of the coconscious society, the saturnalia, the constituents wore animal pelts, and so they were no longer recognizable, either by sight or by smell. And in the spontaneous abandon of the panto-mime and masque there had taken place not merely the loss of personal idiosyncrasy (the sense of separateness) but there was the experience of an identification with all life.

Tragedy, on the contrary, seeks to give numbness by the tourni-quet of detachment. It has removed itself from direct touch and is, by becoming a spectator, only being affected by a spectacle. But the tension that produces this attempt at aloofness is temporary because what is being projected is an arc of consciousness. At the start, with the breakdown of Comedy, with man's inability to go on laughing off a growing self-consciousness, there arises the boast-ful hero, who condignly punishes any attempt to laugh him out of his pompous braggadocio.[b] The hero will not be laughed at. Neither will he permit the beaten-up jester to laugh off *his* punishment. But the hero, largely because he will not acquire the objectivity, pro-portion, and perspective given by humor, cannot, as we have seen, stand failure. One of his ways of avoiding suicide is to see himself as the tragic figure, sacrificed for people too stupid to recognize him as a social savior.

Hence, there is not much room for tragedy in the process which changes man from hero into ascetic. As a matter of fact, it lasts in its classic form, the Hellenic, for only three generations. This is the century-short span that always lies between the break-

[b] Cf. Napoleon's anxious query of Talleyrand: "Power, surely, can never be ridiculous?"

down of tabu and the beginning of objectivity. For when the proto-hero breaks in on the magical matriarchal society, the last phase of the traditional society, he destroys it utterly. He calls all its ways unspeakable, vile, and accursed and he forbids its beastliness ever to be mentioned again. On pain of instant death the former foul practices must be forgotten in absolute silence. The hero's ways: violence instead of craft, blows rather than words, of a father's unbrooked authority, a woman's subservience, and a son's submission: these, the only right ways, must be the only possible ways for a man who is worthy to live.

But, of course, this vain hope of an individualist, that he might revive the unquestioning acceptance with which the preindividual accepts the immemorial tradition, is bound to fail. A tabu, when it is real, is part of an entire system of total awareness and disregard of every possible behavior save those which fit in with the group's closed interpretation of every experience. The hero, by his emergence as a destroyer, has made such unquestioning consent impossible. His rule is by martial law and martial law is, at base, no more than an attempt to legalize anarchy: the rule not of the code but of the sword. In consequence, tragedy marks the end of the Heroic Age.

The three phases of heroical man's retreat from belief in his own rightness are delineated by the three masters of the Attic drama. We can watch, in their work, the growth of the critical spirit, its search for detachment, and its desire for objectivity. Their successive dramas show man coming apart from his environment. For tragedy is only possible during that brief time between the traditional aeon, when the tabu cannot be mentioned, and the age of critical self-consciousness. Tragedy emerges as a form of transitional therapy for the short spell of three generations when, intellectually, men feel a new doubt of and even skepticism about the tabu, but when their emotions still register something of the old emotional horror-thrill.

After a century, the emotions catch up with the intellect. For it was the emotional reaction of disgust that was the first step toward the awareness which must turn into concern and end in interest. At the start, Aeschylus had intended to show that pride goes before a fall, and that Nature herself punishes any man, however great, who interferes with her sway. In point of fact, however, Greek minds (when they were told to notice how vengeful Fate could be) began to attend to Natural Law. Would large-scale engineering always arouse Fate to destroy such impiety? So when Sophocles succeeds to the station of philosopher-dramatist, his audiences are shown not a god striking the incestuous Oedipus but the psychotic hero himself putting out his own eyes. And, finally, Euripides leaves the Athens of his humane triumphs and goes to live in the Macedonian north, there to show, in his Bacchae, that only by intoxicating frenzy could even women recover their abandon and lose their critical self-consciousness.

Thus, the work of these three dramatists effected, in just under a century,[c] the transition of tragedy whereby the Heroic pattern of prestige could be modulated from the early success story and yet not turn into despair, skepticism, or cynicism. Tragedy was an attempt to show that the grand man could and indeed would fail, but that in facing this fact we, the onlookers, need not become life-rejecting or question as to whether or not life is worthwhile. Failure could be so spectacularly elegant that it could make life actually meaningful. For even the hero himself could live in the hope that men in the future would look back and up to his sublime frustration and appreciate such majestic futility. This is, of course, an attitude of spectatorship, whether of looking on at a dramatic sacrifice or of looking forward to one's own deification. We have already seen a franker diagnosis of the human situation. Homer was more realistic and honest with the speech that he puts in Achilles' mouth, "Better be a poor man's slave than king among the dead."

Tragedy, which begins by being a speculative blueprint of human values in a rapidly changing moral and psychological climate (as self-consciousness becomes concentrated), ends by being drama, an artifice for entertainment. Catharsis turns into elegant estimation and the tears are no longer purgative, postponing the seizure of

[c] Aeschylus, born in 525 B.C., produced his first play in 499 B.C. and Euripides died in 406 B.C.

despair; they are gracious tributes, symptoms of a sophisticated sensibility that wipes its eyes of drops that sacred pity hath engendered.

No longer, now, could these questions be postponed: Is virtue (courage, good sense, the conscious avoidance of fault and trespass) enough to assure a man happiness and a life of worth? Is a man who thinks that his thews and high spirits are enough to win him the good life only a boastful child? Is the world (instead of being a fair field with no favor) but a deceptive sward, concealing a morass? Therefore, Tragedy passed, and with it went the pretense that fine writing can alter hard facts. A skilled description of ruin and despair, with the victim going down to defeat either defiant or submissive, may be enjoyed by some onlookers in a quiet theater seat or readers in a quieter study. But it is no answer to the riddle of life. It cannot explain the unavoidable processes of old age and death that are the experience of every human being. Still less can it speak to the developmental process that we can detect today, now that the vast curve of human history lies extended before our eyes. Looking on at tragedies or writing them may give a temporary and slight catharsis. It does not and cannot permanently alter conduct, character, and consciousness. The real contribution of the Hellenic genius to the actual education of man's evolving consciousness was not made on the stage and by the drama. It was made at the birthplace of Aeschylus, but not by a playwright, however inspired. Aeschylus was born at Eleusis, the small town a dozen miles from Athens, and it was there, in the Eleusinian mysteries, that the Greek mind blended with the pre-Hellenic, prepatriarchal tradition of preindividual man. This was the tradition of the great Mother and Daughter Goddesses: Demeter, the very life of Earth and power of the Moon, and Kore Proserpine, Demeter's undying daughter who ruled the underworld. Hades, the realm of Kore Proserpine, was thought by the first frightened *individuals*, the heroes, to be the Kingdom of the Dead where all things are forgotten and from whence there is no returning. But originally it had symbolized, to *preindividual* man, that hidden base from which all life springs and returns perennially. This basic concept of the underworld was preindividual man's intuitive solution of the mystery of life. At Eleusis, however, sometime during the rise of proto-individualism, a rite that had been completely intuitive and spontaneous became specific and shaped to the needs of men whose dawning self-consciousness was beginning to make them fear the dark of death. This solution of the main problem of individualism was, however, never put into wide circulation. On the contrary, it was sealed up under the specific spell-name of *mystery*: a word that did not originally mean a puzzle, but meant a voluntary muting, a vow of secrecy, on the part of the initiate not to repeat what had been told him. For what had been revealed to him was the secret that delivered him from the death fear, a fear that is inherent in the ignorance of individualism. Any person could apply for this enlightenment. But it was a private liberation and, while it did remove the fear of death (if we are to trust contemporary reporters), it did not elucidate the riddle of life.

At this stage of further contraction into individualism, what was being sought by the condensing mind of man was an answer to the acute question as to whether life can be lived at all with any certainty of dignity. The hero's crude conviction that only the prison and shackles of the preindividual tradition kept life from being fun, that being free of obligation one would naturally be happy —such a childish misapprehension was amply disproved. The midindividual had appeared. Self-conscious man, who in his early stage had realized that he was distinct from the group and had felt a reactive anger at the group's restraints and exploitations, now, in this third, middle term of the contraction of his consciousness, becomes not only aware of himself but aware also of his helplessness as a lonely creature pitted against an unfriendly Nature. He is also aware that this terrible and alien Nature is not only vastly aloof and indifferent to the individual's fate, but (so it seems to the self-consciously self-blaming midindividual) she can rise, like the snakes round the doomed Laocoon, wrap herself around the small protesting private will, and make the helpless, vainly resisting creature do *her* will.

Here, then, is the base of the Ascetic epoch, the third stage of mankind's psychological history. He discovers that he must find a method of disciplining himself. For not only is *outer* nature unpredictable, powerful, dangerous, and uncontrollable but his *own* nature betrays him. The Universe is unfriendly and man is fallen. His one hope is to escape *this* situation and *this* vehicle. Man becomes life-rejecting and, by denying the body, seeks a state in which, after death, he will be free and bodiless. He now begins to believe that in this present life not only will suffering exceed happiness—there is no armor against fate—but that enjoyment involves one in further suffering, that pleasure is bait that lures and traps the soul into a fresh round of misery. Birth, illness, old age and death—all these all men must endure and all are suffering.

Asceticism, as athletic training, was inevitable and right when man's psychological evolution, the condensation of his consciousness, reached such a degree of concentration that he became detached from and critical of not only his fellows but from and of himself. Discipline and training were necessary and certainly paid. The organized, planned, and forecast life made the ordered city (with its storing and distribution, its integrated crafts, arts, and administration) able to ride out barren years and cataclysms of weather that were fatal to more feckless communities. While, when it came to war, the drilled phalanx soon showed the free fighting hero that he was as anachronistic on the field of battle (which he thought was his native heath) as he was in the complex of the city streets.

But the mid-self-conscious man could not be content to add self-training to his defenses and, being so armed with surplus resources and the power to foresee and guard against eventualities, feel that he now held the initiative. This was because the more his foresight permitted him to be forewarned, and so forearmed, not only was he confronted with a wider range of uninsurable risk, but it appeared to be all the more certain that in the actuarial dates against which he provided there must be an increasing number that carried increasing risks. And in the end there would be one date on which he must lose all that he had.

The midindividual who, because of his self-blame, is already

uneasy as to whether he is worth his keep (the guilt sense) and as to whether it is worthwhile keeping on in such an unbalanceable world (the death wish), begins to long for release. Liberation must be not merely from outer molestation but from inner weariness and frustration. The hero felt shame at losing face, at not being outstanding among his fellows whom he could emulate and surpass. The ascetic felt guilty at his lack of anonymity. He began to long to be lost, obliterated. He began to fear that death might only be the gate to another round of such impossibly demanding and conflicting lives as his present one. The dread of reincarnation, of repeating, endlessly, this predicamental experience, of finding himself once again possessed by passions that only created more craving and more guilt—this fear engrossed increasingly the mind of the midindividual. All appetite must be shunned, all possession eschewed, all position abdicated.

But addiction and appetite are two different things. It is untrue to say that all appetites grow with eating. In point of fact, all those appetites that sustain a healthy life are self-terminative. There can be no private salvation from the self which is morbid precisely because it is private, that is, self-centered. The desire for liberation can itself become a fetter if it is for a self to be released into a condition where it will gain self-satisfying ends.

Again, this was clearly understood by the few. We shall see in Part III that the crisis-transition from the coconscious preindividual to the protoindividual had its own therapy whereby that dangerous passage could (and can) be achieved and that, in the event of mishap or miscarriage, it can be remedied. And we shall see that as, in turn, the crisis-transition from the protoindividual to the midindividual also had (and has) its remedial therapy, so too the midindividual epoch did discover the appropriate praxis for bringing the psyche safely through this stage of development and into the succeeding stage, that of total individualism.

But what we have noted of these first two crises is also true of this third one: the therapy was personal and private. It might deal with pioneers, sporadic advanced types. It might keep them from wholly seceding and even make some of them into seers by giving them not only freedom from adolescent self-blame but also, prophetically, precognitionally, freedom from those two further crises which mankind was yet to reach: (1) the manic depressive derangement of Humanic man and (2) involutional melancholy, the final failure of nerve that now threatens twentieth-century man.

However, the greater number, by far, of those who were capable of reflective thought did not find the appropriate method that would give them a state of consciousness that was contemporary. They did not find the technique of that dilation of awareness that would solve the particular psychological problem of the midindividual who was conscious of self-blame for his inadequacy to love the community and who could not deny that community's right to demand loyalty. Although as we shall see in Part III, in India, the source of many such techniques, methods were certainly devised that would make those willing to be trained able to become contemporarily conscious. That is, they would be able not only to understand the stage to which human psychological evolution had reached. They would be able to become themselves trained persons whose psychophysical phase of energy was predominantly adrenaline and no longer the nor-adrenaline of the previous protoindividual; the self-assertive character (see Part II) who could be self-critical without guilt, without life dread, or despair.

Still, the ascetic failed (just as the Hero had failed before him) although he did have a temporary success. The man who renounced (who disciplined himself, who was uniformed, closely drilled, and always under orders, who was always flouting his self-love) soon became a force in society. Just as the exiled protohero, for a while the lone wolf, quickly gathered around him a gang of adventurers, so the protoascetic soon found postulants. The monastic order arises. It has a new if temporary inherent strength from its repression. It is explicit, propagandist; and it preaches, continually pointing out two things that its listeners are ready to allow. First, that the boastful hero has proved a failure. He ends personally in a dismal demonstration that the undisciplined are contemptible. Besides, and secondly, even if he ever were admirable as a knight errant, now, in a world of police forces and magistracy, he is out of date, an anachronism.

The ascetic therefore demotes the hero from his position of being the pattern of prestige. He shames both the exhibitionist brawler and also the lazy, sensual man. His discovery of energy generated by repression, his use of propaganda, drill, and uniform are practical discoveries that the new state can employ against its subjects and against its less modern rivals. Diplomacy and coordinated armament are by-products of this second level of individualism, of a self-consciousness that can be made efficiently loyal by exploiting its sense of guilt. Thus the state can largely depend on its subjects to denounce themselves.

And, just as inevitably, the creation of a monastic autocracy (some of those who began as persons seeking anonymity become autocrats) leads to further questioning in the midindividual mind. Guilt turns into despair and the best seek to escape from life itself. Large numbers were drawn into monasticism by leaders who seemed to have both knowledge and strength; and the dilution of enthusiasm, caused by this influx, led inevitably to the relaxed orders. The ascetic, as the pattern of prestige, is discredited and mankind seeks still another standard (16).

4

The total individual
[Humanic, self-sufficient man]

In this chapter, as we consider that contraction of consciousness that has been most intense and has called itself modern man, we must also contract our purview. Up to this point we have been able to consider the human process as a homogeneous whole. The first step in this process, the coconscious preindividual state of man's consciousness, when he had emerged from animalhood into a creature with a culture, may be said to cover all that there then was of a mankind. Both the number of groups and their possible habitats were very restricted. With the next stage, the Heroic, the increase in area and the restlessness of the personality made for more wandering but *ipso facto* for more communication. The Heroic Age and the feudal companion condition that shares its exhibitionist ideals of honor and dispute broke out at different times in different places. But it was the same movement and caused by the same force: a contraction of consciousness that was provoked by the same outer pressure of an ankylosed priest-kingly tradition.

All the cultures of the past (save those very few that were protected by complete isolation, as for example, the Aboriginal Australian and Papuan cultures) have arrived, sooner or later, at stage two of man's consciousness: the protoindividualism of self-assertive man. And, in turn, all these Heroic cultures, because they were precipitated by self-conscious, challenging men, had of necessity to challenge themselves. The young heroic prince, born in the warrior caste to rule an army-girt kingdom, becomes the Buddha. The ideal of the ascetic now becomes widespread: as widespread as the ideal of the hero had been.

But humanic man does not supplant the ascetic so readily; at least not yet. In this phase of sense-of-separateness growth, the West outran the rest of the world, pushing to the utmost the limited knowledge of the outer world given by a criticism and analysis that are confined by the narrow conviction of reason, and neglecting the inner world. Only now are Asia and the rest of the world reaching the psychological crisis brought on by such one-sided physical discovery and striving to keep it from shattering society, which it must do if further *psychological* discovery is not made.

The West is now emerging from that phase and is already learning that economic and scientific advance without equal psychological advance must be disastrous. Asia, which during the ascetic phase did much to teach Europe about the dimensions of the psyche, must now learn from the West as the Indic and Mongolian peoples go through the humanic phase and the West emerges from that phase of total individualism. Asia stayed behind, short of the total individualized psyche, because the center of her thinking (India) remained attached to the renunciatory other-worldly-ism of the ascetic phase. This, of course, was due to her absorbed interest in the psyche, in the inner world rather than in the outer. The thought of Western man, resuming the self-assured individualism that asceticism had compelled the hero to abandon, appeared to India to be so preposterously irrational as to be impossible.

On the other hand, China, for an opposite reason but with equal force, rejected the return of the hero now armed not with traditional weapons but with scientific armament. Her concern with society made the independent, irresponsible superindividual appear to be a monster. The *chung tzu,* though in an essentially urbane way, is as self-effacing as the ascetic. Therefore, when China needed expert answers to the ultimate problems of life and the nature of things, she did not send for the West's technicians. She had already imported what her socially minded masters felt would serve their purpose: Buddhism (40).

In this chapter, therefore, we consider the culminating contraction of consciousness into self-sufficient man as it is illustrated by the West. This is not provincialism. The foreconsciousness of Western man was almost completely insulated from his deeper total consciousness and this drove him to the search for objectivity. The search for objectivity centered his interest in the outer world and led to his discovery of the scientific technic. This gave him (1) the physical powers that permitted him to threaten all the world and conquer much of it, (2) the economic increases that allowed him to raise his biotic standards, and (3) the physiological information that gave him the ability to get rid of much disease, multiply population, lengthen his life, and increase energy and output. Such apparent victories made it possible for him to believe in progress and an earthly Utopia. Now the West, by its very striving to discover objectivity, has reached psychology and is trying to study the self, which constructs the environment it would modify. While the East, with scientifically armed assault and with scientifically discovered and commended aid, turns to attempt the humanic phase and to abandon asceticism. In studying the West's experience of the humanic phase of extreme individualism we are, then, studying not the private story of aberrant occidental man but the first attempt of mankind to be a complete individual. And this is an inevitable step in the evolution of the human consciousness as it strives toward complete understanding.

The ideal of denial and abandonment lasted on as the pattern of prestige in the West until the fifteenth century. True, the last great ascetic enthusiasm, the Franciscan, was rapidly degenerating by the time that Dante had written his *De Monarchia* (1310–1313). This was the book that was to offer the Papacy terms of circumscribed authority, which it promptly rejected, putting the book, when it was published, on the Index of forbidden reading. The Revival of Learning was well on its way but, until Constantinople fell to Mohammed II in 1453, men had not awakened to the fact that they were in a new epoch. As always, and as it is today, human character has already changed for a considerable time before human consciousness becomes aware that this is so.

The ideal of the man who sacrifices himself to save others (into an afterlife from a world that must always be sorrowful) had become, from the Atlantic to the Pacific, the noblest concept for thoughtful, sensitive, responsible men who were capable of that degree of self-consciousness which can blame itself. Though China revered Confucius, she had to allow that the Buddha held the answer for those whose sensitiveness drove them to ask those most searching of questions: "What does life mean? Where does it go? Can this world be enough in itself?" So the two great ideal images that dominated the midindividual consciousness of self-accusing man are both other-worldly. The Eastern figure sits in self-losing salvational contemplation under a tree. The Western figure hangs on a tree in an ecstasy of self-sacrificing, salvational offering. Both call men away from a temporal world of suffering to an eternal world of peace.

But the mind of man alters because his consciousness evolves. The protoindividual, self-assertive man admired the hero, thinking that men could win happiness if only they had the courage to break with the cowardly fears of the ancient group tradition. In turn, the midindividual mind, in its growing self-consciousness, became self-accusing and admired self-denial, submission and renunciation. But, as once again man's consciousness contracted still more, he no longer felt guilt. This further concentration of awareness gave him a greater degree of detachment, both outer and inner.

Outwardly, he began to question the ascetic authority's right to give him a sense of guilt, and in this respect he recapitulates the heroic protest, but more self-consciously. Unlike the primal tradition, the ascetic order had used argument. For the hypnotic power of the coconscious pattern of culture over its constituents could no longer be exercised. The Heroic Age had served the purpose of destroying the primal magic. And argument, the use of the syllogism, the analysis of words came to be used more and more both in East and West, whether in Buddhist Taxila or Late Scholastic Paris. This was necessary in order to prove and convince because direct psychical experience was increasingly lacking. The new Man of the Renaissance, the man of recently intensified self-consciousness, aware of his distinctive and separative individualism, was keen to reason and sharply equipped to argue. The Church had admitted the authority of Aristotle, the inventor of the syllogism. And Aristotle had ruled that there is nothing in the mind that is not first in the senses: a pronouncement favorable to the thinking of modern sensory man. Consequently, modern man not only felt it to be natural for him to debate with authority, as an equal, and to have no sense of guilty temerity in daring to question its answers and challenge its conclusions. He also challenged it to test and experiment as to whether its conclusions could stand up under actual examination.

In the West, this revolt, this secession from the ascetic tradition had started. The opening of the way for experimental, empirical science had already begun with the triumph, in the medieval schools, of the Nominalists over the Realists. Words were not things. Species did not exist, they were abstractions. The only reality was a number of separate objects. "Entities must not be multiplied" unless you could show that each name did apply to and describe an actual, definite thing. This, to repeat, was projection. It was man's new acuteness of self-consciousness, his new sense of being a totally separate person, being projected onto the outer world. Nominalism has been the basic philosophy of natural science because it is the self-evident conclusion of the fully self-conscious mind. The semiconscious mind of the midindividual cannot dismiss species, or other collective nouns, as being unreal. Authority is something more than an average or majority of private opinions, and tradition is not necessarily superstition but often contains inspired intuition. The collective mind is not necessarily a delusion and certain wholes may be apprehended by precritical, preanalytical minds although those same integral wholes become imperceptible to the critical individual intelligence and attention. With the disappearance of this apprehension of fields, of areas in which objects behave coordinately (a behavior only to be understood if the presence of a field is recognized), the total individual becomes incapable of apprehending any relationships between himself and other beings except that of physical contacts.

Such was humanic man's outward detachment. And he was able to exercise that outward detachment to such an extreme degree because his inner detachment was equal to it. The tie that still held heroic man and ascetic man to the community was their social conscience. And it gave the community its modifying power over the assault of the one and the secession of the other. The hero wished to be outstandingly famous and so feared to be shamed. The ascetic feared being expelled and hoped to be forgiven his guilt. The total individual now saw not merely no reason why he should prefer the pricking of his own finger to the death of any of his fellows who were of no use to him, but no reason why he should feel either shame or guilt. He viewed the oddity of his emotional behavior, whether asocial, antisocial, or absurd, as one more subject for his curiosity, neither to be censured or lauded but to be observed as intriguing entertainment. So humanic, self-sufficient man, believing in reason alone, can be amused by the extravagances of his own nature, viewing from the citadel of his private intellectual detachment not merely the ridiculous antics of his fellows but the carnivals and carousing carried on in the streets of the self's own town and watched with humor from the battlements of the central keep: the completely self-conscious psyche.

This self-sufficiency meant, at the beginning, a great release of energy. Ascetic man had given his attention to and had spent his repressed drive in striving to expunge his guilt and to escape an afterdeath doom. But that attention was now held by an interest in the outer world, and that energy was now employed in modifying the environment. His efforts were now turned to an attempt to understand not only the human situation but the human physique, not merely the field of vision but the viewer. The very energy of penetration outward was, however, due to and a symptom of a contraction within. The attempt to find and fix objectivity, complete definition, and a final hardness of focus led to the restriction of and final denial of all midterms and indeterminacies. Renaissance man, because he was aiming at being without shame, guilt, or any irrational, nonphysical tie with his fellows, was also the first man (and, indeed, the first creature) ever to attempt to live without intuitive knowledge and acknowledgment of his preterrational nature. Humanic man had no specific exercises for contacting and working with his deep emotive being. And toward the traditional exercises of the past his attitude was skepticism tinged with aestheticism, a contempt for superstition that was kept in check by the antiquarian's appreciation of an object or of a process precisely because it belongs to an extinct culture. His attitude was well stated by Adam Smith, the vastly influential eighteenth-century economist whose *Wealth of Nations* furnished the economy on which humanism was to be based. Smith proposed, as a self-evident policy for mankind, that reason should always be followed and that enthusiasm (the powerful waves of the emotive life) should be dismissed.

Toward the end of the humanic phase, when man's critically minded enquiry brought him to study not only his economy and his physique but also his psyche, he discovered that, whether it was regrettable or not, reason did not rule man's interior life. It could not alter his conduct, character, and consciousness, while the emotions could and did. Humanic man, in his phase of some fifteen generations (from the mid-fifteenth century to the beginning of the twentieth), went through a cycle that started with keen elation and ended in considerable discouragement. Because his total individualism made him examine critically all the areas of experience, he had, at the start, an unparalleled success in handling what first came to his attention: the outer, molar, inorganic world, the province of astronomy and chemistry. And he made almost as striking advances in understanding his physique.

When, however, in his contracting investigation he reached the psyche, because of his method of approach by detachment and analysis it presented him with a problem as insoluble as it was distressing. For the psyche, because it is the subject, cannot be understood by making it an object. Nor, because it is not a machine but a field-of-wholeness (as is a work of art), can it be understood by reducing it into its constituent parts. Self-sufficient man, the total individual, therefore became subject to a fluctuation of mood. Instead of the shame-fear that haunted the hero or the guilt-fear that brooded over the ascetic, humanic man alternated between two states of mind. On looking forward, he considered himself to be a machine that could be made to mesh in perfect gear with the environment and so produce a totally satisfying utopia. On looking back, he regarded himself as an animal that, because of its beast-hood, could never be rational nor hope to conceive of the nature of an objective world, a creature whose intelligence only armed it the more lethally to destroy its own species.

Emotionally, then, humanic man could not be stable. His epoch is brief because he had a psyche that was even more strangulated than that of the ascetic at his most schizophrenic extremes. His personal consciousness was almost completely cut off from his deep, personal preterconsciousness. And the traditional methods of keeping the two in touch, of penetrating through the barrier of the limen (religious procedures such as the Mass) he mainly regarded as being, at best, of antiquarian, romantic interest and, at worst, a superstition that still prevented his release into personal happiness. The critical, analytic method was the only means whereby the hyper-self-conscious, individualistic intellect could conceive of the meaning of understanding and could hope to attain to it by achieving the detachment of complete objectivity. The intensification of this critical, analytic method drove humanic man, as we have seen, to studies that lay closer and closer to himself, and finally led him to the discovery of his own preterconscious.

Still pursuing objectivity, however, he could not recognize that this preterconscious was part of himself and that it was the complement of his personal, objective consciousness, that it was the link between him and his past, his tradition, and his fellows: between him and all life. He must still look on it as being a power that was alien and hostile to his one means (reason) and his one aim (personal happiness). No wonder, then, that Sigmund Freud, the popularizer and not the discoverer of this sunken continent of consciousness, could only regard it as being the permanent frustrator of reason, good sense, and generous behavior and, therefore, could describe man as being "a base, ungovernable beast." No wonder that H. G. Wells, the popularizer of humanist history and the missionary of man's salvation through physical science, could declare, after the Second World War and the discovery and use of the atom bomb, that the mind was "at the end of its tether." For, of course, to him the mind was the critical, analytic intellect of humanic, individualistic man. It would have been a better simile to say that the surface mind, like a yacht with canvas crowded to the topsail, had dropped off its balancing keel and so was capsizing.

Nevertheless, even though Blake may be too hopeful when he says "If the fool would but persevere in his folly he would become wise," we can say that if the mind will but persist in its criticism, penetration, and analysis it will come upon expansion and integration. Like circumnavigators of the globe, by consistently going away from our point of departure we find ourselves returned to it. Man, in seeking the absolute detachment of complete objectivity, found the roots of his attachment to the whole. And so he had to admit that although objectivity was impossible orientation *was* possible. Orientation, in this context, means the realization that he and the universe cannot be separated, that he and it are two poles between which there is a constant interplay: an interplay that precipitates creation. Therefore, detachment is an impossibility. Man cannot now regard life with a cold curiosity; he must realize that he and life are one.

Neither Freud, who took part in the beginning of the transition from humanic, totally individualistic man to postindividual man, nor Wells who was concerned with history and saw the transition more than half completed, understood what was going on. Tied to the assumptions of an epoch that was practically ended while they were still alive, they failed to see that the discovery of the preterconscious (together with the subsequent realization that objectivity and detachment were impossibilities) was one more step in psychophysical evolution.

It is an interesting fact that since the seventh century A.D. the changes in Western culture can generally be detected as being crescent by the last quarter of each century, and at half moon at the century's turn. Greek is rediscovered by Western Europeans about 675. The Revival of Learning takes another decisive step when, about 775, the great Scriptory Schools are founded by the Frankish kings. Each change in the development of style in architecture throughout northern Europe (Romanesque, Lancet, Decorated, Flamboyant, and/or Perpendicular) may be dated at about the seventy-fifth year of each century from 1075 to 1375.

In our own epoch we can now see, looking backward, that by 1875 the intellectual-emotional climate was beginning to alter. Until then, the chief concerns of man's practical-theoretical thought had been with economics and a biology slanted by economic assumptions. Charles Darwin has left it on record that Malthus' work on population and its pressures had turned his mind to seek an explanation for the evolutionary process and that it had channeled his thought toward finding that explanation in the blind struggle to survive. Karl Marx, impressed by the support that Darwin's theory might be made to give to the class struggle, wrote to Darwin. Naturally, but not rationally, Darwin shunned the possible application. A quarter of a century after the publication of *The Origin of Species* its popularity was established with the practical reading public, but the growing edge of Western thought was turning from bioeconomics to psychology.

The modern age, the age of the four revolutions, had begun with the ecclesiastical revolution. The political revolution came next and was, in turn, superseded by the economic revolution, the revolution that was to overturn industrialism and which, toward the end of the nineteenth century, began to be undermined by the oncoming uprising of the fourth, the psychological revolution. By 1873 J. M. Charcot (at Salpêtrière Hospital in Paris), in his *Lectures on the Maladies of the Nervous System,* had drawn the attention of the educated world to the problem of the preterconscious. As discoverers of profoundly original facts usually do,[a] Charcot missed the true significance of his great find. He maintained until the end of his life that this till then unknown side of the psyche was merely a morbid aberration. For instance, he thought that the hypnotic state was specifically a hysteric characteristic. Nevertheless, as an original researcher, he realized that no narrow exploitation of this strange find should be made. He has been blamed, and with some point, for dismissing the hypnotic state as being essentially one aspect of a morbid condition of hysteria or hystero epilepsy. But today we can see that Charcot's insight, that the inrush from the preterconscious onto the foreconscious is leptoid in nature and epileptoid when thwarted, was prophetic.[b] Prophetic also was his foresight when he remarked to one of his pupils, Pierre Janet, about a fellow pupil who already showed a limiting self-assurance combined with an overmastering gift for systemizing, "that young man will put back psychology sixty years." "That young man" was Sigmund Freud.

By 1882 in London a philosopher of eminence (Henry Sidgewick of Cambridge), a Greek scholar (F. W. H. Myers), and a young man who was to be a British Prime Minister (Arthur Balfour) had decided to risk academic disapproval by founding the London Society for Psychical Research.

By 1884 H. Bernheim, Professor of Medicine at Nancy, aided by the work of A. A. Liebeault, published *De la suggestion,* which was a definite treatise on hypnosis. These researchers, reacting against Charcot's physicalism and attempting to consider, empirically, the mind in itself, tried to equate the hypnotic trance with normal sleep. Actually, these two states are mainly polar: for exam-

[a] For example, Priestly, the discoverer of oxygen.
[b] See Part I, Chapter 5; Part II, Chapter 5; and Part III, Chapter 5.

ple, muscular tension is at a minimum in sleep and often at a maximum in hypnosis.

During the next and last decade of the century it was clear, from Becquerel's work in fluorine and the work of the Curies in radium, that physics, the science of greatest detachment, was about to enter a new epoch. Classical physics, with its standard of objectivity (the object's mass and position can and must be known), was to be transformed by the field concepts.

As the nineteenth century passed into the twentieth, Max Planck in Berlin, with his concept of quanta (together with J. J. Thompson, his greater pupil Rutherford at Cambridge, and Niels Bohr in Copenhagen, with their revolutionary notions of the electron and the proton) started concepts that were to lead to the disappearance of what had been the goal of thinking men since the rise of Ionian science twenty-four hundred years before: the goal of absolute objectivity.

Finally, with the Heisenbergh principle of indeterminacy (that if the position of a particle can be known its mass cannot and *vice versa*) man had reached, as Niels Bohr himself summed it up, "the end of a twenty-four-hundred-year search for objectivity."

Meanwhile, the sciences of life were also in travail. The concept of mutation, based on the evidence that living processes could suddenly leap into new forms, just as the electron did, was as radical as the new physics and was received with violent controversy. Ernst Haeckel, a famous and conservative popularizer of simple Darwinianism, shouted in a biological conference that had reached ecclesiastical conciliar heat, "If this ('Mendelism') is accepted, here we go back to Moses!"

Nevertheless, the process went on. By 1910 there went into biological circulation a term that was more significant, though less convulsant, than mutationism had been. Ecology, as much as any science, marked the end of analysis as being the method of finding the final interpretation of life and so signaled the oncoming shift of consciousness from total individualism to postindividualism. The one science to which the Middle Ages would give money was astrology. And the first clear indication that the Middle Ages were gone for good was when star-study changed from astrology to astronomy. This is the first sign that man's concept of himself and his situation is altering. In the ascetic midindividual stage he had conceived of himself as being a creature that was struggling guiltily to have his way against the law of an implacable Heaven whose dooms for him could be spelled out in the stars. When astronomy comes in, it is a symptom that man is becoming content to be a self-sufficient creature that can catalogue (*nomos*) the cosmos but cannot and need not comprehend it. The how of the cosmos he may know, and he may find such detached knowledge entertaining. Its why he cannot know and doesn't need to. All the sciences should then have been termed *nomoi*, not *logoi*. And the science that mattered most to humanic man in his most elational form was economics. (Carlyle called it the gloomy science because in its first phase it was trying to define the *status quo*.) Economics was the faith that you, the detached creature, are free to carve the environment to shape your personal convenience. Therefore, when from actual observation of how living forms are integrated it was seen that each is in field reaction with all the rest, this was rightly called ecology. And we can see a symptom of a new shift in human attention, a new expansion of awareness.

For the sciences were projections of humanic man's highly restricted focal length of consciousness. And as that consciousness, in its intensity, contracted on itself the sciences themselves came under the analytic scrutiny of the method that had extended them. As a young man H. G. Wells himself wrote an essay called *The Scepticism of the Instrument;* thus indicating that he was aware of the question raised by epistemology: "How do we know that we can apprehend an objective world?" (Darwin and Freud both recognized this problem.) And as the analytic sciences were found to be partial and highly selective, men began to discover that it was possible to seek for a further method of understanding; what Radakrishnan, in the nineteen twenties, had named integral thought (see Glossary). At about the same time, the first issues of ecological journals began to appear; the first number of the *American Journal of Ecology* came out in 1922.

Meanwhile, however, such shifts of scientific attention from the critical analytic focus to integral apprehension were not enough to prevent acute psychic distress in Western man. (39) His spirit, for a dozen generations, had been on a deprivative diet. The vitamin of meaning, essential for sanity, had been steadily diminished in his food for thought. He had been able to endure this inadequacy of significance, and so to postpone collapse, by three devices.

We must, then, at this point survey these three substitutes to see whether they can any longer prevent the mutation of the mind; or whether we now have to face the fact that another great shift of consciousness is about to take place—is indeed already taking place. And we must ask ourselves how we may best cooperate with the inevitable, how we may integrate ourselves with life's evolution by learning those exercises whereby we may emerge into the new condition.

The three methods whereby modern man has sought to prevent (and has succeeded in postponing) his psychological collapse are these: (1) utopianism (progress), (2) reactionaryism (counterprogress) and (3) detensionism. Earlier in this chapter we said that humanic rationalistic man was the only creature that had ever attempted to live with no information other than that given by the rational exercise of the senses. This was certainly the hope of the person who felt himself to be the self-sufficient, total individual. Very soon, however, there were many secessionists from such a notion. It is true that since the writing of *The Cloud of Unknowing* (circa 1350) there had been no treatise written in vernacular, and by a mind that was up to date with the psyche of its age, which could serve as a guide for a consciousness that was shifting from the stage of the guilty, midindividualistic ascetic to an ultraindividualistic, nonguilty state of mind.[c] The succeeding

[c] For example, see the *Cloud's* attitude toward the banishment of the sense of sinfulness.

best seller, *The Scale of Perfection,* and the widely popular *Imitation of Christ* are rightly called books of ascetic, not mystical, theology. But almost as soon as humanic man emerged, an answer to this need for a guide book was produced by the counterreformation, which threw back the Protestant Revolution and contained and remolded the Renaissance. The Jesuits, who were better disputants and finer scholars than the reformers, better psychologists and better trained than the humanists, used self-consciousness to conquer itself. The core of the Ignatian answer to humanic man's revolt against asceticism lay in the *Exercises* which, although he did not invent them, Ignatius did put into circulation.

For a time, this method proved to be highly efficacious for mastering the emotions of even the most critically minded. In consequence, Ignatius could recruit men of high humanist culture and yet keep them loyal and indeed subservient to an ascetic point of view. For there was a large number of those, even among the intelligentsia, who wistfully wished to feel again the close supporting convictions of the Ages of Faith, if only it were possible. Humanism was still far from certain of its frame of reference and hesitant about framing its own distinctive philosophy. The conservative reformers of the New Learning wished to repair the ascetic tradition, not to reconstruct it; to correct ancient slips of the pen, not to add new information. Galileo has often been cited as being the hero of Renaissance science. But now in his definitive study Giorgio de Santillana has shown that he was only a very muddled and even petty man who was motivated far more by emotional and indeed irresponsible resentments than by a consistent and practiced philosophy; an unprepared, vacillatory person who wanted to preach Copernicanism and at the same time to be recognized as an orthodox Catholic.

The ancient ascetic Orders dreaded revolutionary license and anarchy and feared their own nature. The Ignatian *Exercises* gave intellectuals who wished to serve this ancient order a method whereby they might recreate their own belief, whereby they might feed down into their sunken preterconscious those instructions that were in favor of the past: a thing which the conventional methods of attending Mass and listening to sermons seemed no longer able to do. The success of the system, however, depended on two things. First, the man must desire the point of view of the past, the ascetic position; and second, he must also believe that it is intellectually valid—that is, it is both desirable and true. Heaven is the only desirable goal, a goal that is attained by denying the body and dying to this world. And this desire is, within the frame of reference, unavoidable. For after a few years at most, the soul is faced with an irrevocable situation. If life here has been sufficiently mortificatory then there is the reward of eternal bliss. If life here has been carnally minded, an expression of the appetites, then, as St. Paul says, there is death or, far worse, eternal torment. Naturally, that being the state of affairs, it was inevitable that men should *wish* to believe in order to be saved. It might not be possible to think with desirous vividness of a heaven the charms of which were unimaginable to the senses. And it was equally impossible to conceive of a Deviser of that Heaven Who, although He was said to be Love, used as His alternative method of extracting obedience and restraint from His creatures the threat of and practice of torturing forever those who, during their brief life here, had failed to satisfy His demands. But fear could do most of the work—a fact that Ignatius well knew and on which he acted. As a very thorough individualist, honestly ignorant of human symbiosis and solidarity, he was convinced that men did best when they were driven. He knew and understood why four fifths of the visions of those authorities which he studied (the mortificatory Saints) had been of Hell and only one fifth of Heaven. And his action was based on their indications together with his own convictions and experiences. His exercises are visualist. Things are to be seen with terrific, mind-etching vividness and the things that are to be basically branded on the consciousness are the torments of an irremediable, interminable Hell. These two facts, the subject and the method of memorizing it, account both for the immediate success of the *Exercises* and for their subsequent failure. Only an ascetic world, wherein the conflicts of repression had been projected until self-hate became hate of others, could wish to believe such a doctrine. Only a world in

which fear for one's own salvation made a man frantic with suspicion and hate against anyone who by his doubt might increase
and make indiscriminate God's rage against man could believe
such a doctrine to be true.[d]

And as to the method: it could work only with people of such
visual power of projection that they could generate eidetic imagery:
that is, such visualizers that they literally see before them, as an
autonomous vision, what they are imagining. And only a society
in which such a type is common could successfully practice this
system of autosuggestion. There is reason to suppose, from the work
of the brothers Jensch (Dr. Jensch and Professor Jensch of Mar-
bourg University) that such eidetic imagery is most frequent in
children whose parathyroids suffer from a deficiency of lime. And
there is a strong probability that this deficiency is the provocative
condition that makes the state possible. As dietary conditions improved in Europe, it is then likely that these powerful hallucinatory
aids to the ascetic belief faded at the very time that not only the
intellectual climate but the emotional atmosphere was changing.
The humanic epoch, by the beginning of the seventeenth century,
had begun to pass from being a request for reform of the ascetic
system and an appeal for tolerance to belief that an alternative
system might replace the old interpretation of nature and of man.
By the close of that century's first third, the last war of religion has
come to an end. By the close of the second third it is possible to
detect humanic man's new aim: humanitarianism. Charles I of
England and his Long Parliament that fought and defeated him
agreed on at least one point of greater importance than all the
issues they disputed: they both abolished torture as a part of judicial
procedure. By the time of the Restoration, the historical student
finds references to compassionate conduct as being something not
saintly but of common decency. At the very beginning of the
eighteenth century we find (as J. B. Bury (7) points out in his
The Idea of Progress) the first statements of the belief in the

[d] Philip II of Spain, as he lay dying in great misery, came to the conclusion
that God was plaguing him because he had not burnt enough heretics, although he had certainly burnt all those he could lay hands on.

indefinite improvability of man. The great Ignatian system had lost its pristine power; this remarkable psychological method was no longer relevant. For a time it postponed, almost singlehanded, the humanic process, and headed off the full emergence of the total individual who would know no world but this one, have no technic but reason, and depend on no providence but his own resources. Now the order that had seemed so irresistible that its opponents feared it more than its own side admired it was itself in trouble. By the time of Ignatius' successor, Laynez (1556–1564), the power of the General, which had been great to begin with, was increased. By the reign of Claude Aquaviva (1581–1615), mistakes had been made that made the still increasing material success embarrassing to many conservatives.[e] As an authority has said, the evil reputation was surpassing the good. When, under the generalship of Vitelleschi, the Order reached the end of its first century—at the completion of those three generations which so often have marked

[e] In this work politics is not being considered save insofar as symptoms of frames of mind, states of consciousness, projections of various degrees of self-consciousness. From that point of view, the Jesuit rise and fall was inevitable; its initial success and subsequent failure was natural. It had a skilful technique whereby the ascetic, other-worldly point of view was contemporized into something that looked like humanism: a humanism in which the firmest authority was modernized so as to appear, to the cultured, to be gentlemanly ease. More, the Society itself became an arbiter of taste and an innovator in art. However, this praxis did not arrest individualism or make it nonsecular. In 1590 Philip II of Spain, of all people, recognizing this fact complained to Sixtus V, urging the Pope to alter the Society and even give it another name, and the Pope was prepared to do so just before his death. Individual Jesuits inevitably went on playing the most violent politics in spite of the wise and emphatic order of the Fifth General Congregation (1593–94), commanding "severely and strictly" because of past scandals, that no Jesuit touch public affairs in any way, even though he might be invited to do so. Next, they abandoned the excellent and free education that had brought them real renown, devoting themselves to control of the consciences of autocrats. After that they took to trade; and some groups amassed such wealth that in 1741 Pope Benedict XIV had to make special regulations against this scandal. By 1773 Pope Clement XIV had dissolved the order. Resuscitated in 1804 after 31 years and formally reestablished in 1814, it is now only a shadow of its original powerful self.

the failure of spectacular success—it had 36 provinces, 800 houses, and 15,000 members. But by 1647 the Pope censured it severely at home and by 1651 even abroad the retreat was evident. The Society and the Christianity that it taught were driven from Japan while in Europe it was approaching its eclipse at the hands of the Papacy. And in what were the roots of this decay? If men's actions are consequences of their life process, of their basic consciousness, then the Jesuit movement was fighting a rear action; and having fought that action the retreat from asceticism to a more prepared humanism could be made. When, in 1773, the Pope dissolved the Society it had served its purpose, and when it was re-established in 1814 the human climate had altered. The humanic epoch had attained to its humanitarian phase. The psychology behind this remarkable reaction, the reaction to the process of evolving consciousness, seems to have been the subconscious realization that mortificatory asceticism had had its day. The Ignatian *Exercises* had shown those who practiced them that Hell awaited the immoral, especially the sexually loose. But the Jesuits were always generous with salvation. No example of their resentment is more striking and more comprehensible than their attack on the Port Royal Jansenists, who certainly made salvation very hard, and indeed precarious, with their revival of Augustinianism and the issue of predestination. The self-tormenting eremite was suspect in the eyes of the Jesuits who wanted the world to enjoy a cultured urbanity under their sophisticated cosmopolitanism. Although they didn't consciously realize it and so never made it verbally explicit but did render it obviously manifest in their outstanding art, their aim, then, was to revoke and, with the young, prevent the super-individualism of the humanic phase: not by returning the psyche to adolescent asceticism, or even to boyish heroism, but to pan-esthetic infantism. Of this, one unmistakable evidence is their most remarkable achievement: the transformation of the classic Renaissance architecture (self-consciously masculine with its rectilinear strength and honest athleticism, wide-shouldered in its trabeated muscularity) into Baroque.

Baroque has rightly been called the architecture of the counterreformation, the style of Jesuitism as shown emphatically in their first church, the Jesu in Rome. It has also been rightly called psychological architecture by its ablest defender, Geoffrey Scott, (74) in his *The Architecture of Humanism*. Although Scott skilfully defends this form against the charges of pretension, vulgarity, and dishonesty, it is the brilliant defense of a lawyer who is more concerned to gain an acquittal than to understand the defendant's motives. He does not even use that profound insight of Michelangelo, the founder of Baroque: "He may never understand architecture who has not mastered anatomy."

That statement contains the clue to Baroque and shows it to be the revealing symptom of the Jesuit's unconscious psychological strategy. For the Baroque forms are romantic. But they are not the romantic, fantastic, aspirational extravagance of the Gothic building, such as the Beauvais' arches, which outraged the adolescent engineering of the time, shooting up spires that too often collapsed and crushed in ruin the shrine they were to protect. The counter-reformation style produced false domes and sham vistas suggesting avenues and perspectives of horizontal order to bring delusively near a friendly, broody Heaven. But back of these delicious illusions was all the latest engineering skill, even to vast concealed iron chains trussing and corseting the maternal corpulence. In short, as the style of Gothic is ascetic, aspiration-escapism in stone (as the style of Madura, Puri, and all the pure Indian architecture is exuberantly phallic) so the Baroque is infantic. These great curves are projections of both the progenitive Mother and, even more, the baby form, all belly and head. The architecture was the most significant symptom of this daring though unconscious psychological strategy. The strategy, however, is confirmed with emphasis by the Jesuits' radical modification of the angular, syllogistic argumentation of Thomism in favor of their own construct (Francisco Suarez, 1548–1617) which was far more ingenious, flexible, and indeed modern.

For example, Grotius, the founder of international law, had a high appreciation for Suarez' work. Suarez is preparing for a world where men will have to learn to live together, sin and die with some sort of moral agreement. The prose style is therefore also urbane and florid. This pleader would rather win over by oratorical charm than by the force of clinchingly hard argument. Again, instead of a polemic aimed at confounding opponents, making rivals surrender, and presenting a clear case for the destruction of the obdurate, we have psychological insight, or rather flair, which is directed toward making of its listeners children who are willing to be guided and who need to be given security and rightful pleasures.

But the question, "Who guards the guardian?" has as its complement "Who teaches the teacher?" The Jesuits honestly wished to save man from humanic total individualism by restoring him to infantic innocency. But (1) they had nothing but the outer methods that used symbols and patterns, with which to reduce the contractive pressure of intensifying self-consciousness; their exercises were fear-compellers, not soothers. (2) They had no method for assuaging their own intensifying individualism. Power inflames the desire to dominate; fear precipitates the desire to be secure. Ambition and, next and more pathetic, the love of money made the Church authorities, and indeed the Order itself, anxious and scandalized. Anxiety and shame, however, cannot stop a subconscious passion (repressed fear and a longing for security) from working itself out.

The counterreformation ended in being no more than a counterattack. It had delayed, and perhaps rightly in its aims though often wrongly in its means, the too rapid emergence of total self-consciousness. It had tried to give mankind contemporary psychological exercises as part of a total modern education for the new type, humanic man. But the exercises were based on fear and they were also imagist.[f]

Humanism, therefore, went on into secular humanitarianism. This, we have seen, was the second means—if not method—whereby modern man postponed the oncoming total individualism. Even David Hume did not believe in his own rationalistic egotism:

[f] The Jesuits ruined Molinos and the Quietists, who rejected images, any visualistic or auditory aid, and any use of the surface will with its danger of producing Baudoin's psychological "law of reversed effort."

"There is no reason why I should prefer the pricking of my finger to the death of a hundred people." And the fine society of the second part of the eighteenth century prided itself more on its sensibility than even on its good sense or its reasonableness and rationality. Yet, as noted above, this sensibility was, to the very men who could not help their growing sensitiveness, wholly groundless. They were convinced, in their minds, that their hearts were irrational and mistaken; though these seats of emotion made them act with pity and give rights to the poor. For example, the French Revolution was started by the sensibility of the intelligent well to do who were inspired and urged on by Rousseau. But after a reign of terror in which (as in Russia later) nearly all the reformers executed each other or had to fly for their lives, it ended with an autocracy which, in turn, ended with a reaction to the ancient regime. And so France entered on an oscillation of reform (for example, Louis Phillipe, the citizen king) and reaction (the Second Empire) down to the almost autocratic government of today.

In brief, the promise and disappointment of humanism illustrates humanic man's predicament. Humanitarianism was a symptom that humanism was losing faith in its individualistic rationalism. The appearance of sensibility indicated that good sense had proved to be psychologically inadequate. For individualistic man to feel humane is a frustrant sensation, for it has no reason to guide its gush. Indeed it appears to be utterly irrational, contrary to the truth of things, a flying in the face of the facts, as unnatural as a society for multiplying malarial mosquitoes. Hence, humanitarianism becomes sentimentality, the autosensualism of the soul, the enjoyment of feeling for itself, and by oneself. Thus, the cruelest tyrants of the Modern Age have marshaled their forces in the name of sensibility, caring for the mistreated and suffering, championing the underdog. And note the description of this: "For whom one's heart bleeds" (metaphorically), "the flesh of one's opponents shall bleed" (actually and plentifully). The humanitarian pities a creature that has failed. But the creature is a crushed cur which, at heart, he despises. For when he pities without understanding and therefore without any hope that this thing of the gutter could become a colleague, the humanitarian can feel only contempt for this animal that he is going to tame and parasitize. Humanitarianism sends out missionaries who insist on turning natives into their own guilt-ridden, God-fearing, costume-shrouded, inhibited selves.

Thus humanism has ended in a despotism that will employ any outrage, not only on the body but on the mind of those men who, by questioning its methods and enquiring about its ends, dare to show that they have a right to be colleagues and an inability to become slaves.

A suppressed rage was felt by the poor as their lot grew worse. Take as an example (even a fairly favorable area) eighteenth-century England and the driving of the people from the countryside into the cities by the enclosures of the common lands. This indignation was sublimated by Wesley through the catharsis of a conversionism that was not, in basic nature, different from the technique of Ignatius (whom Wesley studied) (18). Rage turned to guilt; and guilt that was balanced, if not quashed, by redemption from Hell to Heaven relieved the social pressure here on earth. In this later case, however, the technique worked only on the uneducated classes: those persons who could upset but not lead society. And it left unaffected that class on which Ignatius had drawn, those who could be patterns of aristocratic prestige and leadership. The conversional procedure was also convulsional. It was not gradual, still less pertinacious. It was an attempt to reduce a dislocation, not to initiate the growth of a new faculty and type. As William James (47) pointed out in his classic study, *The Varieties of Religious Experience,* though it was rapid it was frequently only temporary. But it did permit time to be gained while the laboring classes educated themselves for gradualist reform and while the growing sensibility of the governing class permitted them to offer themselves and be accepted as leaders of such melioration.[g] The rising standard of life, the spreading distribution of the benefits of large-scale production, the exploitation of non-European areas and peoples, together with humanitarianism at home and some abroad, tended to make utopianism a distraction from the growing con-

[g] For example, the Earl of Shaftesbury.

tractive pressure in the psyche. Hence, economics dominated Western thought, from the ending of the political revolutionary phase in the Napoleonic fiasco to the rise of the psychological revolutionary phase which, we have already seen, begins to be visible in the last quarter of the last century.

Then when sensibility and revolution, humanitarianism and class war come into manifest opposition, enquiring minds perceived that here must lie a profound psychological conflict, a conflict that was repressed by the religious and disregarded by the secular. People began to doubt the possibility of attaining individual happiness in a highly bureaucratized state, a state that was necessary to give the economic security demanded by the individual who has become self-consciously self-conscious. For it is clear that the individual demands two incompatible things: security and liberty. Because he *is* an individual he feels insecure and demands protection. But equally because of his individualism he desires to be free. His state of mind makes him simultaneously an agoraphobiac, fearing to be exposed and alone, and a claustrophobiac, fearing imprisonment and restriction.

Meanwhile, to precipitate the crisis of psychological contraction there came also, and inevitably, the contraction of loyalty. At one time, in the Hellenic Roman Empire and the Chinese Empires, men had known a real veneration for an organized political-cultural power that was coterminous with civilization, and had felt a warm loyalty to their city or district where the range of the senses was the focus of the affections. In Europe, during the nineteenth century, Western man's loyalties became chaotic. Nationalism, which now became the substitute for religion was not only a secession from civilization and traditional morality. It was also itself hopelessly unstable. Alternately, it desired to expand into a world empire or to shrink to a xenophobic group that would exclude all those who did not find native the local dialect. Men so distressed—their retreat to an earlier state was cut off, the counterreformation had failed, and their hopes in humanitarian sensibility had been defeated— men in such distress hence sought psychological aid.

It was clear that they were under increasing stress and therefore the obvious therapy would be to detension them. At the end of the seventeenth century, when the diet of the well to do improved and better coaches and roads meant less of the hard exercise of riding and walking, men swelled with overfeeding and under-exertion. Blood pressures mounted and apoplectic strokes became about as common for the rich as heart attacks are for the executive of today. Bleeding, which for long was fancied by the physicians as being almost a panacea, certainly relieved vascular high tension temporarily. In much the same way, psychiatry today gives temporary emotional relief and can "cleanse the stuffed bosom of that perilous stuff that weighs upon the heart." And the success of the method seems to be just as fleeting. Digestive trouble cannot be permanently cured by emptying the stomach every time indigestion is felt. The cure will end in death—by starvation. A more apt simile is that of birth. The task of the obstetrician is not to abort, to terminate a pregnancy as soon as the potential mother shows signs of an inconvenience, but to make possible a full delivery without damage or dangerous distress.

So it is with man today as his humanic phase ends and his hyperindividualist epoch begins to give rise and birth to the next condition of consciousness. He has tried reaction: skilled retreat to an infancy where he will be provided for and guarded. He has also tried humanitarianism—which ends too in the creche state; but of civil instead of ecclesiastical provision and guardianism. This means that the state becomes his guardian and provider, replacing the church. Thirdly, and finally, he has attempted a psychic abortion by means of a therapy of retreat, which could only bring about a miscarriage of the evolutionary process. Dr. William Sheldon once called an old-fashioned psychoanalytic processing "animectomy," an extraction of the soul. It might be more exact to call it de-foetation, the constant reduction of passionate experience to point-less pleasure that leaves life, it is true, without urgency but also without aim. We must therefore conclude this historical sketch of man's psychological story by bringing it down to the present day and its fifth epoch.

5 The postindividual
[Leptoid man]

Up till now we have been dealing with four distinctive epochs of mankind. And not only have these ages been recognized by historians as being successive sections of man's social development; the directive force shaping them can now be seen as being due to changes in human consciousness. First, it is now clear that before historic record, but well illustrated by superb pictures, there was a culture that was preindividualistic and to some extent coconscious[a] because it was under a comprehensive suggestion by imposed interpretation and rule. And even today there are fragmentary societies which (as in Australia and Papua) still seem to preserve much of the same cohesion and precritical amalgamation of psychological value and economic profit. Secondly, there is the Heroic Age, which helped to destroy the preindividual condition and which is itself only protoindividual; only crudely critical of the old order; child-

[a] To what degree there must always be considerable latitude in our judgments.

ishly ignorant of its own weakness and faults; boastful, displayful, and un-self-conscious in any sense of objective awareness. It did not understand, it simply reacted. Thirdly, this second stage is succeeded by one of self-questioning and criticism that produces a desire for self-improvement, self-discipline, and finally self-reduction. Then, with struggle, this ascetic, midindividualistic condition passes into the fourth stage when individualism attains totality. At first, man's self-consciousness made him criticize only the tradition-bound group. Then it made him criticize himself. And now, in his complete self-confidence, he no longer sees any need either for boast and shame or for guilt and gratitude. He sees himself as neither condemning nor approving, as being the flawless mirror of the world that is as orderly (and so as repetitively aimless) as he is rational and inventively comprehending.

These four phases have therefore given rise to four distinctive types: (1) the nonpersonal group constituent, (2) the hero, (3) the ascetic and (4) the humanic. And that, until the beginning of this century, seemed to be the culminant end of the story. At last, man had become a critically minded individual who attained complete objectivity. He saw the environment and it was reality finally perceived with no shadow of illusion on it. He was completely detached from it. It was totally mechanical and he could handle it as he wished. He was self-sufficient.

Of course, as was mentioned at the end of the last chapter,[b] men very quickly discovered that this was wishful thinking. For from both ends came disquieting doubts. Advanced physics denied that objectivity had been attained or could be attained. Depth analysis in psychiatry showed that the findings of psychophysiology had been right. There was no reason to suppose that man could apprehend reality. His senses were biologically confined instruments of apprehension for finding food and a mate, for learning to avoid damaging physical contacts, and for finding those contacts that served his greatest drive—to survive physically. And there was much evidence to show that he had little or no desire to find anything else. What he called reality was a sensory construct that he wished

[b] See also Appendix A.

to contact not for the sake of truth but for physical and racial satisfactions. Hence, after these facts had had the necessary generation-of-digestion time, the distress became psychologically acute. That the instrument was inadequate to comprehend an outer world that was really a construct and that was made out of unknown data handled so as to meet the requirements of projected needs, symbols, and imagery—this alone was upsetting. The inadequacy of reason to control the deep demand-making nature was even more awkward.

The protopsychoanalyst thought only of reducing conflict, allaying disturbance, and restoring to man his thwarted nature: thus to let him be, at least in erotic expression, an uninhibited animal in the hope that this would detension him. But this was really as mistaken as and failed even sooner than the Ignatian effort to restore the climate of dogmatic, persecutory faith and make men other-worldly ascetics. Still, this primary and primitive psychiatry of Freud did serve, as we have seen that the Ignatian system had served, to modulate this new crisis. It would not have been possible for a mechanistically minded medical profession, in spite of their failure to deal with mental trouble, to have accepted psychotherapy unless that therapy was presented as being, at base, not too great a departure from medicine's current assumptions. Freud accepted, with a devout and highly reassuring belief, the axioms of Darwinian evolution that man was a beast that had risen to intelligence by a combination of lucky breaks and ruthlessly cunning exploitations of those opportunities. By agreeing with these postulates he was able to do something to reduce the pressure on the psyche. At least he saw that rational individualism could be no goal for man with his many-layered consciousness. And so he advocated the search for freedom, even though he thought that that liberty could only be license, atavistic behavior at the cost of the social restraints of a civilized society.

The idea, then, that self-conscious individualism is the end of the evolutionary process and that through this self-consciousness, at last, we attain to objective control of our environment and can direct our destiny, came to be doubted increasingly. And along with that idea, the popular notion of progress also fell into disrepute. Two world wars for establishing peace; an anachronistic economic revolution that spread not among artisans but among peasants and that in the name of human freedom removed the individual's rights, setting up ruthless tyrannies—such major events of this century convinced even the hurrying man in the streets that individualism was defeated and done for. Forecasting essays and utopianist science fiction saw man as a potential termite. Samuel Butler's neglected nineteenth-century *Erewhon*[c] became, to many mid-World-War-I forecasters, a prophecy to be heeded. And there were some psychiatrists who had troubled to inform themselves about modern anthropology and modern evolutionary theory. These men knew, therefore, that such works as Freud's *Totem and Tabu* were out of date because Freud had depended, for his anthropological conclusions, on Sir James Frazer's out-of-date *The Golden Bough*. And these men felt not only that individualism was passing but that it must now be brought to an end.

To cite one example, as late as 1955: The late Douglas M. Kelley, Professor of Criminology (the existence of such a chair is suggestive) and who was the psychiatrist chosen for the Nazi trials at Nuremberg, told the Texas Medical Association at Fort Worth that Freudianism, in order to save a child from the psyche scarring of a strict (he meant castigatory) discipline, had let it grow up without self-control. Thus, immature childhood behavior has been carried on into later years by the young who are so left untrained. In adults infantile conduct is psychopathic and destructive. The nor-adrenaline energy that projects all the infant's frustrations in rage, and must do so at that level if it is to survive and emerge into self-consciousness, has not given way (at the dawn of self-consciousness) to the adrenaline that turns the child's anger back onto itself. Hence the increase of crime and juvenile delinquency. Kelley had hoped to find a middle ground. He owned that if we use more punishment on the young we shall only produce more neurotics. That, he held, is the price of the safety of the state which, as the

[c] *Erewhon* is *nowhere* spelled backward. Butler took the idea from Thomas More, who had coined a word from the Greek, Utopia, which meant nowhere.

Roman legalist put it, is the supreme law. Kelley also warned that at present we have no clear line of action, no training rule; we have no way of knowing the exact amount of pain that will produce least neurosis and most obedience. However, he still does not make it clear that while punishment may produce only a servile neurosis in the docile and malleable, it can turn the vital into those "heroically" all too attractive rebels who create gangs, build up "parties," and become dictators. Faced with the problem of the individual and the community, Kelley could only see them and their rights in constant conflict. In short, the socio-historical outlook of this able psychopathologist, whose main study has been the criminal, is still that of the poetic British Educationalist, Mathew Arnold, and his equally eminent contemporary, the eloquent biologist, T. H. Huxley. "Mad man or slave, must man be one?" cried Arnold. "Defy the cosmic process," was Huxley's antiphonal answer.

However, this dilemma, like most of these either-or impaling horns, has proved to have a way between its two deadly choices. "The mind of the Universe can count above two" used to be a cheerful warning of the still open-minded H. G. Wells when people gave way to premature and immature despair over this stalemate of either-or. And we can, with more precision, now trace this middle path.

First of all, ecology has shown us that the relationship between the life of the individual and the field in which he lives is more of a reciprocity than a competition. Secondly, it has been found that much of what was thought to be parasitism is, in fact, commensalism (lives living at and contributing to a common table) and symbiosis (two or more organisms forming a joint organism of the highest value to its constituents). Such facts show that even at animal level there can be a cooperation that does not sacrifice the constituent to the group. Thirdly, we can now see that the idea that man's society, in aiming at efficiency, must turn into a human termitary is a complete misapprehension.

The social insects differ diametrically from man. Termitary, anthill, and beehive all derive their completely specialized workers by atrophy; and in almost every case from atrophied females. Thus, by a reverse process, the insects have built up a society completely instinct-bound and thus incapable of enterprise, invention, or even change.[d]

All this is completely alien from human history and especially from man's present pass. The new concept of human evolution shows that man's structure is that of a creature of unique sensitiveness. Not only does he have a physique that is the reverse of that of the social insects—they have a hard outer husk (exoskeleton); man has an inner skeleton on which sensitive flesh and skin are stretched, a highly impressionable form that he shares with almost all the noninsect forms of life. But in this direction he goes quite the farthest. Lacking scales, as do nearly all mammals, man disposes also of hair. He is born and remains mainly naked.

This leads to the new psychophysical concept of the process of man's evolution. Not only is he not a callous creature, a pachyderm, a creature that is insensitive because of the thickness of its hide; man's particular advance is precisely coordinate with and made possible by his becoming increasingly sensitive. And this sensitiveness is made possible and achieved by the force within him taking an increasing risk in unprotectedness—the risk of prolonging the period of helplessness so as to extend the age of teachability. All mammals are "fetalizings" of the reptilian form. That is, they carry on out into the afterbirth state an unspecialized, uncommitted structure that is abandoned by the reptile at hatching. This is possible because the mammal is specifically the creature which, because it takes care of its young after birth, can give it, in its fetal helplessness, the extrauterine protection without which it must perish. And, in turn but far more strikingly, man is the fetalization of the mammal. Yes, as Louis Bolk pointed out, man is the fetalization, even, of his primate cousin next below him on the ladder of life, the ape. The mammals gave to life the extended possibility of learning and of freedom that a comparatively lengthy and protected infancy can bestow. That power and desire to protect the helpless young and to extend the period of their irresponsible

[d] It would seem from fossil evidence that the social insects' patterns may not have altered since at least the Oligocene.

curiosity and learning has been extended even further by man. To man-the-mammal's capacity for the specific stage of infancy has been added man-the-human's endowment of specific childhood, an enormous enlargement of the time and area of education, the stage of paidomorphy.[e]

Such, we now know, is the biological history of man. He is master of the world because he knows more, understands better, and acts more purposively than any other beast. They are all better armed. He has won because he is better informed. And he knows more precisely because he has been cared for more, protected better, given greater freedom, and a longer span of time in which to learn. His group, far from enslaving him and atrophying him, loves him and is proud of his initiative. It encourages his adventures and departures. And it wishes to leave him at large, at least as long as he remains a child—even if at adolescence he is put into harness.

However, although these facts may be allowed (for they cannot be denied in the face of the evidence), they have yet to convince almost all statesmen and, as we have seen, the influential majority of psychiatrists and sociologists to whom the statesman increasingly defers. They are influenced not by biological history but by the brief individualistic phases of history—written history—the crises of Heroic, Ascetic, and Humanic epochs when, during each of which, individualism is steadily diminishing suggestibility; during each of which governmental control is becoming increasingly difficult and thus increasingly coercive. Therefore, it is in this partial picture of man (man-the-rebel, man-the-deserter, man-the-cold-cynical-exploiter) that most historians and sociologists have thought there is to be found the realistic analysis of the human being. They have assumed that this is the true description of humanity, given by itself of itself through its catalogue of its actual behavior, its violent acts, and its dishonest boasts. Most of them would still say that man alternates between revolt into anarchy (against an order that has become a tyranny) and a reaction from that anarchy back into the rigid peace of despotism. The totali-

[e] See also Cope's *Law of the Elimination of the Specialised.*

tarian state or the *librum veto* of the individual, the loathing of oppression and the horror of chaos—these are the poles between which mankind has oscillated since he became individualized and yet remained incapable of asocial living. And the sophisticated humanic man has given us a world that is no more secure or noble than the world that was given by the rule of either tyrant or inquisitor.

We have seen, however, that history is not such a pointless and weary shuttle. It is a spiral. In the first age of self-expression (the heroic, protoindividual) the very contraction of the focus of consciousness that made the hero revolt against the preindividual groups leads in turn to criticism not of society but of the self. Still further contraction of consciousness leads again to criticism of the ascetic, self-criticizing society. Now, without the shame-fear of the protoindividual or the guilt-fear of the midindividual, man's totally individualized consciousness can consider, with dispassionate detachment, both its record and its origins. Hence, humanism, the capacity to choose eclectically and combine styles to suit a widely tolerant taste, is followed by humanitarianism, the interest in human beings regardless of the type to which they may belong. So extensive was this enquiry that humanic man was able, first, to conceive of his animal origin and kinship and, next, recognizing his unique extension up from and beyond any animal condition, he was able to see that *he* was unique. And thirdly, he was able to perceive that the power by which that uniqueness was achieved lay and lies in a continual extension, first of infancy and then of childhood.

We have seen, further, that the final contraction of consciousness, which produced the total individual striving as never before for objectivity, leads to the knowledge of his own temporarily repressed and concealed nonindividual nature.

When man first conceived of himself as being biologically an animal, evolutionary doctrine held that he must have survived by violence and cunning. But now it has switched to the point of view that man survives, is supreme, and advances because he is, by his prolonged infancy and childhood, preserved in his unprecedented sensitiveness and awareness. And so it has been with psychiatry.

Psychiatrists, too, began by thinking that the deep, submerged consciousness was merely a subconscious, a residue of frustrated revenges and brooding revolts. In turn, psychiatry today has found that there is also a superconscious of unspent creativity awaiting release. Man's energies, as we shall see in Part II, Chapters 1 and 2, are *pure* energies. That is, they are neutral. Given release they bud; met with repression the bud turns into a thorn.

We can see, then, the vast hope and acute risk with which man today is confronted. We are the first generation of self-conscious mankind to become conscious of the nonself-conscious. And we can see that totalistic individualism is finished. The huge cycle that extended from the rise of the protoindividual, out of the preindividualistic group, to the total individual, has now completed that loop of the spiral. We are in the postindividual age and world.

What does this mean? First, it means the end of the apparent conflict between the rights of the constituent and the survival of the group. We are symbiots, linked by our common preterconscious. Secondly, it means that we can understand and command creativity through the amalgamation of integral thought (see Glossary) with analytical thought. Thirdly, it means that our interactions with our fellows need no longer be based on violence and competition but on cooperation. For all fear sterilizes creative thought, and inspiration is possible and only possible when there is mutual understanding and appreciation.

That is not to say, however, that this fifth stage of man is easy. This age has come upon us swiftly, and it is also demanding of us a step greater than the one from the heroic to the ascetic, or from the ascetic to the humanic. For these steps called only for an increase in individual self-consciousness, an intensification of self-awareness. Our age has to surrender its isolation and experience a vast dilation. For some four thousand years man has been learning to live increasingly and more powerfully in himself. Now the process must go onto the other tack of the spiral. The huge impersonal nonindividual force that he has sighted, lying back of him and out of which he emerges like a lonely crystallization of the great flux, he now finds mounting up in him from time to time, and momentarily reintegrating him with himself. Suddenness characterizes this experience and it is revolutionary, mutational. Therefore, the term *leptoid* (suggested by the Greek word *lepsis,* which means the leap) has been chosen to describe or at least to distinguish it.

Man, in his first age, when his coconscious society lost its capacity to assimilate new data, became imprisoned and buried in the tribal system. He became arrested at a puerile level.[f] In his second stage of protoindividual protest he became paranoid when utterly frustrated. In his third stage, of midindividual self-disgust, his mental danger was schizophrenia. In his fourth stage of total individualism his mental risk was manic depressive insanity.

But surely in this his fifth stage which man has now reached, the specific symptom of collapse would be that failure of nerve, that sense of being at his tether's end, that melancholy out of which he cries "*vanitas vanitatum.*" This has been the indicative terminative disease of earlier societies and civilizations. The West's only attempt at a culture that was coterminous with an administrative civilization, the Hellenic Roman, did sink into such a decline. Its failure of nerve was shown not only in corruption of its administration, increasing inadequacy of its economy and weakness of its political integration, but also in a degeneracy of its crafts, sciences, and arts. Senile paralysis was evident long before the barbarians took over. But with our age this certainly is not so. The age of humanic man has passed and his picture of a world united by men of good sense and bright reason certainly seems, at best, pathetically premature. But although our confusions are terrific they are not those of liquidation and decay, but rather of explosion and overabundance. Earlier civilizations were daunted by scarcity; we are embarrassed by surfeit. The anarchy of nationalism and the immorality and inhumanity of fanatic ideologies would seem to be enough to make the creative mind withdraw and abstain. But as a matter of fact, applied research and pure research, experiment, exploration, discovery, and invention have never, in the world's

[f] W. R. Thompson and Ronald Melzack (85) discuss the permanent immaturity of dogs that have been sheltered in total isolation for their first seven to ten months.

best times of the past or under humanism's most generous patronage, approached the present pitch. The cultures of the past died
of a spiritual pernicious anemia. The peril of the present is a risk of
death by convulsions. The specific crisis of this fifth epoch of man,
postindividual humanity, is caused by the release of power that is
too great to be handled by a frame of meaning and application
that was devised to be run by, to express, and to deploy far smaller
resources.

We can see this in four areas. Economically, we are aware of
the problem as we pass from an economy of scarcity, wherein saving was a primary need, to one of plenty when spending power
must prevent glut (62). Politically, we are aroused by the fact that
speed of communications and range of striking power have made
frontiers more absurd than walled cities and have made defense
an impossibility. And our emotions, made only more suspicious by
this involuntary impaction, still cling to our fatally anachronistic
limits, from which foci we would exercise sovran (that is to say,
anarchic) power. Religiously, the power of insight into other systems of devotion alien from ours has weakened our assurance of
our own rightness. Psychologically, as we discover our other levels
of consciousness, the importance that we have attached to our personality grows less. And all these erosions of our convictions are
because of our knowledge, and power derived from that knowledge,
which continues to advance like a tide, flooding the locks, sluices,
and harbors of our old beliefs.

Ours is assuredly a world not of tired melancholy but of almost
frantic stimulation; in a word, a leptoid age. And we are aware
of our precarious disbalance: of our persistent and ever-increasing
production of power and our inadequacy of purpose; of our critical
analytic ability and our creative paucity; of our triumphantly efficient technical education and our ineffective, irrelevant education
for values, for meaning, for the training of the will, the lifting of
the heart, and the illumination of the mind; of the boredom that
haunts our extending leisure and the futility of our recreation. No
wonder we have at least one in ten who is in acute mental distress.
No wonder that there is hardly one of us out of a thousand who is

able to diagnose the situation in contemporary terms, still less who is able to propose an education, a training, a psychophysical praxis whereby we may become adequate to handle our powers; whereby we may be able to release ourselves in creative action and be capable of making those field associations with others that will allow us to explicate the evolutionary pressures that today may otherwise drive us toward racial destruction.

Such then, in the briefest possible terms, would seem to be the outline of man's history as a psychologically driven creature; that is to say, as a unique animal which, because he has (instead of instincts) an unequaled teachability, develops first by a social heredity: a coordinate series of developing reactions, which are satisfying, at least economically, to the constituent and the group. When that system has hardened and man has broken out of it, he proceeds to educate himself, first by exploring the outer world and testing the old assumptions by new personal experiences. Next, by questioning himself and testing his own limits. Later he attempts a two-sided exploration, trying to gain a complete objectivity toward the external and the internal worlds, toward the seen universe and toward himself as its seer. This the humanic education, critical and analytic in its method, leads man to learn that objectivity is impossible because it is a misapprehension of himself and of the universe. Man, therefore, attains a new clarity of vision in regard to his problem of education. Recognizing self-consciously his nonself-conscious, he realizes why till now the individual has been able to gain physical power but not to alter his character and consciousness. Henceforward, he may hope to do even this and so, having become conscious himself of his station and purpose, take part, by his self-education, in the evolutionary process that has produced him.

II

THE PERSONAL
PSYCHOLOGICAL STORY
OF MAN

[The five ordeals]

1

The ordeal of birth and infancy
and its specific mental breakdown
[The trauma of birth]

In Part I we have attempted to show that the human story is one of progress, of man's advance; that there is unmistakable evidence that man has risen to his supremacy through his capacity to remain sensitive and so teachable; that he can be developmentally changed because he remains, for so long, an impressionable child; and that this evidence is not canceled out by his historic behavior. Man has advanced by understanding, by his increasing capacity for being taught, and that advance has been in a spiral. When, at the close of the first culture (the preindividual epoch), the interpretations and explanations that had once faced and fitted all of the known facts grew too rigid to allow the acceptance of any new data, man was bound to break out, to shatter the suffocating husk of tradition, and explore the outer world. And this reaction, when it became excessive, provoked the complementary counterreaction. Man tried to reimpose order on the new data that he was now confronting.

Chief among these new facts, he discovered himself to be confronting a lawful, powerful, but apparently unfriendly Nature on the outside and strange irrational passions within himself. This new self-conscious knowledge in turn led to a further self-conscious examination of Nature. Finally, this objective-subjective dualism (wherein power increases but self-control decreases) is transcended by insight into the whole problem of the seer and the seen.

Henceforward, man may hope to gain a knowledge of his *total* nature and by doing so achieve a total education. This, as we have said, will mean that evolution is continued consciously by a creature made conscious in order that the process may now be intentionally explicated.

But if this is so, if such a further development is to be possible, then the contemporary individual must now be a creature such as can be capable of this conscious educational-athletic training. For the vast processes of life may miscarry; the greatness of a promise does not guarantee its fulfillment. And even if the process that has brought man so far, and built his endowment so firmly into his nature, is not to be frustrated it may be postponed. In the past, great insights that seemed about to dawn over all mankind were not accepted at once. The seed that appeared to be due to sprout immediately lay dormant through century-long winters of brutal stupidity. For example, there was the failure of the Hellenic Roman world to understand the mathematics of Archimedes (this was not to be grasped until the nineteenth century) and the centuries-long delay of the Chinese in accepting the Confucian teaching.

But is there any evidence that man today, the present personal self, is a creature who is equal to this opportunity; that he is a being of material that is adequate to be fashioned by the training that is now due and possible? The tempering processes that turn iron into steel cannot turn clay into knives; nor can the best teaching make a mandrill into a mathematician. There must be a substance suitable for the intended shape.

It is the discovery that the individual today is not only prepared for such a training but that without such a training he must go to pieces—and indeed *is* going to pieces—that gives such strong confirmation to the psychological interpretation of history. It may be said that all our history is vitiated by selection. Indeed, it is often adduced as being a reason for maintaining that human history shows no pattern or process. Most historians believe that we do not and cannot accurately survey the true human record since (1) all that has survived of the past are the fragments that a few exceptional persons chose, for their own reasons, to record; and (2) these fragments are further selected and distorted by our attempts to interpret them, not even in terms of the meaning that they may have held for those who recorded them, but in terms of the particular meaning that we who study them wish to give them (92).

Much the same argument was used against those who, in the mid-nineteenth century, were trying to establish the fact of physical evolution. The record, it was maintained, was so piecemeal that the linkages it suggested could be dismissed as being hopeful leaps. Then the connection between phylogeny and ontogeny was detected. The fact that the individual fetus can be seen to recapitulate the life of the vertebrate phylum—the evolution of the back-boned animals—made embryology a vital adjunct of paleontology. The fossil record of the phylum's history (phylogeny) could be confirmed and elucidated by actual physiological study of the individual embryo's development: that is, by ontogeny. Of necessity, however, this dealt only with the physical development. Although, as we shall see later, the child's growth in the womb is not merely recapitulatory; it is prophetic. During the fetal months in the womb the brain of the embryo is much larger, in proportion to the rest of the physique, than it ever is after birth. This would seem to indicate that the human brain has yet to reach its full development.

However, what is of immediate and decisive importance, in helping us to decide whether or not human history is a rapid extension of evolution and whether or not it shows evidence of evolution and advance by social heredity, is the application of the physiological discovery of the correlation between the life of the race and the growth of the fetus. For this lends psychological insight into human progress.

G. Stanley Hall and Arnold Gesell, Cyril Burt in Britain, and a number of child psychologists in other countries have now made it sufficiently clear that just as our physiological evolution is sketched out in our fetal development, in our growth up to birth, so does the infant, after birth, recapitulate the coconscious, preindividual age of mankind (see Introduction). In some thirty months it relives that whole stage of man's development which, although it lasted some four hundred thousand years, was nevertheless a vast acceleration over the speed of the evolutionary process by which man emerged out of animalhood. This acceleration resulted from social heredity taking the place of physical heredity.

Today, these findings seem to have been largely accepted by child psychologists as being an illuminating insight into child behavior. But unfortunately, owing to the lack of psychologically interpreted history, psychologists in general have not extended this interpretation to the post-infant stages of the individual's life. And, conversely, neither have social historians availed themselves of this master clue for understanding history.

Stanley Hall, Burt, and his fellow discoverers were aware, as are all educated men, that man had gone through a prehistoric phase during which he was neither a group-animal nor a self-conscious individual. These child psychologists, therefore, were able to recognize that this stage of preindividual consciousness was being recapitulated by the infant. As the infant was symbiotic with the mother, so prehistoric man had been symbiotically coconscious with his group. But both the specialty of their study (which was mainly concerned with the vastly important first couple of years) and their unawareness of the growth of protohistoric studies prevented them from seeking in the next stage above infancy—that is, in childhood proper—the child's résumé of the protohistoric (the Heroic Age), which succeeded the prehistoric. Still less could these experts in the growth of the individual child-mind be expected to detect, in the successive stages of personal development, recapitulations of historic man's successive epochs: the Ascetic and the Humanic, the mid-individual and the total individual, as did Gesell.

Nevertheless, once their first correlation was made the succeeding three (and indeed, as we shall see, the fourth) fall into place. The psychological understanding of human history (as being a spiral shift of human consciousness from the coconscious to extreme self-consciousness and so on to a self-consciously coconscious condition) can be greatly clarified and made even more convincing by our being able to trace these shifts in the individual life. And we can then see (*a*) how, by a series of crises, the individual emerges into fuller consciousness until he is completely contemporary (that is, he reaches the present leptoid stage) and (*b*) he is thus ready to be recruited and fashioned into the new type.

The Gesell team (Arnold Gesell, Frances Ilg, and Louise Ames) in 1956 added a new study, *Youth: The Years from Ten to Sixteen* (30), to their first two parent-shaking books, *Infant and Child in the Culture of Today* (31), and *The Child from Five to Ten* (32). This means that the third epoch of the individual's history is now recognized as being a natural growth phase and that sooner or later historians will have to accept this recapitulatory contribution to our understanding of the record of historic and prehistoric man (homo loquens).

In this and the next four chapters, we shall then outline the five stages of birth and infancy, childhood, adolescence, first maturity, and second maurity through which the individual passes; and we shall examine the stresses endured, the damages sustained, the palliatives that are offered, and the levels attained.

That birth is a challenge for a human being has been recognized today. Owing to the exceptional development of the head in man (the mammal with the hypertrophied brain), delivery would, in any case, present difficulties that the smaller brained mammals escape. And today, certainly, the self-consciousness of the mother greatly increases the trouble. Having foresight she dreads pain; and her fear provokes the very contractions that cramp and cause the agony of labor as the voluntary muscles try to hold back the action of the involuntary delivery muscles.[a] Further, the woman, seeking to allure and tame the male by her show of refinement, dreads throwing herself, without inhibition, into the indecent abondonment

[a] See Grantly Dick Read's (69) *Childbirth Without Fear,* and the further developments in France and Russia in these methods.

that is necessary for a powerfully effective delivery. Still further, our elevation of the pleasure-pain principle to the position of being the final criterion of worth misleads the mother. The naturalistic theory, that every organism inevitably seeks comfort and shuns disturbance, makes travail appear to be the most morbid of experiences, something to be avoided with anesthetics, something that cannot be transmuted and transcended.

The child, therefore, experiences a very bad passage and even when it escapes physical damage it is apparently general for most children to show marks of this distressing experience.[b] Nor does the evidence for this rest solely on psychiatrists' deductions from child behavior and the interpretation of hypnotically raised regression memories of experiences that are probably birth emotions. Isaac Shour of the University of Illinois College of Dentistry reported, in the spring of 1937, the discovery of growth rings in human teeth and that such rings show the incidence of glandular disturbances and other illnesses. Outstanding is the ring called the neonatal ring that marks the stress of birth.[c] Many child psychiatrists are inclined to regard this traumatic shock as being one of the main sources of such psychosomatic complaints as asthma. The psychological effect of so severe an introduction to the outer world is, to some degree or other, to provoke and sustain a profound subconscious desire to be able to return to a condition previous to this stress and the terror that it has produced. For this terror, as long as it cannot be raised to consciousness, may remain unresolved and so possess an undiminished power to check initiative and to create fear. The child, therefore, strives not to grow but to return to the womb. As Margaret Ribble (71) has pointed out, the frightened infant, instead of breathing, may actually go back to womb lung reflexes, refusing to fill the

[b] Indeed, Theodore Reich maintains that the trauma of birth is the largest cause of mental trouble in later life. See, also, Nandor Fodor (24), and Otto Rank (68).

[c] See report on meeting of American Association of Anatomists at Toronto in 1937. Shour reported that the rings can be detected under the microscope after the use of a special stain. Every ninety-six hours a ring is added in the human tooth; one every twenty-four hours in those of lower animals.

lung with air and forcing the emptied lung down on the diaphragm. This is the reflex whereby, in the prenatal state, the fetus helped to draw in more oxygenated blood through the umbilical cord, but which now in the postnatal state can only result in suffocation. Dynamic tender loving care; much playing with the infant; the tickling that results in laughter, which increases the sugar in the blood and so feeds the growing brain; the rousing of the baby to react with the exercise, particularly, of its chief member of exploration and understanding, the mouth: all these will bring the child through this crisis. Otherwise it may remain arrested. As Ribble has also pointed out, unless the child is permitted constant sucking-manipulation with its mouth the growth of the muscles round the head, which are brought into play by the exercise of the jaws, may be defective; brain growth may be retarded and, even more easily, too little use of the mouth may lead to defective speech. Then, too, when the child reaches the babbling stage and vocalizes for the sheer love of it, this vast range of sounds must be encouraged and allowed to pour, like a melt of metal, into the casts of specific language. If this tide is not taken there may be permanent retardation.

Birth, therefore, is man's first ordeal. And in this generation we have certainly come to rate highly (indeed, in a way that earlier scientific periods would have thought absurd) the perils and possibilities of this initial test. Yet this high rating has been a faulty one, not because the beginning of life is not of intense importance, but because of the overcompensatory emphasis that has been given to the birth experience and has made us tend to believe that this is the *one* significant ordeal; and that if it were properly handled the rest of the life process would fall into place and flow as an untroubled sequence.

This, however, is not so. For man has to face not one but five ordeals. If we rid the injured child mind of the trauma of birth we shall do it harm, not good, should our intention be no more than to return it to freedom from conflict. Now that we can correlate our individual development with that of the race, we see that there were some societies that managed to adjust to change of environment and the increasing complexity of their culture without intensifying the quality of their consciousness. Such seems to have been the Indus civilization. In a lesser degree this has befallen the Australian and Papuan premechanical cultures.

The task, then, of facing the first ordeal is now seen to be doubly difficult. Today the new-born child emerging from the pre-personal, unseparated life of the womb still feels, under the stress of the alien situation, two conflicting drives. One is to stop this dif-ferentiation by elaborating a web of dependency ties with the mother (if not to behave so recessionally as to reattempt fetal breathing) and re-establish an external womb situation: the situation of the ankylosed tribe whose inflexible tradition can now have no place for enterprise. The other drive is a protest and defiance that regards any thwarting of its impulses as an outrage: the attitude of the protoinvididual hero who regarded the traditional tribe not as a matrix from which to rise but as a prison to be wrecked. Hence, at the beginning of our self-consciousness lies the fissure of man into conservative-reactionary and rebel-revolutionary. Therefore, the task of human education today must start at this base by helping the infant to balance these conflicting drives and to create a compre-hending initiative, an enterprise which, by understanding, renders the traditional cohesion into a liquid asset and interprets it as con-temporary conservation of wholeness.

The growing infant consciousness has to be led along a knife-edge path. As we have seen, laxness may be as fatal as strictness. Quietude can prove to be as dangerous as overstimulation. But, now we know that the child is recapitulating the first human crisis, we can determine the amalgam of encouragement and challenge that it needs to temper its mind and make it capable of agreed initiative, of enterprise blended with communication, of adjustment with originality.

At this stage, when his racial infancy began to pass into the childhood of the race, when the challenge of further intensification of consciousness confronted him, man became divided and began to follow two divergent paths. The reaction of the primary group was to elaborate further and make the social pattern more explicit and more complex. Everyone should have particular parts to play and functions to perform but no one should extemporize or create a solo air. This led to the heroic revolt in which all orchestration of a comprehensive theme was temporarily lost in a bedlam of soloists, each trying to drown out the rest.

Today we can see that the child need not and must not be faced with the choice of madman or slave. But the middle way is even harder. For it leads to an advance into an ever more consciously reciprocal symbiosis with the parents, with the sibs, with the group. And there is no clearer evidence that progress through learning by conducive, tempered challenge is the inherent drive in man than the discovery that, whereas premature exposure to unexplained contradiction can be fatal, conversely the screening and protection from all enigmas and surprises can arrrest the child in an infantile state (85). Even dogs, when they are given a completely contained and sheltered early life, do not emerge into full growth with the scarless curiosity of the puppy. On the contrary, they show suspicion, alarm, and resentment at every unfamiliar object. Most psychologists have reacted against the careless and unkind handling of young things in early life, which leave scars of fear and resentment. Consequently, most of them have assumed that every organism longs for rest and quiet because its entire behavior is directed toward preserving its stability. But as Thompson and Melzack point out, this assumption has proved to be untrue. No creature can live normally or fully if it is not challenged. Without challenge not only will it never grow up, but it will sink to the state of being a febrile alarmist that is capable even of rest only in a completely artificial, non-stimulating environment.

Today, then, the fissure of consciousness that took place historically must be healed in the individual child. He must be shown and directed onto the midpath that combines the enterprise of the hero with the intuitive, traditional wisdom of the tribe. He must leave the womb and exchange the mother love, to which he needed only be receptively passive, for a relationship of an increasing give and take. He can do this, and thus meet the demands of his growing nature, if encouragement is always given with every challenge. For encouragement makes it possible for him to regard failure as being a negative experiment, not frustration: not the closure of an answer but the opening *through* and *of* a new question.

If, however, the birth trauma has been severe then it would seem that only the regressionally recaptured and relived experience can set him free. Experiments in that direction (by hypnosis and other methods of depth analysis) are, we know, being conducted now.[d] Increasingly it is being proposed that no person can be considered to be free of deforming subconscious maladjustment who has suffered damage at that depth and not had the damage remedied and canceled by its having been raised to consciousness. No doubt this would prove to be valuably ameliorative.

Nevertheless, we must remember that the undertaking is both more worthwhile and also more difficult than psycholonalysis has, up to the present, conceived. For we are no longer able to think of such treatment as being solely to aid the patient to adjust to and consent to society. He must be prepared to contribute a skilled release to an inherent nature that insists on growing. And this nature insists on growing in a way that not only combines the art of communication with the passion for exploration (and so remedies our social birth trauma that still tries to make us choose between being a rebel-hero or a submissive ascetic) but also, by its growth, leads him as a person toward a new threshold with its new challenge: the offer to become a new type of character.

In the third part of this book we shall see how thorough such a rebirth procedure has been. And in the Epilogue some suggestions will be made as to how such a procedure might be applied today. Meanwhile, one hopeful fact may be noted before we pass on to Chapter 2 of this second part. Apparently, psychologically speaking, it is never too late to mend. In the physical growth of the fetus in the womb, a failure to advance, a delayed or deviant step in the growth process cannot be remedied. Stockhard has pointed out that ten minutes' chilling of an embryo results, generally, in an irremediable malformation. This does not seem to be so with psychological

[d] At the present time, according to L. M. Wolberg (98), *Medical Hypnosis*, Vol. 1, the consensus is that regression actually does produce early behavior in a way that obviates all possibility of simulation.

growth. It is possible to penetrate down into the depths, thence to regress the consciousness to where the blockage took place and so, reliving the event and making the sunken consciousness loose its paralyzing grip on the evil memory, start the total person anew.

But, we must repeat, that totality of consciousness cannot be won by only one delivery-experience, from the trauma of birth. There are four others. And the procedures whereby this fivefold freedom is won and crowned by the fifth and culminant freedom are more profound and transforming than, at present, even our most extensive psychotherapies envisage.

2

The ordeal of childhood and
its specific mental breakdown
[Dementia praecox becoming paranoia]

We now reach the second stage of the personal psychological story of man. The individual has recapitulated man's first crisis. For better or for worse, the process has gone through its primary stage. Since growth, the manifestation of the life process, waits for no man, all men must become increasingly implicated or increasingly explicated. Mankind has not yet lived well but he might have lived worse. He has certainly lived better than any other animal. None of his forms has degenerated into beasthood. And only a small minority of humans have chosen a life wherein tradition is rigid and initiative is practically impossible, such as the Australian Aborigines whose tribal law has swallowed enterprise.

The Heroic Age was wasteful and overexuberant but it was not valueless in itself. Its epic art forms were unique and of high quality. For in them the hero was constantly asking, with passionate emphasis, this question: "Why is the courage of the heroic will not enough?" Through its expression of energy and initiative it gave drive to the ages that were to succeed it. The individual, then, as he leaves infancy (mother and child symbiosis) and enters childhood proper, is generally viable, albeit considerably distorted, thwarted, resentful, and unhappy. Though, like the leaning tower of Pisa, he is out of plumb because of poorly laid foundations, the subsidence is not so severe that he cannnot, in most cases and by some compensatory if costly adjustment, be prevented from collapsing. Nevertheless, far too often total ruin does take place; and even where it does not, flaws, faultings, and cleavages continue to cause stresses which may, if not at this stage, later provoke disaster. The specific child has won to the station of its age group, to the elevation that permits the growing mind to confront a far wider purview than the strictly mediated environment of the nursery.

But here we need to ask, "How is this done?" The view of most embryologists and paleoanthropologists does not allow any firmly based hope about this further venture of man, once he takes leave of his station as an animal. The common summary that closes any thorough account of the fetus' life in the womb is that at birth we took leave of (or were abandoned by) the marvelous and inherent mastery which, up to that point, had directed and shaped our amazing development. Maybe a few modern pediatricians would allow a small extension of that happy and deft intuitiveness after birth, for that dozen or score of months during which a perfect mother relationship can give the infant an enlargement of the womb's protective response to its growing demands and to which it can instinctively respond and grow. Thereafter, we are humans. We are now creatures who have abandoned intuitive understanding, spontaneous interior knowledge, for vocal communication (that conveys symbolic information) and for tentative exploration of an outer world. From thence on man's social heredity has carried and will carry him on a warp of tradition into which the painful shuttle of experience will be continually thrusting threads of new knowledge across the web.

In his "Fossil Man and Human Evolution," Loren Eiseley (21), Professor of Anthropology at the University of Pennsylvania, has pointed out—and he is quoting the long accepted judgement of Leonard Sillman—that "no other species comes into the world with so few fixed reactions for survival, knowing less, inherently, about how to maintain itself" as does man. It is this new brain (denuded of precise, instinctive responses, growing in a curious, mighty spurt during the first few months after birth) that has created man and set him off from his nearest relative.

The factor that was overlooked by Charles Darwin and his critic and codiscoverer of natural selection, A. R. Wallace, was the decisive part played by social heredity in the ascent of man. This second invisible environment replaced man's lost instinctive adjustments. Institutions could take the place of instincts because of the ability of all men to use language: the one great socializing instrument.

Such a viewpoint is hopeful. Speed and intention, a rapid progress in intelligence are now considered to be present in the evolutionary process at its growing point, man. But unfortunately this point of view, where it is accepted, is taken to mean that man must expect no help from his nature. Indeed, progress was possible (so runs the argument) solely because man had already been stripped of his instincts. If his prehuman drives remain in him they will bar his ascent and he must fight them, reduce them, nullify them.

Now it is clear that if the word instinct is used with exactitude—that is, as signifying behavior that is not dependent on the individual's past experience nor his interests but which serves the needs of the species—then it is true that man has no such inbuilt patterns of conduct. But he certainly is subject to innate drives to precipitate action, which distort his judgment and overwhelm his reason and which, combined with his intelligence, can make him the most dangerous of animals. These drives are glandular; and that pair of ductless glands whose hormone secretions most disturb understanding and dislocate society is far away from the brain's controls. These twin glands of conflict, of stress, are the suprarenals that drive the animal to self-forgetful rage: useful for the beast, essential for the carnivore (see later), but fatal to one who must survive by taking thought. True, the brain has grown marvelously in its power of thought and of that worldwide vocalized thought, language. But of what use is this if the emotions (the movers to action) are violent, divisive, anarchic? Then intelligence only sharpens the knife with which humanity cuts its own throat.

Suppose that evolution has simply provided us with a brain that can think up new schemes for mastering and upsetting the environment; suppose that evolution has given us a speech center that can shape only slogans. And suppose that those slogans were used to make one mass of men (who have no quarrel with others) take up arms and rush to destroy all those who will not submit to their masters. Then, of course, a big brain, because it is a social instrument, is a social disaster; it is society's self-produced destruction. Even if the peace of terror and the fear of annihilation keep mankind on the brink of extinction, at best he must always live in interior conflict, "willing to wound but yet afraid to strike"; fearing to fire but longing to end the intolerable tension; hating his Leviathan state-master but dreading that if the despot were dethroned, he, the little man, might in the scramble for the loot be trampled under foot by those in the stampeding mob who were tougher than himself.

Surely, it was a mere freak of the tongue that gave him speech. It gave him a premature power: the power of the spell, the intricate snares of the lie with which he could trap those of his fellows who could avoid all other ginns and lures. From pious fraud to election promises, from investment circulars to patent medicines the word has proved to be the chief weapon of the deceitful seeker after power, and the chief peril of society. At best there must always be in man an increasing interior conflict between what he perceives and what it is wise to say; between what he knows and how this knowledge can be fitted in with the current pattern, the going concern.

Such, certainly, would be our insoluble dilemma if it were true that only man's brain had grown and that his tongue had become his chief means to power. But the full truth is far more hopeful. We have seen that if man's glandular system is still such as can operate only in the conditions of a prehuman world then all that his reason can do will be to rationalize what his endocrine drives direct; all his unprecedented intelligence will submit to make him only an unprecedentedly beastly animal. But if we examine our endocrine (ductless gland) system we shall find two pieces of evidence that are as striking as the growth of the human brain, and complement that growth of intelligence with an equal growth in the emotions.

The first has to do with the endocrine balance in the present human body. The second, and even more important, deals with the changes that go on in the glands of stress (the suprarenals) during the growth of the present individual. In the first place, it is clear that man's endocrine balance has been modified as much in favor of the reasonable life of sustained cooperative effort toward long-distance goals as his brain has been turned into the path-maker toward those goals and the lens through which he sees them. Compare the endocrine balance of a tiger with that of a man. In the tiger's case, the suprarenals (the energizers for attack) are gross and the thyroid, the gland of sustained effort, is small. But with man this disbalance is reversed: small suprarenals and big thyroid is man's endocrine setup. Indeed, glandular research has now led to our being able to find a similar division that distinguishes all the peaceful animals from those who assault and destroy, the carnivores. J. Reusch (the work is reported by W. S. von Euler of Sweden), working on the adrenal glands of African wild animals, found that the aggressive beasts (the lion and others) had a high amount not of adrenaline but of that nor-adrenaline that (see below) is the quintessence of the rage-creating glandular component, while in the glands of the animals that survived through flight there was found a preponderance of adrenaline. Von Euler had already discovered that this changeover (from a preponderance of adrenaline to a preponderance of nor-adrenaline) in the secretion of the suprarenal medulla (the core or pith of the gland) could be brought about by stimulating different parts of the hypothalamus, the old brain, the center of the emotional drives. And Nobel-prizeman W. R. Hess of Zurich has mapped two areas in the hypothalamus, one of which, when stimulated in animals, produced rage while the other produced flight. From this glandular evidence we see that it is the hypothalamus, the seat of the emotions, that triggers the animal organism either to flight or fight. Also, it is clear that even in animals—at least in mammals—there is the possibility of choice, for the two centers that direct attack or escape are present also in them. But animals that live by aggression and those that survive by flight are slanted either to rage or fear by their gland balance in favor of the nor-adrenaline of fury or the adrenaline of panic.

This is important. But even more important for our understanding of our human condition and process of development is the further research into this suprarenal balance in man himself. From the work of D. H. Funkenstein (Director of Clinical Psychiatry at Boston Psychopathic Hospital), H. G. Wolff (at New York Hospital), Bernt Hokfelt, and G. B. West, it is now clear (28) that the small child's first reaction to thwarting is rage and that that rage reaction can be correlated with the particular secretion then found in the core—medulla—of the child's suprarenals. This secretion, at that age, has more nor-adrenaline than adrenaline. In later childhood, and from the influence of its group upon it, the child not only learns to blame itself for mistakes, with the resulting appearance of anxiety, shame, and finally of guilt, but at the same time this older child's gland secretion alters. It is at this age that adrenaline becomes the main secretion in the core of its suprarenals. Further evidence of this important correlation comes from the study of the insane. Those who suffer from paranoia regress to childish behavior. And it is in paranoics that the suprarenals are found to be secreting excessive amount of nor-adrenaline. Conversely, there is a preponderance of adrenaline in the suprarenal secretions of those patients with acute anxiety and the guilt sense that drives them to the hopeless attitude of the schizophrenic

Further, the results with (*a*) the mood-changing drugs (for example, Librium) have shown that violent carnivores such as the lynx and the leopard can be reverted to the caress-seeking friendliness of a kitten as long as the drug is active in them; while (*b*) the same results have been achieved by E.S.B., electrical stimulation of specific, pinpointed brain areas.

This is the second piece of evidence that makes us have hope of man because of (and not in spite of) his glandular structure, his basic emotional drives. Here we have evidence to indicate that man is, and has been since he was man, evolving not only intellectually but emotionally. Here we can obtain the physiological data that confirm the meaning of man's past history: that it is a spiral development of consciousness up from the preindividual who is co-conscious with his fellows, through the protoindividual of the Heroic Age, on through the midindividualism of the Ascetic Epoch, and up to the total individualism of the humanic period. And, on the other hand, these physiological data, just because they are physiological, indicate most clearly the fact that each of us today recapitulates, after birth, man's history since he became the creature with the biggest brain, the needlessly large mind. Our glandular development can now be seen to indicate, in at least three of our five stages (childhood, adolescence, and first maturity), the way in which the life within us urges us to grow emotionally to a psychophysical competence that is equal to our intelligence.

It was mentionad above that even the glands of conflict are now shown to be subject to evolutionary development. The secretion which is at first predominantly nor-adrenaline, a secretion making for instant, unreflective reaction, attack, protest, does become as we grow up and begin to leave childhood for adolescence, predominantly adrenaline. This adrenaline makes not for fight but for flight. Fear comes in. Fear is, of course, intuitive misgiving, doubt of one-self. The anger that first flashed out against others is now painfully held. It turns against the self and the longer it is held the stronger grows the feeling of resentment at one's own foolishness in getting oneself into such a fix. It may be assumed that during these times of stress there grows, in the mind, a capacity to examine its past actions and their proved inadequacy. The gland of sustained effort (the thyroid) may be coming into action. Certainly trapped men, seemingly cut off by their pursuers, have time and again, under such stress, shown inspired ingenuity in effecting an escape.

So to the structure of man another floor is added. On the ground floor of simple protest and defensive attack against another molesting species (even among peaceful animals and clearly among mankind), there has been built a second story, the rapid and increasingly skilled retreat from assault. And this fear is the beginning of

wisdom, for it makes the creature judge itself, estimate its deficiencies, and criticize its stupidity and rashness. Then on this second
story man has reared his third: wariness, the foresight of understanding avoidance.

This third addition has negatively been called apprehension
and anxiety. But wariness is the better word. *Beware* need not be a
command to flee. Rather it means be awake and advance with circumspection. Constant awareness, the constant vigilance that is the
price of freedom is no doubt fatiguing. Only a creature that is
largely and rightly thyroid-energized (as Hans Selye (77) puts it)
can sustain such steady exertion. Further, only a creature that can
put implicit trust in its fellows can have those releases from being
on watch without which the appetite for constant circumspect investigation sours into that indigestion of the mind and body that we
call anxiety or *angst*. Hence Renaissance man (called here by the
wider title humanic man), because he was at the apex of individualism, the extreme of self-consciousness, could not sustain his keen
awareness as a constantly growing critical curiosity. So he fell into
anxiety: that *angst* which, as it has been pointed out, marks and
mars all the active countenances rendered by that superartist-genii
of the conflicts, Michelangelo.

So important are these glandular discoveries and their confirmation of man's socio-racial evolution and individual growth
development that here (where these new endocrine discoveries are
in this chapter being mentioned) for the first time we have had to
forestall the argument. We must now show how this glandular
development provokes (if it does not produce) not only the child's
propensity to attack its environment but, as we shall see in the two
succeeding chapters, the adolescent's inclination to self-suspicion
and the incessant anxiety of first maturity that fluctuates between
impudent interference and anxious apprehension.

To return, then, to the ordeal of childhood: we can now see
from the evidence of endocrinology that the child (as did the hero
whose phase the child is recapitulating) needs to be charged with
nor-adrenaline in order to break from the suckling cycle, "full of
repose, full of replies," be weaned from the extension of the womb's

condition of dependence and develop initiative toward new experience, be curious about the anomalous, and feel adventurous toward the enigmatic.

Further, in this particular section of our enquiry, and specifically on the psychosomatic action and reaction of mood and function, of physique and state of mind, research in pathology lends additional weight to the evidence that the human being does go through a series of mind-body developments, and that arrest at any one of these levels can be disastrous. We have now known for some time that failure of the individual's emotional life to grow up and out of the childish nor-adrenaline rage-states of projected fury can and often does culminate in paranoia and its expression, homicidal frenzy. But what we have learned only in the last couple of years is that there is a psychosomatic correlation between cancer and paranoia. The paranoid have been found to have a cancer incidence no less than four times in excess of the cancer incidence among the general population. Also, the cancers start with the paranoid at an earlier age and, in their growth, resist all means of holding them back. Unfortunately, there is nothing surprising in this grim correlation; indeed, it is only one more confirmation that the paranoid condition is a state of emotional arrest wherein the psyche has become confined at a childish, heroical level. That frame of mind, being one where rage is projected and so never thought about, still less understood by its experient, is, of course, that level of most rudimentary self-consciousness, protoindividualism. At this level, in consequence of this lack of self-awareness, a person is most liable to psychosomatic illness. And if, as MacCurdy (57) in his *War Neuroses* and many psychiatrists since have pointed out, an army conscript, and not an officer, is the person most able unconsciously to give himself incapacitating illness (conversion neurosis), then this would indicate that the protoindividual's desire to kill those who have coerced him turns on himself. He who would be an anarch finds his own cells catching his mood; they attack and anarchize his whole body. Cancer is always swiftest with the young, always deadly with the children; and the paranoid is an arrested child.

Conversely, and confirming this as we shall see in the next

chapter, the cancer rate among schizophrenics is much lower than in the average population.[a] Schizophrenia, of course, is the specific mental breakdown peculiar to adolescence, that stage of development in the individual which recapitulates the third stage of development of social man: the ascetic, the midindividual who blames himself.

It was mentioned above and it is, of course, a commonplace that the relation between hormone and mood is reciprocal. Indeed, it is now being proposed by competent researchers that mood may precipitate hormone as hormone can project mood. Certainly every emotional state may be very easily overdone and set up its emotional resonance. What was a good starter, a real source of inspiration, can become simply a bad habit, an addictive behavior pattern, a conditioned reflex. It is clear that at the stage of childhood the individual confronts the issue that the heroic age, on the whole, failed to face: how is independence to stop short of anarchy and initiative short of irresponsibility? Freedom must not take leave of composition nor must private conviction and personal assurance abandon communication, persuasion, and interpretation of as well as respect for and appreciation of the insights of others.

Again, as they have gotten through infancy, most children get through this second stage after a fashion. They are partly damaged, considerably deformed, but not sufficiently to turn the growth process predominantly morbid. They are under increasing stress and living less and less to their full capacity. Their happiness diminishes

[a] See *Psychological Variables in Human Cancer,* by J. Gingerelli and F. J. Kirkner (35). See also the equally impressive studies entitled *Cancer and Atheroma Explained by a Basic Phylogenetic Pattern in Disease,* by Lang Stevenson, M.D., F.R.C.S. (81), Surgeon at Whipps Cross Hospital, Leytonstone (Essex), England. In these reports the author indicates that one of the causes of neoplasms is a reaction of the organism, when under psychosomatic shock, of a far earlier evolutionary level in the phylogenetic tree (for example, the crustacean damage reaction of abandoning an assaulted limb and regrowth of a new one on the old site). Cancer can thus be regarded as a surviving power to restore renewal by producing reproductive cells. After the crustacean level, the second completing step, the capacity to build up a new limb, is, however, lost.

and their spontaneity, welcome, and creativity are growing poorer, but they get along by a series of shifts. Their curiosity has sunken to a conviction that they can debunk everything. This is a very dangerous state and all the more so because it seems to be at worst only subacute. Here is a latent condition which, like fire-damp in a mine, a spark will ignite. It is from these partly paranoid, puerile types that dictators recruit their youth gangs. And lately, as is pointed out further on in this chapter, we have been able to detect that there is a delayed psychosomatic cost for this miscarriage of energy when it degenerates into rage.

We have already found the way (see Chapter 1, Part II) whereby the infant may be kept from regressing and can be induced to release its pent-up energies in a joyous friendship and with laughter. By cheerful challenge and entertaining puzzlement the force, which if balked would become frustrant or destructive, becomes adventurous. Between fear and rage curiosity is disclosed. The desire to shrink becomes the wariness that is the beginning of awareness, circumspect estimation, detached objectivity. The desire to attack becomes the wish to investigate, to contact; and this is the beginning of interior understanding.

But when we come to the education of the postinfantile child, we are far less successful. Most persons, however, are unaware of how greatly the educational situation degenerates after the progress made by a good infancy induction. We are unaware of it because of a fundamental confusion in our own minds as to what the good life is and as to what the procedure and progression of the life process is. Psychotherapy has now made us realize that the child may well become a severe and costly failure unless we give it, for its first two years, that inspiring invitation to generous living. However, such a way of life is not ours today. It is not the climate of our adult world. The child psychologist and trainer is not, as yet, an average person of our life and times. And this teacher-sculptor is molding a substance—the infant mind-body—which is far more eductile than the substance of most adults. The success of the new infant training, which has been in practice for twenty years now, has, therefore, not had the impact that was hoped of it. Indeed, it has in one way made our conflict more acute.

For as our adult society still accepts the idea of struggle and competition as being the way of survival and the procedure of evolution, this outworn aspect of Darwinianism still dominates our mores and education. The present attitude of those who control education is then a compromise. Granted, they would say, that one must not begin to toughen up the infant too rapidly, any more than one should try to teach an embryo to goose-step. Still, as soon as the easy way of early training has brought the young to where they may have practical instruction, the sooner they are taught to be aggressive the better for their success and our security. The infant is, in the main, still considered to be an unprepared, prematurely born creature, representing an unviable type with whom, therefore, one must have patience until this plastic has hardened sufficiently to be hammered into weapon-shape.

However, the new concepts of neoteny, of fetalization and paidomorphy (see Glossary), now acknowledged by evolutionist and child psychologist alike, provide us with a profound insight. For in these concepts the callous is considered to be the decadent and it is recognized that the capacity to keep tonically sensitive is the mark of evolutionary advance and the indication of man's unparalleled success. But this is yet to be recognized by those who still set the standards of our mores of maturity. Hence, in those cases in which the infant has had an induction to life in accord with really contemporary concepts of the life process and the evolutionary development, this child is even less prepared to confront the stage of childhood, as it is now lived out, than one whose infancy was less encouraging, whose parents were less able or willing to let the psyche open out into generous, unguarded welcome (75).

For just as we know that a child could be born with a too disproportionately advanced head and brain to survive in the present conditions of our contemporary knowledge, so it is evident that advanced infant training that is not accompanied by an equally advanced neoteny training of the other age groups—childhood, adolescence, and first and second maturity—can expose a prematurely opened creature, provided with no defenses, to other groups that are still mainly aggressive. Hence, at this child period when the individual recapitulates the rough and tumble of the heroic bedlam

there is all too great a chance that the tragedy of the epoch of boastful brigandage will be repeated. Nor is the child psychiatrist himself
wholly without some share of blame for this confusion. For too many
of them have failed to realize the profound implications of the concept of neotenic evolution.

Hence, such experts and specialists failed to see that as essential and basic as was the proper explication of the ordeal of birth,
this was but a first step. There were four others to be faced and
taken. Only then would a person be complete. To bring an infant
through the first phase and then to leave the child unprepared for
the second was as frustrant and disastrous as to have exposed it to
callousness and callousing from the start. Maybe it would become a
beast of prey but otherwise it was only being prepared to be the
prey of the beast.

However, when the childhood ordeal and initiation is not properly provided for and undertaken, the main disaster for the child is,
in its most acute and therefore most unmistakable form, dementia
praecox. For those psychiatrists who follow the present tradition that
labels psychic misfortunes with classic Greek names, this might be
called the Ajax complex. The child psyche is not attacked by a guilt
complex but a shame trauma. Its attempt to show generous love (if
it has had a modern infant training this will be its display initiative)
or its attempt to show off its prowess (if it has had the careless,
callous, or selfish bringing up) is rejected, snubbed, mocked. Hell
hath no fury like a lover scorned. Dementia praecox, essentially the
child-age-group insanity, is, of course, the extreme state, the full and
immediate reaction of the rejected child.

Earl Loomis thinks that it emerges in its full form, as we might
expect, in children of high awareness and uncommon hypersensitive-
ness. If it cannot be cured this nor-adrenaline rage will become paranoia and the homicidal maniac results. The actual number of children that so suffer is tragic but not sufficient to constitute in any
wise a threat to society. What is far graver, because of its social
peril, is the great number of those who carry on, up from a semi-
dementia praecox stage, the paranoid cast of mind. This will lead to
passionate aggressiveness (see next chapter) if it is not caught up

with and eliminated by the time the child has reached the next stage: the pure adrenaline state that makes possible anger-with-the-self instead of anger-with-others. Because of its lack of experience and foresight, uncalculating violence is released in the child; and because it lacks any sense of opportuneness and has little freedom, the violence is often thwarted and the possessed creature is put under restraint. But if the charge is fed back (after maybe only a few exhibitions of that admired role, "I'll beat up anyone who crosses me,") until the man has learned to nurse his wrath, then there will be grave trouble. He may, like Hitler, reach such demonic repression concentration that he learns, through speech and with violent sounds, how to create such a resonance of paranoia in large masses of similarly afflicted men that they, smoldering in their sense of wrong, are willing to have the homicidal experience under his leadership, and he can use them as his instruments of mass murder.

And indeed for many child psychiatrists this is the whole story. Themselves still nursed in the tragic concept, they are under the limitations of a despair that tries to make itself acceptable by giving those who face up to it a sense of superiority over those who feed on the opium of wishful thinking and self-deceiving optimism. For them, even if they cannot render themselves and their work totally futile by accepting man as being "a base ungovernable beast," the child is completely neutral. There is in the creature no natural drive toward understanding and cooperation. The inherent evolutionary process that has brought it to mammalhood in the womb is regarded as being a series of accidents. These flukes of fortune have resulted in a creature whose high adaptability no doubt made for animal survival. But this adaptability in a group creature whose social cohesion depended on common cries led to complete suggestibility. Any slogan would catch on.

Education, therefore, when it works on the emotions and the will, is nothing but sloganization. Some cries are the auditory rhythms of common pleasure. In this way we find ourselves feeling good, saying that we are right and asserting that the nature of things means us so to be and so to succeed. Most cries are the vocalizations of fears, warnings, and vetoes; of defiances and excommunications.

Man the suggestible is therefore far more likely to become a creature of retractive fear-hate than of enterprising love-curiosity.

History, therefore, has genial spells when events have, for the time being, gone well enough for the main chorus to be cheerful. At such times most children find themselves subject to a happy family feeling-tone, a social euphoric mood. Children have the highest chance of survival and of reaching adulthood who are born and reared at times of tribal plenty and prosperity, stability and openness. The adults' experience is, however, far more likely to enter on a series of grim happenings. Happy living or quick dying, which were the two most likely probabilities for the child, are not the only ones for the adult. There is, for the mature, a third alternative: an unhappy life that endures until it longs for death. Gloom and suspicion form in man's mind; his tone and chant become dismal and forbidding. Finally, the more man becomes conscious of his inevitable fate the more the carrying wave of all his communication is minor and miserable. On the whole then, man may at best oscillate manic-depressively between elations and despair; or perhaps, what is more likely, succumb to a growing retraction of courage and spread suspicion which must end (when he discovers nuclear power) with the opportunity to destroy his entire species.

This view, though unjustifiably pessimistic, is still popular in most scientific circles. It is supported by two natural but faulty reasons. In the first place, the scientist is increasingly a specialist. His actual work has, in consequence, an ever-shortening focus. General significances, long range comprehensive views concern him less and less. He does not, then, feel able or willing to bring within the orbit of his study those peripheral effects which, although they may not be of immediate concern to him, nevertheless do affect his particular subject. Indeed, he believes himself to be obligated to rule out any *general* considerations because he is a *specialist*. Yet his studies and restricted conclusions are used in parallel studies (as anthropology is used by sociology and bionomics by economics) to give them collateral support and general significance. Further, the specialist, because besides being a specialist he is also a community member, must make some generalizations. He is a citizen who has constantly to conform with, develop or reject the present rulings of tradition and the trends of social heredity.

As Donald Hebb and others have pointed out, perception is largely due to and in terms of social significances, though the researcher may not be aware of this force as a comprehensive field that suggests and modifies his hypotheses.[b] Charles Darwin, we know, was largely influenced, in the general orientation of his thought, by T. R. Malthus' theory of population.

Therefore, in making his generalizations, the scientist, on the whole, tends to come to conclusions not too alien from current expectations. That does not mean that these conclusions have to be palatable to either the conservative or the progressive. A period which assumes, emotionally, that tragedy is the highest form of art and that art is superior to religion; and which believes, intellectually, that increase of means has relieved it from the necessity of a superstitious faith in Providence—such an age's ruling minority is not surprised, indeed it is interested to learn that it is a unique freak without responsibilities toward a creator or obligations toward creatures.

Meanwhile, in regard to his particular branch of study the researcher inclines to support those first hypotheses around which his own science was precipitated. Hence, in the sciences of life, the old nineteenth-century notions still rule the greater part of scientific opinion: the old notions that life is a blind struggle; that survival lies in the victory of the best competitor (the most cunningly callous) instead of in the victory of those most increasingly aware; and that the life process is an exhausting process rather than a process of creative, emergent evolution. And these notions persist in spite of such radically new and different assumptions as that of neoteny (now present in biology) and that of open systems and their freedom from entropy (now present in physiology and biochemistry). At present, the neotenic concept (the concept of the infant, the growing edge of the life process, as being an emergent type and a

[b] "Concepts come before percepts." *Patterns of Discovery* by N. R. Hanson (39); "Nothing can be seen unless it has already been recognized." *Art and Illusion* by E. H. Gombrich (36).

unit of increasing awareness that strives—until it is destroyed or discouraged—to manifest and express a still further capacity to understand and cooperate) is hardly built into the philosophy and premises of the child therapists themselves.

We need not, however, give up hope. Indeed, we may expect that as this completely new notion has been in circulation for only some twenty or thirty years, not only the child psychiatrist but psychiatrists in general are about to recognize the decisive relevance of this concept to their work. Then, instead of the more advanced therapists having to be on the defensive and striving to preserve such enclaves and reservations as the new therapeutic mental hospital, the new child clinic and neo-progressive school and the new psychiatric developmental centers, they can, must and will issue forth from these special fastnesses. Therein they have accumulated their ammunition of confirmatory data. And with these data they can challenge the still calloused and callousing patterns of behavior, such as the drill systems of the tough professions: the military police and penal institutions. They can appeal to the paying public to decide as to which system, the old or the new, does produce the human character that is best able creatively to handle itself, its fellows, and the whole human situation.

There is no reason for the new neotenic psychiatry to defend itself, still less to retreat. It must now (and it can) plan its advance. So and so only will we make the world open for life, through cooperating with life's process, neoteny. For neoteny can make life open, safe for itself and with itself only by neotenics, the training of the person so as to know how he may, by refusing to loose the hold on his unspent endowment of fresh response, continue to be creative. And this training must be spread up from the child-age groups until it covers all five stages of the entire human life process.

In concluding this chapter, we must repeat that there is one strong ground for hope and for hope in our own time. As we have seen, owing to the fact that our past still lives in us and that our future is also present in potential, we can, unlike the embryo, relive our past mistakes and release ourselves from our former wrong developments. As we increase our therapeutic processes of deep penetration and, from that depth, regress back to the source of miscarriage, we may hope at any age to untangle the strangling web of the life that has been lived, bring back each of its five cardinal choices, and restore each of them to their original state of freedom from any force or coercion.

And what makes this discovery in the technique of neoteny significant and timely is that this recovery of consciousness is to be made not merely in order to restore the individual to a lost happiness, although this is good—not merely for the individual but for his group. For it removes his debit load on the group's resources and re-establishes him as an asset. But as valuable as that may be, an entire release of the individual psyche holds a far greater promise for society and mankind. For we have seen that the individual, when he is put through this psychic recapitulation, this total recall of consciousness, relives with initiative not only his own personal history but that of the race. And so we may hope, by this new education, to restore directly to the consciousness of the individual (as he passes through each phase of his personal life) the initiative of each corresponding epoch of human history but not the frustration.

Collingwood, the historian and philosopher, in his repeated attacks on the theories of progress maintained that they were all false because the only real progress would take place if it were possible to conserve all the insights of the past while advancing into new awareness. This demand can now be met. At last there can be a generation in which the entire richness of the past not only exists as an unconscious endowment of reactions and drives, but is consciously appreciated. The contemporary individual may at last know, by direct interior knowledge, that he is the growing edge of life.

It is clear, then, that this process is no mere therapy for restoring those who have been damaged and returning them to the more or less vicious circle of current affairs. This is a training that everyone must and will wish to undergo. It is a fivefold birth whereby each person explicates and summates evolution. And as this evolution is now consciously pursued, not only is it so accelerated that each generation can advance an aeon but each may emerge into a new and vaster frame of reference.

3

The ordeal of adolescence
and its specific mental breakdown
[Schizophrenia]

We have now seen how two great stages of the individual's development do recapitulate two great ages of mankind's history. These two epochs—the preindividual, coconscious, traditional aeon and its successor, the protoindividual, aggressive, heroical era—make a recapitulating, summarizing appearance in the early years of every person; save in such rare isolated and ankylosed cultures which themselves have hardly, if at all, left the traditional aeon.[a]

[a] The culture of the Australian aborigine may, perhaps, even be called by that too easily used epithet, decadent. Konrad Lorenz has pointed out, in his study of the dingo (the feral dog of Australia), that these tribes seem to have entered that continent bringing with them the domesticated dog. But the tribes became so weak in enterprise that the animal deserted them and resumed a purely wild life of adjustment to and conquest of its new environment. However, in 1961, an expedition of Melbourne anthropologists did discover an isolated tribe that called themselves the Bindibi and who were living in the Great Sand Desert that is on the border of Northern and Western

We have also seen that each of these epochs (prehistoric and historic) and each of these individual age-stages was and is attended by a crisis. There comes to every person an ordeal that can be made to be a specific test rather than a sudden onrush of spontaneous pressure for which he is unprepared. If this ordeal can be presented to the individual in a way that is adequate to the inherent psycho-physical, mental-emotional needs of the growing psyche, then the ordeal results in an initiation. And this initiation is a new birth into a fresh quality of consciousness, for it is a further depth penetration that releases energy levels now repressed. They are repressed because at the historic period of their first emergence they found only partial or frustrant expression and because, since then, we have devised no explicit methods for dealing with these crises in the development of the individual life.

So far, what seems to be the main norm of human history is this: the ordeal has been largely accidental and brought on by outer pressures, which triggered into an explosion inner repressions that have long been accumulating as the standardizing, prestige-giving patterns and instructional interpretations given by society grew increasingly inadequate to balance the growth of actual experience. Hence society and the men in it have blindly, and at great cost, psychomutated. Many, perhaps most, have been destroyed by the strain of the disordered, uncomprehended changeover. And those who have survived have only been able to construct—inadvertently and largely by mere reaction, in blind revolt and resentful recoil—a society whose standards must be mainly negative because they are precipitated and energized by protest and almost devoid of comprehension. Further, under this unforeseen and unprepared-for stress

---

Australia, some five hundred miles west of Alice Springs. These people were of so low a culture economically that they had no agriculture, nor houses, nor tents. At night they sheltered themselves from the cold (for they wore no clothes and had no weaving or pottery) with heaped windbreaks made of small withered bushes (like the tumble-weed of the semidesert states in the Western United States), which they piled around the hollows where they slept. In their hunting they used the dingo which, it would seem, they had either never lost touch with, or had reattached to themselves.

many individuals, though their intense inner vitality prevents their becoming wholly liquidated, nevertheless do become mad.

In the first phase of this mental constriction they manage to make themselves impervious to the inner-outer process of change-growth. They stabilize at the level of the total conservative. Any change in the tribal pattern is treason.[b] These are the type that produced the first gerontocracies: that iron rule of the arthritic-minded elders, of those old men who can neither live nor die. They are fruit that has dried on the branch, refusing to fall to the ground and preventing new shoots from sprouting. Such elders are killing the last preindividualistic tribes in Australia today.

Later, in the second phase of their madness, monomaniac conviction changes from being broodingly fanatical (and excommunicating all development) to paranoid attack; and the raider-crusader emerges. His mission is no longer to keep his own world and social circle spellbounnd under the magic of his arresting command but to launch his feudatories out on an annihilating attack.

But on the whole, though at a cost in suffering that must seem appalling to the humanitarian, the process has worked, the progression has explicated, evolution has continued. And it has continued with the prodigious acceleration first made possible by the slow and tentative exchange of physical heredity for the rapid oscillating exchanges of social heredity whereby what begins as question-and-answer sports into criticism and creation, the working equation, and the challenging absurdity. In spite of cruel mistakes and crueler convictions, callous ignorance and frenzied fanaticism, man has come, first, to challenge, criticize, and remold his unconscious tradition, then to test, explore, and manipulate his environment and thirdly, to be aware of, to question, and to gauge himself. Repeatedly, and because man delayed in giving his rising nature adequate

[b] Men of later epochs have reverted to such rigidity. The Median Persian Empire prefaced all its laws with the phrase "The Law of the Medes and Persians which cannot be changed." And even the city-state of Megara, neighbor of Athens, had in its constitution that whoever would suggest a change must do so with a noose around his neck. He was to be hanged if he failed to carry his motion.

release and contemporary expression, there has been such tectonic stress that mutational revolution, not evolution, has seemed to be the unavoidable rule. The violence of the moments of contorted delivery has been so shockingly memorable and the welter of wreckage left from the explosion so obliterative that chroniclers and their moralizing amplifiers, the historians, have felt hardly able to pay tribute to man's capacity to recover or to pay attention to the long-range results.

And yet there is a process and it moves in a discernible direction. For man is not merely the most viable of all creatures, he is also the creature that rapidly and sustainedly gains in consciousness. The process of gaining awareness, though it turns the corners with such violent switches that myriads are flung off at each bend, does survive this vertigo. Mankind does emerge onto another and higher traverse of that tremendous effort, the expression of his inner nature in regard to his comprehension of outer nature. Men's unawareness of their psyche growth has therefore left them unprepared for its sudden delivery pains because the awareness of the psychic pregnancy was repressed. The new births were brought on by forces driven to become increasingly subconscious.

Hence, temporary spastic chaos. But that chaos has not been collapse and death. It has been a birth, however clumsy and damaging. Some inherent power has kept man going and after each convulsion has swung him not merely back onto disciplined acceptance but thrown him up onto a higher level of challenge-exertion and outlook. In Appendix D we shall enquire as to whether, beside an inherent preterconscious drive, there may also have been present among rare individuals in hidden groups an esoteric practice that was designed to keep alive, consciously, the flame and light of an authentic inspiration. But before reaching that point, we must try to discern how the individual today, in the process of his personal life, confirms by recapitulation the progression of history, illustrates its physical significance, and indicates where and how education can and must cooperate with the explication of the evolutionary process.

In this chapter we therefore trace in the individual the oncoming of the third great crisis wherein and when the young still have to recapitulate mankind's third great change of consciousness. The infant, we have seen, today has the new child psychiatry to aid him in the birth of his psyche during the first two or two and a half years. He is now cheerfully challenged, laughingly roused to react and explore. But we have also seen that when the child begins to enter his next stage and to recapitulate that further condensation of consciousness that will be his first awareness of separate individualism, our paidogogy is still proving to be inadequate and mainly unhelpful. Whether or not half a truth is the worst lie, preparedness half done is surely the worst defense, especially when that preparedness has stripped off the defensive armor of growing callouses and wariness but has failed to replace these rigid defenses with the alerted vitality of initiative and understanding. If a sedentary organism discards its shell without gaining agility it becomes a prey of its foes far more easily than if it had remained shut up in its immobile armor. To prepare infants to be happily responsive in the world of today is not to prepare them for life but for a despairing disappointment. For in the stage of childhood, the next phase into which they must, by their growth process, inevitably move, they will find that generous creativity is considered to be sissy. And the adolescents, the next group to which they must go after childhood, regard blasé indifference and Don Juan sophistication as being proof of maturity. Once the skin has been made capable of keeping its resilience, it may lose the power of acquiring a defensive callus and so be able to respond to constant irritation only by producing a malignant sore.

The infant, we have seen, is charged with nor-adrenaline that remains with it for its first years of tremendous brain expansion, adaptation, and growth. But by the time it reaches the threshold of adolescence this glandular slant should be beginning to change to adrenaline, or at least to balancing the nor-adrenaline with spells of adrenaline repentances (28). As Piaget has pointed out in his classic studies of the child, it is not until the age of seven that the child ceases to use the intuitive emotional apprehension of a situation (and/or a relationship) and begins to apply reason and logical analysis.

This is a vitally important sequence of facts; it should make us realize that the change that takes place at the oncoming of this third crisis (the first sign of the dawn of adolescence, which Arnold Gesell and his colleagues place at about the age of ten) is as grave and critical as birth, as testing an ordeal as were the two earlier ones of birth and childhood. The growing psyche has been brought through birth and infancy and protected from collapse-retreat into idiot infantilism. Next it is brought through early childhood and dawning adolescnce. At this point it is guarded from dementia praecox by letting the nor-adrenaline energy (which might turn into the poison thorn of homicidal rage if it is balked) bud into a fully developing wish to explore, experiment, construct, and communicate.

How tragic it is, then, that at this point, of all places, contemporary Western society (the confused survivals of Heroism and Asceticism with a smattering of Humanism that still constitute, so largely, the amalgam that we call our social heredity) takes over the adolescent and tries to toughen him up. For it is here, when we try to make him surrender his generosity, that we first suggest to him that he is shameful and guilty. Our schools, with their competitive and aggressive sports, as well as premilitary training, try to turn the adolescent into a series of reflexes that are driven by fear of shame.

The religious bodies whose tradition is ascetic can substitute guilt for shame and so keep up the struggle for the distressed soul of the adolescent. And the humanic notions of the specialized sciences, when they attempt to generalize, can give him the paralyzing anodynes of materialistic skepticism. This condition is, of course, an extremely grave threat to adolescent sanity.

Why should we be surprised at the high incidence of juvenile delinquency? Such fuel put into any machine would make it corrode or explode. Such a diet fed to any organism would give it convulsions and lead to prostration. Nevertheless, although a basic drive toward growth (in this case the great mammalian movement toward advance through increasing awareness, progress by neoteny) may be periodically thwarted and temporarily distorted, it cannot be brought to a standstill except by destroying the species that carries the basic aptitude of teachability. You can bewilder most of mankind for part of the time and mislead part of mankind most of the time. But you cannot delude and deceive all mankind all the time about his true nature. You can expel nature now and then with bayonets; nevertheless she will return as inevitably as a dammed stream will erode the barrier that has been placed in its path and resume its predestined course.

So it is that when the problem of juvenile delinquency is examined thoroughly we find grounds for hope. When with our most advanced techniques of detection we study the energy rhythms of delinquents, we turn up evidence that this is a social disease that is attacking a psyche of promise. To quote again Grey Walter (93) (page 210 in *The Living Brain*), 70 per cent of youths who, beween the ages of ten and seventeen, had given this kind of trouble were found to be giving off the delta waves from their brains when they were tested under electroencephalogram instrumentation.[c] As Walter indicates, these boys were not lone wolves, solitary brigands. On the contrary, they appeared to have failed to grow emotionally. They had remained malleable rather than becoming resilient. Hence (as did the Nazi youth) they became material for gang assimilation. Our society did not give them a modernized heroic group modus and style; and as no man hired them they sold themselves for nothing.

Of course, the Boy Scout Movement did much and the Big Brother therapies have also done a great deal to aid. The problem, however, will remain stubborn until its nucleus can be transmuted by skilled use of the therapies of specific catharsis by which adolescence is given its particular ordeal and initiation.[d]

Then our education will resume its now limited and arrested process of drawing forth the entire man. Having achieved the basic success of a full and healthy birth and infancy, it will then follow

[c] The delta wave has also been described by Walter as being the wave of oncoming birth effort. It has been given the name—the letter D in the Greek alphabet—because of its association with the initial of the four cardinal words of major stress: disease, degeneracy, death, and defense.

[d] See Part I, Chapter 2 and Part II, Chapter 2.

the rightful extrapolation of that first part of man's growth. It will attain to the practice and technique of releasing the paidomorph, the form of psychophysique that is the next step in neotenic development.[e] The child will become heroic but no longer be boastfully afraid of being shamed or attempt to conceal uninformed and mistaken initiative by calling his temporary setback tragic when it calls for reflection.

The stage of protoadolescence can then be safely entered. For now the secretion from the suprarenal medulla, which has been predominantly nor-adrenaline, becomes predominantly adrenaline. The energy that was formerly projected out onto the world and onto others (and, if not rightly engaged and entertained, turning into destructive rage) now alters its objective. The adolescent awareness now turns in on itself and corrects the unexamined conviction that outside of itself lie all its tasks, problems, and conquests. It begins to explore, criticize, and attempt to order itself. The task of conquering the conqueror is begun.

Now we are able to recognize how the Ascetic Age inevitably succeeds to the Heroic Age. We also perceive the recapitulating process whereby the individual repeats (and through education may remedy) the psychosocial record of the race: human history. And these two insights permit us to see how a fully informed emotional psychophysical education would give the adolescent age group that contemporary version of strenuous, tempering athleticism (which, of course, is the original meaning of asceticism) whereby this age group may express its inherent need phase, yield its particular service, and integrate with the age groups behind and ahead of it. Then when each individual of the adolescent age group has become fully, completely and neotenically adolescent, he may pass safely into the next phase the age of first maturity.

And here again, in adolescence (as we also saw in the previous chapter when dealing with the childhood stage) we have biological

---

[e] The paidomorph is that form of psychophysique which, for a longer time than ever before, will remain undifferentiated because not yet committed to the polar differentiation of the sexual opposites. See the work of Louis Bolk, the Dutch anatomist, and *The Human Animal* by Weston La Barre (51).

evidence that the whole physique prompts and cooperates with the psyche in the growth of consciousness. Thus we see that, in each of these stages of psychophysical growth that man goes through, our racial nature is striving to accomplish its further evolution. So great is the glandular drive that the entire bodily structure is mobilized to assist and, if we will not cooperate, penalize and eliminate. A vital force is shaping man; a force far more form-pervading and comprehensive than simply the growth of an enlarged brain that can be taught because the bodily instincts have been reduced.

For remember, as we mentioned in the last chapter, that the paranoid, with his psyche arrested in its simple, projected nor-adrenaline rage, tends to have cancer four times more frequently than the average person who has made our current adjustment to life. Their cancer attacks them earlier than usual in life and grows rapidly and uncontrollably. And this collapse of the body's controls over its own cells is precisely the psychosomatic hit-back or conversion neurosis that we should expect of one too simple to do other than project its unmanageable charge of energy.

Conversely, we should expect the reverse of this process in the adolescent, ascetic, self-blaming type. And so a study of *The Psychological Variables in Human Cancer* shows the case to be. For whereas the paranoid have a fourfold excess in cancer, the schizoids have only half the incidence common to those who, in our society, are called the sane. Further, the attack period comes at a later age than is normal for the rest of us. And as cancers in later life are nearly always slower growing and often show signs of arrest[f] there is much greater hope of retarding them.

Once more, we see how aberrant our departure from life can

---

[f] Autopsy studies of males who had died of miscellaneous causes have revealed that from 20 to 46 per cent of them had cancer of the prostate. Most of these growths had remained stationary or had regressed and the individuals had lived a normal life span, though actually they had had cancer for twenty or thirty years. The same appears to be true of women. Mass surveys for detection of early uterine cancer show that in only 20 per cent of the cases where

be and how deadly are the consequences of not using the forces in us for growth into further conditions of psychophysical awareness. Once again, evidence from the field of pathology indicates that the life process is still sustaining a pressure on its growing point: man. Still further, it would indicate that, as that growth process has been the achievement of consciousness, now this consciousness must cooperate with the life process by conscious development of even greater awareness. If it will not and refuses this cooperation, then the human organism will not stabilize or even continue to increase in powerfulness. It will be destroyed by the disruption of its own homeostasis, by the inadequacy of the psyche to control the cell growth, to command the cooperative loyalty of myriad coordinate cell lives, lacking which it must rapidly degenerate into corruption.[g] Cancer is not, in the same sense as other complaints, a disease. It is a resumption, by the cells, of their primal right (eschewed for the sake of a larger life) to reproduce themselves regardless of any greater discipline or purpose. And just because of these two facts, it now seems that cancer may supply convincing negative proof that man can and must continue to evolve.

Not only does the evidence of pathology indicate that adolescent asceticism, with its capacity to blame itself and to judge itself against a universal law, is psychosomatically more healthy (more in accord with the homeostasis of the entire psychophysique) than is the nor-adrenaline, heroical, child phase. It is even more healthy, in this profound respect, than the stage beyond it, the age group of first maturity. The fact that there is four times more cancer among the paranoid (the arrested child type) than among the ordinary

---

cancer was found did the tumor grow and require treatment. In the rest they receded and disappeared. So, the report continues, we are faced with the startling possibility that any cancer that becomes grossly evident and finally kills may actually be an exception. The opinion of this Symposium would suggest that the emotions of the patient are among the forces that influence the course and outcome.

[g] See *Man's Presumptuous Brain* by A. T. W. Simeons (78); see also footnote, Part II, Chapter 2, footnote *a*.

adult population would seem to indicate that the first maturity and second maturity groups are considerably less disbalanced and more sane than those arrested, un-self-aware types whose constant reaction is to blame others. Conversely, the fact that most of us, the so-called sane, composed of the first and second maturity groups, have twice the cancer rate of the schizoid, suggests that the ascetic adolescent's midindividualism, the individualism that blames itself because it cannot live up to a universal law, may be biologically more sane, more balanced in its sense of responsibility than is humanic man, the total individual who believes in no universal law requiring personal responsibility to it (78). Although second maturity is today subconsciously aware of first maturity's inadequate outlook on the outer world (of its mistaken notion of objectivity) it has as yet put no alternative faith in the place of the humanic. Hence, while its conscious mind inclines to involutional melancholy, its subconscious, having no faith in a universal law of being, cannot maintain mastery over the cell secession: cannot control the physiological anarchy of cancer.

To return, then, to the adolescent and what must be done to explicate his condition: it is clear that his sense of universal law and the individual's obligation to it is an evolutionary contribution, a growth gain. What must be done today in the new outlook of psychophysical elucidation, eductive education, is to prevent this conviction from leading to self-immolation through the further conviction that it is a law that must execute all who fail to fulfill it.

In the heroic, childhood phase, it is necessary to save the child from becoming caught in the primary oscillation of proto-individualism, the fluctuation between boastfulness and shame that explodes into paranoid rage. Just so, in the succeeding adolescent phase, the training requirement is to prevent the youth, the stripling, from abandoning further growth by degenerating into a fruitless fluctuation between guilt and expiation. He desires now to be trained and to submit, to be drilled and to be habited, to be uniformed. These desires spring from his new self-knowledge as his increasing self-consciousness turns in on itself. As far as this self-consciousness can be kept as a rightful skepticism of the instrument, a checking up of its actions in comparison with its estimates, of its behavior in contrast to its convictions, a desire for an objective and for outer opinion on performance and on views, this is growth and progress. When, however, disappointment at the self's conduct and capacity becomes unbalanced and obsessional, then there is a failure of nerve. The guilt-ridden seek to suffer for suffering's sake. Pain is not merely the cost of becoming tempered and the price necessary to remedy excess and correct trespass. Suffering now is to anaesthetize the sense of sin in and by physical anguish. Such sufferers must then correspondingly seek to find an outer authority, an infallible rule, not to add as a necessary balancing judgment to their own conviction and to strengthen their capacity for informed cooperative, contributory initiative, but to relieve them of all the pain of making choices. Just as they yearn to humiliate the body, for whose appetites they feel disgust, by exposing it to debilitating punishments, so they correspondingly long to sacrifice intelligence, curiosity, and will. Their submission, to satisfy this mortificatory craving, must be to some authority that is just as domineering, presumptuous, and bitterly exclusive as the spirit that unconditionally surrenders is abject, questionless, and without any reservation. Thus they only project the will they long to renounce.

Hence the ascetic, when he arises from a stock that has produced the tragic hero, the suffering servant, becomes the backbone of the persecuting churches and, as the asceticism is persisted in for its own sake and for life-rejecting, mortificatory purposes, the repression is increased. The appetites are further restricted and strangulated. The primal, undifferentiated appetite that began by being panaesthetic, the basic cutaneously suffused sense of reassurance and of belonging that the infant must have by total uninsulated contact with its mother's body (or be damaged psychologically), is now severely confined and denied to all but infants.

During the heroic, childhood phase, when the ideal behavior is manifested through physical activity and display, this type (which William Sheldon first called the somatotonic and now calls the mesomorph or muscular type) is still largely diffused, sensorily, through muscular development and exertion. Man's attention does not begin to concentrate on specific sexuality as long as struggle and contest are his chief delight and rage is his principal auto-intoxicating emotion. Sexuality per se can be brought to its obsessional pitch and made into the prime cause of guilt only when rationalism begins to ask questions about pleasure and, disregarding panaesthetic sensation, concentrates on the genitalia and the orgasm, neglecting or condemning all the other aesthetic (erogenous) zones; and when heroicism has regarded all tenderness as being weakness, any caress as enervating, and gentleness as effeminacy.

When, therefore, the muscular violence of heroicism and its delighted rage in destruction is over and banished by discipline, the more acute individual, the midindividual, enters a specifically erotic phase of intense sexuality. Inevitably, his sense of guilt seizes hold of this as his main conviction of sin and main offering as expiation. The aim (and goal) of life is made to lie beyond death and the drive to attain that unimaginable condition is found, in the East, through fear of returning to this world, and in the West, through fear of eternal physical suffering in a world to come of eternal torment.

Naturally, that drive today, that schema of the mortificatory mind is fading out. Half a millennium of increasing skepticism extends from the time when this schizoid other-worldlyism was able to hold the mind and conscience of thinking man. That is why the adolescent today does not seek the mortificatory life or even the ascetic way, though he is an ascetic at heart. The educated Protestant churches do not understand the ascetic way, so they cannot, save in dwindling Fundamentalist communions, generate the energy-conviction of ecstatic repression.

Protestanism, although it is becoming aware of the need for a psychiatry, is now mainly a temporary and temporizing mixture of apologetics and good works. Catholicism, too, as we see by the increasing nonenclosure of the modern orders and the increasing hygiene of the ancient ones, is what the Ages of Faith would have called more and more secularized and fatally relaxed. And even so, the number of vocations in proportion to the population is steadily declining. Neither the Second Coming—the end of the material world and of Time—nor hell fire and eternal anguish are stressed any longer. Hence, the adolescent seeking for his rightful phase-expression (*askesis*), has to turn from the ascetic ideal back to the heroic. And instead of serving, with his highest and utmost loyalty, a universal religion that regards this life as an essential phase in spiritual growth, he has to give his devotion to a nation whose standards, values, and goals are at best only heroic.

Still, even in this national religion he is looking and must look for an absolute. His attitude toward the State cannot be the same as that of the humanic gentleman. The eighteenth-century Man of Reason, with a civil loyalty well on this side of idolatry and as a free, uncoerced partner, was able to support the State. This he did just as much by constructive criticism of the nation's executives and veto against their interference with private rights as by his willing defense of his nation against those who might trespass on *its* legitimate rights. Today, in consequence, there has arisen the frantic, fanatic, racist nationalism that has twice imperiled civilization in this half-century and whose example has seriously corrupted and intimidated the freedom of citizens in those democracies which still do not consider the title shameful.

Clearly, however, this atavistic heroicism of nationalism is such a psychological anachronism that it cannot last. Twice (three times, if the Japanese militarists' lunatic and paranoid attack is considered a separate manifestation of this madness) having seized the initiative after deliberate preparation, these racists have nevertheless suffered a disastrous defeat, even when confronted by a divided and uninstructed civilization. Because it stems back behind asceticism to heroicism, this frenzy of nationalism is paranoid.

The real danger today lies, therefore, in some religion or ideology that would really satisfy the ascetic drive of the adolescent by claiming inevitability, universality, and supremacy over racial morality. The churches cannot provide this because they are divided and what the ascetic adolescent is seeking is an absolute authority. The nation, the total state has tried to claim this total authority but it has failed. No person of even sufficient mental competence to keep modern machinery going can for long prevent his critical intelligence from challenging and corroding the completely unsubstantiated superstition of race, and the equally insane notion that a sovereign government or people can be above the general principles of humanity.

In the Communist ideology, the three requirements of the ascetic type are answered, albeit falsely: utter anonymity for the subject, historic inevitability of the process (the fulfillment of man's story and the finality of his striving) and world universality. Here, and again, we see the pressures being attempted which in the great ascetic age produced (1) the man who accuses himself, denounces his own actions, and informs on others: "the right-acting man"; (2) the examiner of conscience and the spiritual judge, the ideal; and (3) the one revelation, absolute and final, the code to which utter submission must be made in the name of *quod semper, quod ubique, quod omnibus*. And today Russia and China are split.

The heroic and pseudo-heroic, when they crack, become paranoid. The ascetic, when he goes to pieces, becomes schizoid. And here we have two correlations that lend further support to the hypothesis that the adolescent is recapitulating the ascetic epoch. The first is the fact that the nor-adrenaline child, representing ontogenically the Heroic Age, if it goes mad will tend in its specific madness, dementia praecox, to the madness of the hero, paranoia. The second is the fact that the adolescent, in turn, when he goes mad will tend mainly to the specific ascetic madness, the schizophrenia that seems to be a split of the mind brought about by the pressure on it of a code that is conceived to be one, infallible and all-embracing, but which, nevertheless, the individual finds he cannot keep.[h] Here is guilt madness, while in the earlier heroic phase there is the madness brought on by intolerable shame.

The educational, remedial, and developmental method for dealing with this adolescent stress (which, if it becomes extreme, can end in collapse) is through showing the adolescent how he may further develop his paidomorphic trends. For man today is a creature that is rapidly evolving through growth of awareness,

[h] In the Middle Ages suicide was most common among monks (16). Today schizophrenia is the mental disease most often attended by suicide.

and this awareness can and must now be deliberately expanded and drawn out by the construction of a social heredity that favors and explicates neoteny. Man needs the encouragement to accept that type of dedication which most often appears in adolescence. He often feels that to accept that role would be both pretentious and unsophisticated. The urge has been so misrepresented and exploited that now it is debunked. And the need that the adolescent feels for athleticism must be met by a psychophysical training that avoids the blind alley of specialized competitiveness. The need that the adolescent feels for discipline must also be met. Today, our education of the almost mature youth, the upper teen-ager, is at best an amalgam of scientific skepticism, the uninformed and straining discipline of heavy intellectual, informational and technical instruction (for example, engineers, physicians and surgeons, lawyers, managers) plus a faint flavor of sophisticated culture. This means that courses in literature are given engineers to remedy the fact that they have become so specialized in the study of stress in materials that they are totally ignorant of how nervous stress in themselves and their fellows has rendered communication almost impossible.[i]

As we have seen, the concept of the gentleman that at one time tried to substitute for the hero and the ascetic is, with the passing of humanic man, no longer relevant. For the gentleman's temporary ascendency as a pattern of prestige depended on a type of consciousness that no longer exists. Into that we shall go a little more fully in the next chapter when considering the next age group, that of first maturity, and its specific standards and risks. For it is that age group, and not the adolescent, that recapitulates the humanic epoch.

Meanwhile, to finish with the adolescent phase, it is clear that only through neotenic education, which teaches insight into one's self by humor, can the keen self-criticism of adolescence be kept

[i] At one world-famous institute of technology the culture cure for this serious deficiency was to give these quite unprepared adolescent minds the task of reading *King Lear.* The Elizabethan tragedy was dismissed by one of the brighter embryo engineers with the comment, "a medieval shot at *Life with Father.*"

from producing a schizoid condition. The tempering tensile strength to produce this dynamically balanced endurance will be achieved by that reconciliation of toughness with tenderness whereby these states of the psyche are seen as being complementary and not as being mutually exclusive antitheses. William James, who did so much to reconcile apparent opposites, nevertheless on this important issue made one of his few great and tragic mistakes. The world is not divided into the tough who can act because they cannot feel and the tender who, because they feel, cannot act. For as the child becomes the preadolescent, the plasticity that it still retains from the healthy responsiveness of the infant must be gradually replaced by the elasticity of the adolescent. Psychophysical elasticity, in contrast to plasticity, is the capacity to react with the combining reply which brings its own contribution to the blend of informational opinion. The tenderness, which at the start is a delicacy of impressionability, does, as it thereby develops, become capable of that tensile strength without which there is no retentiveness; otherwise each new impression obliterates the one before. Retentiveness requires that the new be blended with the old. This is a demand for a resilience that accommodates fresh data by composing the present findings in the basic conception. Significant form is preserved while it is constantly enlarged. This is the principle of all growth. Toughness, seen in this way, is polar to callousness, for the callous is the rigid. Toughness is tenderness grown to a full equality of response to stimuli; for, to take its dictionary definition, it is strong but not brittle, yielding to force without breaking, capable of resisting great strain without coming apart.

To sum up then: in this third athletic-ascetic phase, the personal psychological story of every man calls for an immediate new advance. We have begun a modern psychophysical diagnosis and therapeutic education of the first two phases, infancy and childhood. But as yet we have done nothing significant toward a similar psychophysical diagnosis and education for Phase 4, first maturity, and Phase 5, second maturity. And we shall do nothing as long as we do not provide Phase 3, adolescence, with a new training, a fresh therapeutic education. Further, as we have said before, as long as adolescence remains uninterpreted and unexplicated, the successes of the new training in the first and second phases of infancy and childhood remain anomalous. That is to say, they are successes that temporarily alleviate the conditions of infancy and childhood but do not affect the over-all mores of society (which are those of arrest), still less those of the State (which are coercive). But once we win over the adolescent phase and make it resilient, not callous, once we can give it its rightful place as the third step of a sane series of natural development that is begun with infancy, then we have a majority of the five phases of the individual's life now constructively slanted and in favor of a developmental and creative psychophysical training. That is why the new therapy for adolescence must be carried out now; that is why, if it is carried out, it can prove to be decisive.

Meanwhile, there is reason to hope that this new step (which will shift the balance of society from denial to affirmation, the authority of the community from veto to inspiration) is being taken. As we have just mentioned, diagnosis has made its next advance. With the psychophysical chart of the individual's life brought up to the span of the third octave (from the age of ten to seventeen), we now have the map of organism behavior in our hands. We have a skilled estimate of the quality and release rate of that phase of human beings which, when it was the high tide mark of man's urgency, the great middle phase of individualism, the ascetic epoch, produced the superb desperations of Fakirism, the Thebaid and the Dervish. It produced the rocket aspirations of Beauvais and the equally unstable agilities of later scholasticism. And still, even after that magnificent failure and the reaction back to the horizontal perspectives and level horizons of the humanic phase, it appears in the lives of each one of us. A potent spirit from our past, it rises and complains that it was wrongfully dethroned and submerged; it calls on us to re-express its mis-stated need or otherwise it will, with its fanaticism, make nonsense of our reason and our science and shambles of our steel-wrought cities and teeming populations.

When the domesticated reindeer herds of the Finns have grazed contentedly and obediently for months, they will one day begin to sniff the arctic air. The owner-herders must perforce follow their stock for the annual sojourn in the far north. Man is a migrant of eternity. The culture that does not provide for these rhythms of infinitude will be wrecked by the force which, had it been expressed, should have given replenishment.

4

The ordeal of first maturity
and its specific mental breakdown
[Manic depression]

If the principle of recapitulation that we have posited is valid, then it should carry through all the age groups. If the new-born infant, the child, and the adolescent recapitulate the social history of man (the top section of human evolution since man became psychosocial) then when the individual develops on past adolescence into his first maturity we should find him recapitulating that stage when mankind first tried out the concept of personal self-sufficiency; when he alternated between the optimism that came out of the certainty that he could now attain utopia and the pessimism that arose out of the feeling that he was only an animal.

And of this we do find sufficient evidence. First, if we follow Bernard Hart's[a] classic estimate of madness as being such a magnification of the normal web of life that tolerable eccentricity becomes insane aberration and departure from the viable pattern, then in

[a] See The Psychology of Insanity.

each epoch and age group we should find a characteristic madness. The type of mental collapse should give us a clue to the total character of that epoch and group. Of this we have found evidence in (1) the trauma of birth of the new-born, (2) the dementia praecox (ending in paranoia) of the child that is heavily charged with a nor-adrenaline that is not rightly channeled, and (3) the schizophrenia of the adolescent who is collapsing under a sense of guilt, longing for an over-all authority whose incessant total demand he feels he cannot meet.

These forms of madness do appear in other age groups, but when they do it is because the person's emotional life has not advanced beyond the level where that specific insanity is endemic; his emotional age does not correspond with his biological age. Hence, when he breaks down he produces the insanity that belongs to his emotional age. Thus, dementia praecox is the disease of a child mind that is showing off, and schizophrenia is the illness of an adolescent mind that blames itself. Yet today the main impact of these specific miseries appears in the age groups of the child and the adolescent. Similarly, we find that the fourth great mental disaster, the manic depressive madness, makes its principal invasion into the area of first maturity.

As the late Louis Cholden remarked, the manic-depressive form of insanity might well be regarded as being a temporary effort to escape from the schizoid state. As the sense of a universal law that can be neither denied nor fulfilled becomes intolerable, the psyche hopes to avoid this agony by making its own self-consciousness so acute that it may become wholly independent of the law. The changeover of the ascetic movement into the humanic is the outward symptom of man's consciousness striving, by further contraction, to escape the sense of guilt. But, basically, this only aggravates the condition, for guilt itself is a symptom of growing self-consciousness; just as, before ascetic guilt, the primal self-consciousness of the hero was manifested in his sense of shame. Shame, guilt, and skepticism are three successive symptoms of an intensifying sense of separation. The Age of Humanic Man, therefore, is a transitional and comparatively brief epoch. The total individual either regresses back to authority and expiation or goes on into that melancholy of second maturity that only the leptoid state can eliminate.

The problem of assigning actual years to these age groups is a difficult one, at least in all but the two earliest. We can say that most individuals have completed their psychophysical birth by the time they have reached the age of two and a half years. By then their emotional life has taken on its contours. And although a severe neurosis may still be inflicted, a good start during the first thirty months probably means that the danger of a psychosis springing from traumatic pre-self-conscious experiences is past. We can say, too, that the specific age of childhood, between infancy and adolescence, ranges from the age of two and a half or three years up to ten or eleven.

But adolescence is far harder to fix in terms of specific years. As we have seen, Gesell has provided a map of adolescence that follows the modern accepted span of ten to seventeen. However, in our rapidly growing neotenic extension of consciousness this may omit those who, though they are not average, are most specifically representative of our present age group distribution. Undoubtedly, a number of individuals remain arrested at adolescence and, indeed, many at childhood level. But though many may still be growing emotionally, the rate of growth may be slower than at other times. For example, it has lately been discovered that many men who have been given life sentences for murder can safely be released after the age of forty. They had been homicidal because the nor-adrenaline of infancy (the hormone of aggression needed at that age) had lasted on into adolescence and early manhood. Some mistake in their early handling had prevented them from adequately using the nor-adrenaline for the effort to live, grow, and expand, and then, its purpose achieved, from being able to develop the adrenaline necessary for social growth.[b] However, after having continued to

[b] A useful analogy here is the elimination of the thymus as the child's growth proceeds. The thymus is the gland in the chest that ceases to function as adolescence approaches. Research into the thymus, in these first years of the Sixties, has indicated, however, that although as a growth-activating gland

function (but atavistically; that is, murderously), the nor-adrenaline did at last diminish. When at length the social level of adolescence and first maturity was reached, the individual was under the endocrine control of pure adrenaline and at fifty the person had the contrite amenability of the adolescent and the required responsibility of the mature.

Further, this whole problem of age grouping and assigning year-spans to each group is made far more complex by the fact that there is much real retardation among present-day groups. Not only are there many individuals who are laggards, gravely retarded, but the whole issue of neoteny makes it doubly difficult to say whether an individual's delay in becoming mature is due to a morbid arrest (such as the above example of a person's emotional life still being in acute nor-adrenaline conflict) or to a paidomorphic retention of an early uncommitted openness and flexibility that may appear to be irresponsibility. Under the Kentish Saxon law of "gavel-kind" a male was considered to be mature at fifteen; the Australian aborigine is said to attain maturity at twelve and an ape is mature at three.

We must expect our present-day youth to take longer and longer to grow up. If, as J. B. S. Haldane has said, urged on by the neotenic drive man is heading for a growth retentiveness that will permit him to postpone committing and uniting his thought to speech until he is five, and that will allow him to learn until he is forty, then human beings will still be adolescent at thirty when, at present, almost half our life expectancy is over. It may not, then, be inaccurate to advance the year span of the three later age groups of adolescence, first maturity, and second maturity and so find, as some modern authorities believe, that from the twenties even on

---

it is in manifest activity up till the age of eight or ten years (after which its growth slows until by fourteen it starts to wither and disappear) it has another use in keeping up the body's immunity. This find suggests that there may be some truth in the Yoga statement that dilational thoracic breathing with the expansion of rib cage and sternum (for the thymus lies just behind the sternum) does reactivate the thymus and add to the health of the practicer.

to forty there may now be an incidence of schizophrenia: that is, the retention of an adolescent-ascetic self-blaming frame of mind. And the succeeding phase of first maturity (the humanic stage) may not come into action until between forty and sixty. Certainly there are psychiatric authorities who hold that the specific manic depressive state of mind is mainly endemic in that score of years of the fifth and sixth decades.

The ordeal of first maturity, as it is recapitulating the humanic phase, will then consist of two stress factors. In the first place, as we have seen, it will be subject to the conflict between the relief of independence and the distress of isolation. The man is now responsible. He may and must make choices. As an adolescent he might and often did break down into schizophrenia because he was faced with one all-embracing, all-exacting law that he must acknowledge and revere but could not obey. The very humility that made him accept it made him confess his inadequacy to fulfill it. As a completely self-conscious individual his breakdown risk lay in the opposite direction. He was now in danger because he now saw himself as a person who could seek no final authority to give him the true and complete law. But at the same time he saw that he must, out of many findings, numerous opinions, manifold dogmas, and even conflicting hypotheses decide for himself as to which were the better ones and as to how, from these possible advices, he could best guide his own life. Such a state of mind is the seedbed soil of manic-depressive insanity. And it is made more acute by this frame of mind having been accompanied by the complementary stress of critical education which it has, itself, largely brought forth. The humanic phase, as we have seen, was the epoch which, in the West (its real home), produced the new learning. Tradition and reason itself, in its form of Scholasticism, were put on trial. Tradition was demoted from its office of supreme judge. Reason was ordered to take on experimentation as its vicar or suffragan. Dogma and argument could stand only if supported by experiment.

Therefore, not only does the individual who out of adolescence enters first maturity have to undergo the ordeal of finding himself in the position of having to reject the hope of one utterly trust-

worthy authority and of having to choose between experts, specialists, and a variety of devotedly closed minds. He has to face the
even more distressing fact that his is no longer the simple will of
the hero who knows that the past was futile and wrong and that
the present is here for the strong-willed to take. He realizes that
certainty may never be possible for anyone, least of all for himself.
Skepticism offers the only possibility of knowledge; and skepticism
will not work unless it leaves the skeptic free to find that if the
facts show that no answer is obtainable nothing can be done.

The first maturity of the fully self-conscious individual, therefore, is very different from the assured defiances of the proto-
conscious heroic individual, the nor-adrenaline child. He realizes
that he must reject authority. Moreover, he sees that even he himself is not adequate to be an unbiased authority for his own conduct,
since he has neither sufficient information about the outer conditions nor sufficient understanding of and control over his own inner
states. Nevertheless, he knows that by experiment he must and can
do much to produce powerful, predictable, and profitable results
in the outer world, among and with his fellows and on and in his
own physique. Conscious, experimental education therefore becomes
his concern.

It is this aspect of the humanic first maturity, its growing
belief in experimentally established instruction, that ushers in man's
next phase, crisis, and ordeal. For the isolationism of complete self-
consciousness, which produces this skepticism of first maturity, leads
such a type of mind to jettison every belief and practice that cannot
quickly and obviously be shown to be experimentally accurate. It
even leads to the rejection, without experiment, of every practice
for which a mistaken explanation has been given (for example,
the efficacy of prayer or the anomaly of extrasensory perception).
Hence, man disregards his preterconscious and refuses to give attention to any data that are anomalous within his confined category
or sensory judgment. This naturally produces an increase of repression, misgiving, and fear. Thus, those threshold pressures are generated in the psyche that make the total individual, the man of

first maturity, aware that he is something more and other than an individual.

Still further, as we have seen and will note again later on, as the process of evolution works through the extension of paido-morphism, the man who is coming into first maturity will naturally (but inexplicably to those who do not grasp the neotenic process of evolution) dislike being called on to accept maintenance respon-sibility. As was mentioned earlier, J. B. S. Haldane (as well as N. J. Berrill) has pointed out that even now biologists can foresee the time when men will not become adult until they are thirty or thirty-five. It is not an escapism that makes the young adult object to being called up to administer codes that he questions and that also cause the young scholar to doubt the current belief in the increase of means as being a criterion of progress. Intuitively he feels, through the evolutionary urge within him, that he must have more time, room, and freedom to grow; that man's future lies in an upward growth in quality of consciousness and not in a crude extrapolating, horizontal advance in gear and economics.

For first maturity, the fourth stage of the individual, repre-sents, tallies with, and is the parallel of the fourth stage of the human social heredity. Today, however, we are in the fifth stage, the leptoid age of the postindividual; although that stage has not yet been recognized, still less has it achieved a pattern of prestige. And so, as our society still regards itself as being humanic, individ-uals in first maturity are still regarded as being the age group of executive authority, the focal range of power. Therefore, our society, precisely because it is itself predominantly manic depressive in its outlook,[c] welcomes the manic-depressive man.

Hence, the overly energetic young man of today can escape into action. He can project his conflict on others in that confusion of misunderstandings and thinly disguised ill-will called politics, and in espousing that patriotism which, because of its element of paranoid heroicism, Doctor Johnson in a moment of understand-able exasperation called "the last refuge of a scoundrel."

[c] As Ruth Benedict (3) indicates in her *Patterns of Cultuure.*

Although the reckoning with reality is thus postponed, with the aid of frequent transferences of mental conflict into such psychosomatic diseases as ulcers and coronary seizures,[d] nevertheless the individual does meet, in second maturity, the disregarded Sphinx returning with accumulated vengeance. Not only this, but he finds that society itself, now becoming increasingly either leptoid or melancholy, with corrosive satire debunks the impudent opportunist and seeks for his superseder, the truly mature and contemporary person.

It is clear, then, that the evoluionary process of our consciousness calls for a new step in education. As each of us individually passes through first maturity we need to learn from the experience of humanic man, from the stress he had to endure in becoming a total individual. It was a two-sided stress and projected itself, alternately, as a challenging skepticism of the tradition (the tradition that the ascetic had tried to resuscitate and make into the all-comprehensive, infallible authority of veto and repression), and then as a challenging skepticism of himself. The education that begins as being critical and analytic at last arrives at the self; at which point integral constructions, creative methods are required, not the reductional technics of skepticism. And this involves a re-examination of the tradition. At this time, too, when this re-examination has become requisite we discover that the tradition has already been found to be, in origins and at base, not repressive and ascetic, but expressive of the total mind-body consciousness plus the individual group-consciousness as a psychosomatic whole, that is, the life religion.

Originally, the tradition was the extreme growing edge of evolution, its most highly accelerated part. Mind and body were being developed together by neoteny, by (biologically speaking) the rapid extension of infancy and, next, the even more rapid intercalation and extension of the specifically human phase of childhood, paidomorphy.

The fourth ordeal in the individual's life process, the ordeal

[d] Research in 1962 into the average life expectancy of the high executives in the advertising business showed that it stands at 61 years.

of first maturity, is then the first life phase wherein specific critical teaching becomes part of the test whereby the individual is driven to make three specific growth discoveries about himself. (1) He has to reject all the tradition that does not conform with his experience and experimentation. (2) Feeling himself to be an individual who is purely physical, he confines his critical faculty of evaluation only to data that come to him through the "five senses." (3) This confinement-isolation in turn leads to a skepticism of his physiological instrument as being an adequate apparatus for apprehending the continuum, and to an even greater skepticism of its ability to understand or to control itself. And so those in first maturity discover intuitively, and by the negative process, that the concept of total individualism is a misapprehension.

The critical analytic method of education must be supplemented. For under this ordeal of growth some try to retract and return, to get rid of their total individualism by retreating to the ascetic totalitarian authoritariansm, whether it be of a church or a commissary, ecclesiastic, communistic, or fascistic. To some degree, today this must mean a schizoid state. Many become manic depressive, while others, avoiding withdrawal, nevertheless hang on with no keen pleasure in the present or hope of the future. So they are transferred, by the inevitability of the biological process, into second maturity. Physically, they are carried on but, being psychologically uneducated and unequipped to cooperate with the process, they are bewildered and it is compulsive. As old age comes on what should be second maturity is in danger of becoming involutional melancholy; the fear of death becomes the basic phobia, unbalanced by any compensatory desire, let alone significance. The life declines from being even the pretense of a rear action into a rout. Every observer now realizes that without an adult education of the emotions first maturity only sows the seeds of a harvest of futility which, in second maturity, must be reaped as a suicidal despair; for the increase in the incidence of suicide follows the increase of age.

5

The ordeal of second maturity and its specific mental breakdown [Involutional melancholy]

We have now reached the at present final state of the individual. We have come to old age, the phase that Wartin, in his *Old Age*, has called the period of involution. These are the terminal years when the organism begins to shed and diminish its structure and the mind must become either senile or detached. And in considering this fifth ordeal of man's, which today has given rise to the new science of geriatrics, we must recognize a vital fact that may give significant help to gerontology.

Up to this point, we have seen that the recapitulatory relationship between the life process of the individual and the five stages of man's social heredity is discernible in the postbirth stages of psychophysical development (just as it was in the uterine prebirth physical stages). In this fact we have an invaluable clue to interpreting and elucidating each age group.

As we have also seen, (1) the insights that anthropology has given us into the preindividualized mind of cave man, and those cultures that until now have preserved much of his outlook, have aided us in understanding the state of consciousness that individual infancy still recapitulates. (2) Protohistory, in turn, with its elucidation of the Heroic Age, permits us to understand the child's exhibitionist urges. (3) Religious history, with its central theme of ascetic other-worldlyism and the sense of sin and guilt, allows us to orient the adolescent's self-blame and longing for discipline. (4) Sociocultural history (especially the history of experimental technology, scientific method, and critical apparatus) and in particular, modern history of Western Renaissance man (with its specific pattern of prestige—the critically minded, power-loving individualist) has given us the clue to the major drives of the individual's first maturity, the tableland years between the climb of adolescence and the decline of second maturity and old age.

But at this point (and it is this which makes the problem of old age uniquely difficult) our guide rail ends, our psychophylogeny gives out. We have no pattern of prestige up to which the age may live. It is true that in the past, from the Stone Age cultures of Papua to the exquisite aestheticism of China, there have been societies that had a place for and gave authority to the aged. But, under this retractive influence, such societies always became arrested. For better or for worse, the old have had to be dismounted (just as they have been) if man's development was to continue.

The problem of second maturity is as severe and acute as it is precisely because there is no traditional pattern with which to meet and into which to fit the old. Later on, we shall see that it is just this lack of a pattern of prestige that is today holding up neotenic evolution in the younger groups.

Meanwhile, as we saw in Chapter 5, Part I, it is clear that our epoch has yet to find itself a name. We have begun to realize that it is post-Renaissance, post-Humanic, postindividual. We begin to suspect that its character will be of that specific cast given by the experience and realization that it is the first generation of self-conscious men to find themselves conscious of their unself-conscious. Also, among those who have accustomed themselves to such an estimate of the present human constitution, there is a feeling that this change has been brought about through a mutationally swift alteration in awareness: not merely a shift in values and compositional capacity, but an enlargement of consciousness. As yet, though, no pattern for post-Renaissance man has emerged; there is no design in which it is possible to imagine the stature and orientation, the place and profile of the postindividual person.

However, we can clearly recognize that the units, the members, the raw stuffs for such a new integration and new age class, which can have its specific vision and value, have emerged. We now have a fifth estate, a new extension of the life process, a new category of the biological process. Nor is it made up of stragglers and worn-outs, or of those stubborn, dried-up integuments that did, in the past, cause those social arrests called gerontocracies. It is, in its way—which is more wary but not one whit less minatory—as rebellious and as mutinous as is adolescence. The adolescent, if frustrated in his deep desire for service, sacrifice, and discipline, will literally gang up on us, just as the Hitler youth yahoos did. Similarly, the sullen and reactionary old (who are jealous of the young, bitter at lost opportunity, and fearful of an immediate future) will seek revenge by retaliatory punishments, repression of liberty and exploration, and the persecuting suspicion that corrupts all free government. The ancient gerontocracies respected and incarnated tradition. This new class of the old, unless they are given vision, can only respect themselves, as did Stalin. The damage that, today, the rebellious young can do to the community is great. It is smaller, though, than that harm that can and must be wrought by the growing mass of a new class of elders who have a greater sense of political power and a deeper selfishness because they have a more profound, far better founded hopelessness and fear toward a tomorrow that holds for them no promise: only negation.[a]

Hence, since we find that each of the growth phases of the individual is marked by a particular type of breakdown at the time

[a] The greater part of all the wealth of the richest nation in the world is now in the hands of elderly women.

when the person should pass into the next phase and fails to do so (that is, womb retreat trauma, dementia praecox, schizophrenia, manic depression), it is not surprising that, later on, second maturity is marked by its specific mental risk and all too frequent culmination, involutional melancholy. And this mind disease, which is peculiar to the aged, is doubly significant. First, because of its stubborn resistance to therapy and, secondly, because of its clear association with and relevance to the fact mentioned above, that the advanced elders of today have no traditional, inherited pattern of living, while all the other age groups have. This great category of the healthy grandparents is such a late comer, so unprecedented among social phenomena that it has, as yet, no libretto, no part written for it in the play of life and human process. As the old of today, like the newly rich, do not know what to live for or how to use this new endowment, these unparalled years of freedom, and as the community with its traditional, standard fourfold code that ends short of this newly added section knows no more than the newcomers do, everyone is at a loss and painfully embarrassed.

Further complications are added by the very success of our economic system. For instance, vast amounts of our surplus wealth have gone into medical research and the development of new medical and surgical techniques that prolong the life span.[b] As a result, there are more persons above the age of sixty still living than at any other time in man's history. But at the same time our successful economic system also means that fewer workers are required. And the old are not wanted as producers. Naturally, the required cut in the labor force comes first in the upper age brackets. The oldster's tempo is not suitable for turning things out. However, they can still serve as consumers: as an army, not of hands but of mouths, for getting things out of the way and preventing the ship of prosperity from being swamped by the following wave of glut. Nonetheless, the more alive the old are, the more alive they are to

[b] For example, prostatectomy has been raised from being an agonizing exceptional success to an equality with tonsilectomy. Both operations are introductions: one to adolescence and the other to second maturity.

this situation. They do not want to be banished to pensioneerdom, that reservation fenced round with the eyes of their guardians who are vigilant lest these prisoners should try to break back and flood into the labor stream, who are watchful with hope that death will evaporate these useless and dangerous snowdrifts of time. So pathetic has this situation become, so futile the pension-and-get-rid-of-them method, that some firms let them seep back into their business circulation, as kindly drivers will risk a skid and even a collision to avoid running over a blind dog that is crossing the street. In the past, the only pattern for the old was that of the man who had had so much experience that he could be referred to in every crisis. For life was repetition and he had seen all of it.

Today, of course, life is not repetition. Even encyclopedias now become out of date in a decade. Nor are the oldsters sound bases for mummification. The elders of today are more alive than ever before and in a new extension of life. And this new aliveness is even more disquieting to our conventions than their mere survival and their wish to be in circulation. They don't want to be treated as dignified, immobile, antique statuary that is set in the background, against the hedges of formal gardens and at the end of blind alleys. Nor do they wish to be considered as busts of the ancients that are ranged on the top of library bookshelves. They don't feel that they are in arrested animation, or laid out on the cooling board and awaiting the embalmer's hand. Just as King Saul on Mount Gilboa, after his army's defeat and while he was still unwounded, felt that "it repented him that his life was still whole within him" and committed suicide, so, as we said at the end of the last chapter, the suicide rate steadily climbs and increases in the higher age group. And the old, we must repeat, are themselves as ignorant about their condition as are all their juniors. They feel their unprecedented aliveness but they cannot, any more than can the other age groups, explain it or know what to do about it. They are without any pattern of behavior, without any particular prestige-giving standard of conduct.

Therefore, feeling their life still whole within them, they can only do one of two things. In a last echo of manic-depressive alternation, they may fluctuate between a nervous elation and a chilling despair. Or they may, with finality, turn in on themselves and, burying the mind because the body will not die, sink into the specific madness of the aged, involutional melancholy.

And it is a significant fact that not only is melancholy endemic to old age, but it is, of all the psychoses, the most stubbornly resistant to all treatment. New medicaments are all highly promising aids in the treatment of other mental diseases. Yet psychiatrists are all too aware that these drugs, shock treatment, carbon dioxide plus oxygen, or the more patient therapies can do little to shift this final dark cloud of the spirit. Why?

The answer to both these questions—why is the psychiatrist helpless before this despair and why does it attack the old most heavily?—is the same. The other mental collapses can be challenged as being irrational. The rage and suspicion of paranoia (which rises from the person's being balked), the schizophrenic's conviction of inadequacy and guilt and his withdrawal (arising from a too perfectionist desire to fulfill a too little understood law), and the manic-depressive extremes of the man in first maturity who recoils into premature depression because his undisciplined temerity has led him into overplaying his hand: these complaints are all subject to challenge by reason, and to reinterpretation by good sense. First win the attention of the patient. This is what the new tranquillizing drugs do; while shock treatment does temporarily jolt him out of his obsessional attention to his private plight and out of his personal conviction that his problem is an insoluble one. Recover for one who is mentally ill his capacity to listen to another's evaluation of the situation and he can be shown that his view was wrong, that the sensible view of sane men is accurate.

But this is not so with melancholy when it comes to the aged. Even if it strikes in the younger age groups, it is not really to be answered by modern psychiatry, though its challenge may be deflected and postponed. The protoindividual can be given the euphoria of exercise, the anodyne of the healthy appetites. The midindividual can find respite in romantic attachment to a person or cause. And the total individual can take to the amassing of means, the exercise of power, and the intoxicant of recognitional praise. But even when these are available—and generally they are to be had only in strictly limited amounts—they are, by their very nature, only temporizing palliatives. Sooner or later, and inevitably with old age, their power to distract sinks to the vanishing point. In the present picture of the life process that still gives scale, map, and chart to public opinion and professional psychiatry, there is no place for age. Still less is there a place for a new extension of age.

The Freudian position, which because it was first is still the most popular with a profession that felt its chief enemy to be asceticism, still regards detensioning of sexual pressure as the one sound therapy. The socially amalgamated therapies of Stack Sullivan and Eric Fromm mix biological release with the promise of a juster society and the concept of man as a being whose sanity must be social as well as personal.

The Jungian position is more helpful. For it admits that the history of man consists of more than biological and social records. There is also a psychological record, which is discernible in the study of the archetypal images. And this teaching permits man to make some peace not only with his racial inheritance, his appetites, and his socio-economic heredity, but also with humanity's standards of value and significance. But even the best psychiatries aim at little more than adjustment; most of the men who practice them are still looking backward. Very few if any of them foresee psychological evolution as being the future of the race; so we are still waiting for them to make any real contribution to the problem of geriatrics. Have any of them successfully challenged melancholy (in any of the age groups)? Have they been able to deal with it when it forecloses on those who have bought it off, when it triumphs as involutional despair?

But is there anything really to be said to the old, this new and latest class that nature has permitted? For they are the embarrassing and accidental resultant of new realistic, specialized medical and surgical skills that have been irresponsibly worked out and, so far, are being employed by a sentimentality that is equally irresponsible and unthinking-out of the consequences of its emotional pity. Similarly, and at the other end of the line of life, infant hygiene has permitted the results of unrestrained and unplanned-for breeding to survive beyond our means of subsistence. If a headlong increase in population is all that has been brought about, if we have simply disregarded earlier checks and balances of society and Nature and have admitted, without foresight, a flood of lives for which our scale of life has no place, use, or purpose, then there is nothing to say to the old.

But in the schema we have set out in this thesis, and which can now be detected in our actual history, it is clear that the sequence is still incomplete if it stops short of this fifth stage of second maturity. Very few thinking persons today are willing to go along with our proposal that man, since he has been man, has gone through the first four great psychophysical epochs and that each person recapitulates these four stages in his own life. However, even if we do allow that this is true, and in spite of the studies of such men as Peter Drucker,[c] Roderick Seidenberg (76), Friedrich August von Hayek (90), which show that the age of humanic, total-individual man is over, we still seem to be unprepared to recognize the implications. The emergence of second maturity, the large class of healthy grandparents, can be understood and be availed of only if we see that this fifth phase is inevitable; that it is the essential requirement for the manning of a fifth category of mankind, the fifth age of man as a race and as a person. Involutional melancholy is caused by the fact that although this fifth rank and estate of man has been recruited today, nevertheless it has to wait about for its equipment, office, and accouterments. For though we knew that humanic man was no longer the growing edge of the life process, we were not able to think out what the new type would be and, therefore, what its specific contribution, standard, and behavior should be.

So involutional melancholy will remain to consume and challenge us until we learn how to burn it out of the system. We must

[c] See *Post-Renaissance Man* by Peter Drucker.

recognize it as being a symptom of unreleased, damped-down forces, just as flame-suffocating fumes are indicative of fuel that is only turning into gases below ignition point. We can answer the riddle it poses when we can see it for what it is, for what all the mental illnesses have shown themselves to be: symptoms of balked disposition, or energies that have not been given their appropriate expression.[d]

We have said earlier that these new elders shock the old-fashioned pension planner by their failure to enjoy their pensioned freedom, or even remain sane, when they are "put out to grass," when they are taken from the shafts of social traffic and left to browse, doze, swell, and run to seed. Not only this, but they scandalize their concerned juniors even more by their refusal (or inability) to behave as the drained aged used to behave; to carry on, at best, either as fossilized tables of the law or in a chrysalis of comfort and so "shut up in measureless content," rewombed, and readied for the tomb. The new and latest age group wishes inevitably to live, but neither they nor their juniors know how that may be done.

Hence, as there is no part written for them and they must play something, they can only go back and attempt to replay old stock parts. They not only long to be recalled to power, they wish to resume or continue (with their still valid potency) personal relationships. This is a theme that has often been dealt with by authors in the last few years. It is both pathetic and exasperating. But it will remain as incurable as it is inexplicable until we put our knowledge of the point at which mankind today has arrived (the age of post-Humanic, postindividual, regeneralized, whole-conscioused man) together with the personnel, the manning, the new age category with which the evolutionary process has now provided us. For if the principle of neoteny (the increased capacity to comprehend the experience of living through an ever new, youthful, fresh, childlike approach) is the aim of life, and the process of paidomorphy is the means whereby neoteny is made possible, then we should find

[d] The well-known psychoanalyst, Andras Angyal, has pointed out that at the root of all neurotic defensive structures there lies the fundamental urge for self-preservation and for the protection of personal integrity.

neoteny actually working precisely where the newest step is being taken by the life-process today: in second maturity.

The main tragedy of this vital and new old-age group is that, because it feels that its growth is not over and that it is not at its *Nunc Dimittis,* it imagines that it must return to a repetition of those activities which belonged to its first phases and now belong to those who are in those first phases. The present mind of the man in second maturity can conceive of only two alternatives: death or repetition, elimination or recurrence. The third alternative is, of course, the way between the horns of the dilemma; the spiral that, on a higher level, re-dilates and emerges to a recovery of unspecialized function. In addition to the *Rajas* of activity and the *Tamas* of resigned inertia there is the *Sattvas* of understanding composition (see Glossary).

What, in actual terms, does or can that mean? Are we not compelled by such a suggestion to fall back on Nicodemus' protest against the statement, "You must be born again"? "How can a man go back into his mother's womb?" he asked. He cannot, but he can and must recapture the freedom of the young. The first step to understanding how this process can and does work, if we will understand it and cooperate with it, is to be able to conceive of the life process of every individual as being a spiral, just as the life process of the race is a spiral. The neotenic process works out from a high degree of unspecialization to an apex curve point of specialization and, that achieved, back once more to unspecialization, generalized expression. To put this in the simplest terms, the new-born child of today is the least specialized of all creatures; more potential and less actual, more of promise and less fulfilled. It is an uncommitted, fetal creature. Yet, as we have seen, even now it is not able to be born as completely unenclosed as the fetus is in the sixth month.[e] But after the prolonged infancy that belongs to it as a mammal (another extension of uncommittedness that is its birthright as a

[e] Some additional and confirmatory evidence on this important point is provided by findings that seem to show that the brain cases of children born by a successful caesarian section are less contracted than those delivered by the natural delivery. See also footnote *g*, this chapter.

primate), followed by the particular and uniquely human stage of childhood (a third enlargement of freedom and opportunity for spontaneous learning and experiment, curiosity), the individual does begin to specialize. In adolescence, the diffused generalized interest-affection begins to focus. Particular interests begin to canalize the mind's radiation of curiosity. Just as the small child in the second year of infancy, having spontaneously vocalized and experimented (just for the sake of expression) with the whole gamut of all sounds ever used in any speech, now begins to confine itself to those speech sounds (its mother tongue) that produce results and permit communication, so it is later in the mental-emotional life of the adolescent. The youth begins to specialize his intellectual pursuits. Similarly, and at the same time, his emotional life also turns from being a tide into a stream, and begins to carve out its bed. First, instead of a generalized companionship, particular persons become a concern. Intensity, with its complement exclusiveness, begins to appear. And next, a particular person begins to epitomize satisfaction, the fulfillment of demand, the absorption of devotion, the embodiment of ideal, the inspiration and purpose of all endeavor.

However, we know that this is not a final stage. Only in the romantic fairytale that dates from the last phase of the Heroic Age (when the woman hopes to glamorize and spellbind the wanderer to her side) does the formula of "and they lived happily ever after" terminate the plot. The focal intensity of reproductive passion, passing from suppliance to dominance, passes on again to companionship, division of concerns, and an awareness of other and alternative associations. The late Ralph Linton, the anthropologist, and many other students of the social sciences have pointed out that because our civilization has accelerated community and social interrelatedness the requirements of education and hygiene have restricted the familial phase to an ever fewer number of years. As our years of life expectancy have increased, as the ages of maturity are extended, the years of the marital-parental phase that used to cover all the first maturity have contracted. At the present pace it may well happen that as the child, for its right emotional and physical growth, requires some parent to be devoted to it for the first three or four years (and a devoted foster parent is better than even a dutiful but vocationless begetter or child-bearer) the home phase may be confined to those who have the inborn gift of home-making. Being "in love," it has always been known, does not last in its exclusive and others-eclipsing phase. And jealousy, the oxide of a mono-devotion in the corrosive atmosphere of a possessive-exclusive society, eats away the inherent strength of a truly loving relationship that is by its nature nonpossessive. Mothers snatch and fasten; fathers elide and elude. These painful symptoms are simply negative proofs that the personal life process is a spiral, not a straight line.

It is natural and also social that, at his present stage of development and with his extended life span, man should find, beyond the marital phase, a period far longer than was the premarital and in which he must make at least as distinctive patterns of value-bearing behavior as the period of parenthood (marital period) had permitted.

This is, of course, only to say that second maturity is neither a rest-house annex nor an extension to "real living"; nor is it a paddock in which to cool off before being led into the dark stables of death. In its own right second maturity is a creative epoch of life. Indeed, it is an epoch of such unique potentialities that, because it is not an echo or an encore of the achievement of any other and earlier phase, we have found it hard to believe in and to develop. For in this stage of second maturity, because it is evolution's latest gift to man, he is given, in still larger measure than it is given to any other epoch or any other age group, life's greatest gift to man: the liberty to *choose,* freedom of choice. Throughout the history of all mammals and particularly throughout the history of the primates, we can see that gift of choice, that power of selection, being increased. Natural selection's culminating test is selection of the best by giving all promising candidates themselves the capacity to select. Choice and the way it is used, to gain or lose liberty, is the supreme criterion of character, the swiftest and most searching method of picking the creative type who believes in a meaning that he, the chooser, must explicate and exemplify.

This flexibility of choice is possible only if the person is left inherently free. That is, as we say descriptively but still with an uncomprehending bewilderment, if the person is left at a loose end. In order that the mammals should have the first inkling of freedom, the close-stitched selvedge of instinct (the web tucked neatly in upon itself) had to be partially unraveled. A further fraying made the minds of the great apes capable of curiosity and anxiety.[f] The curiosity with which we come into this world can endure years of disapproval by timid oldsters and punishment by security enforcers before it is wholly cauterized. Now, with old age and at the upper end, Nature restores freedom of choice and permits, once again, that rightful irresponsibility to enquire and explore regardless of consequences. Being relieved of the armor of authority and the enforcement instruments of command, those in second maturity are once more at liberty to enquire rather than to order, and to question rather than reply.

A promising sign of this is that several original minds, having held high administrative office and then been honorably retired, have expressed delight not only at the release from executive detail but at the deliverance into a liberty in which they are free to think aloud and to say what they notice. For as private persons, in a State that still declares that it guarantees freedom, they need no longer fear that what they say will be taken as being more than the opinion, the obiter dictum of an individual insight. This, of course, is a very simple but quite hopeful example of the spontaneous and indeed almost unconscious de-crystalizing development of the mind of Second Maturity into its rightful and unique liberty.

To go back to an earlier, cruder simile, which was used to illustrate this latest phase of life: after completing first maturity, after the administrative phase has followed the parental-familial phase into the past, after retirement from office, the tracks of social life end, the known and well-trodden paths of typical behaviors, the sequences of character-parts run out and are finished. This is dismaying to the routineer and authoritarian. But, once show this new class of the old that they *are* a class and that they can find a specific

[f] The gorilla and the orang are *angst* types, while monkeys are almost inexhaustibly curious.[8]

cooperative consciousness, that they are not only the latest class, the growing edge of life, but that they are therefore free, as no other class is, to write in their own unique and original part, to lay out the new pattern of creative liberty—and at least a large number will desire to live up to this stimulating offer. So being able comprehensively to consider the historical life process and the individual life process, they will see, first, how they can regard themselves as being the latest though not necessarily the last step in that process. Secondly, they will see that as they are the latest achievement of the life process, a creature of choice and initiative, they may and must now consciously cooperate with it by specific conscious development—that is, self-education.

The basis for that education is first a clear realization as to the aim and purpose of that education. What kind of person are we hoping to produce? (1) Clearly such an education must aim at a further development of the whole person, the entire psychophysique, for the full release of that being's still hardly realized potentialities. (2) That release-development can be, and can only be, by further deliverance from those specialized commitments, those individualized characterizations and stations (of profession and office) which reach their apex in history with humanic man, the total individual, and which reach their climax in the personal life history at the last stage of first maturity, retirement age. (3) And that further deliverance is only possible if the principle of neoteny and its process paidomorphy are willingly and comprehendingly applied by the latest age group, the unstereotyped personality, those in second maturity whom the State and the community must leave free to pioneer because no social pattern, today or in the past, has had a place for this new and advanced variety of vitality. The question of Nicodemus can be answered, not esoterically but socially and biologically. Those that are most mature need no longer harden up, callus, crack, flake away, and die, identified with their husk. They need no longer attempt to repeat their past phases of adolescence and first maturity. They can regeneralize. And what in actual fact that will mean, how they may perform this metamorphosis, we shall see later.

For before we consider this next evolutionary step we must answer the practical question of what possible use to society and to the life process such a regeneralized type could be. Its function is clear when, for a moment, we reconsider what the evolutionary process has now become. The first factor, we must stress again, is the process of heredity as it actually works with man, the growing edge of life. Once a creature was evolved who advanced no longer by physical hereditary modifications, but by the exchange of vocal information, by speech, then social heredity had begun. And, through the exchange of new findings and the collecting of these findings into traditions of skill and behaviors, not only was social heredity a growth far more rapid and purposive than any physical hereditary improvements. The very growth of these gainful skills, uniting behaviors and defense powers, permitted the infant to be born increasingly in an unprotected state of body and therefore of unprecedented responsiveness to teaching.[9] Later, the steady extension of these protective resources and capacities permitted the infant's sensitiveness to new stimuli, and its welcome toward original experiences, to be further extended until true childhood emerged.

This was the period between the symbiosis of the infant-with-the-mother and the allotted service of the adult (and in our society, to some extent, the adolescent) to the tribe, the stage when the child is free to move on its own but not yet called on to use its main activities for the community's needs.

Meanwhile, *pari passu,* a third factor was added to and accelerated human evolution. The growing tradition-by-speech permitted first the infant and then the child (who were the recipients of the

[9] H. F. Fleure has pointed out that the sustained openness of the infant's skull and so its unconstricted brain were largely dependent on the availability of cow's milk for a prolonged lactation period and the postponement of the development of the jaws and the jaw muscles that run up onto the skull:—a development that was necessary if a hard, tough, masticatory diet was to be assimilated. And G. R. Levy (53) has observed, in her *The Gate of Horn,* that even in the Paleolithic (Magdalenian) cave drawings there are pictures of penned and kept cows. See also Kirk's reference to expansion of skull in caesarian-born children, footnote *e,* this chapter.

tradition) to grow in receptivity. And under this reciprocal growth of finder and receiver, of widening knowledge in play with enlarging capacity to understand, there arose the beginnings of understanding for its own sake. This was the start of comprehension that welcomes new data as contributions to an enlarging frame of general understanding, a view of Nature as a whole. Here lies the source of the mythos. Here we see the first faint dawn of *religio,* that total interpretation of experience in one embracing meaning, the weaving, into a totally significant whole, of the entirety of events. This task of keeping the social heredity always sufficiently flexible, of having always a sufficiency of wonder, curiosity, and a delight in composing new things into the picture of the whole—this gift must always have been of the highest social and survival value. For the tribe that needed least to reject new discoveries, because they could find a place for the anomaly in the *nomos* (the law of things as they are), was the tribe that must advance ahead of all others and become their teacher. For example, there was the triumph over the dread of giant wild beasts through the concept of totemism (53). And it is now thought that knowledge of the wonderfully improved technique in making flint implements by "pressure flaking" (it was called the Solutrean and was one of the final phases of the Old Stone Age) was spread, most probably, by the handing on of a new idea that was commended by its inherent superiority, and not by conquest as had been assumed.[h]

And such a gift would, of necessity, tend to shine most brightly in those minds that, most neotenically, could retain the child's gift of pure curiosity. Hence, there would be a natural selection in favor of those who could thus remain young, who could fend off the arthritis of fear by the constant suppling activity of curious interest. So the seer-shaman type would tend to be selected. This is a type

[h] "Most workers [archaeological excavators] are quite prepared to accept the Solutrean as being due to a diffusion of certain specialized ideas, not to the invasion of new peoples with superior weapons." *Anthropology Today* edited by A. L. Krober (50); see especially "Old World Prehistory: Paleolithic," by H. L. Movius. See also Zotz (99).

that (a) specifically and developmentally carries on the social heredity and instructs the open-minded young in the comprehensive meaning of the circle and cycle of events; and (b) he selects from those young such as show neotenic capacity for this compositional curiosity, this search for the new that will enrich the tradition. We can now clearly recognize this seer type in history and prehistory's preservers, the pre-urban and even pre-agricultural societies. Social heredity and physical heredity, the way of the God-possessed and inspired and the way of the property-possessed and gear-involved, soon become distinct though complementary, a reciprocal relationship of contemplatives and actives. And further, it is discovered that the seers must remain paidomorphic for another important reason. Seership, the extrasensory power to foretell, has been persistently and highly prized by tribes whose rudimentary economy could hardly afford to retain members whose only function was a fancy one and whom natural selection would punish with extinction for a very moderate number of mistakes. In view of this fact, we are now less inclined to disregard evidence for the faculty and more inclined to research and to find confirmatory data.

This gift was always supposed to be correlated with youth and to be commonest and brightest in prepuberty. During the ascetic phase, this traditional opinion was construed to mean that erotic feeling destroyed this capacity for apprehension and, further, that violent mortifications could release the gift. It is now well understood by researchers that there are various assaults on the psychophysique (such as intense strain, great anguish, the acute but quickly depleting stimuli of the relatively large sheathed nerve fibers that carry keen stinging pain, fasting, sleeplessness, rapid breathing, and any tormenting denial), which may jar the normally fixed focus of ordinary biologically valuable consciousness and give glints of another frame of reference. Under such stress, and especially when it has been damaged and wounded to the extent that it assimilates such toxins as its broken-down protein and infection by-products, the body will give rise to apprehensions, all of which are not always illusory.

This subject must be dealt with more fully in Part III. However, it is raised at this point because of the misinterpretation made by asceticism of the pre-ascetic, traditional finding: that the capacity to shift the focus of consciousness from its fixation on that focus which is of immediate biological importance to a wider range (for instance, the range that permits a certain degree of precognition) is a capacity, a state of mind much more easily fallen into by the young than by the mature. The fixation of attention on the biological construct of experience, the concentration on the utilitarian view of things and persons contracts as first maturity reaches its height. This is necessary, for it is correlated and synchronized with and may be provoked by that concentration of the emotional life which, in the beginning of maturity, fixates it on one person for reproductive purposes. As Freud noted, and plenty of other observers before him, eroticism that had been diffuse in childhood becomes concentrated on the genitalia in adulthood. Freud, in one of his case history examples of how the sensation is thus restricted, tells of a man who regularly had congress with his wife while the midday dinner was being heated. The procedure had become so routine, so conditioned that the man would often ask his wife, after they had eaten, whether or not they had copulated before the meal.

We can then see that the high incidence of extrasensory perception in prepuberty must be because of the paidomorphic openness and freedom from biological fixation at that time of life and not because of a lack of erotic feeling.

We shall deal with the further and fuller implications of this distinction in the Epilogue. Meanwhile, we shall conclude this chapter by pointing out, and as a summary of the argument so far, that second maturity is a return from the reproductive focus of first maturity, which had been narrowed in two ways: first, in its marital concentration and, secondly, in its administrative concentration. Second maturity is a return to a regeneralized outlook emotionally and intellectually, a resumption of generalized response. Hence, it can be the state in which it would be natural for the capacity of seership to be attained, to re-emerge. And, with that capacity, to regain a generalized affection, good will, and anxiety-free concern and vision into the nature of time that would explicate death by uniting the mind with eternal life.

This may seem to be a surprising solution to suggest in answer to the problem of geriatrics and the riddle posed by the emergence of a new class that is without any recognized social part to play, or any present standard of prestige to fulfill. But such a denouement may appear to be less improbable when we recall the three main elements of our present situation. The first is the unprecedented speed of our advance, a speed that is not only greater than that of any change process before, but that accelerates with arithmetical progression. The second is a convergence of pressures. Our social heredity has reached the psychological revolution and the total individual has discovered that he is more than an individual. An increasing number of individuals, those who are in second maturity, find themselves to be a new class, a fifth estate, for which there is no place in the former classification of mankind. The very intensification and triumph of individualism, it is clear, culminates in first maurity, the age-group out of which they, the postindividuals, have emerged. Thirdly, this sense of not being wanted has provoked a specific and serious mental disease, involutional melancholy. Because there is no place for them, this new category of mankind, these latest of the mature, instead of dying off become an additional burden by turning into mental patients, whom we are not callous enough to kill nor understanding enough to cure.

Something, then, must be done. Further, something certainly could now be done if we could find, for this new contingent, a real place and purpose. But what must be done must be done quickly. It, too, must be mutational. It must forestall degenerative collapse, involuntary elimination, despairing decay. This is why I have called the postindividual leptoid man. Schizophrenia has been fought with electric current and other relief agents—clumsily at first, but now with an increasing aptness that opens the blocked way so that the force of encouragement may be thrown into the beleaguered citadel of the spirit. Even so, the second attack of massive despair, the later melancholy now can and must be tackled by a surge treatment. The

particular methods whereby this therapy might be applied are outlined in Part III, Chapter 5, and in further detail in the Epilogue.
Here we need only say that after those who are in second maturity
have been intellectually assured of their position, their condition,
and their promised contribution, after this informational education
then they would be prepared to submit themselves to the psychophysical therapy whereby (1) the two aspects of their consciousness
can be combined, (2) their thinking can be made integral (which
is the modern concept of seership) and (3) their explication made
voluntary, intentional, expert, and desired.

III

THE DEVELOPMENT
OF INITIATIONS
OR PSYCHOPHYSICAL
RELIGIOUS EXERCISES

[*The five mysteries*]

Introduction

In Part I we have traced, in outline, man's history as a psychological five-act drama of development. We have seen the evolution of his consciousness following a spiral path. For first he becomes increasingly self-conscious and so attempts to educate himself in skills, to modify the tradition in the direction of efficiency and to control and alter the environment in favor of his individual desires and needs. And then he discovers his own preterconscious and realizes that he must educate himself so as to modify his self-consciousness and be able to cooperate with his setting.

This is man's five-phase psychological sequel to his embryonic recapitulation of his evolution from the first vertebrate into man; the specific and unique development of the one creature that has not only modified his environment but has vastly extended it, and has done so by the preteranimal, invisible instrument of speech, the intangible grapple of ideas.

In Part II we find this theory is both confirmed by evolution and made immediately apposite by the fact that the recapitulation and extension of phylogeny (in the five stages of man's social heredity) can be recognized as being ontogenically evident in the developmental growth of the individual. The psychophysical unit, the person, the constituent of the group, the representative of the race also goes through the five stages through which the race has traveled. As in the womb and before birth he recapitulated the vertebrate record, the development of the backbone aligned creature, so after birth the person runs through the story of mankind. In consequence, today the race and man, the person and society have each reached the same crisis of consciousness. Man and the individual are both at the ends of their tethers if individualism and its rational use of the five senses (or the twenty-two channels of apprehension) to master an objective, aimless, unconscious outer world is the goal of evolution and the senses are the one means for survival.

However, we have also seen that this is not the only possible prospect. Man, today, may hope to understand his total nature and, through that means of understanding, he may educate himself. Through his preterindividualistic consciousness, he may reconcile his individualism with society and also with his environment. But that education, though it be conscious and informational, must be total to be efficacious in this task. It must be a psychophysical developmental therapy, a mind-body hygiene.

For that reason, and to confirm the fact of our psychological evolution whereby instinct was turned into tradition and tradition into education, we must and can trace a third thread in the human process. Beside the obvious story of mankind and its recapitulatory résumé in each individual's life story, there is another sequence, an esoteric series that follows the five stages and epochs of human history. And this third aspect of man's story has made it possible for the violent social mutations of mankind, which we have called catastrophic revolutions, to lead to an evolution of consciousness.

This has been obscure until late. Now, however, anthropology and historical psychology (especially the Jungian *Eranos* investigations) have laid bare sufficient parts of this neglected record. Its significance becomes evident when we perceive that in this sequence, also, there is a fivefold development. And these five stages of the process do correspond, as a therapeutic reply, to the five developmental crises of historical mankind and to those five developmental crises of the individual, each of which, when not corrected, shows its complete destructiveness in a specific form of madness.

Further consideration of the data and investigation of the process certainly suggest that it was, and indeed is, due to these remedial psychophysical processes that man's development, though it has been spastic and convulsive, has not proved to be catastrophic or fatally disastrous. It is true that time and again large areas, entire branches of man's social heredity have collapsed in confusion under noncompensated stresses and disbalanced growth. But always, after a delay, there has been not merely a resumption of growth and an increase of power, but an increase of comprehension as well; not merely of capacity but of vision too.

In Part I it was suggested that all five of the "mysteries" of ordeal and initiation may not have existed since the dawn of man's culture and the beginnings of his religious rites. Indeed, if each "mystery" is a therapeutic reply to a particular contractive crisis in man's development, the contrary might be argued. It might be maintained that as only today has mankind produced the fully manned fifth class, the class of those in second maturity, the veterine with their peril of involutional melancholy and their specific therapy of electric surge treatment,[a] the fifth ordeal and initiation would not emerge until now. But this is certainly not so. For the ordeals and the initiations

---

[a] The response of the melancholic aged to such a drug as Equanil or Miltown is interesting and promising if it is used as an initial and introductory alleviant for anxiety. Like Tolserol and other meprobamates, Miltown is basically a muscle relaxant. The first step is to un-freeze the physique, which is involuntarily shrinking from oncoming decrepitude. After that, however, the subject must be recharged. As always, sedation only gains time for advance to be resumed.

of the mystery sequence are fivefold and, as we shall see in Chapter 5 of this Part III which deals with this final initiation, this fifth mystery called ether, or the finer fire, is electric surge treatment.

The truth in this obscure matter would seem to be that whereas mankind has advanced, roughly speaking, in three divisions, (1) spiritual pioneers, early developers, exceptionally early seers and sensitives, (2) the main body of average men, and (3) laggards, then, throughout history, we should expect an advance column of experimenters and explorers to be at least one stage ahead of the main body. The entire sequence of the fivefold mysteries may then have been worked out by a spiritual elite. By the time of the rise of Asceticism, these pioneers may have reached what is here called the initiation of transformation: that fifth initiation of which those in second maturity stand in need.[b]

However that may be, there can be no doubt that mankind does develop in the above mentioned divisions. And there can be no doubt that in the past, when the average man was thinking only of cathartic asceticism as being the highest life (and the laggards were still playing anachronistically at being heroes and producing militarism), the most advanced were considering those stimulations that are intenser than mortification and more informative than critical analytical knowledge.

Today this entire fivefold series is needed as an explicit therapy. For today we have not only the entire fivefold series of mankind at last present, with each of the divisions fully manned, but also we have reached the fifth stage of human history, the postindividual phase that has brought us to a self-conscious knowledge of our unself-conscious. What was esoteric and intuitive can now be exoteric and explicit. What had been a traditional ritual may now become an experimentally verified science.

Until now, this complete knowledge and praxis were confined to the few leaders, a sparse and generally hidden number of seers. Their inspiration and guidance had to be fed cryptically, if not clandestinely, to those leaders (administrators, judges, kings, gen-

[b] Psychological discoveries made in an ascetic age lead to the volatilization of the advanced out of society, and so to social collapse; for example, India.

erals) who were obviously in control. And these advisory powers were exercised chiefly as an inhibiting power over violence, a conservational minatory force rather than a message of initiative and creativity.

Now, however, this secret of a complete and elucidating education, of a process that can alter conduct, character, and consciousness, can be employed openly for the birth-delivery not only of each present stage of mankind but of the stage in the epoch that lies ahead of postindividual man, for the conscious forwarding of the evolutionary process.

1 The initiation of rebirth
[Earth]

We now know that the five mysteries, certainly since the Ascetic epoch, were developed to produce successive states of increasing release and awareness. The basic mystery is rightly called that of earth; the second is that of water; the third that of air; the fourth that of fire and the fifth that of aether (that is, electricity).

Correlating these both with the five epochs of mankind and the five recapitulating phases of the individual's life, we see that the first initiation is to remedy the trauma of birth. This trauma has its two aspects: one social and historical, the other personal and immediate. We find its socio-historical aspect in the fissure, the faulting that occurred when our prehistoric coconscious social growth (which was advancing too slowly) was broken by the eruption of our proto-self-conscious, heroic revolt. Its personal aspect lies in the fact this event has to be recalled in order that it may be gone through again, recapitulated intentionally, accepted consciously. This process of psychic regression is now a commonplace of psychotherapy.[a]

However, only now can its full significance and value begin to be appreciated. We had to understand that each individual is recapitulating human history; that his frustrations are its tragedies still calling for explication in a contemporary interpretation, in a third act of metacomedy (see Glossary) which can now be written to follow that second act that semed so futile, so unresolvable, so final that it was called tragic. With that understanding this third act can now be conceived. It can be more majestic than the second act of tragedy and more hilarious than the first act of comedy, more significant than any personal drama.

In this chapter, then, we must deal with the primal ordeal of birth and its initiatory therapeutic process whereby, getting down to base, to earth, a firm rebuilt foundation is made for the four other and successive re-elevations of the human psyche. Racially, anthropologically, we now have clear evidence of this rite and its therapeutic value. The trauma of birth echoes and indeed recapitulates the racial crisis that occurred when animal intuition and anxietyless immediacy began to be interfered with by the cross light of reason and the tension of expectancy and apprehension. And this deep stress point and faulting require remedy.

As studies of the Arunta and other Australian aboriginal tribes have shown, those who would be the wizard tribal leaders must undergo this earth rebirth. The cave is the womb and the tomb. As we know, it bore a similar duality in the consciousness of paleolithic man. From its opening one emerged to do battle with the tundra beasts. Into its depths one penetrated and sank, there to die to human identity and become merged with the life forces, to become one with the common basic life power, the universal soul out of which beasts and men (men pelt-garbed as beasts and beasts anthropomorphically souled as men) loomed and mingled in mystic communion in the wavering dimness (53).

From thence onward, we can recognize the cave burial, the

[a] See footnote, Part II, Chapter 1, footnote d.

yawning dark mouth that leads down into a sightless world, as being *mors janua vitae* (the death gate of life), the strait between the inland sea of life and the outer ocean of death. Even when man no longer was compelled to seek shelter on the cave's lip and in the cavern's forecourt, still he brought home his dead to be reborn in those fecund, transforming depths. The protopatriarch of the Hebrew people, Abram, purchases the cave of Macpelah in which to bury Sara, his wife. The later editor of the account has to rationalize this rite by making the father of the Hebrews say "that I may bury my dead out of my sight." By then, man's concept of his soul had become so personalized and body-identified that the crumbling of the corpse meant the evaporation of the spirit. Therefore, as this materialistic concept gained ground flesh became the awkward, embarrassing and, in the end, foul element; while spirit was the sweet, elusive, evanescent spectrum. Thus death became a penalty of ultimate degradation, and the faint spirit itself remained only a wraith, a ghost, a last echo of the sigh of ultimate despair, the last groan of irremediable defeat.

As Henri Frankfort has pointed out, the Egyptian civilization held so firmly to the reality of the spirit, and to the reality of the body as its wholesome expression, that the dead were supposed not to haunt the night but to sleep comfortably in their tomb house, rising with the sun and, while others had to work, spending their day carelessly, seated like a gay plumaged bird in the leafy branches of a tree. Because the dead were living a so much fuller and more relaxed life than those still in the first hard working stage of human existence, the yet-working living used to come to the tomb's door for their picnics, there to enjoy a foretaste of liberation from hard labor and in the company of those who had arrived at that cheerful station. Thus the Nile culture was able to resist the despair that comes in with the Ascetic phase until, in the third century A.D., the epidemic of mortificatory eremitism found its fastnesses in the Libyan Desert.[b]

Egyptian civilization very early formed around the powerfully binding mythos of death and resurrection, of the tomb being

[b] See Appendix A.

also the womb, of burial and procreation being parts of one act. The rite of Isis and Osiris, at Abydos, is known to be very early because of the fact that this brother-and-sister marital couple were moon deities, not sun gods. Therefore, they date from the lunar monthly calendar that precedes the solar annual chronology. They are also earth (chthonic) deities, not day-sky gods; and they belong to the phase of human consciousness when the dark is the time not only of fecundation but is also recognized as being the time of psychic vision to which day vision is only detailed foreground, present-time supplementation. The myth describes how, when Set the enemy has slain Osiris and scattered his limbs over the land, Isis reassembles his body and, having buried her recomposed brother, is fertilized by him while he lies mummified and subsequently bears their child Horus, the Sun God, who incarnates as the reigning Pharoah. Indeed, so quickly, powerfully, and comprehensively did this cosmological-political conception grip the mind of the Egyptians that, though there were feudal periods when Heroicism did appear, it never destroyed the basic social heredity founded on the pattern of death and resurrection and the idea that the tomb was also the womb.

Nor should we so state the reciprocal polarity of the two apparent extremes of this conception as though death were the master theme (as though tragedy were the bed-rock fact with redemption being an afterthought, a desperate contrivance whereby, at frightful cost, victory is snatched out of defeat) with the issue lost here and the remnant, though annihilated in this life, by heroic sacrifice rescued from the stricken field and translated, Valkyrie-wise, to a nonhuman heaven. For even in our own Anglo-Saxon tongue the word *Hella* in no wise referred to a place of retribution or even a realm of the lost, any more than, as we noted earlier, was the Hellenic Hades other than the underworld. *Hella* was simply the hidden place, the dark area. And the dark, as we have seen and shall see again further on, is the prerequisite of seership.

As we have noted earlier, in the Eleusinian mystery Persephone, who was the wife of Pluto (King of Hades), was supposed to have risen again from her married state in the underworld to rejoin her mother Demeter. When considering this most famous of the classical mysteries (*The Mysteries;* see especially "The Eleusinian Mysteries"), W. F. Otto (65) points out that Persephone cannot be thought of as being the seedling that dies in the earth to give rise to the new plant. The appropriate image, Otto goes on to say, would be one of fertilization or impregnation, not of death.

The midindividualist ascetic thinks of birth as committing the soul to death. And the two other phases of individualism, the heroic and humanic, think of death as being the final frustration, the annihilation of consciousness. The coconscious know that death, voluntary and understood, is right rebirth. It is a second birth that explains, explicates, and elevates the first birth, which had been an involuntary, psychophysically distorted birth, a miscarriage.

In short, the first of the mysteries, that of earth, consisted in a burial, either in a cave or an artificial cave: a dug grave. The individual was given back to Mother Earth, restored to his seminal state in her fruitful womb, and then, with the mistaken husk of his calloused selfhood shed, he was reborn rightly. Therefore, in the power of endless life he lived forever, free of wrong time and of mistaken identity. He was deathless, for henceforth every change would be no destruction or defeat but a further and voluntarily undertaken expansion and growth. To experience this earth mystery of voluntary death and resurrection was, we know clearly, present as a requisite of the Egyptian Pharaoh's right to reign. After a certain number of years on the throne, he who was the incarnation of Ra, the Sun, nevertheless shed his golden insignia, was wrapped in the grave clothes, placed in the sarchophagus, and buried. There is no reason to suppose that, at the beginning of the Pharaohonic sacramental rulership, this was a mere pageant: at best a miracle play to recall a past magical event; at worst a cynical method whereby an aged ruler, by pretense, claimed to have restored his sexual virility, lacking which he would be killed by his subjects. As Frankfort points out, there is no evidence that the Egyptians sacrificed their king when his reproductive potency disappeared. On the other hand, there is plenty of evidence of the intense group suggestibility of every person in an early traditional society. There is also evidence from India (from early dates down to the present time) that by hypnotic suggestion, and sometimes by autosuggestion, catalepsy is induced; that in this state the subject is buried with mouth bound, body ceremented, nostrils and ears plugged with wax; that he can remain so, in suspended animation, for as long as thirty days; and that when he is resuscitated it is claimed (he maintains it and his behavior would certainly suggest it) that his consciousness has been changed and that the sensory ego has disappeared or has been vastly modified.

Let us grant then (1) that there have been some persons in the past who retained, to a large extent, an earlier quality of consciousness: a preindividualistic psyche that had not become divided by a threshold into a personalized foreconscious and a preterconscious, and that such persons used the earth mystery of burial and resurrection to cleanse the mirror of consciousness from the oxide of personal and immediate concern. Let us grant further (2) that ancient societies (even cultures as explicit and complex as the Egyptian) employed this method to restore to the priest-king his sense of universal identity, which old age was corrupting and contracting into body identification. Then it is possible to see the primal place that the earth mystery and its ordeal and initiation have held in man's history and so holds in his preterconscious today.

We can see that it has been an essential psychosocial therapy in man's developing culture. For as individualistic consciousness increased, birth, in consequence and as it does among all individualized peoples, becomes a dreaded and sinister event.[c] And the mother catches the contagion of panic. She contracts (literally trying to shrink from the delivery process) and the child, inevitably having a bad passage, carries the trauma of birth in its subconscious. The person who would be freed of this birth-death fear had, therefore, to undergo a regression, repassing through the process and so,

[c] For example, the horror tabus in all the heroical cultures: that is, the woman defiles and is defiled; her menstrual blood is foul and wicked and parturition is filthy.

Persephone-like, rise again from the cave womb-tomb to become an immortal one who knows that birth and death are two names for a single process.

We can see also that the individual today, if he is to be emotionally educated, psychophysically taught, must have the repressed memory of his misbirth raised to contemporary consciousness and relived constructively. There is great hope that this can now be done and that a generation can now be reared that will be basically sane because it is freed of this earliest, most deforming and unnerving fear.

Even forty years ago, this hope might have seemed far-fetched and vain. "Those who can do can't know, and those who can know can't do" seemed to be the modern form of the well-known Taoist dilemma, "Those who know don't say, and those who say don't know." As C. Kerényi (49) has put it, in his "The Mysteries of the Kabeiroi," "arreton" (ineffability) "is the more exact word for 'mystical.' " For there are no words to describe the mystical experience: none are needed, although sounds can be and are used in the third mystery, the initiation of air and inspiration. Not only this, but wordy explanations and the disputes into which they degenerate render the creative process impossible. The state of mind is literally unspeakable; for speech is a calling across to someone else who cannot otherwise understand—while the mystical experience, at the very start, is the sense of that chasm being closed; a sense of being taken back and restored to the original symbiosis with the mother who is Earth; a sense that a primal unity has been re-established. As Kerényi says, even Plutarch, the devout practitioner of the Eleusinian Mysteries in the tolerantly appreciative, syncretic climate of the Hellenic Roman Peace, lived when "atmosphere had changed to object" (*ibid., supra*); when what had been an unquestioned field of timeless experience had to be objectified in a relic and a rite.

But the very fact of the outrageous stresses to which Western youth was exposed while the psychological revolution was dawning and the postindividual type was emerging (the First World War of 1914–18) led to an acceleration of advance in psychiatry, owing to the outbreak of war neurosis. This led to the discovery that men broke along a line of previous fissure; and this, in turn, led to the tracing of these fissures back to infantile traumas, the primal and most profound of which was that of birth.[d]

Nor did these discoveries end simply in diagnosis; they led to remedial therapy. For it was then that the therapy of regression began (see before). This sprang from work with apparent paralysis, blindness, deafness, and other psychosomatic disabilities. It was soon noted (1) that these disabilities occurred almost entirely among conscripts and/or simple, unthinking buck privates. They were very rare in the officer class (57). A higher sense of responsibility made this subconscious mechanism of autosuggestion-escape almost impossible. The officer, when his nerve broke after long strain of intensified anxiety, could only commit suicide.[e] (2) By using the electric detector on the conductivity of the skin it was possible to show the patient that he could and did see, hear, and feel, although his unconscious deep controls could prevent his showing visual, auditory, or sensory reaction. This method, very moderate in its usefulness, afterwards became vulgarized as the lie detector and has now become refined as the polygraph examination. (3) Hypnosis then showed that the deep consciousness that had caused the inhibition could be spoken to and, in some cases, could be persuaded to revoke the escapist device.

During the Second World War these techniques were advanced and improved. For example, pentothol sodium and other drugs were used to put the patient into a suggestible sleep. He was then regressed to the moment of the traumatic shock when he would have a convulsive horror shock as the fear block was raised to conciousness, after which the psychosomatic inability (paralysis or the like) was removed. However, it was soon realized that just to strip off this defense was of even less use and more damaging than tearing off the scab from an unhealed wound:—reinfection is very

[d] See earlier reference to the growth rings in children's teeth, Part I, Chapter 5, footnote *c*.

[e] Army officers, together with white collar workers, professionals, white men and city dwellers, all have a higher suicide rate than do conscripts, laborers, artisans, Negroes, and country dwellers.

likely to follow. The deep area of weakness had to be strengthened or collapse must be repeated whenever the patient was exposed to fresh stress.

Here, then, we find psychiatry today. The map it now has of the mind shows that misintegration of early experience, shock and faulting when the character is coalescing, must mean a basic flaw and weakness that makes the subject liable to collapse under strain. Therefore, psychotherapy now stands faced by the fact that all further advance in power education, in mastery of the environment (technical equipment and the like), all intellectual instruction, all executive and administrative skill (indeed, all understanding of the management of men) may prove to be worse than useless [f] as long as the emotional life is untrained and the psychic life is still subject to and motivated by infantile fears, resentments, panics, and rages.

The psychological revolution is about to move out of its first phase of theory and experimental private therapy into the mass fields of corporate action and sociopolitical ruling. As the child psychologist, the criminologist, and the psychiatrist find their work interlocking and their conclusions converging, the demand for preventive measures made by these three experts should prove to be irresistible. For their three fields, put together, cover education, law, and mental health: a vast area, in which the consequences of disregarding expert advice are demonstrably disastrous.

The argument is greatly strengthened when we realize that prevention is not merely the avoidance of felony and insanity, of neurosis, psychosis, and criminal psychopathy. It is not merely the damming back of flood waters into reservoirs less demonstrably inefficient and harmful than are prisons or even mental hospitals. Nor is it merely the detensioning and release of balked energies into comparatively harmless channels of expression. Prevention can now be considered to be focused deflection, the carrying of forces that are otherwise destructive not down to the entropic ocean of desirelessness but through the turbine dynamos of enlightened control to a new level of creative energy. In brief, the real hope of adequate prevention lies in a far higher value-developmental creation. At

[f] The IQ's of the top Nazis were remarkably high.

length a truly progressive education is possible because at last a true progress is possible: a progress through a psychophysical training that can purposively release the emotions, and so be the conscious deployment of the evolutionary drive.

Nor need the consequences of this revolution be slow in becoming apparent. We are not compelled to await the arising of a new generation that is freed from the trauma of birth, that has been brought into the world by mothers who have been taught how to bear a child without damaging it. For, although physical misgrowth in the womb is largely irremediable, it seems that if the right method is used psychic misgrowth can always be corrected. This means that the first initiation, the rebirth through regression to the mistaken birth, and the reprogression from the recovered birth memory and its misapprehension to a true understanding of birth and a voluntary acceptance of the psychophysical beginning, can be reinitiated; that is, gone into again.

It is now necessary, therefore, to see how this may be done and what actual step in this process psychiatric and psychophysical research already suggest. We have already seen that a rebirth by burial has been used throughout history, at least to the rise of the Ascetic Epoch and, in Egypt, down to the end of the Pharaohonic priest-kingship; while in India this rite has lasted on among some sects to the present day. We have also seen that our psychiatry, now that our own culture is in the psychological revolution that ushers in the postindividualistic epoch, sees the importance of and applies the method of regression while the subject is under either hypnosis or a dissociative drug, or both.

This new therapy, however, is not as yet general; still less is it part of the emotional education that is the necessary complement of intellectual education. It is employed almost solely for those who have indicated serious psychic maladjustment pointing to some traumatic birth experince. Nor does the method as now employed seem to avail itself, as yet, of the indications given by study of the past employment of this primal mystery of earth and sepulture redelivery. Again, neither are we yet incorporating, in regressional therapy, such research findings as have now been made as to the effects of what has been called "limited environment," the recreation of a womb situation. Whether it is the method used in the royal Egyptian Sed Festival procedure, or the one today practiced for entombment by the Hathi Yogin in a suspended animation that has been brought on by self-induced catalepsy, either by auto-suggestion or hetero-suggestion, the traditional method would seem to aim at insensibility brought on by breath control. The tongue is swallowed, blocking the throat, and the heart's action slows down to the point that, although a minimal supply of blood is kept in the brain, a heart beat cannot be detected except with the aid of X-ray, which shows not an actual beat but a slight movement in the valves of the heart (96).

We should note here that our psychiatry, reacting from the failure of chemicalized medicine to "minister to a mind diseased" and "pluck from the memory a rooted sorrow," has tended to neglect the physiological side of the psychiatric problem. It is true that a number of sedational drugs have all had much initial promise.[g] However the Menningers and others believe that these can only assist at most some 10 per cent of those requiring instant aid. The concept of using a therapy which would go beyond both drug and doctrine is still unfamiliar. Psychoanalysis has grown in expression and communication techniques from speech (words) through drawing and now on to psychodrama. From the other side, out of simple massage there has been emerging the tentative procedures whereby the subject, with his attention confined to his physique, is communicated with and released by tactile rhythms.

If, however, as the correlation between the fivefold stages of man's developing social heredity, his individual recapitulation of that process, and the initiation series suggests, we are today at an age and crisis when our psychophysical history, our individual psychophysical development, and our psychophysical research all indicate that we must consciously cooperate with and elucidate this process, then we should be able to outline the procedure and method of a modernized mystery.

As the first mystery is that of earth (burial and resurrection),

[g] For example, Reserpine, Thorazine, Librium, Melleril, Stelazine, and others. And new ones are regularly being developed.

we shall conclude this chapter with a tentative sketch of the procedure in a modern version of this initiation. The first and prefatory step, naturally, must consist in explanation to the subject. As we have seen, regression has been of great interest to therapists and thanks to the success of Morey Bernstein's (4) *Search for Bridey Murphy* (a case based on regression under hypnosis), it was for a time a popularized notion. The trauma of birth is also a familiar concept to anyone who is acquainted with psychotherapy. And as we have mentioned earlier, dental evidence of the severity of this shock is now available. There can be little doubt, then, of the fear block, of the repressed distress, resentment, and panic that, from this birth level and throughout their lives, is distorting the basic emotional reactions of all but a very few. Once this has been explained, and the need and method of release has been shown to the person, the researches of Donald Hebb (of McGill University, Montreal) and John C. Lilly (formerly of the National Institute of Mental Health, Bethesda, Maryland) become highly relevant. Their work with the limited environment has indicated the profound modifications of feeling tone, of body image, and indeed of ratiocination, that are brought about when a person is so comfortably confined that no major stimuli or familiar contact is experienced.

Stretched out on his back, with his hands in large, roomy containers, his body resting in great softness, the only light coming through a filtering visor, sound reduced to a minimum by the soundproof sarcophagus in which the couch was enclosed, the person was rewombed. After a few minutes, the effect was most striking. Active athletes seemed to suffer the most. The sensation of isolation rapidly became distressing, and when the mind began to function in an unfamiliar manner, the distress became acute. The new type of imagery was at first alarming and finally terrifying.[h]

[h] For further details of the Hebb and Lilly work see Appendix D. Other researchers in this field have been Meyers and Murphy of the Army Research Project in Monterey, Jack Vernon at Princeton University, and Jay T. Shurley at the University of Oklahoma. And although they have used variations of the limited environments designed by Hebb and Lilly their results were the same: a distinct and sometimes profound modification of consciousness.

It is clear that if this encapsulation were undertaken by an instructed and prepared subject the results could be quite otherwise. The instruction, the reasons for the treatment, we have considered above: the therapy is to bring about a regression to the moment of the trauma, a rerememberang and a reprogression. The preparation should include presuggestion, to see how far the subject is easily suggestible. If there is a resistance to hypnosis, light suggestibility and an introduction to the preterindividual conditions of consciousness may be aided by 25 micrograms of LSD. Then it is best that the subject make a tape recording of his own voice, which should be quiet, relaxed, and assured. In this recording he should tell himself that he is now going to be regressed to his birth experience; and he should then instruct himself to look on at this event with interest and without any alarm, to watch as both spectator and actor. He should further instruct himself that, should he at any point become aware that the delivery he is re-enacting is changing from a vigorous struggle to frustrant panic, he will correct the story; that he will witness and experience the delivery as something in which he can retake the initiative and as something which he can perform with a dynamic realization of its purpose and outcome.

This experience is much more than the mere witnessing of a crisis from the past, much more than the reliving of distress which releases repressed fear and ends subconscious conflict. Considerably more than a mere return to normalcy can be effected and by this method will be achieved. The fully accomplished rebirth releases a vast fund of energy that permits further evolution. The consciousness that both looks on and also releases, untying the knot of tangled birth and delivering the soul, is more than the personal consciousness, far more than the individualistic aspect of the psyche. The relived birth, in that presence and through its invoked power, means the first step toward bringing forth the total consciousness, the complete man who is the aim of evolution.

When this tape has been made by the subject he goes into his confinement. However, to the conditions of limited environment, as described above, are added two further aids to dynamic recovery. The first is the means, which is now known, whereby respiration may be suspended and yet lung aeration be maintained.[i] Yes, a consciousness remains, which is not only clear but is possessed of a steadiness, a lack of distractions and minor fluctuations, that is otherwise unknown and probably unknowable.

For any full regression, the advantages of this are clearly great. For in the first place, how is an adult, respiratory, alternating consciousness really to recapture the fetal prerespiratory consciousness if the body-mind is still being disturbed by the wave of inhalation-exhalation?[j] The attempts to achieve the necessary stillness, through an encoffined limited environment, are largely frustrated by this steady, fluctuating internal disturbance. Secondly, how can the subject attain the detached, reconstructive interest of the onlooking, remolding self (the consciousness of the scanner of Penfield, the organizer of Spiemann, the causal self of the Vedanta Sara) if he is still a respiring creature whose respiratory rate automatically accelerates with any alarm and whose alarm is reciprocally aggravated by the respiratory increase? Further, the heart action (which combines with every alarm to accelerate and further distress the emotions) is itself cut down by one third when respiratory breathing is exchanged for still-lung aeration. The state of mind now achieved is one of a serenity that is utterly unfamiliar to the present-day, high-pressured man-of-action. Nevertheless, it has proved to be delightful. Especially noticeable is the cessation of those small restless movements of the hands and feet, which most of us continually make with as little purpose as a cat twitches the tip of its tail. Perhaps even more remarkable is the total disappearance of any wish to smoke. The two package per diem semiaddict no longer fidgets for a fag. For hours, the hands are still, the body position easily maintained without any movement. The mind, even of the most active person, appears to pass into an effortless contemplation which is peaceful, somehow significant, and strangely satisfying to those who are at odds with themselves.

[i] See Morey Bernstein's account of his experience in "an equalizing chamber which enables the patient to stop breathing," in *The Search for Bridey Murphy*, pages 42–44.
[j] Cf. Yogi practices of breath control.

It is obvious that such a state is a powerful adjuvant to that of the limited environment. For, in the space of a few heartbeats, it changes the forbiddingness of isolation into a welcome vacation. Further, it is not a state of vacancy but of creativity. It creates that frame of mind which the Stoics called *ataraxia,* the God's-eye view that permits one to be constantly interested and highly concerned but incapable of anxiety or the lower sympathy of distress or, still less, of heartbreak.

And now something more can be added. While the entombed, expired subject lies motionless in body and with steady, unwavering mind, and after his own prerecorded voice has spoken its instructions and encouragements to his totally attentive ear, the other senses can be brought into cooperative play. Set at the speed that will give the precise flicker that is needed to rouse the encephalogrammic delta wave, the stroboscope can stir again the nerve energy which was present in the infant's brain at birth.[k] And certain subsonic vibrations (which can be felt as well as heard) do produce a sense of awe. In the unprepared, this sound wave generally causes dismay, as do mescaline and lysergic acid; while in a person who is prepared for it, it induces a vast sense of wonder. The olfactory sense, with its direct access to the very base of the brain, should also be employed. With a corrective use of the indoles (the chemicals both strongly stimulating to the olfactory center and also associated with chemicals that shift consciousness, for example, lysergic acid) those odors which are considered to be repulsive may be adjusted to be evulsive, leading to an exultation and transmutation of revulsion. (For instance, the first violent scents of the mother's ammonia, made harsh by her panic and her blood, may have led to pathological disgusts and aversions.)[l]

[k] See previous reference to Grey Walter's *The Living Brain.*
[l] It may also be noted here that not only is incense still used in the celebration of the Mass, but the first mention of its use in religious rites occurs in the Egyptian *Book of the Dead.* Here is given an explanation of its meaning which throws some light on its evocative use. We are told that when the worshipers in the dark of the shrine smelled the aroma, they knew that the God was not only present but benign. For the sweat of a friendly man is sweet, and smelling it they felt at peace.

So, in modern psychophysical and psychochemical terms, the birth process can be not merely relived and rendered innocuous, like a lanced abscess, but it can be relived in terms of a process that transcends the personal, private individual and renders him reborn, enabled then to go on to further stages of new growth. Now possessed of a true and full birth, he is prepared and equipped to grow.

It is certainly a gain that the patient has now attained freedom from the dead hand of a misunderstood, dreaded, and repressed past. However, it is considerably more that he is now possessed of the free use of the energies that were locked down within him in the effort to hold back his primal fear. Still, this is not enough: far from it. We cannot rid a man of wary fears, set him free with new energies, and not let him know where he is going under this released steam, and how he is to handle his new powers in the fuller categories of enlarged living. This would only be to make the psychological revolution a dreary repetition of the three preceding ones: the ecclesiastic, the political, and the economic. This would only end in another weary round of the tyrannies of sects, of parties, and of ideological fanaticisms, only this time armed with an apter violence and subtler weapons with which to subject the soul.

It is a fact (and it has awakened much comment in psychoanalytic circles) that although tens of thousands have undergone successful analyses during the last forty years, these large numbers of freed individuals have not affected society, still less have they become even a leaven that is slowly altering it. Further, in the last generation, even larger numbers of children (many now adults) have been brought up with a careful avoidance of those harsh and violent methods that caused traumas. And these undamaged recruits have proved to be no more efficacious socially than their restored and recovered elders have been.

However, in the light of the facts that we have been considering, this is not surprising and should have been expected. Successful analysis may release and clear up damage done to the psyche in the portentous first forty months. It can, however, make little impression on the physical shock of the actual birth when this delivery has been from a mother who was contracted in panic. To cure that a far deeper, more actualized re-experience is required. Talking about it and so merely recalling it is not enough. And even when the birth trauma is raised and its repressed complex is released, this is only one fourth of the full and necessary recovery. A successful analysis may teach a man not to be frightened of his deep emotional life, but if this release of the infantile fears is not followed up with a release from his childish, heroical rages, then his shrinking has only been exchanged for aggression and assault. Too many of the well analyzed have turned from being timid retreatants into callous-conscienced persons who feel free of any compunction about enjoying themselves, if not at the expense of others at least with a disregard of public benefit. The community gains little, if it gains at all, when, in exchange for members who are fearful, it is given persons who consider loyalty to be a crippling inhibition.

Therefore, the very success of the ordeal and initiation of the first mystery applied to modern, postindividual man would demand that we render and apply the other four mysteries in equally modern terms. Then with these four explicated we should be able, at last, to produce that complete man who alone is adequate to life's demand and the situation's challenge. In the next chapter, therefore, we shall deal with the next step: the reintroduction to the specific child crisis and the reinterpretation of the heroic ideal.

2 *The initiation of catharsis*
[Water]

The initiation of rebirth leaves the individual not only free but recharged; not only with his adhesions removed, his inhibitions loosened, but with a new zest for the larger living that is now made possible. For it has brought the psyche out of its historical and individual infancy. The actual historical process, when man was born out of the coconscious aeonic life of the tribe into the proto-individualism of the Heroic epoch, was a miscarriage. Or rather, it was a kind of auto-caesarianism whereby the child tore itself out of the mother-matrix that wished to deny it birth. He was delivered through his spasm of hatred, revolt, and revulsion against the tradition that he spurned as being suffocating and foul. And this scar-trauma in our tradition still remains in our mind. In our conscious mind it is our repression and deliberate ignorance of the preheroic phase: and so we have interpreted history, until today, in terms of exclusive individualism, physical force, competition, and violence.

In our unconscious mind it can be seen in the destructive or tragic character that typifies our images and patterns of prestige.

Hence, every infancy (the first psychological history-recapitulating phase) has also been damaged: first, by a bad parturition inflicted by a panic-stricken mother, and then by the inflammation of the child's race memories, generally by the passions of the parents. We are born into national hatreds. This scar tissue (of the bad birth of the child's social heredity and of the child's own psychophysical bad birth) can, we have seen, be removed by the ordeal and initiation. It can be taken away by the test and going in which, when it penetrates in, down, and back, replays the misrendered birth drama.

Man then has new liquid assets with which to start again. He can now have a proper respect for the primal aeon of coconscious conscience and consent, for the social heredity as a growth process, and also a proper evaluation of his psychosomatic freedom to forward that growth. He can advance—but whither? He has recovered his infantile plasticity and has at his disposal the potentiality of generalized response and awareness. He can have the panaesthetic alertness if he will, and if he knows how to employ it.

But, as we mentioned at the close of the last chapter, this is only one quarter of the human task today. Indeed it is only one fifth of the regrowth and on-growth that man must achieve if he is, by complete initiation, to win a complete initiative toward the human situation and complete cooperation with the life process. Those who have achieved this first freedom will only face defeat if they are taken no further. If with their sensitiveness they are left to confront others who have themselves failed to grow, in blind defensiveness these newly free may even produce thorns instead of buds; stings instead of egg ducts; weapons of destruction instead of tools of production.

So if the first liberation is to be worthwhile, and this correction of miscarriage itself not miscarry, it must be the first of a series. And however remarkable be the gain, if it is to be harvested it must be looked upon as being only a beginning. Certainly the mysteries, as we have now been able to uncover them, are a fivefold series; although in various epochs men have been content with two: for

example the Eleusinian and Samothracian initiations of the Greeks [a]
and, in more modern times, the conversion and second blessing of
the Methodist praxis. Still, there seems never to have been a time
since the Heroic epoch, and for the peoples that have gone through
that protoindividual stage, when less than two was considered
adequate.[b] For although the first initiation was an essential initial
step, it called for a further advance. All it could do was to deliver
the subject from the consequences of a wrong emergence; from the
consequences of an involuntary, panic-stricken, resentful expulsion
out of a condition where though things had become restrictive no
other life is conceivable. The end of a golden age is imprisonment
in fetters of gold. Every question has its closing answer and life is
locked in inflexible replies. A state of suffocating security is the
fetus' condition during the last month in the womb. Oxygen
shortage and intolerable congestion, consequences of its successful
growth, have turned the sheltered paradise into a trap.

Then the infant, with its birth struggle over, able to breathe its
fill and be suckled amply, begins again to adjust and settle down to
the all-found-for-you utopia of the mother-matrix external womb.
Against this indolence, as we have seen, the healthy child has to
struggle with its nor-adrenaline charge. And, historically, the later
hero struck out destructively against the blandishments of the
mother-deity city cultures.

The second initiation, therefore, is to correct and reconstruct
this not unnatural but mistaken reaction. The first initiation teaches
the psyche how to be born into distinctiveness, from unison to
harmony. The second initiation is to teach the psyche how to correct the excessive reaction, that the race and the individual made
and still make, against a too long retention at the level of possessive
motherhood: whether this be in a religious cult or in a nursery
climate.

[a] Both of which had a primary and a secondary ordeal and initiation. At
Eleusis these two ordeal initiations were separated by a period of three
years.
[b] The Stone Age Australoid cultures, when they were discovered, seemed
not to have reached that psychic level.

And as this second stage is a correction of a personal excess, a protoindividualistic, destructive revolt, this initiation has in its procedure something more active and, indeed, more penitential than the first one. The returning to earth, as a symbol of return to the womb, demands only a gentle resignation, a reteaching of the initiate so that he may consent to have performed for him a rightful, peaceable birth to take the place of the spastic, violent expulsion that had so wounded his soul and overwrought his body. But the second initiation differs from the first in demanding more of the person. For it is dealing with a new state; a state in which there must be choice and a new act: one of revolt. An individual, however rudimentary, has struck out for himself and has raged against restriction. This second process of redemptive deliverance, therefore, requires more than that the postulant should go within himself and be relieved by reliving a repressed nightmare. What is now necessary is an act of repentance for a mistaken act of the will, a definite surrender of willfulness. The individual must emerge and he must have the nor-adrenaline charge to do so. But that charge must be *Raj*, the Sanskrit word for force that is controlled by discipline; not rage, the blind reaction of destructiveness.

It is clear, then, why the second mystery after that of earth is that of water. But as we now preserve it in a traditional, atrophied form, consisting of the sprinkling of a few drops or at most a quick dip, it is naturally difficult to recognize why such a gently dampening procedure should have been considered adequate to quench the flame of anger or to smooth the contortions of rage. However, a study of the research evidence can leave us in no doubt that in the water initiation there was once a power to reduce fury: a power that was as demonstrably strong as the power of a physician to reduce a dislocation.

First there is archaeological evidence to consider. For example, the most striking features of the great twin cities of the Indus civilization (Mohenjo Daro and Harappa) are its huge baptistries. This would seem to indicate that a tremendous importance was attached to the water initiation by this civilization, which retained longer than any other culture, and raised to a higher level, a premilitary, nonphysically coercive, hypnocratic way of life.[c]

Secondly, the philological evidence indicates that the actual process was no idle swimming pool exercise or elegantly appointed ceremony such as we see, for example, in the decadent form of the Sed festival in Egypt. Nor was it the empty pageantry of the Venetian Doge wedding the sea with a ring that he cast into it; or Queen Victoria having her son and heir sprinkled by her Archbishop with a little flask of water from the Jordan. Baptism, by the time the word took its present Greek form, did mean to dip. But in its ruder root it meant something much more strenuous. In Old Norse, the language of the tribes that went northwest while their fellow tribes went southeast into Greece, the word that the Greeks turned into *baptein* is *kafa*, to dive and, more, to swim under water. Further, this word for strenuous effort and risk is linked with the minatory verb *kvefja*, to suffocate.

Thirdly, anthropology throws a confirmatory light on this sequence of dive, swim under water, suffocate. In his thorough study of shamanism, Shirokogoroff points out that the man or woman becomes aware of his or her vocation to become a shaman between the ages of fifteen and twenty-one through experiencing spells of excitement and trembling. However, although this may convince the individual personally it falls far short of persuading the other members of the tribe that he will be of psychic use to them. As a first test, not merely of his sincerity but of his stamina, he is told to go out (or is driven out) into the Siberian forest to live alone and as best he may. After he feels adequate to face the tribe's further testing and "because he has won some spirit-mastery," he has to recite, accurately, a list of the spirit names. Then, however, come the real ordeals of water and of fire. The fire we will leave until,

[c] A hypnocracy is a society that is so completely subject to a traditional, comprehensive social suggestion that, as with a hypnotized subject, orders are implicitly obeyed even when the one who gives orders is not present and has neither threatened nor rewarded those who have been given the orders. See Gerald Heard (40).

in Chapter 4 of this Third Part, we come to consider this particular aspect of a possible recharging: the initiation of illumination. Certainly, the water test is sufficiently severe; indeed, it is a kill or cure, a dissolution or a transformation.

The postulant is taken to a frozen river. Here he has to dive through one ice hole, swim under water and emerge through another hole in the ice which is a considerable distance away. This he may be called on to do as many as nine times. It is not a surprise to learn that some drown. One would certainly not be surprised to learn that most seminaries were closed for want of ordinands if such tests were used to discover whether or not our candidates for the ministry or priesthood had the conviction and stamina to face such ordeals. And, just as certainly, one cannot regard these shaman cultures as being composed of credulous creatures ready to accept anyone who is odd enough, or sufficiently impudent, to claim supranormal powers.

The initiation by water, we can then say, has always been the great method of bringing the protoindividual to a coordinant balance of mind wherein his individualism, his personalized consciousness, may be able to work with his generalized nonpersonal consciousness. The force that would otherwise express itself as violence culminating in homicidal rage is thus turned back and given release through the desperate struggle to survive drowning. If the subject can struggle through, this ordeal is intense enough for the personality to be dilated until it discovers its superpersonality. The ordeal by water, then, even when it proved to be fatal, might prove to be socially valuable. For those who were strong enough to undertake it would be types of such energy that if they did not attain to knowledge of their superconsciousness they would become ruthless power types.[d] Here, then, would be a socio-natural selection removing those who were powerful enough to mutate psychologically and who, if they failed to do so, would become public enemies.

[d] For example, Genghis Khan, who sprang from a shaman culture, murdered his spiritual overlord and created a destructive empire that vanished with his death. Chaka, the founder of the Zulu militarist empire, did the same thing.

So, in the stage of consciousness in which he might otherwise fall into heroics, defiance, denunciation, and destruction, the individual can become the seer, the eyes of his community. He can give to his fellow beings that open vision without which there is chaos and sanctionless activity; without which, as the writer of the Hebrew Book of Judges says in describing a period of heroic chaos, "Every man did what was right in his own eyes."

We now know what is being aimed at in the training of all seers, of the shaman, of the rishi (to use the Sanskrit name for him), who can either prevent or reorder the anarchy of a Heroic Age. It is to make it possible for both sides of the mind, the conscious and the preterconscious, to work at once.

Two steps are necessary for this. The first, being considered in this chapter, is the reduction of the passionate egotism of the proto-individual who, if left unharnessed, becomes the stallion that kicks the chariot to pieces. The next step, which we shall consider more and more in the three following chapters, is the increasing of the power to balance the energies of intuitive, whole, total understanding-insight against the polar energies of specific, particular, immediate communication and instruction. This will then make it possible to answer the practical questions: What do we do now? What is the next step to be taken from here? What is the future of mankind at present?

We have now considered, most briefly, the outward purgation, the catharsis. (1) There is the removal of social support, of sustenance from the world of the ordinary warm human atmosphere. There is the banishment into the wild: into an exercise ground, a natural gymnasium where the postulant, denuded and sundered from mankind, wrestles with unseen forces, hoping that they will give him the nonhuman power and insignia-stigmata of being able to defy his nature's basic need for a modicum of warmth and a minimum of breath. (2) The ice-capped water is again a womb; but it is not a quiet tomb where, closely held in suspended animation, the psychophysique may intuitively understand prebirth and birth and come forth reborn, refreshed, and re-energized. The postulant is now choosing consciously to abandon a private wilfulness: the conscious wilfulness of the child, of the protoindividual who, through its self-awareness, is far more set in its separateness than the embryo can be. This stage, then, requires definite renunciation, specific retraction of an already emerged and committed egotism. Swimming under the ice is the immense effort of an ego which knows that if it cannot transmute, and transmit into active skilled effort the superhuman powers it has attempted to release and league in its own interest, then it must suffocate, drown, die. If the "spirits" refuse to aid, refuse to recognize that this creature is willing to be their instrument and vehicle, then it must perish, having gone out past human safety but fallen short of superhuman power.

So the rebirth, the initiation through water is now a stage more active than the first rebirth of earth. And although the postulant desires to slough off the mistaken protopersonality of the hero and the angry child, he must not retreat or hope that just by surrender and leaving himself to be rehandled and remolded he will be brought back to an effortless innocency "full of repose, full of replies." He suffers, voluntarily, to the edge of death in order that he himself may become the troubled oracle who struggles to convey the ineffable universal, in temporal terms, to aid the action—or at least to limit the mistakes—of those who are involved in temporary contriving.

Yet, as the full rite of initiation by water shows by its very name, catharsis, an outward cleansing is not enough. By itself, an outer exposure to and drenching by water, however overwhelming, still is only external and only one half of the purgation. For man is a creature of two surfaces, external and internal. And, as all teachers have pointed out, he can be defiled more deeply, more lethally if less perceptibly, by inner foulness than by outer stain. Hence, in the Yoga practices of India, the internal purging by water is even more essential than outer cleansing. Nor is this purgation merely a matter of physical hygiene. The Yoga methods never take mind and body apart; no therapy that really works ever does. Millennia before Freud the Yogi therapists of India realized that grasping, retention, avarice, and self-defensiveness are reflected by visceral clutching. Hypertonic sphincters are symptoms of (and, in turn, provocative of) a psyche that is determined to hold its ground and not to give or to yield. Embryology confirms this intimacy by showing that the viscera and the genitalia spring from a common area of the fetal protostructure. The tradition retains this intuitive knowledge by maintaining that the bowels are the center of compassion and that the hard, shut heart goes with a costive fear and refusal to eliminate and release. The deep lavage, the colonic irrigation, has been known ever since the second mystery was found to be the next step in the deliverance of man. It has been used ever since the catharsis of water was discovered to be the method of restoring to the individual his binary nature, to be the remedy for his wrongfully asserted protoindividual ego of revolt, through purging him of his defiant destructiveness, his secessionist assault, through liquidating his congested, impacted recoil and restoring him not to the stagnant pool of conformity but to the current of an out-flowing life.

Therefore, and as we did at the close of the last chapter, we must now ask "How, today, could we apply such a therapy?" If such, then, is the mystery tradition in its second phase and we could, through this water ritual, correct the mistaken heroic phase; if we would permit the enraged child now buried in our repressed subconscious (just above the birth-wounded infant) to release its pent-up energy—what, in modern terms, would be that procedure? As we did in the first mystery, we first need right knowledge. The postulant must be intellectually informed and convinced that he is part of the living process (phylogenic and ontogenic, racial and personal) which, willy nilly, must grow. Further, this process, once self-consciousness has emerged, must be understood and then an active, conscious cooperation with it must be undertaken. Otherwise the process is bound to be largely frustrated by ignorant and inhibitory fears of the individualistic foremind seeking a false homeostasis by arresting all development. Even before the emergence of the proto-individual, we have seen that the traditional, preindividualistic society had reached the point where, more and more, fear of growth had rendered the social heredity as fatally rigid, though no longer as competent, racially, as animal instinct. With the rise of individualism, increasingly the foremind must be informed if it is to remove its veto on any modification of its instrument and matrix. In the first mystery, because it deals (through regression) with reduction of the psyche to a preindividualistic, preargumentative condition, the verbal procedure need be no more than affirmational.

In the second mystery we have to work with a personality that has its case and is prepared to assert its wrongs and to claim its rights. The subject, therefore, has not merely to submit; he has to put out skilled effort to heal or reduce his own dislocation by relocating himself. All psychoses and neuroses are, to some degree, basic atavisms, anachronisms, inabilities of personalities (in varying degrees) to live contemporary lives: a wilful determination to take refuge in some emotional state that crystallizes out of the past.

After this instruction, this explanation of the process and this giving to the subject his bearings, we can go on to the procedure itself, the outward conditions in which the therapy can be performed. We can now see that these conditions must be a further development of that definably limited environment that was the frame of the re-enacted birth process. The research that led to immobilization of body and retraction and dilation of mind, in the burial, close-contact process, has led to experiments with immersing the body in a tank of water.[e] With the tank water at a neutral temperature, the subject was equipped with a mask and a breathing tube (snorkel) and his naked body completely submerged. He was anchored to the back of the tank by a light harness. Even with these simple conditions the alteration of consciousness has been reported as being striking, and for the unprepared, alarming. The change from solid contact to fluid apparently modifies the sense of the frontiers of the self even more remarkably than does the burial experience.

The condition, however, seems to be too passive to act as the best medium for the emergence of the protoindividual, nor-adrenaline-charged level of consciousness. The possibility of rhythmic effort in a liquid medium would seem to be the condition that would give best results. It may be that immersion in a deep, dimly lit tank of

[e] See Appendix D.

tepid water and the use of some form of aqua lung would allow such extension.[f]

There would be a distinct risk, however, in using the aqua lung. For even those who are stimulated by the cold have, when they have descended beyond a certain depth, experienced a dissociation from biological consciousness. This was accompanied by either elation or an indifference that made them neglect their respiration. In some cases it would seem that divers have actually removed their mouthpiece and so were drowned. However, these states seem to have been experienced only at very considerable depths, of one hundred feet or more. And such depths seem to be unnecessary for the experience of liquid suffusion of the frontier-signifying and self-defining internal and external surfaces. The reduction of congestion, the loss of self-contained alertness, the loosening of unconscious defenses and resistances—these psychophysical undoings and releases seem to be of the nature of a nondebilitating catharsis that is free of self-pity. And in comparison with this the nonpsychophysical catharsis of drama is little more than a literary simile. Tragedy, at least Greek tragedy, Destiny playing with the self-ignorance of man, could, as we have seen, undoubtedly give a cautionary release. For it was a religious rite, with the audience taking a visual and auditory part in the self-induced sufferings of a hero whose individualistic pride led to an infatuation that ended in death or mutilation. Deep pity could be stirred in the person watching his sufferings and commiserating with him. Deep fear could be released through the realization that the worst had been witnessed.

But not only was such catharsis really faint; it was not actually felt. It was, we must repeat, also adulterated. There were present the two alloys of the surrogate situation and projection. So there was self-pity masked as sympathy, and there was that repressed and secret elation that pities in order to patronize, the *schadenfreud* that covertly rejoices that the proud and noble are brought low.

[f] The Yoga practices enjoin floating in a stream, with the sphincters held open in order to irrigate the eliminatory area. They knew of no way of total immersion.

The actual procedure of the water initiation would, then, involve first an immersian, naked and in a tank of circulating water kept at body temperature, and wherein the body would be irrigated exteriorly and interiorly. The eyes could see, through a glass visor, the water-suffused and wavering light that should probably also have rhythmic light patterns given it by the use of a stroboscope. The ear should be vibrated by sound rhythms of a comparable frequency sent through the water, which is a better sound-carrying medium than air. In this medium and state the postulant should first be floated. But after ten minutes the water in the tank would be made to begin a pulsing, vortex movement. And against this whirlpool he would have to struggle until exhausted. At this point he should achieve a further loss of self; he should emerge into an enlarged state of consciousness.

The ordeal by water, the initiation by catharsis, is then the psychophysical therapy whereby the nor-adrenaline, paranoid child rage, the dementia praecox which in a spasm of contractive revulsion is homicidal, is reduced. At the same time the energy of the protoindividual stage of consciousness, which caused the tragedy of the Heroic Age, is rerouted into productive channels. This leads, without convulsion, revolution, or reaction and by evolutionary development, on to the next stage of the pure adrenaloid, self-blaming type.

With the release of that type, through its specific initiation of air, the next chapter deals. It will be indicated how there can be an *askesis* without self-hatred and how self-criticism, by being made to be creative, will not provoke the despair arising from a sense of irremediable guilt.

3 The initiation of inspiration
[Air]

In this chapter we consider the third mystery, the third process of ordeal and initiation through which the earliest psychophysiological therapists worked out a technique that would remedy mankind's third mistake of excess. Excess of conservatism had led traditional coconscious society to lose way, to cease to continue coordinating new data in an expanding, flexible frame of reference. In turn, the excess of protest generated by this repression had led to destruction and pointless violence (the Heroic Age). And this social chaos had, in turn again, led to just as intemperate a reaction, from projected anger to self anger, from revengeful shame to expiatory guilt.

But these psychic pioneers, these torch bearers of the race, had themselves gone on ahead. They were the first to practice on themselves the rebirth therapy when they had found that the traditional coconscious tribe was strangulating itself and suffocating the new life to which it should be giving rise. Again, as forerunners they had devised the initiation of the second mystery whereby, through catharsis, passionate protest might be prevented from turning into infatuated rage. And then, after having practiced their method of delivery on those who were struggling to emerge from an arthritic tradition and those who were seeking a way out from their own imprisoning rage, they devised a process that made it possible for self-criticism not to fall into the abyss of guilt, self-detestation, and despair, but with clear sight to balance itself on the brink.

Therefore, these therapists, these midwives of the soul, were prepared to salvage those who were caught in that convulsion of contraction, that schizophrenic revolt of self-revulsion, which appears in history as the great mortificatory movement, the flight from life. And because they were prepared by their own pioneer experience they were no reactionaries. They had learned to understand the three reactions of blind clinging to tradition, the blind defiance and rejection of it, and the blind desire to rage against and destroy the raging self. They had learned to understand that blind as these three reactions were still they were not death throes or vain, convulsive efforts to return to an ease that only existed, even in the womb, in the early fetal months. This was a natural insight: first, you mustn't lose intuitive coconscious understanding, you must conserve contact with the preterconscious; secondly, you must have freedom of expression; and thirdly you must attain that disciplined skill that combines energy with empathy and enterprise with comprehension. In short, these spastic movements were mishandled parturition contractions, as the spirit of man sought a delivery that would permit him to be born whole, with his every endowment, faculty, and member preserved, developed, and expressed into a fuller stage of being.

Therefore, understanding all of this, the mystery therapists knew that the ascetic movement was not a reaction to primal, coconscious tradition. They saw, on the contrary, that it was a further development of individuality, a further conscious knowledge of the separate self and a wish to master it. And they realized that the earlier mystery methods of rebirth-burial and catharsis-immersion could not be used as the specific therapy for the midindividual, the adrenaline, self-blaming person who is in peril of schizophrenic collapse.

The ascetic must go through the rebirth-burial and water-catharsis. But he specifically stands in need of a third release, an inspiration that he must be given or the other two are for him in vain, not speaking to his actual, immediate, and urgently critical condition. The ascetic type, therefore, after having been delivered from birth trauma and catharized from pathological rage, must have his particular treatment. As earth-burial permits the righted rebirth of the psyche into a cooperative empathic society, and as water-catharsis is the means of reduction for the strangulated, anger-distended ego and the way of turning the duellist into the pioneer companion, so the psychiatry of air causes the ascetic to correct his drive to mortification and life rejection.

And the ordeal phase, the first stage in this mystery process, has its specific test. The raising and removing of the first fear block, by the first mystery ordeal, was and is achieved by reliving through the birthdread of death by confinement. In most births the heart is in danger of stopping as the umbilical cord is jammed by the pressure of the mother's muscles, cramping in panic and refusing to open the womb channel. Hence, in all the mystery procedures that we can trace in some detail (for example, the Eleusinian), we find this repeated pressure. At Eleusis we can still see and go through the narrow, dark birth passage through which the postulant had to work his body or be thrust.

The raising and removal of the second fear block by the ordeal preliminary of the second mystery initiation was through the fear of drowning and, simultaneously, the fear of being washed out and away, of being drained of all substance and of being purged of any power.

The ordeal of the third mystery, that of air, is less physical but certainly not less terrifying. For air in its psychophysical aspect is a mixture of gases: by volume, 78 per cent nitrogen, 21 per cent oxygen, 0.94 per cent argon, 0.04 per cent carbon dioxide, 0.001 per cent hydrogen, 0.002 per cent helium, neon, krypton and xenon, with variable amounts of water vapor.[a] This mixture is brought into the lungs and there mixed by them with the blood. This gas-loaded blood then delivers its charge to the brain. So fueled, the brain is then able to select and construct, from its twenty-two channels of sensory apprehension, that comprehension of experience that is necessary for biological survival. And as we all know in this generation of anaesthetics, analgesics, anodynes, sedatives, and stimulants, a slight modification of the brain's diet will cause it to experience a change of impressions. The biologically necessary view or construct of the environment, mistakenly called reality, will alter. Not only is this alarming to those who assume that any possible construct other than that of the biologically useful one must, ipso facto, be insane. It can be highly dangerous. And not merely because it may well be illusory; because the impressions may not answer to any reality or may not be an accurate interpretation of any external experience; may be sheer delirium.

There is another risk and one that can be even more perilous. Some range of experince, some new awareness of a condition or conditions usually unapprehended and in some way out there, may have come upon the soul. The experience itself may be valid; it may be more potent and portentous than any event transmitted to the mind from that range of data (or sensa) of which the mind, when in a waking state, generally is biologically aware. But whereas the body-mind has more or less learned to make the responses that are necessary to keep its body-mindedness adequately tending to its business of physical survival, the mind by itself has no such learned reactions to another range of experiences and events. Hence, the delusions and fanatic convictions of the enthusiast who (without instruction and after his first fear that confirms for him that the experience is wholly external and imperative) translates his "revelation" in terms of his own prejudices. He is certain that God has spoken to him, giving him an authoritative revelation or a sentence of eternal doom. It is an important fact, therefore, to note at this point that work with the insane has always shown that no madness is more grave and has an uglier prognosis than the disturbance that

[a] See *Chemistry for the New Age*, by Robert H. Carleton, 1954.

begins with the patient hearing voices. One would think that visual
hallucinations would be more serious. It seems, however, that the
hypnotic and suggestive power of the ear bears more on the will
than does vision.

The air mystery does not ignore this danger but faces it; and
by treating it as an ordeal can make it of necessary profit to those
who under guidance endure this trial. The sense of being lost, the
wandering in one's mind is usually associated with the delirious
states of high fever and of mental decay. But this wandering (and
we know this from Apuleius, Plutarch, and the others who went
through the Isis initiation as it was practiced in the Hellenic Roman
Peace during the first two centuries A.D.) was an essential part of
the ordeal that preceded the initiation of true inspiration.[b] And
that a shrewd mind could utterly lose its bearings, that a reasonable
intelligence could wander—lost, without rhyme or reason, memory
or intention, pestered and bewildered by false voices, threatening
and insane words, absurd and outrageous terms and sounds—this
was an experience that reduced personal pride. This grave disturbance, which had to be endured in the dark where the ear can give
no proper sense of distance or direction, undermined the self-confidence of common sense, the assurance that the ego is master of
itself and its situation if only it keeps its head, believes in its own
competence, and knows that the senses give it contact with reliable
reality. Then the spirit becomes aware that it is not the ego; that,
as Heraclitus said, "The senses are bad witnesses" and that the soul

[b] Stobaeus quotes an earlier author, "The first state [the ordeal stage of
the air and sound mystery] is nothing but errors and uncertainties, laborious
wanderings." The misery of amnesia was also indicated and probably induced. As Colin Still has pointed out on page 151 of his *The Timeless
Theme*, "the search for the lost child Persephone," which was a central
part of the Eleusinian ritual, "is the search for the Lost Word." This is
the mantram which, catalytically, not only gives the clue and solves the
riddle but actually makes the mind mutate. It is the *Aletheia*: the sudden
truth that inevitably comes with the disappearance of the ignorance (the
Lethe intoxication), the truth that the illusory personality now perishes
(Persephone means death-bringer) in order that the true eternal self may
emerge.

must realize its communion with others. And it must be saved by putting its confidence in these others who not only do not want it to be a subservient slave, but who wish to deliver it through this third birth. They wish to bring the struggling soul into the new life of true inspiration where as an intelligent, critically minded being it may yet know its deep non-self and the powers of revelation and communication that belong to this group-spanning consciousness.

As we have said above, we can trace this third ordeal and initiation through the references that have survived from the classical and preclassical mysteries, from Greece, Egypt, and the Levant. Indeed, we know, for instance, how sound in darkness was used in paleolithic times (and by the surviving Stone Age Australoid tribes today), through the use of the bull roarer. This is an orificed stone fastened to the end of a leash. And when it is whirled in the air it produces a whirring, throbbing siren ululation, with resonance, in a cave. And when we come down to Eleusis we find that the appearance of Persephone, the sudden flash of vision, took place when the postulant, after being through a long period of darkness that was filled with minatory whisperings and sinister echoes, suddenly heard the note (probably of a particular pitch) of a massive bronze gong being struck. The pulsating rhythms of such gongs play a critical part in Chinese and Japanese ancestral (and now Buddhist) ritual. This gong was also sounded when a Spartan King, at the moment of his death (still identified with his body by the Lacedemon obsession with physical violence), must be shaken out of his body. At Eleusis when that shock air-wave burst on his anxiety-strained eardrum, the postulant knew that he was confronted by the goddess who was both Queen of the Dead, sovran in the realm to which he and all mankind were irrevocably bound, and also whom he must now take as a bride. Even though the Hellenic mind had no naturalist's knowledge of those families of creatures wherein the male is consumed by the female as he fertilizes her (he is her impregnator and her nourishment), it is no wonder that in the Greek language the word *telos* is used for both marriage and death.

So much for illustration of the air mystery, with air used as the vehicle of sound waves to affect the mind through the eardrum.

The Greeks also employed air mixed with carbon dioxide as a pulmonary method of altering consciousness. The Sybil of Apollo at Delphi was first put into trance (dissociated and sometimes extrasociated consciousness) by being made to breathe the carbon dioxide fumes that came up through a cleft in the Delphi temple floor; and then, when that gave out, by having her head held over a hot copper bowl in which laurel leaves were being scorched.

But the full and late development of the mystery of air is seen most clearly in India where it is still present today in the yogic practices of the Sanskrit and pre-Sanskrit tradition. There, it has not been the main aim to use sound either to shock the eardrum or to give hypnotic suggestion in the dark. Sound—the air wave— is used, but almost entirely in an interior way. The use of the syllable OM (pronounced AUM and giving, as the instructors in its use say, the whole rhythm and gamut of sound from open mouth to closed mouth, from alpha to omega) is to vibrate not only the eardrum but also the thyroid and, some believe, the skull bones sufficiently to tremor the pituitary and the pineal. The main use of air by the Yogin has to do, however, with the control and extreme modification of respiration. This discipline is to teach the postulant how to alter consciousness by control of breath. The normal rate and depth of respiration give the brain, through the oxygenated blood, the gas fuel that makes it possible for the mind to make that biological construction of the environment, and of its own physique, which is necessary for it to operate in the everyday world. By shifting that normal rhythm of breathing this common-sense construction is dissolved. The Yogin is then free to seek for or devise another construction. The rapid breathing exercises, by intense acceleration of the respiration rate, produce hyperoxygenation of the lung and so permit considerable pauses without need of respiration.[c] In Chapter 1 of this Third Part, we have seen the importance of these rest

[c] See K. T. Behanan (2), *Yoga*. Behanan is an Indian by birth and a graduate of Yale University on a Sterling Fellowship. To study Yoga, he went back to India where he was trained by a North West Indian Hathi Yogin whose religious name was Kavalyanda. Behanan says that "the main feature of all Yogi varieties of breathing which are claimed to have spiritual value" is the pause between inhalation and exhalation.

pauses for keeping the mind one pointed and free of distractions; and we also saw the value attached to respiration cessation by the Yogic traditions.

It is also worth noting here that that unique mixture (unique in the modern world) of an intellectual genius and a psychic sensitive, Emanuel Swedenborg, left it on record that "my breathing was such that I could respire inwardly for some time without aid of external air and so converse with spirits." He goes on to remark that "this tacit breath" he first experienced as a child in prayer and "lately, when thinking deeply."[d]

However, other students of respiration have pointed out that rapid and/or deep breathing may and, indeed, should increase the carbon dioxide in the blood. And this would lead not to clarity of consciousness but to visionary experience: delusions rather than inspirations, fantasies instead of insights. As we shall see in a moment when, in the second part of this chapter, we are discussing modern therapies and research that employ and explore varied respiration mixtures, apparently the preparation, intention, and attention of the subject is a primary factor in deciding whether the experience will be dissipatory and delusional or concentrative, constructive, and truly explorational.

[d] See *Emanuel Swedenborg* by Signe Toksvig (86). In his "Spiritual Diary" Swedenborg says, "I sometimes scarcely breathed by inspiration at all for the space of a short hour and merely drew in enough air to keep up the process of thinking."

In his first volume, *Africa Dances*, in which he reports on the psychophysical exercises of several tribes on the West Central Coast of Africa, Geoffrey Gorer (37), the anthropologist, notes that after hearing that the Moll fisher folk, a shore tribe, could remain under water for long periods he asked one of these divers to demonstrate. Gorer reports that the man dived in and lay down at a considerable depth on the sea floor. He remained down while Gorer kept the time by his watch. After twenty minutes, and with no sign of distress, he came to the surface and asked whether that was a satisfactory demonstration. Gorer, who had watched him all the while through the water, noticed that only on occasion a bubble of air rose from his mouth. When Gorer asked him how this breath retention was managed he remarked, "by fish breathing," which, as Gorer comments, was not informing.

We must also remember the particular purpose for which the postulant, in this air ordeal and by means of altered respiration and held breath, was seeking inspiration. The purpose of this was to save the man when, in his midindividual stage, he falls into self-hatred (pure adrenaline) and when, seeking for an infallible authority and a completely repressive discipline to which he may become slave and victim, "like a corpse in the hands of his Director"[e] he becomes schizoid. Having asked for law that is inflexible and without exception he finds that he cannot keep it when it is given to him. Like a completely closed suit of armor with no chink, it encloses, defends, and supports him, but it also suffocates him. The all-embracing, all-confining iron law kills with its clauses that shut down on every avenue of growth and deny every expansion of living or lifting of the heart.

First, then, the mystery of air, of respiration, was a therapy to restore the adolescent mind, the midindividual personality, from that self-hatred that seeks an outer law for the sake of security and to destroy its self-will, only to find itself invaded by guilt because that law condemns it for not abiding by the rigid principles which alone can save. As Paul of Tarsus says, the letter kills but the spirit makes alive, and the spirit is, at root, the pneuma, the breath that inspires and exhilarates. The basic therapy was, then, to remove guilt and prevent schizophrenia by showing the postulant that he was not totally depraved, that in him there was the living breath, but that, owing to his individualism, he had lost inspiration and was subject to illusion. He must, therefore, open himself to the cleansing breath. Then his biologically confined consciousness (which was, at least in the beginning, racial good sense and the desire for racial survival, and which is now only a selfish, cowardly concern for personal escape) will be raised to the knowledge and insight of the true preterconsciousness.

There is a further significance in this the third initiation, the air mystery. As we have seen, the age group and epoch that this third mystery was developed to serve is the midindividual, the

[e] This was the way it was phrased by St. Francis of Assisi and confirmed by Ignatius Loyola.

adolescent. And, as noted in Chapter 3 of Part II, it is at this age that the individual (just as it was at this epoch that man did so) becomes specifically sexual; particularly and almost exclusively aesthetically and sensorily aware of the genitals as being the source of pleasure and release. This concentration and consequent loss of the panaesthetic euphoria led to frustration and next to the sense of guilt. The air exercises, by concentrating on the lungs, first raise the sensory awareness from the viscera and the genitalia. Secondly, they give respiratory euphoria and thirdly, by expanding the rib cage and convexing the sternum, they increase the pectoral area and awake the thoracic nerve centers.[f] Hence, there is both a tonic restriction in the abdominal musculature and also a complimentary tonic dilation of the upper chest and neck. It is possible that by such exercises, and the carriage that they induce, the thyroid is stimulated.[g] And there is some evidence that the thymus—the mid-chest ductless gland that prevents premature sexuality and in average cases atrophies after puberty—may be brought into action. This would help restore the paidomorphic panaesthetic sensorium, which, in turn, would restore the generalized euphoria and prevent a disbalanced sexuality, concentrated on the genitals. And as they are a neotenic zone of dilated sensibility, the breasts, when they become the center of the body's alertness, aid in removing that shrinking, self-centered attitude that is the pose of the self-accusing and which, as attitude increases mood, aggravates the abject state of mind.[h]

Having finished this brief account of the traditional air mystery,

[f] See work of Szent Gyorgi. Also see Part 2, Chapter 4, footnote b.
[g] Ibid.
[h] See the James Lang principle in regard to the effect of attitude on mood.

It is also worth observing here that the Negro Galla tribes in mid-Africa, which have adopted an aggressive militaristic social pattern, have two main ordeals in their puberty initiation rites for boys. The first is circumcision: a rite that most psychoanalysts now regard as being a substitute for castration, but which may be considered, with more likelihood, to be a callusing of the glans so as to make sexual feeling less peremptory and, therefore, battle-rage the preferred sensation. The second is excision of the nipples. The Galla maintain that these nerve centers make for compassion and that a man, to be sufficiently heartless, must be rendered incapable of such emotions.

we can now turn to the subject of the second section of this chapter: What might this ordeal initiation of the third mystery be if it were performed under present conditions and with today's psychophysical knowledge? As in Chapters 1 and 2 of this Third Part we saw what practical steps are being taken, and could further be taken to apply the psychophysical releases and developments that the ordeals and initiations of earth-rebirth and water-catharsis suggest, now, in concluding this third chapter on the ordeal and initiation of air, we must see what steps are being taken in modern therapy to explore respiratory methods.

As we have seen, this the third mystery has never, like the earth burial and rebirth mystery, become lost. Nor has it, like the water-catharsis, become diminished and atrophied into traditional baptism. Through the East Indian interest in yoga, the mystery of air has had constant exoteric, explicit practice. And although yoga, especially in its Hathi and Tantra forms, uses other psychophysical exercises along with breathing (especially that of raising Kundalini and other techniques for activating the ductless glands and increasing the electric charge on the brain) still the changing of consciousness mainly by respiratory control has been the principal yogic technique.

Nor was the West without evidence that in between the final expiration of death and normal respiration there did exist many other states of consciousness, many conditions resembling sleep but, on examination, found to be radically different. There was hypnotic sleep, discovered by Mesmer (1733–1815), in which normal attention could be so altered that severe pain, such as caused by amputation, was unnoticed. However it was not a sleep of relaxation, as is normal sleep, but of high muscular and nervous tonicity.[i] But normal attention was altered; it became so absolute that in hypnotic sleep the subject was rendered completely oblivious to the most intense agony. And unfortunately for pure research it was this physical anaesthesia, and not any change of consciousness, that alone concerned the doctors who were using hypnosis.

Meanwhile, Humphrey Davy, the chemist, experimenting with

[i] The hypnotized person is not simply *inattentive;* he is entirely *attentive* to *one* thing, that is, the hypnotic suggestion.

"the airs," gases other than the mixture we call ordinary air, discovered nitrous oxide. Chloroform and ether followed. Research into hypnosis, had hypnosis been the only anaesthetic, might have been pursued by medicine and so come to be a detached study, a pure research. But it was fanatically attacked by that ugliest and most dangerous, because it is the most dishonest, alliance of superstitious conservatives (who think that suffering is good in itself provided that they are not in its grip) and materialistic specialists who believed that the mind was a vapor given off by the brain. Very few troubled to inquire further into this enigma of consciousness, although the medical profession was constantly being reminded, with every major operation, of how much consciousness was altered by changing the gas that was given to the lung. They were only concerned with rendering the body insensible. Their one interest was to make the patient temporarily as dead as possible. And his frequent accounts, on his return, of the experiences he had when breathing these gases were regarded as being tantamount to the ravings of a lunatic.

Now, however, research in hypnosis is being pursued, although lack of an adequate hypothesis of the structure and range of consciousness delays our being able to coordinate all the data. Further, even in the West, breathing exercises, at least in moderate forms, have gained considerable attention during this century. And it is an attention that owes not a little to the West's interest in operatic singing, the need to study breath control. And still further, in the last couple of decades psychotherapy has become specifically interested in respirational treatment.[j] After a number of experiments, a mixture of 30 per cent oxygen and 70 per cent carbon dioxide was found to be the gas blend most suited to bring on a shift of consciousness. After five breaths most subjects—and I am included among them—experience a sense somewhat similar to the first couple of breaths of nitrous oxide. After ten breaths, and with the eyes closed, vivid, iridescent rainbowlike effects are seen and these rapidly become decorated with moving jewellike prisms and other

[j] See *Carbon Dioxide Therapy* by L. J. Meduna (60), who was Professor of Psychiatry at the University of Illinois, College of Medicine, Chicago.

crystalline forms. Those who have practiced in training themselves
to do so can retain consciousness of the outer world (biological consciousness) even up to twenty breaths, but this is rare. Most persons
pass out between ten and fifteen respirations. Also, there is generally
distress, partly because of the strangeness of the breathing mixture
to which the lung and, indeed, the throat are not accustomed, partly
because of the inconvenience of the nasal-oral mask on the face
and partly, no doubt, because of the traumatic, subconscious birth-
respiratory memory. The system is used by Meduna and other
psychiatrists to raise repressed memories and fear blocks that are
due to past psychic damage. It became very popular for a couple
of years. Lately, however, many psychiatrists have turned against
it. There is a feeling that it not only adds to the distress of the
patient but that it does not—or very seldom does it—permit him
to raise his repressed fears. Also, it may release such fears too spas-
tically. As the patient is out of normal consciousness at the time,
the shock of recollecting a deep traumatic experience, under these
conditions of loneliness and nightmare fear, may be too severe. The
rapidity of the process does cut costs of long conscious analysis, but
the price may still be too high.

This work, however, is only in its initial stages. The effect of
previous informational instruction, given to the subject by the psychiatrist, is very great. Also, the attitude of the psychiatrist toward
the subject appears increasingly to be of importance, and all the
more so if both of them are not conscious of the tie. This, of course,
is in keeping with the mystery process, when the postulant is rendered
wholly dependent on his trainer and hierophant, one who has already
been sent through the tensions of liberation and so attained to
enlightenment.[k]

[k] It is important to note here the steady growth, in psychoanalysis, of companionship between the patient and the analyst. Beginning with the extreme
of detachment, as shown in the original Freudian attitude toward the analy-
sand, the Jungian method of treatment shifted from having the therapist
crouched out of sight and the therapee sprawled on a couch. Now they
face each other. In the Karl Rogers nondirective approach the patient takes
the initiative and the analyst listens as though being instructed. In the
Moreno psychodrama several persons act out an issue with the psycho-

As, then, respiratory methods of psychotherapy are clearly part of the air mystery, and as the air ordeal and initiation are specifically for dealing with the midindividual, the person in training, the adolescent, athletic, ascetic mind whose specific mental peril is schizophrenia, it seems reasonable to suggest, in the light of these facts, two proposals for obtaining better results.

The first is definitive: that is to say, we should stress the respiratory method particularly with that specific age group, or emotional-mental category, which has already, by regression to the limited environment (burial and rebirth), been freed of the trauma of parturition; and which, by the catharsis of water, has been released from the paranoid, heroic, projected rages of the small child emotional reaction. For the guilt sense of the midindividual has back of it the primal, panaesthetic dilation of infancy, which, when it reached childhood and was rejected, became rage. That rage has now become guilt and is largely, though not wholly, composed of the sense of sin. The original, primal desire for general cocharging has now, in mid-self-consciousness, shrunken to a confined sexuality.

For, as we have seen, in the heroic person and the child, as in the coconscious man and the infant, sexuality is not dominant or ripe. It is the ascetic, the midindividual with his sense both of separateness and yet of obligation (that semi-independence that seems to be banishment and exile rather than liberation and enterprise) who is specifically sexual. That this guilt cannot be dealt with by vetoing the act and repressing the emotions, all now agree. But absolution cannot give peace of mind. For absolution, which is bought at the price of promising never to repeat the act, cannot provide certainty that the act will not be repeated and so rekindle guilt. Nor can the mere recollection of the deed cure the guilt,

---

dramatist serving as a kind of conductor of an unrehearsed, extemporized chorus or play. With Robert Lindner and other pioneers came experiments in identification. Sandor Ferenczi, although he remained true to the basic child-traumatic discovery of Freud, did introduce a loving, inspiring intimacy that restored the relationship of the mysteries, of the hierophant psychopompus to the postulant and neophyte going through his ordeals-initiations.

even though the person may be temporarily salved by being told that it is rationally trivial. For the guilt springs from a profound disappointment with the self, a profound feeling that specific sex—the genitally centered orgasm—is so far from being the promised whole that it seems a bitter, shameful travesty.

Here we must repeat that in spite of the value of Freud's insight into the great unrecognized part that the trauma of birth—psychic damage sustained in the first thirty months—inflicts on the psyche, his belief that the infant is a polymorphic pervert was a grave mistake. If accuracy is to be maintained there must be a distinction between specific sexuality (which, as the productive rhythm, is only specific when it centers in the genitalia and culminates in the orgasm) and eroticism. The body has a number of erogenous zones and this condition of suffused libido and dilational euphoria does not need to center down in the genitals and culminate in the orgasm. As Ivan Bloch (6) pointed out fifty years ago, specific sexuality is the confining and restricting of a generalized tickling and tonic sensation that is primarily and generally suffused. The child, therefore, should not be called a polymorphic pervert, for it cannot yet achieve sexuality. It should be called a panaesthetic transit as long as it is in symbiotic relationship with its mother (or mother surrogate) (84), and a panaesthetic exvert as it explores and activitates its various hyperaesthetic areas.

Therefore, we come to the second recommendation: besides raising the memories of adolescent ascetic-erotic failure, the therapist must also interpret them. He must be able to explain, not explain away, the guilt-disappointment by showing the postulant (1) what the life process is and what it is aiming at, (2) where actually, in that embryo growth, the midindividual finds himself to be, and (3) how he may cooperate with that process and recover this lost wholeness by neotenic fulfillment.

This the therapist does first by rational discussion, showing the intelligent critical surface mind that this explanation indicates the meaning of the life process, the sequence of evolution, and the particular position in this sequence that the patient himself occupies. Next, when the patient is under the respiratory treatment, and so transferred from biological consciousness, he will be witnessing and experiencing his adolescent shames and disgraces. And in this state, which we know is also a state of high suggestibility, he can and should be given the inspiration that will grant him the assurance and energy to handle his separateness, not only without guilt, but in the clear belief that, after he has gone through the reproductive phase (the marital phase of first maturity), on the higher level of the spiral he will be able to recover the panaesthetic condition that is the psychophysical aspect of neotenic development.

Such then, in bare outline, seems to be the ordeal and initiation of the air mystery. This treatment, then, of breathing gas mixtures close to but other than air we may regard as the specific therapy for the ascetic, self-accusing man of schizoid tendency.[1] By breathing this mixture he is transferred to a state of consciousness other than the biological, wherein with the aid of hypnotic suggestion not only are his repressed emotions raised but they are reinterpreted and reconstructed, not dismissed. And the midindividual may now go on, untrammeled, into his next two stages of psychophysical growth, that of total individualism and that of postindividualism. In the chapter that follows, therefore, we consider the stage into which those who have been healed by the air mystery must then pass and how its specific ordeal and initiation may be undergone.

[1] It is, of course, assumed that he has already been brought successfully through the first and second mystery ordeal-initiations.

4

The initiation of illumination
[Fire and light]

We now have to deal with the fourth therapy. For if the first therapy, by regression, cleared the basic infancy level of consciousness and made it possible, through the second therapy of catharsis by water, to deal with the paranoid frustrations of childhood so that in turn the third therapy of auditory explanation and encouragement can be worked for those who are going through (or are still held by) the adolescent, self-accusing phase, then we are now ready for the fourth therapy. And it is essential; for not only have the other three led up to it, but for us today this fourth stage is more critical, more apposite than the earlier ones. Each of them serves a specific purpose, for each can, when it is achieved, refer the freed person to an appropriate and, for the time being, fulfilling pattern of behavior. The boy of today can have, as his specific standard, a contemporary rendering of the heroic behavior that thrills him—for example, the interplanetary explorer, the space man who will soon travel to our close satellites.

The adolescent, in turn, can have as his ideal the selfless, anonymous member of a research team on an assignment full of unknown risks (for example, X-ray and nuclear study) and with the laurels going to the Lab and to no one person.

The man in first maturity, however, is our contemporary type, the modern executive. He it is who has to decide what adventures are to be planned and assigned, who has to order the advance and to pick the pioneers. And it is this key man whose problem is second only to that of second maturity, who is of first concern to most of the concerned today. For immediate power is now in the hands of first maturity. And he has no authority above him; second maturity is not producing social vision but only self-commiseration. The man in first maturity, the most acute example of the intensifying triad of the individual, is now cruelly torn.

Always, from the time that the Chinese achieved the great Confucian pattern of culture, the conflict between the family and the State has torn the heart of the administrator. Today this manager is key man in a secular State made up of routineers, engineers, and managers, but which lacks seers (41). So he must be his own guide, for his social and psychological experts tend to tell him that conscience is, at best, a tradition that is largely out of date, and, at worst, a conglomerate of wholly misguiding tabus. Nevertheless, he who is most acutely an individual is the person who has all the principal controls of the community in his hands. He has to double the parts of lookout-man and administrator. And his pattern of behavior is based on the humanic concept of a mankind that is completely self-seeking because it is completely individualized into separate physiques that can have direct knowledge of only their own private pain and pleasure, inferring but faintly the feelings of others. Such a race of ingenious animals, each able to see and to seek his own advantage, must be kept in combination with each other by appealing to their separate interests. Such, of course, is modern democratized Machiavellianism, the latest edition of Hobbes' *Leviathan*.

No wonder, then, that the more intelligent and contemporary are those in first maturity and the more they strive to have principle and achieve statesmanship, to avoid opportunism and the mere playing of power politics, the more they find themselves under the strain that has brought this age-group into the main killing range of coronary heart disease. There must be found one preventive therapy that is aimed specifically at relieving their tension. Nor is the search hopeless. But it presents difficulties that are greater than the earlier therapies. And, as we have seen, even these preliminary treatments are anything but easy to apply.

One of the main obstacles in the way of this fourth therapy is the acute self-consciousness of the subject. The patient who is at an extremity of individualism puts up the most intense intellectual and emotional resistance to any therapy. He looks on himself, for better or for worse, as being the type picked by natural selection to have the highest survival rate. For does he not out-climb all the rest? Though he reaches the top only to fall stricken. Considering himself to be a master at managing others, he scorns (and fears above all) being managed himself. Well masked to look what others like, he is naturally full of well hidden misgiving should anyone suggest prizing off his visor. The skin is always most raw under the scab and the callus. He is inexperienced in viewing his character, for he finds it best not to know his motives too precisely, and to believe in the pretenses and defenses he makes for his actual conduct. Hence, he suffers mainly from conversion psychosis, the transference of subconscious conflict out into physical functioning. And so he often dies from heart rupture or brain artery lesion before he knows he is ill; long before he could have been brought to any mind-body knowledge, let alone any mind-body renovation. He may believe that psychotherapy can do something for the young. For instance, it may help to solve the problem of juvenile delinquency. But for the mature, in their armor of success, what release is possible, feasible? A recreation tour, a discreet or at least clandestine love affair, a fairly heavy sedation in which alcohol is still the main ingredient—these are the only let-ups from the strain.

And still the strain is growing. There is a steady increase in the hours of unavoidable vigilance and decisiveness, management, adroit adjustment, and subtle maneuver. The psychosomatic disease incidence mounts. Mature man is running himself wrongly and, in his extensive study, *The Stress of Life,* Hans Selye (77) has gone far to show just how wrongly.[a] Man today is driving himself (naturally enough, once we allow the humanic premise as to what man is) in a way that must lead to breakdown. Kicking himself along with the suprarenals, the glands of combat as they have been called, modern man fights off depression with aggression.[b] The thyroid, the gland of sustained effort, is neglected. And lately it has been discovered that not only may a too active suprarenal system provoke heart disease, but that a too lethargic thyroid may make the body fail to deal with the chloresterol that sludges the arteries and, in the end, will cause blockage.

Meanwhile, for those mature who are too self-awarely intelligent to misinterpret a warning from the psyche by transmuting it and projecting it into a psychosomatic disease such as a coronary or rupture of an artery in the brain, there awaits the mental disease of the manic depressive. He is the one whose life has to be run on a megalomaniac, self-believing elation that is paid for by catastrophic bouts with suicidal despair.

Yet the resistance of the total individual, the humanic man who believes that he is mounted in the saddle of life with the reins in his hands and with a generation of mastery ahead of him, remains highly formidable. In all that he can affirm, he is a positivist. It is only in the world that he perceives through his senses that results can be achieved. Negatively, he denies any other possibility for the future. He regards himself as being the apex of growth. Up to this point the vague impractical generosities of the boy and the superstitious self-blaming of the adolescent had to be outgrown and brought to the keen cutting edge and fine penetrating point of a skeptical individualism. This is the culmination of consciousness. This is man's final comprehension, his final and completely com-

[a] See also *Man's Presumptuous Brain* by A. T. W. Simeons.
[b] In classical English, aggression is a reprehensible form of conduct, in American English it has become prestigious.

petent grasp of circumstances. After attaining to this stage there remains only the problem of making one's mastery more automatic until at length the younger generations, coming up into maturity, push the elderly into retirement.

Hence, at this point any therapy can only be restorative, not developmental. For with the age group of the first mature every sign of change must be evidence not of yet another stage of growth, but of decline and decay. The psychophysiological therapist or counsellor is dismissed as a quack if he suggests that just as adolescence led to this maturity, so this maturity itself is a preliminary stage for a further, even more mature condition. The whole notion is utterly alien from the assumed psychology and physiology of today. We may propose that old age need not be and should not be decay and yet, at the same time, affirm that the hope does not lie in rejuvenation. We may point out that the foreconscious, critical mind of the individual, with its concomitant self-consciousness, with its awareness of separation and its desire for objectivity, has, by its growth and intensification throughout written history, given necessary power. But at the same time we must insist that individualism, having now done its work and made its mistakes, must, when men have completed the spiral curve, develop beyond individuality, objectivity, and self-consciousness. However, such propositions seem to be pure paradox; metaphysics brought back, masked and made up as some Newer Thought nostrum.

Yes, it is difficult to persuade the man in control that he must grow. Such a suggestion to the young mature (with his maintenance physicians honestly grooming him to avoid any further development; they, as much as he, believe that first maturity is the end of growth) raises in him the resistances of both greed and fear. For even if he did believe that there was another stage ahead of him and that he ought to grow into it, he would resist any call to leave his enjoyments. It is hard enough to make the too happy child put away its toys, or the too successful athlete stop his games. Still and all, they have the pressure and command of society to call them up to further trainings for further development. But who can call the leaders of society and order them to undergo a still further training for a still further development? See how impossible it has been, in spite of medical advice, to get the central power executives, the chief politicians and the chief judges to allow a ruling that, at certain advanced ages of say sixty or sixty-five, a general check-up should be made of their involutionary processes[c] and that this estimate be available to the electorate who has to decide on their capability to stand the strain of office. Greed, therefore, makes men cling to power, which is the chief lure of the total individual.[d] Then the fear of what lies beyond makes even those for whom the exercise of power has become a wretched fatigue, and executive work a task to be shirked, dread to resign, to vacate a seat however stormy and to step down into the dark.[e]

But if acute self-consciousness can, at best, hardly conceive of a state of mind beyond individualism and if, therefore, the young mature, at the height of self-consciousness, can seize power (for society thinks that those in first maturity are at the peak of human possibility and the Western World, being ignorant of the seer, knows no category of social value above the manager), then there is little hope of getting the total individual even to consider further growth.

Nor does the task appear to be any less improbable when we consider the specific technique which is, in the mystery tradition, employed at this fourth stage (at the crisis when those in first maturity must pass into second maturity) in order to bring about the new quality of consciousness. As mentioned above, today's regression therapy for curing birth trauma and the techniques of restricted environment actually re-establish the ordeal and initiation of second birth (rebirth) by burial (rewombing) and resurrection. Also, today's water-catharsis treatment can deal with rage states, eruptive or repressed, and deliver patients from the mistaken child reactions that prevent emotional maturity. While thirdly, the hypnotic techniques, yoga breathing, and such respiratory psychotherapeutic treatments as the use of carbon dioxide are the ordeal initiation of air,

[c] As Wartin of Ann Arbor calls the second part of the aging process.
[d] Compare La Rochefoucauld: "I have seen men leave love for power, but never leave power for love."
[e] For example, Konrad Adenauer.

practiced in modern form. All these means can be and are being accepted; for although they are sometimes shocking, psychically, they are safe; any physiological risk is nonexistent. In these first three, only solids, liquids, and gases (all at comfortable temperatures and at familiar pressures) are being used. The customary innocuous tangibles (for even a gas can be felt) are being employed. But, further, the ends for which they are employed can be approved by the therapeutic authorities: that is, removal of the trauma of birth, of the possible repressed paranoia of childhood and of the schizophrenia of adolescence. So, in turn, the adult leader can approve such therapies for, through their use with the young, he may hope to be given more dependable future members of the society he rules; members who are returned to normalcy once more accepting the reality that he controls. But not only will he reject any therapy that is aimed at altering *him*. He will be able to dismiss the traditional technique of the fire initiation as being absurd, utterly impossible, and to be vetoed as clearly dangerous: indeed, highly damaging if not lethal.

And what is even the most openminded researcher to make of the fourth mystery? True, the others have established their value. But how can this one? Fire is a destroyer, not a stimulant. The ordeal by fire, practiced under Anglo-Saxon legal procedure as a method of establishing innocency, has always been regarded as being the survival of a cruel use of credulous belief in magical superstition in order to assure a conviction. Here there was no hint of giving the defendant any recharging, any initiation, any resistance. The innocent person, it is callously assumed, will be able to receive protection against the fire from God, Who thus indicates the person's innocence and so vindicates his case. This is akin to, indeed it is worse than, the utter injustice of flinging into water a bound woman who has been accused of witchcraft, and assuming that if she sank she was innocent and that if she floated she was guilty.

It would seem, then, that the association that we have now traced between (1) the psychophysical phylogeny of man—his history since he was homo loquens, homo fax-factor (the torch maker), (2) the psychophysical ontogeny of man (the life stages in which the individual, from birth to maturity recapitulates human history) and (3) the successive particular insanity risks that threaten each of these successive developments, here breaks down.

The preindividual, coconscious infant, the protoindividual of childhood, the midindividual of adolescence—each of these, we have found, can be brought past its particular danger (of the trauma of birth, dementia praecox becoming paranoia and schizophrenia) by (1) a regression to birth and reliving of the experience, by (2) the catharsis of unreflective rage and its transmutation into tears and fearful awe and by (3) psychophysical inspiration through pulmonary salience that helps to restore the panaesthetic sensory awareness and so lifts the body-mind out of its despairing disgust. These three technique-therapies specifically meet the struggling person at his successive personal and ancestral crises and bring him through and into a new age.

But when we reach the age of total individualism, the period of office and power, that cresting moment when energy is not yet past its apex and skill is close to its climax, then we have no answer to the problem of its particular process of ordeal-initiation. The issue of first maturity seems to be insoluble. For although second maturity exists today, it is, as we have seen, without power, purpose, or plan. It is the stepping-down stage, the declension that is sedated so as to break the fall into the grave, the dietary training to teach the unwanted that, though go they must, we spare them the time to take two bites at the bitter apple of death rather than make them bolt it at one gulp.

In the face of such fact, then, the mysteries' offer of a fire therapy as being the technique that is apposite to and for those in first maturity (the age group which, of all the age groups, is the most critical, the most powerful, the most assured, and the most individualistic, and so the least conscious of its preterconscious and its psychosomatic linkage) seems worse than mistaken. It discredits all the others. The other therapies might work for the other classes. This one is absurdly out of the question.

And it is true that only a few of the scholars who have studied them have been able to view the mysteries as being anything but ankylosed and romanticized fertility rites. Even fewer have been able to regard them as having a possible or real therapeutic value; at least to cultures in which such rites were indigenous. But even of these rare researchers most have fought shy of the fire mystery. And as very few of them distinguish between the air-fire and the aetheric-fire, the air-fire is usually considered to be the final mystery. Further, their way of dealing with it has been to regard it as being a mystery not of fire but of light, the visionary by-product of fire. The final rite (for example, at Eleusis) was a matter of seeing; it was purely psychological, not physiological. "They see something," said Aristotle, "they did not learn but were moved." Up to this point, our few informants all agree, the postulant was in the dark: masked, blindfolded, groping, stumbling, ear-straining to catch echoes and cudgel his bewildered brains over enigmatic, threatening sounds. Then, when this stage drew to a close, there was the encouragement of inspirational affirmations. But all the while not a thing was seen, no authority appeared. The whole experience might be a delirious dream, a private nightmare. And the ear is one of the worst guides, the most rumor-creating of the senses. Seeing is believing.

So suddenly—and of this there can be no doubt—the postulant, after all these strivings, wanderings, blunderings and recoils, instantaneously saw. What it was we cannot be sure. That it was dazzling light we know from Apulieus. "The sun shining at midnight" is his well-known phrase. Surely the postulant was both startled and relieved, both shocked and delighted.

This was, therefore, called *Epopteia.*¹ The Homeric hymn says "Happy is he who has seen it." It was vision-producing ecstasy. The *epopt* is the postulant now, in a flash, made a seer. As we have seen in Chapter 3 of this Part, here at this moment and climax of the process a bronze gong sounded. Speech and auditory instruction, listening and trying to make sense of paradox—all of this was ended. Now, with a crash the veil of darkness was rent and the postulant, instantly initiate, saw.

¹ "The climax was a vision." See Walter F. Otto's (65) Bollingen Foundation-sponsored *The Meaning of the Eleusinian Mysteries.*

PSYCHOPHYSICAL RELIGIOUS EXERCISES

And then? If he were going through the rite for the first time,[g] then when the light broke he saw Demeter, the Earth Mother of the dark mysteries of fecundation and birth travail. If he were there for the second time (generally several years after the first time) he saw the Great Mother's even more terrible daughter, the Bringer of Death, Persephone of the even deeper dark—a dark not of the womb and the earth but of the tomb and the realm of the dead.

So fire must be considered to be simply light, and the clear vision to be that given by light. So and so only can the critically minded total individual accept such psychotherapeutic symbolism. For does it mean more, need it involve more than believing (a belief very welcome to the individual) that in the end a man must, if he is to be a leader, take leave of secondhand authority, go beyond being a dutiful listener, see for himself, and have his own vision?

And if it is maintained that this insight is more than seeing one's way through argument to understanding, more than the self-satisfied, self-congratulatory "Eureka" when one has made the solitaire card game come out or adroitly fitted the clinching piece in the jigsaw puzzle; even then the modern individualistic master can be persuaded to undergo a little mind training that pays off highly. He can honestly and respectably accept the phrase, a flash of inspiration. All executives who employ expert managers have now heard of integral, creative thought; the complement and indeed the crown of analytic, critical thinking. After wrestling with a problem, you put your mind into a suspension, into a kind of blind, uneasy incubation. You wait in the dark and suddenly the light breaks; the answer shines, daylight clear, before you. So Tesla worked; he was the seer and creator-inventor of original machines that were worth millions.[h] And so, from Descartes down to Henri

[g] Going through the water ceremony of washing in the nearby inlet, receiving auditory instruction, and passing through the series of dark sanctuaries and claustrophobic passages.

[h] Tesla often remarked that he actually saw, in the air before him, a picture of the machine he was afterward to construct in the solid.

Poincaré and the supermathematicians and physicists of today, the breakers-through into new realms of understanding and power have made their spectacular advances (38). Thus illumination (as indeed the word has now come mainly to mean) would simply stand for a particularly bright moment of understanding.

Today, of course, with the new attention that is being given to the processes of insight,[i] we know that we have to learn how to dilate the mind, increase its span and grasp. The process is quite difficult for the critically minded man of strong convictions and quick decisive action. For it lies in knowing how to stop arguing and analyzing and to await in alert passivity. And he finds it bafflingly difficult to keep the mind so open. But it pays to learn it, for it makes for a further step toward efficiency. However, that means, as a matter of fact and inevitably, a further step toward making the man of executive power, who is in the upper rank of first maturity, more definitely and inescapably what he has been and what he now (if he continues in outward growth only) should and must cease to be.

But might not this revolution in the technique of the humanic man in first maturity, while bribing him to use it in the name of efficiency, lure him into self-knowledge and self-growth? This certainly seems to be what, in actual fact, is now happening. Methods employed to increase profits (or, at most, to advance insights into the outer world) may tend to advance a true progress toward enlarging consciousness.

Just look at the advance during the last ten years in the new sector of restorative medicament, which may be called that of the psychiatric wonder drugs. They are certainly proving to be as promising as—and, indeed, more promising than—the magic molds, the many bacteriophages and antibiotics. Beginning with the barbiturates that finally yielded the sedative Seconal and, on the other hand, such tonics as Dexedrine and the tension-reducers such as Tolserol, a new advance is now under way with still finer aids: for

[i] See *The Art of Thought* by Graham Wallas (91); *The Creative Process*, edited by Brewster Ghiselin (33).

example, the drug distributed under the names Miltown and Equanil. However, all these lead up to work now being done with vegetable extracts which, it has become clear, lead to far more extensive, profound, and releasing effects on consciousness. Further, we now see that this process can be considered to be part of the tradition's method of giving illumination. And, from the present practical, empirical standpoint of psychophysiological research, it is the part that gave to the mystery its efficacy.

Obviously, then, at this point we must ask: Did the traditional practitioners of the mysteries, and especially the self-conscious Greeks, have any physical aids that they used in changing the focal length of consciousness? Did they employ any means other than darkness and confinement (claustrophobia) and a complete sense of wandering and being lost (agoraphobia) followed by the sudden auditory and visual shock that imprinted, in an impacted association, an image of majestic terror and a feeling of assured discovery and insight?

Undoubtedly they did. From the early times when the Indo-European tribes were up on the Iranian plateau they had found the soma plant. However, and although the Veda saying runs "I have drunk soma and become a god," it was apparently highly toxic and death, it would seem, often resulted from drinking it. The plant became extinct, but later Herodotus reports that the Scythians (on the plains region north of the Black Sea) used sweat houses and, probably, Cannabis Indica (Indian hemp) as aids to their shamans in achieving ecstatic states. We know that at Eleusis the drinking, by the postulant, of a special potion made of a number of herbs was part of the rite of initiation. And Plutarch mentions the *leucophyllus* as being the plant principle in the draught given to those about to be initiated into the Mysteries of Hecate (Demeter). This potion, however, was employed to act as a truth drug, purging the candidate of his sins by driving him to make a full confession, not merely of his past deeds but also of any guilty intentions. It was a preliminary catharsis; a frenzy, it would seem, of fear and remorse and, therefore, not a direct aid to illumination.

Still, we must allow that this mixed potion may have aided the critically minded Greek to become capable of recovering integral feeling-thought.

Certainly the work now being done on the psychedelics, those chemicals which render the mind able to see and hear with the attention and insight of the artist and apprehend with the comprehension of supreme intuition, has shown that, under the influence of this completely nontoxic medicament, minds of the highest critical intelligence do have experiences of an intensity, assurance, and completeness that leave on the consciousness a lasting impression of dynamic significance and coordinant initiative. Nor do these chemicals seem to be confined either to mescaline, which was first discovered in the peyote button cactus and is now made synthetically from gallic acid, or the lysergic acid which is derived from ergot of rye. The mushroom cult, it appears, was widely distributed from the Levant to China and was later known to the Norsemen of the Icelandic culture.[j]

Then there is the Yage snuff, which is employed from Cuba to Patagonia. When taken in small amounts it also seems to give (as do mescaline and lysergic acid) a sense of communion and 'at-peacefulness' with one's fellows, while in larger amounts it gives the similar sense of an equal communion with all of Nature. Indeed, as anthropology abandons its preliminary attitude of patronage toward all cultures other than that of its own humanic phase, it is being found that there are cultures, now widespread throughout the old and new world, which employ the aid of some psychedelic medicine to assist the mind in viewing the world with unpossessive, unexploiting charity and delight. Still (and this seems to be the important point in this enquiry), research in the therapeutic use of the psychedelics seems to indicate with increasing clarity that the value of these medicines lies in the fact that they provide two preliminary aids to attention.

In the first place, they remove distractions—those incessant

[j] Note that the psychedelic element of the mushroom has now been synthesized and given the name of psilocybin.

animal-alertings that the human mind involuntarily makes to any irrelevant stimuli, outer or inner.[k] It has been known to all trainers-in-attention (for example, spiritual directors and psychiatrists) that these dissipating interferences only intensify when the surface will is employed to banish them. Four decades ago, Baudoin of Lausanne well named it the Law of Reversed Effort. The psychedelics smooth away such irrelevances and attention attains to that wholeness of focus which is as flawless as that of a person under deep hypnosis. But there is this profound difference:—the hypnotized person attends totally to the instruction of the hypnotist, while the person who is freed from distraction by a psychedelic is perfectly free to attend to whatever area of interest on which he may choose to concentrate. He can range, at will and with equal totality of attention, over the whole phenomenal field, over everything across which his vision passes.

This brings us to the character of the second contribution that the psychedelics make to that attentiveness which is the essential preliminary to preter-analytic, meta-critical insight. Not only are the distractions removed. But, and this is more important for it is a further step toward insight, the observational construct (the way we have of instantly seeing the world around as being a series of separate objects, an assumption that is useful enough for exploiting our environment) is corrected. For though this observational construct is convenient and, indeed, necessary to us if we are to prise loose bits of the continuum and consume or store such fragments for personal use, it is not, in point of fact, an accurate picture of what is out there. What is actually out there is an unbroken series

[k] In the animal world the inability to attend for any length of time is a built-in safeguard necessary for survival. For instance, if a bird in the grip of one of the most powerful of instincts (the nesting instinct) were to become absorbed in what it was doing it would fall easy prey to its natural enemies who could then approach it undetected. On the contrary, a nest-building bird will stop every ten or fifteen seconds and scan its horizon 360 degrees.

In humans this biological leftover, no longer necessary for survival, is a hindrance and is overcome only through great effort and discipline, and the unique human power of being selflessly interested.

of events in a variously accented panorama. The artist, with native realism, has always seen the Nature around us as being a design that is made, as Constable said, "by light falling on light." And this is where art and science differ. For art is always composition while science is always bent on analysis. As Adelbert Ames and H. Cantril of Princeton have shown, this modern, scientific, humanic way of instantly fractionating the total presentation *is* perception, but it is a perception that is so largely influenced and distorted by instantaneous assumption (that is, construction-interpretation in terms of use and convenience) that it is constantly misleading the perceiver when he would comprehend.[1]

With the corrective aid of the psychedelics the mind is presented with a world that is commanding in its unbroken coherence, arresting in its flawless intensity of color and form, startling in its immanent aliveness. But it must be repeated that these aids are and can only be preliminary. Spectacles can only assist defective vision; they cannot give sight to the blind. They cannot make the world appear friendlier to one whose myopia is a psychosomatic symptom of a neurotic wish to shun and disregard strangers. The psychedelics can correct our utilitarian deformation of what is around us. But, as tens of thousands of experiments with thousands of subjects have shown, though everyone has the same intensifying of experience, though to many it is one of amazement, to a considerable number it is one of dismay, alarm, distress. While to a few minds, well trained in modern philosophy and at the acme of critical defensiveness and denial of wholeness, the removal of the imposed barriers can be resisted and the arbitrary distinctions and abstractions still regarded as continuing. What the subject makes of the experience is what he brings to it. All that the psychedelic biochemistry can do is to remove the barriers to attention and permit the observer to consider the scene without the assumptions regarding it that are currently made by humanic man.

We may say, then, that although it would now appear that

[1] See *The Ames Demonstrations in Perception* by W. H. Ittleson (46). See also *Patterns of Discovery* by N. R. Hanson (39), and *Art and Illusion* by E. H. Gombrich (36).

when he has become self-consciously critical and individualistically analytic toward his surroundings man has often employed psyche-delic medicine to cleanse this oxide of utilitarian assumption off the presented scene, these aids are only preliminary. At best they can only assist the onlooker to have an experience that will be con-structive or daunting according to whether his cast of mind is open and curious or defensively assured.

We are back, then, at the point where we started when we were attempting to explain away the fire mystery of ordeal and initiation as being nothing more than illumination; nothing more than a new-found conviction that somehow life is more than (and can be enjoyed as more than) personal success, economic mastery, and the psychophysical capacity to enjoy life—for those in first maturity—and a sedated calm for those in second maturity who are undergoing a painless elimination.

True, our present psychophysical diet may neatly taper us out of life without dismay to ourselves or embarrassment to those who wait, needing the room we occupy. But not only is this no true solution to the problem, the riddle of second maturity. It is simply a slow, sentimentally rendered, inefficient way of getting rid of the unwanted whom (were we frank and rightly urgent) we would, with true kindness to all concerned, euthanatize as soon as they fail to be effectively productive or enjoyable to themselves. The method itself, it becomes increasingly clear, cannot work unless it is accu-rately and fully as psychological as it is physiological. For not only do these mental wonder-drugs do no more than bring the subject to the threshold of a new experience. Even if we are to bring him thus far and render him able to regard and profit by this new presentation, numerous experiments are beginning to show that the subject, the postulant, must be prepared, accompanied, and led by those who have already advanced along that path. They must know (from their own experience) and they must tell him why he is being so processed. Illumination, if this is all that the fourth mystery can yield, must at least be used honestly. It cannot be based on a pretense, a device the real purpose of which is to get the old out of the way.

It is clear, then, that the psychedelic aids, when given by devoted and experienced guides, can prepare those in first maturity for their next beginning, their next entering in.[m] Having, in the phase of first maturity, become completely *self*-conscious, they can, with this new help, penetrate down through the layers of their being and recover their knowledge of the *whole* consciousness that works in them. But it is equally clear that this is only a preparation.

We return, then, with additional assurance that we are right in pressing further our enquiry into the real nature of the mystery of fire—this mystery for which the first mature, when they have completed their phase, must be prepared and which can give the second mature a personal and social significance. We cannot, in honesty, any longer say that information or even inspiration, insight, or illumination is the final answer to this riddle, the truthful interpretation of this fourth mystery.

Formerly the other three mysteries were dismissed as being as nonsensically impossible as this one. They were play-acting: first by men who couldn't distinguish between fantasy and fact, pretense and reality; and secondly, by actors, pretenders, and frauds.[n]

But we have found that each of these three successive, traditional therapies do fit in as an apt remedial measure for each of the successive miscarriages of development that man, as a race, had suffered and that the vast majority of men repeat as individuals. First, there was the failure of the primitive coconscious society (and its constituent, the preindividual) to permit psychological growth and to keep alive and flexible a tradition that was able to comprehend a widening circuit of events. Secondly, there was the failure of the heroic society, and the protoindividual consciousness, to be protesting (critical of others) without becoming paranoic, to be independent and yet not to be anarchic. And thirdly, there was the failure of the ascetic society, and the midindividual, to be self-

[m] *In eo*, to go in, is the basic meaning of initiation.

[n] For instance, as we have mentioned earlier, an aged Pharaoh would have himself put through a sham burial and rebirth in order to make his duped subjects believe that he had come out of the womb for a second time and would now live forever.

critical without a sense of guilt and to be disciplined without becoming mortificatory.

Each of these three excesses was in turn sufficiently corrected for man's psychosocial evolution to continue. Man did not stay arrested, still less did he collapse into a feral condition. His consciousness continued to intensify. Some degree of initiation was given him: not enough to resolve his conflicts but enough to prevent them from reducing him to chaos, and enough to permit him to continue making discoveries. And this degree of disciplined understanding, this extent of resiliency of mores was due to a minimum of leavening being given to the congeries of mankind. At each of the three crises there were rare, unnoticed but catalytically influential individuals who were able to undergo, fully and successively, the appropriate mysteries: the earth mystery to free the coconscious, the water mystery to make liquid the assets of heroism that were in danger of paranoic spasticism, and the air mystery to give a capacity for true inspiration.[o]

The correction of each excessive deviation was, however, only sufficient to permit recovery from mistake and the most painful progress. Any one who studies history cannot but allow this. It is true that man not only survived; he also advanced to a keener definition of his problem and a more intensive and extensive study of his situation, mistakes, and predicaments. Yet what he was actually doing was this: he was carrying forward his unresolved conflicts in a growing suspense account that was increasingly forced below the level of conscious awareness. And this repressed suspense account, *pari passu* with the growth of his new focus of self-consciousness, was becoming a new and corresponding area, the subconscious. The suppressed conflicts with compound interest increased his liabilities. As we can see, the ordeal and initiation of each mystery did permit him to go on; but only into an increased condition of psychophysical stress, an increased sense of separateness, an intensification of self-consciousness and so of individualism. Each ordeal is a more severe strain and centers in on a more immediately urgent area of awareness. Earth is mainly muscular and cutaneous release;

[o] See Appendix D on the underground tradition, Tantra, Adamites, etc.

water is muscular and visceral stimulation and unbinding; and air is respiratory transference. Yet none of them reduces the conflict and leaves man at last balanced and whole, one with his whole self, his community, and life.

Hence, a still more strenuous experience and stimulant is demanded. "Nothing fails like success" is too simple an epigram to interpret the problem and process. We might better say that a partial success, a particular answer, because it lets the one who makes the answer get by, always adds to the depth of the total enigma. The complete self-consciousness of the humanic phase is, as we have said, completely cut off from the total consciousness, from those layers of integral awareness that have been forced down and out (along with unresolved conflicts) and so have become the subconscious. Among other disadvantages of unawareness, this results in the fully self-conscious mind being able to treat its body as only a machine. It cannot purposely affect, cooperate with, and aid its body through intuitive use of emotion, frame of mind, and attitude. So individualistic man, regarding his physique as a chemical still, tries to keep himself in good health (energetic euphoria) by the use of drugs, diet, and excisional surgery.

Hence, our immediate situation (the predicament of humanic man today) compels us to hypothecate some further procedure, some fourth process of development. For three reasons a specific treatment is required for the present dominant type, the totally self-conscious man, the person of first maturity. (1) Cut off from his own deep, intuitional mind, he must suffer increasingly from a subconscious anxiety. (2) Cut off from interior knowledge of his own body and function rhythms, he must be increasingly attacked by psychosomatic illness. (3) Cut off, psychologically, from the society whose granulation into separate cells he acutely expresses and coercively commands, he must create an international anarchy.

Up until now a tiny minority of men has been able to correct these three excesses by undergoing the three ordeal-initiations of burial for rebirth, of catharsis for reducing pride, and of inspiration as an absolution for banishing guilt. And this small group has, in each age, kept the main line of man from straying too far from the road of growth.[p] And today we find that as the individual, in his personal growth, ontogenizes the phylogenic growth of psychosocial man (man the creature of conversation around a fire), each of us recapitulates these three stages. And all of us (or at least nearly all of us) need a corrective process that is specifically designed to remedy our ill-performed developments at birth, in childhood, and in adolescence.

Finally, when we trace these psychophysical therapies that were esoterically named mysteries, we find that they were not completed with the third one. That this could not be so we can see clearly. For up to the third mystery the entire triad together can only release and reinduct (1) a social pattern that has reached the ascetic phase of midindividuality (midconsciousness) and (2) an individual who has reached and is arrested in a misdeveloping adolescence, and whose self-knowledge turns into a guilt that makes him despair of progress and long for a schizoid imprisonment, a submissionist escape. Neither the individual nor the social pattern that the third mystery can achieve is complete or contemporary. If left there the individual would remain (as so many do today) only half-mature, one who must seek a peremptory leader imposing a dogma. And so the society would also be an arrested medieval form: pre-experimental, precritical.

The fourth ordeal and initiation is then called for by the phylogeny and also the ontogeny of man—as an individual necessity but equally so as a social essential. Personally and socially we cannot be sane and cease from mutual destruction (let alone develop) if we cannot solve the problem of the total individual, the age group now in control. Just to set free the other three more preliminary age groups is to do one of two things. It is to give more flexible material for his delirious aims to the total individual of the power class, the man of frustrant, unexplicated violence who is still caught in his destructive self-ignorance.

Or it is to cause such an internal conflict between the master and those who cannot or will not obey him that (because he has the whip hand of concentrated violence) he will destroy his chal-

[p] See Appendix D on the underground tradition.

lengers and himself. They might serve him; they may defy him. But they cannot supplant him, for they are not in the age group that can take power.

Enough, then, has been said to show that this fourth ordeal and initiation is required, that the creators of the mysteries understood this and that, whether it was for a tiny minority or an influential élite, they did try to provide such a psychophysical therapy. But although all of this can be made unavoidably clear, the great difficulty remains. Earth, water and air can be used as contact materials for psychophysical therapy. But nearly everyone will still maintain that fire cannot be so used. To them we must state the challenge as we truthfully must and can, as a clear question. "Is there any evidence that man can go through flames given off by blazing logs and the temperatures emitted by a bed of brightly glowing charcoal and not even be burned, but actually be refreshed?"

First, however, we must ask whether back of the ordeal by fire there was a method which, at one level of culture and for one type of consciousness, did act as a test of the acquisition and possession of extraordinary and protective resistances and controls? To refer again to Shirokogoroff's thorough study of shamanism in Siberia: in addition to the severe water ordeal (previously referred to in Chapter 2 of this Part III), the shaman also had to show his resistance to fire. After he had gone through the preparatory self-training, undertaken when he went to live in solitude in the forests, the candidate had to walk on heaps of hot coals and, immediately afterward, show that his feet had not been burned.

But the fire walk is not confined to one culture. Nor is it practiced only by those unusual persons who have an odd and rare psychophysical balance; adolescents who between the ages of fifteen and twenty-one have shown symptoms of a possible vocation; who, further, have been able to endure severe isolation and who have also cultivated some form of extreme auto-suggestion which utter solitude favors. Even now the fire walk is practiced in India, in Japan, and in the Pacific Islands; it is a part of the procedure in the rituals of certain Buddhist, Brahmanistic, and Islamic sects.

As Ruth Benedict (3) points out in her now well-known

Patterns of Culture, page 176, in British Columbia the ecstatic worshiper dances with glowing coals held in his hands and at moments puts them in his mouth. Olfert Dapper (17) reports the same practice in South Africa, in *Description de l'Afrique.* Lane (52) (*An Account of the Manners and Customs of the Modern Egyptians,* page 467 f.) witnessed Islam Sufis doing the same. J. G. Warneck (94) (*Die Religion der Batak*) studied the identical fire rite in Sumatra and Adolf Bastian (1) (*Die Volker des Oestlichen Asiens*) describes it in Siam.

In 1956 there appeared two careful reports on the fire walk as it is still practiced in Europe.[q] One of these reporters, Martin Ebon, is editor of the quarterly review of psychical research called *Tomorrow.* The other is Admiral Angelo Tanagras, a student of long standing and high reputation in psychical research. Both of these researchers, Ebon in 1956 and Tanagras on May 21, 1940 (the feast of St. Constantine in whose honor, and of his mother St. Helena, the rite is performed), witnessed the fire walking; Admiral Tanagras at the village of Mavrolefki, Mr. Ebon at the village of Aghia Eleni (St. Helena). These two villages and the nearby country (it is a district in the Macedonian mountains some forty miles from Salonika) are populated by a sect of Paulicians, a Christian heresy, which has always preserved fire-walking as a mystery rite. The two observers note that the rite has about it no fraudulence. In both cases careful examination was made of the dancers' feet after they came off from dancing in the glowing beds of charcoal. The feet were not calloused nor were they inflamed; still less were they blistered or burned.

In the ceremony that Mr. Ebon witnessed two men and three women took part. Each went over the glowing charcoal not less than five times; one of them went over it fifteen times. The dance in the

[q] See *Fate* magazine, April 1963, page 22, Curtis Fuller's column "I See by the Papers . . .," paragraph headed "Before 15,000," which is an account of a firewalk (performed by 30 people) in Argentina, and witnessed by 15,000 people, including Armando Vivante, professor of anthropology at the Universities of Buenos Aires and La Plata.

fire continued for some twenty minutes; the dancers were barefoot. Previous to the actual firewalk a service of chanting began at about 5:15. From 6:30 until past 7:00 the pyre was kept blazing. Then about 7:15 the pyre was spread into a floor of embers, and the dancers, carrying icons and the scarf covers of the icons, now executed their dance (which they had been performing for two hours already) on the live charcoal.

Admiral Tanagras notes also that besides the quietly ecstatic dancing to the sober rhythm of the music the dancers take deep respirations while they perform. This is so striking that, for this reason, they are called anastenarias (or nestinars for short) which, in Greek, means sighers. Before this rite in the evening there has been a Mass, general dancing, and the sacrifice of a bull. Admiral Tanagras also notes that, on the occasion which he observed, when the pyre was level enough to be danced on the coals were nearly a foot thick over an area of some twenty-five square feet. In this case the dancers were three women who bore the icons.

Admiral Tanagras believes that this rite is a survival from the classical Greek worship of Dionysus. This certainly seems probable; for the worshipers of Dionysus did so perform: a fact to which Euripedes bears witness in his play *The Bacchae*. Also, in the present-day rite a bull (which is the beast sacred to Dionysus) is sacrificed, not the lamb sacred to Christ. And, since the dancing of the Maenads was a chief feature of the Dionysia, the preliminary ecstatic dance and the fact that the fire dance is not undertaken until ecstasy has been attained, is an additional confirmation of the Admiral's theory. Even more, we know that the musical instruments still used today (the lyre, the flute, and the drum) are the orchestra that was employed by the worhipers of the ecstatic god to raise themselves to *ecstasis*.

A number of careful studies have shown (*a*) that there is no fraud in the rite. The heat of the fire is enough to ignite a piece of paper thrown into it. The initiate goes through real flames and walks on live, red-hot charcoal. These studies have also shown that (*b*) calluses on the soles of the feet are not the explanation of the protection from burning, (c) that there is a careful, preritual method of preparation, and (d) that the rite is intended to heighten health, strengthen vitality, and restore damaged body tissue.

Also, as we have seen, the anthropological literature dealing with this subject is not small. *The Journal of the Society for Psychical Research* contains several full and careful accounts by qualified observers. Particularly remarkable are two cases. One is the account of a fire walk as it was conducted by a Moslem initiate. This account was written by a British banking official who took part in the procession when those in attendance at the ceremony were permitted to walk the length of the fire trench, treading on the burning logs and the live charcoal. The other case was from the Pacific Islands. There the white observer did not himself walk in and along the fire trench, but he tested the temperature by throwing pellets of paper onto the glowing embers and clocking the length of time it took the pellets to break into flame. A couple of seconds and they were fully ignited. The bona fides of both of these observers, and their competence to judge the experience objectivly, do not appear to be in doubt.

However, I would like to add to this evidence two cases, witnessed by two authors, both of whom are known to me personally. The first is an account, given to me in a letter, by Joseph Campbell (11, 12). He is author of the important anthropological studies, *The Hero with a Thousand Faces* and *The Masks of God;* he is the editor of Zimmer's outstanding *Philosophies of India,* co-worker with Dr. Zimmer and also editor of the volume entitled *Papers from the Eranos Year Book.* Campbell had lately completed a year of anthropological travel and study in Asia; and his experience with the fire walk occurred in Japan. The following quotes I make, with his permission, from an account that he wrote for me at my request.

The ceremony took place in an area behind a small Shingon temple in Kyoto. The Buddhist sect that practices this fire therapy is called "Yamabushi." In a roped-off space of this back lot of the temple a large square pyre had been built. Outside the ropes and on three sides, a congregation sat and there was an altar covered with flowers and fruit. Over fifty Yamabushi priests were in attendance, chanting as they circumambulated the altar. Next three principal priests recited prayers in front of the pyre, after which the pyre was ignited from two sides. One of the principal officiating priests now seated himself on the ground before the pyre, pointing two wands at the pile from which smoke was now pouring. The smoke swirled out, as though the pyre were the center of some vortex, forming a cloud that drove sideways following a circular path twice around the burning pyre "nearly smothering all of us each time it came our way." Then, with the increasing conflagration, the smoke gave way to flame and the whole pyre was one blaze. Nearby, some bundles of wooden votive tablets had been stacked and these were now fed to the fire. Then, with long rakes, the mass of blazing wood was formed into a trench some fifteen feet in length. The bigger logs, ablaze but not yet broken up by the fire, were arranged crosswise in the trench, above the bed of flame made by the pieces that had broken down into small brands and bright charcoal. So a kind of cattle-guard or corduroy walk was made, through which grate or grill the flames rose. The priest with the wands, who had sat before the fire while it was being lit and brought to full conflagration, had now moved and sat at one end of the trench with an assistant seated at the other. They stayed sitting like this for a few moments, after which all was ready for the therapy. The first to walk the length of the trench was one of the chief priests. By then a considerable portion of the lay congregation had been brought near and lined up. Old people, the middle-aged, and youngsters—between seventy-five and one hundred persons went along the trench. Dr. Campbell himself went in his turn. He reports, "I deliberately stepped on some nice fat flames, smelled the hair burning on my legs but found the flames were cool. When I put on my socks again I found that my right ankle, which had been swollen and sore from a strain acquired at Ankor Vat some weeks before, had gone down to normal and no longer hurt. The next day I walked some nine or ten miles and the ankle was still OK. The skin of my feet had not been damaged in the least— not even reddened by the flames. . . ." Dr. Campbell adds, "The Yamabushi priests are particularly celebrated for their handling of fire."

The second account is given by Mr. George Sandwith, a Fel-

low of the Royal Geographic Society, who also carried out an extensive anthropological travel-study tour, more especially in Polynesia.
His experience of the fire initiation was at Suva; the rite being performed by an East Indian priest who was the officiant of the Maha
Devi Temple there. The deity worshiped in this temple, so her priest
said, was the goddess who gave fertility as well as the goddess who
could protect from burning. She could be called (indifferently, for
all the names meant the same thing) Devi, Kali, or Mariammam.
These titles only indicate a manifestation of the Divine Power that
is available to everyone of any race or creed who believes sufficiently
to undergo the essential preparations. Fear and guilt must go; driven
out by love for the Divinity who was here called the Universal
Mother.

It is worth noting that here we have the same image of the
terrible and also benign All Mother that appeared in the therapy at
Eleusis as Mother Demeter and Daughter Persephone. And this is
not all. For Demeter (who is also the dreadful Hecate, the moon-
power of the dark and night side of life) appears in what is perhaps
the earliest myths regarding the beginning of the Eleusinian mysteries as the All Mother Goddess who can give mortals immortality
through bathing them in fire. She roamed the earth in disguise, so
the myth runs, seeking her daughter. She comes to Eleusis and the
local royal couple take her into their house as a nurse. Every night
the goddess puts their child to bathe in the glowing ashes of the fire,
until the Queen discovers this and rushes in. The goddess then reveals herself and tells the mother that she has prevented her son
from being made immortal.[r]

---

[r] Though the Greeks at Eleusis lost the fire ordeal and initiation as the
fourth mystery (or retained it simply as light after darkness), as we have
seen, it lingered on in the worship of Dionysus. At Eleusis even a water
initiation was retained only as a bathing preliminary performed in the small
bay outside the Temple precincts. So they were puzzled by the Demeter
story as it hung on around the great shrine of the Mother and Daughter.
This part of the Mother myth therefore split into two versions. In one
the child of King Celeus and his wife Metaneira is called Demophon. Demeter feeds him ambrosia, a preparational rite, and then applies fire to his
mortal parts. At this point Queen Metaneira breaks in and Demophon is

One of the particularly interesting observations made by Sandwith, in his study of the rite at this Tonga temple, is in regard to the
methods of stepping up the tonicity or resistance of the postulants.[s]
The first method is water purification. The postulants bathe in a pool.
Next, an object of concentration is made. It is called a *khalasam*
and it is a kind of monstrance made of a water-filled pot crowned
with a peeled and pierced coconut held in place by a skewer which,
like a dowel, goes down into the pot. The postulants stood circled
around this object, concentrating. Suddenly they shouted. A young
man sat down, crosslegged, before the priest. The priest took up six
bamboo skewers, three of which he pressed through the boy's cheeks
until they were completely penetrated. Then, in the same way, the
boy's arms and pectorals were pierced and the skewers left in place,
transfixing the muscles. The postulant did not wince and no blood
appeared.[t] At this point, attendants went around laying their hands

---

burned to death. Demeter then takes the younger child, Triptolemeus,
teaches him all the arts and crafts, and sends him, in a magic chariot, to
spread civilization throughout the world. In the other version this Triptolemeus is the only child in the story and though he is not made immortal
(because of his mother's intervention) he became the benefactor of mankind
and also the founder of the Eleusinian mysteries.

[s] They often come in order to be healed of complaints; especially paralysis
and insanity.

[t] A description given to me by Roger Fry may throw further light on the
level of heightened concentration that must be reached before this psychophysical condition is possible. When traveling in North Africa, Professor
Fry was permitted to be present at a meeting of a dervish group in a
small mosque. Having been brought in and seated near the conductor, he
was able to watch closely how the conductor tested the preparedness of
the performers. These dervishes were dancing themselves into dissociation.
As they circled round and passed before the conductor they held out their
hands for him to give them, from the heap before him, the lances and
knives with which to penetrate their muscles and the hot irons which had
been heated to a red-hot pitch in a small brazier. This conductor told
Professor Fry that as long as he could see the pupils of their eyes it was
not safe to give them the weapons. But when the pupil was so contracted
as to be invisible then he handed them not only the knives but the red-hot
rods which Professor Fry saw the dancers put in their mouths. He could
hear the saliva hiss, but there was no wincing and, next day, no scars.

on the foreheads of the other postulants. This roused some of the group to dancing and singing, while some fell to the ground, foaming. (Clearly, a leptoid seizure had been precipitated.) One became violent and had to be held. Cold water was then thrown over all of them. After that each one was able, with quiet elation, to be pierced and have his muscles transfixed as had the first boy. They gathered in a circle and drum rhythms were begun. The priest, putting the *khalasam* on his head like a crest, called loudly on the goddess. Chanting, he led the procession carrying a long whip in his hand. At intervals one of the followers would come abreast of him, hold out an arm which the priest would lash furiously. No blood ever appeared nor did any weal arise. Instead the postulant laughed and asked for further stimulation. The procession took two and one half hours and all the time, in the midday heat, the pierced performers kept up their vigorous dance. Behind the Devi temple forty tons of firewood had been burning for fourteen hours and was reduced to a pyramid of glowing charcoal. Poles fifteen feet long were used to rake the heap into a trench. Police, doctors and members of the governor's family were present in addition to a large group of onlookers. The fire was hot enough to make the sweat pour from the bodies of the men raking the trench. The priest went to the edge of the trench, stopped, prayed, and then walked slowly along the live charcoal. As soon as he was near the further end the postulants were allowed to follow. They all walked the length of the trench twice and then returned, unscathed, to the Temple. The fire was certainly of considerable heat for, when the initiates had gone, some Europeans, certain that it was merely auto-suggestion, tried to walk the trench in their boots. But they were burned as the leather soles peeled off rapidly in the high temperature.

This case has been noted at some length because it indicates that not only can fire be endured and not only, when it can be stood, is it a high stimulant, but that it is a culminant therapy that can be taken only by those who have stepped up to this intensity. True, in this case and even more so in the Kyoto Yamabushi case of Campbell, the officiants can and do exert, vicariously, some kind of stimulation control and suggestive hypnotic power on behalf of those whom they conduct. Nevertheless, we see that there is a degree of preparedness and that this points to the fact that the fire mystery has always been the fourth: an accumulant and a culminant experience for those who would complete their psychophysical education, their psychosomatic, developmental therapy.[u]

[u] Max Freedom Long reports seeing a film on firewalking that was shown, with an accompanying lecture, on February 21, 1935, by John G. Hill, Professor of Biblical History at the University of Southern California. The place was an island in the Tahiti group and the fire ordeal was first being used in the medieval legal way: a man charged with a crime was forced to attempt to prove his innocence by being able to walk unscathed along the fire trench. If, as seems clear, preparation and lack of fear are essential to immunity, it is not surprising to learn that he suffered bad burns. Those others, however, who of their own desire went through the trench in order to obtain health were completely uninjured. After the ritual walking was over, Dr. Hill tried putting his own hand within three feet of the rocks. After eleven seconds the pain was so great that he had to remove his hand. One of Dr. Hill's companions accepted the priest's invitation to make the walk. Even his shoes, which he did not remove, were uninjured though his face was slightly scorched and in the next few days peeled considerably.

It is not uncommon to find, in the popular press, articles by writers who, with considerable satisfaction to themselves, explain how they have found out what really lies behind the ceremony of the fire walk. They describe how they have demonstrated the very simple nature of the apparent immunity to fire. They claim, and there is little doubt they have shown, that they can place and press for a moment or two the palms of their hands or the soles of their feet on a surface sufficiently heated that if cold water is poured on it the water turns into steam. Their explanation, they believe, lies in the fact that if the hot plate has a temperature of sufficient height water coming into contact with it does not immediately pass into steam but granulates into a series of minute globes resembling liquid mercury, and in that state, for a small space of time, these globules run about over the hot surface. These explainers point out that this can happen with the sweat in the palms of the hands and the soles of the feet, and that it is because for a few moments the skin is so cushioned and insulated that the person walking on a hot iron plate, or one who clasps a piece of hot iron, is not immediately burnt. However, it is clear that this does not explain how (in the case of Dr. Campbell and many others) it is possible for a person to be exposed for some time to the direct heat of a flame. Nor does it explain the equally well authenticated evidence of unprepared persons being burnt when they attempted to walk through a fire trench

The earth burial, the water catharsis, and air respiration are indicated now, by research therapy, to be apposite when by regression and reprogression they deal with the trauma of birth, the revolt of protoindividualism, and the despair of midindividualism. So is it possible to suggest, then, that total individualism, with its threat of manic depressive collapse, might yield to radiation therapy? Infrared, heat ray treatment is highly stimulating, curative, and restful. The intensity of the radiation can, step by step, be increased. And infrared, unlike ultraviolet short wave radiation, is not a cancer-provoking risk. Work with hypnosis shows that resistance to heat damage can certainly be heightened to levels that would be considered impossible were the body-mind at what is now its customary slackness of coordination. Certainly here is a line of research that we cannot neglect. For racially and individually, phylogenically and ontogenically, we have reached a state when acute individualism of the power-desiring and power-holding type will ruin us. And it will frustrate both the evolutionary and growth processes unless, to the other three therapies, we can add this fourth one.

---

when others who *were* prepared had done so and emerged unscathed. Something is projected from the skin to protect it, but this does not seem to be the momentary shield provided by globulated droplets of sweat. This momentary phenomenon of the sweat-shield has been demonstrated since the nineteenth century. Edward, then Prince of Wales and afterward King Edward VII, visited a famous laboratory and watched the chief technician put his hand into a large crucible of molten lead without harm. Edward followed suit and also without harm. Of course the immersion in the molten lead was only for a moment.

5 The initiation of transformation
[Electricity]

In Part I we traced a record of the psychological development of social man. And we saw, at the close of that section, that man today is no longer in the humanic epoch. He has passed out of that phase during which he considered himself to be a complete being, a finished product, the fully rational, objective, individual self. We are in a postindividualistic period. For we are now aware of the fact that we can no longer regard personal self-consciousness as being a final irreducible state, a condition that cannot be analyzed further. We see that we are, and must know ourselves to be, parts of a field, nodes in a web of patterning forces, synapses in a whole of inter-communicating ranges of consciousness.

This post-humanic epoch was clearly detectable by the beginning of the twentieth century. And indeed symptoms of the oncoming change, we can now see, were increasingly evident during the last two decades of the nineteenth century. Therefore, it is now apparent that mankind has reached another phase in his history beyond any that he has so far known, an epoch of a state of mind that lies above and beyond individuality.

This is hard to realize. For up until now we have extrapolated. That is to say that up until this generation we have naturally assumed that individuality has always been the characteristic of human consciousness. It is true that studies of the great paleolithic cave art galleries did compel us to realize that in our prehistoric ancestors there was a quality of awareness, a type of consciousness, essentially different from that of the three historic phases of individualism. Still, to most individuals even that gave no insight into the evolution of their own consciousness. It seemed to indicate only that primitive man was still largely possessed by an animal consciousness and that his art was akin to the spontaneous musicianship of a bird or the architectural skill of a bee. The millennial and score millennial creep of craft development in the prehistoric paleolithic epochs seemed to be proof that, although they were in their way as ingenious as birds or insects, the capacities and awareness of these men could hardly be called human. Naturally, then, man has felt that he was right in being critical and analytical, he was right in shunning integral states of mind. For the only true and valid humanity (the only possible progress) that could emerge would be insofar as man gained in intensification of self-consciousness and definiteness of individuality.

The notion, then, that the path of progress might be a spiral, instead of going straight on in simple extrapolation, has been very hard to accept. But it is also difficult to see how individualism could be intensified further or, if it could be, what would be gained. Certainly, our present perils that are due to lack of awareness of others would be mortally increased. Even so, a new concept of consciousness, the ideal of another quality of consciousness, is clearly inconceivable to nearly everyone. We can now detect other levels of consciousness in ourselves, outside of our self-consciousness, and many of them show greater insight and power than that self-consciousness. Yet we still cling to the ego as being the ultimate unit, the only possible final value.

And there are two further symptoms to indicate that we are at the end of individuality, that it is not the final term. In the first place, we have enough evidence that man in his first maturity, the shrewd power type that is now the main manager and executive sector, is no longer sufficient to handle the human situation. The rational critical intelligence, shrewd and decisive in its own realm of the sensory world, today sets up, in the psychophysical world, conflicts it cannot understand. As long as materialism was held, by the Western World, to be the ultimate explanation of reality, the practical individualist, with his mechanist faith, could not be withstood. Today, however, resistance is growing against his blind faith in a purely physical view of life. As yet, men have little to put in its place, but the power type's conviction no longer gives him control over them. His high-handed action, his drastic surgery on the body politic is like that of the pre-aseptic surgeons. "Operation successful; patient succumbed," is now the verdict on much coercive social planning.

The very fact that communication now has to become a science shows that the mere announcing of orders and directives is a woefully inefficient way of getting things done. The resistances to and stoppages of the flow of idea exchange are found to be due to pararational, subconscious hostilities. These hostilities are provoked, without his being aware of it, by the rationalist, power-type efficiency manager through his absence of insight, his basic belief that he has fought his way up in strenuous competition with the rest. Hence he is incapable of cooperation. Meanwhile, not only does this deep-seated attitude block the efficiency of his team, it exacts a heavy price from the man himself. His repressed hostility creates in him a psychosomatic bad conscience which, more than the excessive pace at which he lives, provokes such psychosomatic diseases as cardiac, respiratory, and arthritic trouble. In short, the total individual, the humanic type, the man of first maturity is no longer adequate. A new person must be produced.

In the second place, we have already seen (in Chapter 5, Part I, and Chapter 5, Part II) that just as in the history of the race the postindividual epoch succeeded to the total-individualistic,

Humanic Epoch, so in this century a new age group has appeared that is above and beyond the first maturity age group. At last, instead of semi-solitary survivors from a generation the vast part of which has perished, we have a large new class of oldsters. And they are in no wise senile, unless they wish to be. They are in the new category of late, postfamilial second maturity, the veterine type. But they are utterly untaught, their education is completely neglected, their part is unwritten, their pattern of behavior unprovided, their contribution unknown.

All the age groups today need a specific emotional training. Evolution will continue only if we, understanding its drive and direction, provide those exercises whereby we may express its urges. The child must still strive to be heroic, the adolescent to be anonymous, those in first maturity to be critically wise and personally responsible. Enterprise, discipline, conscientious supervisorship— these three successive standards of conduct exist and only need to be adjusted to the present situation. But the new class of those in second maturity not only has no class solidarity, it has no standards, it has no role.

We have, then, a threat, a hope, and a demand in this new human category, this latest age group that has been produced by what seems to be a series of accidents in hygiene (the prolongation of life through medical advance: surgery, diet, and drugs), but which clearly might be the particular class needed to be the new racial epoch-making type, the postindividual type. The threat is now unmistakable, for geriatrics draws attention to an acute danger. We need not repeat those serious views, expressed by experts in the grave problem of old age, which were referred to in Chapter 5, Part I, and Chapter 5, Part II. These experts agree that they can warn but that they can do little else. Solutions to the problem remain stubbornly unobtainable. And they evade us for the double reason that society can honestly see no *raison d'être* for the senile and that the old can just as honestly see no reason why they should hold back from senility as long as they are unwanted, as long as they are not provided with some specific purpose to fulfill.

The hope, of course, is that the history of man, the force of the species' drive, the urge of evolution—the aim of life—all point to the production of this new class. No one knows the upper limit of a human being's life expectation. At present there are stocks in our species that can be traced back even to Hellenic Roman times and whose natural viability extends to one hundred and more years. So we should be prepared for a large new age group of the hearty aged, those in second maturity, as we continue to put a check on the accidents of wear and tear.

Further, not only is mankind today postindividualistic in psychophysical development, with the present population producing and carrying this new and growing original class that demands a new category for it to fulfill. But the great traditional therapies, which when esoteric have been called mysteries, are not merely four but five.

The four mysteries, as we have seen, do cover the four categories: the four epochs of the race and the four age groups of the individual. Until today, save for comparatively rare cases, mankind was contained within these four great stages of the traditional psychotherapy. But there must be and there is a fifth mystery.

It was, no doubt, confined to the most advanced.[a] Very few would go beyond the fourth mystery. For until today the only thing that lay beyond was the rare situation of the lonely seer who can look back on life from the station of one who is already above the battle and left without contemporaries. Already he is aloof from action, already dead to and departed from the drives that involve the younger age groups.

But today the fifth mystery is the fifth freedom for the new fifth age group of man. By regression and reprogression, the four former cramps and adhesions can be released and broken. So there is achieved: (*a*) a voluntary birth instead of the actual birth trauma and protest, (*b*) a voluntary childhood of energy and enterprise without rage, (*c*) a voluntary adolescence of discipline and self-criticism without guilt, and (*d*) a voluntary maturity of ambition-

[a] See Appendix D, *The Timeless Theme,* by Colin Still (83).

less responsibility that voluntarily accepts office for the general good (Plato's wise ruler), instead of arrogant, elational authoritarianism alternating with loss of nerve.

The fifth voluntary acceptance of the fifth phase is, of course, voluntary relinquishment of all specific personal status, of all executive authority. All that is retained is an advisory influence; but even so no specific rulings would be given. This person is consulted only because he can give the inspiration of true seership; he can give a true picture of the process as a whole, in which frame of reference all the executive functions must operate or they must in the end miscarry. Yet his influence is all the more authoritative precisely because he exercises no personal coercion. He must be obeyed because instead of his having to enforce his rulings the nature of things carries out the enforcement. The authority of those who really know the laws of life and nature is self-sanctioning. No pilot who wishes to live thinks of disregarding a warning from the weather tower. Patients who wish to recover know that the diagnosis and prognosis of the great physician must not be flouted. Those who are aloof can see further than those who are involved in action. Foresight is an increasing need as the immediate issue grows in complexity.

Therefore, the fifth ordeal initiation is the elimination, the explication whereby the person (who from birth to first maturity has been intensifying in individuality and self-consciousness) now re-expands, redilates, becomes regeneralized and finally, completely released, can pass liberated from all the ties of appetite, possession, and recognition into a state of consciousness in which he no longer requires particularity, locality, or a specious present. This sequence is shown in the Sanskrit phases of life. The child phase is succeeded by the period of the dutiful youth (Brahmachari) after which he becomes the householder, the Gratha, the man of first maturity. In turn, that focus,[b] that concentration on social and racial obligations being over, the man and wife, following the way of the fathers, begin their education for second maturity, for rising out of the "cycle of births and deaths," and aim to go on to the nonreturning way of the gods. Then, having learned this path out and up, the solitary life

[b] Focus means hearth.

begins. As a forest seer or *rishi*, having nothing but wisdom, home-less and begging for his food, the gymnosophist, the wise man utterly denuded, the man who has cast all the husks is ready for voluntary death and complete volatilization. This Indian view of life is even more realistic and eliminatory than that of the Chinese.[c]

But how can either of these traditional answers to what Bud-dhism calls the fourth dislocation be made apposite today? The old need help, and society must find it for them on the double utilitarian demand made by sound economics and by psychosocial hygiene. We have seen that their increasing power of consumption (not merely of ordinary consumers' goods but of those skilled medical services that should go to keep producers in cheerful action) is a grave and increasing strain on civilization.

On the other hand, we are expending our finest therapies just to keep alive those who are now made unnaturally to endure. We are extending the consuming uselessness of those who are holding on not to be an inspiration but who are clinging on out of fear, and so spreading depression. This exhibition, from the psychosocial point of view, is the worst kind of pattern of prestige to give all the age groups below second maturity.

The boy can be a hero, the adolescent can become the disci-plined, obedient member of his team, the man of first maturity can be a critically minded administrator, but what lies ahead for the old? This head contingent, which can neither go on nor clear out, is a miserable snarl that is jamming the traffic on the bridge of life instead of leading it forward to the other shore.

Is it possible to shed any light on this problem that would be neither wishful thinking nor brutal realism? Must either the com-munity or the individual be sacrificed? If the prestige patterns of our race present no specific, socially valuable ideal for the postindividual,

[c] In pre-communist China the great-parent, head of the whole compound, was an honored load that was carried into senility, for care of him guar-anted that those who cared for him would, in turn, be cared for. Under the influence of Buddhism, even in China it was permissible for the head of a house, at the age of sixty and if it was so desired, to leave the highly honored position and retire into a cloister cell.

this fifth category of mankind; and if the four age groups of today can offer no place for the old (for in second maturity we are producing no type that serves a specific social function; that has energy, vision, and enterprise; that knows its purpose, its contribution, and its direction), then what are we honestly to say?

However, two possibilities remain to be examined. In addition to the life of the race and the life of the individual, we have seen that there is another pair of sequences that indicate the course of human development. (1) There are the specific breakdowns that each epoch and each age group has suffered when it failed to achieve the stage of development next above it. And (2) there are the specific therapies (mysteries) that were devised to remedy these breakdowns and permit the resumption of human development.

We have seen that the particular insanity of second maturity is involutional melancholy. This breakdown is of particular interest, for in the first place it is rational. Melancholia at any age, it is admitted by all psychiatrists, is the hardest to handle of all the mental complaints, and the psychoanalyst shuns it. It is one of the prime provocants of that baffling and stubborn addiction, alcoholism, which, therefore, analysts also shun. For the melancholic is asking the basic question that always arises when the life of irrelevant appetite fails: "To what end?" Such is the question that drives all the ascetic movements to attack the unreflective, boastful heroic. Even the intensely vital Jew reaches that wall across the easy, unreflective way of life when Koheleth, speaking for Wisdom, gives as the final verdict, *vanitas vanitatum, omnia vanitas.*

For the melancholic does not have illusions. He is not the paranoic, thinking that if he could slay his persecutors he would be happy. Nor is he the schizophrenic, drawing away from a challenge he feels he cannot answer. He is not manic, in a phase of groundless optimism, nor depressive because his dream has proved to be baseless. He questions those who conform and who claim to make it possible to persuade those who cannot conform to come back, to readjust, to face up to reality and to accept conformity as sanity. He asks them "Do you believe that life has any meaning? Can you say, even, that our senses let us contact reality? Do you think that man is capable of rational action, that he possesses free will and that society is run intentionally, let alone nobly? What are your own arguments for establishing that the world, as we perceive it, is not a tale told by an idiot with sadistic tastes?"

The materialistic analyst has no answers to these questions. The vast majority of psychiatrists accept, via Freud or some other channel, the nineteenth-century notion that evolution is a result of chaotic randomness. Naturally, the man who has, with critical intelligence, asked these basic questions and, through his responsible sensitiveness, been depressed by finding that most psychiatrists believe that there is no answer but the worst, ceases to discuss and withdraws into himself.[d]

Melancholia, if it is to be looked on as a disease, should then be regarded as being a psycho-deprivative complaint. Our society is deranged because although it is intelligent it cannot give an intelligent reason for living, or at least for living well. No society has lasted that did not have a psychotherapy. As we have mentioned before (Chapter 4, Part I) the humanic society is the only one that has attempted to live on the deprivative mental diet of a rationalism that was ignorant of the preterconsciousness. So we must regard melancholia not as being a disease per se, but rather as being an acute condition of thwarted appetite, such as thirst pains, hunger pangs, or the vitamin deficiency of the alcoholic whose diet, in consequence of his heavy drinking, is a deprivative one that brings on delirium tremens as well as bodily breakdown.

By sound psychosocial prognosis we might have expected, then, that in a still humanically oriented society a new age group, those in second maturity, would slip out of gear. Finding that they were not needed by society and that society is convinced that life ends in inexplicable futility, such a group as those who are in second maturity must regard their melancholy as being all too rational. Howard

---

[d] Already we are finding with schizophrenia and with catatonia that the patient falls into silence and becomes inaccessible because he realizes that even the psychiatrist (not having had the patient's experience and even if there were words in our common language for it) could not understand this condition, which lies outside any "common-sense" category.

Fabing, out of his great experience, has said that the will to live depends mainly on the capacity for interest, the conviction that life is worth living. There is dismal proof that the collapse of old age is not the fault of the body. It bears us into these advanced years with patient efficiency. It is not the worn-out weakness of a brain that is finished that is the main cause of second maturity's failure. And, as John Pfeiffer (66) has pointed out in his *The Human Brain,* there is no evidence that the brains of the second maturity group are in any way inferior to those who are still in first maturity. The body grows less capable of muscular exertion, but the mind appears to be just as able to learn if it can see any reason why it should.

Second maturity's defeat, the collapse of the veterine, is a problem of the intelligence, a failure of the understanding. It is a lack of purpose, the absence of any creative function by which the old can find that they have a rational right to go on living. It is the lack of an insight, an experience that can convince them that their advanced sector of life's great line demands of them a unique service, leadership, and message.

We can no longer shirk this problem. For beside the dark cloud of despair that now settles in a spreading eclipse over increasing numbers of the old, we can also see the widening pit above which that cloud hovers. The latest figures show that today the rate of suicide increases in each decade of life. The incidence of suicide among the old is five times what it is among the young.

The rate of suicide is lowest among those who accept, with implicit obedience, the orders of the authoritarian religions. Orthodox Jews have the lowest number, then Roman Catholics, next Protestants, and after them secularists.

The ancient religions do not argue; they order and threaten. But today the educated must have their questions answered and their fears honestly faced and truthfully removed. Possibly we could continue to make men, who are filled with the futility of life, hang on to their bodies for fear of worse misery should they let go. But fear cannot drive out fear. We might prevent suicide from spreading among the obedient and the ignorant. But if we cannot convince them that they are needed, that they matter, we cannot prevent them from going out of their minds. And we must recall Sargant's (73) grim warning (see his *The Battle for the Mind*) that a frequent cause of suicide today is precisely the fear of going mad; the supreme fear of having to go on living in a tangible nightmare where every value and joy has turned to dust.

The specific mental disease of second maturity appears, then, to be as significant a symptom of a failure to develop rightly as the madnesses of the other age groups have now shown themselves to be. Mental disease—all insanity that is specifically psychological[e]—is a state of mind, a failure of nerve, a failure to find the way onto a higher level of comprehension and more adequate response.

Having seen the direction in which this fifth insanity points, we can now see how the traditional therapy dealt with this demand for the next stage of higher sanity and wholeness. We have already mentioned in this chapter that above and beyond the ordeal and initiation required to bring a man through first maturity there seems to have been a fifth mystery. It was rare, because few lived to need it; and it was esoteric because the experience turned the individual into the lonely seer, who was often blind and always much aloof from life. The Greeks seem to have known of it, but mainly, one judges, by hearsay. So their description has in it not merely mythic confusion but meteorological misapprehension. The Hellenic cosmogeny tended to be ranged round the atmospheric levels of the snow mountain that they knew best, Olympus. The Greeks recognized that there were two levels. There was the basic level where trees could still grow and animals could live. But above that was rock and snow; the air was rarer; you panted and were chilled to the bone as well. Here, therefore, dwelt the nonhuman gods. The gas that we mortals breathe is a thick, vaporous stuff (*aer*), but the breath of the gods is *aether;* and there in that thin, fine medium everything is clear, keen, and cold.

But what has this to do with fire? Dazzling light is there, but though the mountaintop is nearer the Sun himself, the cold is greater

[e] That is, insanities in which no lesion or callus of the brain can be found. And according to *The Human Brain* (66) this is the state of 80 per cent of the brains of the insane after death, even after a long period of madness.

than below. Zeus (Daos) the shining one ruled there. And everyone who has climbed mountains knows that besides those fine days when the peaks can be seen rising in the clear, hard blue, often the summits can wrap themselves not only in mist but in thunder cloud. Zeus is just as much the thunderer and the slayer-by-lightning as he is the Light of Heaven. Further, anyone who is on a mountain during a thunderstorm is in considerable danger of being struck by lightning. And even if he is not struck he will feel electric shocks of various intensities, for the whole rock is charged. He will see the glow and hear the hiss of St. Elmos Fire, the static electricity being given off by his own body, and when he steps off the rock of the mountain peak onto earth he will feel a very distinct electric jar. The Greeks knew, as did the Sanskrit Aryans about their sacred peak Mount Kailas, that there are two fires: that of the flame, from the sun's heat and the volcano's fire (the heat of molecular activity), and also that of the lightning flash.

What, then, would be the fifth therapy? Only of late have we been able to be sure. The final initiation, the one that alone can cure melancholy, enlarge consciousness, and release the psyche into its final explicatedness is electricity. This is clear from the growth of electric shock therapy during this century. It is significant that as we have moved out of the humanic epoch and, at the same time and for the first time have produced, but provided with no role to play, the fully manned class of second maturity and their specific mental disease, involutional melancholy, we have also introduced the strangest of all the therapies, a degree of electrocution. The steps whereby this came about are also instructive.

In the thirties it began to be recognized that epilepsy was, for all practical purposes, the state that was polar to melancholy. Freud wrote an essay on how epileptic seizure could be postponed by emotionally moving the subjects so deeply, by pathos, that they would break into tears and the fit would not take place. Electric shock treatment became so popular a way of dealing with withdrawn and gloomy states as to be almost routine. And it was soon recognized that this was a way of bringing about a controlled epilepsis. It was also recognized that although this treatment permitted the patient to resume his customary and normal life, the effect might fade; the tormenting questions might return and the shock would have to be repeated. In some cases the shocks became a routine part of such subjects' lives. There were also cases where this routine treatment produced, in the end, the same result as did persistent epileptic seizure: the brain itself was injured by the shock and the subject died insane.

Here, then, we have a temporary cure for melancholy, but with two distinct disadvantages. (1) It can be physically damaging if repeated. (2) Psychologically (and this is the reason for its repetition if the patient suffers a relapse), it does nothing to answer the questions that caused the melancholy; it simply disregards them. It is regressive but not reprogressive.

However, before going on to consider how this method has been further developed as a palliative therapy and individual relief (and also noting parallel lines of pure research in electric shock that suggest further progress), we should see what can be learned from the traditional esoteric mysteries, insofar as they may throw some light on this fifth stage of life and its specific ordeal and initiation. The Sanskrit psychophysical researchers, we now can recognize, not only had become aware of the ductless glands by detecting the fields of energy around them (called chakras or wheels). But they realized that this series of glands, from the interstitial in the genitals, through the suprarenals, past the thymus,[f] on past the thyroid to the pituitary and culminating in the pineal, is a sequence coordinated with and branching out from the spinal cord.

Now we know that central to all yogic exercises is the raising of Kundalini. And if breathing exercises (especially in the intense form of the breath retentions of Hathi yoga, the yoga that is mainly the physiological rather than psychological method of changing consciousness) are the primary technique in the yogas, then we may say that the raising of Kundalini is the final goal of such disciplines. Kundalini is no longer an unfamiliar term now that anthropological

[f] Which they, together with some modern researchers, believe can be activated in maturity by proper exercises. See also Part II, Chapter 4, footnote *b*.

investigation and psychophysical research have been able to exchange their findings. Kundalini, literally the coiled serpent, is that stored nexus of electric energy which, according to the Sanskrit theory, lies congested at the base of the spine and especially around the perineum. This may be raised by such specific exercises as (1) breathing rhythms, (2) breathing rhythms with other physical contractions, (3) glandular pressures, or (4) physical contractions and tensions by themselves. Others hold that constant mental concentration accompanied by strict sexual continence will make this surge of energy take place of itself. The customary and traditional theory is that this energy, when it is triggered and released, runs up the spinal cord and flashes into the brain, making it superactive but also unconscious of the sensory world. But Vasant G. Rele (70), known for his *The Mysterious Kundalini,* and some others trained in Western physiology, who themselves are also trained in this yogic technique, hold that the current does not run up through the spinal cord. They believe that the impulse, the energy, and the effect on body and mind are due to the vagus nerve[g] and its automatic functioning being altered and brought, to some degree, under conscious control.

Whichever theory may be true, there seems to be no reasonable doubt as to the following facts, for they are backed by a great deal of evidence from a large number of qualified observers. By specific exercises the yogin can bring on a surge of energy that rises up from the perineum area into the brain. With the aid of this surge the yogin can put himself into suspended animation, catalepsy—and, what is more, he knows how to bring himself back from this state of arrested vitality. The yogin claims that this condition not only permits him to remain without breathing, anaesthetized, unaware of the physical world, but it also permits him to enter other levels of consciousness that are not restricted to biological time, and to enjoy a state of health that is unknown to us who are running on more sluggish rhythms. He can endure stresses under which we would break and succumb. With all these certified data, the psychophysiologist today is less inclined to cavil. The psychic claims still await rationalization in an acceptable frame of reference.

[g] The nerve that ends in the epigastric region.

But we can now understand how the physical modifications that the yogin manifests could be explained in terms of biological energies that modern physiologists are already prepared to recognize. The electrical field of the body is at present well gauged and mapped. All nerve impulses are electrical, the spine does channel these charges to the brain, and the brain does handle these surges. Further, if and when these waves become breakers, the brain is swamped. The rhythmic energy, which should drive the dynamos of purposive action, has become an inundation. The brain, like a flooded irrigation system, its sluices gorged by too high a tide, is lost to sight under tumbling waters and all control is lost. This, as we have seen, is what takes place in an epileptic seizure.

Therefore, the yogin's claim, that he can at will both induce and also control and feed into his brain the full leptic energy so that it will not stun him but, instead, will give a superdrive to his consciousness, does not seem improbable today. And an epileptic seizure is what takes place when the organism gives itself its own self-generated shock treatment. Haunted by the futility of remaining confined to our present sense-limited knowledge, to such weak and jejune emotional experiences as the senses as we use them can give (and especially such as the panaesthetic current can give when restricted to sexual-genital sensation), the mental-emotional life seeks an enlarged, dilated experience. This is specifically so when the reproductive cycle is over or unrequired; then it is that the consciousness longs for the larger frame of awareness and the enlarged power of response.

But epilepsy—because it *is* epilepsy and not prolepsy; because it comes as a leap upon, an attack, a tidal wave from outside the victim's awareness; because it is not a surge that is induced by a prepared consciousness that can then ride this wave, as the surf-rider breasts the breaker, is still a disease. Often, as Penfield and other researchers have demonstrated, the fit is brought on by a purely physical blockage. A callus or scar tissue has formed on the brain as the result of some past skull injury. This callus bars the flow of electric energy over the brain and, the energy blocked, the rhythm thwarted, the convulsion follows. The channels of the brain having bars in them, the blocked current no longer surges but bursts through.

But, just as a blocked streambed may be flooded by a moderate rainfall, so a clear streambed, adequate for an average rainstorm, may be wrecked by a cloud burst. Should the spinal cord send an exceptional charge to the normal brain that is accustomed to only average disturbance, and so unprepared for such a shock, then *pro tem* the normal man would go into a state of seizure. And this condition we now know can be provoked in persons otherwise never subject to fits.

Metrazol is a chemical that makes the nerve channels more sensitive. Give a person who has never had a seizure of any sort fifty milligrams of Metrazol (orally) and then let him look at a flickering light—a stroboscope—and he will begin to twitch. But give the average, normal person a dose of less than fifty milligrams and he will show no abnormality; none of the healthy reactions will be disturbed. On this basis a very valuable scale has been worked out. At the top of this scale is the fifty-milligram dose required to disturb the normal person. At the other end is a dosage of from zero to ten milligrams, which is the amount, together with the stroboscope, that will bring on a seizure in the epileptic. At zero there is the person who is a victim of the grand mal, whose fit may come on at any time and who can be put into a state of seizure by looking at the stroboscope. Then from zero to ten there are those who suffer from the petit mal, those who, when seized by it, do not fall to the ground and foam, those whose seizures may be brought on by stress, fatigue, or a dosage of up to ten milligrams of Metrazol and the stroboscope.

However, the illuminating fact that has unexpectedly emerged from these researches has nothing to do with the damaged and weak who cannot handle these tides that are brought on by the Metrazol-induced heightening of their nerve channels. It has to do with the healthy and the strong who can handle them and do. The French psychophysicians who conducted these researches studied a number of ace test pilots. These pilots, of course, were men who had been picked for their job only after going through the most strenuous and most thorough laboratory and field tests.

They were selected because they had been proved to be men of the finest and most advanced control and initiative. Their reflexes and their power of making decisions were equally swift and sure. Yet on the Metrazol scale test they came out as being at twenty-five! It took only twenty-five milligrams of Metrazol to disturb their normal reactions: twenty-five milligrams less than the average, normal person and only fifteen milligrams more than the epileptic. Their nerve sensitivity was double that of the person who was found to be normal.

In short, persons who acquire adaptability to strange experiences and quickly learn how to react originally are not normal. The routineers who can never be excited are no use on the speeding edge of modern advance. Our need today is the person who has been given a high charge and been taught and learned how to handle it. At the same time, if he is to serve in the present crisis he must be no daredevil. That is why, since originality of mind and daringness of speculation are today more needed than sheer physical courage and unquestioning élan, this problem of lepsis is one for old age. For as Grey Walter (93) has shown in *The Living Brain,* when the system is facing a severe challenge the brain produces the special Delta wave, sign of the mobilization of organized defenses. It is present when brain areas are being attacked by growths or are deformed by scars. Yet it is also always present in the first year of life. The electroencephalograms taken from the fetal brain as it presses against the mother's abdomen show this wave; and sometimes even the full wave and spike that is characteristic of epilepsy. We can see then that this lepsis[h] (this superpulse of electric energy on the brain) is not itself a disease but a spur to a new leap out into a larger frame of reference. It attended our birth out of the womb. It comes again to summon us to a second birth.

Also, we must not disregard the high association between genius and epilepsy. This, too, makes it difficult to avoid looking at the leptoid condition as being a progressive state of mind, a condition of the nervous system that is culminant and, therefore, can

[h] See page 161, *The Human Brain* by John Pfeiffer (66).

be the next step in evolution. It is a newly stepped-up pressure that is seeking for a new and adequate vehicle of expression, a new energy that destroys if it is not allowed expression but, given that expression, builds up new faculties, a new character, and a new quality of consciousness.

It is clear, then, why I have given the name leptoid to this latest age group of humanity that stands in need of a treatment that can deliberately rouse and canalize this energy. For the controlled surge is the therapy answer to this age group's specific mental distress and disease: involutional melancholy. The electric shock treatment is now being increasingly modified to the point where (with the weaker and more prolonged current that is being used and the antecedent sedation and anaesthesia that have been added) it may now be called surge treatment rather than shock.

Further, it is now being realized (*a*) that though one surge may give temporary remission, repeated surges are required to lift the patient to a level where the counter down-flow and rip-tide of depression will not suck him back into the abyss. And (*b*) it is rapidly becoming evident that all that the surge can do, as it is now administered and understood, is to throw the victim out of the sea and onto the beach. Once there, he must be secured, made fast, and raised above high tide and storm danger, by persuading him to take hold of life and its larger interests and by giving him such rational encouragement as he and his counsellor can believe to be valid. Even when modified, as it has been, into surge therapy, shock treatment, as Dr. Menninger of Topeka has said, can aid only some 10 per cent of the mentally sick. The remainder must have a far more comprehensive therapy. We may hope that when this therapy is fully worked out it will incorporate the surge as part of an entire "pro-lepsis"; in other words, a leap forward.

And as has happened with so many therapies, we can see how this modified treatment also may and indeed must be shifted from being a last resort (or even a curative method once melancholy has set in) into being not merely preventive but developmental, as all truly preventive methods must be when they are intended for a growing creature. If second maturity is a new class that is waiting for a new experiential discipline, then we may look to electric shock treatment for the therapy that will take the energy that will otherwise sink, thwarted, into the frustration of despair, and transmute it into a new quality of experience, a new superpersonal, postindividual consciousness.

Have we any further insights as to how this may be done? We have seen that electric shock (or what we may now call electric surge treatment) was not a product of pure research. It grew up out of the simplest empiric attempts at palliative and relief measures for dealing with those insane who had sunk into incommunicability. Yet it has brought into clear light the polar relationship between melancholy and the leptoid condition, and between the leptoid condition and electric surge treatments. Meanwhile, and converging with this practical research, a series of studies have been made that, from another aspect of restorative therapy and from pure research, may give us some insight into how a fifth developmental therapy may be devised. These studies may give us some idea as to the nature of a fifth ordeal and initiation, which would give those in second maturity a specific quality of consciousness, a specific social position, and a specific service to the community.

After an accidental electric shock the victim, although not mortally injured, generally dies of a respiratory failure. The breathing reflex has been thrown out and is not spontaneously resumed. This, again, is due to fibrillation of the heart: the muscle fibers twitch but no beat is produced and, after a short time, all cardiac activity ceases. Therefore, death by electric shock was presumed to be practically instantaneous. But twenty-seven years ago Stephen Jellinek, giving shock to monkeys under anaesthetic, obtained cardiograph records which showed that although the heart did stop beating and begin to twitch, frequently it resumed its beat again. The lower animals certainly succumb to weaker shocks. But—and this is highly significant when we consider vitality and a large central nervous system together with the effect of electric stimulation on them—the larger the creature's brain the greater is its tolerance. Jellinek (48) (who was professor of electropathology at the University of Vienna) has pointed out, in his *Dying, Apparent*

Death and Resuscitation, that there are on record cases of men being struck by four hundred volts of direct current, being certified as dead by a physician, and yet after persistent artificial respiration being brought back to life. In fact it now seems clear that electrocution is anything but instantaneous: a thought that should be disquieting to those who retain capital punishment by electric shock on the ground that the criminal does not have to endure a lingering death. As long ago as 1934 at the International Life Saving Congress at Copenhagen, experts gave it as their judgment that a victim of electrocution may remain alive for at least an hour. Some of them even judged that death might not take place for as long as three or four hours. I know, myself, of a man who tripped, fell on a live cable and, as the current could not be shut off immediately, was subjected to strong shocks for some moments. Although he lay as one dead, he recovered and later reported that he had been conscious but incapable of movement or speech, and that as long as the current was flowing through him he felt a strange heat. In short, as Jellinek points out, the victim is in suspended animation and is in no wise dead. He gives as proof the evidence of autopsies. They indicate that victims of electrocution frequently have not died instantaneously but slowly and by asphyxiation. And in a lecture in London which I attended, Jellinek established the fact that even the burns produced by electricity (and their subsequent healing) are different from the burns and their healing produced by hot gases and ordinary molecular activity. Electric shock, then, is neither a physical blow though it feels like one, nor a burn by flame though the aftereffect looks like it. The discovery of such a strange distinction between the effects of an electric shock and such an apparently similar damage (cell destruction by flame, bone fracture by a blow) led Jellinek to investigate further. He arrived at striking and (I believe) illuminating results, especially in the specific line of enquiry being dealt with in this chapter. When he had observed the odd fact that the more highly developed nervous system had a greater resistance to damage by electric shock (certainly a startlingly unexpected correlation—

indeed, the very opposite of what might be expected), Jellinek began an extraordinary experiment. Considering the fact that the more highly developed the brain (though it be more elaborate) the better did it withstand shock, Jellinek felt himself driven to assume that a psychological factor must be involved here. Somehow mentality and not mechanism must make this difference, which was so completely contrary to what might be expected. Like all good researchers he decided to experiment on himself. Although he knew that forty volts of direct current could sometimes be fatal, he felt that this was a very low level for a healthy man. For he also knew that far higher voltages are frequently taken without damage. Wishing, then, to detect the danger threshold, he started with one hundred and ten volts taken through the hand, and found that it was possible gradually to build up his resistance to the point where he could sustain four hundred and forty volts direct current without any damage. This is certainly a lethal dose for most human beings.

Realizing now that the mental factor was involved and that it must lie in the training, in teaching the subject to prepare himself for the shock, he instructed a number of electricians in how to train themselves. None of them met with bad effects. Finally, a meteorologist friend of Jellinek's, caught in a thunderstorm on a Swiss peak, used the method. Having braced himself against the possibility of being struck, he was hit three times by lightning. But although his clothes were torn and his skin broken, because he was prepared he was neither stunned nor did he suffer anything but the surface abrasions.

Electric shock can then be vastly modified simply by knowing that it is coming and by having learned how to prepare for increasing voltages. But what is the factor that makes this possible? Jellinek consulted a fellow Viennese physician, Sigmund Freud. Freud agreed that this was a factor of the psyche, and made the interesting comment that in preparing for the blow one is preparing oneself against fear; and that thus psychic resources can be and are summoned, which do hold up or transmute the violent shudder. He added that it was not possible to avoid the conclusion that electricity and the field called the psyche were somehow aspects of the same thing.

We have now seen that electricity can be taken as a tonic, a tonic of consciousness. And just as a person can be prepared for the fire ordeal so that the experience becomes not destructive but stimulating, so electricity (which is the breath of the brain, the warmer of the intelligence) can be given in gradually increased charges and become, as it were, a transfusion of superenergy. But how may this be still further developed? Could this energy be used as a real re-energizer? Jellinek's work does suggest an extension of this research, an extension that would link up with the *aether* ordeal and initiation and supply a cross reference to those tribes which, in their development of the fifth mystery, use the severe shock given by the electric eel. However, we must remember that this fifth mystery was—as is our still rudimentary electric shock treatment—an attempt to produce a death of the old anxiety, fear, and foreboding and to start the person off with the *tabula rasa* or fresh rhythm of a new emotional attitude and outlook. Somehow, the old record, the old matrix and stereotype has become hopelessly corrupt, corroded, and defaced. If it is possible, as it now is, to take the sounds from a worn record and rerecord them on a new disk or tape, then it should be possible to raise the electrical field of consciousness off the old disk, the old tape of the brain and, after resting the mind and cleansing the brain, resettle the consciousness on a refreshed matrix. We cannot even put it beyond the bounds of possibility that this field need not dissipate on being separated from the brain but could be induced to continue in a state that could be contacted, at least for a while.

This, of course, sounds like science fiction, but some additional evidence that Jellinek gives certainly seems to point in some such direction. The important fact is that these further results were obtained with animals, as indeed they could only have been. But that a creature so low in the mental scale that it can be completely stunned and probably killed by a sixty-volt electrical charge should show the following amazing reaction makes the report all the more significant. The phenomenon was quite unexpected. For humane reasons hogs in a Vienna slaughter house were electrocuted before they were hung up, head down, their throats cut, and their bodies drained completely of blood. The bloodless carcasses were then thrown into tanks of water that had been heated to one hundred and seventy degrees Fahrenheit. As they sank into the scalding water the animals first shuddered violently, then righted themselves and, for some seven seconds, proceeded to swim. As Jellinek says, this coordinated swimming was quite other than the spasms of animals just killed. Further, it was quite different from the usual reaction of hogs that had had no electric shock before their throats were cut and their bodies drained of blood. Must we not suggest, then, that in the case of the electrocuted hogs the electric field on the brain, instead of being dissipated by the electric shock, had been congested onto the brain and the creature was not dead but in the suspended motor animation of shock resulting from too much stimulant? Therefore, when the blood was removed this did not produce death. For the immediate function of blood, circulating in the brain, is to carry to the brain its food, which, together with glucose, is oxygen. And, in turn, the oxygen is the medium through which the brain keeps its electric field running. So to remove the blood, and so remove the oxygen, need not mean death. For if (in spite of the fact that the normal essential sequence of steps for producing it have been removed) the electricity could itself be kept present on the brain, then the creature without blood or breath would be alive. And the shock of the scalding water would activate its sensory and motor centers, make it struggle for its life, strike out and swim. But the electric field of consciousness, so crudely retained on the brain, would not, of course, endure save for a few moments in such a damaged vehicle. However, the fact that for some seven seconds it remained present and could cause coordinate life-saving effort shows that such a strange noncorporeal survival is a possibility.

If, then, we compare the data of this experiment with the diagnosis of the human psychophysique that is given by the Vedantasara, of the Sanskrit tradition, we may find a significant correlate.

Here it is recognized that in addition to the gross body or circuit, the biochemical physique, there is the subtle body or circuit that we now know as the electric field of the body. Can it be that electric shock, and especially when employed as electric surge, can produce in those prepared for it the rising of Kundalini, the raising of consciousness until it can first be kept at this superphysical level and then later, and at will, be raised and detached to function in its own right and independence?

How then, from these indications, might we hope to see the fifth mystery devised today? How could it be constructed in a modern form that would give ordeal and initiation to those who need and desire to be raised to complete postindividual consciousness? What can we suggest as a contemporary technique, one which would serve the immediate and double demand of our age? First, we need a developmental therapy for this new age group, those in second maturity, simply for their own sake. But we also need this therapy because it is from this group (when it has developed its postindividual consciousness) that we could obtain that pattern of prestige, that specific function and service that humanity now requires.

Naturally, such proposals can only be tentative suggestions, extrapolations from our present convergent lines of knowledge. But if we summarize these findings we see: (1) that the most advanced types are and must be highly strung, highly charged. The stolid cannot help the advance of life any further. They are maintenance men, not pioneers, creators. (2) We see that this great natural charge must be given expression; channels of constructive release must be found for it, or it will either break the system by its pent-up pressure or, if it is finally crushed, the person must sink into melancholia. (3) We see, further, that owing to the kinship between vitality and electricity, between the psyche and the biological field and charge, it is through rightly directed electric stimulation that the balked energy can be lifted in a way that will raise the psyche from its melancholy and sense of futility at having exhausted all earlier experiences, from its weariness of the physiological round, and yet avoid throwing it headlong out of all coordination into convulsion. It is true enough that without knowledge of it as a growth process life is a knife edge between boredom (security) and catastrophe, between lethargy and frenzy. And man, when he is ignorant of his true purpose, must and can only oscillate between the two.

But, as Shirokogoroff has pointed out, even the shaman culture had discovered that whereas it is necessary to raise the normal biologically diffused (and indeed dissipated) consciousness to total attention (the one-pointedness of the Sanskrit disciplines), that intensity must be tempered so that it can be sustained without collapse. As we mentioned earlier, Shirokogoroff shows that not only must the shaman not take refuge in the hysterical detensioning of tears or laughter,[i] but, as he is raised to the leptoid level, neither must he o'erleap himself and crash on the other side in the epileptic seizure. In short, the shock must be made a surge treatment. And this surge must be so adroitly and gradually fed into the system that, as Jellinek says, the subject may learn to cooperate with the charge, blend it with his own charge and so, balanced on the crest, not be thrown but raised.

We may now propose the following procedure: first, the subject must be informed. The person in second maturity (and those in the earlier age groups if they are prepared by already having gone through the preceding therapies) must first of all learn intellectually about the process and why it is required. Every indi-

---

[i] The Sufis, to attain states of extrasociation, not only practice on the semicircular canals the centrifuge effect by means of the spinning dance but also often take *cannibus satva* (hashish) to attain this dilation. They are reported to warn the postulant that as the oncoming proleptic condition, the rising pressure of the experience is felt, the psychophysique will first seek the relief of catastrophic weeping, then the relief of hebephrenic laughter, and finally the detensioning of epileptoid convulsions. And the postulant is instructed that each of these releases must be denied. Then, it is said, the trainee will be able to experience the manifold world around with the flexibility that permits him to compose every event and, living with complete awareness of initiative, know what Milton named "The sober certainty of waking bliss." (See Vett (87), *Seltsame Erlebnisse in Einem Derwisch-kloster.*)

vidual will come to the age when he will require such therapy. Otherwise the futility of the life process will lead to some form of melancholia, which is either acknowledged or repressed. Every responsible person of today must arrive at this conclusion: that the new age group, second maturity, with the aid of this fifth therapy can make their true social contribution. And that without this development their lives are as useless a miscarriage of life's purpose and the community's needs as is a stillbirth.

After this instruction, and having acquired the intellectual insight and conviction that it can give him, the subject will undergo the specific training. The aim is, by the administering of a series of gradually increased electric impulses, surges, to make it possible for the subject to experience an elation that can be held clearly in uninterrupted consciousness. The person must not be stunned or in any wise shocked but must be lifted into an increasingly intensified quality of awareness and sense of vital interest.

For a considerable time it has been known that the nervous system can be trained, right down to its deepest reflexes (for example, the Pavlovian techniques). It is possible for the conscious will to be taught how to obtain complete control over reactions caused by physical disturbance: reactions which, if the person is not trained, have always resulted in his being completely incapacitated and which, in consequence and if he is in an unprotected situation, often lead to his damage and possibly his death.

As far back as 1933 (and read before the annual meeting at Leicester of the British Association for the Advancement of Science) MacCurdy reported, in a paper, that he had devised a successful method for training air pilots to be able completely to disregard the vertigo caused by large disturbances of their semicircular canals. The derangement of these, the controllers of our sense of balance, will in any ordinary person cause him to be unable to stand and, even when lying down, to feel helplessly unbalanced. So deep and primitive are these centers that it was taken for granted that they could not consciously be controlled, and that if they were behaving abnormally not even the visual, rational evidence that the floor was neither tilting nor slanted could help the person to disregard the delusory feeling. Nevertheless, MacCurdy discovered that after three months' training practically any pilot could acquire this unsuspected mastery. We may therefore assume that the ninety-day term (which has generally been the span of time found necessary for the acquisition of a skill, a language or any other psychophysical achievement) is the period best suited for this preliminary training.

Two further suggestions would seem to be proposed by the Tantric teachings. (1) If the electric physiological current, which this therapy re-enforces and combines with the ordinary electric current, is flowing up the spine and its main residue is at the base of the spine, then the place where the external current should be sent into the body and onto the central nervous system should not be through the temples and into the fore-brain (the customary practice). It should be fed in at the base of the spine (or the perineum) and so conducted up into the brain stem. Indeed, as a preliminary this surge should first be mediated through the body's main muscle and cushion of the spinal nerve base: the gluteus maximus.

(2) If the physiologically generated electric current is in every practical sense the same as that generated by coil and magnet dynamo and stored in batteries, then surely, as some Tantric practices suggest, it would be wise (at least as an initial practice and preliminary treatment), to pass the current first through another person who was more prepared by training (and actual experience) and from him let it pass to the postulant beginner. Indeed, it has been suggested by some practitioners that it is possible for a linked circle gradually to step up its own joint charges so that, finally, without the auxiliary contribution of battery or dynamo they can give a postulant sufficient current for him, cooperating with it, to experience the dilation of consciousness.

In closing this chapter, which ends our enquiry into the mysteries' fivefold sequence of intensified therapies of ordeal and initiation, a word should be said as to the twofold purpose of this culminant therapy. The aim is not merely to remove the phobia of death, which is the chief misery and mortification of the large and growing class of second maturity. It is not merely to remove a social nuisance, a biological scandal, and the worst possible example (for the younger age groups) of the meaning of life, the triumph of biology, and the achievement of civilization. It is to attain a development that is as useful to society as it is necessary for the individual. The usefulness for society is to produce a type, a social class, an age group that has reached the position where integral and analytic thought are combined. At this point the mind, made accustomed to postindividual consciousness, can function with conscious control of the extrasensory apprehension. And this is possible because the individual consciousness and the preterconscious are in touch. In consequence, a far larger specious present is comprehensible, a more extensive time-binding (Korzybski's phrase) is possible. And yet these insights can be conveyed down to our sensory-bound society for its use, or at least to warn it.

The needed usefulness for the individual is twofold. This is an experience in which there can be first a frequent and then a constant awareness of life that is necessary for the percipient at that level; that is, it is an experience in which the field of consciousness is always at high pitch and kept at the highest level of the psychophysical frontier. Secondly, when this has become regular and easy, the consciousness, its center of gravity already above the physical nexus and fulcrum, will have achieved its physical experience and service. Then by a voluntary act it can lift itself free to function as a field that is no longer dependent on an entropic structure, on an organism that is subject to decay.

Epilogue

THE PSYCHOPHYSICAL FUTURE OF MAN

[Evolution resumed]

The aim of this study has been to see whether it would be possible to discover any method (or methods) whereby men might educate their emotions. All who reflect on our present predicament agree that this is our supreme need today. Further, enquiry now shows that it is possible to change not only conduct but character and indeed consciousness; that though the deep emotional life is not altered by reason and argument—or at least it is altered only slightly and slowly—the basic forces of a man's nature can be and are molded and channeled by psychophysical experiences and exercises.

Again, investigation shows us that the advances of humanity and its recovery from periodic reactions of frustration and collapses into disorder have been due to successive discoveries made in this area of emotional training. The majority of mankind has repeatedly—to be exact, five times—failed to keep its emotional responses abreast of its growing mental powers and so each time has come to temporary ruin. Nevertheless, there has always been a series of inexplicable recoveries. Now, however, with modern psychological and anthropological insight it is possible to detect the cause and reason for such restorations. Today, we can trace throughout history a series of five such procedures whereby a small but decisive minority of mankind was able, at each crisis of human development, to devise a discipline through which the new balanced order could emerge and so that the gains and powers of man's outer achievement should be salvaged and extended. At each of these crises, because of man's indolent unpreparedness, because of his inability to cooperate with the growth of his consciousness and keep his emotional capacity equal to his intellectual power, there was a temporary submergence of civilization, an international anarchy. But, each time, the gains of the past were carried forward to future generations by the esoteric praxis and organization of the seminal few, an élite of the spirit.

Finally, enquiry along these lines has shown that not only has man's progress followed an oscillatory spiral as he alternates between the exploration of his environment (and the expansion of his power over it) and investigation of his subjective being (and an attempt to achieve peace with it); but that that spiral has accelerated greatly in the speed of its ascent. In consequence, man, by following a process of detached investigation, has in this generation (and for the first time) become a self-conscious creature that is conscious of its unself-conscious. This fact, which has been the core of the psychological revolution, the mutation in thought that ended humanic, total-individualistic man, the alteration in consciousness that has produced leptoid man, this discovery by man of his whole self made it possible to recognize the actual force operating in human evolution.

As long as individualism was intensifying and man was able to define himself only by making his personality entirely separate (by regarding the ego as the one real unit of consciousness) he could only regard the life process as being one of competition and a blind struggle for separate survival. But once man could recognize himself as being part of a field, as being a nexus in a larger whole, then economy (see opposite) turned into ecology, and co-operation (symbiosis and commensalism) took the place of competition as the directive activity of increasing consciousness. In turn this discovery of the symbiotic field led to a further insight into the process as it culminates in man. Louis Bolk's principle of fetalization (that the young and flexible, the uncommitted and open-minded inherit the earth) led to Cope's law of the survival of the unspecialized. As the mammal is the fetalization of the reptile and retains some of the generalized features the reptile lost when it specialized out from the amphibian; as the primates neotenically retain fetal freedoms that the rest of the mammals have lost; as man remains an infant longer than the ape and, to his infancy, adds another span of uncommitted freedom, his specific childhood; so this principle of paidomorphy is now seen to be the power of human evolution and the capacity and promise of its further advance. Applied to specific human history this insight makes comprehensible the vast acceleration of the growth of consciousness since the rise of man. For as man has no instincts he holds together and advances through social heredity. Hence, the human advance has been and must always be through the reciprocity of the two parallel lines of man's physical heredity and his social heredity. The social heredity is the die that stamps its pattern of developing behavior on the matrix of the human brain. While the physical parents beget, bear, and rear increasingly impressionable, teachable young, the begetters of the social heredity have to keep themselves young and open so that they may creatively accept new data and incorporate the new evidence into those new comprehensive conceptions that can feed the fresh, open minds of each generation.

There must, then, be achieved a seer type. This type, we can now see, was obscurely recognized in the shaman, the witch doctor, and the prophet. But theirs was an esoteric dark art, mainly wrought by dangerous stresses and self-violence, and in the interests of the past and the old. Conservation became conservatism. The mysteries were a subterranean stream sunken so deep that we cannot even tell whether there was an unbroken succession of psychophysical knowledge and practice containing and composing new knowledge of means and power and, step by step, compensating for the automatic behavior of the outer world. (See Appendix D.)

Today that knowledge and practice must be neotenic. It must work toward a balanced progress, an enlarging vision. It must never deny but affirm; never arrest but release. The intuitive artist, afraid of losing his conviction if he altered or even explained any detail of the tradition, can now become an explicit, forward-looking scientist. And now this consciously understood method can and must (because of the fact of neoteny) be in the hands not of conservative and reactionary elders but controlled by those who best retain the faith, hope, and cooperative trustfulness of the undamaged young.

In concluding this enquiry, I shall attempt to indicate what these contemporarily unspecialized persons would be; how they could be preserved and retained; how they could be kept open and trained to be the carriers of the immediate social heredity, the producers of comprehension, the feeders of understanding. But first we must glance, in a final résumé, at the exoteric methods of emotional education and character training that have been used in the past, tracing them in outline down to the present day.

We have seen that no society has ever been so complacent as to imagine that its young could acquire adequate psychological equipment either through contagion-suggestion (simply by living with its elder kin) or through being left to learn by themselves. We know now that in the cave life of the coconscious there was pictorial instruction and organized ritual exercise.[a] With the rise of the hypnocratic urban organization,[b] the ritual instruction was obviously elaborated. Even at the time of the heroic explosion, the young were still instructed not only in martial exercises and con-

[a] For example, the paleolithic cave under Montespan shows the imprint of a ritual dance; and there is the picture of the magician in the cave of the Three Brothers.

[b] For example, the Indus civilization as shown at Harappa and Mohengo Daro.

duct worthy of a man-at-arms, a hero, but also there were inculcated those precautions necessary to keep pride from going too far. Naturally, the ascetic age gave persistent warnings, and engraved inhibitions on the growing mind. For by then, man's increasing self-consciousness had made him increasingly frightened of his repressed emotional nature. When the ascetic ideal could no longer serve as the master pattern of prestige and the total individual emerged, there was an attempt to get rid of fear, to form character and direct emotion by an appeal to reason and by a demonstration of its personal advantages.

However, we have seen that this appeal and argument were, naturally, quite incapable of dealing with the preterrational mind; especially was this so as the critical mind had now thrust this aspect of consciousness down to become a vast rebellious subconscious. Hence, the Ignatian attempt at psychological education. Unfortunately, as this was a revival of the ascetic frame of mind, it had to be based on fear. And it was aimed at defending the past, not at explicating and inspiring the present—still less at welcoming the future. The Jesuit exercises were the great attempt of the sixteenth century to balance, by psychological training, the physical and critical advances of humanic man.

In the mid-seventeenth century the English-speaking Protestant world was momentarily affected by another religious genius, George Fox. Fox happened on the fact that a silent meeting of devotees, who were compacted by a common experience and the common peril of being outlawed, could generate a force. The Quakers, as long as they quaked,[c] did generate a current. When this procedure led to seizures, however, they repudiated it and disclaimed any connection with the Holy Rollers and other paroxysmic ecstatics who were practicing it. Therefore, this uncharted power, unchanneled and suspect, had largely left the Quakers by the middle of the eighteenth century when they had become wealthy, socially concerned, and interested in education. They did not become ascetics or rationalists. They were neither guilt-stricken nor materialistic. Their persistent inbreeding led to a good deal of insanity.

[c] See Robert Barclay's *Apology:* "Without quaking there is no Quakerism."

Otherwise, they were exceptionally balanced. They were aware of the need of cultivating a deep interior life. But by the seventeen hundreds the movement had come to resemble Judaism in some respects. It acquired new members still, but its hard core was the birthright membership. And for some generations it practiced the excommunicatory persecution of driving out those members who married outside the society. They claimed, with complacency, that they were a peculiar people and were content to be a social enclave, wearing archaic dress, using archaic speech.

By the middle of the eighteenth century (the rococo phase of humanic man's sensibility) the new attempt at altering conduct, character, and consciousness springs from the missionary zeal of an Oxford lecturer in Greek. John Wesley carried on the Ignatian tradition: the ascetic fear-therapy. He studied Ignatius Loyola and worked out a system. About this system, Sargant, a well-known London psychotherapist who was brought up in Methodist traditions, points out: first of all, it brings on a panic-crisis that destroys any self-security, and then offers vicarious deliverance, the relief of an unexpected, undeserved salvation. This violent repentance (or rather *metanoia,* change of consciousness) (1) not infrequently fades, sometimes completely.[d] (2) It works, in the far greater number of cases, with simple, uneducated people whose critical faculties are undeveloped and whose emotional and passional life is strong.

Wesley, therefore, had his great success with the poor and dispossessed; he failed with the educated.[e] He was opposed not only by the skeptics but also by the quieter pietists and mystics[f] who mistrusted and shunned the fear emphasis and undesirable theology of eternal damnation. Wesleyanism, as had Jesuitism and Quakerism, turned increasingly to organization and educationalism.

[d] See the classic study of seizure salvation in William James's (47) *The Varieties of Religious Experience.*

[e] See, particularly, accounts of his visit to the Southern States in the United States.

[f] William Law, for example, who was mainly influenced by the writings of Jacob Boehme.

The follow-up methods that characterized the new order (or company), the new sect, the new church, were necessary to shape the softened-up character of the convert and give it lasting form. But Jesuits, Quakers, and Wesleyans alike all took to critical education, scholarship, natural science, and ultimately to big business. The psychophysical evolution of man was arrested, deflected. The opportunity that Quakerism and Wesleyanism might have had to make a contribution to the emotional education of man and to the progress of consciousness was lost.

After Wesley (and his successful prevention of the French, the political revolution spreading into England, a key country) there is no advance in psychological education. The milder mystics, such as William Law who tried to make a nonfear-motivated psychiatry out of Jacob Boehme's hell-warmed visions, never worked out an empirical method. Subconsciously, they feared ecstasy, apprehending that it might become erotic. They had, then, no driving force equal to the Ignatian-Wesleyan fear of hell. Swedenborg's revisitings of Boehme's limbos made a mélange of psychical research and evangelical piety in which hell was retained as a very powerful forced draught. The consequences of this strange insight have been the rise of a small church based on these revelations. However, this religion, because of Swedenborg's own notions of hell, has not been able to free itself from fear-pressuring undertaken to avoid unpleasant after-death consequences. Therefore, it makes no contribution to a modern education of the emotions.

During the nineteenth century, evangelical revivals repeated, but always less memorably, Wesley's attack. From Charles Simeon (of the Church of England, who reintroduced the Wesleyan method) through Booth (the founder of the Salvation Army) on to the varieties of Southern States conversionism and American missions to Britain (from Moody to Graham), fear-generated repression worked with decreasing performance. Psychoanalysis, though it was not prepared to consider the emotional development of the "base, ungovernable beast," was ready and able to debunk the old energy-generating or energy-compressive terrors and so hamstring the nightmare. The patient was to be detensioned; and the detensioned will seldom if ever explode into conversion. In the Southern States, Southern Methodism still works with considerable method; not only to bring on salvation from hell but also the "second blessing," the experience of pentecostal outpouring, possession by the Paraclete. The pressures are high and in many ways generate intensities that produce the paraleptic condition at which the shaman and the witch doctor aim: the parallelogram of the two forces, the epileptic tension and hysterical expression. But again, the generators of such paroxysmal power do not know what to do with it.[g]

Meanwhile, these methods are marking time and, it must be owned, losing ground; for they are, at base, ascetic, fearing the body and ignorant of evolution. And since these churches are defenseless against scientific education, since they cannot handle insanity, and since they fail to answer either psychiatry's criticism or its offer of an alternative therapy, another education of the emotions has arisen.

We have noted earlier that psychiatry itself is as helpless against that extensive complaint, alcoholism (and the powerful neurosis of which alcoholism is the symptom) as is Evangelicanism or any of the other ascetic disciplines. Each can gain only an occasional success: none really makes any recognizable headway against the disease. It was the extent and intensity of this addiction that gave rise to the first of those peculiar and specific methods which have been the particular contemporary contribution to emotional education in the last couple of decades. In studying them, I came to the conclusion that they are best described as *ad hoc* churches. For as an *ad hoc* hypothesis in science is an arrangement of a particular group of data so as to give a provisional explanation of the interrelationships of such incidents, and as an *ad hoc* committee is one charged to enquire into and report on a single, specific issue, so it is with the *ad hoc* church. It is an association of persons concerned with one challenging threat and peril. They are not, and

[g] Howard Fabing, who has studied the bringing on of the conversion at Southern revivals, is certain that the spiritual shock treatment of the final stage of the conversion process brings on some kind of seizure that is not epileptic.

in their condition cannot be, concerned with collateral dangers or ultimate goals, any more than a drowning man is able to be interested in the sun-stroke casualties on the beach, water contamination problems, or by-laws of shore behavior.

When we consider our heavy reliance on alcohol, it is only natural that the first *ad hoc* church, the now worldwide Alcoholics Anonymous, was for alcoholics. But although it was a method for addicts, a method that has effected more cures than any other system (whether by drugs, by therapy, or straight religion), it could not work for a group that seems so much the same: the takers of habit-forming drugs, the narcotic addicts. A second organization (or better a salvage system run by those who have suffered from the same attack) had to be founded and put into action for drug addicts. A third one of such self-help associations had, again, to come together when, beside alcoholics and drug addicts, the insane had to undertake getting themselves sane. Psychotics Anonymous now lives and grows alongside the elder AA (Alcoholics Anonymous) and the younger AA (Addicts Anonymous), which is sometimes called NA (Narcotics Anonymous). There are, to my knowledge, at least fifteen other leagues of sufferers joined to meet and take disaster with the strength of that unlimited liability that is given by actual experience, both of the full weight of the attack and the full strength of united resistance.[h]

We have, then, the interesting phenomenon of a general associative method of psychophysical salvage (not only from addiction but from many sorts, maybe all sorts, of emotional peril and defeat) which is, we must recognize, at the same time always specific. In short, the same procedure is employed but each specific sufferer can only be helped by this procedure if the specific helper has been through the same specific defeat.

Before we can hope to propose why this unexpected limitation should appear (and all limitations, being definitions, guide

[h] For example, there is an Anonymous for mothers who have borne an idiot child; for parents whose child is dying of cancer; there are a couple for cancer patients themselves; one for epileptics; and one for those persons who get least understanding or sympathy, the heavily overweight who have to fight an unbalanced appetite for carbohydrates.

us to understanding the method and its way of working) we must first note the procedure, study the steps. Alcoholics Anonymous has twelve. From these it becomes clear that what we are viewing in this ladder of deliverance is the traditional mystery discipline. There is the ordeal, there is the guide who has been through it before (the heirophant) and there is initiation (the rebirth, interior understanding, illumination) that not only explains but empowers.

But the procedure is *ad hoc*. That means that it is curative and restorative. These two practical limitations mean that the *ad hoc* church comes into action only when the ordeal is already half over. For the disaster of addiction, breakdown, or despair had to drive the victim to the edge of destruction, to the point where he or she was ready to seek any possible aid. No *ad hoc* church seeks to act as a general guide for unaddictional characters who desire to grow. These associations rightly stick to what they know. Further, they have found that they must wait until the drowning person calls; and, still, most of those who are drowning drown before they call.

So the *ad hoc* churches cannot prevent. Their function is cure, salvage of the sinking, not teaching people how to swim or how to sail without capsizing. Nor can they do other than restore. Knowing their job, knowing that they are life-savers who have learned how to make the shore, each one of these rescuers who has won free from a suffocating addiction, fear, or collapse aims at retrieving and relanding one who had ceased to swim. The task is to return the victim to the shore circulation and see him back safely high and dry. For the *ad hoc* churches, being *ad hoc* and directing their efforts toward immediate salvage, can have no comprehensive philosophy.[i]

[i] It is a proved policy of the AAs never to have any contact, *as a body,* or any specific association with a particular religion, sect, or party. If members desire to return to a religion, they are advised to try again the faith they had failed to make solve their problem. AA exists to help a man stop drinking. He is then free to give his support to any policy or theology he believes to be true.

They cannot load themselves with a theory as to life's over-all meaning. They cannot answer the basic questions of where we are, whence we came, and whither we are going. They cannot, therefore, give rules as to how we should live, as to how we may grow, as to how we should be prepared and developed, as to how we should educate ourselves. They are not dealing with humanity and its problem and destiny, but with anomalous persons and their predicaments and disasters. The concern is personal and primarily private. When, then, the victim is rescued, his future is with similar victims. He keeps able to make the shore while having often to be swimming in the ocean (that is, he retains his sober life of responsible sanity though often being with the irresponsible and the immoral) by keeping his moral muscles in trim through the constant practice of life-saving, of rescuing others. To change the simile: a fire-fighting team cannot spend its time insisting on rebuilding people's houses with fireproof materials. Once a fire has started, the job of the team and its equipment is to put it out. They have no right, even, to go round soaking people's drapes to lower fire risk.

The *ad hoc* church, therefore, has to let disaster have the first move.[j] For these rescue squads have to depend on the threat of imminent destruction to generate the necessary intensity of demand for retraining. That the peril has to be acute is shown by a fact often observed by AAs of long standing and with distinguished records of salvage service. Now that AA is widely known many persons join who, though they are drinking far too much and are aware that the habit is getting out of hand, are not within a short distance of complete disaster: death or loss of their minds by alcoholic poisoning. They are gravely concerned but not yet desperate. Their motivation is preventive rather than salvational. So

[j] See "Alcoholics Anonymous: Cult or Cure?" by Arthur H. Cain (10). Even in the latest of these salvage efforts where with a more collective procedure (for example, living together in a hostel for the purpose) a movement called Synanon takes in alcoholics, drug addicts, neurotics, potential suicides, etc. Still the ends are the same: to restore to social circulation, to adjust—not to develop, to grow.

their ordeal is not yet sufficiently severe to produce a mutation of consciousness, a real *metanoia*. Hence, there is not an initiation. A bad habit has been arrested; they return to their past norm but they do not develop further. A number of these persons, after some years, finding life too dull resume their drinking.

Thus, since the starting ordeal has to be a specific disaster, in order to salvage the victim the specific device or method of overcoming that particular disaster is then needed. Give all children a full vitamin and protein diet and rickets disappears, tuberculosis incidence sinks, and many other diseases shrink toward vanishing point. But fail in this preventive dietary hygiene and then all kinds of special surgical and medical skills must be called in to deal with the many and varied pathological conditions, with the particular diseases that have arisen as a result of the deficient diet.

We see, then, why each *ad hoc* church is confined to one particular type of patient. In spite of the fact that once the patient calls he is given the same restorative treatment, each patient can only call out of some specific hole or pocket of the abyss. The method is that of the mysteries but with these two definitionary limitations. The patient must ask, and to ask he must have fallen into acute disaster. His ordeal cannot be prepared for, balanced, tempered. Already, he has been through an infancy and childhood which has, in nearly every case, left damage in his subconscious. And this damage, because it has not been remedied, may well be the deep root of his alcoholism, drug addiction, or nervous breakdown. It hits him as a line squall hits an unwarned yachtsman. He capsizes. The chances of salvage are at best slim.

To use still another but more helpful simile, this is curiously like the first stages of modern medicine when preventive medicine was dawning. When the pandemic of smallpox hit Europe as the seventeenth century was ending, when it was said that no woman dare call her child her own until it had been stricken, no prevention was known. Then at the close of the eighteenth century, Jenner discovered that a cowpox serum used as a prophylactic, a vaccination, gave immunity with very small risk. General preventive medicine is still seeking for a panacea miracle drug that would so raise general resistance that every disease would be held at bay. And it seems increasingly likely, as psychosomatic medicine advances, that this elixir will be found only when the psychophysiology of man is well understood: so well understood that the psychophysique can be brought to such coordinated, comprehensive functioning that the entire person will have become so alive that every attack will only rouse the organism to greater resistance and initiative.

The *ad hoc* churches must continue their unique services and their specific salvages. But the very particularity of their success points up the need for the extension and enlargement of their process. The first step, of course, is to decide to forestall attack and not wait to be overrun before striking back. This requires an over-all strategy. And this preparedness cannot be merely defensive, a plan of prevention. It must be a process of initiative and development. We are now prepared to be told that we must make such comprehensive preparation if we are ever to gain the initiative in the struggle wherein the *ad hoc* churches put up not only gallant defensives but remarkable rear actions and counterattacks. For those who know because they have been there—the ex-alcoholic, the ex-addict, and ex-psychotic—all recognize that the specific breakdown is the final phase of a reaction, of a balance, of a growth process that was never properly fulfilled.

The craving for alcohol, narcotics, and/or the relapse into psychosis is an escape from a situation that has become acutely stressful but out of which no one has offered the patient any way. They must conform and they cannot. As Earl Loomis has pointed out in regard to the dementia praecox children (see earlier), they are often of high intelligence but are also intensely sensitive. They are therefore too frequently stung to passionately resentful reactions by slights, disregards, and roughnesses that do not actually madden children of average toughness and resilience. In short, as almost all experts in the addiction psychopathies now agree, we are, in these destructive categories, dealing with men and women whose sensitiveness would not let them endure our incoherent and pointless way of living. Their addiction is an anodyne adopted to staunch a purposeless pain: the exasperating futility of aimless living.

Once the situation is so diagnosed and understood, the next step toward prevention is evident: education. And as the addicts and psychotics are different from the rest of us only in the extremity of their reaction, since we all must be to some extent frustrant in a society that cannot say in modern terms and rational language where it is going and why it so conducts itself, this education in understanding must be available to us all. We must act on some such hypothesis of history and some such picture of the individual's growth as I have proposed in this thesis. As we have seen, the psychophysical development today cannot be begun unless it has as its premises a rational, empirical instruction. Man must be shown whence he has come, where he is, and whither he may go. He must realize that his present stress (which reaches breaking point with the addicts and psychotics) is due to a force that cannot find fulfillment unless he provides it with that process of expression; a force which, if he will not give it a procedure of development, must destroy him. To attempt the readjustment of an individual to a society which itself is out of gear because it does not know where it is going (and when that individual has become deranged for that very reason) is like trying to cure a consumptive, who has fled a slum, by putting him back in the infected air with the pious hope that he will learn to build up resistance and adjust to reality.

Having arrived at this intellectual agreement, then, we can see, as the inevitable third step, how we may act to implement our knowledge. It is clear that every child, and, in turn, every adolescent, every person entering first maturity, and every person becoming veterine must have his specific ordeal and initiation. By these means, by psychophysical training, and specific raising of initiative, we may and can and must do for the emotional life of man, for his psyche, what preventive medicine, development diet, and exercise-hygiene have done for the physique. Then, and then only, will our mental health equal our physical health; then will our age of revolutions and reactions be over and our evolution be resumed through man's intentional cooperation with the force within him.

Therefore, this essay can now conclude with a hypothesis of social development through psychophysical education. Such an education, by following and explicating the principles of evolution that are now understood, may enable man to achieve a new progress and to develop the potentialities in himself which, until now, have been thwarted. The idea of progress has been written off by the microscopic historians who believe that a tapestry can be understood by chemical analysis of its threads. The design of the future has been left to embittered satirists, such as we now know Orwell to have been. With a dislike and ignorance of the human animal equal to Swift's (but without the excuse of Swift's insanity) they project their hatred on "the damned race," as Frederick of Prussia named it, under the disguise of righteous protest. But as John Pfeiffer has pointed out, these "Base Late Worlds," these dismal perspectives of degeneracy are purely perverse fiction. The opposite of all this satire is first the rational expectation and then the reasonable extension of our present knowledge of human evolution.

As La Barre (51) has stressed, the more we study the infancy of apes and men the more unmistakable and outstanding does Louis Bolk's principle of fetalization appear to be. And as John Pfeiffer has pointed out, man's nature and the society that human nature constructs is utterly unlike the ant and its hill, the termite and its termitary, or the bee and its hive. These insect prisons are all precipitated by creatures that have atrophied until they have become automatized by instinct.[k] Human society springs from a creature still so generalized that he is inexhaustibly inventive because he is insatiably curious. Cope's law of the survival of the unspecialized works through life. But it reaches its overwhelming vindication in man, the incomparable creature. J. B. S. Haldane the biologist, we must repeat, points out that this neotenic capacity has paid man so prodigiously that the man we are in process of becoming will remain free of the commitment of speech; will still be vocalizing with unrestricted variety of sound responses and auditory experiments, until

[k] See von Frisch (89), *Bees,* and Lindauer (54), *Communication Among Social Bees.*

he is in his sixth year. See also *Man's Emerging Mind,* page 290, by N. J. Berrill (5).

And so it will be with man's learning; it will extend into his fifth decade. Not only are some of the nerve centers that served us with lightning-flash reflexes and powerful passionate drives showing signs of atrophy. But other areas, the ones that learn most easily and quickly, where curiosity reigns and wonder inspires, the ones that are the foundation sites of freedom, invention, and creation, seem to be growing. As John Pfeiffer points out, it certainly looks as though the very life in our bodies is making us ever more easy to inform and to persuade, ever harder to deceive and to coerce. And as La Barre has remarked in his *The Human Animal,* man has no innate pugnacity. The one innate characteristic he has is teachability.

That, however, puts a unique responsibility upon the teaching and the teachers. For without psychophysical teaching of the most thorough sort this birth of a new type of consciousness will not be achieved. We have to make clear to ourselves both the goal that we can now see and the means that we now know are the way to that goal. That goal is the increasing capacity to retain and to express the vast potentiality that is in the brain of the embryo and which, we must always remind ourselves, has not yet been able to be born at the height of its fetal promise. Just as the gorilla fetus, when it approaches birth, loses roundness of skull as the brain is compressed by the jaw muscles and muscle-keel that run across the skull-dome, so to a much less degree (but still to a serious amount) the proportionately vast brain case of the human embryo has to be reduced before birth.

To permit such a child to be born and grow, this creature (see earlier for the negative side of this, the collapse into dementia praecox) must have an environment of dynamic stimulation, generated by the tonic loving delight of a parental field that believes in the child's tremendous promise and that keeps it in an optimum, unwavering atmosphere of cheerful expectation. There is no sentimentality or soothing repose in such an environment. It is one of constant courageous wager and tempering challenge. Indeed, in the future it may well come to be that this stimulation will be started while the child is still in the womb. If, as we have seen, its leaps are really evulsive (plus shudders, spastic exultations as it prepares to throw off a now cramping security for an energizing risk), soon it may be possible to send back into it a responding rhythm.

It has been found that on the human brain there are, as it were, very fine recording tapes. And those areas that record sound can hear music when all that is being transmitted to them are the electric impulses used to carry musical sounds and record them on magnetized tape. No sound wave travels; it is only an electric impulse. Considering the effect that deep sounds and parasonic vibrations have on the brain,[1] certainly the possibility of such a method of both soothing and bracing the central nervous system of the embryo for its oncoming challenge should not be neglected.[m]

When the child is born, then, it is clear that it should feel, taste, smell, hear, and see only such sensa as reassure and stimulate. It should have only those contacts to which it will respond with delight (such as caressing and tickling); tastes that attract and intrigue; scents, sounds, and lights that rouse and fascinate. We now know that the mood of the mother or foster-mother (according to whether it is friendly, anxious, sullen, or angry) affects the infant: bitterly, if the mood is negative; stimulatingly, if it is positive. And, a little later, the parental group together with all others in contact with the child (which has yet to acquire its protective filters) can profoundly help or hinder its growth. Their mood, involuntarily expressed by their scent and sound even when they are at a distance from the infant, can make it prematurely harden and close or can help it to keep supple and open its consciousness. This is all the more impressive because these involuntary influences are involuntarily accepted by the defenseless infant.[n]

---

[1] Referred to in the chapter on the earth ordeal and initiation of rebirth.
[m] Any reference as to specific instruction of the preborn is here omitted. The evidence, advanced by one therapist, that the fetus can understand language seems unsatisfactory and, considering the fetus' position and brain capacity, very highly improbable.
[n] The milk of the modern mother is often made too acid, by her constant anxiety and impatient frustration, for the infant to digest.

After this preliminary treatment of welcome, given to all children, then it would be possible to estimate inborn aptitude, revealed at this point because the child has expanded freely in such an atmosphere. We must remember that because the progress of man now depends on two unique, reciprocal human factors, two complimentary types must be prepared that are as interdependent as the two sexes have been throughout bisexual evolution. Man, since he now advances by social heredity, requires two representatives to forward that heredity. The first is the type that composes. Every generation, every decade, every year, those who value a true and living morality should bring the ruling mores up to date, should be continually adding new and fuller knowledge as to how we could behave more effectively. This seer-coordinator is constantly taking new data and using them to construct a wider frame and range of reference from which to deduce an ever more significant and creative way of feeling, thinking, and acting.

However, these inspiring conceptions together with the behavior patterns and processes whereby they are performed and actualized have to find a perfectly responsive matrix: a subject, a recipient, who can absorb and practice what is given. This double gift seems to be what evolution has bestowed on man. On the one hand, he is the most suggestible, the most teachable of all creatures. On the other, he is the most original, the most constructive. The teacher-seer must then be picked; and to that selection and training we shall turn in concluding.

But prophets have always spoken in vain if there were lacking those who can hear, apply, and produce the superfine material adequate to take the impress, who are adequate to express in actual form the new vision. Nothing has caused more discouragement, disingenuous casuistry and, in the end, hypocritical cynicism than those hyperbolic ideals that spring mainly from the guilt complex and life-rejecting revulsion of the ascetic. By what may only be called the "whitemail" of shaming people into a "potlach" competition in surrender, they have made countless numbers attempt to live a life described as that of perfection without proof of results, without process of specific instruction, or without first getting rid of their subconscious traumas and repressions.

The chronicle of Salimbene, a Franciscan who was born in 1221 (five years before the death of St. Francis) and who spent his life as a Friar, shows how rapidly success and degeneracy came upon the great Friars movement. It set as an ideal a life of ecstatic detachment that was to be lived out in the actual world.° However, not only must the lofty ideal be worked out in contemporary terms. Two preliminary factors must be clear and proved: the steps by which it may be attained, and the manner in which material capable of being worked into that shape may be produced.

What in Sanskrit is called "The Way of the Fathers" is to produce and rear children under those optimum conditions we have just mentioned, so that they may be more flawlessly responsive, flexible, open, and aware than any other creatures before them. This is the basic receptive aspect of neotenic evolution. It is the essential premise and ground without which vision cannot be actualized but must remain only a heart-breaking ideal. We must repeat, this is the matrix that can take and retain the full impress of instruction.

Once, however, such receptivity exists then it is equally necessary that there shall be not only a message and an instruction but an exemplar and trainer who is penetrating and comprehending enough to fill the full stretch and capacity of such suppleness. In the Sanskrit tradition, the seer, the teacher, the trainer, is said to go "The Way of the Gods." The fathers produce ever more open, teachable, inspirable children. The trainer produces an ever apter, wider, more inspiring doctrine: one that is wholly realistic because it is wholly apposite. This picture, of a parenthood that is able to produce ever finer psychophysical stuff and, reciprocally, a teacher-hood that is able to bring forth ever more stimulating training techniques and character ideals, meanings of life and goals of con-

---

° The man who succeeded St. Francis as head of this organization, Brother Elias, was picked to make a viable corporation out of a waning enthusiasm. He ended by being deposed because of his use of power politics.

sciousness, is, of course, the development and culmination of the neotenic conception of evolution reaching its apex in man, the paidomorph.

We see now that the particular characteristic of man is this: he is the social creature which, of all the social creatures, has succeeded in building a highly functionalized and indeed specialized social structure without destroying the adaptability and curiosity of the individual constituent. All the social insects that have raised the most elaborate social structures have done so at the price of all initiative and by the complete subordination of the individual unit to the consequently rigid group pattern. Their worker type is an atrophied form, generally a female. Man has a vastly complex set of inventive societies and an expanding, unfinished concept of civilization. These may be dangerously diversive, but certainly they are not arrested. Their very confusions and anarchies are evidence of their inherent vitality-of-variety; and their story, as we have seen, has been one of convulsive advance, spastic progress.

From the start, then, man's process has been through neoteny; and as his history has gone on, its progress has been through increasing paidomorphy. Through retaining increasingly, and to ever later ages, the child's curiosity and desire for adventure, the result has been societies that are increasingly inventive, constructive, and enterprising. There have had to be, and there have been, plenty of reactions. Life leafs off the husks that lose flexibility, and as they stiffen inevitably they try to throttle the force which, since they will not expand, breaks them and casts them off. The new living shoot, as it thrusts off the old husk, can itself be deformed by the dead rind that it struggles to discard. The task of civilization (and its instrument, education) is by insight and foresight (by developmental therapy) so to supple the whole process that the old, instead of clinging on and deforming the new, will explicate their own elimination. The violent, oscillatory process of revolution and reaction, of martyr-prophet and counterreform-conventionalist, must and can be made to cease its spastic alternation. Then progress-with-conservation can take over.

The society that can be foreseen (the civilization that, with such knowledge as we now have, may be extrapolated) would then be a restoration, or rather an explication, of the primal trinity: father, mother, and child. Wordsworth's phrase, "The child is father to the man," was much more true than he understood. In Taoist tradition the same basic idea is expressed. Lao Tzu, the traditional founder, is called the young old one, the ancient boy. Complementing the parents who produce the flawless supereducatable young there has, of necessity, to be the advanced neotene. For he is the one who can take the perfect material and feed into it that complete diet of charging stimulant, tonic encouragement, and open inspiration whereby it becomes a completely contemporary creature of constant growth. This image of the divine foster-parent, the god-parent, has been present in man's archetypal consciousness since the basic social heredity ritual was put together at Abydos in Egypt. This was a rite of *religio,* of total meaning and comprehension which, as Egyptian civilization grew, was able to contain and compose all the vigorous gear of a highly elaborate and developing nation for two thousand years.[p] For the story of Demeter (visiting Eleusis in disguise, becoming nurse to the son of King Celeus and Queen Metaneira, almost succeeding in making the young prince immortal) must certainly derive from the far earlier account of Isis. She too wanders the earth in disguise, seeking a lost loved one and doing a precisely similar (and similarly misunderstood and spoiled) service for alien mortals who befriended her.[q]

To sum up then: first, we must have a parenthood capable of begetting and rearing a child that can be born and be viable with the extreme neotenic promise shown by the fetus; a creature of unprecedented uncommittedness, unspecialization, and receptivity, of intense openness, sensitiveness, and responsiveness. Next, we must and can produce from this very type a trainer, an educator who can instruct and inspire this child not merely to adapt to and serve the present, but to advance into and create the future. Here again, from the very limitedness of the complete social insect societies'

[p] See Henri Frankfort (27), *Ancient Egyptian Religion* and *The Human Venture,* by Gerald Heard (40).

[q] For further analysis of significant detail of this mythos see Appendix D.

reaction to grave challenge we can gain a hint as to how, with our knowledge, we may react in our present crisis: not to preserve the defenses of a threatened pattern but to rise to a new level of initiative and progress. The most deadly peril that can confront the beehive is when the Queen, through some accident, has failed to lay royal grubs, or the grubs have died in their cells. This supreme danger rouses the worker-tenders of the grubs to a rare reaction. A few common grubs, which under ordinary feeding would emerge as workers, are fed the royal jelly and transmute into queens.

The most deadly peril that confronts mankind today is lack of contemporary seers; for lacking these we have nothing but a tradition of fossilized ideals, irrelevant disciplines, and vestigial praxes. We could now know how to take the at-last-full-born child and, out of those who show the highest neotenic development, to raise and rear a creature that will be a complete, viable paidomorph.

It is clear that such a being could, if given the whole range of even our present psychophysical knowledge (endocrine stimulation, dietary supplementation, body-mind exercises, profound suggestion) attain to the capacity to use the entire resources of the body-mind, both lobes of the brain, all and wholly the endocrine system, and every aspect of consciousness. Such a creature would retain its perfect generalization to full growth and never lose it. The wide compass of association, the complete freedom from prejudice, that would go with such a range of comprehension would render this paidomorph not only able to see and forecast correlations and conjunctions that must appear abstract or prophetic to our limited minds. But with the authority of superknowledge would go the persuasiveness of one who understands and empathizes with those he can instruct.

Human evolution must be so regarded. The present data of fetalization, paidormorphy, and neoteny do not permit us to see the process of man in any other terms. The risk, of course, is terrific. But it always has been, if a higher station is to be won. And, up to the present, the risk has been taken and the new station attained. Besides, we have seen that even among the apparently completely rigid social constructional finalities of the social insects, even in the beehive when the peril is sufficiently acute, the challenge sufficiently desperate to be beyond the flawless repetition of the instinctive pattern to fulfill or to solve, daring invention (for example, the use of the royal jelly) saves the system that is otherwise doomed.

However, the possibility that we will accept this new way and undertake this new experiment will turn on our having some concept of our goal. For we are creatures who act with originality only when we can have some hypothesis, some vision of whither we are going, of how that end will fulfill and not make futile our past strivings and earlier experiments. So, first, can we visualize how such a reciprocal process of development would fulfill man's past attempts to live the binary life (social and individual) of biological survival (persistence) and also permit him to go further by an ever larger actualization of an ideal?

From the earliest ages, from the cave rituals, there seems to have been a leader-magician. In the Heroic Age there was not merely the hero type but also, keeping him in bounds, the *vates* and heralds who set forth the limits and molds in which exuberance must be shaped. Even more strikingly, in the Ascetic epoch there are the two lives: (1) that of the contemplative who surveys and envisions, and the clerk through whose canon law the scale of values, the scheme of life, the plan of creation and salvation that has been envisioned by the seer can be applied; and (2) that of the lay folk who supply the means, secure the foundation, and implement the findings of the clerical side of life. Humanic man alone (because he was cut off from knowledge of the paraconscious by his total individualism and its entire dependence on his individualized senses) neglected the binocular vision, the inner and outer sight, the integral-plus-analytic thought that until then man had never wholly ceased in some wise to attempt and never anywhere utterly disregarded. Because he is a creature that can exist, not to say advance, only with and through a social heredity, man must require, and increasingly require, the seer who can weave a web of purpose out of those ties and linkages of energy and data that would otherwise be only destructive and baffling. This is a new belief but its roots are to be found in man's tradition. And this long sustained, often frustrated hope for a meaning that would coordinate all means, for a purpose that would embrace and order all powers, for an understanding that could interpret, give significance to, and derive value from all experience, today has a greater possibility of fulfillment (as well as peremptory demand that it be fulfilled) than ever before.

We must have a type to reassemble and reissue our canon of meaning, our plan of significance, our chart of value-charged purpose. And now at last we can conceive of an exemplar type. He will have the initiative of the hero without his egotistic *hubris*. He will be as anonymous as the ascetic but without his paralyzing guilt. He will have an even wider circumspection than the greatest humanist but without the humanist's self-limited frame of reference, without his confinement to sensory data as being his only substance and to reason and critical analysis as being his only instrument.

Also, we can now propose and estimate a goal that is not, on the one hand, other-worldly: a nonphysical, nontemporal condition. Nor, on the other hand, is it utopian. That is, it is not simply an extrapolation of quantity, an infinite increase of means, an ever further elaboration of apparatus without any development of the human faculties. As a first step toward conceiving the further evolution now open to man, to us humans of the twentieth century, let us note the extension developments that seem probable to evaluators of the human endowment as research today has been able to estimate it.

In his admirably concise summary of man's specific expression and instrument, his brain, John Pfeiffer (66) remarks that a majority of researchers seem to expect the brain to go on growing Grey Walter (93), of the Burden Neurological Institute in Bristol, England, believes that areas of the human brain may be now increasing. About this theory of Walter, Pfeiffer makes the evident but significant comment that the enlarged brain case would make its wearer look childlike. We might go further and say they would be infantic. Pfeiffer also remarks that the human brain already uses double the amount of oxygen that is required by an ape's brain, and that one quarter of all the oxygen taken in by the human lung goes to the brain. Four minutes of lack of oxygen from the brain involves the collapse and ruin of its highest centers.

The brain, the instrument of the mind, seems to be asserting an evolutionary right: as it is the largest unspecialized mass of tissue in the body it can be the growing edge of the life process. This need not mean degeneracy of the rest of the organism. The brain needs the entire physical apparatus to keep itself going and growing. What this does seem to propose is that the brain, as the instrument of thought, the culminant expression of feeling, and the psychosomatic fulcrum of development, should be expected to throw its decisive weight in favor of rendering the entire physique as generalized as itself. In other words, this spearhead of evolution (and especially of human advance) must aim at ever further development and fulfillment of this law of the survival of—and, we may add, the dominance of—the unspecialized.

As Grey Walter has pointed out, the sense of touch seems to be almost independent of the brain's control and ordering; and he adds, as illustration, that the reproductive process seems to proceed on its own, disregardful of the mind that receives the tactilely conveyed messages but can do little if anything about them, unless, as he stimulatingly suggests, we should train our mind tactually. Indeed, this has been explored by the German studies in haptics, which derived from studies on the apprehension of their environment by those who were born blind.

But further, we must note that at the beginning of this century Ivan Bloch (6) drew attention to the fact that the specific sexual sensations are derived from and concentrated-contracted in from that suffused sensory dilation which in this essay I have called the panaesthetic neotenic psychophysical tonus.

The brain, then, may be extending the further evolution of man. It may be a connative organ, a center that is striving to establish a paidomorphic structure. In and through this structure it may express itself; it may inform itself in and about its environment, about its fellow body-minds and about its present field. So it may be moved to undertake further enlargements and modifications not only *in* that field but *of* that field. Certainly the brain has already reached such a complexity that man can no longer hope for peace by settling down; any more than an animal with a large stomach can hope to rest by leaving its digestive areas empty. The brain insists that we keep on the go. The younger and more nimble we become the better we shall satisfy our rider, enjoy the exercise he insists we take with him and, in the process, utterly outstrip any who might, while we were drowsing, have taken our place in the van of life.

This is how the neotenic drive may fulfill itself. First there may be a minority with sufficient expert knowledge and authentic authority to inhibit violence, to guide the future by the accuracy of their insights, the surety of their forecasts, and to control and liberate education by producing and inculcating a valid contemporary psychophysical morality, a mental-somatic social hygiene. So, at length, a race able to be free might be produced. Then this minority might become the balancing moiety of mankind; alongside the "Way of the Fathers" there could march not a comparatively exceptional élite but another complementary column in the human procession. These would be neither superathletes nor superascetics. Human life, as it has developed, has produced an increasing variety of response-types. And as the neotenic type or types emerge, we may find a species of man that lives its whole life naturally, without ever narrowing down to the no longer necessary confinement of the specific sexual focus and no longer confined, intellectually, to one professional expertism. In fact this type must emerge in view of the threat posed by the present population explosion.

The widening of apprehension could at last lead to a race which, comprehending the purpose of life and the meaning of time, could complete its history. For the individual can achieve voluntary death as a further liberating birth; and the individual is the epitome of the race (its phylogeny henceforward following his ontogeny). So the race, its physical process completed, could translate itself into another field and transmute itself to function in another medium, at a higher frequency.

In closing, however rash it may seem, honesty suggests that if a researcher believes there is now detectable a clue that runs through history and points to a process that has repeatedly held societies together and reknit them when men had ruptured their intuitive cohesion, then he should indicate how that process may be made to function today—how it may be used to heal our individual and social fissures. If four times the intuitive reactions of man to his outer environment and inner racial depth broke down, and if four times a specific procedure reknit a minority that was sufficient to prevent the temporary failure of nerve that proves fatal, the collapse of society into total anarchy and a-moralism—what now?

Any informed person is now aware that we are in the psychological revolution. This is the last of the four revolutions (the religious, political, economic, and psychological) that comprise that epoch of revolutions which we still call the modern age. But more than that, we are aware that with the explication of this psychological and psychiatric revolution we pass out of the epoch of revolutions. For revolution is the resultant of the trough of the wave (the subconscious intuitive value system) not being kept in balance with its crest: the critical foreconscious directed to accumulate data in regard to the outer world. Discovery of the unconscious integral mind now permits this balance to be re-established. Psychologically, integrally detected values can now be in coordination with critically detected outer data. Revolution (the advance of sense-data knowledge beyond the compositional capacity of the retarded inherited value system) has always been followed by reaction (the retraction to earlier mores and resistance against new data). But now this revolution-reaction breaker or cataclysmic comber conclusion of the social wave process need no longer occur.

Our psychosocial evolution can be resumed in a balanced advance of the intelligence and the emotions. Being the first generation of men who are both self-conscious and also now aware of the non-self-conscious, we can now educate those implementers of action (the emotions) and so close the fatal gap, in the individual, between his intellect which works by critical reason and his reflexes that are trained by athletic conditioning.

We are also well aware that the progress in psychiatry has not only detected the way whereby the repressed emotional life may be brought to the surface and so given relief. We have added two further important discoveries to our knowledge of ourselves. First, we have learned that there have always been four cardinal turning points at which the human living process, whether that of the race or that of the individual, faces a crisis of change and may be derailed. Secondly, we have come to see that no therapy, no education of the emotions can be sound and lasting if its aim is to return the individual to normalcy and only render him able to submit to the present rapidly collapsing mores. He can be taught to adjust, to make mutual adaptations with his altering society. But he can do so fruitfully, and with a new sanity toward himself and his society, only if the therapy of psychophysical hygiene that he is given is more than curative, more than preventive. It must be developmental.

Already we have seen the results of such a therapy when employed with the first great age group, that of infancy. We are now at the stage when we can see that these processes of development therapy (through education of the emotions) must continue. The subject of juvenile delinquency may be too much colored at present by the time-old prejudices and subconscious jealousies with which elders have always viewed the impetuous young. Today, too, the speed of change, which is far greater than in any other generation, tends to prove that the old were wrong in trying to prevent the young's rapid response to altered circumstances and increased knowledge.

Nevertheless, here is an issue of great acuteness today, and for two reasons. First, the rate of revolt is rising (23). A radio report the other day gave the figure that 50 per cent of cars stolen were purloined by boys between ten and seventeen years of age, and that 19 per cent of all acts of criminal violence were committed by the same age group. The "rebels without a cause" (to use Robert Lindner's title) in this age section are hostile to discipline and suspicious of esprit de corps. As Lindner (56) has pointed out, repression can only increase the pressure and provoke full neurosis and psychosis. J. A. M. Meerloo (61), who was an expert witness of the trials of brain-washed American prisoners of war in Korea, states that the failure of loyalty was caused, basically, by the fact that the soldier who yielded had generally never been given a fully valid, character-convincing instruction in that voluntary and joyful self-giving without which loyalty is only conformity. The enforced service of a conscript is always in conflict with such dedication; and psychology may yet prove that the two are incompatible.

The second reason why some method of training the adolescent emotions is necessary comes from the other direction. "If we don't train adolescent emotions," says the conservational sociologist, "they may wreck our society." The age group psychologist has an equally strong reason for urging that this third great life crisis shall be rightly handled and those in this third birth be helped to achieve a healthy delivery. For the infancy therapist points out, as mentioned earlier in Chapter 3 of Part II, that a child toughened by a harsh infancy (if it survives and does not become antisocially psychotic) is more suited to survive in a tough Junior High, and hence go ahead as a callous, self-seeking competitor, than one trained to welcome and to cooperate. Margaret Mead is today's most influential anthropologist. In her latest and most important study (59) she twice asks this searching question: If the life of the grown-up is to be based on self-interest and if friendship must be disowned when personal profit becomes the standard of adult prestige, would not these now mature persons be better adjusted if they had never known the happy carelessness of their early years? "If ignorance is bliss, 'tis folly to be wise." But conversely, "A sorrow's crown of sorrows is remembering happier things." In a fighting world he survives best who never heard of peace. Our helping the individual through his first ordeal and initiation (of the full psychophysical birth of some thirty months) may be worse than useless if he is to be exposed to deforming atavistic pressures in childhood and adolescence.*

The child is easily bored and as easily contemptuous of convention and finish. He needs action. Theodore Reich writes of the adolescent's subconscious need for compulsion and confession and the demand for punishment. These adolescent needs are not basic; they are symptoms, for they can be analyzed into deeper causative

---

* In passing, it should be noticed here that delinquency seems to stem from two types: (*a*) a child type that is an exuberant prankster and (*b*) an adolescent type that, newly equipped with the critical faculty, like a child with a new knife practices on anything that cuts up easily.

conditions. They are the miscarriage of an innocent constructive urge toward intense, exertional, agonic effort, toward a positive heightening endurance of a tempering process. For adolescence is also a birth that requires, as did the first two births, the rousing of intense latent vitality, which not only drives the craft through the narrows of parturition but also sends it out with an initiative drive.

So as the infant is roused, by play and bright challenge, to go ahead and avoid the lethargic danger of hebephrenic arrest and inertia, the child and the adolescent must also be helped to keep moving and to keep growing. By skilled ordeals in which we may suspect (if the past ordeals are any guide) that increasingly strenuous water exercise such as swimming, diving, and underwater effort would be a central term, the individual in later childhood may experience not only a catharsis, a purging of congested psychophysical pressures. He may also experience anarsis, that further stringing, tautening, and acquisition of muscular tensile tonus and strength whereby he becomes ready for adolescence.[s]

Education at this third stage (the stage of the ordeal and initiation of air) would probably involve learning a number of the now tested and efficacious yogic breathing exercises. These increase oxygen utilization, keeping the brain at a peak of activity and the bodily circulation high. The corresponding enlargement of the rib cage and convexing of the sternum not only increases lung room but there seems to be some evidence to suggest that it also affects the mass of tissue situated back of the sternum. During early childhood (generally to about the age of six) this mass of tissue acts as the thymus gland and holds in balanced check the ripening of the reproductive organs.[t] It is possible that this gland may be brought again into endocrine action and assist the adolescent in preserving,

---

[s] The optimum condition to which each ordeal should be raised is called Right Effort. Right Effort is the Sixth Step in the Noble Eightfold Path of Buddhism. It is generally illustrated by the tuning of a stringed instrument, each string of which must be brought to perfect pitch—neither slack nor overtautened, neither sharp nor flat.
[t] See Part II, Chapter 4, footnote b.

as long as it is desirable, the panaesthetic dilation before he temporarily enters the phase of specific reproduction.

First maturity in turn would then have its radiant heat therapy treatments. By this still higher form of strenuous stimulation, the executive type would be kept not only releasing his full energy, but acutely vital so as to be able to look forward to the further and higher stage of second maturity with the interest and appetite with which the adolescent looks forward to his oncoming adulthood. To such a person in first maturity, administration would not be the final station. It would be an education toward a still higher experience and more efficacious authority in second maturity, just as athletic achievements and academic ratings and recognitions are not the final station of the adolescent.

The specific treatment for second maturity would be short-wave radiation. It would seem possible that by this means those who have discharged their obligation to life and learned its purpose, might be freed from what today is an all too common blind and desperate clinging to bodily existence. This wretched and irrational fear-cramp seems too often to increase, not lessen, as physical resources become spent. The old could have much to give but they are commonly shunned because to listen to complaints is always exhausting. And to be with even the secretly frightened is profoundly fatiguing. If when a person entered second maturity he began to be given high frequency treatment as a part of advanced adult education and psychophysical hygiene, three highly beneficial consequences seem possible. In the first place, his unspent energies (his frozen assets of vitality) could be released. He might become a person of such extended outlook that his counsel would be sought and his presence would give peace and encouragement instead of misgiving and dismay. Secondly, he himself might become increasingly psychophysically aware not only that his consciousness (his electric field) is distinctly superior to that field's precipitate (the material body) but that this consciousness can be independent.

Thirdly, after some years of such hygienic exercise he might be able to understand how to detach this essential noncorporeal field, freeing it increasingly from its entropic system. This would lead to an awareness that (like the tree with the leaf) all the essential essence in the outer vehicle has been resumed into its original volatile condition. Then with an act of intentional initiative the consciousness principle could discard the unwanted residue.

Appendixes

THE HYBRID PSYCHE

*[The transitional blend of heroic mystic and lawful
ascetic, which produces (1) the city state,
(2) the nation state, and (3) the empire state]*

One question remains: How does this historical schema describe
and explain, in its psychological diagnosis, the mental energy that
produced the ancient civilizations?

Surely, neither the destructive, paranoid hero nor the schizoid,
escapist ascetic can account for those achievements in administration, law, economy, and art that the ancient civilizations produced
and which, because of their impressiveness, have seemed to most
historians to be the highest fruit of mankind's intelligence. If the
psychological hypothesis outlined in this study of history is the basic
diagnosis of the force that has been shaping mankind, if successive
alterations in the human mind are the persistent cause of the
changes throughout successive phases of human culture, then under
each of these cultural phases we must be able to detect that specific
phase of human consciousness that was the cause of that change in
culture.

It is true that in a number of cases in history (for example, in the fourth and fifth centuries A.D. in Ireland) there is given evidence that there is a conversional moment in history. The mutation in consciousness, the contraction of the soul on itself, on these occasions took place with spastic speed. For there are records of heroes in the very heat of battle, at the pitch of their paranoid frenzy, being compunction-pierced, of their having a sudden sense that their violation of the natural law, "Thou shalt not kill within thy species," convicted them of murder. They fled headlong from the bloody field, knowing the curse of Cain, and not only forsook the sword but excommunicated themselves from society and abandoned the world, henceforth to live only to die, to expiate their guilt before, after death, it would fall upon their souls with the pitiless avenging fury that they had dealt out upon their earthly foes.

Nevertheless, this swift reaction from paranoid, childish, homicidal rage over into schizoid, adolescent, mortificatory guilt has certainly not been the only possible path of human development. Take, for example, the classic case of the emperor Asoka (264–227 B.C.). His conversion took place the night after the culminating victory in which he had completed the conquest of all India proper. In a dream, he is walking over the won field and he sees that all the faces of the dead are his own face. And though his conversion compels him personally to adopt the regime of a monk, publicly he retains his administrative and, in fact, his legal punitive powers.

He is a psychological hybrid. His private conscience is set on saving his own soul. His public obligation is tied to the discharge of his duties through the exercise of legalized violence. For example, capital punishment is kept in force. Condemned law-breakers have their date of execution postponed for one day if that date falls on a holy day in the Buddhist calendar. He has not the peace-keeping mana-power of a priest-king in an hypnocracy. He is an armed executive-emperor. He cannot assure his own royal succession. His son is recorded to have risen against him and to have had militarily to be crushed. Finally, the Buddhist religion, which he made that of the State, endowed and privileged by such patronage (like the

Christian church when similarly bought by Constantine), degenerated and modified its teaching. For instance, on the Asoka pillars there is no mention of Nirvana, the one aim of Buddhism, the deliverance from all physical and all individual life in a state that means the disappearance of the whole material world. What is commended and commanded, in these edicts, is a life of good social deeds to be rewarded after death with the conventional paradisal pleasures.

Here, however, we must note that the Indian and the Irish heroes were late.[a] Already there had been, centuries before, that Eurasian-wide outbreak of the private conscience, the desire for personal salvation (compare Karl Jasper's *Axis of History,* Breasted's *Rise of Conscience*), the ego guilt that can only conceive of liberation in an escape from all existence.

We must ask what, then, of the protohero? When he broke out and blasted the hypnocracies, did he wreck all society and leave

[a] The five stages of consciousness are gone through by all mankind. But, as Carleton Coon has indicated, it is more likely than not that Homo sapiens has emerged out of Homo erectus not once but five times. The starting up of man's social heredity, therefore, could have taken place five times. Therefore, at least five different times men may have emerged from group coconsciousness. And, next, most of these entered the protoself-consciousness of heroic barbarism, "gangsterics." Some of these types, however, remained arrested in a set balance of inner and outer, of psyche and economy: for example, fossil societies such as were still found in the *culs de sac* of inner Australia and Papua. In turn, some of those in heroicism did not go on into the total individualism of modern man. The greater part of Africa is still arrested in the psyche limits of the chief-led tribe. The talk now fashionable in the cosmopolitan democracies about Africa and Papua being "swept in a decade from the Stone Age to the Modern Age" is only rhetoric. As Jung put it, and as the behavior of those peoples on whom the imposture of democratic procedure has been pushed clearly indicates, their subconscious is still tribal, not national. In fact, then, their psyche, which is still heroic on top and black-magical at base, is an amalgam of witchcraft crossed with the martial law of a Pretorian-guarded tyrant. In short, the phases of human consciousness are gone through at different times by different social heredities. So while the Roman Empire had by A.D. 200 reached ascetic life rejection, when Patrick, preaching this life-rejecting Romanism, reached Ireland he found the Irish still in heroism.

only a desolation haunted by life-rejecting eremites? Clearly not: there arose city states that were not hypnocracies and, more, nations composed of many cities and their reservoir lands, and, in the end, empires with supercapitals, coordinated provinces. What held these congeries together up to the point when varied races lived subject to one imperial law?

The city states came first and failed first. We see why when we study their psychosocial cohesion. The hero could not continue ruling by the sword, by martial law, by throwing spoil to his gang and holding down, while trying to live off, terror-stricken serfs. For example, the Homeric hero has to marry the daughter of the priest-king he had murdered and she, in turn, carrying out the ancient law of magic, kills him as soon as he is helpless and unarmed: for example, Agamemnon, Homer's King of men, is murdered by Clytemnestra, with the aid of her native lover, Aegistheus. They, in turn, are killed by her son.

The blood feud continues until sacred kingship is replaced by an armed oligarchy alternating with brief spells of democracy. This mutual private convenience holds in uneasy consent-of-advantage the tiny territory where the mobile tribe gang had grounded. These minute groups were so weak in psychic cohesion that they could not extend fibriles of common loyalty to their fellow racists, men of the same blood, tongue, mores, and religion.

Neither in Sumeria nor in Greece did the city states, so vivid in curiosity about the outer world and so ingenious in ordering that world, succeed in making any psychosocial federalization with their companions. On the contrary, in both areas they fought each other till they fell prey to outer forces, which imposed order, though never consent.[b]

In short, the city state remained psychosocially merely a lakelet, a bright puddle left where the torrent of heroic barbarian invasion, as its force was spent, settled into these sundered pools. Their drama was arrested at tragedy, their art fixed at the age of adolescent

[b] See Henri Frankfort (26), *The Birth of Civilization in the Near East,* on the Sumerian stubborn clinging to an autonomy as blind as that of the Hellenic anarchy.

athleticism, their religion set at a polytheistic anthropomorphism, their philosophy caught and frozen in skeptical pessimism (for example, the Socratic elenche) on which hard ice there shimmers an other-worldly idealism (Platonism).

The next stage, the nation, did better. We see it, at present, best illustrated by Egypt's record. Here are the first predynastic hypnocracies: the Badarian, Tasian, Gersean. And here we see the first signs of the attempt to construct social cohesion, to match technical advance in the know how with an equally advanced concept of the know why. As there increased the critical mind, which produced improved technics, there had to be answered, more definitely, the newly emerging questions as to values, purposes, goals. The master invention or composition made by the social psychological thinkers in the Realm of Ends was the Abydos mythos. Therein a frame of reference and an avenue of comprehension were provided that would hold an increasingly technicalized and granularized population in a condition of consent, the good goal of each person interpretatively balanced with the good state of the whole society.

The equation held in poise nature, society, and the separate soul. Osiris, the fertile earth whose sister is Isis the moon, has coitus with her while he lies buried, and from this fertilization is born Ra, the sun, who manifests himself as the Light that is righteousness, the Hawk, which is the all-seeing eye, and the reigning Pharoah, who incarnates as the presiding man-god.

With amazingly sustained ingenuity millennium after millennium the priesthood extended this right, of the increasing number of those who became self-conscious, to be granted personal immortality. While at the same time they, with a corresponding control, kept the Pharaoh arrested as a priest-king. His nails and hair, his bodily functions—coitus and elimination—and his every activity were all under constant priestly surveillance and control. On occasion he would break out with a band of the priests' armed guard. But even Tutmoses the Third's great venture was no more than a giant raid. Egypt was a holy nation. Its mana could be made to endure along the Nile. Its great mythos with its cohesive power was for Egyptians alone. It had no purchase on mankind in general.

What, then, does Egypt show us in regard to psychological evolution, in respect of that great curve of intensifying consciousness which is the invisible field precipitating the five great frames of reference in which and through which mankind has successively lived?

It shows that there have been occasions when the horde leader could be arrested before, having smashed the hypnocracy, his destructive rage of frustration turned in on himself and he went eremite. The destruction of the priest-kingly matriarchate by the Achaean northern invaders in Greece and the Greek Islands (for example, Crete) was thorough enough to leave, as we have seen, only midget, mutually repellant, and internally disruptive city states.[c]

In Egypt, however, the consent-producing, obedience-enforcing mythos was of sufficiently tough elastic to net the fighter and reduce him to the form and function of a priest-king. The retiarius-priest won against the gladiator-king.

Still, although Egypt was a nation and it did master the anarchy of city statism, it could not spread to an empire.

We must ask, then, this question: If heroism, with its mores drawn from the fighting epic, resulted on occasion in the Hellenic city state, and if that unit was, inevitably, politically unviable and psychologically unstable; if heroism, when it was captured by a priest-kingly myth, was able to be turned into an amalgam of social suggestion (religious hypnosis) and military control and this made a Nile nationalism enduring some three millennia: What is the amalgam that produced empire?

The first empire, the Persian, is made of the military and the mana alloy. But as it is to embrace, keep in communication,[d] and in considerable liberty, a number of different nations, Cyrus and his successors are not reduced back to priest-kings. Instead of a king

[c] The city state of Athens shows in its history that an aboriginal element survived in the population; and that syncretism gave some mana of consent through the female God Athena and her synoecistic rites.

[d] The first great highway in history is the one that the Persians built from Persepolis to Ephesus, a distance of one thousand miles.

of two natures, there was made a constitution of two authorities, a binary system in which the system of laws was always called the Laws of the Medes and Persians. In this partnership the Medes, though the Persians had conquered them, were nevertheless always mentioned first. For they were the magicians, the society of magic and mana.[e]

So the striking power of the Persian military machine was hilted and sheathed in what alone could produce consent, the seer's authority. Meanwhile both partners in the administration of their rule had back of them the Zoroastrian cosmological ethic in which the ruler was the armed servant of Ormuz, the Light of Righteousness, and all this servant's wars are in the name of this Light, and to push back the Darkness Ahriman.

The psychological history of the Roman Empire illustrates the same problem. The Imperator first known as master of the legions cannot sustain his authority with his forces demobilized. Hence, when Julius Caesar crossed the Rubicon into the homeland of Rome with his legions still under arms and so, by breaking the law of security of the government from a general's coup d'état, showing himself wholly dependent on violence, he had to seek for the psychological sanction of kingship. This move being checkmated by assassination, his successor Augustus has to combine with his control of the army the office of chief priest (the Pontifex Maximus) and when the mana of Roman religion, too debilitated by militarism, was too weak a cohesive, the master of the legions had to be made a god.

The two offices, still failing to make an amalgam, failing not merely to sanction a lawful peace throughout the empire but even to guarantee the god-general from assassination by his own guards, had to be taken apart. The killing of a commander-in-chief by his staff shakes discipline in the army. A god murdered by the army is a blow to all social cohesion, an open invitation to anarchy. The emperor must (as did Cyrus) find a god above the battle, a ruler of Heaven whose agent on earth is the commander-in-chief. Hence, Constantine's shrewd pact with the Christian church. Its mana was

[e] The Greeks regarded the Persians as more than half magicians by virtue of this partnership.

just strong enough to make it able not to submit to flat coercion but to hold out until the purchase price offered it power to use the state to destroy its religious rivals while the state, in turn, used it to help crush political revolt.

The end of the empire was, therefore, postponed, its deliquescence extended. For what mana the church had was already ascetic, life-denying, society-deserting. The heroic barbarians' relentless invasion steadily encroached, while, internally, bureaucratic corruption debased the currency and ruined credit, and while slave labor under the whip exhausted agriculture.

In the end, as the barbarians now manned the legions, inevitably and soon these heroic-level fighters move in with a king of their own kind. The transitional phase between paranoid hero and schizoid ascetic is over. Monasteries and militarists, celibate, anathema-loaded bishops and loose-breeding, sword-wielding chieftains divide loyalty and provoke anarchy. This confusion endures until this alloy of other-worldly dreams for the sensitive, with this-worldly gains for the tough, leads to the uneasy balance of crude, crescent nationalism with decrescent, ghostly cosmopolitanism, that is, the Holy Roman Empire.

At last the psychic conflict is resolved. The inconsistency of a combination of practicality and ideality in which both are compromised is abandoned. Man, seeking for a force more apt than clumsy violence and a relationship subtler and stronger than dogma, therefore concentrated on means and immediacy. And so he finds that not only do his powers multiply but his sense of independence is made clearly conscious and manifest. Modern man, the fully self-conscious individual, depending on reason (measurement), intelligence (choice), experiment, and critical analysis has appeared. The fourth type of consciousness has emerged.[1]

---

[1] The modern age itself divides into four epochs. Four convulsive revolutions are its specific symptom and so it should be called the age of revolutions. Now that the age is over, "modern," we can see, is not a descriptive term. These revolutions are caused by the frame of reference (the realm of ends, the subconscious keel or trough of meaning, of know why) not being kept in balance with (not going along with and so not bearing) the realm of

The initial aspect of the first revolution took place in physics (for revolutions always begin in the mind) (42). When the physics of the Church (for example, the Aristotelian geocentricity) was challenged the ecclesiastical revolution resulted.

The second revolution was when polity (sociology, social heredity, civil law) challenged the traditional law (for example, the theory of the divine right of kings). The result of this was the political revolution.

The third was in economics. The principles of laissez faire, private enterprise, and free trade challenged mercantilism-capitalism. This complex of ideas then found *itself* challenged by biology. Darwinianism, the natural selection idea of evolution, refuted not only the Adam Smith concept of human nature (with its concept that free enterprise would of itself lead to general wealth and happiness) but also struck at the basis of the political revolution, equality of man.

Today, we are in the psychological revolution, the fourth and last which, of necessity, ends the modern age. For now the critical mind seeking objectivity has to turn on itself in order to examine the instrument whereby it attempts to define objects. First, finding that it has confined itself to such an instrument ("Nothing can be in the mind unless it is first in the senses") the human intelligence next arrives at the conclusion that this instrument itself is strictly

---

means, the conscious sail or crest of powers. Through the Middle Ages the political deadlock of priest and king, of secular nation state and holy church universal, at least allowed some slight adjustment of inherited values with observed data (for example, the relaxation of the tabu of usury, and the ruling as to what was a just rate of interest, and the approval by Pope Clement IV (1265) of Roger Bacon's chemical researches and study of scientific procedure). Indeed, it grows increasingly evident that with the steady infiltration of Arab scientific work, which arose from their study of Aristotle, the eleventh, twelfth, and thirteenth centuries were more open to physical discovery than was the fourteenth. Later scholasticism offered only a rigid syllogistic resistance to discoveries. Hence, the keel was dropped, the matrix left behind. Natural knowledge, study of the outer world, rushed ahead. Knowledge of the inner world was arrested and the old theories denied.

confined to select and construct electromagnetic impulses (radiation) to yield the impression of an environment in which and on which an animal can subsist. This psychological insight has led to further developments in the method casually called science.

The first phase of science was threefold, a process of definition, abstraction, and experimentation. In the second phase, while the first and third terms were retained, the mid-term was altered (39). Instead of abstraction, hypothesis is now employed. Abstraction's aim is to build up a proposition, every step and statement of which is based on an already established finding. But, to produce such a confirmed coherence, a certain number of anomalous findings must be excluded to preserve the symmetry of the resulting pattern, for example, the natural law.

Hypothesis, on the other hand, rejects none of the findings. It incorporates them by extrapolation, by placing them in an open-ended system. Instead, then, of tying itself to the pretentious and brittle idea of natural law, hypothesis in this the second phase of the scientific method uses the gauge of probability. By statistically arrived at degrees of probability it establishes the likelihood that by extending investigation in this direction, the anomalous data will be found able to occupy a station in this flexible and enlarging design and, in turn, the data so incorporated will show whether new findings will come to light.

To summarize the answer to the question of why is not the great civilic epoch of man (the age of the creative city states, the inventive nation states, the administrative empire states, an outburst of external activity and mastery) traceable to a specific phase in man's intensifying psyche: this controlled outburst was produced by the transitional combination of a couple of these basic psychological phases.

The hero in decline, the ascetic in ascension; in this conjunction was produced a type of mind still longing for the fame of victorious battle but growing aware that looming up behind the hero's projected image of the Gods of Battles was the vision of an uncapricious, indeflectable law. This hybrid consciousness, this transitional psyche had then either to become the servant of this living law, the executive of righteousness (and this is the frame of reference in which the Chinese and the Western empires sought and found sanction) or, in the longer lasting but smaller societies of the nation, the ruler had to be co-natured with the God.

The Roman emperors' flirtation with deity never became a marriage. For if a man is to be dowered with divinity the inherent God must prove his presence by evidencing his mana. And the more the man-master of the legions uses armed violence the less is it possible to believe he is possessed of any other force. Nothing more thoroughly disproves religion than religious persecution. Egyptian society and the kingship that crowned it lasted longer than any other nation because the Pharaoh was more often and more nearly divine than any emperor, any king, or any pope.

The search for consent, for an uncoercive authority had still to be made by the last supernational empire, that of Napoleon I. When Talleyrand warned that victories won no consent ("Everything can be done with bayonets save to sit on them") and Napoleon ("My cannon can defeat the Austrians but not their hatred of me") then the extreme advice of Sieyes, the constitution maker, alone seemed to offer any settlement. Napoleon had sneered that Austria's claim to the manifest of the Holy Roman Empire was to assert a power that was "neither Holy nor Roman nor an Empire!" But he crowned himself (with the Pope present and giving his blessing) Emperor of the West and claimed for his son, by the daughter of the Austrian emperor, the title that the son and heir of the Holy Emperor had by right of birth: the King, not of Paris or Aix-la-Chapelle (Aachen, the capital of Charlemagne), but of Rome.

In spite of all these efforts to reprecipitate loyalty, Bonaparte's empire lasted only that dozen years (1800–1812) that marked Alexander's and Ghengis'. Certainly, modern man, humanic man, could not solve the problem of human cohesion, the issue of a nonviolent cosmopolitanism. And it is clear why this psychological adhesive, this organic binding is lacking.

For the cosmos that modern cosmopolitan man postulated was

a machine, and the only ethic deducible from a cosmo-machine is (as we have seen) that which regards man as a machine and his behavior as not intentional but imprinted, a series of imposed conditioned reflexes. Not only are intention, purpose, and responsibility dismissed, but consciousness itself is denied.

As a historical fact, as the analytic-critical method of the primary form of the science process increased in its capacity to break things down and so to multiply means, plurify power, and accelerate transit, the units of psychosocial consent, the limits of loyalty, of spontaneous cohesion, have as rapidly shrunken. All empires are in ruins and where the primary scientific method was most forwarded (the states around the North Sea), as indeed had happened before with the first, the Hellenic, outburst of science, the wider the thought the more cramped the feeling. Scandinavia is divided in four pieces; the Netherlands into three—and, with Belgium splitting, would, if self-determination was not coerced, be in four, the fourth being the Walloons. Let choose, three nations (Esthonia, Latvia, Lithuania) emerged round the southeast of the Baltic. Left free to choose, Alsace and Lorraine would secede from Germany or from France. France itself would be in pieces if a fanatic out of the thirteenth century did not coerce her. Even small anachronisms such as Ireland, fixated on an anarchic past (an angry alloy of guilt-haunted heroes and mortificatory ascetics), has its northeast section, Ulster, seceded from it.

B

ON FURTHER DIRECTION OF

PSYCHOPHYSICAL EVOLUTION

It may seem strange that our present brand of prophets—the authors of our modern apocalypses, the writers of science fiction—have not availed themselves of present biological views as to man's indicated future and the potentialities in him by which he may attain it, although some of them have been biologically informed. The process of neoteny through fetalization and paidomorphy has been recognized for almost a generation. Louis Bolk, the outstanding Dutch anatomist, named the process forty years ago. And the same process was recognized by Max Hilzheimer (45) in his essay "The Dog: the Foetalization of the Wolf." H. G. Wells, one of the great popularizers of science, gathered a worldwide audience with his *Outline of History*. Then in his *The Science of Life*, published about thirty-five years ago, he introduced the lay reading public to Louis Bolk's conception of "man, the foetalization of the ape."

Let us grant that every stage in the advance of life has been due to fetalization; this has been stated in minimal terms by Cope in his "law of the survival of the unspecialized." Let us also grant that with man this process of the neotenic extension of generalized form and function, physique and behavior, has added to the infancy stage (which no reptile has) the stage of childhood; it has added to the fetalistic postbirth stage the stage of the paidomorph. Then we may say, as Haldane had said, that man will now begin, must begin, to add a still further extension of his retention of generalization. In short, the man of tomorrow, the man we must have as the only type that is psychophysically adequate to handle our psychochemical powers, must be as much the paidomorph of the man of today as man today is the paidomorph of the apes.

The person of the future who will carry on and keep the social heredity up to date, who will make a constantly expanding interpretation of a constantly expanding knowledge, must have the child's freedom of association and curiosity. He will find delight both in new facts and in making new sense of those facts.

It is out of such a type that a completely contemporary form of the seer can spring. Every epoch of mankind has required and produced this type. The magician of the cave culture, the herald-bard-prophet of the heroic epoch, the mystic-contemplative of the ascetic age, the scholar-sage of the humanic era,[a] no period has been wholly without that specific discerner of standards, that designer of values, that framer of the prestige pattern that directs endeavor, molds enterprise, canalizes energy, shapes behavior, and instructs taste.

Today, our convulsive culture is subconsciously aware of this need. Our very desire to keep young, our pathetic effort to remain juvenile is a symptom of our blind reaction to a deficiency disease caused by the loss of purpose and coordinant drive in the way we now live. Still and all, and certainly in the light of such an interpretation of man's history as I have tried to outline in this discussion, we can propose an aim. We can suggest the type of man who

[a] In the West the scholar becomes the pedant, or at best a specialist, and is despised as an egghead that does not even hatch out atom power. Only in China did this type become authoritative.

could be the pattern of prestige for this leptoid age. However, to suggest a pattern of prestige is not to say that everyone must attain to it. An orchestra cannot be composed solely of first violins. Indeed, the more human life advances the more it gives rise to variety. And this variegation is strengthening because variety increases the capacity for multiform enquiries and responses.

The pattern of prestige has always been a theme, a leitmotif, around which and on which man, with an ever growing orchestrational capacity, could compose symphonies out of a constantly enlarging experience. Besides this there is another factor of variety that is perceptible in human history. From earliest times, from the crystallization out of the coconscious, two possible modes of human conduct seem to have been recognized. In the ascetic epoch they were called the Precepts of Universal Obligation and the Counsels of Perfection. The precepts are the five natural moral laws. They are to be observed at least up to the standard of justice by everyone, and up to the standard of equity by those in control of the group's policy.[b] This means that the two basic classes of society, the maintenance men and the inventors, the applied researchers and the pure researchers, the routineers and the pioneers, are in a constant reciprocal relationship; a relationship as close as the lichen symbiosis in which a fungus (which finds its purchase and nourishment on a rock) and an alga (which feeds on air) combine together to form a single living organism.

Future human evolution, therefore, would be marked by three characteristics. First, there will be a tendency for increasing psychophysical generalization of each constituent of human society. Secondly, there will be an increasing tendency toward a racial fanning out into a variety of these unspecialized types. And, thirdly, there will be an increasing width of qualities of consciousness, of apprehension and comprehension. We now have a number of arts, such as music and poetry for the ear; painting, ceramics, and sculpture for the eye; dancing and gymnastics for the body. But we may

[b] For a detailed analysis and interpretation of the five natural moral laws see *The Eternal Gospel*, The Ayer Foundation lectures given at Colgate Rochester Seminary by Gerald Heard (43) in 1945.

develop new arts for, say, scent, taste, and touch. We may develop new sciences in sensory detection, extrasensory perception, and integral thought.

In brief, the really possible Utopia would be this world experienced by a psychophysique at full aperture.

C

ON THE CATACLYSMIC CHARACTER OF
THE SUCCESSIVE EPOCH CHANGES

From a study of the places where each of the four epochs in man's history ended, and of the time when each of these epochs ended and its successor rose to power, it would seem that every epoch first begins in a particular area and then spreads until its influence is felt, sooner or later, throughout the Eurasian land mass and in Africa. The heroic epoch seems to have taken on its specific pattern of culture (its epic ideals and its phobias, its mobility and its destructiveness; its exercises and its additions) when the hold of the originally coconscious society had become arthritic. That is to say, what had first been unquestioning submission to an immemorial tradition, which had its own millennial growth, was now repression under a rigid penalty-laden social structure.

This hardened legalization of tradition seems to have taken place first in the Near East, where writing and mathematics first emerged. It provoked the mobile-minded to move out onto the new grasslands that were appearing north of the Caucasus, there to cultivate horsemanship, and finally, in the second phase of the heroic ages, to depend on a pastoralist rather than an agricultural economy. Therefore, this heroic culture could, because of its mobility, diffuse itself to the limits of the great Eurasian-African plains.[a]

In turn, the ascetic movement seems to have arisen in the upper basin of the Ganges about 750 B.C.[b] and thence to have spread, by a series of missionary waves, west, north, and east. At first they were disciplinary. In their second phase they were mortificatory. By the time (510 B.C.) that Cyrus, the founder of the Persian Empire, had extended his frontiers to the Indus, Indian asceticism (disciplinary controls of the appetite), quickly to be followed by Indian mortification (the denial of appetites), could spread to the Mediterranean. Thirdly, when in the fifteenth century A.D. the ascetic prestige pattern was challenged, the rise of humanic man takes place in Italy. In its initial stage of rational and critical individualism it spread through Europe. In the nineteenth century humanic rational criticism becomes materialism and materialistic economics. In this form it spread, and is still spreading, throughout the world.

Fourthly, in this century in the arc of culture stretching from Scandinavia (through Germany, Austria, Lombardy, and France) to Britain, the leptoid, postobjective complex of concepts and praxes has superseded the humanic total individualism. Certainly, the speed

[a] For example, the Greek heroic figure of the winged horse, Pegasus, is found in high relief on the back of Chinese bronze mirrors.

[b] However, Dodds (19) thinks it may have started with a shamanistic culture on the steppes north of the Oxus Sea. (See Appendix D.) It is true that arctic hysteria may have abetted this ascetic movement among migrant Mongolians, some of whom may have brought the doctrine of denial down to the Indus and Ganges headwaters. (A Mongolian skull was dug up in the ruins of Mohenjo Daro.) To date, however, it seems somewhat more probable that a heroic culture, having come up against one that was sophisticated and discouraged—for example, the Aryans meeting the Dravidian culture in the Ganges basin—would turn from shame and projected anger to guilt and self-blame, and that some such inner-seer as Gautama (the Kshatrya who, though an Aryan, became a Buddha) would be one of the launchers of the doctrine of denial.

of ideational change seems to be spastic, or perhaps one should say mutational. Right back to the sudden rise, on the lower Nile, of the Pharaohonic civilization out of the pre-Dynastic cultures, we note this increasing abruptness of change.

As to the position of the scholar-sage, his lack of authority in the Renaissance and his extraordinary prestige in China, let us first look at him in the West. Here we can find four reasons for his ineffectiveness. (1) He was purely a literary, concerned with the resuscitation of a dead language: Greek. (2) The Churchmen still claimed all psychological authority. (3) The natural philosophers, the incipient scientists, claimed all authority in the fields of research and experimentation. And (4) the apparatus of scholarship, meanwhile, was totally inept as an instrument whereby to initiate a psychological therapy.

We can account for the Chinese sages' failure to achieve a Renaissance because of their indifference to psychology and their disregard of physics and physiology. The Chinese heroic age did enter on an ascetic phase with the introduction of Indian Buddhism. The sage culture, however, kept the alien asceticsm in check. Therefore (according to C. C. Chang) in China it is to Taoism and Mahayana Buddhism that we must look for a psychophysical underground that carries on a cryptic practice based on an esoteric doctrine.

ON THE EVIDENCE FOR AN ESOTERIC MYSTERY TRADITION IN THE WEST AND ITS POSTPONEMENT OF SOCIAL DESPAIR

Because of their very nature the ways of an underground are exceedingly difficult to trace. History, it has been said, is documentation. But secret sects keep their records hidden; proscribed heresies destroy theirs. Yet on the Scilly Isles it has been possible to prove that the present Little Archipelago is a series of hilltops (that were left after the original single island submerged) through the discovery that roads starting on one islet, and going under the sea, may be found emerging on another shore on the further side of the sundering strait. So in history we can make similar tracings.

The rise of the ascetic, life-rejecting religions meant the persecution and repression of the libidinal life-accepting religions. The heroic protoindividual had not liked them. His creed was that of a male fighter who sacrificed the victims of his victories to his warrior God. Blood and flesh were the sacraments fit for a masculine God of Battles. The heroic blood-shedder denounced the gentle religion of the matriarchies and its beliefs and rites: its sacraments of milk and semen, of life foods that were given willingly and not torn from a murdered fellow man. He denounced it as unclean; and often, when looting these industriously wealthy societies, massacred its peaceful practitioners.

But persistent persecution, cruel inquisition, and crueler punishment were the uglier behaviors of the midindividual, whose eroticism was more acute than that of the protoindividual and whose guilt-motivated cruelty was also greater.

It is probably at this point that the mysteries began to be concealed. In the forcing house of the Nile we know that at a certain time the idols were broken. This is when individualism had developed beyond the protoindividual level in the ruler and his associates. Aknaton, the weak, has been married to Nerfertiti, the strong, blue-eyed daughter of the far northern Mitanni Kings whose steppe religion had rid itself of images. But the statues of the gods were again set up in the swift reaction that followed. However, one former prime favorite was omitted. This was Min, the god of fertility, whose images were phallic. After that, initiation became a specifically secret thing. And it became secret not because, as formerly, the unitive state of mind (the condition of coconsciousness) *cannot* be expressed in the increasingly concrete terms of a language that is becoming one of separative definitions. These states where the new antagonism of mind and body was banished *must* not be spoken about. For the new schizoid dogma rules that spirit must always be at war with its enemy, flesh. Soon then, in the West, there was no place in the open daylight world for the unitive mysteries. Even in India, the original mysteries that refused to be asceticized had, in the end, to be concealed.

India has certainly had an esoteric underground. Since the Mohammedan invasions in the fourteenth century, Islam, a puritan religion, began to persecute Tantra. And finally Akbar, the great Mogul who controlled a large portion of the peninsula, although he was tolerant of other cults (mainly because Brahmanism had become almost as prudish as Islamism) made persistent drives to stamp out this ancient life religion.

China, too, has had its secret methods in Taoism. Arthur Waley feels sure that back of the gnomic paradoxes of the *Tao Te Ching* is a yoga technique of training consciousness by psychophysical exercises. The most famous of its absurdities—those who know don't say and those who say don't know—is not meant to stultify all exchange of knowledge. It is to point out that the Way is not to be found through rational information. Exercises, not propositions, open the mind, permit it to see the way things truly are, and to go along that path of illumined understanding (95).

But it was in the West that repression was the most fierce and persecution was set on annihilation of the old religion. The Hebrew prophets, whose religion was a blood sacrifice cult, succeeded in making their small, exclusive, and politically unviable people believe that the failure of its attempt to become a great power (or even to survive as a territorial nation) was due to the anger of their tribal god. He was angry because they worshiped divinity in a life symbol of the phallus: the sacred pillar, which the prophets were always cutting down. The prophets were like most persecuting critics. They were far more effective as denouncers than they were as consistent creative instructors. Some of them, such as Jeremiah, declared that Jaweh never did want blood sacrifices. Behave ethically, they said, and all will turn out well. It didn't. But of course it was possible to say that if only the moral standard had been high enough then it would have. Other prophets (for example, Malachi who concludes the book of the canonized seers) maintain that if the blood sacrifices are kept up then Jaweh will fulfill his promises of national glory for his people. Nevertheless, although the sacrifices were kept going the Jews lost, for more than two thousand years, the land they coveted.

After the final destruction of Jerusalem under Hadrian, the Jews seemed to have taken to the psychology of the day. They were known, employed, and feared as magicians. The cabala is viewed with almost as much disfavor by orthodox Judaism as was the witch cult by medieval Catholicism. But these strange texts, containing alchemical-astrological references and purporting to give methods for obtaining power, may refer in cryptic form to psycho-

physical methods for controlling the emotions and altering consciousness (as we shall see in a moment with contemporary Greek writings
of the second century).

Like the ethical Jewish prophets, the Greek moral philosophers
also began their thinking with the assumption that the moral law
was self-evident and self-rewarding. *Dike,* justice, is of the nature
of things; and man, being a reasonable creature, is sensible enough
to follow such an advantageous way of life. Protagoras, like Confucius, believed that virtue could be taught; that the emotions were
as open to argument and as influenced by logic as was the reason
itself. Then a profound change came about.

Until lately, it was generally supposed that the Greeks were
"the young, light-hearted masters of the waves," alien to pessimism
and despising asceticism. It was thought that although in India the
Indo-European culture, after going through the Heroic Age (of the
Vedas), arrived at the Ascetic Age, this did not befall the other
Aryan culture, that of the Achaean Greeks. We now know that this
is untrue. The true Greek Heroic Age, the age that so named itself,
was that late Bronze Age (1000 B.C.), which Homer made un-
forgettable. This age was boyish (as was that of the Vedas) with
its boisterous gods. But its unreflective nor-adrenaline culture,
whose one check was shame, not guilt,[a] did not last. The age that
succeeded it (the Archaic or Helladic), whose poet was to be
Hesoid and which was to be given its final summation in the
archaistic drama of Sophocles, has already exchanged shame for
guilt and in its inmost conviction is as life-fearing as Buddhism.[b]

With Socrates, what budded as poetic despair and flowered as
dramatic tragedy fruits in logical discussion leading toward intellectual skepticism and individual emotional detachment. And with
Socrates we reach a dividing of the ways. He still believes that
reason can guide a man so that he will live righteously. He refuses
to be initiated into the mysteries. But he finds that he has to listen

[a] Even *aidos,* as Dodds points out, though it has in it a certain sense of
"We are all mortal," has in it even more "What will the neighbors say?"
[b] For instance, the final comment of Sophocles is "Only truly blessed is he
that never was born."

to a daimon, an inner preterrational voice whose rulings must be obeyed. Further, and most significantly, this arresting conscience is negative. It never tells him what to do; it vetoes what he thought of doing. And he reported that it was totally silent when, at his final crisis, he had to decide whether to flee or to die.

These items in the life of a man who was so largely decisive in causing the division between cosmology and morals, between science and religion, are highly informative. For it would seem that the mysteries offended the good sense (the rationalism) and probably the moral sense (the sexual repression) of a mind that was already sundered into a logical intelligence and an emotional subconscious, and so subject to further psychic inhibitions (the daimon voice). Hence Greek philosophy, instead of trying to understand them, tried to reject and repress the irrational and emotional. And so, cut off from creative integral thought, Greek thought became skeptical. Phaedo, and Pyrrho after him, establish the Eleatic School of complete skepticism, derived from Socrates' *elenchos*.

Though then Socrates is still mainly a rationalist, both his skeptical method of argument and his own awareness of his interior preterrational guide (his daimon) show that thinking men are becoming aware that there is something in nature and in human nature that may require more insight than common sense (the rational use of the five senses) can provide. Still they remain individualistic puritans, fearing their dark side and the unlit aspect of nature. So they rejected the mysteries, (1) because the mysteries taught (and their practitioners understood intuitively) that that dark side of one's self is dreadful only if repressed; if it is expressed it will add its energy to creative living. (2) Because the mysteries kept the panaesthetic rites going and these were shocking to the rational puritan. Thus the mysteries had to become esoteric.

However, this doubt as to the adequacy of the five senses to provide human nature with sufficient insight was made explicit by Plato, Socrates' pupil, interpreter, and fulfiller. He saw also that such skepticism was doubly perilous. It must excite the mob to one of two evils: either to lynching the enquirer or to personal license. Also it would paralyze the intelligentsia. As Plato remarked to

Phaedo (his fellow pupil under Socrates, and the founder of the school of complete skepticism), he cleared the ground but never built. A razed site only invites erosion. Because he was socially concerned, Plato's own teaching therefore became increasingly esoteric. The wise, The Guardians, must know, not only intellectually but also by direct experience; they must have been initiated. And further, they must be repeatedly refreshed by being given direct knowledge of that intuitive world which is not comprehended in those biological states of mind-body consciousness that are all the unenlightened man can know. E. R. Dodds (19), in his valuable volume *The Greeks and the Irrational,* traces in Plato's mind this realization that there had to be a secret doctrine and that this esoteric teaching was more than rational information. It had to change conduct, character, and consciousness. For, if it did not, then society would cleave asunder into an ineffective curd-film of rational culture afloat on a sour whey of superstition, with the cream finally being swallowed up in the fermenting sludge. Dodds gives good reason to suppose that Plato in his extremity[c] came across the Pythagoreans in South Italy or Sicily about 390 B.C. From them he borrowed much of their psychophysical system to propose a method of training for that level of character which we now call the unconscious or semiconscious emotional life. Dodds believes that this method of training, or Plato's adaptation of it, is the foundation of the esoteric social structure that Plato describes in *The Republic* and further accentuates in *The Laws.* The Guardians of the State, it seems clear, were to undergo some regime that would do much more than inform their intelligences and confirm their self-assurance. They would be shaped in their inner man, as Paul of Tarsus puts it. Or in our current language, their semiconscious and subconscious emotional life would be given profound, character-molding suggestion therapy.

That the actual procedure would be kept secret would not have surprised the Greek world or awakened suspicion. The vow of absolute secrecy was always imposed by all the mysteries and, as far

[c] Socrates having been killed, himself in voluntary banishment, his thought facing this sphinx question.

as we know, kept by the initiates. Plato, however, seems never to have put his scheme into practice. His mind appears to have been too grandiose. For him nothing would serve but a recreated oligarchic Athens set in the amber of his eloquence; or a Syracuse over which he would rule through his vicar, the tamed tyrant Dionysius. He was incurably political, high-handedly impatient of experiment and research. That Plato's great mind never rid itself of the pre-Alexandrine Greek dependence on *a priori* argument (and so the fatal disregard of controlled experimentation) accounts partly for his limitations; and, added to his aristocratic contempt for the common people, it goes far to explain his practical failure. However, there was a defeatism in his emotional life. The Pythagorean movement is the rise of asceticism in the West, the appearance of guilt (instead of shame) as the driving force and the sense that man is a creature who has fallen into a lower world. Empedocles, the Sicilian philosopher (c. 490–430 B.C.) who certainly was influenced by Pythagorianism, is the first Greek thinker to denounce marriage and all sex. At heart Plato could hardly feel that it was worthwhile spending one's life in an attempt to understand this misapprehended world through the misshapen instrument of our fallen state of mind. His fastidious puritanism made him regard the two horses of the soul's chariot as being really irreconcilable, and feel that the only hope lay in the white horse drawing the chariot up into heaven while the black one flung itself down into the Pit.

His great pupil and contrast, Aristotle, did make a start toward the experimental psychology that would have no prejudices but only make observations.[d] He was clearly interested in man's non-rational psyche and concerned that, through empiric study, its nature should be understood and its cooperation enlisted. Most unfortunately (and most probably this was the basic reason for the final collapse of Hellenic Roman civilization) Aristotle's proposals for this vital study were never followed up. By 200 B.C. the fatal division had taken place: the natural sciences (special study of the working of the outer world and what Kant called "The

[d] See page 239, *The Greeks and the Irrational* by Dodds (19).

Realm of Means") confined themselves to objective phenomena. These students of molar physics naturally accepted, increasingly, the handy hypothesis of mechanism as being in fact the universal law of materialism. And they accepted the even handier and more dubious assumption that our senses, as we use them, present us with a wholly objective world. When from mathematics, physics, and astronomy such scientists went to physiology, the notion that the body also was a machine, or at best a chemical still, could hardly be avoided.

On the other hand, "The Realm of Ends" was left to the professional specialized philosopher who used logic and rhetoric to convince the mind and inspire the emotions. As Dodds (19) remarks, "After Empedocles the seer and the naturalist fell apart."[e] Zeno and Chrysippus are the two thinkers who shape Stoic thought (from 304 to 205 B.C.) and make popular, with all men of character, a pattern of prestige: the Stoic philosopher who was to rule the conscience, and at times the law and legions, of the Roman world. But certainly these vastly influential founding fathers of intellectual nobility have no concept of psychophysical or psychological training. They are simple rationalists[f] and hence, as Toynbee and others have pointed out, at the end the Stoics have a frankly materialistic cosmology.

It was inevitable, therefore, that neo-Platonism should return to the problem of psychology and to this question: If our present focal length of consciousness gives a highly inaccurate picture of things and an inadequate insight into ourselves, could there be any methods whereby we might apprehend reality more accurately and conduct ourselves better?

Plotinus is, of course, not only an ascetic, not only one who regards this world as being at best a therapeutic prison.[g] He is also an ecstatic. And he values these experiences of ecstasy not only as being much more convincing than argument but as having a much

[e] See page 146 of *The Greeks and the Irrational*.
[f] See page 239 of *The Greeks and the Irrational* by Dodds (19).
[g] He would not allow his birthday to be observed, remarking that the less said about such a painful date the better.

more efficacious effect on character. However, he does not know nor, as far as we can learn, does he investigate in order to know, how these highly desired, transforming states might be regularly obtained.

Plotinus was suspicious of anything that might degenerate into magic. He did not despise method. He thought that music and mathematics were good preparations for philosophy. He certainly wished to explore, but it is surely going beyond our data about him, and the limits which we know he set himself, to say as Geffcken says, "he investigates." True, he attended a seance but with almost the aloofness with which Ramakrishna is said to have sat out, in trance, a Tantra performance. It seems more just to say that if specifically ethical philosophy flowered with Socrates and its stoic fruit fully set in the Meditations of Marcus Aurelius, then with Plotinus' *Enneads* the condensed and mature kernel was formed from which sprang the tree of medieval monastic contemplation. Socrates served as a soldier-citizen; Marcus Aurelius ruled as a philosopher-Emperor. By Plotinus' time the thinking world is ready for the cloister where, protected from the raw actualities of social life, the thinker, by contemplation, seeks in trance to make the "flight of the alone to the Alone." Philosophy had come to where it could only teach escape. The natural sciences had for three centuries (200 B.C.–A.D. 100) found increasingly that understanding of nature and power over the environment were obtained by regarding the universe as a vast machine. No wonder that when the only two possible choices seemed to be "flee to the dear fatherland" (heaven) or "clear your mind of cant, you and all mankind are basically beasts, conscious automata," nearly everyone thought that man is a pawn of fate and that human nature cannot be changed.

And yet society did go on; and though the structure of the state collapsed, a concealed, re-enforcing network of community endured. There was a minority that neither ran away to the desert nor threw away the armor of its soul. Epicurus had probably been right in expressing his contempt for culture. The oxide of pedantry was spreading over the bright intelligence of scholarship. The pursuit of learning regardless of significance was stultifying understanding. His ironic dismissal of natural science unless it can yield knowledge that helps men attain to Ataraxy, the God's eye view of complete objectivity, is also comprehensible.

To put it mildly, to what end (and certainly our age is asking this question) if natural science gives us the power to flash all matter into energy and we are still subject to passions that make us stampede like panic-stricken beasts? The Stoics were even more anxious, and their success in winning politically powerful recruits made them more concerned, to have a system that would unfailingly give *apatheia,* invulnerability. These keepers of the consciences of proconsuls and emperors actually opposed, and helped largely to get rejected, the heliocentric view of the cosmos for fear that this larger cosmology would disturb their system of arguments, the proofs they adduced for the truth of their philosophy.

Yet we know that their systems of discipline, and those of the Epicureans, were painfully inadequate. Epicureanism sank to be synonymous with hedonism and Stoicism shrank until it was indistinguishable from despair. But we also know that the men who had to keep law and order going (and to fight a rear action with the military system to prevent the legions from becoming leeches on a citizenry that was losing any right to deserve protection) did find a mystery, a masonry, to hold themselves together. After the second century A.D., Mithraism is the cult of the decent army man. Its shrines are found all over the Empire, wherever the Legions were encamped. We do know that it used the limited environment, for the initiation took place underground. There was then the grotto-grave: an earth rite. There was also baptism; and to add to what does not seem to have been a real immersion that could produce some degree of shock, there appears to have been, in most cases at least, the *taurobolium.* The postulant was laid in a grave over which were placed hurdles. As he lay underneath, a bull that had been made to kneel on the hurdles was stabbed and its blood poured down over him. Whether this produced temporary suffocation we do not know. There is even a hint of possible fire worship, in that Mithra himself was in origin a lesser Persian god, a being identified with the Sun by a people that already for some centuries were specific fire worshipers. The use of blood and the forgiveness of sins show, however, that this was a guilt religion with puritan morality and repression techniques. Hence, though it could postpone social collapse, the energy was released only by repression, not generated by cocharging. So Mithraism failed and was superseded by a religion that was confessedly other-worldly, with an acuter sense of guilt, a fanatic hate-fear toward all who did not submit to its view of things and an obsessional belief in blood as the one defense against eternal damnation. Under Christianity the Roman Hellenic world sank into night.

At this point, where in the vestiges of a civilization whose intelligence was about to hibernate must we look for the rudiments of a psychology and psychiatry? The place seems to be in the queer tangle of what is known as theurgy. Theurgy was the name for certain practices through which contact with God could be obtained. The word appears to have been chosen by a certain Julianus who lived between A.D. 150 and 200. He was quite rightly weary of theologians, people who argued about God. He "worked upon the Divine" and claimed he could manifest That. He was the son of a Chaldean philosopher. Is there any clue given us here, which might suggest why hereabouts could be a possible point where psychophysical methods to contact the subconscious might be detected?

The Chaldeans were the people in whose country (Mesopotamia) astrology had arisen (and so the basis of astronomy had been laid). The great astrological library of Assur-bani-pal, the Assyrian King of the mid-seventh century B.C., clearly seems to be the basis of all Western and Eastern astrology. Its basic system is even back of Chinese astrology. Astrology did not merely chart the heavens and there read man's inevitable fate. Why seek to know what could not be prevented? *The Chaldean Oracles,* which this Julianus issued,[h] are astrological. But it is astrology mixed, as it would seem was all astrology, with alchemy. Every star had its chemical and psychological counterpart; for example, Mercury is

[h] It seems that the text was put into hexameters by Julianus. Here he is following the Greek oracle tradition, for the free association outbursts of the Delphic Pythia were worked up into hexameters before being published.

a star and a metal, and mercurial is a temperament. This, of course, seems pathetic or impudent hocus pocus. Still it is strange that a thinker as important in the neo-Platonic tradition as Proclus should have prized such stuff, saying that theurgy can give "the purifying powers of initiation."[i] And Proclus does give at least one reference that shows he was dealing not only with the illusions of sympathetic magic but (and dangerously) with real biochemistry, with drugs that affect the psychophysique. For he remarks that if the eyes are anointed with strychnine (or even other chemicals) they will see visions. Lately, investigation into the odd but constant association of astrology and alchemy has suggested (through research in the middle term, physiology) a solution for this puzzle. Hidden under the oxide of magical superstition there may be purposely disguised attempts, not always fruitless, to reach the subconscious through psychophysical methods.

In the Indian Hatha Yoga charts of the body (see Chapter 3, Part III) the chakras and lotuses undoubtedly refer to the ductless glands. And all of the Hatha Yoga exercises are directed to arousing them.

The trouble with all such research in the ancient world was threefold: (1) most of the magic was simply mistaken science. Like should lead to like. But obvious likenesses are often misleading. (2) Some research went off on a tangent seeking not to help everyone to make peace with his own inner nature but to find and exploit, for purposes of investigation into hypnosis and extrasensory perception, young persons who easily dissociated (mediums). (3) All these researchers wanted quick results. They had, unhappy seekers, to be in a hurry. The Western civilized world, with its tolerance of ancient religions and its emergent sciences, was going into coma. The orthodox church was becoming increasingly stringent in its demands and increasingly cruel in punishing any deviations. Proclus had to flee. The Eleusinian mysteries are proscribed and Eleusis closed by Justinian's decree. Henceforward, all research must be underground.

[i] The Chaldean oracles contain a prescription for a fire cult, so the word initiation may have been used precisely for the great fourth mystery.

Nevertheless, throughout the Middle Ages we do find occasional references to indicate that an underground did exist. How far the mask of magic was merely a concealment for unorthodox psychophysical investigation and for the employment, however fragmentary, of the five ordeals and initiations, we can never be sure. Nor can we be certain as to how far this mask distorted man's outlook and made him fancy that he could control Nature with spells. However, we can detect two deep currents.

The first is what might be called a back-to-Nature cult. Eusebius, the Church historian who lived when Christianity had risen to imperial power, tells us of the Adamites, a sect that met, literally, underground: a restricted environment. Its members appeared nude at their meetings, maintaining that by grace they had been returned to the primal innocency of unfallen Nature. The Church, having already given up its charitic love feasts (the *agape*) and become ascetic, was highly suspicious of such proceedings. Nevertheless, these methods of panaesthetic cocharging apparently went on.

The Church could not wholly forget its own beginning nor brand these practices as being obviously depraved. At the earliest *agapes* such intense releases were experienced that, as Loisy has said, each Eucharist of the Risen Lord had as its regular sequel a Eucharist of the Paraclete. But this first contagion lessened and in the second phase only special persons, individual *prophetes,* could dissociate. Soon, however, this gift also gave out. Paul had ruled, "I suffer not a woman to speak." Hence there appears the interesting psychic phenomenon of the subintroductae. A *prophetes* (who could no longer go into trance himself) took about with him a young woman whom he hypnotized. From her glossolalia he picked out pertinent passages, passages that were relevant to his message. In the early Christian church this common occurrence of hypnotic practice (it went on until the time of Cyprian, A.D. c. 200–258) had an interesting addition. The *prophetes* and his medium slept together, sharing the same bed, but coitus must not take place. Some such panaesthetic cocharging seems to have been continued by the Adamites. Increasing asceticism in the Church and loss of all psychological interests among a lay folk that was becoming increasingly barbarian probably brought such practices to a standstill and certainly made it impossible for such a cult to leave records.

In Byzantine history itself there are one or two references to magical and possibly psychical research. The eleventh-century author, Michael C. Pellus, mentions such matters. The mask of magic certainly bobs about in the background of the theologically obsessed centuries. The only orthodox way of shifting the focus of consciousness was physical self-violence.[j] Hence any sensation that was not dysphoric was suspect. When the churchmen had time and strength to turn against the various undergrounds that spread beneath the rigid life-rejecting pall of orthodoxy, we know that the two enemies the Church most feared, and so most hated, were the Witch Cult[k] in the north and the Cathars in the south.

The Witch Cult was a simple fertility cult. The legal reports of the witch trials give hints that it may have used a water ordeal. For example, a witch was said to be detectable by her dread of running water, an inability to cross a stream, and also by her power not to drown if thrown into water. (Later, this was naturally misrepresented as the power to float on water.) They also—at least at the midsummer Beltane feast—"went through the fire" by leaping through bonfires, a practice retained in rural Ireland into the nineteenth century. They claimed to be friends of the lightning and they said that Satan appeared in thunderstorms, "glowing, hissing, his fingers shooting sparks"—if you touched him you received a shock.

Some rude knowledge of respiratory and sensory control (tested by water immersion, fire, and electric shock) seems then to be suggested. Unfortunately it seems clear that not only did their principal aim become magical power, and mainly for malignant purposes, but the means was thought to be chiefly through the witches being fertilized by the Satan figure. A coven was tradition-

[j] Chiefly by flagellation; especially among the Celtic Churches. St. Bridget's order (she is called the Mary of the Gaels) is often called the order of the rod.

[k] See Margaret Murray's (64) *Witch Cult in Western Europe.*

ally composed of ten females and two males (an old devil and a young devil). There were certain Dionysan dances and there are references to vegetable drugs being taken. The women were then fertilized; often, apparently, with a hollow stone phallus, for they frequently told the court that "his" (Satan's) "nature was cold like spring water in me." There is, in this crude procedure, no hint of any methodic raising of the charge of the body to higher vitality, and the mind to an enlarged and extended focus, by panaesthetic dilation and diffusion.

The Church's quarrel with the Cathars in the south was that they were more ascetic than the orthodox. There can be little doubt that this was a life-denying ascetic movement coming out of the East, passing through Bulgaria and so into South Europe. Their name, Cathars, shows that theirs was a creed of purgation.

The attack of the Church on these two opposite ends of deviation was so ferocious that the two movements disappeared. And there was little if any spirituality, no charity, and not much sincerity in the assault.[1] For the time being "the peace of Tacitus" was established, on the surface, throughout the shattered countryside: *solitudinem faciunt pacem appellant.*

What went on underground? Can it be that this need to make all life a development of consciousness, to be able to treat the seventy-year cycle as being a five-sectioned series of growth stages, is inherent? Further, if this is so can it be that whenever stimulant is increased (and breakdown does not intervene) then with the dilation being heightened the subject not only can endure but requires and finds deep relief in confinement and constriction (the limited environment and cerementing)? Heighten the stimulant even further and when the organism has learned to react to total restriction with passive submission it is ready to struggle with an intense effort against a powerful, moving, and fluid environment.

[1] Innocent III was the pope in whose reign the papacy reached the climax of its power; and he it was who launched this crusade against the Cathars which, under the leadership of a brigand land-grabber, de Montfort, devastated a lovely countryside. Yet, as G. C. Coulton (16) points out in his *Five Centuries of Religion,* this pope himself consulted a necromancer.

Heighten again the stimulant and what began as submission, then went on into wrestling with an outer element, now becomes an interior effort to expand. By breath dilation the rib cage is expanded and the air ordeal raises the psychophysique to a still higher alertness. If the tension can be stepped up once more, then the charged body can endure temperatures which, if the subject were casually relaxed, would have been not merely exhausting and debilitating but destructive. Such temperatures would be actually stimulating and energizing. This would account for the immunity to fire that the maenads and dervishes have when they are at the height of their dance-induced frenzy.

Restriction, catharsis, respiratory dilation, the tonic sting of heat: these four conditions of the ordeal aspect of the four basic mysteries[m] may always be sought and clumsily contrived as the organism, debilitated by *taedium vitae,* dissipated by pointless repetition of indulgence, or nagged by dull aches and pains, strives to fight back, spur itself out of its entropic morass, and rouse its own unkindled powers. This belief that it is inherent in man to seek these tonic liberations (and that lacking traditional knowledge of the mysteries he will and must attempt in some wise to achieve a relief, or rather a release) is not without substantiation.

Colin Still's remarkable study of *The Tempest* seems to make it highly probable that a supreme literary genius, belonging to the close of the first quarter of the modern age, has left on record in his last play a description of these four stages. If this is so then, as Still indeed believes, the fourfold development of man is a demand as inherent in his postbirth nature as the growth of eyes and ears were inherent in his prebirth nature. In his *The Timeless Theme,* Still (83) has put together the fragmentary data that, as we have seen, permit an outline reconstruction of the mystery rites. He has painstakingly correlated these data (1) with the Western Gnostic semi-esoteric tradition (58), (2) with the Western epic poems of

---

[m] As we have said, the fifth mystery ordeal-initiation of electricity may well have come in considerably later and, as we shall see in the following pages, Colin Still, tracing the asceticized rendering of the mysteries, can only regard this final mystery as one of intellectual light.

the primary and secondary phases of the ascetic age—*The Aenead* and *The Divine Comedy*—and (3) with the cryptic plays that culminate in *The Tempest*. He presents detailed evidence to show that all these literary works are veiled descriptions of the triple theme: first, that man is a fourfold creature whose elements may be mystically described as being of earth, water, air, and fire: secondly, that this creature may be restored to wholeness and completion by a method that will recover him from his faulting and fractionation: thirdly, that there are specific steps and techniques whereby this fourfold creature may be made to recover his divine status. Still then goes further and indicates that the reintegration of man the fourfold is by the four mysteries of his nature being released in him through the ordeals and initiations of earth, water, air, and the double aspect of fire as heat and light.

The tradition of the mysteries, as Still points out, maintains that the consciousness of man has to rise through seven planes. This means that each of the four ordeal initiations has, intercalated between it and the one above, a transitional stress phase. This is symbolized (between the first and second mysteries) by the analogy of what he calls mire, a mixture of earth and water. As earth liquefies it becomes morass or quicksand, a midstate on which man cannot walk and in which he cannot swim. It will neither bear him on its surface nor let him float in it. And since he can neither rest on it nor ride it, man sinks in it.

In turn, as water vaporizes it becomes mist, neither clear water nor clear air. Again, it cannot be swum in nor may one safely run or fly in it. The pilgrim is lost in it. This would be the transitional stress phase between the second and third mysteries.

As gases combine with the great gas (oxygen) and burn, there is at first no clear light; the air is full of blinding fumes and wavering images. At this level (between the third and fourth mysteries) man is not given vision but fears that he will be consumed; and if he is unprepared he will be burned. The three transitional stress phases (mire, mist, smoke) are then increasingly severe stress phases because they are phases of transition and therefore of instability.

The former state is outgrown. The new one is still not distinct enough to be functioned in.

It will be noticed that in this description of man's growth in consciousness no place is given to the primary ordeal of birth and infancy, which should have ushered in the first initiation and so been the preliminary stage of the first mystery, the mystery of earth. There is no reference to a conflict as man moves into his primary sensory condition of unreflective physicality, of unself-conscious bodilyness. Birth is assumed to be a Fall. It is not regarded as being itself a mystery with its two parts of ordeal and initiation. Birth and infancy are not seen as both crisis (a test) and opportunity; a trial followed by an equipment for a task; a perilous offer, the offer to be endued with a restricted, specialized instrument of action (that is, a free-moving, independent body). The taking of a body is not looked on as an inmergence, an incarnation that can be taken well or ill, featly or frustrantly, aptly or mistakenly.

Such an omission of the first mystery indicates that in this great literary tradition of the mysteries we have a description not of the original basic therapy but of its supplanter. The first great epoch of the mystery psychophysical therapy springs from the time when primal coconscious man had to submit to the sharpening, intensifying, and defining of the focus of his awareness. He had to become objective. With skilled effort he had to emerge into detachment and immediacy. Trial and error had to become his conscious education. Otherwise his group, repeating with ever more facility its routine solutions, would have sunk—if not into instinct, at least into reflex responses and final answers. This newly separate person must recognize error without dismay, he must remedy faultiness without disgust, and treat solutions as being provisional, temporarily useful, but not irrevocably final.

However, as we know, man's growing sense of an awakening self-judgment and his attempt (through a refreshing regression and rebirth therapy, the earth mystery) to prevent society from ankylosing into a gerontocracy[n] saved only a remnant. The main social

[n] As have the Australian Stone Age cultures of today.

structure stiffened. Inevitably there followed the heroic disruption; and the violent blunders of that epoch led, in turn, to the further contraction and contortion of consciousness. Self-blame and the desire to be punished took the place of shame seeking revenge; rage reacted into guilt and despair. Life became *ipso facto* disgusting and birth of any sort not a specific concentration but a degradation. As we have seen, such an attitude inevitably fulfilled its own fear and revulsion. Birth did become traumatic, leaving on the child's subconscious a stain of panic and a sense of punitive banishment. The woman was taught, "in sorrow shalt thou conceive." Birth must involve anguish and after it she is defiled; she must be purified before she is fit to rejoin unpolluted persons.° Not only could such bruised temperaments only look backward, construing any longing for a fuller condition as being proof of a past paradise from which they had been irrevocably exiled by the sin of growth and en- capsulation in a body. The body became *ipso facto* a foul prison. The life in the body and the lives of the future generations could only be viewed as at best an arrest, but more likely as a steady degeneration (from the Age of Gold, through Silver, on to Bronze and, finally, Iron). The entering into human existence was in itself a fall, a fatally degrading experience wherein a creature enmeshed in a web of animal passions was penned in a vile, sunless crypt. For this reason Plotinus, as we have seen, forbade the celebration of his birthday. Birth was a disastrous deposition. This outlook is other-worldly for it says that life can only be unmaimed, de- corrupted in a transcendental, fleshless, bodiless state.

Indeed, the great epic poets on whom Still relies (to show that they carried on the account of the mysteries) demonstrate by their own characters and master compositions that they, like Ploti- nus, were ascetic-pessimistic. Virgil was known for his melancholy. "Thou majestic in thy sadness at the doubtful doom of humankind," remarks his intense admirer, Tennyson. And Maecenas, patron of

° Even in the Anglican Church the rite of churching the mother of a newly born child continued until this century and may still hang on. The office for this odd social disinfection is still in the prayer book of the Church of England.

Virgil and his fellow poet Horace, used to say that when, as his clients, they regularly dined each side of him, "Here I sit between sighs and tears." Dante's character was that of an embittered man, all whose hopes for himself and for mankind were the other side of the grave. That these hopes were of the most moderate his great work leaves no possible doubt. Virgil (who in his own works had said that it was all too easy to slip into hell and all too difficult to get out again—*"facilis decensus Averno . . ."*) in the *Divine Comedy* acts as Dante's guide through the dismal regions. Dante's masterpiece is a romance in which the greater proportion of the human actors end in eternal torment. To call this a *Divine Comedy* indicates, of course, that mankind is a damned species, that this world is so fallen as to be the common launching ground for hell and that every enjoyment and appetite is tainted with mortal sin.

The fact that the exoteric medieval mystery tradition was a degenerate, life-rejecting form of the original life-accepting, life-hopeful mystery therapy is shown by the absence of the preliminary earth mystery in this later account. Hence, too, the further mistake in regard to the fourth mystery, which we must now note in the degenerate life-denying tradition. Because of the first omission of the earth mystery, the fourth mystery (that of fire) is inevitably misunderstood and so its basic efficacy is lacking.

In extracting the fourfold mystery pattern out of *The Tempest*, and from references in the great ascetic epics, Colin Still, following the basic tradition, rightly divides the fire ordeal initiation into two. But, although (page 23 of *The Timeless Theme*) he owns that the original traditional division is into rainbow (lower fire, prismatic light) and *aether* (fire) and that the rainbow was mistakenly seen as the possible frontier between air and the aether of space, yet he maintains that this "use . . . of the Rainbow needs no other warrant than the fact that nothing exists in the objective world of nature which could serve as well [as a simile] in the . . . seven-fold scale." It is an "age-old system of *imagery*." In other words, he is saying that the mystery is purely symbolic. At best it is a ritual that pre-typifies the state of the soul after death, a sacramental performance that guarantees a life beyond the grave, free of the flesh.

This use of the rainbow, the symbol of hope after the deluge disaster and re-establishment of diplomatic relationships after all deviationists have been drowned, is further evidence that this ascetic form of the mythos is degenerate. It is more evidence that it stems from the dawn of the protoindividualistic age, as the Flood stories do and as also do the stories of a Babel Tower built by men's impious, independent efforts to stand on their own structure above any further inundation.

As it happens, we know that Greek thinkers, watching upper atmospheric conditions, had speculated as to what lay above the common lung-comfortable air of sea level up to timberline height, that region of perpetual snow. This, it appeared, was the home of that uncanny, terrible blue fire that was so awfully, instantly immolating in one blinding, deafening flash: so different from the quiet, licking and cheerful glow of the domesticated red flame of the comforting hearth and the yellow eye of the guiding lamp. The mystery of the two fires, the coarser and the subtler, is then the distinction between molecular, vibratory heat and electric atomic energy.

In the original life-accepting, preguilt mythos there would be, then, five stages or ordeal initiations that we can put in modern psychophysical terms. Between each of these could be fitted the four transitional stress phases delineated by Still and for which he uses the symbols of mire, mist, smoke, and rainbow. This would then give us nine planes of development-growth, through which human consciousness must rise, instead of seven.

(1) The first plane is birth itself; and this is the first ordeal, the first test. Even when there is no trauma, even when the mother's fear-contractions do not physically strain and damage the child, birth must be a severe crisis. For here is the change from the unconscious womb life to sensory separateness and voluntary end-gaining movement. Choice has to be made: to advance or to cling to unconsciousness. So there is conflict between the homeostatic condition, when growth was so involuntary as to be unconscious, and the new demand to move and seek, try and see, err and correct.

(2) The second plane would be the first transitional stress

phase, symbolized by mire, the mixed elements of earth (stability) and water (movement).

(3) However, when the third plane (the second of the five stages) is reached, the new mobile condition of childhood is arrived at. The adjustment to movement is made and the decision to accept initiative is taken. This is the nor-adrenaline state of early childhood, of looking for heroical adventures. This state, in turn, loses its assurance, conviction, and clarity.

(4) Therefore, this second transitional stress phase (the fourth plane) Colin Still calls the condition of mist. This is the one in which contact is half-lost but vision is only half-won, fleeting, enigmatic. Here, delusions (premature constructions made from new, half-apprehended insights) may betray and temporarily destroy: that is, reduce the consciousness factor back to its primary condition, of the will to be, and make it start again from base.

(5) If, however, on the fifth plane the ordeal of adolescence can be met, if the initiation of air can be gone through with proper aid, then vision does become clear. The adolescent, instead of becoming a fanatic mortifier, a schizophrenic, becomes a person of clear seeing who can adjudge and estimate himself. He can understand his station of service not as being servile but as being the undergoing of a training; a training that will be needed, when he is called on to command, in order that he may understand and value his subordinates and be not only their commander but their guide (the *paidogogos*). He can also be the pattern of prestige that even now acts as leader to those juniors who, in the age group under him, are leaving boyish heroicism and entering on their period of confusion, the transitional stress phase of mist.

(6) The adolescent state of vision in turn enters into the third transitional stress phase, the sixth plane. For this state Still uses the symbol of smoke, smoky fire. The clear conviction of the well-adjusted adolescent has to be given up for the capacity to sustain wider uncertainties, to accept the compromises of actual administration and the strain of responsibility for directives, the success and rightness of which cannot be assured.

(7) But the transitional stress phase of fume from fire must

pass into the seventh plane, the fourth stage of lower fire. And the state of first maturity is reached when the smoke of confusion leads to the clarity of flame. It is here that the later rendering of the tradition of the rebirths (ordeals and initiations of the mysteries) shows most clearly its distortion and devitalization under the mortificatory, life-rejecting mistake of saying that birth into a body was, *ipso facto,* somehow a blunder, a fall into ignorance. By those who held to the doctrine of original sin it was assumed that a good birth, which would retain knowledge of the purpose for which a human body was taken, was impossible. Therefore the body, being a fallen body, should be shed as soon as possible. It cannot be developed.

Hence, as Colin Still and all ascetic interpreters of the mysteries must hold, the mysteries must be increasingly symbolic. The earth mystery has disappeared. The water rite has become only a sprinkling. Air and fire ("he shall baptize you with the Holy Breath and with Fire," the saying attributed to John the Baptist) are reduced to metaphors.

Nevertheless, as we have seen in Chapter 4 of Part III, the fire mystery does still exist. It can be practiced and it is employed as a psychophysical therapy.

(8) Having successfully passed through the initiation of lower fire, the individual now enters the fourth and last transitional stress phase, the eighth plane. This is that iridescent phase (for which Colin Still uses the symbol of the rainbow) in which the mind is dazzled.

(9) Now comes the final ordeal of second maturity. This is the grand climacteric when the individual passes not only from first maturity to second maturity, from office to retirement, but also enters on what Wartin calls the involutionary curve; it should be named the exvolutionary re-dilation. This ordeal is marked, as are all the ordeals, by the struggle caused by the individual having to make a new choice, by his having to decide to throw his ship onto a new tack. He has to resolve to terminate an activity that has served its purpose but in which he may be caught by the inertia of momentum, the rhythm of routine, of use and wont. He is

encompassed by final melancholy. The manic depressive madness which, as we have seen in Chapter 4 of Part II, is the specific psychosis of the total individual, humanic man of first maturity, may now also attack in a peculiar, baffling, and distressing form.

For, as this age stage is re-dilational, there comes a return of generalized euphoria. This, as we said in Chapter 5 of Part III, is often mistaken as a return of the reproductive phase. It is more precisely, but usually not more understandingly, called the second childhood. It is the recovery of the panaesthetic sensoriness. I have called it (see Chapter 5, Part I) the emergence of the leptoid condition. It is not a last flash in the pan, a flare of the dying candle. It could be likened to the leap in the womb of the eighth month embryo as the electric force in it makes it shake with the alerting summons toward the adventure of birth. For now that electric field, which in nine months built up the embryo from a single cell and then kept the whole body in repair for its nine-hundred-month life of five stages, releases itself and sheds the physical husk.

Here, then, is a completed cycle, from implicit potential through explicit actual to potential again. "That which drew from out the boundless deep turns again home." But with no revulsion, no spastic struggle to escape the twisted coil, the muddy vesture of decay. Death can and should be sublimation by a perfect volatilization—conscious, voluntary, timely, apt—the converse and complement of the freely chosen, temporary condensation and focus of birth.

The ninth plane, then, is not only the ordeal of second maturity but the initiation of the finer fire, the electric surge whereby (as described in Chapter 5 of Part III) the nervous system, trained to receive high current, rises like a skilled surf-rider and with perfect balance on the shoulder of the comber is steadily borne far up onto the level beach.

Thus we can see a complete cycle of nine planes through which human consciousness must rise to complete itself. For the ascetic midindividual, not knowing whence he came, ignorant of his entire nature, and made egotistic by guilt, could only regard birth as being a fall from blissful awareness into sinful ignorance. So Plato saw it. Sophocles was briefer but more explicit: "Happy is he who dies young; but only truly blessed is he that never was born."[p] Hence, for the ascetic, life in the body is a labor and a snarl; an unintended collapse, not an intentionally and temporarily limited concentration; a trap, not a valve. And death is an escape from a load that could not be eliminated by volatilization. The soul, for its own egotistic ease, hopes to escape and enjoy a personal, unencumbered paradise.

The full self-transforming mystery taught that the entire transcendant self, as manifested in the electric field, chose to take a body and in these two lives out of each of which we must be born (the embryo life and the life in the postwomb experience) to attain a complete awareness of intention and of timeliness. After which it can return to a completely enlightened potentiality.

In addition to the studies of Colin Still, even further evidence has now been brought forward suggesting that there was a traditional underground that preserved, at least in partial form, the original life-accepting religion. There is some reason to believe that at least until the sixteenth century there survived a series of rites that dealt with the body-mind, the soul-flesh unit, as a reciprocant binary system. Fränger (25) gives striking evidence of this in his masterly study of the painter Hieronymus Bosch (1460–1518). Hieronymus van Acken (to give him the name he first carried) was a Flemish artist and he had been chiefly remembered by students of art. For he greatly influenced two masters who have been much more popular than he: Peter Brueghel and Lucas Cranach. His own art was considered too grotesque, too satiric, too literary. This, undoubtedly, it is. And as the need to convey a cryptic message (as in *The Tempest*) can distort a design, even when the hidden meaning conforms with public prejudice since the doctrine to be conveyed is ascetic, even more will obvious beauty be sacrificed to secret sense if the doctrine is not only esoteric but heretical.

[p] Sophocles, who lived to be over ninety, remarked that the one compensation of old age was to be rid of love.

Much of Bosch's work is plainly satire: bitter sarcasm directed at the corruption of the Church, which claimed to be ascetic but which largely was ruthlessly self-indulgent. However, his master-work, "The Earthly Paradise" or "Garden of Delights," is the alternative he offers to an asceticism that had failed and become corrupt. This strange picture Philip II of Spain (apparently quite uncomprehendingly) cherished in his austere bedroom at the heart of his grim palace, the Escurial. No one who reads Fränger's learned study can help being convinced that in this enigmatic master-piece we have an invaluable and (as far as we know) a unique well-shaft down which we can catch sight of the underground river of the original mysteries still going its hidden way when in the upper world the Renaissance had already entered its middle age and the Reformation was at the door.[q]

The picture is in triptych form. The left panel shows Eden. Here, God the Son, the restorative Eternal Love, is presenting Adam (who is just being wakened from a deep sleep) with Eve, the love partner who has just been produced from Adam's side. The para-disal scenery around is inhabited by quaintly monstrous creatures that all carry esoteric significances. The right panel shows a Hell where pride and violence (the robber Knight) and even the cruel hunter are given tit for tat. The reckless gamblers, the gluttonous religious, the pitiless, the rapacious, the greedy are devoured. A hawk-horus-headed monster, symbol of the all-seeing eye set in the mask and armed with the flesh-tearing scimitar-shaped beak of the bird of prey, rends, bolts, and voids his victims through his pierced throne into a cloaca passage.

Yet even this revolting underground sewer has its exit in the great central panel. For since the Cosmos always conceives per-fection, not only does the fool (if he perseveres in his folly) become wise but the depraved, through the peristalsis of their passions, are at length discharged out into freedom again. Even the musicians are strung in a strange anguish on gargantuan forms of their in-

[q] In the latest and definitive study on the Escurial (*The Prado, Madrid,* Abrams, 1956) H. B. Wehle says that Fränger's interpretation of Bosch's work is more reasonable than any before.

struments. Perhaps this is because they used music as an amusement, as an escape and not as one of the sense-trainers to be in play with the orchestra of all the sense-stimulators through which consciousness, using these channels in balanced harmony, attains to ecstasy. However, these mistaken music-makers are being twisted into the right key. They are on the left of this panel wing, close up against the central panel.

Arriving at the center, then, and beginning at the foot, we find this base crowded with exits, emergence orifices. Down in the left corner is, as it were, the master clue, the esoteric signature. For here we find both the portrait of the artist as an initiate and also the portrait of the Grand Master. This is doubly important. Because the face of the Grand Master, here full of humorous kindly power, is the face of the sardonic monster who stands at Hell's center in a swamp, on legs made of dead trees and with an egglike body through which, as through a dismal inn on the road to the cloaca, the penitential souls must traverse. There, looking out at us over his shoulder, he grimly satirizes his own purgative predicament by being douched by his own ignorant followers to whom he had taught an inadequate doctrine. Now, in this re-emergence in the central panel, he understands Blake's wisdom: that folly, if endured to the utmost, gives wisdom.

Further up on the median line we find the principal emergence. Adolescent, transformed males and females are coming up from the purgatory on the backs of giant birds.ʳ We see these resuscitated people coming alive in a Paradise of Delights that, at this level, is the good earth of fantastic abundance (for example, strawberries and gooseberries as big as a man's head). Here, too, are unmistakable Tantra pictures of the rousing of Kundalini.

Above this are people diving into pools of water. Here we reach the level of the great *gymkana* (the mounted dance) in which, astride a number of tamed monsters, the rising humans wind in rhythm. Above this is air through which limpid sky figures, that have now become completely boyish, sail effortlessly. Elevated and

ʳ Through all of mythology the bird is associated with the soul and its migratory flight.

levitated, they soar to where the flights of birds wing through a heaven of fathomless calm and infinite extent.

There is no other work of art that shows us that this underground of the original, ante-ascetic mystery cycle was still extant down to the sixteenth century. As Fränger points out, this picture (which hung before the fascinated, uncomprehending eyes of the greatest burner of heretics, Philip II) was apparently used as a kind of instructive altarpiece when these secret spiritual descendants of the Adamites met to go through their ritual.

Possibly after the sixteenth century this psychophysical tradition perished. Even the author of *The Tempest,* though referring to a rite made respectably ascetic, writes enigmatically. Reason was probably a greater corrosive of the rite than dogma. As it is often said in Tao, the far Eastern mystery that has also degenerated largely into magic, the uninformed man "mistakes the finger pointing at the moon for the moon itself." Unless the meaning of the practices is clearly understood, unless the performer knows that under all the names (and as the meaning of all the ritual) is a psychophysical technique aimed at producing a psychophysical change, a shift of sensation and a dilation of comprehension, then the whole procedure degenerates into superstitious conjuring and/or pointless sensuality.

With the renewed interest in psychotherapy of the last two generations, there has developed an empiric approach to the mind-body-group relationship. Freudianism begins the exploration with a free associating patient listened to by a detached analyst. The Jungian method often makes use of drawing, a release instrument less inhibited than speech. The nondirective therapy of Karl Rogers attempts the less restrained association of a companionship that does not even attempt to explain the subject to himself, extending only the extractive vacuum of a reposeful, sympathetic attention.

J. S. Moreno, however, brings in the social factor even more. His subjects are taught to act out their problems, aided by auxiliary performers. Maxwell Jones, in England, has carried this still further. The therapeutic plays are written, rehearsed, stage managed, and performed. And here we are only one step away from the full rite which (when performed with masks, vestments, and scenery) deals no longer with a personal idiosyncratic accident or episode in the life of an individual but with the race life as it manifests itself in each man. Here, the group therapy of the mysteries could re-emerge and man could be taught how he may cooperate with the life force as it strives to bring him through the five cardinal stages whereby he may attain to reciprocal knowledge, to a full consciousness of the total process.

Fifty years ago, in his introduction to anthropology (*Anthropology*, Home University Library) R. R. Marrett remarked, "Civilized man tries to think out his problems; savage man dances them out." It looks as though human history may have come full circle. With self-conscious man's discovery of the sunken continent of his subconscious, man today may at last understand his amphibian nature and learn how to unite, in binary power, his critical and creative mind, his analytic and integral thought, the intensity of his individual focus with the width, comprehension, and aim of the racial consciousness.

E

LABORATORY EXPERIMENTS IN

LIMITED ENVIRONMENT

In the last couple of years psychologists have been experimenting with what they generally call the limited environment, and they have been studying its effects on the individual who is thus isolated. The first set of experiments to be done fall into the category of what I have called the mystery of earth, the first ordeal and initiation, a womb and birth-recall experience. The best known of these experiments are described in an article entitled "Cognitive Effects of Decreased Variation to the Sensory Environment," by W. Heron, W. H. Bexton, and D. C. Hebb of McGill University in Montreal (44).

The second set of experiments comes under the second category I have used in this book: the second ordeal and initiation, that of the mystery of water, the cathartic rite of immersion. The best known of these are the experiments of John C. Lilly formerly of the National Institute of Mental Health, the U.S. Department of Health, Education, and Welfare at Bethesda, Maryland.[a]

The first set of experiments (those of Hebb *et al.*) were carried out with subjects that had been encased, horizontally, in body-enclosing containers. In the second set (those of Lilly) the subject was floated in a tank of running water. (See note, Part III, Chapter 1, footnote *h*.)

I shall refer first to the second set, because Lilly gives, as a preliminary to the water ordeal, a valuable summary from a good collection of accounts written by men and women explorers who had experienced the strange psychological effects of isolation. The following data throw light on the psychological factors involved in the mystery techniques of changing consciousness. If we consider first Walter Gibson's (34) account (*The Boat*) of exposure in an open boat in the Indian Ocean during World War II, we have Stage 1 of such an ordeal. The boat started adrift with 135 persons aboard. Four survived. To the isolation, which of course was not absolute, were added the appalling hardships of exposure and an agonizing shortage of food and water. As the mortificatory ascetics not infrequently demonstrated, the effect of such deprivation on a powerful physique may be to provoke changes of consciousness before complete physical collapse intervened.

Gibson, however, attributes his survival to a certain psycho-physical preparedness: (1) some years of training under a tropical sun, (2) his capacity to become completely passive, (3) a conviction of survival, and (4) a companion sharing his conviction. The first week seems to have been the worst. This last fact is confirmed by Joshua Slocum (the first man to sail around the world alone) and Filain Bombard, a French imitator.

Two other factors make for survival: a capacity to project helpful hallucinations and encouraging conversations with a mascot, and intense love of living things (29). After such an experience

[a] See the report of Symposium No. 2 on *Illustrative Strategies for Research on Psychopathology in Mental Health* at the meeting of the Group for the Advancement of Psychiatry held at the Berkeley-Carteret Hotel, Asbury Park, New Jersey, on November 6, 1955.

the inner life may have grown so strong that speaking to others is done only very deliberately. In his *Alone*, Admiral Richard Byrd (9) describes the oncoming and immersion in the oceanic feeling. Courthold, the Greenland explorer who was similarly isolated in a polar winter darkness, tells of the same experience. Christiane Ritter (72) describes spells of sixteen-day-long isolation. She found that the preliminary ordeal resulted in initiation, although she had to resist the impulse to walk out into the snow, as the skin-diver, at depths below one hundred and fifty feet, may be tempted to take off his breathing mask. Most survivors report a new inner sense of security, a new integration on a deep basic level.

But let us turn back to the first, and least strenuous, of the artificial restrictions of environment, the tests carried out at McGill University by Hebb (44). These are quietly arrestive and, as we said above, to some degree parallel the rites of earth, the burial regression and rebirth. Donald Hebb and his colleagues used university students as their subjects in these experiments. Each subject was given twenty dollars a day to submit to what would seem to common sense to be at worst a boring way of earning money— by doing nothing. All that was to be done was to reduce patterning of stimuli to the lowest possible level, when surely the healthy, young, money-scarce student would fall to sleep, lulled with the thought that he would wake up automatically richer. To induce this approved and lucrative laziness the subject was laid to rest on a well-sprung bed which was entirely enclosed in an air-conditioned cylinder, a kind of comfortably roofed cradle. Arms and hands had their separate rests in roomy cardboard sleeves. The eyes were completely shielded with ski goggles that admitted a soothing golden light. It might be thought that the subject would feel he was drifting back to a holy innocent's heaven full of repose and so feel shut up in measureless content.

However, the consequences were utterly different. The observer watched through a window and regularly asked the subject how he felt. He was not abandoned. Father was alert by the cradle. And yet after several hours every subject found it increasingly difficult to carry on any organized directed thinking for any sustained period. Suggestibility was much increased and an acute desire for action and stimuli developed. There were periods when the subject, trying to satisfy these needs, would thresh about in the box like a hooked fish. Then there usually came on a state between sleep and waking. Consciousness first diffused and then thought grew confused. After twenty-four hours a number began to quit, finding the condition unendurable, quite unnerved by this mysterious ordeal. Those who hung on for forty-eight hours began to have hallucinations and delusions. The hallucinations were, when they had been present for some time, complete projections: that is, they were three-dimensional and the subject could study their apparently solid volumes and planes by shifting his eyes and his head. While doing this the subject could give a detailed description of the various features of these projections. And carrying on a conversation with the director of the experiment, in which he described these phenomena, in no wise reduced his vision of them. Indeed, at first the subjects who stuck it out until the hallucinations came on found these phenomena a relief from the intense frustration of the two days of acute boredom. But nearly all quit after seventy-two hours. One who lasted out for five days did go into a sudden spastic condition that looked like a seizure. The EEGs taken from this subject's head, however, failed to show the extreme spike rhythm given off by the epileptic fit.

In a completely unprepared healthy youngster, then, this very simple preliminary approach to the earth-burial rite seems to have produced keen distress because of two induced experiences. The sense of an oncoming awareness that his assumed identity of body and mind was not so, that his body was not himself, awoke the first alarm. The second alarm followed when the mind itself began to alter its frontiers and the self-consciousness began to be invaded by subconscious images. The first was due to the loosening of the links with our anchor in space, the body. The second came on because now, like an ice-floe melting in the sea, the surface mind was first drifting from its position in time and, finally, being threatened with the melting-merging of its separate, defined personality in a coastless ocean of indistinct and apparently undirected awareness.

It is clear that if the students could have been prepared this experience would have been highly instructive and therapeutic instead of leading to baffling distress. The images are projections of repressed aspects of consciousness that since infancy have been buried beneath the level of self-consciousness, sealed under by the socially imposed personality-mask-shroud. Released now, as the ice-crust of conformity is thawed, they are floating to the surface. For instance, as the controlled clinical experiments in the use of mescaline and lysergic acid go on it is becoming increasingly clear that whether the experience is instructive and highly beneficial, or humiliating and embarrassing, depends wholly (with sane subjects) on one of two things. Is the subject informed beforehand as to what he is about to go through and then given the medicament by a psychiatrist who understands the therapy and has himself experienced its effect? Or is the subject allowed to enter the condition in ignorance and then badgered or abandoned while he is in it?[b] With informed and instructed subjects, in the mescaline and lysergic acid experiments there are no hallucinations. With the uninstructed, the hallucinations can be intense, apparently solid, and often highly distressing in their grotesqueness.

Some aftereffects were noticed by the subjects of the McGill experiments with this particular form of restricted environment. For several hours after their release from the closed cradle they found difficulty in seeing the world around them as they had seen it before. And in some of the subjects the hallucinations hung on only to fade gradually during the day.

Now, when we consider Lilly's experiments, we can see that in his employment of water immersion he reproduced an ordeal that went a step beyond the relaxed ease of the limited environment of the air-conditioned container. The McGill experiments were "to reduce patterning of stimuli" to the lowest possible level. The aim of Lilly was to reduce "absolute intensity of all physical stimuli" to this lowest level. The subject (Lilly first experimented on himself)

[b] See *Lysergic Acid Diethylamide and Mescaline in Experimental Psychiatry*, edited by Louis Cholden (13). This judgment has been amply confirmed by a wealth of experimental studies made under controlled conditions.

was suspended in a tank of slow-flowing water, the temperature of which was kept at 34.5 C. This is a neutral temperature and so the skin makes practically no reaction to the water. The body is naked save for a head mask that completely blinds the subject, and a very light harness that tethers him by the shoulders. He floats, totally submerged, and his breathing is kept going by the use of a snorkel that extends above the water level. The only tactile sensation comes from the touch of the mask and the tether-harness. The only sounds that reach him are his own breathing and occasional slight water tremors that come from the pipes of the tank. Lilly employed one other subject besides himself. The longest exposure lasted only three hours. Each subject had a full night's rest previous to this immersion. Each had a set of training dips in order to overcome any apprehension as to possible risks: for example, to see if there was to be any distress in breathing, or any physical discomfort.

For the first three quarters of an hour, spontaneous recollections of events lately experienced fill the mind. This is followed by a sense of pleasant relaxation; Lilly is a mature researcher who is much more likely to appreciate quietude (the fruitful acre of the well-sown mind) than is a tonic, kinaesthetic Canadian student. But by the third hour tension began to be apparent and to grow. This stimulated action. The muscles began to twitch and slow swimming motions started up so as to obtain a positive feeling from contact with the flowing water. A strangely satisfying contentment came from stroking one finger against another. When this almost reflex movement of sensory self-awareness was inhibited and then resumed, the vividness and intensity of the pleasure was increased in proportion to the length of time that restraint had been exercised. If the inhibition was made absolute then the tension rose so high that the whole situation became unbearable and the subject would have had to be removed from the tank. Somehow, the self-touching relieved, if only temporarily, the self-generated tension charge. Meanwhile, some of the demand for interest-attention discharge was satisfied by becoming intensely aware of the mask contact and the contact of the suspensory harness until, in turn, these points of awareness in the otherwise nearly total insensibility became almost unbearable. When self-stimulation is inhibited up to a certain point of intensity, then consciousness begins to undergo an interior shift. Directed thinking about actual problems changes into reveries and fantasies that are "highly emotional and personally charged." If this is not resisted the state can be one of relaxed enjoyment. However, if the fantasy is rejected as well as the tactile detensioning, then the projection of visual imagery takes place. Lilly says,

> I have seen this once, after a two-and-one-half-hour period. The black curtain in front of the eyes (such as one "sees" in a dark room with eyes closed) gradually opens out into a three-dimensional dark, empty space in front of the body. This phenomenon captures one's interest immediately, and one waits to find out what comes next. Gradually forms of the type sometimes seen in hypnogogic states appear. In this case, they were small, strangely shaped objects with self-luminous borders. A tunnel whose inside "space" seemed to be emitting a blue light then appeared straight ahead. About this time, this experiment was terminated by a leakage of water into the mask. It turns out that exposures to such conditions train one to be more tolerant of many internal activities —fear lessens with experience and personal integration can be speeded up. But, of course there are pitfalls here to be avoided—the opposite effects may also be accelerated in certain cases.

The aftereffects that Lilly and his fellow experimenter noticed were different from those experienced by the McGill subjects, but not less remarkable. The chief peculiarity after the immersion was an alteration in the sense of time. Apparently some kind of release from the subconscious strain of clock pressure is obtained and a sense of initiative and freedom, of spare-timedness, is enjoyed. Seemingly the subject is able to experience the day as though it were being started afresh; he feels a dawn sense, as Mencius calls it in one of his most intriguing passages. "The subject feels as though he had just risen from bed," with his energy restored by a good night's sleep. We are told that this happy hangover persists so that the "subject finds he is out of step with the clock for the rest of the day"—almost, it seems, in a state of being ahead of time.

Social intercourse also needs adjustment. The subject has slipped not only from the close grip of time but also from the tight clasp of convention. If he is alone long enough (and here these experiments confirm the experience of solitaries) and the levels of physical stimuli are low enough, the "mind turns inward and then projects outward its own contents and processes; the brain not only stays active, despite the lowered levels of input and output, but accumulates surplus energy to extreme degrees. Apparently even healthy minds act this way in isolation. What this means to psychiatric research is obvious: we have yet to obtain a full, documented picture of the range available to the healthy human adult mind." And if we could have more detailed accounts the possible applications to brainwashing and its opposite (psychotherapy) would be more evident.

Since the above was written very considerable progress has been made and increasing interest has been shown in this field of study. Jack Vernon, of Princeton, has made a series of studies with the limited environment wherein the conditions were more rigorous than those of Hebb and his associates. For at Princeton the subject was put into total darkness and confined in an underground room where sound was reduced to a minimum. The subject, however, had some space in which to move about in his tomb, which was furnished with food, bed, and toilet facilities. The subjects, too, were different from those that were used at McGill. They were not Canadian students, most of whom are used to an out-door life and a very strenuous climate. The Princeton subjects were all postgraduates, and most of them had graduated in mathematics. In consequence, having minds trained to think about pure abstraction, the loss of a world of outward images and contacts did not at the start embarrass them. It was only later, when they had exhausted the pure mental games they were able to play with themselves, that the void began to be noticeable, strange and, in the end, distressing. Nor did these minds hallucinate.

Two reasons have been given for this; the first is the nature of the men who underwent this ordeal. For instance, lysergic acid was first called, as was mescaline and, later, psilocybin, a hallucinogen. However, I have experimented with all of these, under supervised conditions, and in none of them found that they were hallucinatory. A mathematician or anyone trained in critical methods does not seem to be able to hallucinate. It may be that hallucination is, as is possibly all dreaming itself, a defense against the mind straying too far outside the frontiers of the ego.

The second reason is exterior. It is possible that men hallucinate more easily in a half light, and with vague outlines, than in a total dark. Certainly, study of children who possess eidetic imagination would show that the pictures they see are built up from the use of hints and themes suggested by outer patterns; for example, cracks in a wall.

A study similar to Vernon's has now been under way for some four years at the Army Research Center, Monterey, California. There Meyers and Murphy have been at work on a large-scale study of the effects of the limited environment on recruits. The set-up consists of a series of cubicles, lightproof but far from wholly soundproof. In these cubicles volunteers—and it was interesting how many applied—are confined. Contact is kept with the experimenters by means of an intercom, and so the subject can ask to be taken out as soon as he desires. His reactions are also being electrically registered all the while. The two outstanding facts that have emerged so far would seem to be that the one man who was able to extend his vigil for several days had been, before being conscripted, a surveyor in Alaska and, therefore, accustomed to being completely by himself, out in the sparsely inhabited arctic, for spells of a week or more. And, secondly, that the time required for these subjects to begin to be disoriented, and often to hallucinate, was surprisingly short, some doing so in a couple of hours or even less.

One of the most significant developments, however, in this inner-outer field comes from a colleague of Lilly. Jay T. Shurley has now been able to set up a type of subterranean baptistery. In the vaults of the Medical School and hospital of the University of Oklahoma he has had excavated a deep cell. In the upper level sits the observer, with his observational and recording instruments. Then deep below this is a circular enclosed tank, or well. In this the subject, stripped and wearing a face mask, is submerged. In his mouth is a small microphone whereby he may communicate with the recorder-monitor seated above. So he is in a giant womb, floating, respirating through the tubes that come into his face mask. The water temperature is at neutral and he naturally floats, suspended below the surface of the water and above the bottom of the tank, in the attitude of fetal balance. The results from these trials have already proved most promising and Lilly himself looks forward with hope that these improved methods will greatly enlarge our knowledge of consciousness, the subject's knowledge of the extent of his own mind, and serve to aid not only pure research but also therapy in all its forms: curative, preventive, and developmental.

Such, then, are the remarkable results that have been obtained from even tentative investigation of the psychophysical effects that are yielded by the limited environment. Further research, it seems clear, should lead not only to further understanding of these states but to command of (or perhaps it would be wiser and more accurate to say coordination with) these conditions. The closed cradle or mummy case procedure has in it the rudiments of the conditioning (activity-suspension and regression) which was traditionally brought about by the first mystery: womb regression, removal of birth trauma, and then rebirth. The tank total immersion has in it the rudiments of the second mystery, of catharsis and the resolving of the repressed rages of the nor-adrenaline child. So it seems evident that now we should not only develop these two basic initiations but also seek to investigate in equally modern terms the remaining three. If the sarchophagic experience, when carried through to completion, can promise to rid the psyche of the birth trauma, and if the submersion ordeal-initiation has as its entire goal complete deliverance from the heroic, childish, baffled rage and suicidal shame, then the respiratory rite can lift from the adolescent ascetic his load of guilt.

Here again, as we have seen, the limited environment has begun to be used for the psychophysical therapy of nonrespiratory lung aeration. Next, research into radiant heat tolerance and adaptation to the supertonic effects of electric surge therapy and stimulation may complete the sequence.

Certainly, from these initial studies in the limited environments, we already have clear promise that experiment with psychophysical conditioning may profoundly heighten the body's tonus and enlarge, reciprocally, the field of consciousness.

F

A NOTE ON (a) THE SOURCES OF FEAR AS IT
EMERGES IN THE FIVE AGES OF THE HUMAN
PSYCHE AND (b) THE WAYS IN WHICH
MAN HAS COPED WITH IT

All creatures have to attain a psycho-environmental frontier.[a] Here runs the axis where the individual's will rocks between confidence and mistrust, adventure and caution, curiosity and dread, exploration and shrinking. The young of every vertebrate large-brained species (and indeed some of the young of lower species such as fish —for example, the stickleback and its parentally cared-for young) begin under parental protection to investigate their surroundings. Curiosity seems able to manifest itself early. This extension of enquiry enlarges its periphery up to that circumference which can be covered by the protectorate of the parent or parents. Beyond that, among the big-brained parents, advance by the young is discouraged, warned against, and often actively censored and forbidden.

[a] See "Critical Periods in Behavioral Development" by J. P. Scott (senior staff scientist, R. B. Jackson Memorial Laboratory, Bar Harbor, Maine) in *Science*, November 30, 1962, Vol. 138, pp. 949-958.

Up to that time, therefore, expansion is commendable, curiosity is the approved drive. Beyond that frontier restraint is counselled, discretion commended: caution is the rightful reaction.

From his first psychic epoch, his first stage of consciousness, however empathic may have been his mind with a world panpsychically intuited, coconscious, preindividualized man nevertheless apprehended a penumbral distinction between what later was to be distinguished as "on our side" (this was if not the profane at least the secular, the realm of physical means), and "on that side," the sacred, the religious, the frame of spiritual meaning, the realm of ends. Coconscious man in regard to and toward that immediate realm of manageable things felt "at home." He could treat persons and objects in this area as familiars, be in play with them, free of formality or protocol. Toward what lay outside that realm he must advance with respect, with pious preparedness. He does present himself but not with forwardness. He is before the unknown: in vigil to detect, if he may, some symptom as to whether It is withdrawn in impenetrable aloofness or might show any hint of condescension.

This is the state of mind toward what Otto labeled as "the numinous." Toward this encircling, incomprehensible presence that constantly envelops him, man, from the first, could not feel familiarity. Curiosity (that intellectual love which reaches out beyond the emotional love felt for all our familial domesticities; that desire to be amused by, to handle and collect the odd, the strange; that desire to play with the peculiar and feel the fantastic to be funny, to feel a humorous lightness toward that which does not fit) is a mood that cannot be sustained toward the indefinable vastness which when it is still seems abysmal, and when moving seems incomprehensible and irresistible.

This reaction, or rather this climate of other-ness awareness, does not contract into the seizure of that panic which was the classical Greek's reaction when sensing, out in the wild, that he was confronted with Pan. The sense of knowing one must not go too far and must, indeed, now cease to go farther, is not a reaction toward flight but an order to wait, petitionlessly suppliant on the threshold.

That sensation is awe. For the awful is not the horrible. It is an apprehension of Presence which fascinates as and because it pervasively enforces on the fascinated the command that he keep his distance.

There are, then, for the primitive, the cosocial, two worlds: one is his world, the other is the world of *That*. But they are polar, they are reciprocal. This world, man's world, is for him to manipulate so it will yield him means and powers. That world, the realm of the Numinous, is not for him to operate. It is for him to draw on as it offers him the unexploitable, incomprehensible range in terms of which his purpose can be extended beyond the visible-tangible, his meaning can be enlarged to an infinite goal.

The Heroic Age snapped that tie. It ungeared from its axis this ultimate polarity. Soon, however, faced with the depth, that void which the thrust of the heroes' armed conquest could not penetrate, the fascination of awe was no longer felt, and its place was taken by craven fear.

For a time the hero attempts to rationalize, condense, and narrow to manageable proportions his ungeared fear, the sense of terror at having overstepped his station and being in trespass on ground sacred to an incomprehensible, unwardable presence. As Dodds has pointed out, and as have all experts on the Heroic Age, the hero tries to control fear by proclaiming that the only thing the brave man fears (for has he not smashed and annihilated the old numinous sacerdocracy?) is shame. His "shame culture" offers him freedom from fear by his demonstrating that he cannot be craven. His honor being established, by the killing of any who question his courage or, indeed, offend his dignity, he holds that he has killed fear itself. The death of a rival, or his own death in such combat, assures him of his society's affirmation of his fearlessness. If, like Ajax in a moment of excessive homicidal frenzy, on recovery he finds he has only killed sheep, and so become ridiculous, he can still rid himself of the fear of mockery by killing himself.

However, this attempt to narrow fear into the manageable, expiatable bounds of shame did not contain the terror of the unseen. Soon it was found that the horror of the avenging Furies haunted the hero whose unbalanced physical violence had torn up the roots of the subconscious reverence, of the biological inhibition against murder within one's own species.

Hence the Heroic Age passes inevitably into the Ascetic Epoch. For now it becomes clear to the reflective, self-blaming type of individual (the next degree of self-awareness, the schizoid in contrast to the paranoid) that by killing another, maybe more fear-trapped than himself, he has increased, not lessened his fear. So whereas shame was the contraction and escape by means of which the paranoid hero tried in vain to conquer fear, to hold the invading, pervading sense of the abysmal unknown, the Ascetic instead of trying to tackle and dismiss the panic attempted to make terms with it.

Instead then of shame, to be flung out by physical courage, the ascetic accepts guilt. And in this term he can approach to an almost real and temporarily personally effective expiation. For now he is, by accepting his responsibility, entering into a renewed relationship contractually conceived between himself and the encircling "Without." As, however, this Without was, in its full emotional potency (in its power to cause fear and require a defense against its otherwise paralyzing, indefensible awefulness), the unseen intangible, men all too naturally assumed that, as they could not make out what it was up to, and so could not gather what it was telling them to do, how it intended them to behave, therefore it was best to abstain from anything that might provoke it.

Further, it seemed reasonable that, as they could not get into direct touch with it or even see it, they must assume it dwelt somewhere beyond their world of bodies, functions, and appetites, and was itself totally inhuman. Hence only if they were total abstainers from all physical life could they contact this power. Not only would it not communicate with the indulgent: you could only hope when you died (and so presumably, having left the body and the body having fallen to pieces, you passed wholly into the realm of the Without) to be at best lost, more likely nightmared, or thrown back into a new human body to repeat the circuit of ignorant folly, suffering, and death, unless you had made expiation for being an appetitive, reproductive creature.

So as the heroic effort to focus and hold fear had failed, in turn the ascetic attempt to make terms with dread also failed. The hero, unable to feel awe, tried to make dread manageable by defining it as shame and confining it to an ordeal surmountable by physical courage. With one's own bodily death in the wager, and so honor vindicated, fear was presumed to have been killed with the death of one's rival.

The ascetic knows how much deeper and wider lie the roots of fear. He cannot, therefore, confine so shallowly-narrowly the span and abyss of dread. He goes beyond the frontier of man's working world into the circumambient Beyond: the vast, enveloping, chartless unknown. But he also feels sadly sure that past experience has shown that these his overtures cannot secure Its favors in and for his actual physical life, that is, bring him good fortune in his this-worldly affairs. Nor can any appeal even assure that It will abstain from intrusion into his small hard-won territory, his homeland of controlled and ordered livelihood. The ascetic's hope is, in the end, no more than to learn (in the same hard way that the hero learned the irresistible, implacable laws that rule visible nature) how to discover and follow the laws that run invisible and intangible nature.

This in turn taught him that he who renounced was not granted any more protection (freedom from pain and loss) than the unthinking who snatched what he could and enjoyed while he might. There was no more discernible a natural moral law which punished the physically indulgent, than there was evidence of a natural moral law that granted its observers physical rewards or protection from damage. In short, the idea of law as supposed to be manifested in punitive karma (with its accent on punishment and suffering being wholly due to the fact that one had a physical body with its natural appetites) was recognized as being still as anthropomorphically distorted as was the idea of law supposed to be illustrated and indeed confirmed by the repeated experience of good luck.

The fourth stage of man, humanic man, emerged. Regarding himself as a total individual, surrounded by his equally completely individualized fellows, and all of them contained within a completely unconscious mechanistic cosmos, Renaissance man not only denied that he had a conscience (if he felt its misgivings he called them hangovers from a disproved anthropomorphic superstition) but that he had any grounds for any sort of fear. "Glory to man in the highest for man is the master of things!"

But as humanic man was ignorant of his repressed extra-individual consciousness he could not define and so confront his fear. He could not rationally conceive awe, for reverence was an atavistic impulse rising from a false, disproved teaching. Shame was even more ridiculous, the craven subservience of an uninformed coward challenged by an even less rational bully, boasting his animal muscular strength. Guilt was only another step down into ridiculous objection. The big muscular bully was projected, hoisted into the vacant, harmless sky and given, in exchange for his club, the thunderbolt.

But inevitably, as man gave up these two methods of condensing awe (which had turned into terror that was first reduced to shame and discharged by courage, and next condensed as guilt and expiated by penitence and absolution) terror once more became pervasive, terror that is unmanageable just because it cannot be defined, confronted, and contacted.

Hence, humanic man has to end. For his specific age, that was to complete man's coming of age, the age of the completely rational, analytic, objective individual, has become the age of anxiety, the age of fear, pervasive, indefinable, inexpressible, unmentionable. And fear, for the creature that sees and surfacely feels itself in itself complete, an all-one, is in fact the confession that he is completely alone.

This must end in intensifying isolationism as this modernic man explores the ever expanding vastness of the macrocosmos shown by his radar telescope, and the hyperintensity of the microcosmos revealed by his hyper-X-ray electro microscope. For as this rack of hypersensory knowledge tears apart the sane, sensual man's world of common sense, man today, forced into postmodernity, finds that he is not merely "a stranger and afraid: in a world I never made." He discovers that there is no one world, made by someone else for something else. He discovers, far more startlingly, that there are as many worlds as there are apprehending systems to apprehend them. He has to face the awe-ful discovery that as his mind grows he can and must apprehend how large a part he takes in composing his cosmoi. The simple dualism of the macrocosm and the microcosm was but a beginning symptom of his mind's expansion.

Therefore, as there are as many ranges of cosmoi as man can make his mind range, out and in, to apprehend them, so we come to understand Niels Bohr's summary of the meaning of the revolution (or rather mental mutation) which we call the end of Classical Physics: "This," said the late doyen of modern Physics, "means one thing for all of us: the end of the 2500-year search for objectivity." There is and can be no rainbow for you when you stand where its onlooker sees it to be touching the earth. Similarly there is no "fact" in itself. The long-hoped-for, basic, atomic, irreducible unit does not and never did exist.

But, conversely, we have simultaneously discovered that we, the field of onlookers, are only one facet of us, the field of finders. "Definition is limitation." But it is also the recognition of the field out of which the find, the fact, has been extracted. Today we are discovering something more than facts. We perceive the continuum out of which we extract them. We explore the setting in which the find, the fact, not merely lies, but functions, performs, exercises, and influences, as an integral feature of an uncircumscribed whole. The atom, we are told, is in a reciprocal-field relationship with the entire macrocosmos.

Finally, this matrix mind of ours, which is in this expanding play with its matrix, the macro-environment, discovers this hyper-environ is far more like the supermind that today we find enfields our full selves than it is an unconscious machine. At the highest reach of our transpersonal mind we discover we are in percolative-osmotic, transfusive contact with a hierarchy of integrated mind-circuits. These pass up in ever intensified frequencies and through constantly increased dimensions, going beyond discrimination, definition, and the all-various modalities of time. Such a compelled conviction alone can now deal with *Angst*, and all fear, by restoring awe. But in that vision the human mind, made for ecstasy and infinitude, experiences a reverence which alone can give purpose to every experience and meaningful delight to every act.

Glossary

AGONIA: Greek. Literally, a wrestling match. Pain which is used to attain to, and is transmuted into, a heightened consciousness.

AIDOS: Greek. An intuitive sense of decency.

ANARSIS: Greek. As catharsis is relief by purging, by discharge, so anarsis is release by aspiration and fulfillment.

ASKESIS: Greek. Athleticism: used here without the connotation either of competitive athletics or of mortification.

CHUNG-TZU: The gentleman of culture, generosity, and obedience (see the *Analects* of Confucius).

DIKE: Greek. Justice.

FETALIZATION: Louis Bolk's principle that in all mammals the form that survives and succeeds holds on to aspects of its fetal structure outside the womb: for example, the dog is a fetal form of the wolf, man is a fetal form of the ape, and the paidomorph is a fetal form of man.

HUBRIS: Greek. Overweening pride.

HYPNOCRACY: A society under the control of a kind of hypnotic suggestion (and, therefore, a psychologically inflexible tradition) as to the purpose and conduct of life: for example, the complex street plan of Mohenjo Daro shows no appreciable change for 1,000 years.

INTEGRAL THOUGHT: A term used by Dr. Sarvepalli Radhakrishnan, the President of India, to describe the opposite or complement of analytic thought.

KUNDALINI: The Yogic term which is interpreted here to mean a power, probably electric in nature, situated in the perineum or at the base of the spine, and capable of being roused (through various exercises) to course upward through the central nervous or through the sympathetic nervous system, thereby triggering the ductless glands, including the pituitary and probably the pineal. The result, presumably, is the highest form of consciousness.

LEPTOID: From Greek *lepsis,* leap: implying an energetic rousing of the aged both to counteract involutional melancholia and to attain awareness of the eliminatory, fifth age of man during which the consciousness must prepare for its birth out of the body via the electrical field, which persists after bodily death.

LOGOS: The divine ruling principle, which is immanent or pervasive in all reality.

METACOMEDY: Literally, beyond comedy. A dramatic form, which would go through and beyond the first act of comedy and the second act of tragedy to a third act in which the protagonist, instead of dying encysted in his egotistic consciousness, would go on to experience his preterconsciousness.

METANOIA: Mutation of consciousness.

METARSIS: As catharsis is relief by purging and anarsis is a relief and release by aspiration, so metarsis is release into a condition beyond, into what Plotinus named the yonder.

NEOTENY: A zoological term meaning the capacity of carrying the larval or child form on into reproductive maturity; also, and especially, of extending the childhood phase of growth, openness, and teachability. See *Embryos and Ancestors* by Sir Gavin de Beer.

NOMOS: A system of laws governing a specified field: astronomy, and so on.

NOR-ADRENALINE: A secretion of the suprarenals, which causes outward-directed rage, as distinguished from adrenaline that causes inward-directed rage or guilt.

PAIDOMORPH: Literally, child-body, a psychophysique not yet committed to the polar differentiation of the sexual opposites.

PANAESTHESIA: Total tactual perception, a natural capacity for total bodily response to stimulation.

PATHEIA: Pain that has become degenerative; sickness.

PHATIC: A term used by Malinowski, the anthropologist, referring to the charge of emotion that is often carried by a descriptive word.

PRAXIS: Psychophysical practice or exercise.

PSYCHEDELICS: Literally, leaders of the psyche; chemical or vegetable products (for example, lysergic acid, mescaline, psylocybin, and the like), which when taken in an agreeable environment produce heightened awareness.

RAJAS: Energy.

RELIGIO: A rite employing all the senses and performed in order to raise its participants to a cohesive, communal awareness of the force that precipitates and guides life in time; literally, a binding back or together. Religion has come to connote merely dogmatic religion.

SATVAS: Used here to mean comprehension, understanding.

TAMAS: Inertia.

The development and refinement of psychiatric nomenclature into its present proportions and complexities make it necessary for me to confine myself to as few terms as possible in order to elucidate the correlations I have seen. Therefore, in this psychological interpretation of history I have used only five categories of mental breakdown. And I define each one as follows:

The trauma of birth:
That state in which the infant refuses to develop into child-

hood, clinging to fetal and rudimentary infantile attitudes and behavior.

That state of rigidity, or ankylosis, which attacked the co-conscious societies, arresting all social growth.

Paranoia:

That state in which the child projects his rage, born of frustration, outward onto others, onto the world.

The berserk rage of the hero-barbarian societies that destroyed the traditional societies and turned the hero into a homicide.

Schizophrenia:

That state in which the adolescent turns his anger and frustration inward, onto himself, when it becomes guilt.

The horror of life that drove Ascetic man to desert society.

Manic-depression:

That state in which the man of first maturity, in a society that lauds aggression, suffers from cyclic moods of provocative elations, leading to reaction into extreme discouragement.

The cyclic madness that makes modern society hopelessly unstable.

Involutional melancholy:

The continuous and increasing mental gloom which, after the climacteric (marked by impotence, poor appetite, and general failure of interests) is an undelusional state of mind in an increasing number of the elderly.

The melancholy that is the harbinger of social despair.

Of the above five states, the first four may appear among later age groups. This, though, is rare and due to the psyche's emotional retardation, which had been masked, to emerge in later life.

Bibliography

1. BASTIEN, ADOLF. *Die Volker des Oestlichen Asien.* Leipzig: O. Wigan, 1866–71.
2. BEHANAN, K. T. *Yoga.* New York: The Macmillan Co., 1937.
3. BENEDICT, RUTH. *Patterns of Culture.* Boston: Houghton Mifflin Co., 1959.
4. BERNSTEIN, MOREY. *The Search for Bridey Murphy.* Garden City: Double-day & Co. Inc., 1956.
5. BERRILL, N. J. *Man's Emerging Mind.* New York: Dodd, Mead & Co., 1955.
6. BLOCH, IVAN. *The Sexual Life of our Times.* London: Rebman, 1908.
7. BURY, J. B. *The Idea of Progress.* New York: Dover Publications, Inc., 1955.
8. BUTLER, R. A. "Curiosity in Monkies" *Scientific American,* February, 1954.
9. BYRD, RICHARD E. *Alone.* New York: G. P. Putnam's Sons, 1938.
10. CAIN, ARTHUR H. "Alcoholics Anonymous: Cult or Cure?" New York: *Harper's Magazine,* February, 1963.
11. CAMPBELL, JOSEPH. *The Hero with a Thousand Faces.* New York: Pantheon Books, 1953.
12. CAMPBELL, JOSEPH. *The Masks of God.* New York: The Viking Press, 1959.

13. CHOLDEN, LOUIS (ed.). *Lysergic Acid, Diethylamide, and Mescaline in Experimental Psychiatry.* New York: Grune and Stratton, 1956.

14. CHOPRA, R. N. and G. S. *Indian Medical Research Memoirs:* Memoir No. 31. July 1939.

15. COON, CARLETON S. *The Origin of Races.* New York: Alfred A. Knopf, 1963.

16. COULTON, G. C. *Five Centuries of Religion.* New York: Cambridge University Press, 1923–50.

17. DAPPER, OLFERT. *Description de l'Afrique.* Amsterdam: Wolfgang, 1686.

18. DIMOND, SYDNEY GEORGE. *The Psychology of the Methodist Revival.* New York: Oxford University Press, 1926.

19. DODDS, E. R. *The Greeks and the Irrational.* Boston: Beacon Press, 1957.

20. EBON, MARTIN. *"Firewalking 1956."* "Firewalkers of Modern Greece" by ANGELO TANAGRAS. *Tomorrow,* Vol. 4, No. 4.

21. EISELEY, LOREN. "Fossil Man and Human Evolution." *The Year Book of Anthropology,* 1955.

22. *Fate Magazine.* Curtis Fuller. "I See by the Papers." April 1963, pp. 22.

23. FINE, BENJAMIN. *1,000,000 Delinquents.* New York: Harper and Row, 1957.

24. FODOR, NANDOR. *The Search for the Beloved: A Clinical Investigation of the Trauma of Birth and pre-Natal Conditioning.* New York: Hermitage Press, 1949.

25. FRÄNGER, WILHELM. *The Millennium of Hieronymus Bosch.* London: Faber and Faber, 1961.

26. FRANKFORT, HENRI. *The Birth of Civilization in the Near East.* Garden City: Doubleday & Co., Inc., 1956.

27. FRANKFORT, HENRI. *Ancient Egyptian Religion.* New York: Columbia University Press, 1948.

28. FUNKENSTEIN, D. H. "The Physiology of Fear and Anger." *Scientific American,* May 1955.

29. GADDIS, THOMAS. *The Birdman of Alcatraz.* New York: Random House, 1955.

30. GESELL, ARNOLD, FRANCES L. ILG, and LOUISE AMES. *Youth: The Years from 10 to 16.* New York: Harper and Row, 1956.

31. GESELL, ARNOLD, and FRANCES L. ILG in collaboration with JANET LEARNED and LOUISE B. AMES. *Infant and Child in the Culture of Today.* New York: Harper and Row, 1943.

32. GESELL, ARNOLD, and FRANCES L. ILG in collaboration with LOUISE B. AMES and GLENNA E. BULLIS. *The Child from Five to Ten.* New York: Harper and Row, 1946.

33. GHISELIN, BREWSTER (ed.). *The Creative Process.* Berkeley: University of California Press, 1954.

34. GIBSON, WALTER. *The Boat.* Boston: Houghton Mifflin Co., 1953.

35. GINGERELLI, J., and F. J. KIRKNER (eds.). *Psychological Variables in Human Cancer: Symposium.* Berkeley: University of California Press, 1954.

36. GOMBRICH, E. H. *Art and Illusion.* New York: Pantheon Books, 1960.

37. GORER, GEOFFREY. *Africa Dances.* J. Lehmann, 1949.

38. HADAMARD, JACQUES. *An Essay on the Psychology of Invention in the Mathematical Field.* New York: Dover Publications, Inc., 1954.

39. HANSON, N. R. *Patterns of Discovery.* New York: Cambridge University Press, 1958.

40. HEARD, GERALD. *The Human Venture.* New York: Harper and Row, 1955.

41. HEARD, GERALD. *Man, the Master.* New York: Harper and Row, 1941.

42. HEARD, GERALD. *The Ascent of Humanity.* New York: Harcourt, Brace & World, 1929.

43. HEARD, GERALD. *The Eternal Gospel.* New York: Harper and Row, 1946.

44. HERON, W., W. H. BEXTON, and D. C. HEBB. "Cognitive Effects of Decreased Variation to the Sensory Environment." *The American Psychologist,* Vol. 8, No. 8, August 1953.

45. HILZHEIMER, MAX. "The Dog: The Foetalization of the Wolf." *Antiquity,* Vol. VI, No. 24, December, 1932.

46. ITTLESON, W. H. *The Ames Demonstrations in Perception.* Princeton: Princeton University Press, 1952.

47. JAMES, WILLIAM. *The Varieties of Religious Experience.* New York: The Modern Library, Inc.

48. JELLINEK, STEFAN. *Dying, Apparent Death and Resuscitation.* Baltimore: Williams & Wilkins, 1947.

49. KERÉNYI, C. "The Mysteries of the Kabeiroi." *The Mysteries.* New York: Pantheon Books, Inc., 1955.

50. KROEBER, A. L. (ed.). *Anthropology Today.* See H. L. MOVIUS, "Old World Prehistory: Paleolithic." Chicago: University of Chicago Press, 1953.

51. LA BARRE, WESTON. *The Human Animal.* Chicago: University of Chicago Press, 1954.

52. LANE, EDWARD WILLIAM. *An Account of the Manners and Customs of the Modern Egyptians.* London: J. Murray, 1860. Fifth Edition.

53. LEVY, GERTRUDE RACHEL. *The Gate of Horn.* London: Faber and Faber, 1948.

54. LINDAUER, MARTIN. *Communication Among Social Bees.* Massachusetts: Harvard University Press, 1961.

55. LINDNER, ROBERT. *Rebels Without a Cause.* New York: Grune and Stratton, 1944.

56. LINDNER, ROBERT. *Must you Conform?* New York: Rinehart, 1956.

57. MAC CURDY, JOHN THOMPSON. *War Neuroses.* New York: Cambridge University Press, 1918.

58. MEAD, GEORGE R. S. *Fragments of a Faith Forgotten.* New Hyde Park: University Books, 1960.

59. MEAD, MARGARET. *New Lives for Old.* New York: William Morrow & Co., Inc., 1956.

60. MEDUNA, L. J. *Carbon Dioxide Therapy.* Springfield, Illinois: Charles C Thomas, 1958.

61. MEERLOO, JOOST A. M. *Rape of the Mind.* Cleveland: World Publishing Co., 1956.

62. MICHAEL, D. N. *Cybernation: The Silent Conquest.* Santa Barbara: Center for Study of Democratic Institutions, 1962.

63. MORET, ALEXANDRE, and GEORGES DAVY. *From Tribe to Empire.* New York: Alfred A. Knopf, 1926.

64. MURRAY, MARGARET. *The Witch Cult in Western Europe.* Oxford: Clarendon Press, 1921.

65. OTTO, WALTER F. "The Meaning of the Eleusinian Mysteries." *The Mysteries.* New York: Pantheon Books, Inc., 1955.

66. PFEIFFER, JOHN. *The Human Brain.* New York: Harper and Row, 1955.

67. PIGGOTT, STUART. *Prehistoric India to 1000 B.C.* Baltimore: Penguin Books, 1950.

68. RANK, OTTO. *The Trauma of Birth.* New York: Brunner, 1952.

69. READ, GRANTLY DICK. *Childbirth without Fear.* New York: Harper and Row, 1959.

70. RELE, VASANT G. *The Mysterious Kundalini.* Bombay: Taraporevala, 1927.

71. RIBBLE, MARGARET. *The Rights of Infants.* New York: Columbia University Press, 1950.

72. RITTER, CHRISTIANE. *A Woman in the Polar Night.* New York: E. P. Dutton & Co. Inc., 1954.

73. SARGANT, WILLIAM. *The Battle for the Mind.* Garden City: Doubleday & Co. Inc., 1957.

74. SCOTT, GEOFFREY. *The Architecture of Humanism.* Garden City: Doubleday & Company, Inc., Anchor, 1954.

75. SCOTT, JOHN PAUL. "Critical Periods in Behavioral Development." *Science,* November 30, 1962.

76. SEIDENBERG, RODERICK. *Post-Historic Man.* Boston: Beacon Press, 1957.

77. SELYE, HANS. *The Stress of Life.* New York: McGraw-Hill, 1956.

78. SIMEONS, A. T. W. *Man's Presumptuous Brain.* New York: E. P. Dutton & Co. Inc., 1962.

79. SIMPSON, G. G. *The Meaning of Evolution.* New Haven: Yale University Press, 1950.

80. SMITH, ADAM. *Wealth of Nations.* New York: E. P. Dutton & Co. Inc.
81. STEVENSON, LANG. "Cancer and Atheroma Explained by a Basic Phylo-genetic Pattern in Disease." London: *The Medical Press,* June 14, 21, and 28, 1962.
82. STEWARD, J. H. "Cultural Causality and Law: A Trial Formulation of the Development of Early Civilizations." *American Anthropologist.* Vol. 51, pp. 1–27.
83. STILL, COLIN. *The Timeless Theme.* London: I. Nicholson & Watson, Ltd., 1936.
84. SUTTIE, IAN D. *The Origins of Love and Hate.* New York: Julian Press, Inc., 1952.
85. THOMPSON, W. R., and RONALD MELZACK. "Early Environment." *Scientific American,* January, 1956.
86. TOKSVIG, SIGNE. *Emanuel Swedenborg.* New Haven: Yale University Press, 1948.
87. VETT, CARL. *Seltsame Erlebnisse in Einem Derwischkloster.* Leipzig: Heitz & Co., 1931.
88. VOEGELIN, ERIC. *New Science of Politics, An Introduction.* The Walgreen Foundation Lectures. Chicago: Chicago University Press, 1952.
89. VON FRISCH, KARL. *Bees: Their Vision, Chemical Senses and Language.* Ithaca: Cornell University Press, 1958.
90. VON HAYEK, FRIEDRICH AUGUST. *The Road to Serfdom.* Chicago: University of Chicago Press, 1945.
91. WALLAS, GRAHAM. *The Art of Thought.* New York: Harcourt, Brace & World, Inc., 1926.
92. WALSH, W. H. *Philosophy of History.* New York: Harper and Row, 1960.
93. WALTER, GREY. *The Living Brain.* New York: W. W. Norton & Co., Inc., 1953.
94. WARNECK, JOHANNES GUSTAV. *Die Religion der Batak.* Göttingen: Vandenhoeck und Ruprecht, 1909.
95. WELCH, HOLMES. *The Parting of the Way.* Boston: Beacon Press, 1957.
96. WENGER, M. A., K. K. BAGCHI, and K. K. ANAND. "Voluntary Heart and Pulse Control by Yoga Methods." *The International Journal of Parapsychology,* Winter, 1962.
97. WHORF, BENJAMIN LEE. *Language, Thought and Reality.* Cambridge: Technology Press of Massachusetts Institute of Technology, 1956.
98. WOLBERG, LEWIS ROBERT. *Medical Hypnosis.* New York: Grune and Stratton, Inc., 1948.
99. ZOTZ, LOTHER FRIEDRICH. *Antsteinzeitkunde Mittel-Europas.* Stuttgart: F. Enke, 1951.